Teaching Children to Read

Putting the Pieces Together
Third Edition

D. Ray Reutzel
Southern Utah University

Robert B. Cooter, Jr.
Dallas Public Schools

Merrill
an imprint of Prentice Hall
Upper Saddle River, New Jersey   Columbus, Ohio

Library of Congress Cataloging-in-Publication Data

Reutzel, D. Ray (Douglas Ray),
     Teaching children to read : putting the pieces together / by D. Ray
Reutzel, Robert B. Cooter, Jr.—3rd ed.
         p.   c.m.
     Includes bibliographical references and index.
     ISBN 0-13-099835-4
     1. Reading (Elementary)   2. Reading (Elementary)—Language
experience approach.   3. Language Arts (Elementary)   I. Cooter,
Robert B.   II. Title.
LB1573.R48 2000
372.41—dc21   99-17100
                                                             CIP

Editor: Bradley J. Potthoff
Developmental Editor: Linda Ashe Montgomery
Editorial Assistant: Mary Evangelista
Production Editor: Mary M. Irvin
Design Coordinator: Diane C. Lorenzo
Cover Design: Diane C. Lorenzo
Cover art: Susan Sturgill
Text Design: STELLARViSIONs
Production Manager: Pamela D. Bennett
Director of Marketing: Kevin Flanagan
Marketing Manager: Meghan Shepherd
Marketing Coordinator: Krista Groshong

This book was set in Souvenir by Carlisle Communications, Ltd. and was printed and bound by Von Hoffman Press, Inc. The cover was printed by Von Hoffman Press, Inc.

© 2000, 1996 by Prentice-Hall, Inc.
Pearson Education
Upper Saddle River, New Jersey 07458

Earlier edition © 1992 by Macmillan Publishing Company.

Photo Credits:
Text: Scott Cunningham/Merrill: 7, 23, 35, 45, 148, 150, 155, 233, 250, 262 (bottom), 282, 311, 315, 330, 353, 356, 529; Todd Yarrington/Merrill: 18; KS Studios/Merrill: 29; Anthony Magnacca/Merrill: 42, 262 (middle), 272; Anne Vega/Merrill: 59, 69, 460; UPI/Corbis Bettmann: 91; Linda Peterson/Merrill: 96; Robert B. Cooter: 492, 494, 553. **Insert:** Scott Cunningham/Merrill: Insert p. 1, 5 (bottom), 6 (top and bottom), 7, and 8; Courtesy of the Wiggand family: Insert p. 2 (bottom); Joseph Nettis/Photo Researchers, Inc.: Insert p. 3; Mary Kate Denny/Photo Edit: Insert p. 4; Jeff Maloney/PhotoDisc, Inc.: Insert p. 5 (top).

Printed in the United States of America

10 9 8 7 6 5 4 3 2 1

ISBN: 0-13-099835-4

Prentice-Hall International (UK) Limited, *London*
Prentice-Hall of Australia Pty. Limited, *Sydney*
Prentice-Hall of Canada, Inc., *Toronto*
Prentice-Hall Hispanoamericana, S. A., *Mexico*
Prentice-Hall of India Private Limited, *New Delhi*
Prentice-Hall of Japan, Inc., *Tokyo*
Prentice-Hall (Singapore) Pte. Ltd., *Singapore*
Editora Prentice-Hall do Brasil, Ltda., *Rio de Janeiro*

To the many teachers and colleagues who have taught me; the young children who have enriched my life; and my wife, children, and grandchildren who have blessed me with their love and support.

    —DRR

For the children, teachers, and families of Dallas. You have reminded me why it is great to be a reading teacher.

    —RBC

ABOUT THE AUTHORS

D. Ray Reutzel

D. Ray Reutzel is the Provost and academic vice president at Southern Utah University. He was formerly a Karl G. Maeser Research Professor and Chair of the Department of Elementary Education at Brigham Young University. He earned his doctorate in Curriculum and Instruction with an emphasis in reading and language arts from the University of Wyoming, Laramie, in 1982. He teaches courses in research design, reading, and language arts for preservice and in-service teachers at BYU. He has taught in kindergarten and grades 1, 3, 5, and 6 as an elementary school teacher.

Dr. Reutzel took a leave from his university faculty position to return to full-time, first-grade classroom teaching in Sage Creek Elementary School in 1987–1988. While in the elementary classroom, he established a model first-grade whole language classroom that has been visited by observers from throughout the country. In 1987, Dr. Reutzel received BYU's College of Education Excellence in Research Award. In the same year, his work was recognized by the American Educational Research Association (AERA) as one of the Distinguished Research Papers at the 1988 Annual Meeting.

Dr. Reutzel is the author of more than 100 articles, books, book chapters, and monographs. He has published in *Reading Research Quarterly, Journal of Reading Behavior, Journal of Educational Research, Reading Psychology, Reading Research and Instruction,* and *The Reading Teacher,* among others. He has served as an editorial review board member or guest reviewer for *The Elementary School Journal, The Reading Teacher, Reading Research Quarterly, The Journal of Reading Behavior, The Reading Teacher, The NRC Yearbook, American Reading Forum Yearbook, Reading Psychology,* and *Reading Research and Instruction.* Dr. Reutzel is an author of the *Literacy Place* program published by Scholastic, Inc. of New York.

Dr. Reutzel lives in Cedar City, Utah, with his wife, daughter, four sons, a dog, and a cat. His hobbies include reading, skiing, fishing, singing, playing the piano, and trying to keep up with his wife and children.

Robert B. Cooter, Jr.

Robert Cooter is a long-time professor of education who is best known for serving as the first "Reading Czar" (Assistant Superintendent for Reading/Language Arts) for the Dallas Public Schools. He has engineered the District's highly acclaimed Dallas Reading Plan, a collaborative project supported by Dallas area business and community enterprises that involves a large cadre of master "lead reading teachers." Dr. Cooter's primary charge: to help some 60,000 children in grades K–3 attain fluent reading by the end of third grade. This has been accomplished, in part, through the training of approximately 3,000 teachers in those grades in his Dallas Reading Academy. In March of 1998, Cooter was recognized as a "Texas State Champion for Reading" by Governor George W. Bush and Texas First Lady Laura Bush as a result of the many successes of the Dallas Reading Plan initiative.

Cooter has worked with teachers and school districts around the nation who seek to create balanced literacy programs. He has taught grades 1, 3, 4, 7, 11, and 12 in the public schools and also served as a Title I reading teacher. Dr. Cooter previously served as Dean of the College of Education and Professor of Reading and Literacy Education at Austin Peay State University, where he taught courses for preservice and practicing teachers, and prior to that as Chair of the Department of Curriculum and Instruction at Texas Christian University. Cooter also directed the prestigious Reading Center at Bowling Green State University in Ohio during the 1980s. Dr. Cooter earned graduate degrees in Reading/Literacy Education at George Peabody College for Teachers of Vanderbilt University and the University of Tennessee.

In addition to *Teaching Children to Read,* which is used at over 200 universities and colleges to train elementary teachers, Cooter has also authored or co-authored several other books, including *The Teacher's Guide to Reading Tests, The Flynt-Cooter Reading Inventory for the Classroom,* and *Teaching Reading in the Content Areas.* His other recent books are *Balanced Reading Strategies and Practices: Assessing and Assisting Readers with Special Needs* and *The Flynt/Cooter English * Espanol Reading Inventory.*

A native of Nashville, Tennessee, Bob enjoys fiction writing, performing Southern folktales for children of all ages, fly-fishing, sailing, listening to good blues, riding his Harley-Davidson "Hawg," and dining on catfish and cheese grits. He lives with his wife (Dr. Kathleen Spencer Cooter, a special education professor and former teacher and school administrator), is the proud father of five children and three stepchildren, has five grandchildren, and is (still) owned by a hound dog of unknown breed and questionable utility.

# Preface

One of the greatest professional experiences we have had occurred several years ago when we decided to leave our university positions and return to teaching children. Our purpose was to try out the various ideas and strategies about reading and writing that we had collected and verify how to practically apply them in the classroom. Our experiences led us to write this book and tell you what we discovered about the need for *balanced reading and writing instruction.*

The field of reading education has been and, we hope, will continue to be in a constant state of flux. Although some view this process as simply a swinging of the educational pendulum between old and new, we believe that current calls for change have occurred for two reasons. First, the language of change represents a fundamental shift in knowledge and understanding of the reading process. It reflects a profound change in how we view the world of language learning in elementary schools. Second, we believe that to revalue some traditions in the field fosters a greater understanding as to why we do what we do as teachers. As Frank Smith (1994) says, examining teaching traditions allows teachers at all levels to move beyond the confines of educational ignorance.

Thus, in the third edition of *Teaching Children to Read* we have culminated our many years of work in the classroom, field, and office, bringing together our collective knowledge and experiences and the knowledge and experiences of many recognized authorities in the field of reading and language arts education. In addition, we have called upon the experience, wisdom, and common sense of our teacher and student colleagues whom we depended on to validate our ideas (or point out what needed to change) for initiating transitions in reading and instructional practice.

In reading *Teaching Children to Read: Putting the Pieces Together,* we ask you to examine closely your own beliefs about reading and writing instruction, and we openly invite you to embark on a stimulating professional journey. This journey may involve a sustained professional move away from more traditional instructional practices and toward balanced literacy instructional beliefs and practices.

A WALKING TOUR OF THE TEXT

Teaching Children to Read: Putting the Pieces Together is a compendium of many of the best teaching ideas presently available to reading professionals. Because of the sheer volume and richness of ideas presented, it will probably not be possible for you to absorb everything at once. This text is intended to be a useful companion as you make your own transitions journey, a resource for you to reference while you teach reading and writing to children. Of particular note is the integration of teaching strategies for developing literacy with *children with special needs* and for *children whose first language is other than English.* These fall into each chapter that describes practice, beginning with chapter 5.

Chapter 1 *Introduces a transitions approach to reading.* Each teacher brings a unique set of experiences and beliefs to the classroom. Part of the art of teaching is drawing on these experiences and connecting new learning to reform your beliefs into best practice. In Chapter 1, you will find *Seven Principles that Support Literacy Development.* These principles encapsulate our reading philosophy and will, we hope, steer you toward the elements of reading and writing you need to examine to move from traditional (and/or whole language) practices to balanced literacy perspectives.

Chapter 2   *Discusses learning theories from which reading instruction has evolved.* It also provides instructional models of the reading and writing processes that spring from reading theories and illustrates each reading model for you.

Chapter 3   *Describes the literacy development of young children and includes aspects of oral, reading, and written language development.* This chapter will help you understand how emergent literacy behaviors are relevant to the development of readers and writers.

Chapter 4   *Provides information on the pros and cons of using basal readers exclusively for teaching literacy.* Through this chapter you will understand the function of basals and concerns for depending on them for teaching reading. In addition, Chapter 4 presents innovative ways to utilize the best qualities of the newer basals and identifies when to deviate from their prescriptive practices to use authentic literature.

Chapter 5   *Explains how to cross the transitions bridge, springboarding from traditional, basal-only teaching toward innovative practices more closely associated with balanced reading and writing instruction.* Three vignettes describe teachers who are at early, intermediate, or advanced transition stages to help you assess your own outlook.

Chapter 6   *Reviews the theory and practice in the study of reading comprehension.* You will come to understand strategies children use to comprehend text and how teachers can facilitate the reading comprehension process through creative and stimulating teaching techniques.

Chapter 7   *Answers questions related to developing vocabulary and recommends skills and strategies for helping children acquire vocabulary.*

Chapter 8   *Identifies skills for part-whole-part instruction.* Thoroughly revised to meet the changing demands of the field, this chapter provides you with the knowledge you need for understanding phonemic awareness, the alphabetic principle, and the teaching of phonics. It was developed to help you understand the importance of teaching word-identification strategies. You will find phonics generalizations and decoding skills and practices that support skills instruction.

Chapter 9   *Details the organizing elements of literacy-rich environments and describes how to design classrooms to engage children in balanced literacy activities.*

Chapter 10   *Features balanced literacy assessment practices.* A key function of this chapter is to explain how to use assessment practices to inform instruction and satisfy typical school district requirements such as student grades. New to this chapter are Literacy Learning Milestones, which identify the skills children in grades K–3 should know before moving on to higher grade levels. In addition, you will find tools for profiling individual students' literacy progress, as well as the progress of the class as a whole, to determine how to group children based on their common literacy needs.

Part II of the text, "Reading and Writing Development: Putting It All Together," describes reading and writing instructional strategies for grades K–2 in Chapter 11, grades 3–5 in Chapter 12, and grades 6–8 in Chapter 13. From one chapter to another, the reading and writing process is set up as a continuum—beginning with emergent readers and writers, to developing readers and writers who benefit from reading and writing workshops, to honing the skills of independent readers and writers, supporting their needs for using content area and reference materials. Chapters 11 to 13 will help you gain a sense of how teaching practices are sequenced to be developmentally appropriate. Because all students do not follow a rigid pattern of reading and writing development, included in these chapters are recovery strategies for students who are not on track and students whose exceptionalities require adapted lessons and activities.

Appendix A, "Balanced Literacy Resources for Teachers," includes ideas for creating reading resource rooms, criteria for determining reading levels of texts, and a listing of Guided Reading selections which have been rated for reading-level appropriateness. Additional appendices include a categorized list of children's literature and BLAST!™: *Balanced Literacy Assessment System and Training* by Cooter and Cooter.

We have attempted in this third edition of *Teaching Children to Read: Putting the Pieces Together* to pull apart the puzzle of literacy development. We hope through reading, studying, and applying the strategies within this text you will have a better sense of how the elements of literacy fit together to create the whole literacy picture. Not all of your students will learn to read and write well. But we believe that the practical nature of this text gives you the pieces of the puzzle you need to become a creative problem solver—and an effective reading teacher.

DISCOVER THE COMPANION WEBSITE ACCOMPANYING THIS BOOK
The Prentice Hall Companion Website: A Virtual Learning Environment

Technology is a constantly growing and changing aspect of our field that is creating a need for content and resources. To address this emerging need, Prentice Hall has developed an online learning environment for students and professors alike—Companion Websites—to support our textbooks.

In creating a Companion Website, our goal is to build on and enhance what the textbook already offers. For this reason, the content for each user-friendly website is organized by chapter and provides the professor and student with a variety of meaningful resources. Common features of a Companion Website include:

For the Professor

Every Companion Website integrates **Syllabus Manager**™, an online syllabus creation and management utility.

- **Syllabus Manager**™ provides you, the instructor, with an easy, step-by-step process to create and revise syllabi, with direct links into Companion Website and other online content without having to learn HTML.

- Students may logon to your syllabus during any study session. All they need to know is the web address for the Companion Website and the password you've assigned to your syllabus.
- After you have created a syllabus using **Syllabus Manager™**, students may enter the syllabus for their course section from any point in the Companion Website.
- Class dates are highlighted in white and assignment due dates appear in blue. Clicking on a date, the student is shown the list of activities for the assignment. The activities for each assignment are linked directly to actual content, saving time for students.
- Adding assignments consists of clicking on the desired due date, then filling in the details of the assignment—name of the assignment, instructions, and whether or not it is a one-time or repeating assignment.
- In addition, links to other activities can be created easily. If the activity is on-line, a URL can be entered in the space provided, and it will be linked automatically in the final syllabus.
- Your completed syllabus is hosted on our servers, allowing convenient updates from any computer on the Internet. Changes you make to your syllabus are immediately available to your students at their next logon.

For the Student

- **Chapter Objectives** – outline key concepts from the text
- **Interactive Self-quizzes** – complete with hints and automatic grading that provide immediate feedback for students

  After students submit their answers for the interactive self-quizzes, the Companion Website **Results Reporter** computes a percentage grade, provides a graphic representation of how many questions were answered correctly and incorrectly, and gives a question by question analysis of the quiz. Students are given the option to send their quiz to up to four email addresses (professor, teaching assistant, study partner, etc.).

- **Message Board** – serves as a virtual bulletin board to post—or respond to—questions or comments to/from a national audience
- **Net Searches** – offer links by key terms from each chapter to related Internet content
- **Web Destinations** – links to www sites that relate to chapter content

To take advantage of these and other resources, please visit the *Teaching Children to Read: Putting the Pieces Together* Companion Website at www.prenhall.com/reutzel

ACKNOWLEDGMENTS

First, we owe a great deal of credit to the parents and children of the classrooms where we have taught and experimented as classroom teachers, especially for the year we returned to the classroom as first-grade teachers. The insights we gain from these learners profoundly influence our growing understanding of how children solve the language learning puzzle. We also wish to thank our teacher and administrative colleagues at Sage Creek Elementary School and Kenwood Elementary School who during that time, through their dedication and risk taking, shared and clarified for us the way of transitions toward balanced literacy teaching. We are grateful also to those many teachers and administrators across the country, and especially at Alpine, Jordan, Nebo, and Provo, Utah, school districts, with whom we have worked in in-service projects and who have helped us clarify our own transitions position and - philosophy.

We owe an enormous debt of gratitude to the Lead Reading teachers, administrators, and other colleagues at Dallas Public Schools working in the innovative Dallas reading plan who have served as active advisors and counselors in this latest edition. They are master reading teachers of the first order and their new ideas are embodied herein. Deserving special attention are: Paula Perez, Barbara Matthews, and Peggy Marrin, who worked on final drafts of this edition. We appreciate their many suggestions and the hours of long suffering they endured with Bob Cooter, who generally made everyone a little daft.

We are deeply grateful to the many students and professors who use our text. We must also acknowledge the insights of the many professors, teachers, and students who used the first and second editions and shared their feelings and ideas.

We are especially thankful for the support of our colleagues at Brigham Young University and Southern Utah University who have been readers of and reactors to our evolving manuscripts of this and previous editions and have offered many hints for improvement. A particular debt of gratitude is extended to Marva Middleton, Kari Gail, and Teresa Moss for their dedication to this project and many hours of careful work, and to Kathy Williams, Starpoint School.

We express our gratitude to Jeff Johnston, our publisher, for sharing our original vision and support for this project. We extend our thanks to our friend and editor, Brad Potthoff, for his unfailing excitement and continuing vision for this text. We are very grateful to Linda Montgomery, Mary Irvin, and Melissa Gruzs for their meticulous attention to detail in the preparation and production of this text. And, finally, we thank our reviewers—Kathy Barclay, Western Illinois University; Carole L. Bond, Memphis State University; Martha Combs, University of Nevada, Reno; Susan J. Daniels, University of Akron; M. Jean Greenlaw, University of North Texas; Judith Mitchell, Weber State University; William J. Oehlkers, Rhode Island College; Timothy Rasinski, Kent State University; James E. Walker, Clarion University of Pennsylvania; Brad Wilcox, Brigham Young University; Alexander Casareno, University of Portland; Laurie Elish-Piper, Northern Illinois University; Kouider Mokhtari, Oklahoma State University; William J. Oehlkers, Rhode Island College; and Peter Quinn, St. John's University—for their words of encouragement, timely insights, and help in shaping the organization and content for this third edition of *Teaching Children to Read*.

D. R. Reutzel and R. B. Cooter, Jr.

Contents

Chapter 3   Emergent Literacy: Understanding the Literacy Development of Young Children   40

Chapter 4   Basal Readers: Determining How to Use Basals Effectively   86

Chapter 5   From Basals to Books: Making the Transition   128

Chapter 6   Reading Comprehension: Focusing on Instruction   174

Chapter 7   Acquiring Vocabulary: Words for Reading and Writing   222

Chapter 8   Decoding Skills: Identifying Words in Print   260

Chapter 9   Literacy Environments: Designing Classrooms That Promote Literacy   304

Chapter 10   Assessment: Determining Students' Progress in Literacy   346

PART II: READING AND WRITING DEVELOPMENT: PUTTING IT ALL TOGETHER

Chapter 11   The Early Years: Reading and Writing in Grades K–2   400

Chapter 12   The Elementary Years: Reading and Writing in Grades 3–5   470

Chapter 13   Middle School: Reading and Writing in Grades 6–8   526

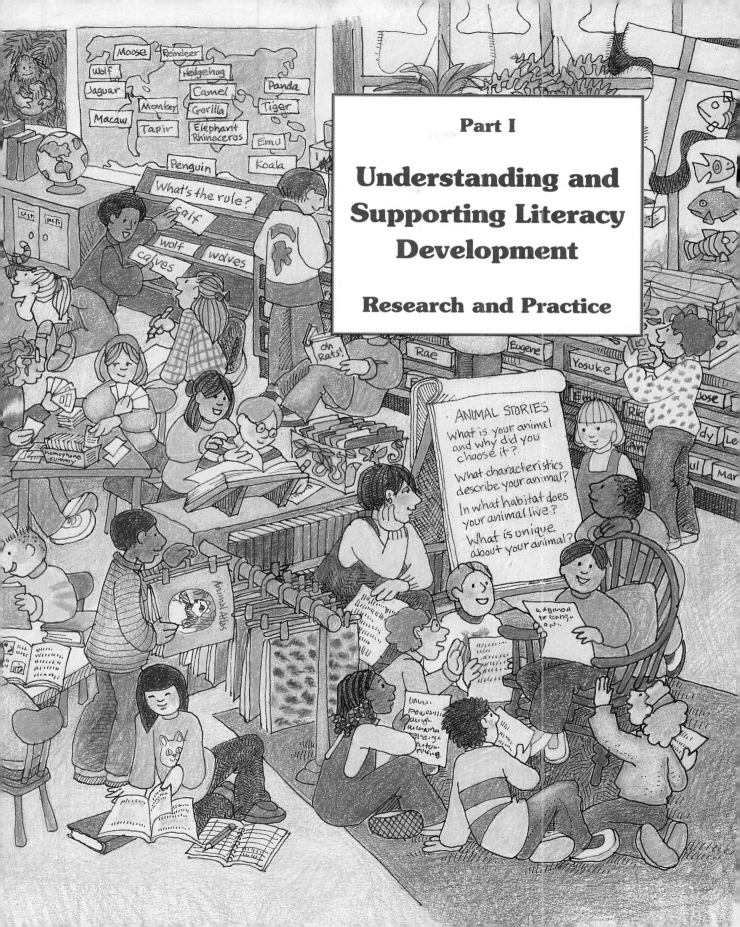

Part I

Understanding and Supporting Literacy Development

Research and Practice

Reading Instruction:

Focus Questions

When you are finished studying this chapter, you should be able to answer these questions:

1. What is the nature of the debate in reading education?
2. What is meant by "balanced literacy" instruction?
3. How does a transitions approach differ from an eclectic approach?
4. Why is it said that making transitions toward balanced literacy instruction is "evolutionary . . . not revolutionary"?
5. At what point in the transition is it appropriate to develop your own system of beliefs? Explain.
6. What are the seven principles for supporting literacy development?

Making the Transition to a Balanced Perspective

Key Concepts

Transitions
Traditional Approaches
Whole Language
Balanced Literacy Programs
Eclectic Approach

Seven Principles for Supporting Literacy
    Development
Preservice Teachers
In-service Teachers

Transitions is a philosophical position that encourages teachers to initiate changes in literacy beliefs and practices by building bridges, not walls, to develop balanced literacy programs in their classrooms. For a number of years, there has been a storm of controversy between literacy educators—some favor traditional direct instruction reading programs with a heavy emphasis on phonics, and others advocate "whole language" approaches. Recently, however, there are those who are instead advocating a position in the "radical middle"—*balanced literacy.*

TRANSITIONS: A MODEL FOR CHANGING TEACHERS' INSTRUCTIONAL PRACTICES

Traditional Approaches

Traditional approaches rely heavily on parts-to-whole skill instruction, worksheets, and "round robin" reading.

For the purpose of our discussion, we define **traditional approaches** for reading instruction as those relying heavily on worksheets, volumes of seat work, either whole-class instruction or ability grouping exclusively, round robin reading, skill teaching from the parts to the whole, and exclusive use of basal reader textbooks. It is also common to find that skill instruction is unconnected to the reading of texts in traditional approaches, what is termed *teaching skills in isolation.*

Teachers drawn toward using traditional basal programs exclusively argue that the basal reader is successful, especially as measured by standardized tests, state-mandated competency tests, and other measures of reading achievement commonly used in most school systems. In addition, many teachers like the structured aspects of basal reader manuals, which save them a great deal of planning time. Thus, many teachers understandably feel that basal readers are efficient classroom tools, help children learn to read, and provide documentation of reading success.

Whole Language

Whole language is a form of teaching loosely adapted from New Zealand, but lacking regular skill instruction.

Whole language, a curious and mostly American phenomenon, is a loosely adapted version of some much heralded approaches to teaching reading developed by successful New Zealand educators. Taking an almost polar opposite stance from the traditionalists, whole language proponents decried the use of worksheets, seat work, or grouping children (other than heterogeneous or "mixed" grouping). They used shared reading and literature response groups rather than ability groups as primary strategies. Teacher-directed, explicit skill instruction was left out . . . even ridiculed by many whole language supporters. Indeed, these educators shun direct skill instruction in any form and believe that children learn skills best by reading or by having books read to them, leaving critics to conclude that whole language advocates believe that literacy skills are apparently learned by some sort of osmosis by children!

"Whole languagers" use only trade-book literature, and all instruction is *whole*—words are almost never broken down or removed from context for analysis. Unfortunately for many students, this sort of incomplete teaching contributed to the virtual collapse of reading programs in California and other states during the late 1980s and into the 1990s. As a result of falling reading test scores in California of an unprecedented nature, a state-level reading task force was assembled, composed of talented reading teachers and other stakeholders. They concluded in their report, entitled *Every Child a Reader* (California Reading Task Force, 1995), that what was needed was a more "balanced" approach to the teaching of reading, an approach that needs to be "research-based and combine skills development with literature and language-rich activities" (p. iii).

Balanced Literacy Programs

Balanced literacy programs are the leading research-based alternative to traditional and whole language approaches.

Balanced literacy programs emerged in the 1990s as the leading research-based alternative to traditional and whole language approaches. Balanced literacy programs teach students skills in reading and writing based on their individual needs, and within the context of appropriately leveled reading materials of interest to the learner. Originally christened *balanced reading* by Don Holdaway (1979) in his book

Figure 1.1   A balanced literacy instruction chart

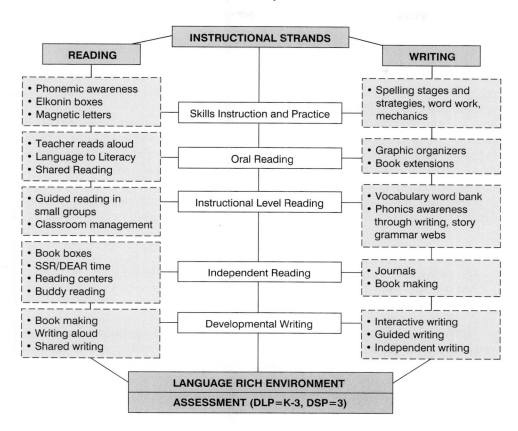

Balanced Literacy Instruction

INSTRUCTIONAL STRANDS

READING

WRITING

• Phonemic awareness
• Elkonin boxes
• Magnetic letters

Skills Instruction and Practice

• Spelling stages and
strategies, word work,
mechanics

• Teacher reads aloud
• Language to Literacy
• Shared Reading

Oral Reading

• Graphic organizers
• Book extensions

• Guided reading in
small groups
• Classroom management

Instructional Level Reading

• Vocabulary word bank
• Phonics awareness
through writing, story
grammar webs

• Book boxes
• SSR/DEAR time
• Reading centers
• Buddy reading

Independent Reading

• Journals
• Book making

• Book making
• Writing aloud
• Shared writing

Developmental Writing

• Interactive writing
• Guided writing
• Independent writing

LANGUAGE RICH ENVIRONMENT

ASSESSMENT (DLP=K-3, DSP=3)

Reading in Junior Classes, balanced literacy programs often use basal readers, "decodable text," and other more traditional programmed reading materials selectively, but they also include daily encounters with fiction and nonfiction trade books. Each day in balanced literacy classrooms, one typically sees oral reading by teachers and children alike, direct skill instruction and practice in guided reading groups (Fountas & Pinnell, 1996), a great deal of independent reading by students in books they enjoy, and "process" writing and spelling instruction. Balanced literacy teachers rely on strategic and ongoing assessment, and their carefully planned classrooms provide a language rich environment for the learners. Figure 1.1 is an example of a balanced literacy scheme (Cooter, 1998) that depicts key instructional strands.

The movement of modern society from the Industrial Age to the Information Age has made the ability to read more crucial than ever. Occupations from convenience store clerk to banking teller to physician all require the ability to read and read well. Drop-out rates and concomitant social maladies are soaring in urban areas and all can be traced, at least in part, to illiteracy. Balanced literacy instruction has taken root in many states and has gained prominence as a political issue. During the 1998 Texas gubernatorial campaign, for instance, balanced literacy instruction was a major plank in the election platform of Governor George W. Bush. The same was so in recent elections in many other states, including California. On the national proscenium, Richard

Balanced literacy instruction has become a popular issue supported by major political leaders.

E. Riley, the U.S. Secretary of Education, likewise pushed to the forefront initiatives that supported balanced literacy programs. These and other trends seem to signal that literacy instruction issues will remain center stage for some time to come.

As we find ourselves in an age of even greater political pressure for greater controls on classroom teaching, many wonder why we don't simply return to traditional basal reader approaches exclusively—a "back to basics" approach. In spite of the popular support of many school administrators and teachers for traditional basal-only modes of reading instruction, discontentment exists among many teachers who feel required to use them. Although basals were substantially revised throughout the 1990s and brought more in line with balanced literacy perspectives, many of the old problems remain. Routman (1988) states that for many years, teachers have been dissatisfied with boring, isolated, and unrelated reading skills, drills, and worksheets; efficient but unfounded teaching methods; and "dumbed-down" stories and textbooks. But because of highly resistant forces and well-established traditions, teachers have sometimes come to disregard their own feelings, intuitions, and expertise as professionals. In some cases, they have been subtly lulled into a state of educational ignorance. Frank Smith (1983) decried this problem in his essay entitled *The Politics of Ignorance*:

> Soft-core ignorance, which tends to be found in schools, is the ignorance of those who feel they need to be told what to do. Many teachers are trained to be ignorant, to rely on the opinions of experts or "superiors" rather than on their own judgment. . . . They express surprise or disbelief when it is suggested that their own experience and intuition might be as good a guide for action as the dogma of some expert. (p. 3)

Overreliance on basal readers can erode the skills of reading teachers.

Shannon (1989), in his book *Broken Promises,* asserted that during the past several decades, teachers have been gradually "deskilled" by an overreliance on basal readers—meaning that teachers lost their ability to plan and make professional decisions about reading instruction largely because of an overdependence on commercially published basal readers. Shannon's assertion was corroborated by Duffy, Roehler, and Putnam (1987) when they reported, "Neither the content nor the instructional design [of basals] offered much structure for decision making" (p. 360). Over time, teachers have become increasingly dependent on published programs to think for them. To make matters worse, administrators have become equally dependent, often mandating the strict and unquestioning use of basal materials and practices.

Balanced literacy programs promote student empowerment.

Given the inherent problems with the exclusive use of basal readers and the virtual collapse of support for whole language approaches, many teachers are making transitions from these practices to balanced literacy instruction. Many teachers feel that a balanced literacy perspective does a better job of empowering students and teachers, accomplished in part through the integration of such activities as reading in real books, teaching composition skills through the writing process, and speaking and listening experiences. These activities are often based on students' own experiences and are assumed to be inherently more stimulating. Preliminary research suggests that teachers and students in balanced literacy programs tend to perform very well indeed in comparison to those using traditional approaches (Wharton-McDonald et al., 1997).

We take a stance of moderation when it comes to making the transition to balanced literacy instruction, especially concerning (a) how quickly the transition is to occur, and (b) whether or not teachers can use some ideas borrowed from traditional and/or whole language perspectives (for us the answer is an emphatic *yes*). Our perspective, like the ideas we present in this book for building a balanced literacy classroom, was formed several years ago when we returned to full-time classroom teaching. We explored the use-

Balanced literacy programs help students become fluent readers, writers, listeners, and speakers of our language.

fulness of many of the balanced literacy program strategies suggested by leaders in the field. So as not to fall into the "throwing out the baby with the bath water syndrome," we also considered traditional and whole language strategies for teaching reading that might have value in a balanced literacy program. A major point of interest in our class-room experiences dealt with the challenges facing teachers moving from traditional and whole language forms of teaching to balanced literacy programs. As a result of these ex-periences, we feel that we have come to a better understanding of the debate between whole language, balanced literacy, and traditionalist positions.

MAKING TRANSITIONS TOWARD BALANCED LITERACY INSTRUCTION

A transitional approach asserts that teachers make changes by beginning from where they are and progressing to where they want to be. Thus, teachers springboard from current literacy methods to balanced literacy practices such as strategic assessment of bench-mark or "milestone" reading skills, teaching interactive writing, direct skill instruction in a variety of formats, the use of popular children's literature and leveled books, and guided reading groups. As teachers experience success with balanced literacy ap-proaches, a new spirit of adventure in teaching and learning enters the reading class-room. Several key elements of transitions are described in the paragraphs that follow.

Transitions Means Philosophical Movement

One aspect of transitions is the notion of *movement*. Over time, most teachers will gradually move toward more balanced literacy strategies and further away from depen-dence on the approaches of the past. Balanced literacy programs as described in this book and others (Fountas & Pinnell, 1996; Mooney, 1990; *Reading in Junior Classes,* 1985) have a long track record of success in English-speaking countries. As has been said so well, "Once you see it in action, you can't go back" (Esch, 1991, p. D1).

One reason the notion of *movement* is important is because it distinguishes the transitions approach from those commonly referred to as "eclectic" approaches. In an **eclectic approach,** teachers simply borrow elements from two or more approaches to create their own approach. Eclectic approaches frequently grow out of what is considered new or trendy, rather than being organized according to an articulated belief system and well-defined practices. Once designed, an eclectic approach is always changing; it is relatively fluid because it is at the mercy of fashion. Transitions approaches, on the other hand, change continuously too, but they inspire one forward in a defined direction—improved balanced literacy instruction and student success.

Eclectic approaches are "blended" programs that lack a consistent theoretical base.

Transitions Takes Time

Transitions means philosophical movement over time toward balanced literacy instruction.

Transitions is also about *time*—time to learn, explore, and grow professionally as a teacher of reading. A transitions position emphasizes and acknowledges the fact that teachers will make changes toward balanced literacy instruction in their own way and at their own rate. Rhonda Jenkins (1990), an Australian educational consultant, commented that teachers in the largest Australian school district were given a 10-year transitional period to learn how to change from traditional to more balanced reading and writing instruction. With this multiyear perspective in mind, one must reasonably expect that teachers will make transitions quietly, little by little, step by step, over a substantial period of time (Routman, 1988). As Lucy Calkins (1986) stated,

> We must remember that it is not the number of good ideas that turns our work [teaching] into an art, but the selection, balance, and design of those ideas. Instead of piling good teaching ideas into the classroom, we need to draw from all we know, feel, and believe in order to create something beautiful. (p. 9)

Transitions Involves Curriculum Integration

Balanced literacy teachers often integrate the language arts and content subject areas so as to deepen students' learning. Integration requires much planning, time, and skill to achieve. One well-known teacher, Regie Routman (1988), wrote about her own gradual transitions toward integrating her curriculum:

> At this point in time I am comfortable integrating the four language modes—listening, speaking, reading, and writing. . . . I don't always use thematic units; I occasionally teach from part to whole (instead of whole to parts to whole—*authors' note*); I am still struggling hard to integrate more areas of curriculum with the language arts—an ideal that is very difficult to attain. I anticipate that this struggle will go on for years. (p. 26)

Transitions Involves Risk Taking

Closely related to the notion of allowing teachers time to make changes at their own pace and in their own way is the recognition that *risks* are associated with making these changes. There is sometimes the feeling that one is "walking the tightrope without a net" when trying somewhat different ideas in the classroom. Silvia Ashton-Warner (1963) acknowledged the risks and frustration sometimes associated with making changes in reading instruction when she wrote:

> If only I had the confidence of being a good teacher. But I'm not even an appalling teacher. I don't claim to be a teacher at all. I'm just a nitwit somehow let loose among

children. If only I kept workbooks and made schemes and taught like other teachers I should have the confidence of numbers. It's the payment, the price of walking alone. . . . It's this price one continually pays for stepping out of line. . . . But I must do what I believe in or nothing at all. (p. 198)

Transitions teachers are supportive of each other and themselves. They build "safety nets" for themselves and others by understanding that transitions toward balanced literacy instruction take time and will not happen all at once. These safety nets are to be not only tolerated but also appreciated as a normal evolutionary step. The movement toward balanced literacy instruction is evolutionary—not revolutionary (Pearson, 1989c), meaning it won't happen overnight. One teacher gradually transitioning into her own balanced literacy program remarked,

Transitions teachers build "safety nets" for students as they make gradual curriculum changes.

The basal program acts like a safety net for me. I've used it successfully for years and I know that the curriculum objectives required by the school system will be met and documented when I use basal materials. But I do want *more* for my students. My transitions program allows me to keep my basal safety net while learning more about balanced literacy. This year I reduced my classroom time in the basal to only three days per week. That allowed me to begin to do more with the writing workshop, whole to parts to whole skill instruction, and children's literature. Next year, I plan to use the basal even less to allow for more balanced literacy practices. (Darlene DeCrane, Bowling Green, OH)

The Transitions Model: A Modest Proposal for Change

Regardless of how, when, where, what, or why teachers begin making transitions toward balanced literacy instruction, there are at least eight interrelated dimensions of this multifaceted process.

Figure 1.2 is a model that shows how transitions involve gradual change along the following dimensions: instructional beliefs, reading materials, curriculum design, instructional grouping, cultural diversity, assessment, classroom environments, and community involvement.

Eight interrelated dimensions are involved in transitions. These dimensions are discussed in detail in chapter 5.

1. Transitions in *instructional beliefs* may range from an initial "combative" stance regarding balanced literacy beliefs to the opposite end of the continuum— an "advocate's" stance.
2. Changes in the use of traditional *reading materials,* while acquiring more authentic instructional materials better fitted to the balanced teaching of reading, make up another dimension of transitions.
3. Teachers' *design of the reading curriculum* may change during transitions from emphasizing isolated skill drills in reading toward integrating reading skills instruction into the context of great books, varied texts (such as poetry, song, raps, and chants), and with the remainder of the school curriculum.
4. Teachers in transition often find themselves moving from a lot of whole-class teaching to such flexible *grouping* modes as needs-based, interest, research "clubs," cooperative learning groups, and, especially, guided reading groups.
5. Transitions in *community involvement* may range from classroom isolation to involving family members and other community stakeholders as important parts of reading instruction.
6. Transitions in *classroom learning environments* range from rigid institutional environments that limit student interactions to more homelike, "language friendly" environments for learning.

Figure 1.2 Dimensions of transitions: A model of change in reading instruction

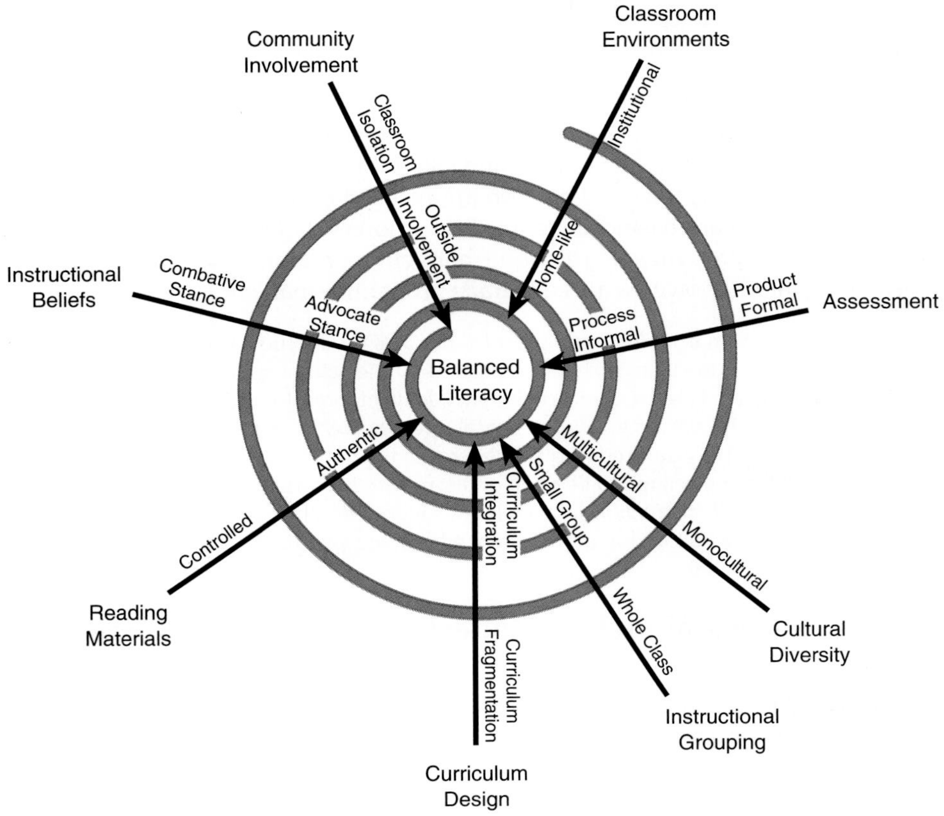

Community
Involvement

Classroom
Environments

Classroom
Isolation

Institutional

Outside
Involvement

Home-like

Instructional
Beliefs

Combative
Stance

Advocate
Stance

Process
Informal

Product
Formal

Assessment

Balanced
Literacy

Authentic

Multicultural

Controlled

Monocultural

Reading
Materials

Small Group

Whole Class

Cultural
Diversity

Curriculum
Integration

Curriculum
Fragmentation

Instructional
Grouping

Curriculum
Design

7. Transitions in cultural diversity involve a shift from what may be termed monocultural and monolingual views of society to a multicultural and multi-lingual outlook in the literacy-learning classroom.

8. Transitions in *assessment* range from *product only assessments*—formal assessments best represented by standardized achievement tests—to including *process assessments*—criterion assessments providing analyses of children's reading and writing development in specific skill areas.

The seven principles provide a springboard for teachers developing a belief system.

To begin making your transitions toward balanced literacy instruction, it is important to settle on a set of beliefs you can use to judge ideas about reading instruction and/or existing program elements. For experienced teachers, new teaching activities cannot be added until some of the more expendable program practices currently in place are eliminated from the busy school schedule. For new teachers, a belief system helps them screen new ideas for "goodness of fit" with balanced literacy program goals.

We have assembled a list of **seven principles for supporting literacy development** for this purpose, along with a description of each. Although this list may not be exhaustive, it should serve as a starting place for teachers to develop their own system of beliefs. We begin with our goal statement, then continue with a list of principles that help us select components for a balanced literacy program.

Seven
Principles
For Supporting Literacy Development

The primary goal of Balanced Reading Programs is to help all students become independent, fluent readers in the early education years, then help them expand their literacy abilities throughout their schooling. This goal has now been adopted by school districts throughout the United States and implies that we have a vision of "every classroom as good as our best." It is accomplished by adhering to the seven principles outlined on these pages.

Principle
one

Begin with the teacher's knowledge of student reading processes. A great deal of research has been amassed over the years that collectively describes stages and milestone skills associated with reading and writing development. A knowledge of these milestones in literacy development becomes the bedrock upon which all learning and assessment activities are constructed and offered to students.

Rely on process and product student assessments that link directly to the knowledge base of reading. Assessment informs our teaching and makes it possible to group children efficiently and effectively according to their learning needs. Classroom assessment should examine students' literacy processes as well as products. Assessment should be used to encourage the learner about his or her progress, not merely to document scores for accountability purposes.

Best assessments are conducted over time and compare students' past and present abilities. This is accomplished partly through the accumulation of numerous learning artifacts using multiple methods of collection. This view of assessment provides a comprehensive view of the learner's progress (Farr & Tone, 1994; B. Hill & Ruptic, 1994).

Principle **three**

Involve families in support of the reading development process.
Parents and other primary care-givers have a profound influence on the development of their child's reading ability. They must be encouraged to become active participants and supporters in creating and maintaining homes that stimulate literacy growth (Rasinski & Fredericks, 1988). Family members can support learning initiated in the classroom in numerous and enjoyable ways. Parents should be encouraged and supported in their roles as "first teachers."

Support Reading To, With, and By students. *Reading To, With, and By* (Mooney, 1990) is a flexible and practical model for instruction that can be useful in creating balanced literacy programs (Reutzel & Cooter, 1999). This model has embedded within it key strands of teaching, including skill instruction and practice, instructional level reading routines, oral reading by students and teachers alike, massive but pleasurable amounts of reading practice, and a great deal of writing instruction and composition. The key practices that occur daily are as follows:

Reading TO Children—Every student is read to each day by a masterful reader. This can take the form of teacher read alouds, reading one to one by a peer or adult, or what is sometimes called "lap reading," most often with a family member.

Reading WITH Children—The teacher reads with students daily. This commonly occurs in small groups during a guided reading session (Fountas & Pinnell, 1996), in "House Calls" wherein the teacher visits one to one with students, in large group choral reading sessions, or during shared reading experiences.

Reading BY Children—Children should have daily independent reading opportunities. It may simply be a time set aside during the day for twenty or so minutes of pleasure reading (i.e., Drop Everything and Read, or "DEAR" time; Sustained Silent Reading, or "SSR"), or it may be in the form of performance reading, as with a Readers' Theater group. Sometimes students read to each other in a buddy or assisted reading period—for instance, a second grader reading to a fifth grade partner once a week.

Principle
five

Integrate the development of reading with writing instruction and composition. In our own classroom experiences, as well as in our work with large urban school districts, we have seen firsthand the power of teaching writing as an essential element of reading instruction. Students who become writers rapidly improve as readers. When learning spelling strategies (part of the *editing* stage), for instance, students learn phonetic elements in words much more easily and become better decoders of words in print when reading.

Similarly, as students learn story grammar elements (e.g., setting, characterization, challenges, resolution, etc.), their reading comprehension soars. Teachers establishing balanced literacy programs see writing instruction as indispensable and embed it within daily teaching routines.

Principle
SIX

Develop reading and writing skills via "whole-to-parts-to-whole" instruction. Children learning to become better readers must be helped to learn certain aspects of print (Sulzby, 1985, 1991). However, that does not mean that instruction in such areas as phonics or comprehension should focus on these elements isolated from meaningful text (e.g., traditional skill and drill instruction). To teach in this way often confuses children as to what real reading is all about and fails to connect the new skills with the reading act (Durkin, 1981b). For example, if reading instruction begins with the reading of meaningful text, the skill to be learned could be taught within the context of the story.

In the final stages of learning, the reading skill or strategy should be taken back into reading and reapplied in other contexts (U.S. Department of Education, 1985). This *whole-to-parts-to-whole* way of teaching skills helps students understand the relevance and usefulness of what they have learned.

Principle
seven

Address the needs of *all* children. A balanced reading program will ensure that most students attain reading fluency; typically, however, some students with special learning needs may require some program modifications. Whether due to physical, language, cultural, or other factors, *all* children should have flexible, quality instruction in the regular classroom. Classroom teachers receive support from reading specialists and special education teachers so that children can escape the stigma of "pullout" programs and enjoy cooperative learning opportunities with peers. A successful balanced literacy program includes all children, recognizing that all students benefit from classroom diversity in ways that carry into adulthood.

CHALLENGES FACING PRESERVICE TEACHERS IN MAKING TRANSITIONS

Preservice teachers, or those studying to become elementary school teachers, face special challenges in developing balanced literacy instruction. Challenges facing preservice teachers are quite different from those of **in-service teachers** (those currently serving as classroom teachers). Preservice hurdles that can be addressed through the transitions approach include the following:

- Disharmony with past belief systems
- Conflicting views among educators
- Overcoming tradition in the schools

Disharmony with Past Belief Systems

Everyone who has ever attended elementary school has some preconceived notions about what reading instruction is supposed to be. To maintain an open mind and overcome mistaken biases based on past experiences, preservice teachers can do at least two things: They should find out what beliefs they currently hold, and then carefully review alternative philosophies and methods for teaching reading. This book is organized to facilitate this process. Once preservice teachers know what they know (and don't know), it becomes easier to begin making mental transitions toward new philosophies and strategies for teaching reading. It is important to remember that (a) everyone holds biases about teaching and learning, either consciously or unconsciously, and (b) we should keep an open mind about teaching children until all possibilities have been explored.

Conflicting Views Among Educators

Another challenge for preservice teachers is the reality that not all educators agree as to the best ways of teaching reading. For example, it is quite possible for students to take college courses from professors whose classroom experiences were very traditional and who feel movement toward balanced literacy programs is not desirable. An important thing to remember is that colleges are organized, ideally, to present many different viewpoints. The purpose of collegiate work is education, not indoctrination. Maintaining an open mind is important if preservice teachers are to become as well informed and effective as they need to be.

Overcoming Tradition in the Schools

Another obstacle is the feeling of inertia or tradition in schools. Many preservice teachers who are practice teaching in schools are intimidated and feel that they are know-nothings. Although it is true that preservice teachers, by definition, lack experience, it is not true that they are uneducated or cannot have useful insights. Preservice teachers are necessarily part of the change process occurring in schools today. Many classroom teachers and administrators are still learning about balanced literacy programs; preservice teachers play an important role in helping other educators stay current and begin their own transitions. Preservice teachers should be seen as change agents who contribute to the improvement of schools while gaining much needed experience from seasoned educators. When

Preservice teachers are people studying to become elementary school teachers.

In-service teachers are educators currently practicing the profession.

Educators often hold differing views of learning and teaching.

Preservice teachers contribute much to the cause of improving reading instruction.

viewed in this way, preservice and in-service teachers become true professional colleagues who can assist each other in making transitions toward balanced literacy instruction.

CHALLENGES FACING IN-SERVICE TEACHERS

Unlike preservice teachers, in-service teachers have had time to get used to the responsibilities associated with daily classroom teaching. The initial feelings of uncertainty have been replaced with a strong desire to find more effective ways of helping children become literate. As in-service teachers begin the process of moving into transitions, they almost immediately become aware of obstacles that can zap one's creative energies unless they are recognized and addressed. Most common hurdles for practicing teachers are related to the following:

- Time commitment
- Comfort zones
- Administrative risk taking

Time Commitment

In-service teachers make significant time commitments when moving into transitions.

Many reading teachers complain that transitions programs require a great time commitment in the early stages. For example, in addition to reading current professional books pertaining to balanced literacy programs (a short list is recommended at the end of this chapter), many teachers need to become better acquainted with popular children's literature, pull together instructional resources (e.g., literacy materials centers), assemble teacher-made books and bulletin boards, order trade books and big books (for primary levels), review computer software and other technology, and perhaps design thematic units. (Note: These and many other teaching ideas are discussed fully in later chapters.)

Teachers also need to find ways of aligning performance objectives required by the school district and state with their own research-based notions of what the curriculum should include. Without a doubt, transitions programs require significant planning time, especially the first few years. But once teachers are off and running, balanced literacy programs become relatively easy to maintain and modify. More importantly, the enjoyment both teachers and children experience in balanced literacy programs makes the effort worthwhile.

Comfort Zones

Another problem is that of comfort zones. That is, it is often difficult to get teachers who have been practicing their profession for even a few years to begin something as different and challenging as making transitions toward balanced literacy instruction. (In chapter 5, we review various attitudinal stances through which teachers seem to evolve as they make changes in the classroom environment.) Ultimately, teachers who continue to experiment and update their teaching strategies throughout their careers tend to have greater success with student development and performance, usually experience fewer discipline problems in these energized classrooms, and enjoy the teaching profession rather than burn out.

Administrative Risk Taking

Finally, a certain amount of administrative risk taking is involved whenever new program changes are considered. Many wonderful, innovative elementary principals are very supportive of classroom change. Some principals (like some teachers), however, are somewhat resistant to change. Successful teachers making transitions view as part of the process the necessity of educating administrators—"bringing them along" concerning how they are modifying their classrooms and why. They find ways to make the administrator part of the classroom family by inviting him or her into the classroom frequently and letting him or her become meaningfully involved with children in balanced literacy activities. It is important to remember that most people become teachers because they like to be around children; principals are simply teachers who have administrative assignments (the term *principal* comes from the title *principal teacher*). Giving your administrator "hands-on" opportunities with transitions will help inform him or her about your new literacy goals and build positive and supportive relationships.

Administrators in transitions schools join teachers and students in becoming risk takers.

Concept Applications

In the Classroom

1. Outline your reading and language arts block schedule or that of a teacher whom you have interviewed. Would you characterize this schedule as favoring a more traditional, basal-oriented approach, or does it include a number of balanced literacy program elements? Hint: Use the *seven principles for supporting literacy development* to validate your judgment if you feel the schedule favors balanced literacy practices.
2. Consider your teaching environment (resources, principal's attitude, school board and central office policies, etc.) or that of an in-service colleague. What are some of the potential "comfort zones"? Will some administrative risk taking be required to facilitate transitions toward balanced literacy teaching? Explain.
3. Draw up a comprehensive list of activities you are currently using in your classroom or those that you plan to use. Next, construct an evaluation checklist using the *seven principles for supporting literacy development* as a guide. Evaluate each of your classroom activities using the seven principles as the standard. Which of your activities qualify under one or more categories? Do any activities fail to meet any of the principles? If so, what should you do? (Possibly you will need to create some new principles!)

Recommended Readings

Au, K. H. (1993). *Literacy instruction in multicultural settings.* Fort Worth, TX: Harcourt Brace.
Fountas, I., & Pinnell, G. S. (1996). *Guided reading.* Portsmouth, NH: Heinemann.
Reutzel, D. R., & Cooter, R. B. (1999). *Balanced reading strategies and practices: Assessing and assisting readers with special needs.* Upper Saddle River, NJ: Merrill/Prentice Hall.

Understanding Reading:

Focus Questions

When you are finished studying this chapter, you should be able to answer these questions:

1. What can be said about the need for reading in our society today and in the future?
2. Why should teachers study and understand the reading process?
3. What are three major learning theories that can be linked to four models of the reading process?
4. What are three reading models that can be linked to three sets of reading instructional practices?
5. Which of the reading instructional practices do you currently believe should be used to teach children to read and why?

The Theoretical Roots
of Instruction

Key Concepts

Aliteracy
Behaviorism
Bottom-Up Reading Model
Subskills Reading Instruction
Cognitivism
Gestaltist Theory

Interactive Reading Model
Skills Reading Instruction
Automaticity
Constructivism
Transactional Reading Model
Balanced Literacy Instruction

Television, newspapers, and magazines boldly proclaim society's failure to develop and sustain literacy as an enticing and rewarding enterprise for both youth and adults. Although many statistics declare that 23 to 25 million Americans cannot read at a functional level, the greater tragedy lies in the fact that many Americans can read but choose not to do so (Chisom, 1989; Kozol, 1985). This problem, called **aliteracy,** is one of increasing concern to corporate leaders and educators alike.

READING IN TODAY'S SOCIETY: A SKETCH OF THE PROBLEM

A large number of adults in the United States were found to be illiterate in a 1993 report issued by Secretary of Education Riley. In addition to these numbers, one must consider the increasing numbers of immigrants who are admitted to the United States on a daily basis (Greaney, 1994; Slavin & Maddin, 1995). Compounding the literacy demands on our society is our passing from an Industrial Age to an Information Age, requiring ever-increasing demands for more sophisticated literacy skills (Bronfenbrenner, McClelland, Wethington, Moen, & Ceci, 1996; Stedman & Kaestle, 1987). In the report *Who Reads Best* (Educational Testing Service, 1988), 55% of low achievers in reading claimed they had access to few reading materials in their homes, revealing a severe lack of support for reading in many homes. Thirty-three percent of low achievers in third grade claimed to read for fun only on a monthly basis or even less frequently. Nineteen percent of this same population claimed they had never read a book just for fun in school or out. Similarly, of adults questioned, only 23% claimed they had read a book in the previous year (Meade, 1973).

E. D. Hirsch (1987), in his book *Cultural Literacy*, claimed that not only do people fail to choose to read, but also their reading experiences in schools have focused so heavily on the development of skills that the transmission of culturally relevant content has been largely ignored. Ravitch and Finn (1987) explain why schools have opted for the teaching of skills rather than content:

Teaching reading as skills risks offending no one, but teachers who choose books or poems may run the risk of offending someone.

> Unlike skill training, teaching the humanities requires people to make choices. Deciding what content to teach risks offending some group or individual, those who prefer a different version of history or different works of literature. How much easier, then, to teach social studies as skills rather than as history, offending practically no one; how much easier to teach the skills of language arts, to fill in blanks and circle words, rather than to bear the burden of selecting particular poems, plays, short stories, and novels and to have to figure out how to make them meaningful. (p. 8)

During the first-grade reading instruction period, children read connected text only about 7 to 8 minutes per day, whereas they spend 49 minutes per day completing worksheets.

In *Becoming a Nation of Readers* (R. C. Anderson, Hiebert, Scott, & Wilkinson, 1985), the Commission on Reading reported that the average amount of time devoted to sustained reading of connected text in the typical first-grade reading instructional period was only 7 to 8 minutes. Forty-nine minutes, or about 50 to 70% of the reading instructional time, were spent in independent seat work completing worksheets (Rupley & Blair, 1987). The impact of the school on reading achievement continues to accumulate. Reading achievement of children in somewhat affluent suburban schools is significantly and consistently higher than that of children in "disadvantaged" urban schools (NAEP, 1995). For example, in one large urban center having approximately 85% of the student population identified as coming from poverty level families, only 37% of the children could read on level at the end of third grade.

Although the preceding information paints a somewhat discouraging picture of literacy in schools and out, all is not lost. Between 45% and 48% of children in grades 3 and 4 report they read on their own for fun on a daily basis. These percentages, however, shrivel to half that number, 24%, in 12th grade (Educational Testing Service, 1988; National Assessment of Educational Progress, 1990, 1995). These data come to light just as societal trends move us rapidly away from smokestack industries toward information-service industries. Our country is quickly becoming one of the largest providers of information services; thus, today's children are growing up in an information age in which reading and writing play a central and critical role both economically and socially (Snow, Burns, & Griffin, 1998). Literacy cannot be oversold in today's economic marketplace. Now as never before, teachers need to understand how children develop into successful readers and writers. More importantly, teachers need to know how they can help children accomplish this goal in their youth and sustain it into adulthood.

THE NEED FOR UNDERSTANDING HOW CHILDREN LEARN TO READ

On one occasion, Frank Smith (1985), a well-known literacy authority, was asked by an exasperated group of teachers just what he would do if he had to teach 30 youngsters to read. He asserted that children have a right to learn to read from *people* rather than from *programs.* Beyond this statement, his response included two valuable insights. First, teachers must clearly comprehend the *general process of how children learn and develop as learners.* Second, teachers must understand the *specific processes of how young children* <u>learn to read.</u>

How *do* young children become readers? This question is likely to provoke a flood of very different and sometimes emotionally charged responses. We asked our students in university teacher preparation courses to respond to this question in their reflection journals. Here is a sampling of their responses.

Reflect on how you learned to read and how you were taught to read in school.

"Little children start learning to read by being read aloud to."

"Kids learn to read from their parents and brothers and sisters."

"I remember learning the sounds of the alphabet letters and discovering how they made words."

"I remember memorizing a favorite book and reading it again and again until the letters and words made sense to me."

"Writing, that's how I learned to read. I asked my Mom how to write my name. That led to more questions about how to write other words and the names of other people."

Next, we asked our students to define *reading.* Here is a sampling of their ideas.

"I think reading is when you make the sounds of the letters and put them together to make words."

"Reading is understanding what is on the page."

"I learned to read from a little book with stories that used the same words over and over."

"Phonics is the first part of reading and comprehension is the last."

"Reading is the ability to put together what you know and what is on the page to understand."

"Reading is tracking the author's footprints in the sand along the beaches of the mind."

Of course, these responses led us to pose several additional questions to our students: What are the aspects involved in the reading process? Are there different beliefs on how children *learn* to read? Are there different beliefs on how children should be *taught* to read? How do these differ? These are critical issues on which to reflect.

Developing a belief system about how students learn to read and write begins with putting theories into practice.

Frankly, your definition and beliefs about how reading ability develops will influence the way you assist children in learning to read. Consequently, the remainder of this chapter is intended to help you understand and define various views on how children learn to read and, as a consequence of views or theories on how reading is learned, how reading should be taught.

READING THEORIES AND THEIR RELATIONSHIP TO READING INSTRUCTION

Focus on several ways theory can be practical.

Theories explain the beliefs teachers and researchers hold about how developing readers use parts of the reading process to become proficient. All instruction is theoretically based, but the theories from which teachers make instructional decisions are often implicitly held; *this means that teachers' theories are seldom examined or explained at a conscious level* (DeFord, 1985; Gove, 1983; Harste & Burke, 1977). Frequently, the mere mention of the word *theory* may cause teachers to dismiss valuable information as *impractical.* On the other hand, Moffett and Wagner (1976) assert that nothing is so practical as a good theory. Teachers, whether consciously or unconsciously, consistently use theories in their classrooms to make instructional decisions among various alternatives to help children become successful readers.

By definition, "a theory is a system of ideas, often stated as a principle, to explain or to lead to a new understanding" (T. L. Harris & Hodges, 1981, p. 329). Major theories of the reading process, at least for our discussion, are grouped into three categories: (a) behaviorism, (b) cognitivism, and (c) constructivism. These three categories of learning theories represent different and somewhat unique ideas used by teachers and researchers to explain the reading process. It is important to realize that these theories have been neither proven nor unproven; they are simply alternative ways of explaining the process of learning to read. They have led researchers to develop various models or verbal and visual descriptions of the reading process. And these same theories have led teachers to a variety of beliefs about instructional choices (curriculum and instructional methods) that relate to helping children develop successful reading strategies.

In the sections that follow, we describe behaviorism, cognitivism, and constructivism. We show how these theories of learning in turn relate to models of the reading process. Finally, we connect these models of the reading process with teachers' choices of classroom practices. We believe by making the link between *theory* and *practice* explicit, we can help teachers come to realize that all instructional choices are derived from personally held *theories* about learning and *models* of the reading process. Teachers who know how theory and practice relate are able to make informed connections between the process of learning to read and instructional choices for teaching children to read.

List two reasons why knowing reading theories helps teachers know how to help children more effectively.

Behaviorism and a Parts-to-Whole Bottom-Up Reading Process

The first American school of thought about learning psychology was the product of John B. Watson known as **behaviorism.** Behaviorists viewed learning as a causal chain of events where a *stimulus* caused a particular *response* in the subject or person, and this response was either strengthened or weakened through reinforcement. In addition, a fundamental scientific idea all behaviorists accept is that complex phenomena must be analyzed into their simpler parts before they can be understood.

One of the first to test the behaviorists' theoretical beliefs was a Russian experimental psychologist named Pavlov. During his lifetime, Pavlov (1848–1936) provided an impressive demonstration of the use of stimulus response relationships known as *classical conditioning.* In the course of his physiological studies of digestion, Pavlov observed that his experimental subjects, dogs, came to salivate when the sound of a neutral stimulus, say a bell, and food were repeatedly paired together. It was concluded from this work that learning was essentially a conditioned response to a stimulus. Later, B. F. Skinner, an American experimental psychologist, identified the elements of *operant conditioning* in work with pigeons, rats, and even his own children. The concept of *operant* stems from the idea that a learner must "operate" on his or her environment; this means that the learner must work or exert effort to learn. Skinner discovered that by rewarding or reinforcing a rat with food each time it pressed a bar in the *Skinner Box* or cage, the rate of presses increased dramatically. The rat had learned the response (pressing the bar), as a result of the reinforcement (food).

In behaviorist theories of learning as related to the reading process, the *stimulus* for reading is the print on the page. Thus, the reader begins with the letters on the page and constructs more complex levels of language: words, sentences, and paragraphs. In this process of stringing together letters into words, words into sentences, and sentences into paragraphs, readers glean the meaning from the print. In a very real sense, behaviorist learning theories describe learning to read as a **bottom-up** reading model: progressing from the *parts* of language (letters) to the *whole* (meaning). Much like solving a jigsaw puzzle, behaviorist theories predict that the reading puzzle is solved by beginning with an examination of each piece of the puzzle and putting them together to make a picture.

One of the earliest bottom-up models of the reading process was the substrata model of Holmes (1953) and Singer (1960). Two other bottom-up models of the reading process associated with behaviorist theories of learning remain popular even today: *One Second of Reading* by Gough (1972) and *A Theory of Automatic Information Processing* by LaBerge and Samuels (1974).

Notice some weaknesses associated with two of the earliest models representing the bottom-up theoretical position.

Gough's (1972) *One Second of Reading* model described how print is processed by entering the mind through the *eyes*, is acted on by the mind in a serial, left-to-right sequence of language processing at several levels of language: first letters, then sounds, then word or concept identification, followed by sentence-construction rules or grammar, and, finally, constructing meaning from the array of visual stimuli. In this model, meaning is produced by Merlin, a magical entity. The presence of Merlin in this behaviorist explanation of the reading process punctuates the magical or unknown nature of deriving meaning from text. In short, the *One Second of Reading* model represents reading as a sequential process moving from the parts of words to the eventual and somewhat magical construction of meaning from the print on the page.

In their reading model, LaBerge and Samuels (1974) describe a concept known as *automatic information processing.* This concept of **automaticity** can be separated into two distinct processes in reading, decoding and comprehension. This model of the reading process hypothesizes that the human mind functions much like a computer, and that visual input is serially and sequentially entered into the mind of the reader. Almost without exception, humans have the ability to perform more than one task at a time. This ability is known as *parallel processing* when applied to computers. Because each computer, and by comparison, the human mind, has a limited capacity available for job sharing, computer or mental attention must be shifted from one job to another. If one job requires a large portion of the available computer attentional capacity, then capacity for another job is limited. This model of the reading process asserts that, like a computer, the mind of the reader has limited attentional capacity for doing parallel jobs.

*The term **automaticity** suggests that readers have limited attention capacity that can be shifted rapidly between the parallel processes of decoding and comprehension.*

The term *automaticity* suggests that readers have limited attention capacity that must be shifted rapidly between the parallel processes of decoding and comprehension. If readers are bogged down in decoding, they will not be able to shift attention to focus on comprehending.

An example is the novice reader who struggles reading each word on the page. She focuses her limited attentional capacity on pronouncing the words. In this situation, attention cannot be shifted to comprehending the message, so she fails to understand the author's message. Like the novice reader, young children just learning to ride a bike focus so intently on balancing, turning the handlebars, and pedaling that attention is unavailable for focusing on concerns about direction, potential dangers, and warnings. Similarly, a reader who is a poor decoder focuses attentional ca-

Figure 2.1 Behaviorist or bottom-up model of the reading process

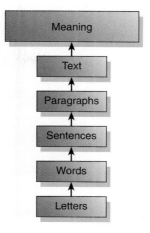

pacity on decoding, which leaves little or no attention for comprehending, and the reading act "crashes," in a manner of speaking.

In contrast, children who are accomplished bike riders can ride without hands, carry on a conversation with a friend, dodge a pothole in the road, and chew gum at the same time. Like the accomplished bike rider, the fluent reader can rapidly shift attention to processing the message when decoding no longer demands too much attention. In short, the LaBerge and Samuels (1974) model predicts that if reading can occur automatically or without too much focus on the decoding process, then improved comprehension will be the result. Behaviorist, or a bottom-up, model of the reading process is represented in Figure 2.1. You may notice that this model begins by emphasizing the importance of the features of the print or stimulus in the reading event (i.e., letters, words, etc.). Important features of this learning theory and reading model are summarized in the left-hand column of Figure 2.3 (see p. 35). Teachers who believe that behaviorist theories adequately explain how children become readers often teach reading as a group of skills or subskills, beginning with letter names and sounds, to be mastered one at a time.

The Relationship of Behaviorism to Subskills or Phonics-First Reading Instruction

According to reading theorists Harste and Burke (1977) and Weaver (1994), phonics, decoding emphasis, or **subskills reading instruction** is depicted as a pyramid, with understanding sound/symbol relationships (the parts of language) at the base and comprehension (the meaning or whole of language) as the capstone. Chall (1979, 1983), a strong proponent of a subskills instructional model, characterizes the first stage of reading development as the initial reading or decoding stage. She describes what children must learn during the first stage of reading development.

> The essential aspect of *Stage One* is learning the arbitrary set of letters and associating these with the corresponding parts of spoken words [phonics]. . . . The qualitative change that occurs at the end of this stage is the insight gained about the nature of the spelling system of the particular alphabetic language used. (Chall, 1979, p. 39)

Subskill teachers, whether they realize it or not, also base their instruction on behaviorist theories and typically focus on systematically teaching children letter-sound

Phonics is the foundation of reading in the subskills model with comprehension as the capstone.

Instruction under a subskills model begins with the letters of the alphabet and the sounds these letters represent.

Figure 2.2 Phonics-first or subskills reading instruction.

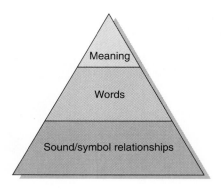

relationships during the earliest stages of reading instruction. Because the most important skill to be learned in early reading is the ability to *recode* the letters of print into the sounds of speech, letter-name and letter-sound instruction often precede allowing children to read words or books independently (as in programs such as CHAR-L or *Intensive Phonics*). Although comprehension is also important in a phonics-first or subskills instructional approach, the ability to comprehend is thought to depend largely on the ability to translate written words into oral language. In effect, the subskills instructional model (shown in Figure 2.2) represents the belief that efficient decoding directly leads to comprehension ability.

Subskills teachers believe that children must be taught phonics first via the letters of the alphabet and the sounds these letters represent *before* beginning to read books independently. Flesch (1955, 1979), among others, cautions that allowing children to attempt to read words or books without knowing the 26 letters and the 44 sounds they represent could lead to reading failure and frustration. Thus, letter names and letter sounds become the basic building blocks of reading within a subskills instructional approach. The use of supplemental or external phonics programs along with phonically controlled (decodable) readers often characterizes the components of this instructional approach. Early books or primers are often made up of words that follow the phonic generalizations the children have been learning, such as short vowel words like *can, man, fan.* This method is well illustrated in the *Becoming a Nation of Readers* report: "The important point is that a high proportion of the words in the earliest selections children read should conform to the phonics they have already been taught" (R. C. Anderson et al., 1985, p. 47). This argument has recently surfaced again in calls for the production and use of "decodable texts" or phonics readers in states like California and Texas.

Finally, teachers who believe in phonics-first or subskills instruction often consider a lack of decoding ability or phonics knowledge to be the fundamental cause of reading disability. Thus, teachers who believe in a behaviorist theory of the reading process tend to make decisions that result in subskills instructional practices. They believe that they can best help young nonreaders learn to read by directly and systematically teaching them to decode letters to sounds, and sounds to words, which are then matched with words in each child's oral vocabulary. Once decoding is mastered, meaning can be derived from the print on the page by referring to one's knowledge of word meanings and oral language. And finally, teachers who make instructional decisions based on a behaviorist theory of the reading process believe that reading skill is built from the smallest parts of language to the whole.

Figure 2.3 summarizes the instructional process associated with subskills instruction as well as the connection between *behaviorist theories* and subskills instructional decisions. Note that *behaviorism* suggests that in order for language to be

Subskills models assume the primary cause of reading disability to be the inability to decode.

Figure 2.3 Theory-driven reading instruction: Behaviorist theories and subskill reading instructional practice

Behaviorist Theories of the Reading Process Reflect a Bottom-up Reading Model

• During reading and learning to read, language is processed from the parts to the whole, as in building a structure from blocks one at a time.
• Learning to read is based on Stimulus–Response chains posited by behaviorists.
• Learning to read is accomplished by reducing the skill of reading to its smallest parts to be mastered one at a time.
• Repetition in reading is focused on practicing the parts of the complex skill of reading to a level of overlearning or automaticity.
• Language stimuli for reading are carefully controlled to represent consistently identified language rules or patterns to be learned.
• Mastery of the smallest parts of reading is assumed to lead to competent understanding and performance of the whole act of reading.
• Automatic decoding of the smallest parts of language is a prerequisite to reading and comprehending connected texts or books.
• Correctness is expected; mistakes are to be corrected.
• Pronouncing words provides access to one's speaking vocabulary to enable comprehension.
• Comprehending words provides access to new vocabulary words and comprehension of text.

Subskills Instructional Approach

• Reading instruction is begun by learning the 26 letters and the 44 sounds.
• Instruction proceeds to demonstrate the association(s) between the 26 letters and the 44 sounds.
• Blending the sounds represented by the letters in a word from left-to-right in temporal sequence or "sounding out" phonically regular words is taught.
• A limited number of high-frequency sight words are taught.
• Texts composed of carefully controlled words that are either known sight words or are phonically regular words are introduced to children for reading practice.
• More phonic patterns, rules, and generalizations are taught and learned.
• Texts are controlled to include new words as application for the patterns, rules, or generalizations learned.
• Control over text is gradually released, allowing phonically irregular words.
• Comprehending text is a direct outgrowth from the ability to pronounce words.

Figure 2.4 The Rubin vase

learned and processed, it must be analyzed into its smallest parts and learned from the parts to the whole. Observe the connection to practice as shown in subskills instructional choices: Subskill teachers begin reading and writing instruction by teaching each of the parts of language as a prerequisite to reading words, sentences, and stories. Notice how the theory of controlling text language results in instructional practices that limit students' exposure to those words that are phonically regular and follow specific phonic generalizations. Finally, notice that it is assumed that if a child masters decoding, then comprehension will automatically follow. Through this cursory examination, one can readily see how this theory relates to and influences classroom reading instructional practices.

Cognitivism and the Interactive Reading Process

Cognitive interactive reading theories place equal emphasis on the role of a reader's prior knowledge and the importance of the print on the page.

Cognitivism is an extension of the previously discussed theories associated with behaviorism, with one important distinction: Cognitivism as a theory attempts to understand and explain how the process of meaning is derived from the stimulus and the experiences of the reader rather than leaving this part of the reading process to mystery, the black box, or Merlin, as discussed previously. Cognitivist theories of the reading process place an equal emphasis on the role of a reader's prior knowledge (what the child knows and has experienced) and on the print (what is on the page). In many respects, cognitivism is a reaction to the constant tension among theorists over pure behaviorist theories of reading. Some theorists believed that one's prior knowledge and experience play as important a role as does print in the reading process. These theorists subscribed to **Gestaltist** psychological views, which became popular in America in the early 1960s. To understand the Gestaltist position, consider the classic example in Figure 2.4.

Gestaltists do not believe people respond passively to physical stimuli like books or stories by simply taking what is displayed in print into their minds.

What did you see? Did you see the vase? Or did you see two persons facing each other? How did you decide to attend to one or the other interpretation of the picture? Did you notice that the stimulus did not change, but your perception of the stimulus did change?

Otto (1982) states that Gestaltist views reconceptualized both the nature of the stimulus and the role of the subject in interpreting the stimulus. According to this theory, stimuli, such as texts, are processed from the whole to the parts. First, the sum

Figure 2.5 Gestaltist or top-down theory reflected in a model of the reading process

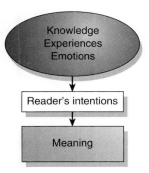

or whole of a text is perceived. Then, one perceives the parts of the stimulus: Sentences, words, and letters are affected by the perception of the whole. People do not respond passively to physical stimuli like books or stories by simply taking what is displayed into their minds. Rather, they actively organize and interpret stimuli. Because the whole of a stimulus influences the perception of the parts, gestaltists claim that the whole is greater than the sum of the parts.

Reading can be viewed similarly. Although reading is composed of several important aspects (e.g., cognitive, affective, and linguistic), these aspects combine in such a way as to be both different from and greater than the sum of the individual aspects of reading. For example, when one reads, the words do not have meaning; rather, the reader brings personal meaning to the text from background experiences. Word, sentence, and text meaning are conditioned, influenced, or shaped by the whole set of experiences and knowledge the reader brings to reading, rather than the text jumping off the page into the reader's head and providing the mind with meaning.

Gestaltist or top-down theories imply that the information and experiences the reader brings to the print drive the reading process rather than the print on the page. In other words, reading begins with the reader's knowledge, not the text. Reading is a meaning-construction process, not merely a process of carefully attending to visual clues or stimuli in the text. Gestaltist theory is represented in Figure 2.5.

To better understand how reading can be driven by a reader's background knowledge rather than by the print, read a few lines from the well-known poem "Jabberwocky," by Lewis Carroll (1872).

'Twas brillig, and the slithy toves
Did gyre and gimble in the wabe;
All mimsy were the borogoves,
And the mome raths outgrabe.

Beware the Jabberwock, my son!
The jaws that bite, the claws that catch!
Beware the Jubjub bird, and shun
The frumious Bandersnatch!

Clearly, one cannot read or understand this poem by simply pronouncing the words on the page or attending more carefully to the visual stimuli on the page. As readers, we invoke all that we know about jaws, claws, and birds to deduce that the Jabberwock is some kind of creature. We also use all of our accumulated knowledge about grammar and language to determine that the Jabberwock is a thing, not an action or a description.

Figure 2.6 Cognitive or interactive model of the reading process

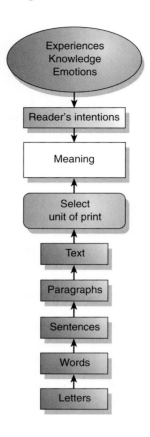

Although these demonstrations are useful illustrations and argue at least partly for Gestaltist reading theories, several authors contend that there can be no pure Gestalt readers (P. C. Burns, Roe, & Ross, 1992; J. L. Vacca, R. Vacca, & Gove, 1995). Readers *must* attend to the print at some point in the reading process as well as use their entire set of background experiences and knowledge to understand the message.

As theorists came to understand the reading process in greater depth, it was clear that neither the Gestaltist nor the behaviorist theories could adequately explain the complexity of the reading process. As a consequence, cognitivists developed **interactive** theories in which the strengths of both Gestalt and behaviorist theories were combined while at the same time minimizing weaknesses associated with either single theory. In short, an interactive theory is a combination theory, as shown in Figure 2.6.

Cognitive or interactive theories of reading are drawn from cognitive psychology and represent a combination of behaviorist and Gestaltist theories.

A cognitive or interactive reading model proposes that readers begin by hypothesizing about the text based on their prior experience while simultaneously processing the print. Readers can begin with print and progress toward meaning or begin with meaning and support their selection of meaning by sampling the print. Processing print information in this manner seems to be most economical in terms of time and resources because elements from both behaviorist and Gestaltist reading theories are combined in interactive theories of reading. From the interactionist's perspective, readers must integrate an array of information sources from the text and from their background experiences to construct a valid interpretation of the author's message. During this processing of text, readers take on active and passive roles (J. L. Vacca et. al., 1995). If readers possess a great deal of prior knowledge about a given text, then they will be more likely to form reasonable hypotheses about the text and, thus, require fewer print clues in reading. This is viewed as an active approach to reading. However, if readers know very little about a specific text, then they take on a passive role, relying more heavily on the information on the printed page, because the absence of prior knowledge limits their ability to predict ahead of the print. For example, many of us have no trouble reading the following passage because we possess the prior knowledge of a birthday party.

CODY'S BIG DAY

Today was Cody's birthday. He was 5 years old, big enough to go to kindergarten that fall. His mother had planned a sledding party up the canyon on the gently sloping foothills of the rugged mountains above. The sun shone brightly that day, and all the children had fun riding their sleds down the slopes. After the sledding party, Cody and his friends played games and opened presents. To top off the party, the boys and girls ate pizza, ice cream and cake. That night Cody went to bed as happy as any little boy could be.

Now, read the following passage. Because you probably know very little about this topic, you may depend more heavily on the text to help you construct the meaning.

But we must be careful not to exaggerate the extent to which a behavioral reinterpretation of intuition about form will clarify the situation. Thus suppose we found some behavioral test corresponding to the analysis of "John finished eating" suggested above. Or, to choose a more interesting case, suppose that we manage to develop some operational account of synonymy and significance. (N. Chomsky, 1975, p. 102)

If you happened to have extensive prior experience with linguistics, this text presented little difficulty. You were able to rely on your prior knowledge and adopted an active reader role to construct meaning. On the other hand, those who know very little about linguistics or transformational grammar have to rely heavily on the text to provide enough explicit information to allow comprehension of the passage; these readers adopt a more passive role. The interactive model of reading suggests that we use what is necessary, either text or background knowledge, to achieve the goal of making sense of text. Teachers who subscribe to cognitive or interactive theories of the reading process will likely adopt a skills instructional approach for teaching children to read.

Readers must integrate an array of information sources from the text and from their background to construct a valid interpretation of the author's message.

The Relationship of Cognitivism to Skills Reading Instruction

Teachers who use **skills reading instruction** see the act of teaching reading like making a tossed salad, in which the ingredients (tomatoes, lettuce, radishes, etc.) are mixed together rather than served in separate bowls. The major ingredients in a reading skills tossed salad are comprehension, vocabulary, and decoding. Even though major reading skill components are mixed together in the tossed salad act of reading, they can still be isolated if necessary for purposes of instruction and measurement. Thus, the act of reading becomes whole when readers integrate the isolated parts

*The **skills model** is composed of three major skill areas: comprehension, vocabulary, and decoding.*

Figure 2.7 A skills instructional approach to reading (Weaver, 1988)

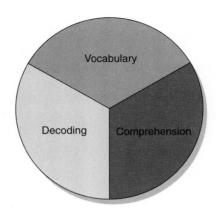

they are taught and practice. Pearson and Johnson described reading this way: "Reading (comprehension) is at once a unitary process and a set of discrete processes" (1978, p. 227).

Weaver (1988) illustrates skills instructional approaches in a circle, where reading is composed of three categories of skill instruction: (a) comprehension, (b) vocabulary, and (c) decoding (Figure 2.7). Decoding knowledge is not shown as the foundation in the model, but rather as an equal part of the reading instructional process. The three reading skill areas become the focus from which individual reading skills can be sliced or isolated for instruction. In fact, the skills model is the most commonly accepted approach for providing reading instruction in schools today, most likely because skills approaches to reading instruction were the predominant form of instructional practice associated with basal reader series. In basal readers, reading skills are typically listed in a scope and sequence chart. The scope and sequence of skills is organized into the three major skills components of reading mentioned previously—decoding, comprehension, and vocabulary—as published in the teachers' edition.

After students read a story, three skill lessons are typically taught—one each on comprehension, vocabulary, and decoding.

A characteristic of skills instruction involves the preteaching of new vocabulary words before reading a selection rather than allowing students merely to discover these words in context (N. Gordon, 1984; Weaver, 1988). After students read a selection in a basal reader, teachers typically teach three skill lessons, one from each of the three skill components of reading. Thus, skills teachers engage students in lessons for comprehension, vocabulary, and decoding. Although these teachers also encourage the reading of stories in trade books and basal readers, reading of the text is usually considered a point of transfer for skill learning or application—from teacher lessons dominated by skill instruction and practice to their use in reading texts. Skills reading instruction clearly focuses on the mastery and application of skills as the means to becoming a reader.

The skills model treats comprehension as a set of discrete skills.

Another distinguishing factor of the skills approach is the treatment of comprehension, which is seen as a set of discrete skills such as getting the main idea, noting details, drawing conclusions, and using context. Each of these comprehension skills is to be taught one at a time and reviewed in subsequent years.

Several assumptions are associated with the skills reading instructional practices. First, reading ability is achieved by learning

$$a \text{ skill} + a \text{ skill} + a \text{ skill},$$

which are interactively integrated by the learner to

$$= \text{reading}.$$

Figure 2.8 Theory-driven reading instruction: Cognitive theories and skills reading instructional practice

Cognitive Interactive Theories of the Reading Process Reflect an Interactive Reading Model

• During reading and learning to read, language is processed by balancing the features of the print with the reader's prior knowledge, culture, and background experiences.
• Learning to read is thought to be the *construction of meaning* through emphasizing information gained from the print and from the reader's prior knowledge.
• Learning to read is accomplished by placing a balanced emphasis on mastering three skill areas: decoding, vocabulary, and comprehension.
• Language stimuli for reading practice are carefully controlled to represent words that are familiar to the child's background and used frequently in the language.
• Mastery of the skill areas of reading, decoding, vocabulary, and comprehension is assumed to lead to competent understanding and performance of the whole act of reading.
• A balanced emphasis on isolated lessons in each of the three skill areas of decoding, vocabulary, and comprehension is assumed to be integrated by each learner.
• Integration of the three skill areas is assumed to enable skilled, independent reading.
• Correctness is expected, although varying interpretations for meaning based on background knowledge are accepted.

Skills Instructional Approach

• Reading instruction focuses on three skill areas in isolated lessons: decoding, vocabulary, and comprehension.
• Instruction begins in all three areas:
  - Decoding: Learning the 26 letters and 44 sounds.
  - Vocabulary: Learning high-frequency sight words in lists, e.g., *the, and, me, look*, etc.
  - Comprehension: Listening to stories read aloud for the main idea, sequence, or details.
• Instruction continues in the three skill areas in connection with the introduction of simple stories in books called "pre-primers."
  - Decoding: Letter–sound associations learned along with some blending and the sounds letters represent in selected sight words.
  - Vocabulary: New high-frequency sight word lists are learned along with attention to new conceptual knowledge focused around word meaning categories.
  - Comprehension: Simple comprehension skills related to short stories in the teacher's edition focus on main ideas and noting details.
• Instruction progresses to the use of a student's anthology of stories (some use controlled text, some use literature-based stories) and instruction in the three skill areas continues throughout the elementary years.
  - Decoding: Prefixes, suffixes, context clues, etc.
  - Vocabulary: Unfamiliar words, multiple meaning words, word categories, synonyms, antonyms, etc.
  - Comprehension: Sequencing, literary devices, following directions, etc.

Second, instruction is designed to teach each of the language-cueing components—decoding, context, and meaning—separately. Third, when these skills are put together by a reader, they function in a unitary fashion. (However, when these reading skills are learned in schools, they are often isolated from their use in text for instruction and practice.) And finally, print contains the author's message, and the reader's job is to construct meaning from the text.

*Because **cognitive** or **interactive theories** of reading balance an emphasis on text and prior knowledge and skills instruction, they simultaneously influence the teaching of decoding, vocabulary, and comprehension skills.*

In Figure 2.8, the connection between cognitive interactive theories and skills instruction is summarized. It is important to understand that cognitive or interactive theories emphasize a blending of the elements of print and the reader's knowledge and experiences. This theoretical stance influences skills teachers' instructional practices. They tend to provide a simultaneous emphasis on developing skills in decoding, vocabulary, and comprehension from the outset of instruction. Language for reading materials is typically controlled to match students' hypothesized backgrounds and knowledge levels as well as to represent the most frequent or common words in printed English. Hence, skills teachers tend to rely on reading materials that limit language in texts to high-frequency words and sight words. Familiar and unfamiliar words are taught from a vocabulary list before reading each text. A purpose is set for reading, and comprehension is checked after reading each selection. The most notable practice in skills instruction is that after each story, three skill lessons are to be taught in (a) decoding, (b) vocabulary, and (c) comprehension. From Figure 2.8, one can readily see that an emphasis on a reader's background knowledge and the aspects of the texts leads skills teachers to focus instruction on comprehension to validate and activate a reader's background knowledge as well as to teach lessons about decoding, vocabulary, and comprehension strategies. This connection between theory and practice clearly demonstrates how the tenets of cognitive or interactive theories relate to and influence the practices of skill instruction.

Constructivism and the Transactional Reading Model

Constructivism is a theory of learning that represents the culmination of several distinct lines of research: developmental psychology, sociohistorical psychology, and semiotic interactionism.

Constructivism is an extension of cognitive theories stemming from three separate lines of investigation and research: (a) cognitive psychology à la Piaget, (b) sociohistorical developmental psychology à la Vygotsky, and (c) semiotic interactionism à la Bruner, Gardner, Eisner, and Goodman. Fosnot (1996) explains, "Rather than behaviors or skills as the goal of instruction, concept development and deep understanding are the foci; rather than stages being the result of maturation, they are understood as constructions of active learner reorganization" (p. 10). The work of these constructivist researchers in relation to language and learning is described in greater detail in chapter 3, "Emergent Literacy: Understanding the Literacy Development of Young Children." Applications of constructivism to learning include the following concepts:

- Learning is not the result of development; rather, learning is development.
- Errors are not to be avoided or minimized but are to be viewed as evidence of seeking to learn.
- Learners organize and generalize their knowledge across experiences.
- Learners represent their knowledge through a variety of symbol systems (movement, song, play), with language representing only one symbol system.
- Talking, conversing, and dialoging provide opportunities for the development of fundamental tools of thinking—defending, proving, justifying, and communicating ideas.

Meaningful learning is at the core of constructivist theory. The unit of meaning and focus of instruction for reading is therefore the sentence rather than the word or letter. For specific word meanings to be correctly understood, a sentence context is necessary, for example, *minute* vs *minute.* Language is initially taught from the perspective of language cueing systems; *syntax,* which relates word order to word meaning, and *graphophonics,* which relates letters to sounds. In short, teaching reading becomes a whole-to-part-to-whole process—language units reduced to smaller than sentence parts returned to their sentence- or story-level context.

Greene (1996) relates constructivist theories of learning to the groundbreaking **transactional model** of the literary process authored by Louise Rosenblatt (1978). Rosenblatt's *transactional theory* declared reading to be a carefully orchestrated relationship between reader and text. A reading *transaction* suggests a special type of relationship between the reader and the text, an act that causes the reader to be motivated to construct a personal meaning for a particular text. Situational conditions, such as *time, mood, pressures, reason, intents,* and *purposes for reading,* influence a reader's *stance* or purpose for reading a piece of literature. Rosenblatt describes two transactional stances—*efferent* and *aesthetic*—to portray this relationship between readers and text.

Constructivist theories of learning are well represented in Rosenblatt's transactional model of reading.

Efferent Stance

When readers focus their attention on information to be remembered from reading a text, they are taking an *efferent stance.* For example, reading the driver's license manual in preparation for an upcoming driving examination exemplifies an efferent stance toward a text. Reading a novel for the purpose of writing a book report to summarize the plot is another example of taking an efferent stance toward text. And when readers assume an efferent stance toward reading a novel as an assignment in school, the focus of attention is on memorizing or gleaning details from the text to pass a test rather than on enjoying and learning from the experience. Obviously, then, there is a need to account for another type of *transactional stance* or motivation for reading a text—an *aesthetic stance.*

When readers focus their attention on information to be remembered from reading a text, they are taking an efferent stance.

Aesthetic Stance

When reading aesthetically, the learner draws on past experiences, connects these experiences to the text, often savors the beauty of the literary art form, and becomes an integral participant in the unfolding events of the text. For example, when a teacher reads Wilson Rawls's (1961) story, "Where the Red Fern Grows," a feeling of reverence and sensitivity interweaves with the reading of the story. The teacher's voice may break a little bit toward the end of a read-aloud session, which deepens the emotions for the children. The listeners wonder how love can sacrifice itself so tenderly, so completely, and yet so sadly that a red fern grew.

Think of a time when you took an aesthetic stance. Can you recall the book and the emotions evoked as you read?

When the teacher closes the book, there is silence in the room, and many eyes are filled with glistening tears. This is the silence of reverent reflection—a silence quite different in tone and mood from the silence in classrooms where every child is working individually on a reading skills workbook page or answering a line of comprehension questions. Also, classrooms rich with literacy tools and props (e.g., books, notepads, message boards, appointment books, pencils, pens, stationery) prompt spontaneous literacy interactions among students (Neuman & Roskos, 1992). Thus, the social, situational context for learning to read and write cannot be dismissed as incidental to the experiences children have as they develop and refine their understanding of reading and writing (See Figure 2.9).

Figure 2.9   Transactional Reading Model

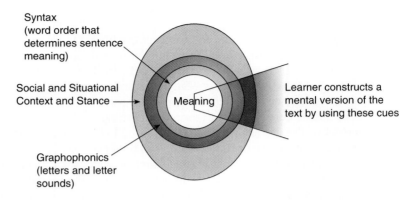

The Relationship of Constructivism to Balanced Literacy Instruction

The elements of balanced reading and writing programs as described by New Zealand and Australian educators (Fountas & Pinnell, 1997; Holdaway, 1979; Mooney, 1990; *Reading in Junior Classes* [handbook for New Zealand teachers, not referenced], 1985) are shown in Figure 2.10. These instructional elements include

- Reading aloud
- Shared reading and writing
- Guided reading and interactive writing
- Language experience
- Working with words
- Supported reading and writing
- Independent reading and writing
- Assessment
- Designing literacy environments
- Instructional planning

In Figure 2.11, the transactional reading model has been penetrated by the instructional elements of a balanced literacy program to explain how teachers can provide reading and writing instruction to young learners. Balanced reading instruction is dependent upon the teacher being knowledgeable about the development of reading processes in children. Instruction begins with careful and ongoing assessment of each child's reading development. This assessment informs instruction and helps the teacher know where to begin.

    An essential aspect of **balanced literacy instruction** is the belief that children learn to read by reading and learn to write by writing (Newman, 1985a). As a direct manifestation of this belief, children and teachers typically engage in daily sustained reading and writing activities using easy, sometimes graded or carefully leveled trade books, enlarged trade or big books, theme units, and self-selected writing projects. Teachers read aloud to children regularly, knowing that reading aloud to children helps them see, understand, and develop appropriate concepts about and attitudes toward reading and language. The environment of the classroom is made rich with print from the everyday lives and learning of the children. The environment and language of texts are designed to provide genuine opportunities for children to read and write for authentic purposes. Favorite storybooks are read and reread in a shared setting that supports children as they make sense of print. Early in the process, children's attempts to

Balanced literacy instruction focuses on helping children learn to read and write by reading and writing TO, WITH, and BY children.

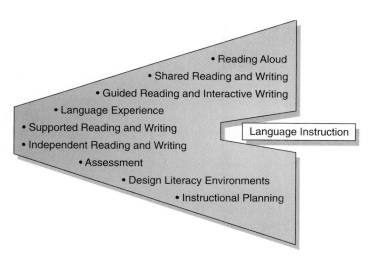

Figure 2.10 Elements of a balanced literacy program

Based on *The Foundations of Literacy* by D. Holdaway. Copyright © 1979 by D. Holdaway. Reprinted by permission of Scholastic Australia.

make sense of print are often assisted with sensitive demonstrations and intentional, explicit instruction on skills by other competent language users, such as older children, parents, grandparents, and, of course, teachers.

Teachers using balanced literacy instruction also believe that children's innate desire to use and learn language to express themselves and to meet their own social and personal needs ought to be respected by using children's oral language as the basis for creating supplemental reading and writing materials. This practice of using children's language and experiences is often known as the *language experience approach.* Teachers who implement this approach believe that children do not begin reading by learning to read and then later on reading to learn.

Balanced literacy practices include the use of carefully leveled emergent reading materials that children can read independently with the help and guidance of the teacher. The object of guided reading and interactive writing is for the teacher to guide, teach, model, and assist children to develop skills and strategies for successful reading and writing as well as to help young learners discover and use the many language clues

Figure 2.11 Balanced literacy instruction

Based on *The Foundations of Literacy* by D. Holdaway. Copyright © 1979 by D. Holdaway. Reprinted by permission of Scholastic Australia.

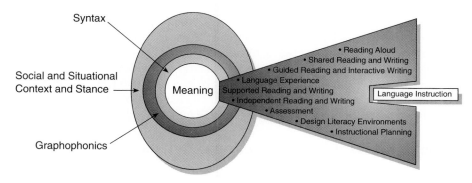

Learner assisted to construct mental text by instruction

found in connected print. Finally, children must be given abundant reading materials and time to read personally selected reading materials independently each day. After all, balanced literacy teachers believe children learn to read by reading.

Similar practices in writing are incorporated into balanced literacy programs. When children write, they write for their own purposes and choose their own topics (Graves, 1983). They do not usually write about topics chosen by a teacher. Teachers demonstrate and reveal to children the many ways in which writing can be used: to tell the story of ourselves, to record ideas, to organize our efforts, to manage others' time and behavior, and so on. Not only are children exposed to these many ways of authoring ideas in writing, but they are helped to understand the form, features, and functions of these various writing approaches through demonstrations and interactive writing activities. Children are given time to write each day. They are encouraged to keep notebooks, lists, and journals. Time for writing independently is provided daily because these teachers believe that children learn to write by writing. In summary, teachers implementing the elements of balanced literacy instruction put constructivist theory into practice by teaching reading and writing strategies and skills in authentic ways that make sense to learners. Such teachers believe that children construct meaning from print; and in the process, they learn to read and write.

The primary goal of Balanced Literacy Programs is to help all children become independent, fluent readers in the early education years, then help them expand their literacy abilities throughout their schooling. The same *seven principles that support literacy development* (see chapter 1) undergird the framework for balanced lieteracy instructional programs.

1. Begin with the teacher's knowledge of student reading processes and literacy development.
2. Rely on process and product assessment practices that link directly to the knowledge base of reading.
3. Support Reading *to, with,* and *by* students.
4. Involve families in the reading development process.
5. Integrate the development of reading with writing instruction and composition.
6. Develop reading and writing skills, moving instruction from "whole to parts to whole."
7. Address the needs of all children.

Think of two ways in which constructivist theory connects with balanced literacy instruction.

The connection between a constructivist or transactional theory and a balanced literacy instructional approach is shown in Figure 2.12. Constructivist theory suggests that children learn to actively construct meaning from encounters with connected texts, in supportive and authentic situations (e.g., bedtime reading). Children's literacy constructions are assisted through people providing demonstrations of reading and writing behaviors, and mini-lessons focused on literacy skills. As such, balanced literacy instruction seeks to create effective literacy learning situations in the classroom: Teachers provide real stories and poems to be read; they present exemplary models or demonstrations of reading and writing behaviors; they offer sensitive and helpful guidance about how to use skills and strategies to read and write; and they create a learning environment and specific classroom situations that mirror other authentic literacy and life-related events.

Defining and Refining Instructional Beliefs

Teachers who do not possess a personal definition and understanding of the reading process are likely to adopt unexamined the beliefs and practices implicit in a given reading program or school setting.

One characteristic of a knowledgeable and masterful teacher is the ability to express clearly and succinctly what he or she believes about teaching and learning. Articulating one's definition of reading is a critical step toward understanding the reading

Figure 2.12 Theory-driven reading instruction: Constructivist theories and balanced literacy instructional practice

Constructivist Theories of the Reading Process Reflect a Transactional Reading Model

• During reading and learning to read, readers process language by constructing meaning dependent on their own purposes, the social and situational setting, and the semantic, syntactic, and graphophonic aspects of print.
• Learning to read is thought to be an event where a reader's response to a text is conditioned by the text, the people, the physical environment, and the cultural expectations of the situation as posited by literary criticism and transactional theory.
• Learning to read is accomplished by creating meaning through the use of semantic, syntactic, and graphophonic cues appropriate to the print, the context, the social or situational setting, and the reader's purposes.
• Language stimuli for reading practice are authentic, uncontrolled, and meaningful wholes including stories, songs, and poetry, as well as leveled books for instruction.
• Approximating the demonstrations of competent language users—often with substantial guidance and support from these individuals—is assumed to lead to competent understanding and performance of the whole act of reading.
• Reading materials are practiced whole and undivided initially. After initial readings of the whole, instruction proceeds to look into the text for what one might learn about how language works and the parts of language. Instruction is tied directly to the text and context of the reading materials and learners.
• Mistakes are expected and seen as evidence of risk taking and progress among young learners.
• Demonstrations and modeling of conventional reading, writing, and spelling are integral for children and adults to learn how to make meaning that others will be able to understand and accept as appropriate.

Balanced Literacy Instructional Approach

• Early reading instruction recreates the bedtime reading or lap reading situation through using enlarged print of stories, songs, or poems often found in "big books" read to and read with young children.
• Instruction demonstrates/emulates how competent readers read and write with fluency, expression, and use the language cues of pictures, semantics, syntax, and graphophonics to process and produce text.
• Instruction focuses on understanding the whole, then moves to understanding the parts, then returns to an understanding or integration of the parts with the whole.
• Because instruction focuses on meaning, language activities are often grouped around a topic, theme, author, or genre.
• Individual interpretations or diverse responses to a text are encouraged. Taking different perspectives on the same text is part of the instructional process.
• Integration of the language and learning approaches across traditional curriculum boundaries influences the use of themed units or thematic studies.
• Children read and write for personal or authentic reasons. Real literature books are read. Topics for writing are chosen by the writer.
• Classrooms resemble busy language workshops filled with literacy tools, print-rich environments, and lively literacy-based interactions between teachers and children.
• Balanced reading program elements include reading aloud, reading together, guided reading, supported reading, and independent reading.

process. Teachers who do not possess a personal definition and understanding of the reading process often adopt, without analysis, beliefs and practices implicit in a given reading program or school setting, which means that they may teach from superstition and tradition rather than from knowledge, experience, and critical evaluation (F. Smith, 1985). Harste, Woodward, and Burke (1984) emphasize the importance of defining and refining teacher beliefs over time in this way:

> We have come to believe that looking at teacher behavior in terms of beliefs held and assumptions made is more cogent and powerful than looking at behavior in terms of the supposed approach being used. . . . What this means practically is that in order to change behavior we must change beliefs. (p. 7)

Transitional Instructional Change Model

*The **transitional instructional model** is discussed in detail in chapters 1 and 5.*

The transitional instructional change model is our way of describing a process currently under way for literally millions of teachers worldwide: movement from traditional ways of viewing reading instruction toward balanced literacy programs. Because so many children are falling between the cracks and failing to become literate via outdated traditional models of teaching, especially in our inner city schools, teachers often feel pressured to make the transition to balanced literacy instruction almost overnight. Yet our research clearly suggests that transitions toward balanced literacy instruction can take from 4 to 7 years to accomplish.

Transitions begin with an understanding of (a) theory that leads to the development of an articulate definition of literacy, and (b) literacy learning "milestones" that children must acquire. Developing this knowledge base helps teachers to consistently select appropriate strategies to assess where students are in their development, and to choose teaching and learning activities targeted to student needs.

Along this transitions pathway leading to the development of successful balanced literacy classrooms, teachers will often find elements within each of the various reading models presented in this chapter with which they agree (Heymsfeld, 1989). That's fine. Balanced literacy instruction, although a very clear and consistent perspective, is not an absolute, "all or nothing" model (Routman, 1988). Rather, the transitions model suggests that teachers are moving deliberately to change the way they believe and engage in reading instruction in their classrooms to be consistent with well-articulated balanced literacy practices.

Summary

A cursory survey of reading habits among the American population today revealed significant problems for teachers, children, families, and schools. Although large numbers of individuals in the United States remain illiterate, the more insidious problem of aliteracy threatens to undermine the general reading habits and attitudes of American adults and children. Although not all indicators are negative, today's teachers need to understand that now, more than ever, the ability to read is necessary to survive and prosper in a rapidly progressing technological and information-oriented society. The goal of producing able readers simply is not sufficient for today's schools. Teachers must become as concerned about developing positive reading habits and attitudes as they have been about ensuring reading achievement and ability. In short, children in today's schools must learn to *love* to read as well as learn to read!

For teachers to achieve the objectives associated with high-quality reading instruction, they must study children and understand how they go about the business of learning about printed language (see chapter 3). They must also clearly comprehend the way language is used by humans to communicate and learn. What is more, they must have a working knowledge of dominant learning theories and how these theories—behaviorism, cognitivism, and constructivism—result in models of the reading process: bottom-up, interactive, and transactional. Teachers must also understand that the assumptions and beliefs associated with specific models of the reading process lead to or drive instructional decisions and classroom instructional practices. Thus, theories of learning frame models of the reading process, which in turn support the reading instructional approaches described in this chapter known as subskills, skills, and balanced literacy. It is equally important to understand one's own beliefs about how children learn to read and how reading should be taught.

Concept Applications

In the Classroom

1. Conduct a poll in your college classes about the numbers of trade books (excluding college textbooks) read by each person in the last year.
2. After reading this chapter, write a brief description of your current instructional beliefs about reading and writing. Then, as you read the remainder of the book, keep a log of information you learn that may cause you to rethink your initial orientation to reading instructional practices.
3. List the major assumptions and characteristics of behaviorism, cognitivism, and constructivism, and summarize each learning theory in writing.
4. List the major assumptions and characteristics of the bottom-up, interactive, and transactional models of the reading process, and summarize each in writing.
5. List the major assumptions and characteristics of the three reading instructional models—bottoms-up, interactive, and transactional—and summarize each model in writing.

In the Field

1. Visit a kindergarten or first-grade classroom. Describe in detail how children are being engaged in learning to read and write. You may also be able to gather some writing samples to photocopy and return to the children. Make a list of the types of books you saw them reading. Which of the major models of the reading process best explains what you saw? Why?
2. Ask a teacher to tell you about his or her reading instructional beliefs. Visit the teacher's classroom, and determine if these beliefs are reflected in his or her classroom instruction. Describe what you saw and how it related to one of the three reading instructional approaches.
3. Visit children in several grade levels. Interview them using questions based on the Burke Reading Interview (Burke, 1987). Ask them:
   a. What is reading?
   b. Who do you think is a good reader in your class? Why?
   c. What would you do to teach someone how to read?
   d. How did you learn to read?
   e. What might you do to become a better reader?

Record the responses for the different grade levels and compare. How do children's understandings of reading differ from grade to grade? Discuss your findings with a peer in your class. Did you notice similar differences?

Recommended Readings

Ashton-Warner, S. (1963). *Teacher.* New York: Touchstone Press.

Chorny, M. (1985). *Teacher as learner.* Alberta, Canada: Language in the Classroom Project.

Holdaway, D. (1979). *The foundations of literacy.* Exeter, NH: Heinemann.

Mooney, M. (1990). *Reading TO, WITH, and BY Children* New York: Owen.

Reutzel, D. R. (1996). A balanced reading approach. In J. Baltas & S. Shafer (Eds.), *Scholastic guide to balanced reading: Grade 3–6* (pp. 7–11). New York: Scholastic.

Reutzel, D. R. (1998). On balanced reading. *The Reading Teacher, 52*(4), 2–4.

Reutzel, D. R., & Cooter, R. B. (1999). *Balanced reading strategies: Assessing and assisting special needs readers.* Upper Saddle River, NJ: Merrill/Prentice Hall.

Routman, R. (1996). *Literacy at the crossroads: Crucial talk about reading, writing, and other teaching dilemmas.* Portsmouth, NH: Heinemann.

Weaver, C. (1998). *Reconsidering a balanced approach to reading.* Urbana, IL: National Council of Teachers of English.

3

Emergent Literacy:

Focus Questions

When you are finished studying this chapter, you should be able to answer these questions:

1. How can you differentiate Piaget's four stages of cognitive development?
2. How does Vygotsky relate children's language growth to cognitive development?
3. What are four affective factors that influence children's motivation to learn language in all its modes?
4. What are stages of children's oral language development?
5. What are stages of children's reading development?
6. What are stages of children's writing and spelling development?

Understanding the Literacy Development of Young Children

Key Concepts

Emergent Literacy
Sensorimotor
Preoperational
Concrete Operations
Formal Operations
Zone of Proximal Development
Internalization
Affect
Behaviorist Theory
Innatist Theory
Interactionist Theory

Preindependent Reading
Independent Reading
Picture-Governed
Print-Governed
Prephonemic Stage
Early Phonemic Stage
Letter-Naming Stage
Transitional Stage
Story Grammar
Environmental Print
Concepts About Print

Very young children discover printed language by observing the world around them. Christopher, a 3-year-old boy, runs down the cereal aisle at the local supermarket and stops abruptly, pointing to a box of cereal, "Look Mom, here's the Fruit Loops! You said they didn't have any!" Amber, age 2, sits on her porch with her doll and a well-worn copy of her favorite book held upside down in her hands. "Now listen while I read you this story," she whispers to her silent playmate. In a local day-care center, Jeremy, a 4-year-old preschooler, is busily scribbling with crayons on a neatly folded piece of paper. The teacher stops, looks at his work. She notices what looks like a picture of a cake with candles with some scribbles underneath the picture. At the bottom of the paper is the carefully scrawled signature of Jeremy. She pauses and asks, "Jeremy, what are you writing?" Jeremy excitedly points to each set of scribble marks and replies with a smile, "I'm writing a birthday card to my Daddy."

ON BECOMING LITERATE

Emergent Literacy

Emergent literacy represents a profound change in how people believe early literacy is acquired.

The **emergent literacy** view of how children learn to read and write implies that becoming literate begins at birth and is a continuous, developmental process. We can observe in the behavior of even very young children evidence of the process of becoming literate. Although their reading and writing behaviors may not be conventional in the sense of those behaviors accepted by adults, young children, regardless of age, maturity or intelligence, are nonetheless learning the uses and conventions of printed language in a variety of situations and contexts. N. Hall (1987) describes the assumptions surrounding the emergent literacy perspectives about how children learn to read and write. Some of these assumptions follow:

1. Reading and writing are closely related processes and should not be artificially isolated for instruction.
2. Learning to read and write is essentially a social process and is influenced by a search for meaning.
3. Most preschool children already know a great deal about printed language without exposure to formal instruction.

Acting like a reader is part of becoming a reader.

4. Becoming literate is a continuous, developmental process.
5. Children need to *act* like readers and writers to *become* readers and writers.
6. Children need to read authentic and natural texts.
7. Children need to write for personal reasons.

From the earliest cognitive studies into language learning begun in about 1956, researchers in language acquisition carefully studied and observed young children to determine how they solved the puzzle of printed language. Durkin (1966) found that some young children could already read and write before exposure to formal schooling and instructional methodologies.

Clay's early work with 5-year-old children in New Zealand showed that "there is nothing in this research that suggests that contact with printed language forms should be withheld from any five-year-old child on the grounds that he is immature" (1967, p. 24). Thus, Clay rejected the notion of reading readiness stages as well as delaying exposure to books and other printed material.

Y. M. Goodman (1986) studied the knowledge of at-risk beginning readers and found that these children possessed a great deal of knowledge about the functions and uses of printed language. Since the time of these early studies about how young children learn to read and write, many researchers have supported and extended these findings. For example, D. Taylor (1983) found homes rich with social and cultural examples of print and print use in the families she studied. In fact, she stated that "perhaps, it is only after children have shared stories and experienced reading and writing as complex cultural activities that they will be able to learn on an individual level through the traditional pedagogical practices of the first-grade classroom" (p. 98). These studies are just a few examples of those that have led to the viewpoints of how young children become literate. In the next section, we discuss how children develop the ability to think and reason, after which we discuss language and how it works. Finally, we describe how children acquire oral language as well as how they develop emergent reading and writing behaviors.

Children may need extensive opportunities to experience books and stories before they can profit from school reading instructional practices.

COGNITIVE AND AFFECTIVE ASPECTS OF LANGUAGE DEVELOPMENT

Contributions of Piaget

To understand child development, knowledge of the relationship between the child's language development and cognitive growth is essential. Piaget (1955) viewed changes in a child's expressive language ability as indicators of intellectual growth and cognitive development. Cognitive development was considered to be the driving force behind language acquisition (Tomasello, 1996). Piaget also asserted that language acquisition and cognitive development occurred as a result of maturational (nature) rather than environmental forces (nurture). These maturational or natural forces directly influenced cognitive growth, which he thought occurred in a predetermined sequence of four stages (see Figure 3.1). Although children were thought to progress through these cognitive stages sequentially, the ages at which they entered or exited each stage varied dramatically. Piagetians call this difference in timing or lag among children in moving from one stage of cognitive development to another *décalage.*

During the first stage, the **sensorimotor** stage (birth to 2 years of age), children's oral language is called *egocentric speech,* meaning speech that is directed mainly at the self or one's own needs. Children at this stage of cognitive development

Piaget viewed language development as a product of cognitive growth.

*Children in the **sensorimotor** stage use language egocentrically to meet their own needs.*

Figure 3.1 Piaget's Stages of Cognitive Development

Developmental Stages	Characteristics of Language Development
Stage 1 Sensorimotor (ages 0-2)	• Once children begin to speak, they use *egocentric speech.* Speech is audible to others but directed at self because children, from a cognitive perspective, do not see themselves as separate from others. • Children may overgeneralize (cars refer to all vehicles) or undergeneralize (cat refers to only his cat) word use.
Stage 2 Pre-Operational (ages 2–7)	• Children use *socialized speech,* language that allows them to interact with others. • Children understand the symbolic use of words, language can be used to represent actual objects. • Maturation must take place for students to understand *conservation* of objects and *reversibility.* Conservation refers to a cognitive understanding that if the shape of an object is changed its mass or substance may not. Reversibility can refer to an understanding of language where a child recognizes that if he has a sister then he is his sister's brother. • By age 3, sentence use becomes more strategic as learned nouns and verbs can be reversed to form questions. • Children begin to develop the ability to keep from centering attention on only one quality or attribute of an object or concept. Referred to as *decentration,* it allows students to relate parts to a whole, important if early reading instruction asks students to identify the parts of words first. • As children mature, sentences become more complex as children begin to cognitively recognize cause-and-effect relationships.
State 3 Concrete Operational (ages 7–11)	• Children develop the ability to solve problems and think deductively. • The use of language increases as children confidently describe and think about their environment, discovering complex relationships of sequence, order, cause and effect, and classification. • The more experiences children have the more opportunity for the development of language.
Stage 4 Formal Operational (ages 11–Adult)	• Children become increasingly sophisticated and able to think abstractly and logically using language to discuss distant concepts, events, and experiences. • Children and adults are able to abstract meaning from text without actually having a direct experience.

Children's preoperational experiences help to develop their sense of how language works.

do not see others as separate from themselves. The ability to take into account the view of others, called *socialized speech,* does not occur until much later, somewhere between the ages of 7 and 8. Although egocentric speech is audible to others, it is nevertheless directed at the self or self-related concerns.

In the second stage, the **preoperational** stage (2 to 7 years of age), children's language becomes social, which means that children now see themselves as individuals, separate and distinct from others. They now use language to interact with others beyond the desire to meet their own needs. This change results from the process of maturation: Maturation changes children's view of the world, and this change is reflected in their understanding and use of language. During the preoperational stage, children begin to recognize the symbolic nature of language. Language can be used to represent an actual object, a concept, or an event. For example, the spoken word *baby* represents a real baby, separate and distinct from a picture. Acquiring this understanding is a critical prerequisite for furthering reading development. Children must realize that a word represents the meaning or identity of an object—separate from the object itself or from a picture—to understand that words are merely symbolic representations of the objects and concepts themselves. According to Piaget, this understanding is associated with the problem of relating and distinguishing classes or categories of concepts and objects.

It is also during the preoperational stage that children learn the concept of *conservation,* that mass or substance does not change when the shape or form of an object is transformed. For example, when a ball of clay is flattened, the mass or substance is not altered by the change in shape. Another concept developed during the preoperational stage of cognitive growth is *reversibility.* Children in this stage do not understand that relationships between events and objects can be reversed. For example, a young boy at this age may recognize that he has a sister but not realize that he is a brother to his sister.

*During the **preoperational** stage, conservation, reversibility, and decentration are cognitive concepts that are beginning to be learned.*

Attaining the ability to conserve concepts and reverse relationships helps young readers generalize their contextually tied recognition of words and concepts read in a familiar book or setting, such as words on a cereal box, to another, less familiar setting, such as the same words found on word cards or wall charts. During the preoperational stage of cognitive development, children develop the ability to relate the parts of an object to the whole. This development is an example of the Piagetian concept of *decentration*—the ability to keep from centering attention on only one quality or attribute of an object or concept. This development is of particular importance because children are often introduced to reading in a manner that requires them to identify the parts of words first. Many children can learn and even memorize word parts before this stage of development, but understanding how these parts fit together to make a word or to access meaning requires an understanding of how the parts make up a whole.

Only when language is experienced whole will the parts make sense to the learner.

In the third stage, the **concrete operations** stage (7 to 11 years of age), children develop the ability to solve problems and to think deductively while continuing their development and understanding of conservation, reversibility, and decentration. Language can now be used as a tool for discovering relationships such as sequence or order, cause and effect, and categories. Piaget maintained that much is learned from interacting with others and manipulating objects in the environment. Actual experience with manipulating objects in the environment has a direct impact on language development. Consequently, experience with language as a whole should precede a study of language parts; only when language is experienced whole will the parts make sense to the learner. Vasily Sukhomlinksy, an acclaimed Russian educator, in his book entitled *To Children I Give My Heart* (1981), clearly believed that experience and language are the fount of cognitive development.

> I begin [sic] to take the children on journeys to the source of words: I opened the children's eyes to the beauty of the world and at the same time tried to show their hearts the music of words. I tried to make it so that words were not just names of people, places, things, or phenomena, but carried with them emotional coloration—their own aroma, subtle nuances. Until the child feels the aroma of words, sees their subtle nuances, it [sic] is not prepared to begin to study reading and writing. And if the teacher begins this too early, he or she dooms the children to a difficult task. . . . The process of learning to read and write will be easy if it is a clear, exciting bit of life for the children, a filling out of living images, sounds, and melodies. (pp. 125–126)

Formal operations allow language to be used to transcend the boundaries of space and time.

In the final stage of Piaget's (1955) cognitive development description, the **formal operations** stage (11 years of age to adult), children become able to think abstractly and logically. Now they use language to discuss distant concepts, events, and experiences. Language has become an important vehicle for transcending the boundaries of space and time. Before this stage, children needed to be in the presence of the object or event to manipulate or experience it; now thought can proceed without the immediate presence of objects or events. This use of language is crucial for reading development: Learning from text requires that the reader be able to abstract concepts, events, and experiences from text rather than from direct experience or manipulation of objects. In fact, it is hard to imagine a child learning from reading who cannot think abstractly.

Focus on two ways Piaget's views support current reading instructional practices.

Language learning, according to Piaget, is determined by increasingly sophisticated thought or cognitive growth; cognitive growth is not determined by language use. Piaget's views lend support to current theories regarding the development of reading and writing in young children. Encouraging children to read and write whole texts and stories early in the schooling process allows them the opportunity of exploring, manipulating, and experiencing meaning in language. Piaget's views also support providing both actual and vicarious experiences to build children's background experiences in preparation for success in reading as well as using children's language and experience in the creation of reading materials.

Contributions of Vygotsky

Vygotsky (1896–1934), a famous Russian psychologist and educator, believed that an individual's cognitive capacity and the range of cognitive abilities among the general population were in large part predetermined by heredity. Contrary to Piaget's beliefs, Vygotsky (1962, 1978) believed that cognitive development was very much affected by language acquisition and its use in the course of interactions with other human beings in society (Tomasello, 1996). In short, Vygotsky believed that language meaning is negotiated in a society. The process of negotiating meaning between children and others in a society expands their ability and tools for thought.

Unlike Piaget, Vygotsky believed cognitive growth was the product of increasingly sophisticated language use.

Hence, unlike Piaget (1955), Vygotsky (1962) maintained that meaning is not created in the mind of the child first and then conveyed to others, but rather it is through interaction with other language users in the environment that meaning arises and is established in the mind of the child. In short, when children find themselves in social situations, they use language as the tool for exploring their world. According to Vygotsky, when children use language to explore, they develop cognitively.

The meaning of language is the result of a social negotiation and agreement.

When Piaget observed children in his research, he assessed their cognitive development in terms of how they could solve a problem without intervention or teacher assistance. From this work, Piaget maintained that there was no point in trying to teach children to perform a particular task until they reached a certain stage of cognitive development when the solution to the task or problem was readily understood. Conversely, Vygotsky assessed cognitive development in terms of how well a child could perform a specific task in cooperation and collaboration with others. The difference between what a child can do alone and in collaboration with others is what Vygotsky called the **zone of proximal development** (ZPD). Frank Smith (1988) described the zone of proximal development this way: "Everyone can do things with assistance that they cannot do alone, and what they can do with collaboration on one occasion they will be able to do independently on another" (pp. 196–197). For a ZPD to be created, there must be a joint activity that creates a learning situation for the child and the expert to interact. The expert can then choose to employ multiple instructional strategies to help the child succeed in the learning situation (Tharpe & Gallimore, 1988). Instead of withholding certain tasks from a child until a particular stage of cognitive development is reached, as suggested by Piaget (1955), Vygotsky (1978) recommended that once the zone of proximal development was identified, a teacher, parents, or peers could help a child perform a task he or she would not be capable of doing alone.

*The **zone of proximal development** is working with a child to accomplish a task he or she cannot yet complete independently.*

Vygotsky also differentiated between school and nonschool learning. Spontaneous concepts (e.g., hot vs. cold, parent vs. pets) are learned outside of the schooling environment and are fairly concrete. On the other hand, scientific concepts are usually somewhat abstract and are learned primarily in the school environment. Scientific concepts are most effectively learned when they are built on spontaneous concepts. However, with time and instruction, scientific concepts become spontaneous concepts, thus continuing the cycle of concept building (Driscoll, 1994). Because Vygotsky valued the role of language use and social interaction as a means for

Vygotsky views social interaction among learners as a primary force for developing cognitive abilities.

enhancing cognitive growth, tasks that are difficult or abstract would not be withheld from children in early schooling experiences. Instead, Vygotsky viewed language use and social interaction as the very vehicle that can support the child through the learning process.

Vygotsky (1978) asserted that external activities, signs, or tools like the processes of reading, writing, and the presence of language symbols must be internalized by the learner from an external source. He wrote, "We call the internal reconstruction of an external operation *internalization*" (p. 56). This process of **internalization** is characterized by three transformations. The first transformation involves an external operation, such as reading, where the external act is *reconstructed and begins to occur internally.* This transformation is well represented by the child who continually asks for the same book to be read aloud again and again by another experienced reader. The second transformation begins when an *interpersonal process is transformed into an intrapersonal one.* An example of this transformation is found when a child uses a book as a prop to act like a reader when he or she is really only looking at the pictures, and repeating what was read aloud on previous occasions. The third transformation (of an external act to an internalized act) *involves changing an interpersonal process into an intrapersonal one as a result of a long series of developmental events.* An example of this transformation is clearly found in the developmental reading and writing descriptions found later in this chapter. The developmental aspects described later in this chapter detail how the externalized act of a more experienced reader or writer is internalized over time with considerable effort by a less experienced learner.

Internalization and the zone of proximal development are depicted in Figure 3.2.

The notion that social interaction plays a significant role in developing a child's cognitive growth and language ability is extremely relevant to current trends in reading instruction. If children are immersed in reading and writing early in their schooling experience and receive support from peers and adults while they are learning, they will begin to internalize certain reading and writing behaviors. Put into practice, Vygotsky's theory, which advocates a child-centered and activity-oriented reading curriculum, enables children to negotiate the meaning of language while using language as an exploratory tool in a supportive learning environment.

Contributions of Affect

Affective aspects of reading include attitudes, motivation, interests, beliefs, feelings, and values.

Young children can often read books about dinosaurs but have trouble reading words like the, this, and that.

Two aspects of the reading process combine to influence whether children will choose to read and how much effort they will give to learning to read. Attitudes, interest, beliefs, feelings, and values make up the **affective** aspects of the reading process; desires, persistence, and motivation constitute the *conative* aspects of the reading process (Mathewson, 1994; Raven, 1992; Wigfield, 1997). Asher (1980) and Corno and Randi (1997) have found that reading comprehension, not surprisingly, was positively affected when children were interested in the reading material. Interest was also shown to be a compensatory factor in reading. For example, some children may struggle with recognizing simple words like *the, at, and,* and *it.* On the other hand, these same children may have little difficulty reading words like *dinosaur* and *tyrannosaurus rex* when they are interested in the material. Interest can also compensate for a child's lack of reading ability (Spangler, 1983; Sweet, 1997). One way to ensure children's interest in a topic, book, or any other reading selection is to begin by enthusiastically sharing new reading materials through reading

Figure 3.2   Teaching model based on Vygotsky's theory
From *Educational Psychology* (4th ed., p. 50) by R. E. Slavin, 1994. Needham Heights, MA: Allyn & Bacon. Reprinted by permission.

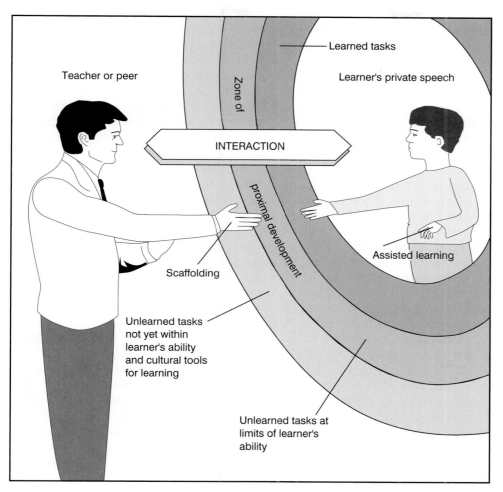

aloud or discussion. Another way is to show children how to self-select books or stories for reading.

Children who have had positive experiences with learning to read will more likely continue to derive enjoyment from reading. Conversely, children who have had negative experiences with learning to read may have found the cost of learning to read too high in relation to the perceived benefit. Children who have had positive experiences with reading at home come to school expecting to learn to read. Parents who read to their children and discuss books with their youngsters create a positive attitude toward reading. Children are also highly motivated by the examples they see: If parents are seen reading and enjoying reading, they can help mold positive reading attitudes.

When schools provide the same caring and supportive atmosphere for exploring language as the home, children form positive attitudes toward reading at school (Ruddell & Unrau, 1997). Sensitive teachers can do much to positively affect children's

Parents and teachers should help students have positive initial reading experiences.

attitudes toward reading. Reading aloud stories, books, poems, riddles, and jingles and singing songs together can immerse children in fun and supportive language activities. Providing time daily to explore, read, and talk about language and books children select themselves can also support the development of positive attitudes toward reading (Guthrie & McCann, 1997).

Think of a time when you selected a book to read. What physical characteristics influenced your choice?

Children's reading attitudes can also be influenced by the format of the reading materials. Print size or style, the presence or absence of pictures, and the type of cover (soft or hard binding) in books all have been shown to influence children's reading attitudes and habits (Lowery & Grafft, 1967; Samuels, 1970). Attitudes toward reading have also been found to influence reading comprehension. Henk and Holmes (1988) and Reutzel and Hollingsworth (1991a) have found that negative and positive attitudes toward the content of reading selections among adults and children can influence reading comprehension. Consequently, teachers should actively monitor children's attitudes and interests in reading so that affectively appropriate selections can be chosen for classroom instruction (Cooter, 1994; Santa, 1997).

Grade level and gender have also been shown to influence reading attitudes. Girls tend to exhibit more positive attitudes for reading than boys in grades 1 to 6 (Parker & Paradis, 1986). Alexander (1983) reported positive attitudes toward reading at the end of grade 1 and continuing through the end of grade 3. Attitudes toward classroom reading showed sharp negative changes between grades 4 and 5 in the elementary school, according to D. J. Brown, Engin, and Wallbrown (1979). Parker and Paradis (1986) found that positive changes in attitude between grades 4 and 5 were related to recreational, library, and general reading materials. It appeared that allowing for student self-selection of reading materials in the intermediate and upper elementary grade levels may play an even greater role than previously thought.

Allowing time for students to choose their own reading materials appears to be increasingly important in the intermediate and upper elementary grades.

Children who have feelings of inadequacy or inability may be afraid to take the risks associated with learning to read for fear they will fail. Students who are constantly corrected by the teacher or who are the object of pointed humor by peers when reading aloud are likely to develop a poor reading self-image. These children often appear to have given up trying to learn to read for fear of failure. Children with positive self-images, on the other hand, attack new and uncertain situations in reading with poise and confidence. These students expect to learn. F. Smith (1988) maintains that children expect to be successful in learning; it is only when they have developed attitudes that they cannot be successful that learning fails.

Teachers can avert the development of poor reading attitudes in several ways. First, they should recognize and respect children's interests and preferences. Second, they can make reading easy by making reading easy (F. Smith, 1983). This means that children can begin reading with very simple and yet complete books like Mercer Mayer's (1976a, 1976b) *Hiccup* and *Ah-Choo*. These books provide complete and enjoyable story lines while simultaneously limiting the difficulty of the text. Allowing children to choose their own books and having a supply of these limited-vocabulary books available can do much to bolster young readers' confidence in their ability to successfully tackle the reading puzzle.

One final way teachers can help avoid the development of poor reading attitudes is to avoid labeling children. Exposing children to needless criticism, endless comparisons to other children, and membership in the low reading group can do much to damage a young child's self-image in the process of learning to read. Children should be supported in accomplishing what they are trying to do (F. Smith, 1988; Gambrell & Marinak, 1997). Read-along tapes, older children, parents, grandparents, and choral reading can do much to support unsure readers while shielding them from criticism and comparison. The use of flexible grouping schemes can also help alleviate the problem and stigma attached to membership in the low reading group.

UNDERSTANDING LANGUAGE

Language is a mutually or socially agreed on symbol system that can represent the full range of human knowledge, experience, and emotions. Children and adults use language as a tool for getting needs met, for thinking, for solving problems, and for sharing ideas and emotions. Language can be both expressive and receptive. *Expressive language* is used when the sender of a message encodes his or her thoughts into the symbol system of the language. *Receptive language* is used when the receiver of a message decodes the symbol system of the language into meaning.

Language study can be divided into at least four major fields of study:

1. *Linguistics* is the study of language structure and how it is used by people to communicate. In linguistics, language is grouped into four categories: phonemes, morphemes, syntax, and semantics.
2. *Psycholinguistics* is the study of how language is used and organized in the mind. This branch of study is mainly concerned with how language relates to thinking and learning.
3. *Sociolinguistics* is the study of how language relates to human and societal behaviors. It is concerned primarily with the social and cultural settings in which language is used, such as regions of the country, churches, or schools, and also how levels of education and social class affect language use.
4. *Language acquisition* is the study of how infants learn and use language to meet their needs and express their ideas.

For the purposes of studying reading, the English language can be divided into three language cueing systems: semantics (the meaning of language), syntax (grammar, or the word order of language), and visual-graphophonics (the visual, letter symbol-speech sound system).

The Semantic Cueing System in Language

Constructing meaning is the central reason for engaging in the act of reading or writing. The semantic language-cueing system relates to the reader's background experience, knowledge, interests, attitudes, perspectives, and present context or situation in reading. R. C. Anderson and Pearson (1984) point out that constructing meaning from print depends in large measure on a reader's prior knowledge and experience with the content of the text. These prior experiences and knowledge are stored together in the mind in something researchers and theoreticians call *schemata,* or *schemas* (anglicized). Schemas are defined as packages of related concepts, events, or experiences. Rumelhart (1980) asserts that schemas are the basic building blocks of cognition—the foundation of the ability to think and comprehend. Readers use schemas to interpret their world, experiences, and print. Each new concept or event we encounter in life is stored and used to help us make sense of our world.

Linguistics is the study of language structure and how it is used by people to communicate.

Psycholinguistics is the study of how language is used and organized in the mind.

Language acquisition is the study of how infants learn and use language to meet their needs and express their ideas.

Semantics is the study of meaning.

Schemas are defined as packages of related concepts, events, or experiences. For example, on reading the word furniture, readers often activate their knowledge related to furniture.

Schemas, or the lack thereof, can affect the construction of meaning from a text in many ways. First, readers may have knowledge about the content of a text yet be unable to access their stored knowledge. Read the following passage from an experiment conducted by J. C. Bransford and Johnson (1972):

> If the balloons popped the sound wouldn't be able to carry since everything would be too far away from the correct floor. A closed window would also prevent the sound from carrying, since most buildings tend to be well insulated. Since the whole operation depends upon a steady flow of electricity, a break in the middle of the wire would also cause problems. Of course, the fellow could shout, but the human voice is not loud enough to carry that far. An additional problem is that a string could break on the instrument. Then there could be no accompaniment to the message. It is clear that the best situation would involve less distance. Then there would be fewer potential problems. With face to face contact, the least number of things could go wrong. (p. 719)

Learning can be inhibited if text information is incompatible with information held in a specific schema.

Did you experience difficulty in locating a schema to help you interpret the text? If you did, you are not alone. J. C. Bransford and Johnson's (1972) experimental subjects experienced great difficulty assigning the content of this passage to a particular topic. Pause for a moment and try to make a mental note of your best guess of what this passage was about. Now turn to page 66 and look at Figure 3.3. Reread the passage.

Were you able to recognize that the passage was a reenactment of the Romeo and Juliet serenade? Did you think the passage was about physics or electricity? Were you thinking about someone making a phone call? Although the word order or syntax was correct and you could pronounce all the words in the text, this was not enough information to allow you to interpret what you read. Once you were able to access a particular schema or set of topical knowledge, however, you were able to interpret the somewhat elusive meaning of the text. Even when the information in a text is relatively familiar, readers often access the most likely schema or knowledge base and later modify their choice as they gain more knowledge from the text.

Read the following sentences and stop and picture what you see in your mind.

John was on his way to school.

He was terribly worried about the math lesson.

Now read the next sentence and notice what happens as you process the new information.

He thought he might not be able to control the class again today. (Sanford & Garrod, 1981, p. 114)

Did you notice a change in the schema accessed to interpret the text? Did your schema change from that of a young boy on his way to school worried about his math class and lesson to that of a concerned teacher?

Not only do schemas help readers interpret what they read, but the text can influence the schema a reader selects. This back-and-forth influence of text on schema and schema on text is known as an *interaction*.

Researchers have found that the more you know about a topic or event in text, the more comprehensible the text becomes (Pearson, Hansen, & Gordon, 1979). They have also found that schemas that contain information that is contrary to the information found in a text can result in decreases in comprehension. Suppose a text was written to persuade you that the world was flat rather than round; you would tend to dismiss that information as incorrect. Thus, texts that are contrary to or that refute a reader's prior knowledge can present comprehension difficulties (Alvermann, Smith, & Readence, 1985; Lipson, 1984).

Finally, the perspective of the reader can influence what is recalled from reading a text. Goetz, Reynolds, Schallert, and Radin (1983) found that people who read a test passage from the perspective of a burglar recalled distinctly different details than those who were instructed to read it from the perspective of the victim.

It is clear, then, that our expectations, experiences, and perspectives help us anticipate and interpret meaning and relate it to our existing knowledge. The more we experience both directly and vicariously, the more our schemas are refined and elaborated, allowing us greater ability and flexibility in interpreting what we read.

The Syntactic Cueing System in Language

The syntactic cueing system concerns knowledge about the order of language. Proper use of the syntactic system results in grammatically acceptable phrases and sentences in speech and writing. In short, a knowledge of syntax is an understanding of how language is ordered and how language works. Using accepted word order in language is important because it relates to how meaning is constructed. Suppose a reader picks up a book and reads the following:

Syntax is an understanding of how language is ordered and how language works.

> a is saying individual the is our aloud ability our in rarely purposes respond reader the silently only skill upon our is word of called conducted reading reading it Most by is private fluent that for element of to to use course one each to. (Chapman & Hoffman, 1977, p. 67)

Although each word can be read one by one, the meaning is obscured because word order is scrambled. When correct word order is restored, the meaning of the passage becomes easier to construct.

> The ability to respond to each individual word by saying it aloud is, of course, only one element in reading. It is a skill that the fluent reader is rarely called upon to use. Most of our reading is conducted silently for our own private purposes. (Chapman & Hoffman, 1977, p. 67)

Syntactic or grammatical knowledge enables readers to predict what comes next in a sentence or phrase. Syntax helps them avoid overrelying on the print to construct meaning. For example, read the following sentence.

Hopalong Hank is the name of my green pet ____ .

Even young children will fill in the blank with a noun. Although children may not be able to state a grammatical rule that accounts for the fact that a noun follows an adjective in a phrase or sentence, they are competent enough to know that only certain kinds of words are allowed in the blank. Moffett (1983) states that by the time children enter school, they have mastered the contents of an introductory transformational grammar text. This commentary underscores the fact that young children have mastered to a large extent the grammar or syntax of their native tongue when they begin formal schooling; and they can, if allowed, use this knowledge in learning to read.

Figure 3.3 The Romeo scene

The Visual-Graphophonic Cueing System in Language

The visual-graphophonic cueing system concerns concepts about how printed language works (directionality, the concept of *word,* word vs. letter, and the relationship between letters and the sounds the letters are intended to represent). *Graphemes,* or letters, are mutually agreed on symbols for visually representing sounds and spoken language. Some graphemic systems use an alphabetic principle, whereas others represent unified concepts or events. For example, English uses a graphemic system that is alphabetic, but Chinese uses a logographic system that represents entire concepts or events with pictures or logos.

A *phoneme* as defined by linguists is the smallest unit in a spoken language. A *grapheme* is defined as a printed symbol representing a phoneme. The English graphophonic system is composed of 26 letters (graphemes) and approximately 44 sounds (phonemes). Opinions on the number of phonemes we use in English vary among scholars in the field. Ruddell and Ruddell (1995) state that English is composed of 21 consonant sounds, 3 semivowels, 8 unglided vowels, and several levels each for pitch, juncture, and stress—the commonly used and understood prosodic features of spoken language. This brings the total to 44 phonemes. In addition to conventional forms of language study, other forms of sending messages involve using facial expressions, gestures, actions, and so on. In written language, punctuation (i.e., periods, commas, exclamation marks, quotation marks, etc.) is a means of graphically representing pitch, juncture, and stress found in speech.

Pragmatics

As children interact with their environment and with significant others in their social circles, they discover that language is power. They learn that they can control the responses and behaviors of others through language. They learn that language can be used to get what they want and need. In short, they learn that language serves a wide variety of communicative purposes.

The study of how language is used in society to satisfy the needs of human communication is called *pragmatics.* Hymes (1964) describes pragmatics as knowledge about language functions and uses that is conditioned by the language environment into which one is born. In other words, children's and adults' language-related knowledge, habits, and behaviors are directly influenced by the culture or society in which they live and interact.

Halliday (1975), in a monumental exploration of cohesion in English, described three aspects of pragmatic language functions in our day-to-day lives: (a) ideational, (b) interpersonal, and (c) textual. F. Smith (1977) expanded and explained in greater detail Halliday's three pragmatic language aspects by describing 10 functions or purposes for which language can be used:*

1. *Instrumental:* "I want." (Getting things and satisfying material needs.)
2. *Regulatory:* "Do as I tell you." (Controlling the attitudes, behaviors, and feelings of others.)
3. *Interactional:* "Me and you." (Getting along with others, establishing relative status.) Also, "Me against you." (Establishing separateness.)

Chapter 8, "Decoding Skills: Identifying Words in Print," provides further information about the graphophonic cueing system.

*A **phoneme** is defined by linguists as the minimal or smallest unit in a spoken language. A **grapheme** is defined by linguists as a printed symbol representing a phoneme. The **graphophonic system** is composed of 26 letters (graphemes) and approximately 44 sounds (phonemes).*

***Pragmatics** is knowledge of how, why, when, and where language is used in acceptable ways within a given society.*

*From "The Uses of Language" by F. Smith, 1977, *Language Arts, 54*(6), p. 640. Copyright 1977 by the National Council of Teachers of English. Reprinted with permission.

4. *Personal:* "Here I come." (Expressing individuality, awareness of self, pride.)
5. *Heuristic:* "Tell me why." (Seeking and testing world knowledge.)
6. *Imaginative:* "Let's pretend." (Creating new worlds, making up stories, poems.)
7. *Representational:* "I've got something to tell you." (Communicating information, descriptions, expressing propositions.)
8. *Divertive:* "Enjoy this." (Puns, jokes, riddles.)
9. *Authoritative/contractual:* "How it must be." (Statutes, laws, regulations, and rules).
10. *Perpetuating:* "How it was." (Records, histories, diaries, notes, scores.)

Once children understand the many uses for language in their own lives, they readily accept and recognize the purposes and meaning of language found in written language. In fact, success in reading depends very much on the degree to which the oral and written language children encounter in their early speaking and reading experiences mirror one another (Bridge, 1978; F. Smith, 1987).

In light of this fact, experiences with quality literature, extended discussions about literature, and opportunities to write and respond to literature become integral to success in early reading. It is in this setting that children begin to make the critical connections between oral and written language uses. When texts support and relate to children's oral language uses and experiences, children can readily discover that written and oral language are parallel forms of language that serve similar purposes for communication.

ORAL LANGUAGE ACQUISITION

After the birth of a child, parents anxiously await baby's first intelligible speech. In the months that precede this event, parents talk to baby, to each other, and to other individuals in their environment. The thought of withholding speech until their infant masters the mechanics of speech production never crosses the parents' minds. When baby finally utters the first intelligible speech sounds, they are often understood only by the parents or those most closely associated with the infant. Not until many weeks and months later will these utterances mean anything to the casual observer.

Several theories have been proposed in an attempt to explain how infants acquire an ability to speak their native tongue. The first theory to attempt an explanation of the origin and acquisition of oral language among infants emanates from the behavioristic tradition in the field of psychology.

Behaviorist Theory

Behaviorists believe that oral language is acquired through a process of conditioning and shaping that involves a stimulus, a response, and a reward.

Behaviorists believe that oral language is acquired through a process of conditioning and shaping that involves a stimulus, a response, and a reward. The stimulus and reward are controlled by the adult role models in the infant's environment. Parents' or other caregivers' speech acts as the stimulus in the speech environment. And when baby imitates the sounds or speech patterns of the adult models, praise and affection are given as a reward for attempts to learn language. Thus, the **behaviorist theory** of language acquisition states that infants learn oral language from adult role models through a process involving imitation, rewards, and rehearsal.

However, behavioristic theories of language development fail to explain a number of important questions associated with children's language acquisition. For example, if a parent is hurried, inattentive, or not present when the child attempts speech utterances, the rewards for the desired speech response are not always systematically provided. Thus, if baby's language acquisition were simply motivated by rewards, speech attempts would cease without the regular and systematic application of rewards.

Another problem with the behavioristic theory of oral language acquisition centers on the fact that young children do not simply imitate adult speech. Imitation implies that when Mother says, "Baby, say Mama," baby would imitate Mother by saying, "Baby, say Mama." Anyone who has raised children knows this is not the case. In fact, baby may not say anything at all!

Behavioristic language acquisition theories also do not account for speech terms invented by infants. For example, one girl used to call a sandwich a *weechie* even though no one in her home called a sandwich by any such name. Although behavioristic theories may explain to some extent the role of the social environment and the importance of adult role models in shaping children's language acquisition, the explanation offered by this theory is at best incomplete and at worse erroneous.

Innatist Theory

A second theory pertaining to oral language acquisition among children is called the **innatist theory.** Innatist theorists believe that language learning is natural for human beings. In short, babies enter the world with a biological propensity, an inborn device as it were, to learn language. Lenneberg (1964) refers to this built-in device for learning language as the language acquisition device (LAD). Thus, the innatist theory explains to some degree how children can generate or invent language they have never heard before.

N. Chomsky (1974, 1979) maintains that children use this LAD to construct an elaborate rule system for generating and inventing complex and interesting speech. Or put another way, just as wings allow birds to fly, LAD allows infant humans to speak. Although the innatist theory provides what appears to be a plausible explanation for some aspects of oral language acquisition, researchers have failed to supply satisfactory supporting evidence. Menyuk (1988) asserts, "Despite the apparent logic of this position, there is still a great deal of mystery that surrounds it" (p. 34).

Innatist theorists believe that language learning is natural for human beings.

Interactionist Theory

A third theory, known as the **interactionist theory,** appears to be a compromise between the behaviorist and innatist theories of language acquisition. Interactionists believe that many factors affect an infant's ability to acquire oral language (e.g., social, cultural, linguistic, biological, cognitive). Like Vygotsky (1962), interactionists believe that not only do cognitive and maturational factors influence language acquisition, but the process of language acquisition itself may in turn affect cognitive and social skill development. Thus, not only do the variables associated with language acquisition interact with one another, but the relationship among these variables appears to be reciprocal. Although children may be born to learn language, as the innatists propose, the language that is learned is determined by the social and linguistic environment into which the child is born and the language role models available. Put another way, the innatist theory explains why babies learn language in the first place, and the behavioristic theory explains why babies born in the United States generally learn to speak English rather than German. Thus, the most reasonable of the three

*The **interactionist theory** appears to be a compromise between the behavioristic and innatist theories of language acquisition.*

theories appears to be the interactionist theory, which blends innatist and behavioristic theories.

Halliday (1975) believes that language acquisition grows out of an active need to use language to function in society. Thus, infants learn language to survive, express themselves, and get their needs met. Holdaway (1979, 1984) discusses approximation with regard to how children learn to speak. He says that *approximating* means that infants respond to speech stimuli in their environment by producing a rough, rather than an exact, reproduction of the speech stimulus. Over time, these crude attempts begin to resemble modeled speech more closely until an acceptable reproduction is achieved. This is what is meant by the term *approximation* with respect to the acquisition of oral language. Holdaway (1984) also makes special note of the fact that parents not only tolerate approximations in oral language learning but meet these unrefined attempts with appreciation and affection.

STAGES OF ORAL LANGUAGE DEVELOPMENT

Teachers should become aware of the stages and average rates of oral language development. They should also bear in mind that oral language developmental rates may vary radically among individual children.

Parents' Baby Talk: One Way of Getting Attention

Parents interpret infants' early language rather than recognize it.

Across languages and cultures, adults use baby talk with their infants.

Parents use a special type of speech called *baby talk* with their infants up to about 24 months of age (Stern & Wasserman, 1979). Characteristics of baby talk include higher pitch and special intonation patterns. Studies have shown that infants respond best to high-pitch levels and to varied rhythms in speech (Kearsley, 1973; Kessen, Levine, & Wendrich, 1979). Other research has shown that the way in which infants react to adult speech affects the subsequent speech and behavior of their adult caretakers. In fact, adults usually use shorter speech patterns with significant periods of pausing to even encourage the infant to respond (Gleason, 1989). Thus, it appears that parents and adult caregivers are intuitively intense kid watchers (Y. M. Goodman, 1986). They seem to scaffold their speech demonstrations carefully in response to the overt reactions and suspected needs of their infants (Harste, Woodward, & Burke, 1984). In conclusion, parents and adult caregivers change their normal speech structures and prosodic features during interactions with their infants to encourage symbolic and verbal interaction.

The First 12 Months: A Time for Hope

Infant speech development begins with vegetative sounds.

During the first 2 months of life, babies cry to indicate their need to be fed, changed, or otherwise attended to in some manner. Because their tiny mouths are almost entirely filled with the tongue, and the vocal cords are still quite high in the throat, children at this age are unable to produce much variation in vocalization. The growth of the head and neck allows infants to vary their vocalizations later to produce sounds already responded to and experienced in the environment. During this early stage of speech development, young infants also make what linguists call *vegetative sounds* such as burps, coughs, and sneezes.

Cooing, crying, and babbling are all means of the developing infant communication with others.

From about 2 to 5 months of age, babies begin to coo, much like the sound made by pigeons, although during this period, they may also begin to vary the consonant sounds attached to the pure "oo" vowel sound typical of cooing. These cooing sounds, along with sustained laughter, typically seem to occur during social and speech interactions with caregivers in the environment. Cooing and laughter, however, may also oc-

Infants experiment with oral language and delight in the reaction they receive from parents and other caregivers.

cur when baby is alone or even asleep. D'Odorico (1984) has discovered that during this period, babies develop three distinct types of crying: a need for comfort, call for attention, and rescue from distress. All of these speech developments seem to provide great pleasure and even a sense of relief and encouragement for parents and caregivers.

From 6 months to 1 year of age, babies enter a period of oral language development called *vocal play and babbling.* This stage of development is marked by the ability to utter single syllables containing a consonant sound followed by a prolonged vowel sound, such as "Maa Maa." Although many other syllables (e.g., "Laa Laa") may be uttered during this period of development, only a few of these syllables will be retained into the next stage (e.g., "Ma Ma" and "Da Da"). These syllables are retained primarily because their use seems to bring a quick and delightful reaction from parents or adult caregivers. It is also during this period of speech development that children begin to use single words or *holophrases,* sounds, or invented words to represent complete ideas (Gleason, 1989). For example, while riding down the road, an infant of this age may point to a cow and squeal in delight "mooooo!" Or this same infant may point at the sink and say, "wa wa," indicating that he or she wants a drink of water.

From 1 to 2: By Leaps and Bounds

Language expands rapidly during the second year of development. Children continue to approximate the speech demonstrations of their parents and adult caregivers to the point of reduplicating their gestures and intonation patterns. Children in this stage continue to make hypotheses about the rules that govern language use. In meaningful

*Infants use two-word utterances called **telegraphic speech** to express their ideas and needs.*

contexts, these children try out and refine these rules in the course of using language. During this year, toddlers achieve a significant linguistic milestone when they begin to put two words together. These words are typically selected from the large open classes of words known as nouns, verbs, and adjectives. Because these two-word utterances sound much like the reading of a telegram, linguists have called this stage of speech development *telegraphic speech*. Typical utterances of the telegraphic type include "Mommy Down!" or "Go Potty?" One recognizes readily the ability of these two-word, cryptic speech patterns to communicate an entire complex idea or need.

From 2 to 3: What Does It Mean When I Say *No?!*

Oral language development continues to progress rapidly during the third year. The acquisition of words during this stage of speech development is remarkable. The broken and incomplete nature of telegraphic speech begins to give way to more complex and natural forms of speech. The use of descriptives such as adjectives and adverbs dramatically increases (Glazer, 1989).

One linguistic discovery made by the 2-year-old is the effect of negation. For many years, baby has heard the expression "No, No." Although over time he or she has learned what this expression implies for his or her own behavior, the child has not yet come to understand what the term *no* means when applied to the behavior of others. When asked, "Does baby want an ice cream cone?" baby responds, "No!" When baby discovers that the ice cream cone to which he or she had said "No" is now denied, he or she begins to cry. Thus, over time, the 2-year-old learns what "No" means for the behavior of others. In a sense, children at this age begin to establish their own identity—separate from others in their environment—and the "No!" response is evidence of this fact. The linguistic transformation of negation by using the words *no* and *not* is an important change in young children's language development.

From 3 to 4: The *Why* Years

*An **analogical substitution** is the overgeneralization by analogy of a language rule although small children rarely receive any formal instruction in these rules.*

By age 3, children begin to transform simple utterances by using complex sentences that include the use of prepositions, pronouns, negatives, plurals, possessives, and interrogatives. Children at this age have a speaking vocabulary of between 1,000 and 1,500 words (Morrow, 1989). Also at this age, children begin to use analogical substitutions in their speech. An analogical substitution is the overgeneralization by analogy of a language rule, which often results in using an incorrect substitute term in speech. For example, a child may say, "Mom, will you put my boots on my *foots*?" In this case, the child has analogously overgeneralized the rule for pluralizing nouns by adding an *s* to the irregular noun *foot*. Another example of an analogical substitution is the overgeneralization of the language rule for changing verbs to their past-tense form. For example, Junior rushes into the house and yells, "Daddy, come quick. I *digged* up that mean bush with flowers and thorns on it!" Language "errors" such as these reveal the language rules children have been internalizing and how they go about refining their language hypotheses.

During this fourth year of oral language development, children begin to transform basic sentence structures into interrogative sentences. Before this time, these same children indicated that a question was being asked by making a statement followed by a rising intonation pattern. Thus, questions were framed without the use of interrogatives or by transforming basic sentence structures. However, by the time the child is 3, parents have become well acquainted with the interrogative "Why?"

For statements that appear to be perfectly obvious to adults, the 3-year-old will begin the typical line of questioning with "Why, why, why?" After several answers to this interrogative, parents realize they are trapped in a linguistic situation that is nearly impossible to escape with dignity. Bill Cosby once gave a solution to a problem similar to this one that has been tried with 3-year-old children with reasonable success. The solution is simple: You ask why first! Regardless of the questioning nature of the 3-year-old, language development during the third to fourth year is an exciting experience for parents and caregivers.

From 4 to 6: Years of Growth and Refinement

At 4 years of age, children seem to have acquired most of the elements of adult language (Morrow, 1989). Vocabulary and syntactical structures continue to increase in variety and depth. Children at this age possess a vocabulary of about 2,500 words, which by age 6 will have grown to 6,000 words (D. A. Norton, 1993). Some children at age 4 or 5 continue to have trouble articulating the /r/ and /l/ sounds and the /sh/ at the end of words, although the vast majority of children are 90–100% intelligible by age 4.

At 4 years of age, children seem to have acquired most of the elements of adult language.

A son of one of the authors, Cody, has provided many examples of imaginative and generative language. One day Cody had purchased with his hard-earned money several plastic clips for his belt. With these he could hang his flashlight and plastic tools on his belt and make believe he was a working man. When his father first saw these clips on his belt, he inquired, "Cody, what are those things on your belt?" He responded, "Those are my *hookers, Dad!*"

On entering the world of school, kindergarten children often discover a genre of speech known as *toilet talk* and *curse words.* One day, a young boy overheard his kindergarten teacher reprimanding some other boys for using inappropriate language. Sometime later during the day, his teacher overheard him remark regarding the subject of taboo words, "She means those words your Daddy uses when he gets real mad!" According to Seefeldt and Barbour (1986), adults find the way in which children of this age group use language imaginative and amusing. We certainly concur with these observations!

Understanding the development of oral language among children can be a source of increased enjoyment for parents and teachers. Knowing how children develop language helps adults recognize and appreciate the monumental achievement of learning to speak—especially when it occurs so naturally and in a space of just 6 short but very important years.

DEVELOPMENT OF READING BEHAVIORS

As explained earlier in this chapter, the emergent literacy model of the developing reader views reading acquisition as a continuum of development: Children pass through certain stages of reading development on the literacy continuum toward becoming independent and skilled readers, much as they do in acquiring their oral language. Although the reading readiness model also describes reading development in stages, the emergent literacy model does not view the beginning of reading as a point or threshold on the literacy continuum but rather as a continuous journey along the continuum. Hence, children are never thought of or talked about as nonreaders under the emergent literacy model.

Under the emergent literacy view of learning to read and write, children are never thought of or talked about as nonreaders or nonwriters.

Some years ago, two teachers had a discussion about what they meant by "he is a beginning reader." These teachers began to gather data to support the construction of a reading development continuum, shown in Figure 3.4 (Cochrane, Cochrane, Scalena, & Buchanan, 1984). They divided the development of reading

(cont. page 64)

Figure 3.4 Reading development continuum

From *Reading, Writing, and Caring* (pp. 44–46) by O. Cochrane, D. Cochrane, D. Scalena, and E. Buchanan, 1984, New York: Richard C. Owen Publishers, Copyright 1984 by Richard C. Owen Publishers. Reprinted by permission.

A. PREINDEPENDENT READING STAGES

1. MAGICAL STAGE
   - Displays an interest in handling books.
   - Sees the construction of meaning as magical or exterior to the print and imposed by others.
   - Listens to print read to him for extended periods of time.
   - Will play with letters or words.
   - Begins to notice print in environmental context (signs, labels).
   - Letters may appear in his drawings.
   - May mishandle books—observe them upside down. Damage them due to misunderstanding the purpose of books.
   - Likes to "name" the pictures in a book, e.g., "lion," "rabbit."

2. SELF-CONCEPTING STAGE
   - Self-concepts himself as a reader, i.e., engages in reading-like activities.
   - Tries to magically impose meaning on new print.
   - "Reads" or reconstructs content of familiar storybooks.
   - Recognizes his name and some other words in high environmental contexts (signs, labels).
   - His writing may display phonetic influence, i.e., *wtbo = Wally, hr = her.*
   - Can construct story meaning from pictorial clues.
   - Cannot pick words out of print consistently.
   - Orally fills in many correct responses in oral cloze reading.
   - Rhymes words.
   - Increasing control over nonvisual cueing systems.
   - Gives words orally that begin similarly.
   - Displays increasing degree of book handling knowledge.
   - Is able to recall key words.
   - Begins to internalize story grammar, i.e., knows how stories go together, e.g., "Once upon a time," "They lived happily ever after."

3. BRIDGING STAGE
   - Can write and read back his own writing.
   - Can pick out individual words and letters.
   - Can read familiar books or poems that could not be totally repeated without the print.
   - Uses picture clues to supplement the print.
   - Words read in one context may not be read in another.
   - Increasing control over visual cueing system.

- Enjoys chants and poems chorally read.
- Can match or pick out words of poems or chants that have been internalized.

B. INDEPENDENT READING STAGES

1. TAKEOFF STAGE

- Excitement about reading.
- Wants to read to you often.
- Realizes that print is the base for constructing meaning.
- Can process (read) words in new (alternate) print situations.
- Aware of and reads aloud much environmental print (signs, labels, etc.).
- Can conserve print from one contextual environment to another.
- May exhibit temporary tunnel vision (concentrates on words and letters).
- Oral reading may be word-centered rather than meaning-centered.
- Increasing control over the reading process.

2. INDEPENDENT READING

- Characterized by comprehension of the author's message by reader.
- Readers' construction of meaning relies heavily on author's print or implied cues (schema).
- Desires to read books to himself for pleasure.
- Brings his own experiences (schemata) to the print.
- Reads orally with meaning and expression.
- May see print as literal truth. What the print says is right (legalized).
- Uses visual and nonvisual cueing systems simultaneously (cyclically).
- Has internalized several different print grammars, i.e., fairy tales, general problem-centered stories, simple exposition.

3. SKILLED READER

- Processes material further and further removed from his own experience.
- Reading content and vocabulary become a part of his experience.
- Can use a variety of print forms for pleasure.
- Can discuss several aspects of a story.
- Can read at varying and appropriate rates.
- Can make inferences from print.
- Challenges the validity of print content.
- Can focus on or use the appropriate grammar or structuring of varying forms of print, e.g., stories, science experiments, menus, diagrams, histories.

into two overarching categories: (a) preindependent reading and (b) independent reading. Within each of these two supercategories, Cochrane et al. describe three more subdivisions. Within the **preindependent reading** category are three subordinate divisions or stages: (a) the magical stage, (b) the self-concepting stage, and (c) the bridging stage. Within the **independent reading** category are three subordinate divisions or stages: (a) the takeoff stage, (b) the independent reading stage, and (c) the skilled reading stage.

The Mystery of Reading: The Magical Stage

Magical stage readers readily recognize print in their environment.

Long before children enter school, they begin noticing print in their environment and learn that printed language stands for words they have heard others use or that they have used themselves. Preschool children spontaneously learn to recognize billboards displaying their favorite TV channel logo. They can recognize a favorite soda brand logo or pick out their favorite cereal at the local supermarket. Although they may not be able to read the print exactly on each of these objects, when asked to tell someone what the soda can says, they may respond with "soda" or "pop."

Children at this stage of reading development love to have books read to them. In quiet moments, these children may crawl up into a large comfortable chair to hold, look at, and tell a story from the pictures of their favorite books. Jeremy, when he was 2 years old, enjoyed the naming of each animal in his favorite picture book. After naming each picture, he enthusiastically made the sounds of each, the roar of a lion or the crowing of a rooster. Parents and teachers of readers who find themselves journeying through the magical stage of reading development may see children who hold books upside down, turn the pages from the back to the front, and even tear out a page unintentionally. Although these actions may concern parents on one level, children who behave in these ways evidence a need for exposure to and understanding of the purpose of books. Withholding books from these children because they do not know how to handle them or read them at this stage would most certainly prove to be detrimental.

Favorite books are requested to be read aloud again and again, indicating how young children want to practice learning to read.

Children in the magical reading developmental stage develop a marked preference for a single or favorite book. Willing adults are often solicited into reading this book again and again. Although parents and others may tire rapidly of this book, the affection and familiarity increases with each reading for the child. Favorite books are often repeatedly read to the point where the child memorizes them. Some parents even try to skip pages or sentences in these books, thinking their child will not notice, but they soon learn their child has internalized these books, and the unsuspecting adult will be caught every time.

The reading of entire contexts such as those found on product logos and in books constitutes evidence that young children prefer to process printed language from the whole to the parts. Reading the entire context of a sign or label and memorizing an entire book are preferred by young children long before they want or need to focus on the details and parts of printed language.

"Look, Mom, I'm Reading": The Self-Concepting Reading Stage

*Children in the **self-concepting stage** view themselves as readers.*

The self-concepting reading developmental stage describes children who have come to view themselves as readers. Although these children may not yet be able to read exactly what the print says, they are certainly aware of printed language and their own progress toward breaking the literacy barrier. Children in this stage will try to read unfamiliar books by telling the story from the pictures and from their own imaginations. Selected words are readily recognized, such as their own name, favorite food labels, and signs on bathroom doors. These children evidence an increasing awareness of words and sounds. They often ask questions about how words begin and about rhyming words. If given a chance, these children can also fill in the rest of a sentence when asked to do so. For example, while reading the "Three Little Pigs," a teacher may say, "And the Big Bad Wolf knocked at the door and said, 'Little Pig, Little Pig'. . . .'" Children at this stage will immediately fill in the hanging sentence with "Let me come in."

Spanning the Gap: The Bridging Stage

Children at the bridging stage of reading development can pick out familiar words and letters in familiar contexts and books. However, they often cannot pick these same words out of an unfamiliar book or context when asked. Children in the bridging stage can reconstruct stories from books with greater precision than can children in the previous stage. In fact, children in the bridging stage can no longer reconstruct the story completely without using the print, although they will continue to use picture clues to augment their growing control over the print system.

Some parents and teachers discount the importance of memorizing books as a step in learning to read.

Children in the bridging stage can also read back what they have written. It has long been a disappointment for us when teachers and parents fail to count these early behaviors as real reading by brushing them aside as cute. Parents or teachers will often remark, "She's not reading. She's got that book memorized." Only by understanding that reading is a developmental process and that memorizing favorite print and books is universal among children will parents and teachers be able to enjoy, recognize, and support the progress their children make toward conventional reading behaviors and skills.

Blast Off!: The Takeoff Stage

If you are an unoccupied adult, look out for kids in the takeoff stage. They are excited about reading and will perform for any reluctantly willing audience. In fact, they want to demonstrate their emerging ability as frequently as others will allow. Children at this stage of reading development have a clear understanding that print forms the basis for reading the story and constructing meaning. Words read in one book or context are now recognized in new or unfamiliar contexts. Signs and environmental print are subjects of intense interest among take-off readers. It seems as if print has a magnetic appeal for these children.

Takeoff stage readers may sound like worse readers than children in earlier stages because they are focusing so intently on the print.

One autumn evening in a parent-teacher conference while one of the authors was teaching first grade, a parent said that her son, Curt, had requested new breakfast cereals. When his mother asked why, Curt responded, "There's not enough to read on these boxes." Mother bought him a box of cereal that seemed to contain enough print to satisfy his appetite.

Oral reading during the takeoff stage may become word or letter centered. Although oral reading before this time may have failed to perfectly represent the print on the page, it was smooth, fluent, and filled with inflection. The fact that words and letters have been discovered at this stage of development may lead to a situation where children appear to regress temporarily in their reading development. Children in this stage need to focus on print details, which leads to less fluent and inflected oral reading for a time. With sustained opportunities to read and gain control over the reading process and print system, fluency and inflection will soon return.

I Can Do It by Myself!: The Independent Stage

*The **independent reader** has developed control over the entire reading process and cueing systems.*

Takeoff readers want an audience, but independent readers take great pride in reading books to themselves for pleasure. The independent reader has developed control over the entire reading process and cueing systems. Reading is now carried on with simultaneous use of the author's printed clues and the reader's own schema for the topic. Fluency and inflection have returned to oral reading. In fact, children now read chunks or phrases fluently instead of laboring over single words. The independent reader is predicting ahead of the print and using context to construct meaning, not just as an aid to decoding (Stanovich, 1980). The ability to critically analyze print, however, has not yet been achieved. Thus, these readers may believe everything they read or may exhibit a tendency toward seeing anything in print as literal, truthful, and absolute.

Independent readers lack critical analysis skills.

Reaching the Summit: The Skilled Reader

Think of a time when you used print to support or extend your own thinking. What were you aware of at that time?

The skilled reader not only understands print but uses print to support and extend thinking. Although this is the final stage of reading development, it is not the end of the process. Becoming skilled in reading is a lifelong journey. The journey to skilled reading involves processing print that is further and further removed from one's own experiences and knowledge. In other words, print is now used increasingly as a means to acquire new and unfamiliar information. The variety of printed media that skilled readers process increases from narratives and textbooks to magazines, newspapers, TV guides, tax forms, and so on. Skilled readers can talk about different types of text organizations, make inferences from print, use print to substantiate opinions, challenge the surface validity of printed materials, and vary their reading rate according to the personal purposes for reading, such as skimming and scanning.

Although more research is needed to corroborate the descriptions offered by Cochrane et al. (1984) in the reading development continuum, this model provides a useful framework for parents, teachers, and scholars through which they can view the becoming of a reader with increased understanding and a good deal less anxiety.

DEVELOPMENT OF STORYBOOK READING BEHAVIORS

Notice two main categories of Sulzby's storybook reading behaviors.

A more scholarly description of reading development is described in the work of Sulzby (1985). In this line of scholarly investigation, Sulzby researched and tested a classification scheme for describing children's emergent reading of storybooks (Figure 3.5).

Picture-Governed

In the earliest stages of storybook reading, children's behaviors seem to be largely governed by pictures. Children's earliest **picture-governed** but not well-formed storybook reading behaviors often includes labeling, commenting, pointing, or even

Figure 3.5   Emergent storybook reading behaviors
Based on E. Sulzby (1985).

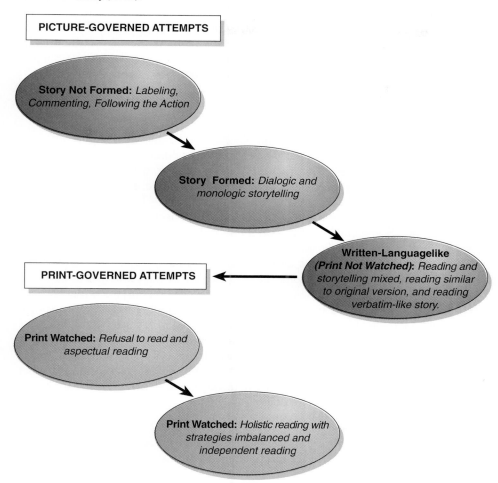

slapping at the pictures. Some children in this earliest stage of not well-formed storybook reading also become so caught up in the action of the pictures that they become part of the story as if the story were happening at the moment. For example, such a child might say, "See, there he goes. He's getting away, and they don't even see him!" At a later stage in picture-governed storybook reading, children's storybook readings become better suited or formed to the story in the book. Children engage in dialogic and monologic storybook reading. In *dialogic* storybook reading, children either create a "voice" for the characters in the story, or they tell the story by making comments directed to a listener of the story. Hence, characters are lived as if the child is in the story, or the child tells the story for the benefit of the listener. In any case, these story readings are often disjointed and difficult to follow. When children shift to *monologic* storytellings, a complete story is told and understood. The story is also told with a storytelling intonation rather than a reading intonation (Sulzby, 1985, p. 468).

After children reach the monologic storybook reading stage, they begin to tell well-formed stories that approximate written language. Children's written-languagelike reading attempts fall into three subcategories: (a) reading and storytelling mixed, (b) reading similar-to-original story, and (c) reading virtually verbatim. Once children enter into these storybook reading behaviors, they tend to focus their attention partially on the print as a means for governing their reading. Consequently, they move into Sulzby's (1985) second supercategory of storybook reading behaviors, **print-governed** attempts.

Print-Governed

Within this second supercategory of storybook reading behaviors, children often engage in three initial responses to storybook print: (a) refusal, (b) aspectual reading, and (c) holistic. In the first response, refusal, children refuse to try to read as they learn that print carries the story rather than the picture. For example, a child might remark, "I don't know the words. I can't read yet. I can't really read—I was just pretending." In the aspectual stage, children focus on one or two aspects of the print to the exclusion of others. Some children focus on memory for certain words, and others focus more intently upon specific letter-sound combinations for sounding out.

The final category, holistic, is divided into two subcategories: (a) reading with strategies imbalanced, and (b) reading independently. In the strategies-imbalanced stage, children might read a storybook by overdepending on certain strategies such as substituting known words for unknown words or sounding out every unknown word. In this stage, children have not yet become skilled in the selection and use of reading strategies during reading. In the independent stage, children have learned to self-regulate their strategy selection and balance the use of these strategies during reading. These youngsters sometimes sound like "word perfect" readers and at other times make deviations from the printed page but continue to demonstrate an awareness and control of the process of reading.

Sulzby (1985) remarks in summary,

> Finally, and most important, the development that was observed in these studies appears to make sense in light of theoretical ideas about general and language development and the findings of other current research. . . . These discoveries about literacy development appear to challenge traditional assumptions about the nature of young children—assumptions built upon a conventional model. (p. 479)

Emergent views of reading development do in fact challenge the more conventional views of the past.

DEVELOPMENT OF WRITING BEHAVIORS

Laura, a 3-year-old neighbor girl, sat quietly on the couch next to her parents with four unlined, white 3- by 5-inch index cards and an old, teeth-marked pencil in her hands as her parents visited in the living room with a neighbor. After about 10 minutes, Laura slipped down from the couch and walked over to the visitor. Timidly, she approached, clutching one index card behind her back. Then impulsively, she thrust the card from behind her back into the waiting hand of the visitor. He studied the marks Laura had made on the card. "Wow! Laura," he exclaimed, "You are writing!" Laura's face broadened into a smile that stretched from ear to ear, "I really writed, didn't I!"

Young children discover that writing has meaning before they know how to write real words.

Laura had demonstrated her developing understanding that writing is a system for recording thoughts and feelings on paper to share with others. She had come to this understanding without formal spelling and writing instruction. By carefully watching others in her environment, Laura had taken the risk to act like a skilled writer and try out her tentative hypotheses about how printed language functions.

Many of us have seen children attempting to solve the printed language puzzle through drawing and scribbling. Just as with reading, however, one may be tempted to dismiss these early attempts at writing as cute but certainly not *real* writing, as shown in Figure 3.6. This attitude may be as dangerous as rooting out a flower in the early stages of growth because the roots do not look much like the flower.

Through careful study over a period of decades, researchers have discovered that young children pass through developmental stages in their writing and spelling similar to those discussed with respect to oral language and reading development. An understanding of these stages will help teachers recognize the "roots" of writing and spelling development and, as such, enable them to help nurture the roots of scribbling and drawing into the flower of writing.

Writing can also be a system for developing thoughts and feelings.

Scribbling and Drawing Stage

When young children first take a pencil or crayon in hand, they use this instrument to explore the vast empty space on a blank sheet of paper. In the earliest stages, children's writing is often referred to as scribbling by adult observers (Clay, 1987). These random marks are the wellsprings of writing discovery. As shown in Figure 3.6, Laura's scribbles appeared to be the result of acting on the paper just to see what happens, without any particular intent. Her scribbles do not evidence much of what adults normally consider to be conventional or even purposeful writing. In Figure 3.7

Scribble writing is as important to writing development as babbling is to oral language development.

Figure 3.6 Laura's scribbles

Figure 3.7 Laura's scribbles as exploration

Figure 3.8 Laura's scribble cursive writing: Christmas list

Laura began to evidence an exploration of alternative forms to her previous scribbles. Circles, curved lines, and letterlike forms begin to appear as a part of Laura's writing exploration.

Sometime later, Laura's scribbles begin to look more and more like adult cursive writing. Note in Figure 3.8 that Laura's scribbles have become linear, moving from left to right. When questioned, Laura could tell what she meant with each of her scribbles. Unlike Figure 3.6, Laura's scribbling represented her meaning in a more conventional way. Because this writing sample was produced near Christmastime, Laura revealed that these scribbles represented a "Christmas Wish List." Often, letterlike writing or shapes as shown in Laura's Christmas list are used repeatedly in early writing attempts. Clay (1987) calls the tendency to reuse and repeat certain scribblings and drawings *recursive writing*. The purpose behind recursive writing seems to be a need for comfort and familiarity as children prepare to move into the next levels of writing development.

Figure 3.9   Laura's self-portrait

Weeks later, Laura produced the writing found in Figure 3.9. Note in this example that drawings have begun to be used to carry part of the intended message. In addition, directly above the head of what appears to be a drawing of a young girl, one can clearly see the emergence of letterlike forms etched in broken detail. When queried about the intent of these letterlike forms, Laura responded, "That says Laura!" Evidently, Laura had discovered at this point in her development as a writer that drawings can supplement the message and that writing is different from drawing.

In another example, Toby, a 4-year-old child, produced the writing found in Figure 3.10. Toby used humanlike forms to represent members of his family in his thank-you letter. One sees the use of letter-like symbols randomly scattered about the page. Near the center, Toby signed his name. By looking carefully, one can see the upside-down letter *b* and what looks like a letter *y,* which Toby chose to represent his name. Thus, one can see that during this initial stage of writing development, Laura and Toby used scribbling, drawing, and disconnected letterlike forms to explore and record their meaning on paper. These children had likewise discovered that writing

Figure 3.10 Toby's thank-you letter

can be used to communicate meaning and that although drawing and writing are complementary processes, they are not the same.

Prephonemic Stage

The next stage of writing and spelling development among young children is often called the **prephonemic stage** (Temple, Nathan, Burris, & Temple, 1993). At this stage of writing development, children begin to use real letters, usually capital letters, to represent their meaning; letters do not represent their phonemic or sound values. Rather, they use letters as placeholders for meaning, representing anything from a syllable to an entire thought. For example, Chaundra, a kindergartner, produced the writing in Figure 3.11. Note Chaundra's use of letters to represent her meaning. Only by asking the child to explain the meaning can one readily discern that she used letters as meaning placeholders and not to represent their phonemic values.

Clay (1975) points out that children in the prephonemic stage of writing development will usually produce a string of letters and proudly display them to a parent while asking, "What does this say?" or "What did I write?" We can remember our children doing this with the magnetic letters we have on our refrigerator doors; they would meticulously arrange a string of letters and then ask what they had written.

*In the **prephonemic stage,** children begin to use real letters, usually capital letters, to represent their meaning; letters do not represent their phonemic or sound values.*

Early Phonemic Stage

During the next stage of writing development, the **early phonemic stage** (Temple et al., 1993), children begin to use letters, usually capital consonant letters, to represent words. Children at this stage of writing development have discovered that letters represent sound values. Words are represented by one or two consonant letters, usually the beginning or ending sounds of the word. In Figure 3.12, Samantha uses only the consonant letters to represent the word *house* in her message.

*In the **early phonemic stage,** children begin to use letters, usually capital consonant letters, to represent words.*

Figure 3.11 Chaundra's pre-phonemic writing

Figure 3.12 Samantha's early phonemic writing: A house

Temple et al. (1993) suspect that the tendency for children in the early phonemic stage to represent a word with only one or two letters is due to an inability to "hold words still in their minds" while they examine them for phonemes and match these to known letters (p. 101). Although this may be true, it is also possible that children at this stage are continuing to learn certain letters of the alphabet. It may also be true that writers in this stage of development have not developed the ability to segment more than the initial or final sounds in a word. Certainly, these possibilities would lead to the incomplete representation of words as found in the early phonemic stage of writing development. This is an area needing much more investigation (Teale, 1987; Templeton, 1995).

Letter-Naming Stage

The **letter-naming stage** of writing development is a small but important jump from the early phonemic stage. This stage is recognized by the addition of more than one or two consonants with at least one vowel used by young writers to represent the spelling of words (Temple et al., 1988). Chris, a kindergartner, produced an example of the letter-naming stage writing in response to his teacher's urgings to write about the rainbow he had seen the day before (see Figure 3.13).

*The **letter-naming stage** is recognized by the addition of more than one or two consonant letters used by young writers to represent the spelling of words.*

Figure 3.13 Chris's letter-naming stage writing: Rainbow

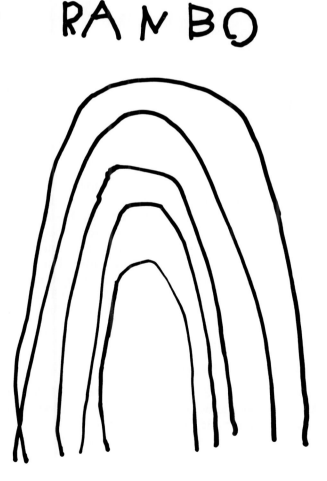

Figure 3.14 Devin's Halloween story

Although Chris continues to use capital letters exclusively, vowel letters have begun to appear in his writing. He had clearly discovered that words are made up of phonemes, both vowels and consonants; that these phonemes occur in an auditory sequence; and that these phonemes are properly represented in printed form from left to right. Although Chris was not yet reading independently, he had made important discoveries about print that nurtured his acquisition of reading; and his acquisition of reading will inform his acquisition of conventional spellings. With continued experiences in reading, Chris's writing will rapidly become more closely aligned with standard spelling and lead to the final stage of writing development—the transitional stage.

Transitional Stage

Transitional stage writings look like English, but the words are a mix of phonetic and conventional spellings.

Figures 3.14 and 3.15 illustrate the **transitional stage** of writing and spelling. Writing produced by youngsters in this stage looks like English, but the words are a mix of phonetic and conventional spellings. Typically, these writers neglect or overgeneralize certain spelling generalizations. For example, the final silent *e* is often

Figure 3.15   Candice's note to her parents

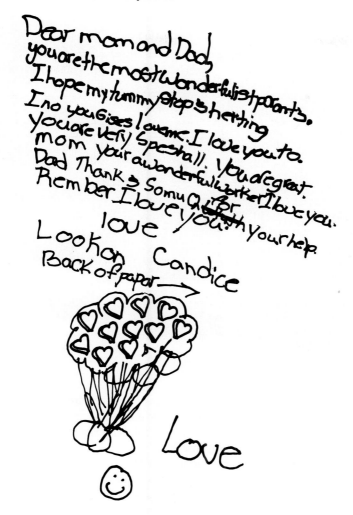

omitted by these writers; familiar phonic elements are substituted for less familiar phonic elements; and double consonants are typically neglected.

Devin, a first grader, wrote the story shown in Figure 3.14 during October. He demonstrates not only some of the substitutions and omissions mentioned previously, but also a top-to-bottom arrangement for his story.

Figure 3.15 shows a note that Candice wrote to her parents during the fall of her second-grade year. Notice the spellings of *parents, hurting, guys,* and *special.* Some of the spellings are unconventional, but the writing of this child looks very much like English and communicates the message well. Candice's writing is also a good example of the characteristics of transitional writing mentioned previously—the mix of standard and nonstandard spellings. Note also that transitional writers have discovered the use of other features of standard writing such as possessives, punctuation, and the standard letter- or note-writing format.

Figure 3.16 Development across the language modes of oral language, reading, and writing

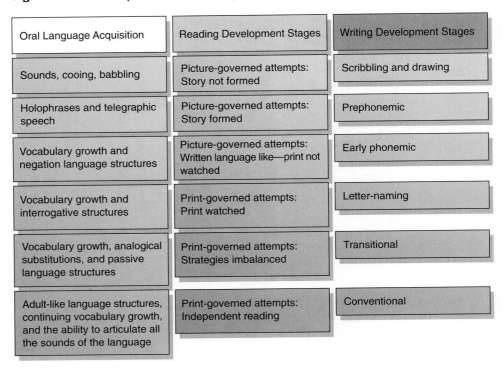

Oral Language Acquisition	Reading Development Stages	Writing Development Stages
Sounds, cooing, babbling	Picture-governed attempts: Story not formed	Scribbling and drawing
Holophrases and telegraphic speech	Picture-governed attempts: Story formed	Prephonemic
Vocabulary growth and negation language structures	Picture-governed attempts: Written language like—print not watched	Early phonemic
Vocabulary growth and interrogative structures	Print-governed attempts: Print watched	Letter-naming
Vocabulary growth, analogical substitutions, and passive language structures	Print-governed attempts: Strategies imbalanced	Transitional
Adult-like language structures, continuing vocabulary growth, and the ability to articulate all the sounds of the language	Print-governed attempts: Independent reading	Conventional

These examples demonstrate the progression of children's writing along a developmental continuum, originating with their early attempts to make meaning on paper through scribbling and drawing to later refinements including the use of conventional spelling, grammar, and mechanics.

One note of caution should be sounded at this point: Although we may discuss oral language, writing, and reading development in terms of stages through which children pass, we want to emphasize to teachers that they should not use this information to try to hasten development or to expect that children will, or even should, pass through each stage of development in the order described. Rather, teachers should use this information as a basis for understanding and supporting children's language learning by providing an environment rich in print and print use, gentle guidance, and enthusiastic encouragement as children struggle to solve the language and literacy puzzle. Just as children learned to speak within a nurturing home environment filled with supportive oral language users, they will develop into readers and writers within print-rich school and home environments filled with the support and encouragement of other competent and caring readers and writers. Figure 3.16 integrates information about oral language, reading, and writing development to show that these modes of language learning are developmentally similar.

Notice at least two ways young children can be helped to develop into readers and writers.

DEVELOPING A SENSE OF STORY

Experience with books and stories has no reasonable substitute for helping children acquire a sense of story.

In 1966, Durkin found that one characteristic common to the homes of early readers was parents who read books aloud to their children. Although we knew from Durkin's research that reading aloud to children seemed to be related to their becoming readers, we did not fully understand how reading aloud facilitated learning to read. During the 1970s, cognitive psychologists began to study the dimensions of how stories and narratives were constructed as well as how children developed a sense of story (Applebee, 1979). Out of this research grew the realization that authors seemed to be writing stories by following a set of implicitly held rules or schemas for how stories should be constructed. Thus, researchers developed a generalized set of rules to describe how narratives were composed. These rules were compiled and resulted in the development of several story grammars (Mandler & Johnson, 1977; Stein & Glenn, 1979; P. N. Thorndyke, 1977).

Story Grammar Elements

The elements found in a **story grammar** roughly parallel the description of the parts or plot of a story. A story typically begins with a description of the setting or location, the introduction of the main characters, and the general time frame of the events in the story. Stories may be composed of a single episode; however, complex stories may contain several episodes. Within each story episode, a series of events has been labeled by story grammarians. The labels may differ from one story grammar to another, but the elements generally include (a) a setting, (b) an initiating event, (c) an internal response, (d) goals, (e) attempts, (f) outcomes, and (g) a resolution.

The setting is described as a location, time, and the introduction of the characters. The initiating event or problem essentially starts the story action. This is followed by the reaction of the main character(s) to the initiating event, usually called an *internal response to the initiating event.* Next, the main character may devise some plan(s) to solve the problem set up in the initiating event, which is a process of setting goals to be achieved by the main character. Next, the main character makes one or more attempts to achieve the goals or solve the problem. Finally, the outcome of the attempts is made known, and the story is concluded by describing the results of the character's success or failure in achieving the desired outcomes.

One question raised subsequent to the development of story grammars centered on how adults had come to know and use a story grammar for writing stories. It was originally hypothesized that adult writers had learned the structure or grammar for stories by reading or hearing narratives throughout their lives. As a consequence, several researchers began to investigate whether or not young children had begun to develop a sense of story. A study of particular interest was conducted by Nurss, Hough, and Goodson in 1981 with a group of preschool children attending a local day-care center. These researchers concluded that preschool children had not yet developed a complete sense of story structure. Other studies (Olson & Gee, 1988; Stein & Glenn, 1979) demonstrated that older children recalled stories more completely and could reorder scrambled pictures and story parts with greater precision than younger children. Thus, a concept of story structure appeared to be developmental in the sense that older children possessed more complete story structure knowledge than did younger children. One reason for this may be that older children had more experience with stories and as a result had more elaborate schemas for stories than did their younger counterparts.

Some researchers have attempted to directly teach a story grammar in the hopes that a sense of story will be imparted more efficiently and effectively to young children; these attempts have met with mixed and often disappointing results (Golden, 1992; Muth, 1989). Consequently, few, if any, reading experts now endorse such an approach (J. L. Vacca, Vacca, & Gove, 1995). Instead, most researchers recognize that

Specific strategies for helping young children develop or elaborate story structure knowledge are presented in chapters 6 and 11.

experience with books and stories has no reasonable substitute for helping children acquire a sense of story. D. Taylor and Strickland (1986) recommend that parents read aloud regularly to their children to help them develop a sense of story. Nurss et al. (1981) suggest that story reading and discussion become an integral part of any preschool, nursery, or kindergarten program to help these children develop a concept of story structure. Morrow (1984) found that having children retell stories to other children or adults can significantly aid their development of a sense of story. Thus, the results to date indicate that children acquire a sense of story structure developmentally, over time, through reading or from hearing stories read aloud frequently.

UNDERSTANDING PRINT CONCEPTS AND THE LANGUAGE OF INSTRUCTION

Making sense of the purposes and symbols of reading and writing is a monumental task for young children. Research has demonstrated that children begin to attend to print at very young ages and come to school already having learned a great deal about the forms and functions of printed language (Y. M. Goodman & Altwerger, 1981; Harste et al., 1984). In our view, children must encounter the meaningfulness of printed language before they can make sense of school-based instructional practices (Lomax & McGee, 1987; Roberts, 1992). Thus, it is important for teachers to study how children develop an understanding of printed language to be able to effectively assist children through their learning experiences with printed language.

Environmental Print Studies

Environmental print is described as printed language on signs, displays, billboards, and labels found in the environmental context of everyday living.

Reading **environmental print** is described as reading printed language on signs, displays, billboards, and labels found in the environmental context of everyday living. In 1967, Ylisto conducted a print-awareness study involving 200 four-, five-, and six-year-old children. The subjects were presented with 25 printed word symbols taken from traffic signs and cereal boxes. The 25 items progressed in difficulty through six steps, from a highly contextualized setting (in a natural setting or photograph) to a more abstract setting (a page of a book or a word card). The youngest of these children were able to identify some of the symbols through each of the six steps.

Romero (1983) and Y. M. Goodman and Altwerger (1981) conducted studies to investigate the print awareness of Anglo, African-American, Mexican-American, and Papago children ages 3, 4, and 5. These researchers found that 60% of 3-year-old children and 80% of 4- and 5-year-old children could read some environmental print. Harste et al. (1984) found that 3-year-old children could correctly identify environmental print or make a semantically acceptable "best guess." Hiebert (1978) found that children made significantly more errors recognizing words when they were presented without the environmental context. In other words, children seemed to be reading the entire context—not just the print. For example, if the word on a stop sign were transcribed onto a box of cereal, younger children would read the word *stop* as the cereal name about 38% to 50% of the time (Dewitz, Stammer, & Jensen, 1980). Thus, according to J. M. Mason (1980), children's early reading of environmental print is highly context dependent.

In another study that supported Mason's (1980) belief, Masonheimer, Drum, and Ehri (1984) found that young readers' errors increased when the unique print associated with a logo was removed from a full context. Even greater increases in errors were found when the unique print associated with a logo was replaced with conventional print. From these results, many researchers believed that children failed to devote attention to graphic detail; rather, children were reading the entire context. However, McGee, Lomax, and Head (1988) found that nonreaders did devote attention, although very limited, to graphic detail in recognizing environmental print. In fact, attention to environmental print is now seen as an important means for introducing children to the world of written language (McGee & Richgels, 1996).

Reading environmental print has been shown to be highly dependent on the context of the print.

Student Perceptions of Reading

When a young girl attending an elementary school was asked about what she could do to become a better reader, she responded, "I would study my vowel rules and my phonics a lot because that's mostly reading" (DeFord & Harste, 1982, p. 592). Jerry Johns (1986) related a time when a second-grade boy was asked, "What do you think reading is?" He responded, "Stand up, sit down!" By this he meant that when he read his teacher requested that he stand and sit when he was finished. These are just a few of the perceptions students have about the purposes of reading.

In a pioneering study, Reid (1966) investigated the understanding of the purposes of reading held among 5-year-old children in a classroom in Edinburgh, Scotland. The children in this class were asked, "What is reading?" Their answers to this question indicated that they had a very vague notion about what reading was and how it was to be done. Some children, Reid reported, were unsure about whether one read the pictures or the marks on the page.

In a similar study, Weintraub and Denny (1965) found that children came to school with widely disparate perceptions about reading, and that 27% of them could not verbalize anything intelligible about the reading process. Johns and Johns (1971) supported this finding with their own research: They found that 70% of students from kindergarten through grade 6 gave vague, irrelevant answers or no response at all to the question of "What is reading?"

In a later and much larger study involving 1,655 students in grades 1 through 8, Johns and Ellis (1976) found that 69% of these students gave essentially meaningless responses to the question of "What is reading?" Nearly 57% of the responses to the question "What do you do when you read?" were judged to be meaningless. In answer to the question "If someone didn't know how to read, what would you tell him that he would need to learn?" 56% of the respondents indicated something that had to do with pronouncing or decoding words and letters. This decoding perspective held among young readers on how reading could be improved was also replicated in a study by Canney and Winograd (1979).

An interesting insight into young readers' perspectives about reading is found in the work of Reutzel and Sabey (1996). These researchers examined how first-grade student perspectives about reading were influenced by teachers' theoretical beliefs about how children learn to read. Children were given the *Burke Reading Interview* (Burke, 1987), and teachers completed the *Theoretical Orientations to Reading Profile* (DeFord, 1985). Responses of students and teachers were examined and were found to be highly related to one another. Hence, students' perceptions of the

Children's perceptions about reading are closely tied to their teachers' beliefs and attendant instructional practices.

act of reading seemed to be subject to the influence of their teachers' beliefs about reading instruction.

From these studies, one may conclude that young readers have only vague notions about the purposes and mechanics of the reading process. Additionally, children's perceptions of the purposes and functions of the reading act are influenced by the beliefs their teachers hold about reading instruction. Finally, as children gain more experience with print, they are able to refine and better articulate their concepts about reading and are more likely to view reading as a meaning-seeking or constructive process.

Very young students rarely perceive reading to be an act associated with constructing meaning for personal purposes.

UNDERSTANDING CONCEPTS ABOUT PRINT

As children have opportunities to interact with print through reading signs, learning the alphabet, or reading books, they begin to pay closer attention to the details of printed language. **Print concepts** typically embrace an understanding of some of the following:

1. Directionality (left to right, top to bottom)
2. The difference between a word and a letter
3. The meaning and use of punctuation marks
4. The match between speech and print on the page
5. Many other technical understandings about how print and books work

Day and Day (1979) found that 80% of 51 first graders they studied had mastered book orientation and directionality by the end of first grade. However, only a small percentage could recognize incorrect words or letter sequences in a line of print or could explain the use of quotation marks. Downing and Oliver (1973) found that young children could not differentiate reliably between a word and a letter. Johns (1980) found that above-average readers evidenced greater print awareness than did below-average readers. Yaden (1982) concluded that even after a full year of reading instruction, some beginning readers' concepts about printed language remained incomplete and uncertain. Roberts (1992) and Lomax and McGee (1987) found that an understanding of print concepts is an important precursor of reading development among young children.

Young children learn as much about print concepts and word reading in a print-rich environment as they do with the addition of direct instruction on specific print concepts.

In view of these findings, Johns (1980) and N. E. Taylor (1986) cautiously recommended that print concepts and the language of reading instruction be explicitly taught to young readers. Other researchers believed children would learn printed language concepts as well in a print-rich environment where they interacted on a consistent basis with meaningful printed materials (Ferreiro & Teberosky, 1982; Hiebert, 1981; Holdaway, 1979; McCormick & Mason, 1986).

Research reported by Reutzel, Oda, and Moore (1989) showed that kindergartners learned as much about print concepts and word reading in a print-rich environment as they did with the addition of direct instruction on specific print concepts. Thus, it appeared that children learned print concepts as well in a print-rich environment with plenty of opportunities for interaction in meaningful ways with printed materials as with the addition of isolated, systematic print concept instruction.

Summary

In many respects, the acquisition of reading and writing parallels the acquisition of oral language among infants and young children. Children process print and speech from whole to parts in supportive language environments. They begin by crudely approximating demonstrations of speech, reading, and writing behaviors and refine these attempts over time to become more like the people they attempt to emulate. Adult language users play a critical role in youngsters' speech, reading, and writing acquisition. An informed teacher can do much to support youngsters in their attempts to become independent, skilled readers and writers.

Concept Applications

In the Classroom

1. Using the information about children's writing development, describe a ZPD à la Vygotsky where a teacher's intervention could be most beneficial to a learner.
2. Using the information about children's reading development, construct a diagram describing reading developmental attributes one might expect to see during each of Piaget's Stages of Cognitive Development.

In the Field

1. Visit 15 minutes with two children of about the same age. Record your visit on audiotape. Write a short essay about the features of spoken language you noted these children had learned well and those speech features for which they may need further demonstrations to support their learning.
2. For 1 week (1 hour per day), visit a kindergarten classroom. Make a listing of invented language used by children at this age. Publish your findings for the other members of the class.
3. Interview two parents about their young children's reading development. Ask them what their children are doing with books and print. Describe in writing the results of the interviews. Which stage(s) of reading development would best describe these two children's reading behaviors? Why?
4. Collect five samples of kindergarten or first-grade children's writing. Label each according to a stage of writing and spelling development described in this chapter. Explain your reasons for categorizing each.
5. Show a child at least 10 food product labels and ask him or her to read them. Record each answer. Ask the child to explain how he or she arrived at these answers. Discuss in writing each answer with respect to how the child answered and why.
6. Ask a child to tell you a story. Record the telling on audiotape. Analyze the telling using a story grammar. Describe in writing the parts of the story included and excluded in the telling. What can you conclude about this child's sense of story development?
7. Hand two kindergarten or first-grade children a book by the spine and upside down. Ask each child to:
   a. Show you where to begin reading.
   b. Show you which way your eyes should progress along the print.
   c. Show you a letter.
   d. Show you a word.
   e. Show you the end of the book.
      Discuss in writing your findings for each child. Describe what each child knows and does not yet know about printed language concepts.

8. Ask three young children what they think reading and writing are. Record their responses on audiotape or in writing. Explain the perceptions these children have of reading and writing in a separate essay or in an entry in your learning log.
9. Ask a young child to read a book to you. After recording the event, reread the description of emergent storybook reading behaviors in Figure 3.5 (based on Sulzby, 1985). Where does this child fit within the developmental stages of storybook reading development?

Recommended Readings

Butler, D., & Clay, M. (1979). *Reading begins at home.* Portsmouth, NH: Heinemann.

Clay, M. M. (1975). *What did I write?* Portsmouth, NH: Heinemann.

Clay, M. M. (1987). *Writing begins at home.* Portsmouth, NH: Heinemann.

Clay, M. M. (1991). *Becoming literacy: The construction of inner control.* Portsmouth, NH: Heinemann.

Cochrane, O., Cochrane, D., Scalena, S., & Buchanan, E. (1984). *Reading, writing and caring.* New York: Owen.

Fosnot, C. T. (1996). *Constructivism: Theory, perspectives, and practice.* New York: Teachers College Press.

Gentry, J. R. (1987). *Spel is a four letter word.* Portsmouth, NH: Heinemann.

Temple, C., Nathan, R., Burris, N., & Temple, F. (1993). *The beginnings of writing* (3rd ed.). New York: Allyn & Bacon.

Vygotsky, L. S. (1978). *Mind in society.* Cambridge, MA: Harvard University Press.

Whaley, J. F. (1981). Story grammar and reading instruction. *The Reading Teacher, 34,* 762–771.

Yaden, D. B., & Templeton, S. (1986). *Metalinguistic awareness and beginning reading: Conceptualizing what it means to read and write.* Portsmouth, NH: Heinemann.

chapter 4

Basal Readers:

Focus Questions

When you are finished studying this chapter, you should be able to answer these questions:
1. How have basal readers changed over the years?
2. What are the major components associated with basal readers? What are five strengths and five weaknesses of basal readers?
3. How are basal readers produced and organized?
4. What are at least three ways in which teachers can take control of their basal teacher's editions; that is, reconciled reading lesson, balanced reading programs, LEA, DRTA, and so on?
5. How can teachers help all students—including those with special language, cultural, or learning needs—succeed with basal readers?

Determining How to Use Basals Effectively

Key Concepts

Basal Readers
Skill Instruction
Scope and Sequence Chart
Decodable Text
Basal Reader Adoption

Themed Units
Literature-Based Basals
Teacher's Edition
Balanced Reading Program
Reconciled Reading Lesson

Basal readers in one form or another have played an integral role in American reading instruction for centuries and are likely to continue to do so well into the future (McCallum, 1988; Reutzel, 1991). According to *The Literacy Dictionary,* a basal reading program is "a collection of student texts and workbooks, teachers' manuals, and supplemental materials for developmental reading and sometimes writing instruction, used chiefly in the elementary and middle school grades" (T. L. Harris & Hodges, 1995, p. 18)

UNDERSTANDING THE BASAL READER

Basal readers are used daily in 9 of 10 primary classrooms in the United States.

A basal reading program is a set of commercially prepared and sequenced materials for providing classroom reading instruction in elementary and middle schools. Research indicates that basal readers are used daily in 92% to 98% of primary classrooms in the United States (Flood & Lapp, 1986; Goodman, 1989). More recent data suggest that 85% of intermediate grade classrooms continue to rely on basal reader instruction (Shannon & Goodman, 1994). These data clearly demonstrate the integral role that basal reader instruction has played and continues to play in contemporary American reading instruction.

The hornbook clearly illustrated the strong religious underpinnings of early American reading instruction.

Current basal readers have descended from a long ancestry of basal readers. The first in this line of predecessors was the hornbook, the earliest reading instructional material widely used and recorded in American history (N. B. Smith, 1986). A cursory examination of the hornbook clearly illustrates the strong religious underpinnings of early American reading instruction (Figure 4.1). Another ancestor of the modern basal published during this era of reading instruction was the New England Primer. Rooted deeply in the religious freedom movement of the American colonists, early reading instruction was aimed at helping children learn the necessary theology to work out their salvation. This goal could be accomplished only by reading the Bible.

McCallum (1988) pointed out that as the American citizenry moved away from government by the church to civil government, moral character, national interests, and patriotism for a new nation influenced both the aims and the content of basal readers. Consequently, the McGuffey Eclectic Readers (Figure 4.2) were introduced to the educational community in the 1830s by William H. McGuffey (Bohning, 1986). In 1912, the Beacon Street Readers were published by Ginn & Co., located

Figure 4.1 A hornbook, with the alphabet, a syllabary, and the Lord's Prayer
Photo courtesy of The Horn Book, Inc.

Figure 4.2 Sample pages from *McGuffey's Eclectic Primer,* Revised Edition, New York: Henry H. Vail, 1909.

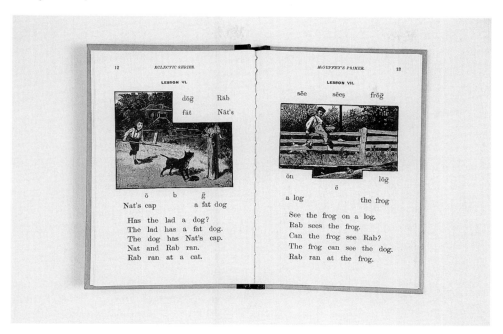

on Beacon Street in Boston. These readers reflected a strong emphasis on phonics, complete with elaborate articulation drills and diacritical markings (Aukerman, 1981).

Some may recall the *Dick and Jane New Basic Readers* (Figure 4.3), principally authored by William S. Gray and Marion Monroe and originally published by Scott, Foresman and Company in 1941. The *Dick and Jane* readers conveyed the stereotypic American dream pervasive in the United States during and following World War II and the Korean Conflict. The family depicted in the *Dick and Jane* basals owned a spacious, white, two-story home in a well-cared-for suburban neighborhood. Mother stayed home while Father worked at a successful career, providing for the family's needs. A car or two and a pet dog and cat also adorned the dream of the American family portrayed in this series. For those who remember the *Dick and Jane* readers fondly and wish to update their acquaintance, we suggest a modern humorous satire written by Marc Gallant (1986), entitled *More Fun With Dick and Jane.*

The basal readers produced during the mid-1960s and through the early 1970s reflected a serious-minded response to a perceived threat to national security by the successful launching of Russia's Sputnik into space. This perception prompted a quick return to basic and rigorous academics in American schooling. The publication of Flesch's 1955 book, *Why Johnny Can't Read,* added fuel to the fire for the hasty return to phonics and basic **skill instruction** in reading.

The basals of the late 1970s and the early to mid-1980s reflected a continued emphasis on a basic skills approach to reading instruction, which was accompanied by a major shift in the composition and content of basal readers. The stereotypic portrayal of men and women in basals was attacked and, as a consequence, revised. The failure of basal readers to represent ethnic minorities fairly was assailed by basal crit-

Observe the language in Figure 4.3.

The basals of the late 1970s and early 1980s reflected an emphasis on back to basics and accountability.

Figure 4.3 Sample pages from the *Dick and Jane Readers*

From *The New We Look and See* by W. S. Gray, M. Monroe, A. S. Artley, and M. H. Arbuthnot, Chicago: ScottForesman. Copyright 1956 by ScottForesman.

Look, Jane.
Look, Dick.
See funny Sally.
Funny, funny Sally.

18   19

Puff

ics. Thus, compilers of the basals of this era reacted by attempting to accurately represent the increasing complexity of modern American society while maintaining a continuing emphasis on back to basics and accountability (Aukerman, 1981).

Then as now, reading instruction was viewed as a principal means for affecting desirable change in American society. As the whole language philosophy became a force for change among reading professionals in the mid- to late 1980s, basal bashing came into style (McCallum, 1988). Basals were sharply criticized by children's literature advocates for devaluing good literature, ignoring the needs of the learner by emphasizing skill instruction, controlling the vocabulary of stories, and prescribing, even usurping, teachers' practices and decisions. On the other hand, E. D. Hirsch (1987), among others, called for the standardization of the school curriculum to produce a literate citizenry and workforce for the future of the nation.

Thus, the interests of the aesthetic and the individual have run head-on into the interests of society, business, and science. Mosenthal (1989b) characterized this situation as "teachers between a rock and a hard place" (p. 628). In fact, publishers of basal readers seemed to be caught in the same hard spot as teachers. In reaction, basal publishers scrambled to meet the divergent demands of this new split in the marketplace. On the one hand, children's literature advocates declared the need for good literature, themed instructional units, natural language in basal stories, and guidance rather than prescription in teacher's editions. On the other hand, school boards, state offices of education, government, and businesses demanded standardized curricula, the use of scientific research findings and standardized test scores, basic skill mastery, accountability, and more, not less, prescription in teacher's editions. So dramatic was the polarization that some publishers actually published two teacher's editions to meet the needs of these two groups—for example, McGraw-Hill's integrated

Basals have been sharply criticized by whole language advocates.

Figure 4.4 Basic skills taught through reading basal readers, as depicted in this 1950's classroom, was the accepted methodology for teaching reading for over 40 years.

language arts edition and basic skills edition (Sulzby, Hoffman, Niles, Shanahan, & Teale, 1989).

During this time, the role of the basal reader became the focus of pointed debates. Two books, entitled *The Basal Report Card* and *Basal Readers: A Second Look,* called for major reforms in both the content and use of basal readers (K. Goodman, Shannon, Freeman, & Murphy, 1988; Shannon and Goodman, 1994). In a point/counterpoint series in *Reading Today* ("Point/Counterpoint," 1989), the bimonthly newspaper of the International Reading Association, the role of the basal reader was hotly debated. More recently, the debate over basal readers has involved concerns related to teachers' professional skills and decision making. Shannon (1989, 1992, 1993) has asserted that basal readers have contributed to a "deskilling" of teachers' expertise and decision making related to reflective and thoughtful reading instruction. Baumann (1992, 1993, 1996) has asserted, on the other hand, that teachers who are otherwise capable and intelligent decision makers are not falling prey to a mindless adherence to basal teacher's editions as Shannon indicates. In fact, Baumann maintains that such an argument is insulting. He asserts that teachers who otherwise think and make decisions do not stop making decisions when they approach basal reading instruction (Durkin, 1984).

Because of the widespread, pervasive, and continued use of basal readers in American schools as the core for providing basic reading instruction (Flood & Lapp,

Teachers and administrators need to understand the basal reader to make informed instructional decisions.

1986; Shannon, 1983; Shannon & Goodman, 1994), it is imperative that preservice and in-service teachers learn to use the basal reader with judgment and skill. The purpose of this chapter is to provide teachers with the information necessary for taking control of their basal reader teacher's editions. Teachers who are in control of reading instruction are empowered to make informed instructional decisions about how, when, and why to use basal readers for providing reading instruction.

ANATOMY OF THE BASAL READING APPROACH

Focus on the core materials that compose basal readers.

Basal readers are typically composed of a set of core materials including the student's text (current series usually include some shared reading or big books as part of the core in the early grades), the teacher's edition, student's and teacher's workbooks, supplemental practice exercises and enrichment activities (usually both of these are in the form of masters that can be duplicated), and end-of-unit or end-of-book tests. Other supplemental materials can be acquired at additional cost, such as filmstrips, picture cards, picture with letter cards, letter cards, word cards, large charts, additional ditto sheet masters, classroom trade-book libraries, big books, and technology including videotapes and CD-ROM computer software. In addition, many basal reading series provide a system for record keeping, management of the reading skills taught and mastered, and assessment. Figure 4.5 shows core components available for Scholastic's *Literacy Place* basal program for grades 3–6. Because many teach-

Figure 4.5   A basal reading program usually includes a teacher's edition, a student edition, workbooks, and an array of supplemental materials
From *Literacy Place: Suggested Core Components,* 1996, New York: Scholastic. Copyright 1996 by Scholastic, Inc. Reprinted by permission.

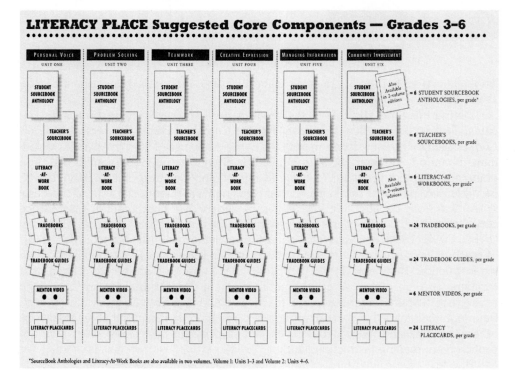

Figure 4.6 A scope and sequence chart showing the range of skills to be taught in a basal program

From *Treasury of Literature: A Place to Dream* (Teacher's ed., Level 3-1, pp. R116–R117), Orlando, FL: Harcourt Brace & Company, 1995. Copyright 1995 by Harcourt Brace & Company. Reprinted by permission.

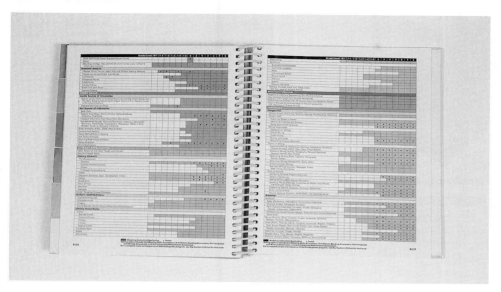

ers will employ a basal series in a school reading program, we will describe each of the most basic basal components along with examples.

The Teacher's Edition

Perhaps the most important part of the basal reading program is the **teacher's edition** because it is often the instructional guidance and in-service support that most teachers receive when they use a basal series. Within the pages of the teacher's edition, one usually finds three important features: (a) the scope and sequence chart of the particular basal reading program, (b) a reduced version of the student's text, and (c) a suggested lesson plan for the teacher (see Figures 4.6 and 4.7). A **scope and sequence chart** describes in great detail the range of skills to be taught in a basal program as well as the order in which these are to be presented. A reduced version of the student's text, or facsimile, is included in the teacher's edition for the teacher's convenience. The lesson plan for each unit in the basal reader is already done for the teacher to save time. More recent editions of the basal reader (1993 and beyond) make subtle changes in the structure of reading lessons. Some basal readers are slowly moving away from the long-revered directed reading activity of E. Betts (1946) toward the lesson structure of the Directed Reading Thinking Activity (Stauffer, 1969).

It is important for teachers and administrators to understand that the teacher's edition is a resource to be used discriminatingly and not as a script to be rigidly followed. Teachers and administrators should not allow the teacher's edition to dictate the reading program. Rather, teachers should be encouraged to decide what is and is not appropriate in the teacher's edition for use with a particular group of children.

*A **scope and sequence chart** describes in detail the range of concepts and skills to be taught in the basal program as well as the order in which these concepts and skills are to be presented.*

The long-revered directed reading activity has been dropped in many current basal readers and replaced with the Directed Reading Thinking Activity (Stauffer, 1969).

Figure 4.7   An example of a 1997 teacher's edition for Scholastic's basal series

From *Literacy Place: Literacy SourceBook,* 1996. New York: Scholastic. Copyright 1996 by Scholastic, Inc. Reprinted by permission.

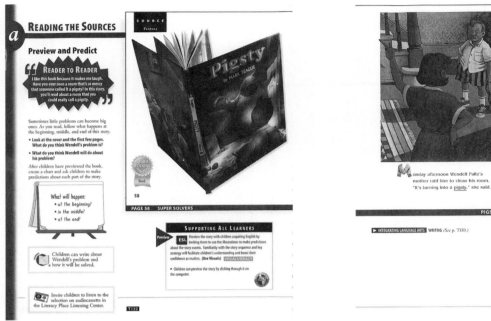

The Student's Basal Text

Although many basal readers include well-regarded children's literature, publishers continue to modify or adapt children's books in various ways for inclusion in basal readers.

The student's basal is an anthology of original and classic stories, poems, news clips, and expository text selections. Some selected original stories have been created expressly by authors for the student's basal reader, whereas other classic selections have been adapted from children's literature or trade books. High-quality artwork generally accompanies the selections. Interspersed throughout the student's text, one may also find poetry selections, jokes, riddles, puzzles, informational essays, and special skill and/or concept lessons. Some basal texts contain questions children should be able to answer after reading the stories. Upper level basal readers often contain a glossary of words that students can refer to when decoding new words or so that students can look up the meaning of new words found in the text.

All of these changes are reflected in current research that reveals how recent revisions undertaken by basal publishers are yielding a "more engaging basal" than that of a decade ago as judged by students, teachers, and reading experts (Hoffman et al., 1994; McCarthey et al., 1994). A close examination of quality children's literature included in the more recent basal reader revisions reveals few, if any, alterations of the authors' language or word choice. However, one disturbing publishing practice relates to cropping or cutting original artwork in children's picture book stories. Because of costs involved in the reproduction and permission for use of original artwork, basal publishers have engaged in cutting or moving the beautiful artwork that supports and sustains the text in many children's books (Reutzel & Larsen, 1995). The practice of cropping or cutting support artwork may be even more damaging than altering the text for young, emergent readers who may rely more heavily on the pictures for support throughout their initial readings of a new or unfamiliar text at early stages of reading development.

A hallmark of past and some current basal reader stories is carefully controlled vocabulary and text difficulty, particularly in the early grades, which allow for the introduction of a predetermined number of unfamiliar words in each new story. Vocabulary control is usually achieved by using simpler words, or words with few syllables, in place of longer words and by shortening sentences. In addition, some basal publishers ensure that lines of text, prepared for grades K and 1, do not break:

Bob went to the barn for Dad

Dad asked Bob to feed the pigs

These practices to control the difficulty of basal reader stories supposedly render a text less difficult to read. Research by Pearson (1974), however, challenges this concept that shorter sentences are easier to read. According to Pearson's research, short, choppy sentences tend to be more difficult to comprehend because explicit connecting or sequencing words such as *because, and, so, then, before,* and *after* are deleted from the text and consequently need to be inferred by the reader.

In some basal reader programs, the earliest books, or *primers,* often contain reading selections known as **decodable text.** Decodable texts are designed to reinforce a particular phonic generalization by using highly controlled vocabulary in their stories. Decodable texts are frequently sold as supplemental books to school districts to augment basal reader instruction. A decodable text example is shown in the following excerpt (*Scholastic,* Book 14, Phonics Readers, pp. 2–7; Schreiber &Tuchman, 1997):

The Big Hit

Who hid? Pig.
Who had a mitt? Pig.
Who did not sit?
Who did hit?
Up. Up. Up.
Who had a big hit? Pig.
Who slid? Pig did!

Although decodable texts can be useful for teaching phonics, children seldom encounter such contrived texts outside of school. As a consequence, the practice of controlling vocabulary to this extent continues to be questioned on the grounds that it tends to result in senseless or "inconsiderate" texts, and tends to cause children to think that reading is primarily a decoding task rather than a search for meaning (Allington, 1997; Armbruster, 1984; K. S. Goodman, 1987; Harste, Woodward, & Burke, 1984). The lack of real content or story in these decodable texts can also cause many children to quickly lose interest in reading if they are overused.

On the other hand, to abandon texts with some vocabulary and language structural controls seems to be, as Holdaway (1979) puts it, "sheer madness." Holdaway reminds us that children continue to struggle to read authentic texts that are far too difficult for them to handle independently. It is clear that basal readers need to provide balanced text types, including decodable, leveled, and authentic texts, in quantities that allow teachers to choose what works best with each child at various levels of reading development.

*In some basals for beginning readers, called **primers,** the language is controlled to produce decodable texts.*

Think about some important criticisms of controlling vocabulary in early basal readers.

Figure 4.8 Many basal reading programs still require students to complete workbook pages devoted to skill practice.

The Workbook

In past years, the most used part of any basal reading series was the workbook (Osborn, 1985). In fact, if any part of the basal reading lesson was neglected, it was seldom the workbook pages (Durkin, 1984; J. Mason, 1983). Although somewhat less the case today, workbook exercises remain firmly entrenched in many classrooms, as evidenced by their continued inclusion as part and parcel of basal reading series.

Workbooks were designed to provide a means for students to independently practice skill instruction provided by the teacher. Also, workbooks often are used for assessing reading skills previously taught as well as those currently taught. In this way, workbooks play a dual role in classrooms, namely, practice and assessment. In some cases, teachers also have found that workbooks can serve a classroom management function: When children are engaged in completing worksheets, the teacher is free to work with individual children or groups of children who most need help.

Past research reveals that students spend up to 70% of the time allocated for reading instruction, or 49 minutes per day, in independent practice or completing worksheets, like those found in workbooks, whereas less than 10% of the total reading instructional time, or about 7 to 8 minutes per day, is devoted to silent reading in the primary grades. In fact, publishers indicate that there is an insatiable demand for worksheets (R. C. Anderson, Hiebert, Scott, & Wilkinson, 1985). Jachym, Allington, and Broikou (1989) reported that seat work using worksheets is displacing many of the more important aspects of reading instruction, such as the acquisition of good books and time spent reading. Based on these findings, it seems obvious that workbooks have been misused and overused. However, when teachers judiciously select workbook exercises to support instruction, workbooks can provide students with valuable practice and feedback on progress in relation to specific reading skills. Osborn (1984) provides 20 guidelines for assessing the worth of workbook and worksheet-type reading tasks:

The cost of seat work has displaced many more important aspects of reading instruction such as the acquisition of good books and time for reading.

Some Guidelines for Workbook Tasks:

1. A sufficient proportion of workbook tasks should be relevant to the instruction that is going on in the rest of the unit or lesson.
2. Another portion of workbook tasks should provide for a systematic and cumulative review of what has already been taught.
3. Workbooks should reflect the most important (and workbook-appropriate) aspects of what is being taught in the reading program. Less important aspects should remain in the teacher's guide as voluntary activities.
4. Workbooks should contain, in a form that is readily accessible to students and teachers, supplementary tasks for students who need extra practice.
5. The vocabulary and concept level of workbook tasks should relate to that of the rest of the program and to the students using the program.
6. The language used in workbook tasks must be consistent with that used in the rest of the lesson and in the rest of the workbook.
7. Instructions to students should be clear, unambiguous, and easy to follow; brevity is a virtue.
8. The layout of pages should combine attractiveness with utility.
9. Workbooks should contain enough content so that there is a chance a student will learn something and not simply be exposed to something.
10. Tasks that require students to make discriminations must be preceded by a sufficient number of tasks that provide practice on components of the discriminations.
11. The content of workbook tasks must be accurate and precise; workbook tasks must not present wrong information nor perpetuate misrules.
12. At least some workbook tasks should be fun and have an obvious payoff to them.
13. Most student response modes should be consistent from task to task.
14. Student response modes should be the closest possible to reading and writing.
15. The instructional design of individual tasks and of task sequences should be carefully planned.
16. Workbooks should contain only a finite number of task types and forms.
17. The art that appears on workbook pages must be consistent with the prose of the task.
18. Cute, nonfunctional, space- and time-consuming tasks should be avoided.
19. When appropriate, tasks should be accompanied by brief explanations of purpose for both teachers and students.
20. English major humor should be avoided.*

*From "The Purposes, Uses, and Contents of Workbooks and Some Guidelines for Publishers" by J. Osborn, in *Learning to Read in American Schools* (pp. 110–111), edited by R. C. Anderson, J. Osborn, & R. J. Tierney, 1984, Hillsdale, NJ: Erlbaum. Copyright 1984 by Lawrence Erlbaum Associates, Inc. Reprinted by permission.

Workbooks, like TV, can be a tool that can assist or inhibit children's reading progress.

Additionally, completed workbook exercises can provide teachers critical evaluative information on the effectiveness of instruction as well as diagnostic information on the quality of students' learning. In short, workbooks can be a valuable resource when used correctly, or they can be a debilitating deterrent to students' reading progress when overrelied on or misused.

Assessment

The subject of testing and evaluation is discussed in depth in chapter 10.

Although workbook exercises can be used for formative assessment of reading skill development, most basal reading series provide end-of-unit or end-of-book tests for summative evaluation of student learning. These tests are generally criterion-referenced tests, which means that the items measured on these tests are directly related to the specific skills taught in that unit or book.

Just as workbook exercises can be abused, so it is with tests. Tests should provide teachers information about the quantity and quality of children's learning to direct future instruction. They should not be used to label children or teachers. No single test score should ever form the basis for making important decisions about children or teachers. Administrators and teachers must be extremely cautious in the use and interpretation of test scores.

Record Keeping

Most basal reading series provide a means for keeping records on children's progress.

*A **skills-management system** allows teachers to keep accurate records from year to year regarding each child's progress through the adopted basal reading program's scope and sequence of skills.*

Maintaining records to document teaching and learning is an important part of accountability. Most basal reading series provide a means for keeping records on children's progress through the skills outlined in the scope and sequence chart of the basal. Most often, the methods of assessment specified are paper-and-pencil testing or worksheet administration. The scores obtained on these exercises are entered into a master list or record available today in CD-ROM form, which follows the children throughout their elementary years. Such a skills-management system allows teachers to keep accurate records from year to year regarding each child's progress through the adopted basal reading program's scope and sequence of skills. Unfortunately, some teachers spend inordinate amounts of time keeping records of this kind, which leads to a most undesirable condition as captured by Pearson (1985) when he stated:

> The model implicit in the practices of [this teacher] was that of a manager—[a] person who arranged materials, texts, and the classroom environment so learning could occur. But the critical test of whether learning did occur was left up to the child as s/he interacted with the materials.
>
> Children practiced applying skills; if they learned them, fine; we always had more skills for them to practice; if they did not, fine; we always had more worksheets and duplicating sheets for the same skill. And the most important rule in such a mastery role was that practice makes perfect, leading to the ironic condition that children spent most of their time on precisely that subset of skills they performed least well. (p. 736)

To this we would like to add the comment that, disturbingly, teachers under this model spent the bulk of their time running off dittos, assigning, correcting, and recording rather than guiding, demonstrating, or interacting with children or books. Although increasingly elegant with the addition of CD-ROM technology, record keeping should go well beyond keeping track of the worksheet type of evaluation. Fortunately, some basal readers now recognize this fact and include process as well

Figure 4.9 Many basal teacher's editions provide recommendations for portfolio assessment.

From *Treasury of Literature: A Place to Dream* (Teacher's ed., Level 3-1, p. T193), Orlando, FL. Harcourt Brace & Company, 1995. Copyright 1995 by Harcourt Brace & Company. Reprinted by permission.

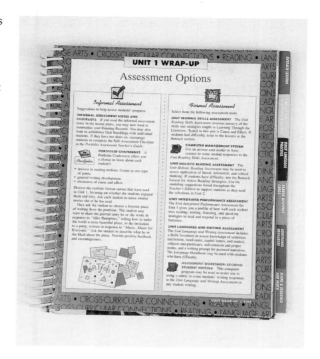

as product measures of children's reading and reading habits. In fact, some basal readers now provide suggestions for designing individual assessment portfolios for each student, including the use of running records. Figure 4.9 shows suggestions for a basal reader student portfolio. Unfortunately, many basal publishers still overrely on paper-and-pencil demonstrations for inclusion in student portfolios. They have yet to become serious about providing means for capturing students' reading processes for inclusion in portfolios. For teachers who want to present students' reading demonstrations to parents as evidence for a reading portfolio, they will need to obtain audiotapes of students' reading and analyze them (as shown in chapter 10 on running records) on their own for the foreseeable future.

In summary, basal reading series are typically composed of a core of three elements—teacher's edition, student text, and workbooks—as well as a host of available kits, charts, cards, tests, technology, additional practice exercises, and assessment/record-keeping systems to supplement the core elements of the basal series. In an effort to compete with trade-book publishers, basal publishers are also producing big books to complement the already expansive list of purchasable options listed previously. Teachers should be careful not to accept these new "basal" big books without careful examination. In some cases, big books published by basal companies are not big books at all—they are big basals!

Although the basal reader approach offers a resource for helping teachers provide systematic and sequenced reading instruction throughout the elementary and middle grades, teachers must nonetheless be careful to supplement this core program with trade books, silent reading time, group sharing, extensions of reading into writing, speaking, drama, music, and so on, as well as provide individual assessment of children's reading progress, behaviors, and attitudes. When this goal is understood and achieved, basal readers can provide valuable literacy tools and resources to

Although many basal readers provide assessment tools, the lack of a high-quality assessment rubric for constructing a portfolio remains a serious flaw.

Notice how teachers can supplement the basal reader core program.

schools, administrators, teachers, and children. In addition, basals provide a safety net for many teachers, novice and experienced, because they make personal and professional transitions toward balanced reading instruction.

PRODUCTION AND ORGANIZATION OF BASAL READERS

Basal reading programs are typically known by the name of the publishing house that produces the basal.

Basal reading series are owned by large, diversified business corporations such as Xerox, Paramount, Inc., Viacom Inc., and Gulf-Western and are produced by a variety of publishing houses from coast to coast. The production of a basal reader is overseen by a managing or chief editor with the assistance of a senior author team, a group of figures in the field of reading who are known and respected as experts. Basal reading programs are often known by the name of the publishing house that produces the basal.

Harcourt Brace	Rigby
Heath	Science Research Associates
Houghton Mifflin	Scholastic
McGraw-Hill	Scott, Foresman
Open Court	Silver-Burdett Ginn

Minor revisions of basal readers occur every few years; major revision cycles occur every 5 or 6 years. Major revisions are usually slated for completion during the same year Texas and California consider basal readers for statewide adoption. Consequently, the "Texas and California" effect is known to exert considerable influence on the content and quality of new basal readers (Farr, Tulley, & Powell, 1987; Keith, 1981). In reading circles, one often hears the axiom, "as Texas and California go, so goes the nation."

Strengths and Weaknesses of Basal Readers

Basal readers contain an organized and systematic plan for teachers to consult in planning reading instruction.

The subskills and skills reading instructional models are discussed in chapter 2.

Readily available tests and practice exercises found in the basal workbooks save teachers enormous amounts of time in materials preparation.

Although basal readers continue to be the mainstay of reading instruction in American schools, the basal reader approach to reading instruction has not gone unscrutinized. Criticisms of basal readers have ranged from the cultural to the literary, from the linguistic to the instructional. Because basal readers are used in over 90% of American classrooms, most teachers will inevitably have occasion to make use of the basal reader approach to reading instruction (Baumann, 1993; Flood & Lapp, 1986; Hoffman, 1994; McCarthy, 1994; Zintz & Maggart, 1989). To make instructional decisions about how, when, and why to use the basal, teachers and administrators must know the strengths and weaknesses of the basal reader approach to reading.

In defense of basal reading series, it must be said that basals possess certain positive qualities that contribute to their enduring popularity in American classrooms. For example, basal readers contain an organized and systematic plan for teachers to consult. Basal readers published more recently often provide teaching suggestions from which balanced reading teachers make decisions about when and how to teach skills that are important to authentic reading-related behaviors. In addition, basal readers are sequenced from grade to grade, thus providing for continuous reading instruction throughout the elementary school years and for continuity both within grades and across grade levels. The readily available tests and practice exercises found in the workbooks save teachers enormous amounts of time in materials preparation. Reading skills are gradually introduced, practiced, and reviewed through the plan provided in the scope and sequence of the basal. The lesson plans found ready made in the teacher's editions also save teachers much preparation time. A variety of literary genres is available to teachers and students in current basal readers. The structure provided in basal readers is often very reassuring for novice or beginning teachers. Administrators can manage and provide accountability evidence more easily by adopting and using basal reading series. In short, basal readers possess several characteristics that teachers and administrators find helpful and worthwhile.

Advantages of the Basal Reader Approach*

- A sequenced or spiral curriculum of skill instruction is provided. Skills instruction is arranged to provide for both initial instruction and a systematic review of skills taught.
- A continuous arrangement of instructional skills and concepts from grade to grade is supplied.
- To save teachers time, a completely prepared set of stories, instructional directions and activities, instructional practice materials, and assessment and management devices is available.
- Student texts are arranged in ascending difficulty.
- Reading skills are gradually introduced and systematically reviewed.
- Teachers are provided lesson plans.
- Students are exposed to a variety of literary genres.
- Organization and structure of basals are helpful to beginning teachers just learning about the reading curriculum.
- Organization and structure are reassuring to administrators and school patrons that important reading skills are being taught.

Limitations of the Basal Reader Approach

- Some new decodable and leveled selections are dull and repetitious.
- Cutting pictures removes support for developing readers.
- Skill instruction is rarely applied in or related to comprehending the story content.
- The basal lesson design in teacher's editions very often fails to relate one part of the lesson, such as vocabulary introduction, to subsequent parts of the reading lesson, such as story comprehension discussion.
- Stories often do not relate to students' interests.
- The format of basals is often less appealing than the format of trade books.
- Censorship by special interest groups leads to the selection of stories that contain little real subject matter content, that deal with few real-life applications, or that present little content that advocates ethical living in society.
- Teacher's editions seldom contain useful directions on how to teach/model reading comprehension.
- A rigid adherence to the basal leaves little room for teacher creativity and decision making.
- The grading or leveling of basal readers promotes the use of traditional grouping strategies.

*From "Understanding and Using Basal Readers Effectively" by D. R. Reutzel in *Effective Strategies for Teaching Reading* (p. 259) edited by B. Hayes, 1991, Needham Heights, MA: Allyn & Bacon. Copyright 1991 by D. R. Reutzel. Reprinted by permission.

- Management demands of the basal program can become so time-consuming that little time remains for students to self-select reading materials.
- Use of the basal reader approach has traditionally been associated with the use of "round robin" reading and ability grouping. Such practices are encouraged by insisting that all children simultaneously attend to the same selection while another child reads orally.

Although popular, basal readers are not without significant deficiencies.

Many of the objections voiced about the stories found in the basals can be traced to publishers' efforts to produce decodable texts or leveled books.

Basal readers have improved significantly in past years. Although in the past, narrative selections in students' basal readers tended in the early grades to be repetitive and boring, recent basal readers have included more high-quality children's literature. However, some have been concerned that high-quality literature is beyond the ability of many students to handle independently (Holdaway, 1979). Thus, recent trends have included demands for "decodable" and "leveled" texts (Allington, 1997). Although the variety of selections found in basals may be considerable, some educators are concerned with what appears to be genre and topic flitting in basal readers. Because of this criticism, most recently published basal readers now organize their selections into similar genres, topic pairs, or themed units. Recent basal readers have included more generous exposure to information, nonfiction, or expository selections in comparison to those of generations past.

Basal readers have also been criticized for poorly representing societal groups and concerns. This problem is often attributable to the censorship of various special-interest groups that enter into the **basal reader adoption** process, particularly in states that adopt statewide (Marzano, 1993/1994). Basal teacher's editions continue to be assailed for poor instructional design and content (Miller & Blumenfeld, 1993; Ryder & Graves, 1994). Durkin (1981a) found that many teacher's editions contained an abundance of questions and evaluative activities mislabeled as instructional activities. What was labeled as instruction was often found to be nothing more than an assessment exercise. Reutzel and Daines (1987a) found that basal reading skills lessons seldom supported or even related to the selections to be read in the basals. These conclusions supported J. Mason's (1983) findings that teachers' reading instruction was, more often than not, unrelated to the text that children would be asked to read. In another study the same year, Reutzel and Daines (1987b) reported that even the parts of the reading units had little relation to one another. Although these conditions have improved somewhat in the newer generations of basal readers, the problems persist.

Eldredge, Reutzel, and Hollingsworth (1996) have demonstrated that reading instruction based on the shared reading approach (Holdaway, 1979) produces significantly greater growth in reading achievement than does the directed reading lesson (Betts, 1946). Despite these limitations, the basal "baby" simply cannot be thrown out with the bath water (Baumann, 1993; McCallum, 1988; Winograd, 1989). Basals have filled an important niche for many teachers and will likely continue to do so well into the future. As they await continued improvements in the basal, teachers armed with an understanding of the strengths and weaknesses of basal readers, as described here, can enjoy the benefits associated with basals while overcoming or avoiding the weaknesses.

Organization of the Basal Reader

Basal readers are designed to take children through a series of books, experiences, and activities toward increasingly sophisticated reading behaviors. Each basal series typically provides several readers or books of reading selections at each level. For example, the *Silver-Burdett Ginn/Literature Works: An Integrated Approach to Reading and Language Arts (1996)* basal provides the following books for each grade level:

Grade 1: Volumes 1, 2, and 3
Grade 2: Volumes 1 and 2
Grade 3: Volumes 1 and 2
Grade 4: Volumes 1 and 2
Grade 5: Volumes 1 and 2
Grade 6: Volumes 1 and 2

An important feature to be found in teacher's editions is the scope and sequence chart, which is a curricular plan, usually in chart form, that includes the instructional objectives and skills associated with a specific basal reading program. These objectives and skills are arranged by the grade levels in which they are to be taught. It is in the scope and sequence chart that teachers can learn about the objectives of the basal program and the lessons designed to accomplish the objectives.

Most contemporary basal readers are organized into **themed units,** with several basal selections organized around a selected theme or topic; still others are organized into arbitrarily divided units of instruction. Most basal readers follow a somewhat *modified* version of the Directed Reading Thinking Activity (DRTA) format developed by Stauffer in 1969. This format can be represented in eight discrete parts or steps in the lesson:

*Some contemporary basal readers are organized into **themed units.***

1. Building background and vocabulary
2. Introducing and setting the purpose of reading
3. Sample the text
4. Make predictions
5. Confirm predictions
6. Comprehension discussion questions
7. Skill instruction and practice
8. Enrichment, integrated language arts, or language extension activities

Building Background and Vocabulary

Activities to build background and vocabulary involve the teacher and students in a discussion of the topic and unfamiliar concepts to be encountered in the story. Beck (1986, 1995, 1996) directs teachers to focus discussion on the central problem, a critical concept, or an interview with or questioning of the author, or to give voice to the story characters. This segment of the DRTA provides students with the necessary knowledge to facilitate comprehension of the story content. Because comprehension of a story is at least partially dependent upon owning the meaning of specific unfamiliar words, teachers might focus on activities designed to help students understand how new vocabulary words will be used in the context of the story.

Notice what teachers should focus on when building story background.

Introducing and Setting the Purpose for Reading

The part of the DRTA devoted to introducing and setting the purpose for reading is intended to provide motivation and purpose for reading the story. Introducing and setting the purpose focus on reading the story title and subtitle(s) and looking at the pictures. Students are often encouraged to make predictions from the titles and pictures. Finally, the teacher typically sets the purpose for reading the selection by directing students to read to find the answer to a specific question. These activities direct students into purposeful reading.

Sample the Text

During this phase of the DRTA, students read to a predetermined point in the basal selection to answer questions or to confirm predictions. Many teacher's editions suggest that the reading be silent reading. Some teachers, however, especially primary-grade teachers, ask that children read stories orally to assess word-decoding abilities.

Make Predictions

Once students have read to a predetermined part of the assigned selection, the group makes predictions about the next part. Predictions are recorded at the board or on chart paper, and the reading continues to another predetermined point.

Confirm Predictions

Students review the recorded predictions with the teacher. Students may be asked to reread portions of the text to justify their assertions that predictions have been confirmed. Once the entire selection has been read, a comprehension discussion ensues.

Comprehension Discussion Questions

After reading, students discuss the basal selection by answering questions about the selection content. Questions for conducting comprehension discussions are found interspersed throughout and following the story in most basal teacher's editions.

Skill Instruction and Practice

Skill instruction, application, and practice focus on developing readers' skills in three areas of the reading curriculum: (a) decoding, (b) vocabulary, and (c) comprehension. Individual skill lessons from each of these areas usually follow the story in the teacher's edition. After instruction, students practice the skills in workbooks and on ditto sheets. Some newer basal readers also provide lessons on writing, spelling, and integrated language use.

Enrichment, Integrated Language Arts, or Language-Extension Activities

Activities concerning enrichment or language-extension activities focus on and extend the selection content. Language-extension activities very often encourage students to go well beyond the content of the selection or skill lessons to pursue related personal interests, related topics, or relevant skills.

INSTRUCTIONAL BELIEFS AND BASAL READERS

Although basal readers may be alike in many surface respects, they often differ with respect to the authors' beliefs or philosophies about how children learn to read and, consequently, how children should be taught to read. Some basal readers, for example, emphasize helping children acquire word-identification skills early and rapidly; other basal reading series emphasize meaning at the outset of reading instruction. In basals created from a meaning emphasis perspective, children are initially taught a stock of sight words and then gradually introduced to decoding skills somewhat later. Thus, the differences in beliefs held by the authors or authoring teams of basal readers are typically reflected in both the structure and content of basal readers.

Although basal readers may be alike in many surface respects, they often differ with respect to authors' beliefs about how children learn to read and, consequently, how children should be taught to read.

Decoding Basals

Basal readers founded on a strong decoding belief place an early and strong emphasis on phonics skills. In fact, these basal readers are often classified as "phonics first," explicit or synthetic phonics basal readers (R. C. Anderson et al., 1985; Flesch, 1955, 1981). Learning the letter sounds and names—usually one at a time until a child has mastered the 26 letter names and the 40-plus sounds those letters represent—is considered a prerequisite to reading words and connected text. Once children have learned these letter names and sounds, this knowledge will allow them to crack the written code. Next, they are shown how to blend these sounds together to "sound out" words. For example, a child learns the letters *a, t,* and *c*. Blending sounds from left to right produces *c - a - t, cat*. Although all basal readers provide some type of decoding instruction, basals that represent a decoding belief can be distinguished by the following features: (a) teaching graphophonic relationships as a prerequisite to reading words and text, (b) teaching the blending of letter-sound elements to get words, and (c) reading phonically controlled or decodable texts written to conform to specific phonics generalizations. Decoding basals begin with the smallest units of language first and progress toward larger, more meaningful units (Weaver, 1994). One example of a componet from a decoding basal reading program is Science Research Associates' (SRA) *Reading Mastery* (Engelmann & Bruner, 1995) pictured in Figure 4.10.

Decodable basal readers founded on a strong subskills belief place an early and strong emphasis on decoding skills.

Notice how skills basals have adapted to calls for changes in basal reader content and structure.

Literature-Based Basals

In response to recent demands of teachers and textbook adoption committees to correct the weaknesses associated with basal readers in the past, many basal publishers have responded by making fundamental changes in both content and structure of their basal programs. These changes reflect a dramatic shift in beliefs, away from a singular emphasis upon phonics first and toward a more balanced literacy stance. Some of these changes include using greater amounts of existing, recognized children's literature. **Literature-based basal** readers, although interested in word identification and decoding skill development, go well beyond the preoccupation evidenced in decoding readers with focusing primarily on pronouncing words to the construction of meaning from print. These basals attend to issues of vocabulary development and comprehension as well as to the requisite skills for identifying words (Weaver, 1994). For example, discussions build experiential background, and demonstrations help children draw on prior knowledge

In deference to decodable basals, literature-based basal readers present comprehension, vocabulary, and phonics skills from the very start of a lesson.

Reading selections in transitional, or literature-based, basals are often organized into themes.

Figure 4.10   Sample page from the SRA *Reading Mastery* program.
From *Reading Mastery I, Presentation Book A* (Rainbow Edition, p. 73) by S. Engelmann and E. C. Bruner, 1995. Columbus, OH: SRA Macmillan/McGraw-Hill. Copyright 1995 by SRA Division of McGraw-Hill School Publishing Company. Reprinted by permission.

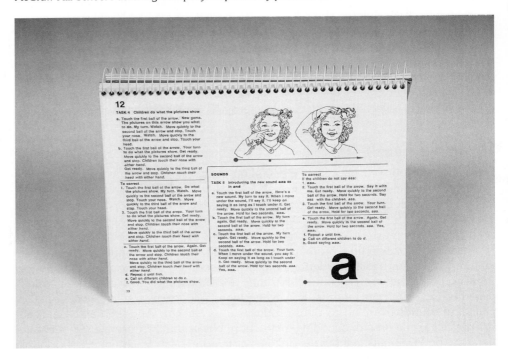

rather than simply teaching a list of new vocabulary words to enhance reading preparation. The Scholastic *Literacy Place* program (1997) shown in Figure 4.11 is one such example. In short, literature-based basal readers present comprehension, vocabulary, and phonics skill lessons simultaneously from the very start of reading instruction, whereas decoding basals delay emphasis on these components until word-identification and decoding skills have been mastered. Some literature-based basal readers are imported from Canada, New Zealand, and Australia. Examples of these imported basals used in U.S. schools include Rigby's (1997) *Literacy Tree Program.*

ADOPTING AND EVALUATING BASAL READERS FROM A TRANSITIONAL PERSPECTIVE

Because many teachers will evaluate one or more basal reading series during their professional careers, they need to understand how to evaluate and select basal readers effectively.

Few professional decisions deserve more careful attention than that of evaluating and selecting a basal reading series. Because many teachers will evaluate one or more basal reading series during their professional careers, they need to understand how to evaluate and select basal readers effectively. Learning about this process will also enable them to help reform, restructure, and strengthen future basal reading adoption processes.

Figure 4.11   The Scholastic *Literacy Place* basal series draws on children's background knowledge to build vocabulary.

From *Literacy Place: Literacy SourceBook,* 1996. New York: Scholastic. Copyright 1996 by Scholastic, Inc. Reprinted by permission.

The Process of Basal Reader Adoption

Twenty-two states have adopted some form of highly centralized, state-level control over the evaluation and selection of reading basals. The remaining 28 states and the District of Columbia allow individual districts and schools to select basal reading series at the local level (Table 4.1). Regardless of whether evaluations and selections occur at the state or local level, the task of decision making is most often placed in the hands of a textbook adoption committee. Farr et al. (1987) indicate that these committees often use a locally produced checklist to evaluate basal readers. Unfortunately, most adoption checklists require the evaluators to determine only the presence of certain features in basals rather than to assess the quality of these features. Follett (1985) estimated that

Notice who is often charged with the responsibility for adopting a new basal reader.

Table 4.1   Textbook adoption policies by state

State Adoption	Local Adoption
Alabama	Alaska
Arkansas	Arizona
California	Colorado
Florida	Connecticut
Georgia	Delaware
Hawaii	District of Columbia
Idaho	Illinois
Indiana	Iowa
Kentucky	Kansas
Louisiana	Maine
Mississippi	Maryland
Nevada	Massachusetts
New Mexico	Michigan
North Carolina	Minnesota
Oklahoma	Missouri
Oregon	Montana
South Carolina	Nebraska
Tennessee	New Hampshire
Texas	New Jersey
Utah	New York
Virginia	North Dakota
West Virginia	Ohio
	Pennsylvania
	Rhode Island
	South Dakota
	Vermont
	Washington
	Wisconsin
	Wyoming

Most basal evaluations amount to little more than a "flip test."

the average amount of time textbook adoption committee members spend evaluating basals is approximately 1 second per page, resulting in what Powell (1986) calls a "Flip Test" approach to evaluation and selection. Farr et al. (1987) proposed several guidelines for improving the basal reader adoption process found in Figure 4.12.

Although many of these recommendations will require major changes, improving the basal reader adoption process can itself contribute much to teachers' understanding of the reading curriculum and, as a result, can enhance the overall quality of reading instruction.

Evaluating Basal Readers From a Balanced Reading Perspective

Only after teachers are sufficiently well informed can they act to correct or adjust the use of the basal to benefit their students.

Although discussions about basal reader evaluations can sometimes be unpleasant, they are necessary to help teachers become aware of both strengths and limitations of the basal reader approach. Only after teachers are sufficiently informed can they act to correct or adjust the use of the basal to benefit their students.

Dole, Rogers, and Osborn (1987) recommend that to improve the evaluation of basal readers, those involved should focus on the following:

1. Identify the facets of effective reading instruction.
2. Delineate criteria related to effective reading to be analyzed in the basal readers.

Figure 4.12   Guidelines for basal reader adoption process

Basic Assumptions

1. The selection of a reading textbook series should not be considered the same as the adoption of the total reading curriculum.
2. Basal reading adoptions should be conducted by school districts rather than by states.
3. The final decision regarding textbook selection should reside with the committee that spends the time and energy reviewing the books.

Selection of Reviewers

1. Reviewers should have the respect of other teachers in the school system.
2. We do not recommend in-service training in the teaching of reading, but we do strongly recommend training for reviewers in the review and evaluation of reading textbooks.

Establishing Criteria

1. The adoption committee's most important task is the determination of the basal reading series factors to be used in evaluating the programs.
2. As the selection criteria are established, the committee must agree on the meaning of each factor.

Procedures in Reviewing and Evaluating Basal Readers

1. Committees must be provided an adequate amount of time to conduct thorough evaluations of reading textbooks.
2. Committees should be organized in ways other than by grade level.
3. Procedures used to evaluate basal programs should be tested before the actual evaluation takes place.
4. Whatever evaluation procedures are used, committee members must do more than make a check mark.
5. Any person who wishes to address the entire adoption committee or any individual committee members should be allowed to do so.
6. Reading adoption committees need to consider carefully how much and what contact to have with publishers' representatives.
7. Pilot studies are useful if they are carefully controlled.
8. When the committee has completed its work, a report of the committee's evaluation procedures and findings should be made public.

From "The Evaluation and Selection of Basal Readers" by R. Farr, M. A. Tulley, & D. Powell, 1987, *The Elementary School Journal, 87*(3), pp. 267–281. Published by The University of Chicago Press. Copyright 1987 by The University of Chicago. Reprinted by permission.

3. Provide a means for carefully recording how well basal readers measure up to the established criteria.

Because many reading teachers are concerned with curriculum changes that reflect a decided move toward more balanced literacy beliefs and practices in basal readers, Heald-Taylor (1989) authored a basal evaluation checklist, shown in Figure 4.13.

Transitional reading teachers can use this checklist to evaluate not only the presence but also the quality of basal features that reflect a more balanced instructional

Figure 4.13 Transitional basal evaluation checklist

	Ineffective	Somewhat Effective	Effective	Very Effective	
Literature How effective is this program in providing for: • quality literature selections? • unabridged literature selections? • variety of literary genre (patterns, poetry, informational, fictional)? • a variety of authors? • biographies of authors? • listings of high-quality literature, supplemental selections?					
Integration How effective is this program in providing for: • the integration of listening, speaking, reading, writing, drama, movement, and visual arts? • thematic organization of stories and student activities? • organizational strategies for the use of activity centers, such as book corners, listening post, drama center, construction area, art station, writing table? • the integration of other content areas, such as mathematics, science, social studies, music, and physical education?					
Instructional Strategies How effective is this program in providing for: • shared reading? • book talks? • choral speaking? • story reading? • storytelling? • listening activities? • co-operative learning? • dramatization, such as role play, puppet plays, mime, improvisation? • debates? • personal dictation? • problem-solving activities? • individualized reading? • encouraging students to use a variety of reading strategies, such as pictures, pattern of the text, meaning, memory, context, and phonetics?					

From *The Administrator's Guide to Whole Language* (pp. 89–92) by G. Heald-Taylor, 1989, Katonha, NY: Richard C. Owen Publishers, Inc. Reprinted by permission.

	Ineffective	Somewhat Effective	Effective	Very Effective
Instructional Strategies (continued) • student use of writing folders? • student use of writing process (prewriting, writing conferencing, drafting, revising, editing, publishing)? • conferencing strategies? • peer conferencing? • experimentation with spelling, grammar, and usage? • revising strategies? • publishing strategies?				
Interpretive Activities for Students How effective is this program in providing for: • interpretive activities, such as drama, role play, improvisation, movement? • interpretive activities, such as discussions or debates? • interpretive activities, such as painting, drawing, cut-and-paste, modeling, and construction? • higher level thinking activities? • comprehension activities? • vocabulary study relative to the literature being read? • a variety of reading strategies, such as cloze exercises, pattern awareness, meaning, memory, picture clues, and phonetics? • phonetic activities that relate to reading and writing, oral as well as written? • skill activities based on the needs of students?				
Evaluation How effective is this program in providing for: • strategies for supporting teachers in observing students as they use language? • varieties of formats for collecting information such as language samples, checklists, running records, etc.? • opportunities for students to evaluate their language growth? • samples of typical language behavior inventories? • balance between standardized and informal evaluation procedures?				

approach. In this respect, Heald-Taylor's (1989) and Sippola's (1994) checklists satisfy many of researchers' recommendations regarding evaluation and selection of basal reading series in addition to considering the relative strengths and weaknesses of basal reading series from a balanced literacy perspective.

TAKING CONTROL OF THE BASAL TEACHER'S MANUAL

Teachers should see their role as an instructional decision maker rather than the implementer of basal programs.

Basal readers were never intended to displace the teacher's instructional decision making in the classroom or to supplant opportunities for students to read a wide range of literary genres (Winograd, 1989). Rather, basals were intended as an instructional resource to help teachers provide basic, sequenced reading instruction for a wide range of student abilities (Squire, 1989). Although some teachers are content to sample or follow the teacher's edition, effective reading teachers take control of the basal teacher's edition so that it truly becomes only one resource among many for the informed and discriminating teacher. Furthermore, moving away from total dependence on the basal teacher's edition is often the first step in beginning the transition to balanced literacy instruction (Altwerger & Flores, 1989). Because this is often a difficult step for some teachers, we offer detailed examples of how teachers can begin to take control of their teacher's editions by using it as the basis for planning along with a variety of reading lesson structures within the familiar confines of the basal reader.

Balanced Reading Program

List the major components of balanced reading instruction.

A **balanced reading program** is described by Holdaway in 1979, in *Reading in Junior Classes* (a handbook for teachers in New Zealand, not referenced) in 1985, and is clearly and succinctly articulated by M. Mooney in her 1990 book entitled *Reading TO, WITH, and BY Children*. Balanced reading instruction centers on using several key reading instructional practices:

Elements of a Balanced Literary Program

- *Reading TO Children*
    Teacher read aloud
    One-to-one reading
    Lap reading
- *Reading WITH Children*
    Shared reading
    Language experience
    Guided reading
- *Reading BY Children*
    Buddy or assisted reading
    Independent reading
    Dramatic/performance reading

Transitional reading teachers recognize these elements of a balanced reading program and attempt to integrate them into their use of published basal reader series. For example, consider how the selection *Tales of a Fourth Grade Nothing*

(Blume, 1972), found in a current basal reader, could be taught by planning a lesson around the three areas of a balanced reading program.

Example Balanced Reading Lesson

Selection title: *Tales of a Fourth Grade Nothing* (Blume, 1972).

Reading TO Children: *Teacher Read Aloud.* To set the context for the selection, read aloud the poem "Sister for Sale" by Shel Silverstein. Have a discussion about younger siblings and their habits that make you want to sell them. Make a list at the board of things younger siblings do to drive you crazy. Make a list of ways you have thought about getting even. Next, tell children that you are going to be reading about a boy whose younger brother is named Fudge in the book *Tales of a Fourth Grade Nothing.*

Reading WITH Children: *Shared Reading.* Begin by reading the first chapter of *Tales of a Fourth Grade Nothing* together. Several versions of choral reading—unison, echoic, one line per child, antiphonal, and so on—could be used to vary the involvement of the group. Next, ask children to respond to the first chapter by sharing their favorite parts with a neighbor. After the discussion, ask children to remember words they had difficulty with during the reading of the story; list these words on chart paper or on a bulletin board. Invite children to add to this list as they read the remainder of the book. Next, determine questions, predictions, and goals for reading the selection; for example, how many chapters or sections will need to be read before the next stopping and responding point.

    Guided Reading. To use *Tales of a Fourth Grade Nothing* as a resource for guided reading, the teacher must have determined the level of the selection. Several leveling schemes exist, including Reading Recovery® levels 1–20, Fountas and Pinnell (1996) levels A–P, and Lexile levels 100–1000. Once leveled information about the selection is available, students who can read 90% or more of the words in the selection independently are grouped together. The teacher gives students a reading assignment and asks all children to read aloud in their mumble voices. With the students seated in a semicircle around the teacher, as each child reads the teacher listens in on the students to prompt, give feedback, or encourage the use of varied reading strategies.

Reading BY Children: *Independent Reading.* Allow children uninterrupted time to read the next chapter or section(s) of *Tales of a Fourth Grade Nothing.* Once children reach the agreed-on stopping point, have several projects they can complete to respond to their reading, such as a Character Report Card or a Literary Passport (see chapter 12, "The Elementary Years: Reading and Writing in Grades 3–5"). Once everyone has completed a response to the chapter or section(s), bring children together for a literature response group meeting to discuss their projects, perspectives, and feelings. Set a new goal for reading, and repeat the responding process. Be sure to note particular language and comprehension skills this book exemplifies for children. Focus on these at the conclusion of each response group meeting.

    When the typical lesson format provided in most basal reader teacher's editions is altered to include elements of a balanced reading program, children experience the modeling of a teacher, join with the teacher and other peers in reading together, read independently, and join together to respond to their reading. In so doing, children and teachers pursue a common reading experience in a supportive social setting.

Reconciled Reading Lesson

*The **reconciled reading lesson (RRL)** reverses the traditional basal lesson instructional sequence.*

Most teachers recognize the importance of building adequate and accurate background information to prepare readers to successfully process text; the **reconciled reading lesson** (RRL) (Reutzel, 1985a, 1991) is useful for this purpose. (However, with texts for which students already possess adequate background knowledge, RRL may unnecessarily postpone reading the selection. In this case, we recommend using the DRTA.) The RRL recommends that teachers begin the basal lesson with the information at the end of most lessons—the language enrichment and curriculum extenders—and then work backward to vocabulary assessment as the last element in the lesson (Reutzel, 1985a). To begin an RRL, turn to the language enrichment and extension section of the reading lesson in the basal teacher's edition. The activities suggested in this part of the lesson are often excellent for building background knowledge and discussing unfamiliar concepts. In one major basal reader, for example, a lesson on the story "Stone Soup" (M. Brown, 1947) suggested that teachers make stone soup and have children write a recipe from their experience. Although these ideas could be used as excellent extensions of the story, the activities may be just as appropriate for background building before reading rather than for enrichment after reading.

The RRL recommends teaching reading skills before reading and relating them to the selection to be read.

The second modification that the RRL proposes for the basal lesson sequence centers on the place of reading skill instruction. The RRL recommends teaching reading skills before reading and then relating reading skill instruction to the selection to be read. If this is not possible, teachers should select an appropriate reading skill that relates to the selection. By relating skills to the stories, teachers help children understand that reading skills are to be applied during reading. For example, the vocabulary skill of categorizing words was to be taught with the story in one reading lesson in a major basal reader; however, the words selected for the vocabulary-categorizing activity were unrelated to the words in the story. One must ask the question, why teach this vocabulary skill in relation to a contrived list of words or using an instructional text snippet (Pearson, 1989a) when the skill could more aptly be applied to words taken from the story itself?

If the story does not lend itself to the reading skills to be taught, then adapt skill instruction to the story.

The decoding skill lesson associated with another basal story dealt with teaching children the vowel digraph /oa/. A quick glance over the text revealed that only one word in the entire text contained that vowel digraph. Even worse, the stories preceding and following the story in the lesson contained no words with the /oa/ vowel digraph. This is just one demonstration of the findings that basal lessons seldom relate skill instruction to the selections children are expected to read (Reutzel & Daines, 1987b). Because of this failure on the part of some publishers, the teacher may often need to make explicit the relation between the skills taught and how (or if) these skills can be applied during the reading.

If the story does not lend itself to the reading skills to be taught, then adapt skill instruction to the story. For example, for the story *Good Work, Amelia Bedelia,* by Peggy Parish (1963), an appropriate comprehension skill to select for instruction would be understanding figurative or idiomatic expressions. If the teacher's edition did not direct teachers to focus on this skill, the professional decision could be made to teach the prescribed skill lesson—such as getting the main idea—later during the year and to teach figurative or idiomatic expressions with this story. Instructional decisions such as these are characteristic of transitional teachers' taking control of their teacher's editions. In summary, the RRL recommends that skill instruction be taught before reading and be explicitly related to and applied in reading.

The third step in the RRL involves a discussion of the story intended to foster comprehension. The typical organization of the basal reader teacher's edition provides for comprehension discussion through a list of comprehension questions following the selection in the teacher's edition. The RRL recommends that guided questioning, discussion, and prediction be included as an integral part of the prereading phase of the reading lesson. Questions usually discussed after reading may be discussed before reading. Children are encouraged to predict answers to the questions before reading and then to read to confirm their predictions. Such a practice can help students selectively focus their attention during reading.

The remainder of the RRL should be very brief. Students read the selection in the basal. Postreading activities focus primarily on assessment of comprehension and skill application. Questions can be asked, such as, Did the students comprehend? How well did students predict answers to the prequestions? Did students revise their predictions as a result of the reading? Do the students understand the meanings of the new vocabulary words as they were used in the context of the story? In short, assessment is the primary purpose for postreading activities in the RRL. Prince and Mancus (1987) and Thomas and Readence (1988) reported that using the RRL significantly increased students' comprehension and recall of text over the traditional DRA as well as other alternative lesson frameworks.

Research has shown that the RRL significantly increased students' comprehension and recall of text over the traditional DRA as well as other alternative lesson frameworks.

Using the Language Experience Approach With Basal Reader Lessons

The language experience approach (LEA) is often used with basal reading lessons by transitional reading teachers for two reasons. First, teachers can maintain their basal safety net by continuing to use the basal reader as the core component of reading instruction while gently making the transition toward more balanced literacy practices such as those found in the LEA. Second, transitional teachers can learn how to make basal lessons focus on integrating children's language and experience into the lesson and thereby make basal reading lessons more child, language, and experience centered.

Jones and Nessel (1985, p. 18) describe how LEA can be integrated with the basal approach. To begin, use the basic steps in obtaining dictated language experience stories:

Using LEA helps teachers integrate children's language and personal experiences into the basal reading lesson.

1. Through experiments, objects, and activities, the teacher provides students with a stimulus that invites student participation.
2. Through discussion with the teacher and other students, the students develop concepts through observations and talking.
3. Children dictate to the teacher an account of the experience or activity. This dictation is usually recorded on large chart paper or poster board.
4. The teacher reads the dictated account back to the children. Next with teacher help, the students read the account with the teacher. The dictated story becomes the basis for phonics, structural analysis, and context usage lessons over the next few days.

5. Students read other books on related topics. They often reread the dictated story alone or in small groups during the day.
6. Learning from reading is reinforced with activities employing the other language skills. Writing and listening activities are used in this way to promote general communication growth.

To integrate this approach with the basal lessons, Jones and Nessel (1985) recommend that the teacher construct an experience to complement the basal story. For example, for the basal story "The Lion and the Mouse," the teacher could tell a story about how a student once helped teach another child. The teacher could describe how even a small child could help and explain that size does not tell us about whether a person can become a good friend. Children could then be invited to discuss how little friends can help big friends or little brothers or sisters can help older ones. These accounts could be recorded on the chart or on small paper for the children to reread during the next few days (Reimer, 1983). Words from the LEA-dictated story could be placed on word cards for practice. Usually, many of the words in the children's dictated stories also appear in the basal story. Thus, new or old vocabulary terms are introduced or reviewed before reading the basal story. After reading the basal story, another story could be created by using words from both the original dictated story and the basal story; this new story provides more opportunities to practice skills and sight words. Finally, reading skills could be taught using these stories to show children how reading skills can be applied to help them read a story.

Using LEA-dictated stories and experiences is an effective way for transitional reading teachers to take control of their basal reader teacher's editions.

Reciprocal Questioning

ReQuest, or reciprocal questioning, is a structure for presenting reading lessons in which teachers and children silently read parts of a text and exchange the role of asking and answering questions about that text.

In 1969, Anthony Manzo outlined ReQuest, or *reciprocal questioning,* a structure for conducting reading lessons in which teachers and children silently read parts of a text and exchange the roles of asking and answering questions about that text. The ReQuest procedure can be used with individuals or with groups. The process begins with the teacher and students reading a preassigned portion of a text silently. Both the teacher and the students close the book after reading. Next, the students ask the teacher questions about the text, and the teacher answers these questions clearly and accurately. By answering the students' questions first, the teacher can demonstrate for students effective question-answering behaviors. Next, the teacher and students reverse roles. The teacher and students begin by reading the next part of the text and then close their books. At this point, students try to answer the questions the teacher asks. At some point in the lesson, usually predetermined by the teacher, students are asked to predict the potential events and outcome of the remainder of the text to be read. A list of predictions is constructed through discussion and shown at the board. Students read the remaining text to confirm or correct their predictions. After reading, the teacher leads a discussion to reconsider the original predictions.

Because children are encouraged to construct their own questions for reading, they become active readers to the extent that they (a) select their own purposes for reading and (b) engage in a proven reading strategy involving sampling, prediction, and reading to confirm or correct predictions.

ReQuest involves teachers and students equally in the roles of participant and observer in the lesson. Teachers frequently serve as the active participant in the lesson while the children spend their time looking on as passive observers. As a result,

ReQuest helps children learn how to compose and answer questions about text through active observation and participation in the reading lesson.

Example ReQuest Lesson

Book title: *Franklin in the Dark* (Bourgeois & Clark, 1986).

Read Text:	"Franklin could slide down a riverbank all by himself. He could count forwards and backwards. He could even zip zippers and button buttons. But Franklin was afraid of small, dark places and that was a problem because . . ." (p. 1).
Student 1 question:	What's the turtle's name?
Teacher answer:	His name is Franklin.
Student 2 question:	What are things that Franklin can do?
Teacher answer:	Franklin can slide down a riverbank, and button buttons, and zip zippers. Oh, he can also count forward and backward.
Student 3 question:	What was Franklin afraid of?
Teacher answer:	Franklin was afraid of small dark places.
Teacher question:	What kind of animal was Franklin?
Student answer:	A turtle.
Teacher question:	Why do you think that being afraid of small, dark places can be a problem for a turtle?
Student 1 answer:	Because then he wouldn't want to go deep under the water.
Student 2 answer:	Because turtles hide in their shells, and if he was afraid of the dark, maybe he wouldn't want to hide in his shell.
Teacher comment:	Those are both good answers. Let's read the next page and see why his being afraid is a problem.
Text:	"Franklin was a turtle. He was afraid of crawling into his small, dark shell. And so, Franklin the turtle dragged his shell behind him" (p. 2).

After reading the second page of text:

Teacher 1 question:	What was Franklin afraid of?
Student answer:	He was afraid of getting into his shell because it was dark and small.
Teacher 2 question:	What did Franklin do instead of getting into his shell?
Student answer:	He had to drag it behind him.
Teacher question:	What do you think Franklin could do so that he wouldn't be afraid of hiding in his shell?
Student 1 answer:	He could take some medicine that wouldn't make him afraid anymore.
Student 2 answer:	He could get a bigger shell so that it wouldn't be so small.
Student 3 answer:	He could use a flashlight to light up his shell.
Student 4 answer:	He could make a window in his shell so that it wouldn't be so dark.
Teacher comment:	You're all really thinking hard about Franklin and his problem. Now let's read on to find out what Franklin does about his fear and see if what we thought was right.

Directed Reading Thinking Activity

*Notice the three steps used in the **Directed Reading Thinking Activity (DRTA).***

In 1969, Russell G. Stauffer developed the Directed Reading Thinking Activity (DRTA) to encourage readers to engage actively in a three-step comprehension cycle:

1. Sample the text.
2. Make predictions.
3. Sample the text to confirm or correct previous predictions.

To use the DRTA, teachers give students a text selection and ask them to read the title and a few sample lines of text, and then examine the pictures to develop hypotheses about the text. Children generate hypotheses as they read from the text and from their own experiential backgrounds.

The DRTA can be adapted by teachers to incorporate the use of narrative and expository texts as well as a variety of reading and shared reading activities.

Teachers can adapt the DRTA in such a way as to sample the most important elements of a narrative or exposition based on the text structure employed. If the children are assigned a narrative or story to read, the DRTA could be based on the important elements of a story grammar or map, as suggested by Beck and McKeown (1981). These elements include setting, characters, initiating events, problems, attempts to solve the problems, and outcomes or resolutions. For example, consider the sample DRTA lesson constructed using the story *Cloudy With a Chance of Meatballs* by Judi Barrett (1978).

Example DRTA Lesson

The teacher begins the lesson by showing the book and saying:

Teacher: The title of the book we're going to read today is *Cloudy With a Chance of Meatballs.* What do this title and the picture make you think the story is about?

John: It might be about an old man that makes a magic spell on the sky so that meatballs come down when he wants to eat them.

Lisa: I think it might be about a place where any kind of food you want rains down from the sky.

Teacher: Let's read and see how close your predictions are.

The students read until the town of Chewandswallow is described.

Teacher: Now, do you still agree with your predictions?

Children: It sounds like it's going to be about a place like Lisa described.

Teacher: What makes you think so?

Jessica: Because they haven't talked at all about an old man, the author only described the town and how food rained down for breakfast, lunch, and dinner.

Teacher: Would you like to live in a town like Chewandswallow?

Susan: I think it would be fun because then you wouldn't have to wait for your mom to cook dinner. You could just catch some extra food and eat when you were hungry.

Tyler: I wouldn't like it cuz what would happen if it rained something heavy like barbecued ribs and you got hit on the head and got knocked out or died.

Teacher:	Tyler brought up a good point. Could there be some problems with living in this town?
Jeff:	It could rain heavy things and hurt you.
Maria:	If there were a storm of ice cream or something mushy, it would get really messy.
Teacher:	Good, now that you're thinking about what a place like Chewandswallow would be like, let's read on to see what happens in the town.

Students read until the weather takes a turn for the worse.

Teacher:	Now what do you think is going to happen in the story?
James:	It's about a town that rains food for breakfast, lunch, and dinner, and then one day the food starts coming down funny.
Teacher:	What do you mean by funny?
James:	I think that maybe too much food started coming down.
Teacher:	What makes you think that maybe too much food started coming down?
James:	Well, in the picture there is too much spaghetti in the road and the cars can't move.
Teacher:	Good, now let's continue reading to see if you are right.

The students continue reading until the story describes a tomato tornado, and then the teacher asks questions again.

Teacher:	So, what happens in the town of Chewandswallow?
Kayla:	All kinds of food start coming down. Some of it is yucky like peanut butter, mayonnaise, and brussels sprouts. And sometimes just too much of it comes down, like when they had a tomato tornado. Everything was a mess because the food was going crazy.
Teacher:	What do you think the town will do about it? Why do you think so?
Frank:	I think that they will hire a magician to put a spell on the clouds so that the weather will get straightened out because sometimes in the stories they can do that.
Harold:	I think that they have to leave if they can, before they all die. That's what I would do.
Nancy:	I think they need to find out who is in charge of making it rain so that they can ask them to stop it and make things go back to normal.
Teacher:	Those are good answers. Now I want you all to decide which of those you think is the most likely to happen and let's continue reading.

The students read the rest of the book.

Teacher:	Did the people do what you thought they would do? Did you like how they solved their problem?
Harold:	Yes, that's what I thought they should do.
Frank:	No, I still think they should've called on somebody to help them so that they wouldn't have to leave Chewandswallow and have to buy groceries in the store.

A DRTA could also be extended for use with expository texts such as those found in the classroom science, health, and social studies textbooks.

TEACHING EFFECTIVE SKILL LESSONS: FROM WHOLE TO PARTS TO WHOLE

Current thoughts on teaching skills involve a process known as "whole-to-parts-to whole" instruction.

Teaching effective skill lessons with basal readers will require some adjustments on the part of the teacher, because most basal teacher's editions continue to approach skill instruction from a "parts to whole" rather than from a "whole to parts to whole" perspective. This means that the skill to be learned is usually taken completely out of context when being introduced, then placed later into the context of real reading by the student. It has been shown clearly in research by Dolores Durkin (1979) that this way of teaching often fails to help students apply the new skill effectively.

For example, one of the strategies students learn for attacking an unknown word in a story is commonly known as "sounding out." That is, when confronted with an unknown word, the student should try to pronounce the word by stringing together beginning, middle, and ending consonant and/or vowel sounds. When the student "sounds out" the unknown word, while also thinking of words that would make sense in the context of the story, he or she can very often decode the word. In the "parts to whole" method of teaching commonly used by most basals, the teacher would begin the skill lesson by immediately talking about how one "sounds out" a word using letter sounds. The students would focus exclusively on the skill or "part" of reading to be learned at the beginning of the lesson. After the skill had been explained and demonstrated by the teacher, then students would be asked to try out the skill themselves in a "whole" text selection—hence, "parts to whole" teaching.

In "whole to parts to whole" teaching, we add a missing element at the beginning of the lesson—"whole" text. This procedure calls for reading a whole text selection first (e.g., a story, poem, song, rap, or chant) so that children can easily envision a real reading challenge. Once the "whole" context of a reading selection is shared, then the teacher would move into the remaining "parts to whole" portions of the skill lesson.

In our earlier example where the goal is to show children how to "sound out" words as a decoding strategy, we might begin by rereading an enlarged version of a basal story recently completed. This provides the "whole" reading context in which a real reading problem can be addressed, namely, "What can I do when I come to an unknown word?" (Note: An enlarged page from the selection can easily be created by simply making a photocopy and transparency of the basal reader page you wish to use with the overhead projector.) Next, the teacher would (a) explain the real reading problem to be addressed, (b) describe the strategy or "part" of effective reading that could be used to solve the problem ("sounding out"), and (c) model how the skill is used. From that point on, students would be coached by the teacher as they tried to sound out words themselves in other "whole" text simulations. This "whole to parts to whole" method of teaching skills has been shown to be highly effective when used with basal readers and with authentic books.

Figure 4.14 shows a kind of generic guide for planning "Basal Skill Lessons" using our "whole to parts to whole" mini-lesson method. (Note: We refer to these as "mini-lessons" because skill lessons tend to be short in duration [about 10 minutes] so as to maximize student attention.)

Skill lessons should be modeled after short "mini-lessons" that focus on application of the skill taught in the context of use.

Planning a skills lesson should begin by the teacher carefully studying the story or text.

Selection and Analysis of a "Whole" Text Example: Analyzing a Basal Selection for Skills to Include in a Mini-lesson

As an example, let us consider a basal story written by Frank Asch (1993), "Moondance," published in the *Imagine That* Teacher's Sourcebook of the Scholastic Literacy Place® program. To begin, read the story to determine possible skills in the

Figure 4.14   Basal skill mini-lesson planning guide: Whole-to-parts-to-whole

I. Selection and Analysis of a "Whole" Text Example
- Choose a basal reader selection to be read.
- Analyze the basal selection for potential skill lessons, using the district or state curriculum guide.
- Decide on skill(s) to be taught *(Name the skill and include relevant numerical code used by the school district or state for accountability purposes)*.

II. Introduction of the Skill or "Part" to Be Learned
- Purpose: Your aim, objective, or reason for teaching.
- Modeling: Demonstrate the procedure, thinking, or behavior.

III. Student Practice and Follow-up Opportunities Returning to "Whole" Text
- Opportunities for students to apply the skill and receive coaching from the teacher.

IV. Assessment
- Gather formal or informal data on how well students understood and used the skill.

V. Supplies Needed
- A listing of necessary materials and preparations.

story that can be matched with: (a) observed student needs, (b) story or text elements that may give children difficulty, or (c) opportunities to teach skills, strategies, or elements of literary style prescribed in the district, state, or program curriculum. Make a listing of the possible skills as shown here:

- Observed student needs
  The use of quotation marks to mark dialogue in reading and writing
  Sequencing
  Using story structure
- Observed potential challenges in the reading selection
  Using and understanding multiple punctuation marks
  Comprehending the concept of coincidence
  Sequencing the events in the story plot
- Observed potential to teach prescribed curriculum elements
  Using quotation marks in writing and reading
  Sequencing story information and events
  Understanding story structure

Once the listing is complete, note that across all three categories of observation—student need, text availability, and curriculum guides—two skills can be appropriately addressed: (a) understanding story plot elements in sequence, and (b) using punctuation marks in reading and writing. A skill lesson on one of these teaching points can be selected for initial attention. For purposes of this example lesson, let's select "using punctuation marks" in reading as the basal skill to be taught in a mini-lesson.

Introducing the Skill or "Part" to Be Learned

- *Purpose: (Your aim, objective, or reason for teaching.)* The main purpose for teaching a skill mini-lesson on using punctuation marks in reading is to improve expressiveness in oral reading and to improve silent reading comprehension. Punctuation marks are visual symbols that indicate a need to change the prosody of oral or spoken language. Prosody, as we learned in chapter 3, involves changes in spoken language signalled by pitch, juncture, and stress. These prosodic elements in language can vastly change the meaning children construct as they read. For example, students who do not notice periods may not pause appropriately at the end of sentences, thus interrupting the normal flow of comprehension. Students who do not observe quotation marks may not realize that someone is speaking in the text. Failure to note exclamation points may lead to dull, expressionless oral reading. In any case, punctuation marks are visual symbols for changes in pitch, juncture, and stress in spoken language—all of which affect what one comprehends as a listener or as a reader. Thus, the selected skill to be taught from this story is "using punctuation marks in reading."

- *Modeling: (Demonstrate the procedure, thinking, or behavior.)* One effective means for drawing student's attention to punctuation in text is an activity made famous by Victor Borge called "Verbal Punctuation." In this activity, each punctuation mark is given a sound. To begin the activity, the teacher reads a portion of a text, giving assigned sounds to each punctuation mark. The children usually laugh uncontrollably, but in the end they are very careful to make note of punctuation when it is their turn to read.

  Next, the teacher calls on children to read the selection aloud using a "Popcorn" reading technique, in which children read to a point, jump up, and call on a peer to pick up where they leave off. Each child reads the text aloud, making sure to give the appropriate sounds to the punctuation marks. Following a reading of a predetermined portion of the story, a discussion follows about how punctuation affects our understanding of a text or story.

Student Practice and Follow-up Opportunities Returning to "Whole" Text

Skills can be isolated for attention as "parts" during the lesson but should be returned to the "whole" text or another transfer text to complete the "whole-to-parts-to-whole" cycle for skills lesson design.

- *(Practice—Part).* In a small-group activity area, an unpunctuated text could be given to a small group of children to read aloud in unison. Once the text is read, a cooperative learning group could be formed to figure out where the punctuation should be placed into the text to make it understandable. The text is divided into three- to four-sentence segments. Children work alone to punctuate their text segment. Next, they check their work with a partner. After this, children read their text segment to the group with the punctuation they inserted. As a group, the students self-check their punctuated text segments against the punctuated original text.

- *(Practice—Return to the Whole).* Students are given another story to read with a read-along cassette in a secluded center or area of the classroom. As they read along in unison, they are encouraged to give sounds to the punctuation marks in the story to highlight once again the importance of attending to punctuation marks while reading.

Assessment

As teachers listen to children read self-selected or assigned texts during the taking of a *running record,* attention can be given to *if* or *how well* students use punctuation marks in reading aloud. Also, comprehension difficulties detected in oral retellings of running record texts should be cross-referenced during later running record analysis with how well children used punctuation in their oral reading. This approach allows for an authentic assessment of the individual efficacy of a basal skill mini-lesson on each child's ability to use punctuation in reading.

Basal skills lessons as just described are effective means for bringing student needs, teaching opportunities in texts or basals, and prescribed curriculum skills into alignment and real application by students. The major emphasis of this type of skill lesson is to meet the needs of students using the available teaching tools, the text or stories in the basals, and to satisfy district, state, or program curriculum requirements. Most important, children are not just told what to do; rather, they are actively engaged in learning and applying their learning independently. Teachers do not just assign a worksheet in this type of skill instruction; they involve students, provide demonstrations, set up opportunities for contextualized application, and assess learning outcomes in the whole act of reading or writing.

Supplies

Supplies necessary to complete the skill lesson should be listed. These might include:

- 1 basal reader story with whole class set or for use in small teacher-determined needs reading groups—"Moondance"
- 1 taped story with multiple copies for independent or small-group work
- 1 unpunctuated story with multiple copies for small-group work
- 1 class set of text segments from the unpunctuated story for small group
- 1 copy of the original story with punctuation for self-checking

HELPING STUDENTS WITH SPECIAL NEEDS SUCCEED WITH BASAL READER INSTRUCTION

Historically, the basal reader has not served very successfully as a tool for reading remediation. There are several reasons for this situation. First, some teachers find the stories in basal readers to be bland and uninviting, especially for problem readers. What is needed most is literature that "turns on" the "turned-off" learner—an order too tall for many basals to fill. Second, if a child is failing to achieve success using one approach to reading instruction, in this case the basal reader, then common sense tells us that what is needed is an alternative strategy—not just more of the same. Finally, basal reader systems frequently do not allow students enough time for real reading. The multifarious collection of skill sheets and workbook pages tends to be so time-consuming that little time is left for reading.

In chapter 1, we discussed seven principles for encouraging literacy, some of which are most pertinent when using basals to help students with special needs. Three direct applications of these principles follow.

1. *Reading the basal straight through.* Teachers working with special needs students recognize that what these children need most is regular and sustained

Notice three ways to support students with special needs by using the basal reader.

reading. We suggest that skill sheets and workbook pages be used judiciously, or even avoided, to allow more time for reading. Children should be allowed to read basals straight through as an anthology of children's stories. The teacher may wish to skip stories that offer little for the reader in this setting.

2. *Repeated readings.* In repeated readings, the teacher typically introduces the story as a shared book or story experience, then students attempt to read the book alone or with a friend (Routman, 1988). If the story has rhyme or a regular pattern, it may be sung or chanted. Repeated readings of stories help children achieve a sense of accomplishment, improve comprehension, and build fluency.

3. *Supported, or buddy, reading.* Many times, at-risk readers are very reluctant to become risk takers. Teachers simply must find ways of breaking the ice for them and create classroom safety nets. Supported, or "buddy," reading allows students to read basal stories aloud together, either taking turns or in unison. By rereading these supported selections, students' fluency and comprehension improve. Another variation is for teacher–student combinations to read together. Similar to the procedure known as *neurological impress* (P. M. Hollingsworth, 1978), the student and teacher read aloud in unison at a comfortable rate. For first readings, the teacher usually assumes the lead in terms of volume and pace. In subsequent repeated readings, the student is encouraged to assume the lead.

Chapter 9 provides more insights into how teachers can enhance the reading–writing environment as they begin making the transition from basal-only teaching to balanced literacy approaches.

Chapter 9 provides more insights into how teachers can enhance the reading and writing environment as they begin making the transition from basal-only teaching to more balanced literacy perspectives and practices. In the process, we will discover numerous opportunities for assisting students with special needs within the elementary classroom.

HELPING STUDENTS WITH DIVERSE CULTURAL OR LANGUAGE NEEDS SUCCEED WITH BASAL READERS

Think about why students should be taught to read in their primary language.

Students who do not possess reading and writing ability in a first language should be taught to read and write in their native or first language to support and validate them as worthwhile individuals. In addition, reading instruction in the first language helps students capitalize on what they already know about their primary languages and cultures to build concepts that can facilitate the acquisition of English (Freeman & Freeman, 1992; Krashen & Biber, 1988). In any case, teachers must be sensitive to these students' special needs, which include (a) a need for safety and security, (b) a need to belong and be accepted, and (c) a need to feel self-esteem (Peregoy & Boyle, 1993).

Teachers should help English as a second language (ESL) or limited English proficiency (LEP) students feel at ease when they arrive in the classroom by assigning them a "personal buddy" who, if possible, speaks the language of the newcomer. This "buddy" is assigned to help the new student through the school day, routines, and so on. Another approach is to avoid changes in the classroom schedule by following a regular and predictable routine each day, which creates a sense of security. To create a sense of belonging, assign the student to a "home group" for an extended period of time. A "home group" provides a small social unit of concern focused on helping the newcomer adapt to everyday life as well as providing a concerned and caring peer group. Finally, self-esteem is enhanced when an individual's worth is affirmed. Opportunities for the newcomer to share his or her language and culture during daily events in the classroom provide a useful way to integrate the child into the ongoing classroom culture.

To help ESL or LEP students succeed in classrooms where basal readers are the core of instruction, Law and Eckes (1990, p. 92) recommend the following:

Describe three things that can be done to support second language learners when using a basal reader.

- Supplement the basal as much as possible with language experience stories (as discussed previously in this chapter).
- Encourage extensive reading: Gather basal textbooks from as many levels as possible. Also, acquire easier textbooks in content areas as well as trade books to encourage a wide range of reading topics.
- Expose children to the many different types of reading available in the "real" world, such as magazines, *TV Guide,* newspapers, product labels, signs.

Summary

Basal readers over the past 2 centuries have become a veritable institution in American reading instruction. As social and political aims have changed over the years, basal reader content and structure have been altered to reflect these changing conditions. Modern basals are typically composed of several major components, including a teacher's edition, a student's reader, workbooks, and tests. For teachers, basal readers represent a structured approach to teaching reading, which can save enormous amounts of preparation time. On the other hand, basal readers can in some instances displace teacher judgment to the degree that the basal becomes the reading program rather than a tool to be used to support the reading program. Basal readers are produced by large, corporate publishing houses. Senior authors on basal series are usually individuals widely known and respected in the field of reading.

Adopting a basal reader is a task most teachers will likely face in the course of their professional careers. Hence, it is important for teachers to understand how basal readers have been adopted in the past as well as to perceive how the adoption process can be improved. Although basal readers can be useful tools for providing reading instruction, some teachers need to make conscious efforts to take control of their basal teacher's editions by changing the way in which they provide instruction. Suggestions in this chapter included using the balanced reading program, RRL, the LEA, ReQuest, and the DRTA. Providing effective basal skill instruction focuses on relating skills to the reading selections, teaching skills before reading the selections, and using a direct-instruction lesson structure. Finally, readers with special needs who may be struggling can be helped by reading the basal straight through, allowing repeated readings of self-selected basal stories, and providing buddy or other forms of supported reading. ESL and LEP students can be helped to feel at home as newcomers in a school environment; the teacher can also take steps to supplement and extend basic basal reader text for these students.

Concept Applications

In the Classroom

1. Go to your local school district or university curriculum materials library. Locate two basal readers. Find the following items in the teacher's edition: (a) the scope and sequence chart, (b) the parts of the teacher's edition lesson, (c) the skill lessons, (d) the workbooks, and (e) the book tests or assessment materials. Compare the instructional approaches and contents of each using a compare/contrast T chart.

2. Compare and contrast the contents of a current basal reader to the contents of the Dick and Jane or McGuffey basal readers. Write a brief essay on the differences you note.

3. Select a basal reader teacher's edition. Using the evaluation checklist in Figure 4.13, evaluate the strengths and weaknesses of the basal you selected. Discuss your findings with a classmate or peer.

4. Select a basal reader lesson and story. Check the lesson for the major parts of the DRTA. Describe in writing how the design of this lesson follows or fails to follow the description of the DRTA.

5. Select a basal reader lesson and story. Redesign this lesson by changing it to make use of (a) the RRL, (b) the LEA, (c) ReQuest, or (d) DRTA.

6. Choose one skill lesson, and redesign it to incorporate the Basal Skill Mini-lesson: Whole to Parts to Whole lesson planning guide described in this chapter.

In the Field

1. Interview a teacher in the field about the strengths and weaknesses of the basal. Find out why this teacher uses or does not use the basal.

2. Visit a classroom in a local elementary school. Observe a teacher teaching reading with the basal. Which parts of the lesson did the teacher use? Which parts did the teacher omit? Write an essay about your observations.

3. Prepare a basal reading lesson to be taught in the schools. Secure permission to teach this lesson in a local grade-level appropriate classroom. Write a reflective essay on the experience detailing successes, failures, and necessary changes.

4. Select a basal reading lesson in a teacher's edition. Adapt the lesson in the teacher's edition by rewriting it using a balanced reading program, RRL, LEA, DRTA, and so on. Secure permission to teach this lesson in a local grade-level appropriate classroom. Write a reflective essay on the experience detailing successes, failures, and necessary changes.

Recommended Readings

Anderson, R. C., Osborn, J., & Tierney, R. J. (1984). *Learning to read in American schools*. Hillsdale, NJ: Erlbaum.

Aukerman, R. (1981). *The basal reader approach to reading.* New York: Wiley.

Baumann, J. F. (1992). Basal reading programs and the deskilling of teachers: A critical examination of the argument. *Reading Research Quarterly, 27*(4), 390–398.

Cheney, L. V. (1990). *Tyrannical machines.* Washington, DC: National Endowment for the Humanities.

Goodman, K. S. (1987). Look what they've done to Judy Blume!: The "basalization" of children's literature. *The New Advocate, 1*(1), 29–41.

Goodman, K. S., Shannon, P., Freeman, Y. S., & Murphy, S. (1988). *Report card on basal readers.* New York: Owen.

A guide to selecting basal reading programs. (1990). Urbana-Champaign: University of Illinois at Urbana-Champaign, Center for the Study of Reading.

Hoffman, J. V., & Roser, N. (Eds.). (1987, January). The basal reader in American reading instruction. [Special issue] *The Elementary School Journal, 87*(3).

McCallum, R. D. (1988). Don't throw the basals out with the bath water. *The Reading Teacher, 42,* 204–209.

Osborn, J., Wilson, P. T., & Anderson, R. C. (1985). *Reading education: Foundations for a literate America.* Lexington, MA: Lexington Books.

Perspectives on basal readers. (1989). [Special issue] *Theory Into Practice, 28*(4).

Shannon, P. (1992). *Becoming political: Readings and writings in the politics of literacy education.* Portsmouth, NH: Heinemann.

Smith, N. B. (1986). *American reading instruction.* Newark, DE: International Reading Association.

Winograd, P. N., Wixson, K. K., & Lipson, M. Y. (Eds.). (1989). *Improving basal reader instruction.* New York: Teachers College Press.

chapter 5

From Basals to Books:

Focus Questions

When you are finished studying this chapter, you should be able to answer these questions:

1. What are eight dimensions of change involved in the transitions model?
2. Which of eight transitional stances about reading instruction best describe(s) your current beliefs and why?
3. What are three levels of curricular integration associated with transitions?
4. How can teachers in transition involve colleagues and parents in reading instructional changes?
5. How does the classroom environment affect children's perceptions of learning to read?
6. What are some notable differences between traditional and balanced literacy assessment practices?
7. How can teachers come to cope with the changing demographics of the classroom?

Making the Transition

Key Concepts

Transitional Stances in Beliefs
Oral Recitation Lesson
Comprehension Interrogation
Standards Based Instruction
Nonnegotiable Skills
Fragmentation
Curricular Integration
Language to Literacy

Flexible Grouping
Homogenous Guided Reading Groups
Institutional Environments
Homelike Environments
Portfolio Assessment
Reading Instructional Continuum

Transitioning toward balance in reading instruction is an invitation to risk change. But *how* can teachers safely but surely move out from between the rock and the hard place associated with reading instructional practices is subject to wide swings of fashion (Mosenthal, 1989b; Routman, 1996). Preservice and in-service teachers need to work through a complex web of changes to make transitions toward balance in reading beliefs and practices.

TRANSITIONS: IMPLEMENTING BALANCE IN READING INSTRUCTION

Preservice and in-service teachers make transitions for different reasons.

Preservice teachers frequently resist balanced reading beliefs and practices because these beliefs and practices are very often incompatible with their own experiences as children in school. In many cases, preservice teachers need to make transitions toward balance to survive student teaching or to gain initial employment in a school that is committed to extremes in reading instructional approaches.

Similarly, in-service teachers risk a great deal when making changes toward balanced reading beliefs and practices: employment security, professional reputation, and perhaps most important, the potential progress and self-esteem of their students. Transitioning toward balanced readings allows in-service teachers to initiate changes in reading instruction with minimal risks and maximal benefits.

> Anyone willing to take some risks can begin the exploration. Any teacher can handle the decision making. Every teacher can create the subtle structures that help shape the learning context. . . . With some support, every teacher can find his or her own way. (Newman & Church, 1990, p. 25)

The philosophy of transitions recognizes, in a very real way, each teacher's need for a safety net throughout the risky process of changing reading instructional beliefs and practices.

The point where teachers begin transitions is a matter of choice.

In addition to risk, making transitions toward balanced reading instruction is a complex process. Because of this complex web of interrelated changes, teachers make transitions in a variety of ways and at differing rates. As discussed in chapter 1, we have identified eight interrelated dimensions of making transitions toward balance (instructional beliefs, reading materials, curriculum design, instructional grouping, cultural diversity, assessment, classroom environments, and community involvement); see Figure 1.2, p. 10.

We have observed that, regardless of the point of entry into the spiral of transitions shown in Figure 1.2, there is a domino effect that leads teachers from one dimension of change in the model to the next. Thus, teachers often begin with a single change leading to the next in a spiral-like movement toward more balanced literacy beliefs and practices shown at the center of the model. Because the point of departure in the model and the speed of the domino effect are difficult to predict, the model can represent only the idea that transitions begin at a point or points in the model and move gradually toward the center of the model—balanced—reading instruction.

Once transitions are begun, teachers go through a series of changes.

The concept of transitions embodies the idea of lifelong professional changes and growth.

In the remainder of this chapter, we explain the dimensions and processes associated with making transitions. We begin this explanation by describing several stances or roles that teachers may adopt with respect to instructional beliefs throughout the process of making transitions. Next, we address necessary modifications of instructional materials and their uses. This section is followed by a presentation on how teaching practices can be gradually changed toward balanced reading and authentic instruction without ruffling too many feathers among colleagues, administrators, and school patrons. Then we discuss desired changes in classroom environments and assessment compatible with a balanced reading philosophy. Finally, we share three case studies of teachers in transition. These case studies are offered in hopes of validating the fact that teachers make transitions at different rates and in very unique ways. What's more, we hope these case studies help teachers relax and enjoy the journey a bit more. Half the joy in embarking on the professional journey of making transitions is the journey itself!

TRANSITIONS IN INSTRUCTIONAL BELIEFS

Teachers approach transitions toward balanced reading instruction in many different ways. Some teachers just jump right in and try to make changes all at once. Others are more cautious, implementing just one or two carefully selected changes before attempting more. In fact, the coauthors of this book approached transitions differently and to varying degrees. For example, one jumped right into implementing balanced reading instruction. The other continued using worksheets and basals as the core of reading instruction but supplemented these with generous amounts of literature, storytelling, writing, and teacher-made worksheets. Consequently, we hesitate to present transitions in a way that prescribes that *every* teacher must pass through specified stages in a predetermined order. On the other hand, we, along with others (e.g., Heald-Taylor, 1989; Routman, 1996), have noted with recurring frequency certain similarities in stances or roles adopted along the way by those who venture into transitions. For this reason, we discuss each of these **transitional stances in beliefs** as we have observed them. Because preservice teachers approach transitions from a different set of experiences, the first stance, "I don't know enough yet to know where I stand," is expressly directed at preservice teacher candidates. The remaining stances are aimed most appropriately at in-service teachers, who approach transitions in the wake of a wealth of teaching experience and tradition.

Transitions in teacher beliefs often pass through several stages or stances. Think of a time you changed your beliefs. What were you aware of at this stage?

"I Don't Know Enough Yet to Know Where I Stand" Stance

Preservice teachers are often confused by the convoluted and conflicting world of reading education and research. From past experiences in school as youngsters, these teachers-to-be remember learning to read in small groups of children with special books. They recall vividly the completion of workbooks and other instructional materials designed to help them learn to read. Their recollections often lead to a belief that these past practices must have been research based, effective, and worthy of continued emulation. Not until they are confronted with conflicting views of reading education in colleges of education and in elementary schools do preservice teachers entertain the possibility that their past experiences may not represent valid educational practice for today. In addition, preservice teachers often spend time as observers or apprentice teachers in elementary school classrooms that exemplify traditional reading instructional practices. Thus, innovative practices very often conflict with the realities of some classrooms they visit. In some cases, students encounter conflicting beliefs in their reading education courses, which sets up further confusion and often a considerable degree of frustration. Hence, many preservice teachers surrender to traditional practices under the weight of confusion and conflict. At this point, preservice teachers often admit, "I don't know enough yet to know where I stand!" Melissa, a preservice teacher, wrote the following about her beliefs:

Many preservice teachers do not know enough about their beliefs, others' beliefs, or their future circumstances to commit to a belief system.

> The stance that best describes my beliefs, since I do not yet have my own class to teach, is the I Don't Know Enough Yet to Know stance. Just because I have this belief now (since I am not in the classroom) in no way means my beliefs will not change to a more balanced approach when I actually do get classroom experience. In fact, I would have to say that once I do have a classroom of my own I may very well become an advocate of balanced reading instruction. I really do love balanced reading philosophy, but I just don't know yet if I can make it work.

The need for classroom experience and an opportunity to test their own beliefs out in the classroom causes many preservice teachers to assume temporarily the "I don't know enough yet to know where I stand" stance. After acquiring classroom experience, however, many of these preservice teachers may be able to skip or move rapidly through the following belief stances as in-service teachers.

Combative Stance

Teachers who adopt a combative stance often feel threatened by change. They may resent a perceived authority figure, peer, or patron for making them feel they should change at all. They may feel cornered, even coerced by circumstances, into change.

Bonnie, a veteran second-grade teacher, had adopted a combative stance when we first met her. For many years, Bonnie had used the basal reader to teach reading and had experienced reasonable success. During summer vacation, however, the school principal and a few of Bonnie's colleagues became interested in balanced reading philosophy and instruction after attending a local workshop. Because of the excitement generated by this workshop, the principal wrote a Goals 2000 grant through the state office of education, which provided funds for in-service instruction to help the staff initiate transitions. But Bonnie was in no mood for this change. During the in-service sessions, she constantly pointed out that she did not feel a need to change. She felt that what she was doing to teach reading worked just as well as what we suggested. In fact, Bonnie just did not seem to want to entertain the very notion of change. When criticisms were raised regarding current school-based instructional practices or basal readers, she rushed to their defense. When ideas were suggested to the other teachers who received them with enthusiasm, Bonnie stood by with the wet blanket of pessimism. She could catalogue a much longer list of reasons why such changes were doomed to almost certain failure than we could conjure up in support.

To sum up, Bonnie was placed in the position of moving outside her instructional comfort zones before she was ready or willing. She was clearly committed to her program for teaching children to read and saw no reason to change. Although the adage "people are generally down on what they are not up on" was obviously true in Bonnie's case, Bonnie was caught in the winds of change unwillingly. To her credit, Bonnie remained open-minded enough to examine new ideas in the privacy of her own thoughts. With time and reflection, many ideas Bonnie resisted at first led to a crack in the wall of her resistance. We have found that, like Bonnie, many in-service and preservice teachers take a combative stance when confronted with philosophical and practical suggestions that are incompatible with their own beliefs, schooling experiences, or long-standing practices.

Tentative Stance

Although Bonnie remained combative on the outside, she began to privately examine her own beliefs and practices. As the days and weeks rolled on, Bonnie listened intently as she overheard her colleagues talking about the events in their classrooms. Secretly, Bonnie confided at a later time, she hoped her colleagues would fail and her position would be exonerated. But this was not to be the case. Children in the other teachers' classrooms were enjoying reading and writing; the need to coax and cajole children into reading and writing had all but disappeared. Bonnie was troubled that she had to coax her students to read a book when they finished their work. These events combined to bring Bonnie to a tentative stance toward transitions. She noted that her colleagues seemed to be enjoying their work more, to say nothing of the fact that their students were reportedly enjoying reading and writing more. Cautiously,

Bonnie began to ask questions of her colleagues about how these new changes in reading instruction were working out. The crack in Bonnie's wall of resistance began to widen. She was now ready to listen—tentatively, but willingly.

Responsive Stance

In the faculty lounge, Bonnie continued to listen to the discussions of her colleagues with increased interest. She frequently asked others what they were doing in their classrooms while openly expressing surprise at their success. Secretly, Bonnie decided to try just one of the activities called *silent sustained writing* (SSW). This seemed to be a reasonably unobtrusive change, even for her. She established 15 minutes of daily SSW in her classroom. Bonnie later confessed that she had made this change for nearly 3 months before telling her colleagues.

Internal changes in beliefs become carefully externalized into selected practice in the responsive stance.

Explorative Stance

During the next school year, Bonnie requested from her colleague and best friend, Ann, materials she might read about balanced reading and writing instruction. She obtained from Ann a catalogue from which she ordered two books. Later that year, she accompanied Ann to a local balanced literacy instruction conference. On returning from the conference, Bonnie decided to make some additional changes—changes in the way and how much she used the basal reader. She invited Ann into her classroom to discuss how she might go about using the basal reader less and become more selective, including reducing her dependency on worksheets. Her primary concern centered on what to do to fill the void created by using the basal and worksheets less. Ann suggested several ideas that she had tried the year before with good success. Bonnie decided on a few, selected strategies she would try and requested funds from the school principal for ordering specific materials to support her continued but carefully concealed exploration.

Active searching for additional information characterizes a teacher in the explorative stance.

An Off-the-Record Stance

After several days of trying the selected strategies, Bonnie was surprised at the success she was experiencing. One day after school, Bonnie told Ann she was trying several of her suggestions and that things were working out fairly well. Then, Bonnie asked Ann several questions about what to do when certain problems arose in her classroom. Ann invited Bonnie to discuss these problems with several other faculty members who met once a month after school to share ideas and problems in a balanced reading study group. Bonnie reluctantly agreed to come. But when Bonnie accepted this invitation to attend a study group meeting, her carefully concealed exploration eventually became apparent to her colleagues.

Practices found during exploration are used without revealing their use to others.

A Cautiously Out-in-the-Open Stance

After attending her first study group meeting, Bonnie's private indulgence in making a transition toward balanced reading instruction was revealed. In many ways, Bonnie was relieved. Now she felt comfortable talking about her experiences—both her concerns and her successes—with peers. During subsequent meetings, she frequently asked questions about discussed beliefs and practices.

    In the months that followed, Bonnie continued to work on practicing and perfecting the strategies she had been using. In addition, she cautiously introduced

A careful public exploration initiated with the knowledge and support of others exemplifies this stance.

Figure 5.1   Transitions toward balanced reading beliefs: Typical teacher stances and behaviors

---

"I Don't Know Enough Yet to Know Where I Stand" Stance

Teachers may

- Express confusion and frustration toward innovations in reading programs
- Express commitment to their own experiences as school students and observers
- Feel a need to conform to current norms or traditions in public and private schools
- Express a concern regarding a lack of experience as teachers in real classroom settings
- Feel unsure of whether they can successfully implement a reading program based on holistic philosophy and associated instructional approaches

Combative Stance

Teachers may

- Demonstrate hostility toward change
- Defend traditional or existing reading programs
- Enumerate obstacles to implementing whole language

Tentative Stance

Teachers may

- Begin to privately examine their own reading beliefs and practices
- Begin to listen in on teacher discussions of changes in reading beliefs and practices
- Begin to ask questions about holistic reading strategies

Responsive Stance

Teachers may

- Ask colleagues about their experiences in implementing holistic reading practices
- Cautiously initiate unobtrusive holistic practices
- Conceal from colleagues the initiation of holistic practices

---

several new strategies and practices into her classroom while continuing to use a few traditional strategies that she was not willing to give up. Bonnie continued the slow but nonetheless directed process of making transitions during the year. At the end of the second year, she was becoming convinced that balanced teaching of reading and language was worth the effort. Finally, Bonnie openly advocated the changes she had made while continuing her ongoing transitions.

An Advocate's Stance

An advocate feels at ease with reading instructional change and supports others through the process.

Three years after we had met Bonnie, she had become one of the most respected reading teachers in her school. Other teachers visited her classroom, came to her with problems, and solicited information. She listened, supported, encouraged, and even offered her colleagues articles and books to read on balanced literacy instruction. Bonnie continued to study and change professionally. She attended reading and language conferences and workshops regularly to gain new insights and information. She shared information and ideas freely and openly with her colleagues.

Explorative Stance

Teachers may

- Request additional information about holistic reading instruction
- Begin to attend conferences with colleagues
- Try additional holistic reading strategies

Off-the-Record Stance

Teachers may

- Share the positive and negative outcomes of the experience
- Begin to ask "what do you do when?" types of questions
- Accept invitations to attend in-school support group meetings

Cautiously Out-in-the-Open Stance

Teachers may

- Begin to perfect the holistic reading strategies initiated
- Begin to offer help to colleagues in transition
- Replace more traditional strategies with holistic strategies
- Show excitement by openly advocating positive results with students
- Continue to use some traditional strategies

Advocate's Stance

Teachers will

- Begin to share willingly with other teachers how holistic reading instruction is used
- Use a predominance of holistic strategies while continuing selected traditional strategies
- Share strategies with teachers who are just beginning
- Read professional articles, journals, and books and share these with others
- Visit other classrooms and receive visitors into their classrooms

Today, Bonnie has largely achieved a balanced reading and language curriculum. She continues to occasionally use direct, isolated skill lessons, particularly those focusing on phonics and word-recognition skills, but alway returns these isolated skills to the context of real reading and writing. On the other hand, Bonnie makes considered use of basal readers and worksheets along with literature books, increased silent reading time, and reading response activities. She encourages her students to respond to their reading rather than interrogating them after reading with a list of questions. More and more, Bonnie integrates reading and writing in her classroom. She has even found that phonics can be practiced in writing and spelling, not just in reading.

Although Bonnie has a ways to go toward balanced reading and teaching consistently from the whole to the parts to the whole, she has made significant strides toward that end. Those who talk to Bonnie today find her professionally vibrant and feeling very much in control of her classroom and curriculum.

Figure 5.1 summarizes the major characteristics of each of the stances in reading beliefs.

TRANSITIONS IN USING INSTRUCTIONAL MATERIALS

An important, even critical, dimension of making transitions is adapting or discontinuing the use of many traditional instructional materials. Using the basal reader like a textbook or script, assigning worksheets as practice for reading skills, and conducting oral round-robin reading in ability groups are examples of classroom practices related to the use of specific reading instructional materials demanding change. Recent reports have pointed out that instructional materials have exerted significant effects on teachers and the teaching of reading for decades (Shannon & Goodman, 1994). K. Goodman, Shannon, Freeman, and Murphy (1988) describe the effect of using basal readers:

> But just as [the basal] must control reading, language, and learning, the basal's central premise requires that it control the teacher. And the control of teachers, far from assuring their effectiveness, limits both their authority and their responsibility for the development of pupils. One of the great tragedies of the basals is the dependency they have built in teachers. (p. 128)

In fairness, some scholars do not agree that basal readers are the *cause* of teachers' elected practices (Baumann, 1992, 1994). In fact, basal readers have been the cause of some recent changes in classroom practices (Baker, 1994). Because of the dependency on instructional materials, particularly basal readers, many teachers are timid about making decisions and sometimes resist taking responsibility for making instructional decisions that could affect change. Duffy, Roehler, and Putnam (1987) contend:

> As more is learned about the nature of reading and the effective teaching of reading, the need for elementary school teachers who will make substantive curricular decisions becomes more apparent. (p. 357)

For whatever reason, many teachers who want to make transitions pursue a cautious and well-thought-out plan for reducing dependency on basal readers as well as other basal-related reading instructional materials. Over time and with effort, teachers can move away from a reading curriculum dominated by basals, worksheets, and tests toward more balanced reading instruction. However, and somewhat paradoxically, to begin this journey, we suggest that the best point of departure for initiating transitions using instructional materials is the basal reader. With this idea in mind, we describe how teachers can use the basal as a springboard toward balanced reading instruction.

Basals as Springboards: Mitigating Weaknesses

Some reading experts recommend that teachers simply cut back on the use of the basal reader as a first step in transitions (K. S. Goodman, 1986). Although this may be a viable approach for some teachers, basal readers have come to fill an important niche in the instructional habits and practices of classroom teachers for well over 100 years (Pearson, 1989c). Cutting back may create much too large a void in classroom practices as a starting point. Besides, simply cutting back does nothing to help teachers think about instruction and make informed and reasoned instructional changes or adaptations in what often is the only instructional material they have on hand for teaching reading: the basal reader. We think a better approach is to rethink or adapt the use of the basal reader as an initial step in transitions.

Using the basal as a springboard for departure from old practices requires that teachers understand several weaknesses inherent in basal readers and several common misuses of basals:

- Reading the basal from front to back, every story in order, as a textbook rather than treating it as an anthology of literature
- Skill lesson overkill: reading instruction as worksheets
- Teaching reading skills in isolation
- Oral round-robin reading: A practice high in risk, low in benefit
- Asking questions: the reading inquisition

Following are suggested ways to mitigate the weaknesses identified that can help teachers begin the process of thinking about and adapting the use of basal readers in classrooms.

Treating the Basal as an Anthology of Literature—Not a Textbook!

"What are basal readers, after all?" questioned a curious college student. "They are a school textbook containing stories, poems, and short informational selections. In a very real sense, basals are anthologies—collections of stories, expository articles, and poetry," we explain. "Are all works in an anthology of literature read in order from the front of the book to the back?" the student continues. "No, not typically! When reading an anthology, readers usually choose a story here or there, based on interest," we respond. The same should be true with a basal reader. Students should not be required to read the basal reader from front to back, every story in order. After all, publishers have never claimed that the selections in basal readers are perfectly sequenced by difficulty. The key issue here is capturing student interest. To capture students' interest, we must allow them to browse and choose interesting reading selections from the basal.

If teachers could envision the basal reader as a small shelf of selected, individual storybooks that students can choose from, then browsing the basal shelf of stories seems to be a reasonable beginning point. We suggest that students be given 20 to 30 minutes at the beginning of each year to browse through the selections in the basal reader(s). They might be encouraged to make a list of their favorite selections. After browsing, teachers should conduct an interest inventory to determine the basal stories for which students seem to indicate high interest. This may be done by reading aloud the titles for each story in the table of contents and asking students to indicate by a show of hands which of the stories they are interested in reading. Another approach is to copy the table of contents, have students put their name on the copy, and mark which of the stories they would like to read. In this way, teachers learn which stories may be skipped in the basal because of little or no interest. After stories have been selected based on interest, teachers can form basal reader visiting groups or interest groups. Some teachers making transitions from using basal readers have actually taken their older, out-of-date basals and torn the covers off, put soft covers on each story as if they were a small, individual books, and placed these multiple copies of soft-bound basal stories into their classroom libraries for students to select for reading.

Learning to think about and use a basal reader differently is an important initial change in reading instruction.

The basal can be thought of as an anthology of reading selections. This concept was also discussed in chapter 4.

Let students choose to read those selections in the basal anthology that interest them.

Basal reader visiting response groups or interest groups are discussed in chapter 9.

Working out of Worksheet Dependency: Toward Reader Response

Worksheets have filled a management role in reading classrooms— keeping children busy.

Several classroom observation studies have found that reading instruction has been dominated by worksheets (R. C. Anderson, Hiebert, Scott, & Wilkinson, 1985; Durkin, 1978). Although this condition may be deplored by experts for important instructional reasons, classroom teachers have come to depend on worksheets for quite a different reason: Worksheets have served a role in the management of reading instruction (Pearson, 1989c). Thus, calls for the complete and immediate cessation of worksheet usage in classrooms may send many teachers into worksheet withdrawal and eventual management shock.

Some questions teachers often ask are "If we don't teach and practice skills with worksheets, how will we know if students are learning?" "How can we give grades in reading without worksheet assignments?" "What will students do without worksheets when I am not working with their reading group?" These questions and many more emphasize teachers' real and legitimate concern over the use of worksheets for managing the reading classroom. How can teachers go about gradually working their way out of a worksheet economy in the classroom—an economy that breeds dependency for teachers? We suggest a three-part process that is aimed at reducing the number of worksheets while simultaneously improving the quality of those worksheets assigned to students.

Notice two things the teacher can do to begin transitions with basal readers.

First, *reduce gradually the number of worksheets assigned during the reading instructional period.* This can be accomplished by cutting out worksheets that emphasize content or skills for which students have already demonstrated sufficient understanding or ability. In place of worksheets, students can be given increased time for reading books, magazines, and drama, and for writing stories of their own choice. Increasing reading time is essential for year-to-year gains in reading achievement (R. C. Anderson, Wilson, & Fielding, 1988; Reutzel & Hollingsworth, 1991). Another means of reducing worksheets is for teachers to ask themselves questions such as "Where is this skill or strategy best demonstrated and practiced—in reading a text or on a worksheet?" Careful consideration of this question leads to the answer that reading skills or strategies ought to be embedded in context: the place where these skills are used in reading and society. Questions such as these will help teachers use worksheets more judiciously while replacing them with increased opportunities to read real books.

Change the nature of worksheet assignments. Use open-ended responses such as those suggested as literature-response activities described in chapters 11 and 12.

Second, *the number of worksheets can be reduced by changing the very nature of worksheets to reflect more open-ended, divergent, or accepting formats.* Worksheets such as these encourage students to write, draw, or otherwise interpret and respond to reading rather than requiring them to provide single answers, convergent or "correct" responses.

Although this recommendation defeats the timesaving advantages of many commercially produced worksheets, one advantage of custom designing worksheets is that other reading materials such as literature books, information books, or newspapers can be integrated into the reading program.

Third, *begin to substitute alternative ways to respond or record feelings about the reading of a book or story.* Students can be asked to use drawing, art, dance, drama, music, or writing to record and share their responses to their reading. Wanted posters, murals, plays, radio readings, or learning logs can be used to engage students in activities that develop and refine skills as well as elaborate interpretations and comprehension (see chapters 11 and 12).

Teaching with Text

Reducing dependency on worksheets leads to the realization that instruction can take place, perhaps more appropriately, within the context of printed language—the stories and books children read. For example, when teaching children about how graphophonic cues are helpful in decoding unfamiliar words in text, the best place to demonstrate this utility is in the texts that children have been reading or writing (Goswami & Bryant, 1990; Hansen, 1987; Strickland, 1998). Specific literary devices or print-decoding skills are better demonstrated with excellent examples found in books rather than on worksheets. For example, helping children recognize figurative expressions is often taught using worksheets. Instead, it seems more reasonable to read stories containing rich examples of figurative language use such as *Amelia Bedelia* (Parish, 1963), *A Chocolate Moose for Dinner* (Gwynne, 1970), or *The King Who Rained* (Gwynne, 1976). Using children's reading and writing to teach specific language strategies makes good sense. We say this because there is no need to "transfer learning" from the isolated nature of worksheets to real reading or writing events.

Teach children reading skills and strategies using the print and books they are reading.

Oral Reading with Basals and Books: Breaking Away from Round-Robin Reading

Perhaps no practice, outside of using worksheets, figures as prominently in American reading instruction as does the practice of having children read aloud one at a time while other students listen and follow along; this practice is known as *round-robin reading.* Hoffman and Segel (1982) reviewed the historical literature on oral reading instruction in American classrooms in an attempt to locate the origin of round-robin reading. After an exhaustive search, these authors uncovered no work that could be used to determine the point at which round-robin reading assumed its prominent place in classroom reading instruction. Recent research on the effects of oral round-robin reading on students' reading achievement in regular classrooms has shown its negative effects as compared to other modes for providing group oral reading instruction and practice (Eldredge, Reutzel, & Hollingsworth, 1996). Because research by Reutzel and Hollingsworth (1993) indicated that the oral recitation lesson is a solid alternative for providing group oral reading instruction, we recommend Hoffman's (1987) **oral recitation lesson** as one approach for breaking away from an overdependence on oral round-robin reading practices.

*The **ORL** helps teachers move away from the practice of oral round-robin reading in their classrooms.*

Components of the Oral Recitation Lesson

The oral recitation lesson (ORL) consists of two basic components with a series of subroutines, as shown in the following outline.

  I. Direct instruction
      a. Comprehension
      b. Practice
      c. Performance
  II. Indirect instruction
      a. Fluency practice
      b. Demonstrating expert reading

Notice two main components of the ORL.

The first component, direct instruction, consists of three subroutines: a comprehension phase, a practice phase, and a performance phase. When beginning an ORL, the teacher reads a story aloud and leads the students in an analysis of the story's content by constructing a story grammar map and discussing the major elements of the story such as setting, characters, goals, plans, events, and resolution. Students are asked to tell what they remember about these parts of the story, and the teacher records their responses at the board. In a sense, recording student responses is somewhat like a language experience dictation of their story recall. At the conclusion of this discussion, the story grammar map is used as an outline for students to write a story summary.

During the second subroutine, practice, the teacher works with students to improve their oral reading expression. The teacher models fluent reading aloud with segments of the text, and the students individually or chorally practice imitating the teacher's oral expressions.

Choral readings can also be used to break away from oral round-robin reading.

Choral readings of texts can be accomplished in many ways. Wood (1983) suggests two that we have found useful for group choral readings: (a) unison reading, where everyone reads together; and (b) echoic reading, in which the teacher or a student reads, and the others in the group echo the reading. To these we add a third, antiphonal reading. In this method, the group is divided into two subgroups. One subgroup begins reading a segment of text, and the second subgroup echoes the first group's reading. In a variation of this approach, the second group reads the next line alternating with the first group. Text segments modeled by the teacher during the practice phase may begin with only one or two sentences and gradually move toward modeling and practicing whole pages of text.

The third subroutine is the performance phase. In this phase, students select a text segment they want to perform for others in the group, and listeners are encouraged to comment positively on the performance.

The second major component of the ORL is an indirect instruction phase. During this part of the lesson, students practice a single story until they become expert readers. Hoffman (1987) defines an expert reader as one who reads with 98% accuracy and 75 words per minute fluency. For 10 minutes each day, students practice reading a story or text segment in a soft or mumble reading fashion. Teachers use this time to check students individually for story mastery before allowing them to move on to another story.

The direct instruction component creates a pool of stories from which the students can select a story to use to become an expert reader in the indirect instruction phase. In summary, ORL provides teachers with a workable strategy to break away from the traditional practice of round-robin oral reading.

Asking Comprehension Questions: The Reading Inquisition

A common practice encouraged by basal reader teacher's manuals is to ask a line of questions following the reading of a basal story or selection. This practice is often mislabeled "discussion." Durkin (1983) referred to the practice of asking a line of comprehension questions following reading as **comprehension interrogation.** Higgins (cited in Edelsky, 1988) referred to this practice as a "gentle (or not so gentle) inquisition" rather than as a grand conversation. Teachers should understand that basal reader comprehension questioning does nothing to improve comprehension; rather, its major utility is to assess comprehension. Hence, teachers should carefully review the practice of asking comprehension questions after reading.

In the real world, people do not discuss a book by one individual quizzing the other with a line of questions. For instance, when someone has just read a great book and is discussing it around the dinner table, those listening seldom ask questions to quiz comprehension (Atwell, 1987). Thus, asking a line of comprehension questions after reading ought to be discontinued on grounds of lack of authenticity, or at least continued on a more limited basis on grounds of "test preparation" practice. Also, asking the line of questions in basal teacher's manuals fails to help children reconstruct the sequence of events in the story. Why? Because the questions in teacher's manuals are seldom, if ever, sequenced in the order of the story! Besides, questions may probe only insignificant parts or details of the story. Consequently, Harp (1989b) warns that questioning may give a piecemeal view of a reader's comprehension of a story. Finally, children do not *want* to discuss answers to a list of questions in the teacher's manual. Instead, they would rather talk about how they felt about the book, a character in the story, the connections they made between their own experiences and those of the story characters, or ask their own questions.

Transitions in questioning begin when teachers ask questions only about the major elements of the story's structure, setting, problem, goal, and so on, and in the sequence these events are found in the story. The second transitional step is for teachers to discontinue the use of question lists altogether and to involve children in interpretive reading response activities, discussions, and retellings.

Comprehension evaluation can be documented using retelling (described in chapter 6) and completing reading response activities such as those found in chapters 11 and 12.

TRANSITIONS IN CURRICULUM DESIGN: STANDARDS BASED INSTRUCTION

Curriculum reform has taken a major turn in recent years away from district and state level curriculum guides, scope and sequence charts, and core curricula lists toward the development and publication of national standards or **standards based instruction.** In the past 10 years, the field of education has undergone an intense period of reform (Commission on Teaching and America's Future, 1996). Researchers, education leaders, policymakers, teachers, and so on, have joined in the writing of national curriculum standards in an effort to identify the best practices in nearly every field of instruction (Zemelman, Daniels, & Hyde, 1993). In literacy, the International Reading Association (IRA) and the National Council of Teachers of English (NCTE) have jointly produced a document entitled *Standards for the English Language Arts* (1996). The outcome of this effort, as well as others, has been to identify best practice recommendations such as:

National curriculum standards identify "best practices" for the teaching of reading.

Less

- time devoted to seat work and worksheet completion
- reading in basal readers and textbooks
- emphasis on superficial coverage of curriculum topics
- rote memorization and drill
- stress on grades and competition
- use of "tracking" or "ability" grouping
- reliance on pull-out programs for students with special needs
- credibility given to standardized and norm-referenced tests

More

- hands-on, active learning
- emphasis on understanding the structure and key concepts of a field of study

- thematic, topic-centered, inquiry-based instruction (problem solving)
- time spent reading trade books—both fiction and nonfiction
- student responsibility related to assessment, record keeping, monitoring, etc.
- collaborative and cooperative learning activities
- attention to including special-needs students
- use of flexible grouping arrangements
- attention to modeling democratic processes in schools
- use of teacher description and informal assessment procedures to document student growth and progress

List the major points presented in the 12 IRA/NCTE standards for teaching reading.

Specifically, the *IRA/NCTE Standards for the English Language Arts* (1996, p. 3) document lists 12 standards for teachers of reading and writing in the nation's elementary and secondary schools:

1. Students read a wide range of print and nonprint text to build an understanding of text, of themselves, and of the cultures of the United States and the world; to acquire new information; to respond to the needs and demands of society and the workplace; and for personal fulfillment. Among these texts are fiction and nonfiction, classic, and contemporary works.
2. Students read a wide range of literature from many periods in many genres to build an understanding of the many dimensions (e.g., philosophical, ethical, aesthetic) of human experience.
3. Students apply a wide range of strategies to comprehend, interpret, evaluate, and appreciate texts. They draw on their prior experience, their interactions with other readers and writers, their knowledge of word meaning and of other texts, their word identification strategies, and their understanding of textual features (e.g., sound–letter correspondence, sentence structure, context, graphics).
4. Students adjust their use of spoken, written, and visual language (e.g., conventions, style, vocabulary) to communicate effectively with a variety of audiences and for different purposes.
5. Students employ a wide range of strategies as they write and use different writing process elements appropriately to communicate with different audiences for a variety of purposes.
6. Students apply knowledge of language structure, language conventions (e.g., spelling and punctuation), media techniques, figurative language, and genre to create, critique, and discuss print and nonprint texts.
7. Students conduct research on issues and interests by generating ideas and questions, and by posing problems. They gather, evaluate, and synthesize data from a variety of sources (e.g., print and nonprint texts, artifacts, people) to communicate their discoveries in ways that suit their purpose and audience.
8. Students use a variety of technological and informational resources (e.g., libraries, databases, computer networks, videos) to gather and synthesize information and to create and communicate knowledge.
9. Students develop an understanding of and respect for diversity in language use, patterns, and dialects across cultures, ethnic groups, geographic regions, and social roles.
10. Students whose first language is not English make use of their first language to develop competency in the English language arts and to develop understanding of content across the curriculum.

11. Students participate as knowledgeable, reflective, creative, and critical members of a variety of literacy communities.
12. Students use spoken, written, and visual language to accomplish their own purposes (e.g., for learning, enjoyment, persuasion, and the exchange of information).

Publishers of national reading and language arts basal reader programs and content area textbooks are making greater and greater use of national standards in the production of their published products. Teachers in transition will be supported in the newer published materials to make transitions toward national standards and best practices as a consequence of the recent standards-based curriculum reform.

Developing a Nonnegotiable Skills List

One problem associated with reading instruction in basal readers and in many school reading curriculum guides is the fragmentation of reading into minute skills and subskills. Because teachers and students spend up to 70% of reading instructional time on mastering a series of skills spelled out in district curriculum guides and in basal readers (R. C. Anderson et al., 1985), several researchers have conducted studies to examine the effect of skipping these so-called necessary skills on end-of-year or end-of-book tests. B. M. Taylor, Frye, and Gaetz (1990) found that without instruction and practice in these skills, many students' performance on skill tests remained high, which suggests that many students could be excused from these skill activities in basal programs and attention could be focused on other reading activities. Reutzel and Hollingsworth (1991b) found that students who were taught skills did no better on criterion-referenced skill tests than did students who had spent an equal amount of time reading self-selected trade books. In any case, it appears that teachers can reduce the endless lists of skills they have been made responsible for teaching without serious detriment to students' reading progress or reading test scores.

Studies indicate that many reading skills may be skipped or omitted without significant harm to reading test scores.

Consequently, one important transitional step is to pare down the scope and sequence of skills to a list of a few important, **nonnegotiable skills.** These skills are judged by teachers to be those abilities essential to becoming a skilled reader. Santa (1990) tells of working with teachers in Kallispell, Montana, in an effort that resulted in creating a nonnegotiable list of reading skills teachers felt students needed to be taught in order to become skilled readers. The process for developing a list of nonnegotiable skills began when teachers met to discuss their grade level scope and sequence of skills with the goal of cutting down to the essentials. Of course, such an effort must be supported by the building administrator if it is to be successful. In addition, reading research may be consulted to determine the most important reading skills to retain for instruction. From several literary and statistical analyses of reading comprehension skills, researchers have identified eight important reading comprehension skills (Rosenshine, 1980, p. 541):

*A **nonnegotiable skills list** is a carefully limited list of essential reading skills to be taught in school reading programs.*

1. Recalling word meanings (vocabulary)
2. Drawing inferences about the meaning of a word from context
3. Finding answers to questions answered explicitly or in paraphrase
4. Weaving together ideas in the content
5. Drawing inferences from the content
6. Recognizing a writer's purpose, attitude, tone, and mood
7. Identifying a writer's literary techniques
8. Following a structure of a passage

This list seems to provide a reasonable guide for judging the relative value of reading comprehension skills in basal or district scope and sequence charts. In addition to these skills, the ability to use graphophonic cues along with other language cues should not be overlooked. In chapter 8, we recommend seven phonic generalizations from among hundreds of phonic rules that deserve selective attention. By combining these seven phonic generalizations with the eight reading comprehension and vocabulary skills identified here, teachers can effectively cut skill lists containing hundreds of reading skills down to a list containing a manageable 15.

After grade-level groups meet and cut down to the minimum list of nonnegotiable skills, then the entire school faculty meets to cut down on unnecessary overlap and repetition of skills between grade levels. The final list of reading skills is ratified by a vote of the faculty; faculty ownership of the process of cutting skills creates greater commitment to the end product. By reducing the almost infinite number of reading skills to a manageable few, teachers and students are released from the bondage of needless skill drill and practice. Teachers are freed to engage in activities related to reading real books with their students.

Levels of Integration: Breaking Down Curriculum Barriers

An issue related to skill lists is the continued **fragmentation** of language in reading and writing instruction by isolating and compartmentalizing the reading and language curriculum. Typically, the reading and language instructional curriculum has been divided into four curriculum blocks, periods, or times, such as 60 minutes for reading instruction, 30 minutes for language arts instruction, 20 minutes for spelling instruction, and 15 minutes for handwriting instruction. This practice was begun and maintained with the best of intentions, including to ensure that each of the parts of the language arts received proper attention in the daily school curriculum as well as for ease of planning and managing instruction. Although these may be honorable motives, we have known for some time that the four modes of language (reading, writing, listening, and speaking) are interrelated and even inseparable in nature. D. D. Johnson and Pearson (1975) remind us:

> We know that language systems—the phonology, grammar, and lexicon—are interdependent. In essence, language is indivisible; yet skills management systems would seem to fractionate it and destroy its essential nature. Because of the interdependence of the language systems, there is really no possible sequencing of skills. (p. 758)

Harste, Woodward, and Burke (1984) warn against compartmentalizing the language curriculum when they state, "The reading and writing curriculum should not be isolated from other curriculum areas" (p. 204). To this end, another important aspect of change to be undertaken in transitions is the reintegration of the school curriculum so that the ideal prescribed by Harste et al. can become a reality.

We have found that transitions toward **curricular integration,** or putting the curriculum back together, generally takes place in a three-phase process, as illustrated in Figure 5.2. The process of integration begins, somewhat paradoxically, with reducing fragmentation. By developing a nonnegotiable list of skills, as described earlier, teachers and administrators can discard some of the curricular artifacts that perpetuate fragmentation and compartmentalization.

The next step is to move to break down the curriculum barriers artificially dividing language-related areas: reading, writing, listening, speaking, handwriting, and

Studies of comprehension and vocabulary skills reveal only eight essential, distinct skills. Combined with the seven phonic generalizations, this yields a manageable list of only 15 nonnegotiable skills.

Fragmentation *refers to the curricular practice of listing, teaching, and measuring reading skills in isolation from other language skills.*

Integration *involves putting skills of language and components of the language curriculum back together with the remainder of the school curriculum.*

Some practical applications of this level of language integration are illustrated by the language routine found in chapter 11, the reading and writing workshops in chapter 12, and the literacy units in the following section of this chapter.

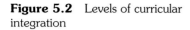

Figure 5.2 Levels of curricular integration

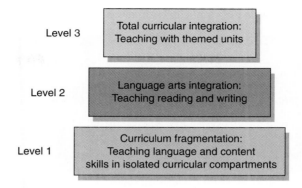

spelling. Rather than scheduling four curriculum blocks for instruction, teachers may begin scheduling a single block of time devoted to *language learning* or *literacy education*. During this single time period, smaller blocks of time can be allocated to shared reading, silent reading, responding to books or stories through writing, discussions, sustained writing, and mini-lessons on reading strategies, writing mechanics, and authoring strategies. Teachers and students can read stories, discuss stories, write responses or summaries of stories, and practice a dramatization. In this way, the language-related curriculum components can become a unified whole again, with subroutines during the period to support each part of language.

The final step is to integrate the language skills with the remaining curriculum areas: math, science, social studies, art, music, physical education, and so on. When language skills are used to learn math concepts, record social studies learning, and document results of science experiments, they become the fundamental tools of learning in the elementary school. This level of curricular integration is very difficult to achieve, and by recent estimates will probably require between 4 and 6 years of concentrated effort (Atwell, 1987; Newman & Church, 1990). Routman (1988) indicated the difficulty of reaching this final level of total curriculum integration when she wrote:

> At this point in time, I am comfortable with integrating the four language modes—listening, speaking, reading, and writing. . . . I am still struggling hard to integrate more areas of the curriculum with the language arts—an ideal that is very difficult to attain. I anticipate that this struggle will go on for years. (p. 26)

When this final level of curricular integration is reached, teachers may wish to teach primarily with thematic units or *inquiry-based instruction* (Short, Harste, & Burke, 1996; see chapter 11). In Figure 5.3, we show some examples of practices that demonstrate varying levels of curricular integration.

Teaching with thematic units is discussed in more detail in chapters 12 and 13.

Language to Literacy Units with Basals and Books

Another program of promise for helping teachers reintegrate the four modes of language into a single unit of instruction is called the **language to literacy** program. Roser, Hoffman, and Farest (1990) describe four basic assumptions associated with this program:

1. Literacy acquisition is a developmental process.
2. Oral language and literacy of printed language interact during development.

Another program of promise for helping teachers reintegrate the four modes of language into a single unit of instruction is called the **language to literacy** *program.*

Figure 5.3 Selected practices reflecting levels of curricular integration

	Reading	Writing
Level 1 Integration Teachers remain mostly (more than 80% of the time) committed to basal programs. They supplement traditional practices with literature strategies and process writing opportunities. Traditional curriculum time blocks for separate reading, language, handwriting, and spelling periods remain intact.	Silent sustained reading (SSR) Open-ended worksheet activities Visiting basal response groups Reconciled reading lesson Direct reading thinking lesson The basal as an anthology Test wiseness units Core books study Directed reading thinking activity (DRTA) ReQuest Language experience approach (LEA) Story mapping	Journal writing Silent spontaneous writing Teacher-directed topic choice Mini lessons on writing skills Sentence-combining practice Word collection spelling lists Handwriting and calligraphy
Level 2 Integration Teachers spend less than 50% of time in basal programs and use literature-based process writing strategies the majority of the time. Curriculum blocks of reading, language arts, handwriting, and spelling have been collapsed into a single period of time.	Supported repeated readings Language to literacy units Author study Language routines: K–1 Reading workshop: 2–8 Sharing literacy Demonstrations and performances Literature response and transmediation Story frames Tradebooks Language experience Portfolio assessment Schema lesson Literature webbing	Writing process Writing workshop Student topic choice Sharing ways to become an author Conferencing and editing Strategic spelling instruction Handwriting models and review Sharing writing Publishing Tips for writing Portfolio assessment
Level 3 Integration Teachers spend less than 10% of their time in basal-oriented programs. They use literature-based reading and process writing curriculum almost exclusively. They have achieved total integration of the language arts and have begun to integrate the language arts with the remainder of the curriculum. Thematic curriculum units are the focus of instruction at this level.	Reading across the curriculum Themed studies Content area reading across the language modes Writing as reading assessment	Writing across the curriculum Logs Reports Projects Reading as writing assessment

3. Literacy is best developed in a positive environment that is opportunity filled, supportive, responsive, purposeful, and highly interactive.
4. Literacy acquisition requires high teacher involvement.

Basic aspects of this program include several components that reflect a trend toward a balanced approach to reading instruction in which literature or basal stories are used as the basis for the program.

- Shared literature
- Writing with literature
- Fluency building
- Personalized reading
- Literature across the curriculum
- Parent as first teacher

Classroom teachers working with university faculty developed several types of language to literacy units (Roser et al., 1990); these included units that focused on authors, topics, literary genre, or themes. An author unit was developed that focused on the books of Eric Carle, *The Grouchy Ladybug, The Very Hungry Caterpillar,* and *The Very Busy Spider.* A topical unit was developed around the subject of dinosaurs. A themed unit was developed around the theme of "Being Different Makes Us Special." A genre unit was developed around the literary genre of biographies. Trade books were located for use in each of these literacy units. We suggest that with minimal effort, basal language to literacy units can be developed using selected stories taken from basal readers similar to those already described. This is particularly true where access to literature is restricted.

For each literacy unit (Roser et al., 1990), teachers read aloud to the children each of the trade books in the language to literacy units. Conversation and response to books were fostered by the use of language charts. An example of a language chart for an author's language to literacy unit dealing with the books authored by Eric Carle is shown in Figure 5.4. In the language to literacy project (Roser et al., 1990), language charts were placed on the walls of the classroom. Children recorded their responses directly onto the language chart. Thus, language charts are a means of encouraging children to write about each of the books they have been reading as well as helping them make the connections between books. Children also recorded interesting vocabulary words onto vocabulary charts displayed on the walls of the classroom. After discussing the books of the language to literacy unit, children practiced reading one book chosen from the unit to an acceptable fluency level, using procedures much like those described in the previous section on the ORL. A tote bag filled with literature was sent home during each 2-week language to literacy unit. This bag was used to invite parents to read a book from the language to literacy unit together with their child. In this way, parents became informed and involved in their children's school reading experiences. Finally, science, drama, social studies, math, and other curriculum areas were planned into the language to literacy units as culminating activities.

A summary of the process of using a language to literacy unit follows:

1. Teacher reads the books aloud to the class from the language to literacy unit.
2. Children discuss with the teacher individual responses to the books using a language chart.

Language charts are used to discuss and record responses to books.

Sending books home involves parents in the school reading program.

Figure 5.4   Example of a language chart for a literacy unit

3. Children record responses about the books on the language chart.
4. Children record selected vocabulary words on vocabulary charts for each book in the unit.
5. Children select a book for personalized reading and fluency building. Children practice the book or a segment of the book until they become expert readers.
6. Children and parents enjoy books read together from the language to literacy unit sent home in literature bags.
7. Culminating activities are planned that integrate the topic, theme, or author study of the language to literacy unit with other curricular areas.

*Basal **language to literacy units** can be developed using basal stories grouped around topics or themes.*

Because basal stories or a limited number of trade books can be used for developing and using language to literacy units, we see this program as one very useful transitional step toward balanced reading and language instruction. Teachers can use their basal stories to develop basal language to literacy units while they acquire an adequate number of trade books to develop language to literacy units. In fact, the development of language to literacy units around selected topics, themes, and author study can directly support the future selection and acquisition of trade books. We can easily envision teachers electing to limit the use of the basal reader to 2 or 3 days per week, and in its place, developing language to literacy units using basal stories or trade books to fill in the gap.

Transitions in Grouping: From Whole-Class (No Grouping) to Flexible Grouping

Many of us recall as children being placed into reading groups with names like "Eagles," "Bluebirds," and "Redbirds" (or maybe even "Buzzards"!). These groups were probably formed on the basis of children's reading ability, hence their name "ability grouping." Ability grouping can be quite convenient for teachers in terms of planning and classroom management. Unfortunately, ability grouping has been found to produce negative emotional, social, and academic outcomes for children. **Flexible grouping** is an effective alternative to ability grouping that has found favor with teachers worldwide. Flexible groups (Reutzel, 1999; Wiggins, 1994) are also a workable alternative to the exclusive use of whole-class instruction, a practice that is overdone in many of our schools (see chapter 9).

Whole-class grouping has become an increasingly popular organizational format in recent years. For one thing, it is an effective means for protecting or "safety-netting" young learners' egos as they try out increasingly sophisticated reading strategies. For instance, children who are practicing their oral reading in a whole-class session are able to read aloud without fear of making a mistake in front of their peers. Whole-class grouping can also reduce some of the negative effects of labeling young learners as "slow," "special needs," or "disabled," as with ability groups. Although whole-class grouping can be used effectively to address the general developmental needs of children in a given classroom, all too often there is no attempt to subdivide the class into smaller, more focused instructional groups to meet individual learning needs.

In flexible grouping, children are placed into *temporary* groups based on their level of independence as learners and their personal interests. Flexible groups are formed and re-formed on the basis of a set of principles like those articulated by Unsworth (1984, p. 300).

During the whole language movement, *many teachers stopped the practice of placing students into sub-groupings within the classroom. This led to the widespread use of whole-class instruction.*

Think about how flexible grouping solves the past problems associated with ability grouping.

Remember, flexible grouping provides for a mix of abilities with a similarity of learning needs.

1. There are no permanent groups.
2. Groups are periodically created, modified, or disbanded, to meet new needs as they arise.
3. At times there is only one group consisting of all pupils.
4. Groups vary in size from 2 or 3 to 9 or 10, depending on the group's purpose.
5. Group membership is not fixed; it varies according to needs and purposes.
6. Student commitment is enhanced when students know how the group's work relates to the overall program or task.
7. Children should be able to evaluate the progress of the group and the teacher's assessment of the group's work.
8. There should be a clear strategy for supervising the group's work.

For flexible grouping to function effectively, the organization, purpose, and tasks must be clearly understood by students. The potential for counterproductive chaos is high in flexible grouping arrangements if the teacher has not carefully prepared the learning tasks and the environment for success. For example, a classroom in which flexible grouping is used to provide for participation in multiple learning centers might operate something like this:

Assume a hypothetical classroom has five literacy-learning centers, established in various locations around the classroom. The first station is an "Alphabet and Word Building Center" where children use magnetic letters and word pattern cards (rimes/word families; see chapter 8) to build words, sort words, and store words in personalized word banks. A second station houses a "Listening Center" where students have multiple copies of a single title to be read with a read-along cassette tape. A third station provides a quiet, comfortable "Library Center" area for reading self-selected books, magazines, comics, and so on. A fourth station is

Writing Workshop Centers provide opportunities for students to conference or edit one another's work as they create student-authored products.

the "Reading Center," which seats small groups of children around a horseshoe- or U-shaped table for guided reading and interactive writing sessions with the teacher. Finally, there is a "Writing Workshop Center" where students can have peer conferences, get and give editing assistance, and prepare student-authored products from greeting cards, recipes, and calendars to newspaper ads, books, and story murals.

Each flexible group can include a mix of reading and writing ability levels, called *heterogeneous grouping,* to avoid the psychological pitfalls associated with ability grouping. These groups can be composed of learners with similar needs, yet with learning materials at varying levels of difficulty and complexity.

Flexible groups often have an elected or appointed group leader to oversee cleanup of centers, operation of necessary equipment, management of supplies, and other tasks. In any case, these groups have assigned tasks to complete in each center. Behavioral and instructional guidelines and goals are clearly established and communicated to each group prior to center time. And, most important, students are helped to know what they may do as follow-up work should they finish before the others. All of this requires careful instructional planning and excellent management skill on the part of the teacher, but the busy and productive activity and learning that come from the flexible grouping strategy makes it well worth the effort!

Another example of flexible grouping is found in the work of Fountas and Pinnell (1996). They describe "dynamic grouping" as a process used to construct **homogeneous guided reading groups.** Unlike the ability grouping practices of the past, guided reading groups are expected to change on a regular basis—at least monthly. Leveled books are chosen for each group from a variety of titles on an appropriate level of challenge (see chapter 11). Skills are taught from the text of the leveled books and not as isolated lessons from a list of skills practiced on workbook pages or duplicated sheets. Reading skills are taught and practiced as a part of reading rather than as a follow-up to reading. Guided reading groups involve all children reading the whole text to themselves, rather than some children listening while others read in a "round robin" or "barbershop" style. Evaluation of student progress is assessed by taking "running records" as students read aloud quietly and the teacher listens (see chapter 10).

TRANSITIONS IN COMMUNITY INVOLVEMENT: SEEKING SUPPORT FOR CHANGE

Making transitions is risky business. On one occasion, Jerry Harste (quoted in Newman, 1985b) warned that trying nontraditional reading and language instruction meant "getting into trouble" with teachers, principals, parents, and even children. Although this may be true, it certainly does not have to be the case. One way to prevent much of the trouble Harste foreshadows is to inform and involve parents, principals, and colleagues in efforts to change the school reading and language curriculum.

Think of a time when you "got into trouble" for failing to seek support from others. What were you thinking of at that time?

Parent Involvement: Information and Volunteerism

Rasinski and Fredericks (1989) asked parents in a survey what they thought of reading instruction in the schools. About 51% of parents surveyed thought that schools were teaching reading adequately; another 36% responded the schools were doing a poor job of teaching reading. The parents who felt schools were doing a poor job of teaching reading were concerned about teaching the basics, especially the need to teach more phonics. A smaller percentage of parents (13%) expressed that the schools were doing a so-so job of teaching reading. Some comments from parents who were surveyed included, "Teachers should read to the class more; and children should get to read what they're interested in." Several parents mentioned that their children characterized reading as "boring." From these responses, one thing is clear: Parents are aware of and concerned about the reading instruction their children receive. Hence, making dramatic changes in reading beliefs and instruction *without* informing and involving parents would most likely mean "getting into trouble."

Making transitions toward balanced reading instruction should include a strong commitment to parent involvement as one dimension of change.

Making transitions toward balanced reading instruction should include a strong commitment to parent involvement as one dimension of change. How can this be accomplished effectively? In an article entitled "Involving the Uninvolved: How To," Fredericks and Rasinski (1990) list 14 ways to involve parents and the community in reading curriculum changes. We have summarized, modified, and added to these suggestions as follows:

1. Provide parents with lots of written and visual informational materials regarding your intended changes over an extended period of time. One-shot information will not suffice.
2. Make parent involvement a schoolwide concern. Individual teachers cannot successfully implement and sustain a parent-involvement program.
3. Provide a good deal of recognition for parents and students who become involved with the school and with school reading instructional changes.
4. Involve students wholeheartedly in recruiting parents to become involved through writing invitations, designing awards, and so on.

5. Encourage participatory projects that involve the entire family. Make reading a family concern. Suggest ways reading can be fostered in and by the entire family.
6. Don't focus school involvement programs on parents alone. Seek to involve other segments of the community, such as the elderly, business, and government.
7. Make the school a comfortable place. Encourage an open-door policy with a liberal and comfortable visitation and volunteerism plan. Let parents see and participate in school reading instructional changes, which will eliminate many fears, doubts, and suspicions.
8. Use the telephone as a means of communicating good news rather than bad news.
9. Find out why some parents distance themselves from involvement with the school and school reading changes. This will take time but can pay sizable dividends in the final analysis.
10. In scheduling involvement activities, provide for flexibility through various options and plans to accommodate those who are willing to participate.
11. Consider offering a "Parent Hot Line" through the PTA or PTO organizations to discuss concerns or provide needed information.
12. Solicit endorsements and advertisements of your school reading program from community business and government leaders, sports figures, and the like.
13. Document the special features of your school reading program through videotaping, photographs, and articles. Make these available to parents.
14. When special events are held that require parent involvement, provide special services such as baby-sitting or escort service. Let parents know that you genuinely care about their attendance and involvement.
15. Survey parents periodically to gather their input. This practice helps parents feel ownership in the school reading program.
16. Hold periodic information or parent education seminars to help parents understand the desired changes in reading instruction.

See chapter 9 for more information on volunteers as an instructional resource.

In chapter 9, we outline resources and provide a recruitment form for starting a school volunteer program.

Small tokens, such as certificates of appreciation or phone calls, have been used to foster a successful volunteer program.

Fredericks and Rasinski (1990) recommended five steps for establishing a quality volunteer program: (a) recruitment, (b) training, (c) variety, (d) recognition, and (e) evaluation. Wasik (1998) recommends eight guidelines for successful volunteer tutoring programs in schools:

1. A certified reading specialist needs to supervise tutors.
2. Tutors need ongoing training and feedback.
3. Tutoring sessions need to be structured and contain specified basic elements (rereading a familiar story or text, word analysis, writing, and a new story introduction and reading).
4. Tutoring needs to be intensive and consistent.
5. Quality materials are needed to facilitate the tutoring model.
6. Assessment of students needs to be ongoing.
7. Schools need to find ways to ensure that tutors will attend regularly.
8. Tutoring needs to be coordinated with classroom instruction.

Because of the diversity associated with transitions, teachers will need to develop and implement their own volunteer training programs; we simply cannot anticipate the variety of training needs for every locale within the scope of this book. It is important to note, however, that recognition of volunteers is critical to the success of any such effort. All of us, parents and students, like to be recognized for our efforts. Although we would like to believe that all people willingly serve others without recognition, this is often not the case. Small tokens of appreciation can go a long way toward sustaining a successful volunteer program. For example, in the school where one of the authors taught, the principal paid for volunteers to enjoy a free school lunch each day they volunteered.

Finally, an annual assessment of the effectiveness of the school involvement program should be conducted. This effort may suggest options to be more effective or possibilities to sustain an already successful program.

Parent education is an almost surefire means for avoiding unnecessary trouble when making transitions in reading instruction (Morrow, 1995; Rasinski, 1995; Shockley, Michalove, & Allen, 1995). Evening sessions, open houses, or seminars can be held to inform parents about how their children learned to speak and listen to language and about how these processes are similar to those the school reading program will be using to help them learn to read and write language. Another session can focus on tips for parents to use while reading aloud to their children. Still another session can focus on ideas that may be used at home to support transitions toward a balanced reading program. Fredericks and Rasinski (1990) suggested several ideas for supporting school reading programs at home. We have selected a few for the following list:

Notice what can be done to better inform parents.

- Encourage parents to work with their children in keeping a family journal. Each member of the family would be expected to make a weekly contribution.
- Encourage parents to make audio- or videotapes of their children's reading. These can be reviewed later and stored as family treasures.
- Encourage parents with young children to obtain wordless picture books. Children can write or dictate original stories to accompany the pictures in the books.
- Send home activities for parents and children to complete with certain books they may be reading at home.
- Send home holiday reading and writing packets to sustain the reading program through holiday vacations.
- Invite parents to share book talks with your class. These may be talks about books they have been reading with their youngsters at home.

To maximize the success of transitions, we need to elevate the sense of responsibility for reading and writing improvement to the level of community concern—it is not the sole responsibility of the schools and teachers (Asheim, Baker, & Mathews, 1983). When we accomplish this goal, our schools will truly become communities of readers and writers.

The sense of responsibility for reading and writing improvement needs to be elevated to the level of community concern—not the sole responsibility of the schools and teachers.

Seeking Administrative Support

The principal plays a critical role in ensuring the success of any curriculum innovations, especially in implementing balanced reading and language approaches (Heald-Taylor, 1989; Wepner, Feeley, & Strickland, 1995). Consequently, teachers in transition need to learn the art of carefully soliciting support and direction from their principals. Teachers can begin this process by simply mentioning an interest in improving classroom reading and language instruction to the principal. They may wish to hint at a particular interest in developing the ability to use the basal reader more

Teachers in transition need to learn the art of carefully soliciting support and direction from their principals.

effectively while incorporating more opportunities for students to read real literature books and to write for their own reasons. At the outset, we want to caution teachers against the use of labels such as *whole language* with administrators. It has been our experience that these labels often become fads or buzz words and tend to lead to greater misunderstanding or resistance by administrators than simply describing the desired instructional changes and reasons.

Nonchalantly sharing books and articles with principals helps them develop a desire to understand current changes in reading research and practice. Teachers should also be patient with their administrators; principals will need time to make transitions just as teachers do. They learn to take risks, seek collegial support, and build a school consensus for change a little at a time, passing through similar transitional stages as teachers.

Once principals become interested in balanced reading instruction, encourage them to avoid mandating curriculum changes in reading instruction. They should seek to work with those teachers who are interested in change until other teachers decide to join in (Tovey & Kerber, 1986). As school administrators begin to ask questions and express interest in reading instructional change, teachers can suggest the need for outside consultant resources to support planning, implementation, and evaluation of potential curriculum innovations. At this point, it is appropriate to invite school administrators to attend conferences, workshops, professional meetings, and support groups to learn more about making transitions and about balanced reading instruction.

Teachers should be sensitive to the financial constraints placed on administrators. However, as teachers purchase fewer worksheets and workbooks and depend less and less on basal readers, funds previously allocated for procuring these instructional materials can be redirected toward the acquisition of real literature books for classroom and school libraries.

Faculty meetings can become a setting for reading and discussing books and articles on balanced reading instruction. Teachers can also investigate the difference in cost between implementing a locally designed literature-based reading approach and adopting a commercially published basal reader program. When teachers help their administrators, they become friends, not foes, of reading curriculum change. And when teachers have the support of their administrators, they can move forward in making transitions with confidence. By listening, providing resources, sharing ideas, encouraging open discussions, and working together, teachers and administrators can form a meaningful network of support for each other as they make transitions toward balanced reading instruction.

Colleague Collaboration: Establishing Support Groups

Because making transitions tends to be a grassroots movement, some teachers feel alone or isolated even in their own schools. To sustain the energy necessary to continue transitions, some teachers have begun to form small, informal study or support groups. They meet to discuss challenges, problems, and potential solutions. They share success stories with each other and help each other work through problems. Sometimes they just encourage each other to stick with it or hang in there in the face of threatening and skeptical colleagues and administrators. We suggest that teachers affiliate with local professional groups such as the International Reading Association or the National Council of Teachers of English. Loose-knit study groups for sustaining transitions toward balanced teaching of reading can be informally constituted at the school or district level. Once administrative support is secured, faculty meetings can begin to take on the characteristics of these support groups, as whole faculties work together through the difficulties of making transitions.

Teachers should be patient with their administrators as they learn to take risks, seek collegial support, and build a school consensus for change.

For example, one elementary school faculty reviews current literature on reading instruction for a few minutes in each faculty meeting.

Some teachers in transition have begun to form small, informal study or support groups to discuss challenges, problems, and potential solutions.

TRANSITIONS IN THE CLASSROOM ENVIRONMENT

In a quiet corner of one home, a mother sits at a desk carefully reconciling the family checkbook register with the most recent bank statement. Two children are in the kitchen, setting the dinner table. Father is sitting in a large overstuffed chair, reading to the youngest child in the family. Each nook and room in this home has its own atmosphere, climate, and function.

Every building, be it a church, court, hospital, or bar, has its own atmosphere. Much like a home, a classroom that nurtures children in a literate environment provides a place that has its own atmosphere, climate, and function. Part of making the transition toward balanced reading instruction involves an increased understanding of the role that classroom environments play in setting the stage for pleasurable reading, writing, and learning experiences (Loughlin & Martin, 1987; Reutzel & Wolfersberger, 1996).

Transitions toward balanced reading instruction involve an increased understanding of the role that classroom environments play in setting the stage for pleasurable reading, writing, and learning experiences.

Institutional Versus Homelike Classroom Environments

Teachers know that classrooms are special places for children and learning; this is evident in the way they adorn the walls, bulletin boards, and windows in their classrooms. But perhaps, the ornaments displayed in classrooms may "only create an atmosphere of inauthenticity, of mere busyness or shallow commitment" (Van Manen, 1986, p. 33). Some classrooms present an image and atmosphere of a department store display window. It is as if the classroom is on display to impress colleagues, administrators, and parents. Colorful but commercially produced bulletin boards seem to say, "This classroom is my classroom, not yours!" to children who enter. In some cases, classrooms mirror the **institutional environments** of our society such as prisons, warehouses, and factories rather than homes (Pino, 1978). Teachers in transition typically initiate changes in the classroom environment that invite children to learn and experience life. Consequently, planning and creating classroom environments to support and nurture children in becoming readers become an integral part of making transitions.

Institutional environments reflect the uniformity and warmth of such societal institutions as prisons, hospitals, and factories.

Classroom environments can nurture and support the development of literacy.

Classroom Design Considerations

When children enter classrooms they can feel the atmosphere—whether it invites and supports or threatens and controls.

> The lived in space of the classroom, its textural and spiritual qualities, first should remind us of what schools are for. School is a place where children explore aspects of the human world. (Van Manen, 1986, p. 34)

In our homes, we carefully create an atmosphere: We consider colors on the walls and in the carpets; we concern ourselves with window coverings and lighting; we experiment with arranging the furnishings to create a sense of invitation and togetherness. Our homes are subdivided into work areas, recreation areas, messy areas, and quiet areas, which in themselves reflect different atmospheres. The same is true in the classroom: Beyond the walls and bulletin board arrangements, the physical arrangement of furniture and other objects bespeaks a certain atmosphere. A transitional approach to balanced reading instruction emphasizes the need to make gradual changes in classroom environments that nurture and support children as they learn to read. For this reason, classrooms need to emulate **homelike environments** rather than institutional environments.

Quality homelike environments are responsive to children's needs for security, support, and collaboration.

When entering balanced reading classrooms, one should immediately sense a climate that is responsive to children's needs for security, support, and collaboration (Reutzel & Wolfersberger, 1996). Display areas in the classroom should act as verification of the *known* and as an introduction to the *new* for learners. Morrow (1993) speaks of preparing print-rich environments for children to learn about how print works. Thus, display areas might provide commonly used words for concepts such as colors, numbers, directions, and labeled objects as well as information about schedules, procedures, and expectations in the classroom. Display areas could also provide opportunities for children to communicate with the teacher, with each other, and with parents. Sign-up boards, message boards, post offices, and the like recognize the need for using written communication in the classroom. Display areas ought to provide models or prototypes of acceptable written language use. Published compositions written by teachers and children, models of how to write personal letters, and models of standard handwriting help children understand the accepted standards of written language in the classroom. Finally, display areas should expand children's access to information beyond that of the home and neighborhood. Pictures of historical figures, time lines, current events, maps, forests, glaciers, and so on remind children of the larger world community to be experienced and enjoyed.

Think of a classroom you have been in that evidenced a homelike environment. What are the qualities you remember?

Many ideas for subdividing the space in classroom environments are discussed in chapter 9.

Classrooms should be arranged and adorned with literacy objects and tools that meet the needs of students as well as the preferences of teachers. For some teachers, classrooms will start out looking rather traditional, with the teacher's desk at the front of the room and rows of desks. Traditional classroom arrangements typically have few, if any, special-purpose areas in the classroom. A transitions approach recognizes the need to subdivide spaces in the classroom for whole-class instruction, small-group interaction, or conferences with individual students, which may mean moving desks out of traditional rows into pods or clusters of desks. It may also mean removing desks from the classroom altogether and replacing them with tables. Decorating the classroom with plants, aquariums, soft pillows, rocking chairs, plush carpet, musical instruments, and bean bag chairs is just one of the possible transitions in classroom arrangements. Like homes, transitions classrooms should gradually be changed to serve the various functions of learning to read and communicate using written language. Play areas such as post offices and kitchens, provided with literacy objects and tools, have a significant impact on the literacy learning of young children (Neuman & Roskos, 1992). (In the final section of this chapter, we illustrate three transitional classroom floor plans to describe how these changes may occur.) The important part of transitions in classroom learning environments is to remember that the classroom atmosphere is, as Van Manen (1986) puts it, a way of knowing and coming to know. Most important, the classroom environment and atmosphere determine for many of us the way we experience and remember schooling and learning to read.

TRANSITIONS IN ASSESSMENT

Changing assessment is perhaps the single most difficult transition to make in reading instruction. Tests are often misunderstood and misused by parents, administrators, and even lawmakers to make inferences about the teaching of reading and reading teachers' performance. Because of the political realities of testing, students and teachers are often obliged to allow their performance to be judged by using traditional and severely limited measures (Cambourne & Turbill, 1990; Clay, 1990). Moving away from traditional forms of assessment is a very scary proposition for teachers. Although an integral part of making transitions means living with the political realities of current testing practices, this does not preclude augmenting traditional testing practices with more balanced and naturalistic documentation of reading growth and progress. Valencia and Pearson (1987) assert:

> What we need are not just new and better tests. We need a new framework for thinking about assessment, one in which educators begin by considering types of decisions needed and the level of impact of those decisions. (p. 729)

Although this is the ideal, teachers in transition will of necessity continue to submit to traditional testing; but they will also recognize the purposes as well as the shortcomings of these obligatory practices. In addition, they will begin to design, create, and use classroom-based and more informal measures of reading progress to inform their teaching and to document student growth and progress in the context of authentic reading activities.

Freedom from the Bondage of Teaching to Tests

Research discussed earlier in this chapter has demonstrated that children's standardized and criterion-referenced tests scores do not suffer appreciably when teachers skip skill lessons or devote increased time to authentic reading tasks. Although one may appreciate these facts at a cognitive level, they may not be fully accepted at a practical or political level. Some teachers say, "If I don't teach all of these skills, my students may not pass the tests." Fear, coupled with a shortage of jobs and the desire to help, not hurt, children, has forced many teachers to reduce the teaching of reading to an exercise in passing prescribed tests. As a consequence of this reality, students and teachers lose the joy of reading and responding to books.

Many individuals take practice tests and pay large fees to attend minicourses to prepare them to take the SAT, ACT, MCAT, LSAT, GMAT, or GRE examinations. One worthwhile suggestion for teachers who are reluctant to withdraw completely from teaching reading skills to pass the tests is to offer an annual minicourse in test-wiseness for their students before administering these tests.

We suggest that teachers obtain alternate forms of tests for practice or produce practice tests that cover the same objectives and concepts in a similar format to

Changing assessment is perhaps the single most difficult transition to make in reading instruction.

Transitions means living with the political realities of current testing practices while augmenting traditional testing practices with more balanced and naturalistic documentation of reading growth and progress.

Offer an annual minicourse in test-wiseness for students before administering standardized and criterion-referenced tests.

acquaint children with the content, format, and language used in these types of tests. We also wish to sound a note of caution: It is considered unethical (and sometimes illegal) to obtain the actual tests to be administered and to practice taking them.

Teachers who have used an annual test-wiseness minicourse have found good success, have been able to help their students prepare and succeed on mandated tests, and have reduced test-related anxiety levels. Thus, offering minicourses in test-wiseness acted as a safety net for teachers as they made transitions in assessment practices.

Portfolios: Movies, Not Snapshots

Portfolio assessment is a collection of evidence that demonstrates students' strengths.

Imagine for a moment your ugliest photograph. Maybe you had braces at the time. Maybe you had just returned from a 3-day camping trip: Your hair was a mess, you hadn't bathed or changed clothes for several days, and to make matters worse, you hadn't slept very well. Now imagine that this photograph would be placed into an album that would be used by a principal to draw inferences about your appearance, personality, mental abilities, and future potential as a teacher. How well do you think such an album would represent you?

Clearly, no one can honestly believe that one or even several standardized or criterion-referenced test scores—like single photos—can capture the sum total of one's life and learning. And yet, schools and governmental agencies insist on relying on one or two test scores per year to represent the totality of a child's progress and growth in reading during a year of school. If this is an insufficient means of documenting reading progress and achievement—and it is—then what is the alternative? We, along with others, suggest **portfolio assessment** (Jongsma, 1989; Valencia, 1998; Valencia & Pearson, 1987).

In chapter 10, we describe in greater detail the reasons for portfolio assessment and how portfolios can be developed.

Rather than relying solely on the snapshot variety of assessment associated with standardized and criterion-referenced tests, teachers ought to gather documentation of students' reading progress similar to a moving picture. This motion picturelike assessment of developing readers' abilities captures their ability to successfully complete a variety of reading tasks, to read and enjoy a wide assortment of texts, and to achieve in a broad array of situational contexts. When teachers build a portfolio, or collection of evidence, they demonstrate their students' strengths and best efforts rather than constructing files documenting students' weaknesses and failed efforts. For these reasons, portfolio assessment has great intuitive appeal.

However, perhaps the greatest appeal for portfolio assessment relates to the balance between instruction, practice, and assessment. Only a fixed amount of time is available for instruction, practice, and assessment of reading progress. Traditional programs of assessment have generally placed a greater emphasis on assessment, which meant detracting from time available for reading instruction and practice. Because portfolio assessment evidence for reading development is taken from authentic reading tasks, texts, and contexts, it does not detract from the time available for engaging in authentic reading activities. Alternatives in assessment are mentioned at this point because a major aspect of making transitions involves teachers in learning to cope with the continued political demands for traditional assessment while simultaneously developing the understanding and skill to document children's progress in reading through the use of balanced literacy assessment tools and portfolios. (See chapter 10 for more detailed descriptions of Portfolio Assessment.)

TRANSITIONS IN DIVERSITY: MONOCULTURE TO MULTICULTURE

One increasingly obvious fact is that the racial, cultural, and linguistic homogeneity of yesterday's classrooms is disappearing. By the year 2000, a near majority of the school-aged population will include people of color, diverse cultural traditions, and a mixture of languages. Gone are the days of the American melting pot; welcome in the days of the "tossed salad," when each part of the culture makes a unique contribution to the American experience (Ramirez & Ramirez, 1994). Because of changing demographics in this nation, teachers who have experienced a monocultural background are recognizing a need to understand and honor the contribution of other cultures to the history, literature, and art of the United States (Taxel, 1993).

There is one danger in recommending that teachers adopt a multicultural view: They may assume that making the transition from monocultural experiences to an understanding of multiculturalism is incumbent only on those people who belong to the cultural, linguistic, and racial majority. This is not true. Because most individuals come from monocultural backgrounds, multiculturalism argues for all peoples to move outside their own cultures to experience, understand, and appreciate the traditions, perspectives, and contributions of others.

Minimizing differences between home cultures and the school culture is a major step in helping children succeed in school. Maxim (1989) suggests that one way to enhance children's self-esteem is to respect their culture. It is suggested that one way in which teachers and children can open the world of multiculture is to read multicultural children's literature (Rasinski & Padak, 1990). From these experiences, monocultural teachers come to better understand children, their cultures, and communities, as well as broaden their view of the world. Harris asserts,

> children of color—African, Asian, Hispanic, and Native American—need multicultural literature. The inclusion of multicultural literature in schooling can affirm and empower these children and their culture. . . . Children can derive pleasure and pride from hearing and reading . . . and seeing illustrations of characters who look as if they stepped out of their homes and communities. (quoted in Martinez & Nash, 1990, p. 599)

We list here several ideas that may be helpful to classroom teachers as they learn about and use multicultural children's literature to make the transition from mono- to multicultural classrooms.

- Encourage children to respond to a story or illustration by sharing connections they make to their own cultures, languages, and traditions.
- Note and list the motifs that appear in different cultural tales.
- Discuss how the literature refers to other cultural groups' contributions to history, art, music, science, and so on.
- Discuss the social traditions of various cultures.
- Produce story-related cultural artifacts.
- Engage in culturally relevant games, traditions, and events through simulations.
- Invite parents of children from various cultures to share cultural traditions, including art, music, and dance.
- Purchase multicultural literature for the classroom library.
- Post lists of available multicultural books in the school or community library.

By the year 2000, a near majority of the school-aged population will include people of color, diverse cultural traditions, and a mixture of languages.

Minimizing differences between home cultures and the school culture is a major step in helping children succeed in school.

Describe five criteria for selecting multicultural literature for transitional classrooms.

Figure 5.5 Multicultural literature by theme

Artistic Contributions
Rising Voices (Hirschfelder/Singer; poetry and essays of young Native Americans)
Neighborhood Odes (Soto; Hispanic urban poems)
A Coconut Kind of Day (Joseph; poetry reflecting celebration of tribal and family traditions)
Alvin Ailey Dancers (Pinkney; history of the famous modern dance company)
The Piñata Maker (Ancona; the life of a Mexican village piñata maker told in Spanish and English)
The Real McCoy (Towle; story of African-American inventor of the automatic oil cup for trains)

Civil Rights Movement
Road to Memphis (Taylor; family saga of racial discrimination in the 1940s)
Plutie and Little John (Edwards; inequality and discrimination in the lives of two young men from different racial backgrounds)
Year of Impossible Goodbyes (Choi; a family's ordeal during the Japanese occupation of Korea)
Devil's Arithmetic (Yolen; family chronicle of the Holocaust)

History and Life-styles
Abenaki to Zuni (Wolfson; illustrated guide to 28 tribes, their customs, habitats, and other useful information)
A to Zen (Wells; alphabet picture book of Japanese events and ideas)
A Migrant Family (Brimner; a photographic essay on the lives of migrant workers)
Mennorahs, Mezuzahs, and Other Jewish Symbols (Chaikin; symbols, ideas, and traditions of Judaism)

Contemporary Children's Stories
Love, David (Case; challenges of mixed-race girl growing up in South Africa)
Hello, Amigos (Brown; photographic essay of Hispanic family life)
Pueblo Boy: Growing Up in Two Worlds (Keegan; adapting to tribal tradition and current American life)
Day of Ahmed's Secret (Heide/Gilliland; young boy in contemporary Cairo finds success in a hard life)

Self-Esteem
Amazing Grace (Hoffman; a young girl finds self-confidence and grows with courage)
312 Valentines (Cohen; gifted and talented black student seeks his own identity)
Year of the Boar and Jackie Robinson (Bao Lord; girl emigrating from China learns to love American life)
Local News (Soto; short stories about Hispanic life in an urban neighborhood)

Folktales, Fairytales, and Legends
Raven (McDermott; Pacific Northwest tale of how Raven found the sun)
The Rainbow People (Yep; Chinese folktales that sustained immigrant laborers)
Lon Po Po (Young; Chinese Little Red Riding Hood)
The Singing Snake (Czernecki/Rhodes; Australian folktale about the invention of the didgeridoo)
The Uninvited Guest and Other Jewish Holiday Tales (Jaffe; a collection of stories providing insight into Jewish life and culture)

Compiled by Livingston and Birrell (1994).

- Note behaviors and beliefs that are universals among all people as well as those that are specific to a cultural, racial, or linguistic group.
- List ways in which certain cultures are stereotyped, and discuss how these stereotypic labels are inappropriate.

As teachers, we must take a proactive role in understanding and effectively dealing with the increasing diversity in classrooms. One way to accomplish this is to apprise ourselves of the available literature and share these books with each other and with children. A short list of multicultural literature for teachers has been compiled by Livingston and Birrell (1994) and is shown in Figure 5.5.

FROM CATERPILLAR TO BUTTERFLY: THE METAMORPHOSIS OF THREE TRANSITIONAL READING TEACHERS

To help in-service and preservice teachers understand different ways teachers make transitions, we present three vignettes of reading teachers and reading classrooms at various stages in transition. The first vignette describes a novice second-grade teacher, Ms. Scott, who begins with a traditional classroom design, whole-group skill lessons, basal reader instruction, and ability grouping. In this *early transitions* classroom, we describe how Ms. Scott has begun to integrate practices and beliefs into her classroom, which are moving her cautiously but surely along the **reading instructional continuum** (shown in chapter 2) toward more balanced reading instruction. In a second vignette, we describe a fifth-grade teacher, Mr. Helms, who has been making transitions for several years and who has been able to successfully integrate some balanced literacy practices and beliefs into his classroom while preserving his basal reader program safety net. We call this developmental stage *intermediate transitions*. In the final vignette, we describe a first-grade teacher, Ms. Valdez, who has been successful in approximating practices and beliefs most closely aligned with balanced literacy instruction, or what we call *advanced transitions*. But as Regie Routman wrote in her book *Transitions,* (1988)

> [This teacher doesn't] always use thematic units, [this teacher] occasionally [teaches] from part to whole; [this teacher is] still struggling hard to integrate more areas of the curriculum with the language arts—an ideal that is very difficult to attain. [This teacher anticipates] that this struggle will go on for years. (p. 26)

EARLY TRANSITIONS: MS. SCOTT, SECOND GRADE

Ms. Scott had just graduated from college with her endorsement in elementary education. She interviewed with several school districts before deciding to accept the offer of Riverside School District to teach second grade. She walked to her empty classroom to look it over for size, furniture, arrangement, and instructional resources. Before arriving in her classroom, she stopped to talk with two teacher colleagues in second grade. They told her that they used a basal reader in the school and that she would be expected to use the basal also. They implied that the principal insisted on following the basal scope and sequence carefully so as to teach children the necessary skills associated with skilled reading. Ms. Scott's colleagues informed her that they used ability grouping by classroom to meet the needs of the children and that she would have the opportunity to work with the poor readers this year. This would allow her to use her recent training in reading.

After her brief visit with her new colleagues and to her new classroom, Ms. Scott began to think about how she could satisfy the expectations her school colleagues held for her professional behavior, classroom, and instruction, and still use what she had learned in her college training about a balanced approach to reading instruction. In fact, she was a bit perplexed by the conflict between her college-based beliefs and the school-based practices she was expected to use. But determined to be successful, Ms. Scott began planning her classroom to conform to the espoused expectations of her school, principal, parents, and colleagues while simultaneously planning a gradual introduction of the balanced literacy practices in which she had come to believe.

First, Ms. Scott sat down and designed how she would arrange her classroom. She realized that she would be teaching an entire class of low readers. Because of this assignment, she thought she might be able to support these children through selected whole-group reading activities. Thus, she designed a large area of the classroom with desks for whole-group instruction. She also knew that not all low readers have the same instructional needs or interests, so she planned a small-group instructional area for guided or targeted reading lessons with children of differing needs and abilities within her low-ability classroom. She also felt children should have a time and place to choose their own books to read silently or with a partner, so she set up a reading nook in her classroom. The result of her thinking and planning is seen in her arrangement of the classroom (Figure 5.6).

Next, Ms. Scott began creating her daily routine for reading instruction. In Figure 5.7, Ms. Scott portrays her daily routine within the framework of a weekly reading plan. Whereas Ms. Scott's beliefs were aimed toward balanced reading instruction, her classroom and lesson plans reflected a more traditional approach. She began her reading instructional time with 20 minutes of sustained silent reading (SSR). She chose this activity because she believed children need to have time to read books of their own choosing. During SSR time, she also read a book—knowing that children learn to read from example. Next, Ms. Scott taught a 20-minute whole-group skill lesson as outlined in her basal teacher's manual. Although Ms. Scott did not quite know whether she believed skill instruction was necessary, her district and colleagues expected documentation for having taught these skills. Because Ms. Scott was unsure of the curriculum and the reading process as a novice teacher, she chose to remain on the safe side of the issue, at least for a while. On Monday, she taught a decoding lesson on several consonant blends. On Tuesday, she had children practice these skills on the assigned workbook pages. On Wednesday, she taught a skill lesson on using the glossary; on Thursday, children participated in a skill lesson on sequencing; and on Friday, children practiced these skills by completing assigned worksheets.

Following the daily skill lesson or practice, Ms. Scott worked directly with her whole class for 20 minutes on a basal reading story. The whole class read the same basal story together because Ms. Scott believed whole-class work supported struggling and shy students. She conducted whole-class discussions and background-building experiences with the group on Monday in preparation for reading as well as preteaching the vocabulary words listed

Figure 5.6 Early transitions, second-grade classroom arrangement

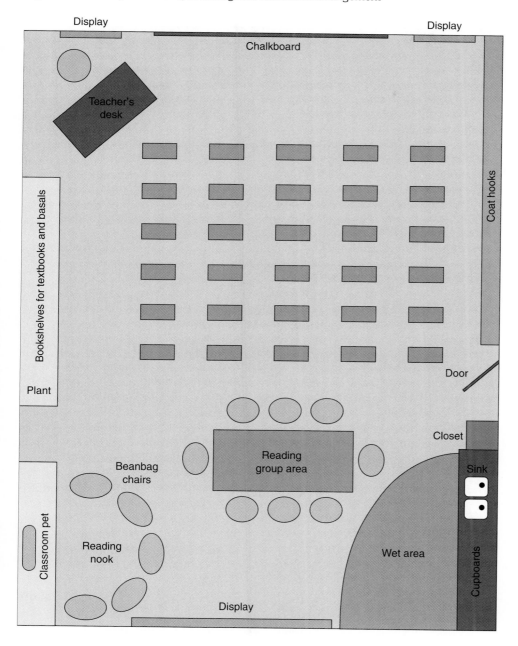

in the teacher's manual. During subsequent days, Ms. Scott provided various repeated and supported reading activities for the whole group or with small groups pertaining to the story The Ugly Duckling, which they had read on Monday. She also taught a skills lesson on Thursday in relation to some of the words found in The Ugly Duckling story. On Friday, she extended the story through drama, music, art, and other language arts activities.

On a daily basis from 9:40 to 10:00 A.M., Ms. Scott read aloud to children, had them share books they could read, sang songs with words

Figure 5.7   Early transitions, second-grade weekly reading plan.

	M	T	W	Th	F
8:40 A.M.	Silent sustained reading →				
9:00 A.M.	Reading skill lesson sn, sm, sc, consonant blends	Practice reading skill lesson Workbook pp. 3–7	Practice reading skill lesson Looking up glossary words	Reading skill lesson Getting the sequence	Practice reading skill lesson Workbook pp. 8–9
9:20 A.M.	Basal Story Introduction: *Ugly Duckling*	Read-aloud together	Read again together in pairs	Skill instruction with story / Word recognition	Extensions into other curriculum areas: Play
9:40 A.M.	Daily language sharing time: LOGOS	Poem: *How Not to Have to Dry Dishes*	Song: *I've Been Working on the Railroad*	Book: *Jumanji*	Sniglets and pundles
10:00 A.M.	Language arts skill lesson: Using commas in a series →	Skill practice: identifying nouns in sentences	Creative writing: Story starter: *Mouse on the Mayflower*	Free writing: Personal topic choice	Creative writing
10:30 A.M.	Handwriting practice →				
10:40 A.M.	Spelling pretest: Unit 6	Spelling practice: Writing list words in sentences	Spelling practice: 6-step spelling strategy with partner	Spelling practice: Spelling bee	Spelling post-test:
10:50 A.M.	Daily journal writing →				

projected on the overhead screen, and played word and language games. She did these activities to help children enjoy the playful nature of language and to broaden their literary horizons.

For 30 minutes, during the language arts instructional block, Ms. Scott followed her teacher's manual carefully. However, 1 day a week, on Thursday, she allowed children a topic choice in writing, remembering this as important from her college training. Daily handwriting and spelling practice were also a regular part of Ms. Scott's day. As a final daily activity, Ms. Scott encouraged her students to make an entry in their personal journals. She encouraged children to share what they had written in their journals with her and the class if they so chose.

Ms. Scott provides an excellent example of a teacher's practices temporarily lagging well behind her belief system until time and conditions change to allow further transitions. As Ms. Scott becomes more sure of herself, her students, the curriculum, and the reading process, she will begin to make additional transitions toward the next stage of instructional implementation, intermediate transitions. In summary, Ms. Scott has carefully and selectively initiated changes in her classroom as well as her lesson plans to arouse little attention from others at the present, which allows her the opportunity to make changes without undue resistance or pressure. This attitude is typical of those in the early stages of transitions.

INTERMEDIATE TRANSITIONS: MR. HELMS, FIFTH GRADE

Mr. Helms has been teaching fifth grade for 3 years at Brookville Elementary school. During his 1st year of teaching, Mr. Helms attended a state reading conference, where he first learned about balanced reading instruction. During the next year, Mr. Helms read about balanced reading instruction and learned late in the year about a group of teachers meeting in a support group to discuss balanced reading instruction. During his 3rd year of teaching, Mr. Helms began attending support group meetings regularly and felt that he was making substantial changes in his reading beliefs and as a consequence his classroom practices. Also during Mr. Helms's 3rd year of teaching, the school district adopted a new basal reading series. He noted that the new basal series contained much better literature than previous editions and that the reading skill lessons were more often related to the stories. Although Mr. Helms had been exploring, implementing, and changing over the 3 years, he still felt that the basal was a necessary part of his classroom reading program. In fact, he recognized that the basal provided a structure and a safety net for his teaching that he still needed. It was also clear that the district supported the use of the new basal and expected teachers to use it. Although Mr. Helms needed and felt somewhat obligated to make use of the basal in his classroom, his attendance at the local balanced reading study group was helping him realize he could teach reading without a total reliance on the basal. As he began planning his 4th year of teaching, he decided to move ahead with further changes.

First, Mr. Helms decided to implement a writing process approach during the language arts instructional block. This meant that he needed to provide time, demonstrations, and locations in the classroom for activities such as drafting, brainstorming, peer conferencing, editing, and publishing. Consequently, he placed peer conference and individual reading conference sign-up boards around the room. Tables were located around the room for conferencing and editing. He arranged desks into pods or groups to facilitate greater interaction among students during drafting. An area for publishing and binding was also added in one corner of the room.

As Mr. Helms contemplated changes in the reading instructional block, he wanted to continue an opportunity for children to read books of their own choosing each day. Thus, a reading nook and SSR remained from previous years. This year, however, he decided to use the basal differently. He had heard his friends talk about not "basalizing literature" in his support group. One teacher who still used the basal raised a question that captured Mr. Helms's attention: She asked, "Do you think I could try to 'literaturize the basal' instead?" Mr. Helms decided to try to treat the new basal as if it were a collection or anthology of literature books all boxed up

Figure 5.8   Intermediate transitions, fifth-grade classroom arrangement

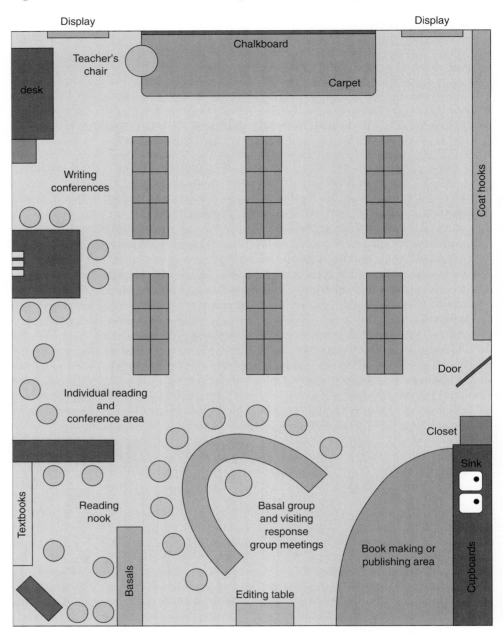

together. He would also treat the basal stories with the respect due good literature rather than just as so much more text to practice reading. Also, this year he would use visiting basal reader response groups with the basal reader, so he established an area in the room for visiting basal reader response group meetings. Because he still felt a need to explicitly teach many of the reading skills in the basal reader scope and sequence, he left the desks close to the front of the room for whole-group skill instruction. The results of Mr. Helms's planning can be found in Figure 5.8.

Figure 5.9 Intermediate transitions (upper grades), fifth-grade weekly reading plan

	M	T	W	Th	F
8:30 A.M.	Silent sustained reading →				
8:50 A.M.	Input sharing time →				
	Singing favorite songs on overheads	Riddles day: Highlights	Spoonerisms fun	Read aloud book: *Ben and Me*	Poetry 1: *A Light in The Attic*
9:10 A.M.	Whole Group	Skill lessons →			
	Dividing words into syllables	The prefix "un"	Understanding figurative language	Locating and noting details	Selecting the main idea
9:30 A.M.	Basal story	Basal visiting response group 1	Basal visiting response group 2	Basal visiting response group 3	Basal visiting response group 4
		Practice: Wkbk 17–19	Practice: Wkbk 20–21	Practice: Wkbk 22	Practice: Wkbk 23–24
	Visiting response groups or skills application and practice				
10:00 A.M.	Writing process (drafting, mini-lessons, conferencing, editing) Time →				
10:20 A.M.	Spelling minilesson pretest	Spelling practice: 6-step spelling strategy with partner	Handwriting: Upper case cursive "W"	Handwriting: Lower case cursive "z"	Spelling post-test
10:35 A.M.	Journal writing →				
10:45 A.M.	Closing Sharing time →	(Author's chair, read-alouds, performances, etc.)			

The next step for Mr. Helms was to plan his daily routine in such a way as to incorporate the changes he intended to make this year. His modified daily routine, shown in the format of a weekly reading lesson plan, can be found in Figure 5.9.

Like Ms. Scott, Mr. Helms began his daily routine with 20 minutes of SSR. At 8:30 A.M., he planned to hold an input sharing time. Mr. Helms realized that just as computer operators say, "garbage in, garbage out; nothing in, nothing out," so it goes with children and language. In Mr. Helms's mind, sharing time was a time for input of reading and writing examples and the literature of the culture. During the week, Mr. Helms shared songs with the words projected onto an overhead screen; read riddles, poetry, and books aloud; and encouraged children to play with language through sharing spoonerisms, changing the initial sounds of two words (e.g., silly boy changed to billy soy). At 9:10 A.M., Mr. Helms presented a skill lesson from the basal teacher's manual. He tried to use examples in the skill lessons from the children's basal reader stories, *library books, and their writing in order to make skill instruction relevant. He taught skill lessons on syllabication, prefixes, figurative language, noting details, and main ideas, to mention just a few.*

At 9:30 A.M., children either practiced their skill lesson instruction on assigned worksheets or they attended a visiting response group meeting. Having selected a favorite story from the basal (see "Basal Reader Visiting Response Groups" in chapter 9 for how these groups are formed and their function), children met with Mr. Helms to respond to their basal story. They talked about how they felt about the story. They discussed where they had experienced trouble understanding. They discussed what they liked best or least about the story. They also discussed how they could extend the story into other language arts such as writing, performing, art, and music.

Next, for 20 minutes each day, from 10:00 to 10:20 A.M., children in Mr. Helms's room engaged in the writing process, selecting their own topics to write about, drafting, soliciting peer responses, editing, and publishing selected works. For 15 minutes after writing time, Mr. Helms conducted spelling, handwriting, or punctuation lessons. He held a firm conviction that children needed to practice the mechanics of accepted spelling, handwriting, and punctuation regularly, although he knew that some of his peers who used balanced literacy instruction did not agree with the isolated teaching of spelling, handwriting, and writing mechanics. Next, for 10 minutes each day, the children and Mr. Helms wrote in their journals. At 10:45 A.M., they met together as a group for sharing time. They shared their books through reading aloud, book talks, and journal entries, and they performed plays for the whole class or read their own published writings to small groups of interested peers.

Mr. Helms is an excellent example of a teacher who has begun to make substantial changes in the way he believes and practices his beliefs in the classroom. Although his practices continue to lag somewhat behind his beliefs, he is becoming comfortable with taking charge of his beliefs and practices despite opposition by both the school system and some members of his support group. As Mr. Helms became more uncomfortable about differences between his beliefs and classroom practices and those espoused by members of his support group, he continued to make additional transitions. Over time, Mr. Helms will progress toward the most sophisticated stage of balanced reading instruction to attain, advanced transitions.

ADVANCED TRANSITIONS: MS. VALDEZ, FIRST GRADE

Ms. Valdez was in her 5th year of teaching first grade. When she graduated from college, she was employed in a nearby school district. The university from which she graduated began a state writing project the year after she graduated. As the newest teacher in her building, she was approached by her school principal and asked if she would like to represent their school as a participant in the state writing project. She agreed to participate. The principal informed her she would need to share the information she learned with her colleagues in faculty meetings.

Ms. Valdez attended the meetings of the writing project and learned a great deal about the writing process. That year and in subsequent years, she was very much involved in implementing the writing process with her first graders from the very first day of school. As she worked more with the writing process, she sensed that her beliefs and instructional practices related to writing were in large measure inconsistent with her beliefs about reading and reading instruction. The daily reading routine just didn't feel right. Ms. Valdez began reading and attending classes at her local university to work on an advanced degree. She signed up for the required course work as well as a class in emergent literacy. In this course she was exposed to recent research on how children develop as readers and to more recent thinking about children, language, and learning. The balanced reading approach fit well with what she had been learning about the writing process. She realized that she needed to put the principles she had once learned in her writing workshop experience to work in her reading instruction. She began reading voraciously anything she could find about balanced reading instruction. She studied, talked, and began trying to implement her balanced reading beliefs and practices in the classroom. In fact, incorporating balanced reading into her reading instruction became her terminal project report for her advanced degree. As she planned for the coming year, after many years of study, learning, and trying, some of the results of her sustained efforts were reflected in her classroom design and daily reading routine.

Ms. Valdez designed her classroom to use various grouping schemes, including whole group, small group, and individual work. She provided specific areas in her classroom for whole-group instruction at the front of the room. Tables with chairs, rather than desks, were arranged around a large carpeted area at the front of the room. Because Ms. Valdez felt that singing songs was a fun and functional way to learn to read, she had an electronic keyboard for accompanying songs children liked to sing. Easels with large sheets of chart paper were used to enlarge song lyrics, poetry, jokes, and riddles, and for taking children's dictation. These easels were located at the front of the room. Another easel was purchased for displaying and reading big books together during shared reading time.

Areas for signing in and writing messages were located next to the door of the room. A book-making and publishing area was located in the back of the room for publishing children's written products. An area for collaborative writing projects and literature response group meetings was established near the center of the room. On the back wall, sign-up boards for editing, peer conferences, and reading conferences were displayed. One bulletin board on the back wall was used to post logo or environmental print that children brought from home to school. Two small tables at the back of the room were set aside for holding writing peer conferences and editing sessions.

A reading nook was provided in a back corner of the classroom; it was complete with a rocking chair, a small chair, a bathtub filled with pillows, and bean bag chairs. Each day, an elderly "reading grandmother" volunteer visited Ms. Valdez's classroom and sat in the rocking chair. She listened to children read to her while they sat next to her in the small chair or on her lap in the rocking chair. Bookshelves surrounded the reading nook. Trade books, big books, child-authored books, personal storage bins, writing binders, and so on were stored in the bookshelves. Next to the reading nook was a librarian area. Here one student was chosen each week to function as a class librarian to check out and keep track of reading materials taken from the classroom reading nook library.

An area of the classroom that was particularly popular was the theme center. Here, children listened to music, made art projects, engaged in science reading and experiments, and played math games—all related to a selected topic or theme. A table with taped stories was also provided for young readers in Ms. Valdez's classroom to allow them to practice old favorite books again and again with support. Next to this area were two chairs for holding individual reading conferences near Ms. Valdez's desk. For 5 years, Ms. Valdez had been gradually implementing her changing beliefs about reading and writing instruction into her classroom. These changes are shown in Figure 5.10.

Ms. Valdez also tried something different this year in relation to her lesson planning. For 2 years she had been using Holdaway's (1984) reading routine including "Tune-In," "Old Favorites," "Learning About Language," "New Stories," and "Independent Output Activities." In spite of this routine, she had been struggling long and hard to integrate her reading-writing curriculum with other curricular areas. During the summer months, Ms. Valdez had designed several themed lesson units using Holdaway's (1984) reading routine, wherein she integrated reading and writing with other curricular areas. The first week's lesson plan involved a themed unit focusing on bears. The results of her planning are found in Figure 5.11.

Each day at 8:30 A.M., "Tune-In" time began. During this time, Ms. Valdez shared with children the enlarged text of a new song, poem, or chant on the easel at the front of the classroom. She pointed to the words of the text as she sang or read the text aloud. The children followed along as she pointed. During this week, four songs and a poem about the theme of bears were introduced to the children.

At 8:45 A.M., "Old Favorites," books that had been read on previous occasions, were read again. Assuming that many children had heard the story of the three bears before, Ms. Valdez chose this book as an old favorite to begin the year. Later during the week, after another book had been introduced in the new story part of the routine, Brown Bear, Brown Bear (B. Martin, 1983) became the old favorite to be read again.

At 9:00 A.M., Ms. Valdez had selected specific experiences she felt might enhance her students' understanding of the theme or the new story for the day. On Monday, the children took their teddy bears on a picnic. On Tuesday, the children predicted from a literature web the plot of the story Hairy Bear. Wednesday, they counted and graphed cinnamon bears. (After the lesson, they ate them!) Thursday, they brought a book from home or borrowed one from the class library to read to their teddy bear. Friday, they drew pictures of their favorite bear of the week.

At 9:15 A.M., Ms. Valdez read aloud, in standard size or in a big book format, a new bear story each day. At 9:30 A.M., independent activity time began. Seven centers or stations were located about the room; children rotated through three of these centers each day. Each child was assigned to a flexible traveling group. A large multicolored wheel with each group on the face of it was rotated at 15-minute intervals to indicate to the children where to move in the rotation of the seven stations.

Ms. Valdez's classroom design and lesson planning exemplify extraordinary effort sustained over many years. Ms. Valdez has worked hard to attain the degree of integration and organization found in her classroom. In many respects, Ms. Valdez's

Figure 5.10   Advanced transitions, first-grade classroom arrangement

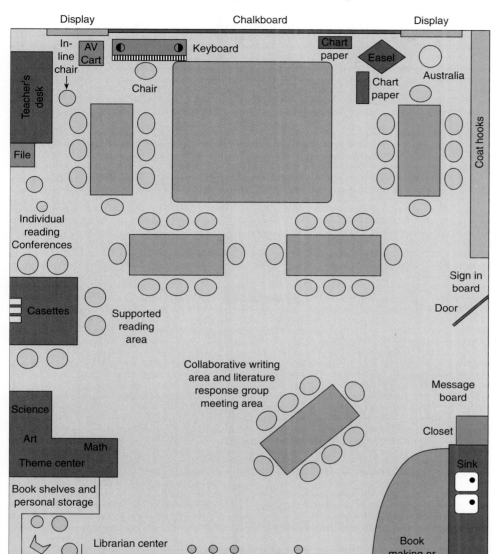

classroom design and instructional practices closely represent balanced reading beliefs and practices. Although it has taken years to make the transition to this point, Ms. Valdez has just now reached the stage of instructional implementation we characterize as advanced transitions.

To a large extent, Ms. Valdez has studied children and the reading process for years to succeed in implementing reading instruction at the advanced transitions level. In chapter 3, we presented vital information for understanding how children develop reading

Figure 5.11   Advanced transitions (lower grades K–1), first-grade weekly reading plan

Theme: Bears

	M	T	W	Th	F
8:30 A.M.	**Tune in:** *Going on a Bear Hunt*	Song: *The Bear Went Over the Mountain*	*B–E–A–R*	*Ten Little Bears*	*T–E–D–D–Y* (Bingo Song)
8:45 A.M.	**Old favorites** *The Three Bears*	*The Three Bears*	*Brown Bear, Brown Bear*	*Brown Bear, Brown Bear*	*Hairy Bear*
9:00 A.M.	**Learning about language:** *Teddy Bear Picnic*	Literature webbing	Counting and graphing # of cinnamon bears	Read a book to your teddy bear	Drawing your favorite part of our bear stories
9:15 A.M.	**New story:** *Brown Bear, Brown Bear* (big book)	(small book) *Ira Sleeps Over*	*Hairy Bear* (big book)	*Bear in Mind: A Book of Bear Poems*	(small book) *Ten Bears in My Bed*
9:30 A.M. 10:30 A.M.	Independent activity: Centers rotation 1 = Writing/publishing center: Language experience dictation stories this week 2 = Writing workshop: Minilessons on handwriting, spelling, or authoring favorite bear posters 3 = Read-along (taped books) with small books 4 = Paired reading of songs on charts, word bank cards, big books 5 = Reading work: Read alone, with Grandma Volunteer or with third-grade helpers 6 = Themed centers work: Work on science, art, and music projects about the bear theme 7 = Response group meeting: Children and teacher meet to discuss a big book read during "New Story" time.				

and writing ability. This information should help preservice and in-service teachers understand how they can support children more effectively as they learn to read and write.

Summary

In this chapter, eight dimensions of change involved in transitions were depicted. Eight transitional stances also were described, ranging from "I don't know enough to know where I stand" to advocacy stances. Springboarding from the basal reader is a good place to begin transitions with instructional materials. Thinking of the basal as an anthology of literature, making careful decisions about the use of worksheets, and doing away with asking a line of questions after reading to evaluate comprehension are some transitional steps in using instructional materials. Constructing and ratifying a nonnegotiable list of reading skills in schools can reduce the teaching of unnecessary reading skills in schools. Involving parents, seeking administrative support, and attending colleague support groups provide important assistance for teachers as they make the transition from traditional to balanced reading instruction.

The significance of modeling the classroom learning environment after homelike environments rather than other societal institutions was emphasized. Developing and teaching test-wiseness units and introducing the concept of portfolio assessment are ways for teachers to cope with problems associated with transitions in assessment. Finally, vignettes of three teachers, Ms. Scott, Mr. Helms, and Ms. Valdez, demonstrated various ways and degrees to which teachers make transitions.

Concept Applications

In the Classroom

1. Describe the transitions in beliefs stance that best describes you. Tell why.
2. Make a language to literature unit for a favorite set of books written by the same author.
3. Design your own parent involvement program for making changes in reading and language instruction.
4. Make a drawing of your classroom arrangement. Explain your reasons for the arrangements, furnishings, display areas, and so on.
5. Make a weeklong lesson plan for your reading–language instruction. Put this lesson plan into a weeklong schedule, as shown in this chapter.
6. Describe in an essay which of the three teachers—Ms. Scott, Mr. Helms, or Ms. Valdez—you most identified with and why. Describe a 5-year transitional plan for your own professional growth.

In the Field

1. After observing reading instruction in a school classroom, make a list of transitions in instructional materials and their uses you would recommend to the teacher.
2. Visit a teacher support group or attend a reading–language conference in your area. Write a brief response about your experience.
3. Make arrangements to visit an inner-city school to visit with the teachers about the types of diversity experienced in these urban settings. Discuss issues of language, culture, socioeconomic status, mobility, achievement, and so on of these schools. Explore with teachers at least three strategies they have found helpful in succeeding with children schooled in these settings.

Recommended Readings

Asheim, L., Baker, D. P., & Mathews, V. H. (1983). *Reading and successful living: The family school partnership.* Hamden, CT: Library Professional.

Goodman, Y. M. (1987). *Supporting literacy.* New York: Teachers College Press.

Loughlin, C. E., & Martin, M. D. (1987). *Supporting literacy: Developing effective learning environments.* New York: Teachers College Press.

Newman, J. M. (1990). *Finding our own way.* Portsmouth, NH: Heinemann.

Taylor, D. (1983). *Family literacy.* Exeter, NH: Heinemann.

Taylor, D., & Strickland, D. S. (1986). *Family storybook reading.* Portsmouth, NH: Heinemann.

Tovey, D. R., & Kerber, J. E. (Eds.). (1986). *Roles in literacy learning.* Newark, DE: International Reading Association.

Van Manen, M. (1986). *The tone of teaching.* Ontario, Canada: Scholastic.

chapter 6

Reading Comprehension:

Focus Questions

When you are finished studying this chapter, you should be able to answer these questions:

1. What is the difference between *teaching* and *testing* reading comprehension?
2. What are the meanings and implications of schema theory and generative learning theory?
3. What comprehension strategies can be taught to students to help them distinguish narrative and expository text structures?
4. What are some types of metacognitive training lessons described in this chapter?
5. What are some strategies suggested for knowledge- and experience-based comprehension instruction?
6. What strategies are discussed in this chapter to make questioning reading comprehension more effective?
7. What are the steps involved in reciprocal teaching?

Focusing on Instruction

Key Concepts

Teaching versus Testing
Schema Theory
Slot Filling
Instantiation
Accretion
Tuning
Restructuring
Generative Learning Theory
Story Grammar
Discussion Webs
Pattern Guide
Content-Text-Application

Cloze
Cohesive Ties
Typographic Features
Prereading Plan (PReP)
Metacognition
Repair Strategies
Think Aloud Lessons
Question–Answer Relationships (QARs)
Wait Time
Reciprocal Teaching
Contextual Diagrams

Reading comprehension is the very heart and soul of teaching children to read (Keene & Zimmerman, 1997). Language parts, such as words and letters, exist only to facilitate the paramount process of comprehending. Although words and letters are easily taught and the teaching of these is easily measured, teachers and children must never lose sight of the ultimate goal of reading instruction and practice—comprehending. From their very first encounters with print, children should expect that books and instruction will make sense.

COMPREHENSION: INSTRUCTION
AND ASSESSMENT

During the late 1960s and throughout the 1970s, reading comprehension was taught in school classrooms by asking questions and by assigning skill sheets as practice for separate reading comprehension skills such as getting the main idea, determining the sequence, following directions, noting details, and cause and effect. During this same period, the process and instruction of reading comprehension enjoyed unparalleled research attention. This interest and attention, spanning nearly a decade of concentrated effort, resulted in identifying several key issues, theories, and instructional solutions that give form and substance to current understandings of how to teach reading comprehension.

During the 1970s and early 1980s, reading comprehension enjoyed unparalleled research attention.

This chapter begins with a discussion of issues that emanated from the comprehension research of the 1970s and early 1980s. Next, the important theoretical understandings gained during this era of research are discussed. This discussion is followed with a presentation of comprehension instructional strategies designed to enhance text-based and reader-based comprehension.

ISSUES IN TEACHING
READING COMPREHENSION

Teaching Versus Testing

Durkin (1978) observed that less than 1% of total reading or social studies instructional time was devoted to the teaching of reading comprehension.

In 1978–1979, Dolores Durkin reported a study in which she investigated the state of reading comprehension instruction in public school classrooms. After observing a variety of teachers engaged in reading instruction in both reading and social studies classrooms, Durkin concluded that teachers spent very little time actually teaching children how to understand, work out the meaning of, or comprehend text units larger than a single word. In fact, less than 1% of total reading or social studies instructional time was devoted to the teaching of reading comprehension. This finding led to another question: What was happening in the name of reading comprehension instruction in America's classrooms? Durkin's answers to this question were both distressing and insightful. She characterized teachers as "mentioners," "assignment givers," and "questioners." She defined a *mentioner* as a teacher who said "just enough about a topic (e.g., unstated conclusions) to allow for a written assignment to be given related to it" (Durkin, 1981a, p. 516). Attention to new vocabulary words was often brief, even "skimpy" (p. 524). Teacher's manuals were usually consulted for only two purposes: (a) to study the list of new vocabulary words and (b) to ask the comprehension questions following the reading of a selection. Classroom reading comprehension instruction was dominated by ditto sheets that were in reality nothing more than informal tests. Thus, Durkin concluded that teachers apparently did not differentiate the concepts of **teaching** and **testing** reading comprehension.

Note the differences between teaching and testing comprehension.

Durkin's research pointed out the need for understanding the difference between asking children to read and perform comprehension tasks and assisting them in their efforts to comprehend a text. She described comprehension instruction as helping, assisting, defining, demonstrating, modeling, describing, explaining, or otherwise guiding students' efforts to construct meaning from text larger than a single word. From this description, we can see that effective reading comprehension instruction involves teachers and students in an active pursuit of constructing meaning from text. This view of comprehension instruction implies that teachers must become far more proactive in providing comprehension instruction. Teachers should feel an ethical obligation to share the secrets of their successful comprehension with students as well as how to monitor and repair comprehension when it fails to take place. Simply asking students to respond to a worksheet or to a list of comprehension questions does nothing to instruct those who fail to complete these tasks successfully. The conclusion to be drawn from Durkin's research on comprehension instruction is that teachers must vigorously engage in instructional processes that reveal for students the secrets of successful comprehension.

Basals Don't Teach Reading Comprehension

Later, in 1981, Dolores Durkin conducted a second study (1981b), in which she investigated the comprehension instruction found in five nationally published basal reading series. Her conclusions in this study essentially supported her earlier study: Publishers, like teachers, failed to understand the differences between teaching and testing reading comprehension. Basal reader teacher's manuals offered little or no help for teachers about *how to teach* children to comprehend text. Instead, basal reader teacher's manuals often presented a preponderance of reading comprehension assessment activities mislabeled as instruction rather than testing.

Basal teacher's manuals offered little or no help for teachers about how to teach children to comprehend text.

Don't Be Afraid to Teach

Although Durkin's comprehension studies made a strong case for active teacher involvement in comprehension instruction, other trends in reading and language arts education have had an opposite effect. Lucy Calkins (1986, 1994) and P. David Pearson (1989b) describe a trend associated with the process writing and whole language movements that may have undermined the role of the teacher in teaching reading comprehension. In an effort to respect the choice and interests of individual readers and writers in classrooms, some teachers have been led to believe that they should never take an active role in guiding or directing students' learning. Thus, some teachers may have become fearful of "taking ownership" of students' learning or "taking over" for students if they, as teachers, intervene in any way.

Calkins gives examples of teachers who have developed sly ways of avoiding teaching by asking questions or making comments such as, "I wonder if there is another sentence you could use as a lead?" (1986, p. 165). From such practices, students often conclude that teachers know how to help them but would rather conceal their knowledge. Calkins is very clear in her admonition to teachers: "We should not relinquish our identities as teachers in order to give students ownership of their craft" (p. 165).

C. J. Gordon (1985) said teachers should take "a proactive rather than an indirect approach" (p. 445) when teaching reading comprehension. P. David Pearson (1985) recommends a new role for teachers in the 1990s:

A trend associated with the process writing and whole language movements of the past is that some teachers have been led to believe that they should never take an active role in guiding or directing students' learning.

> I would like to propose a new model . . . in which the teacher assumes a more central and active role in providing instruction . . . . They become sharers of secrets, co-conspirators, coaches, and cheerleaders. . . . They become willing to share the secrets of their own cognitive successes (and failures!) with students. (p. 736)

Classroom teachers must feel that they have the professional prerogative, even the ethical obligation, to share what they know and have learned with their students. Hence teachers often must walk a tightrope between taking over for students and relinquishing their role as teachers. We believe simply that *teachers ought to be teachers*—people who recognize that they can assist and help children toward better

The key for teachers is to assist students toward better comprehension.

The **zone of proxi-
mal development** is
discussed in chapter 3.

reading comprehension. Vygotsky's (1962) zone of proximal development certainly indicates the importance of the role of the teacher or a more competent peer in assisting children in those tasks they cannot yet complete for themselves. Like Vygotsky (1962), we believe the teacher should gradually release the responsibility for comprehending to the child. In keeping with this understanding of the proper role of the teacher and the learner, Pearson (1985) recommended a model of instruction called the Gradual Release of Responsibility. This instructional model, as applied to reading comprehension instruction, is discussed in greater detail later in this chapter.

THEORIES ABOUT COMPREHENDING TEXT

Schema Theory

A schema is a package of knowledge containing related concepts, events, emotions, and roles experienced by the reader.

In the 1970s and 1980s, **schema theory** led to substantial progress in unraveling the complex and puzzling processes a reader employs to construct meaning from the ink marks on a printed page. Schema theory explained how people store information in their minds and how previously acquired knowledge is used to inhibit or assist the learning of new knowledge. A *schema* (the plural is *schemata,* or anglicized *schemas*) can be thought of as a package of knowledge composed of related concepts (*chairs, birds, ships*), events (*weddings, birthdays, funerals*), emotions (*anger, frustration, joy, pleasure*), and roles (*parent, judge, teacher*) drawn from the reader's life experiences (Rumelhart, 1981).

Each schema contains a set of defining attributes or semantic features, such as wings and feathers associated with a bird schema.

Schemas are composed of defining attributes called *semantic features.* For example, the semantic features associated with a bird schema may include examples of birds such as eagles, robins, and blue jays; characteristics of birds such as wings, feathers, and beaks; and categories into which a particular bird belongs such as birds of prey. Hence, schemas are organized in memory by associations, categories, examples, and meaning rather than by temporal (or time), order, or some other means of organization. Because of this organization, schemas are accessed in memory much like looking up a topic in an encyclopedia. For example, when looking up the topic of *birds* in an encyclopedia, one usually encounters information about birds, including attributes, categories, and examples of birds. Pearson, Hansen, and Gordon (1979) found that children who already knew a great deal about the topic of spiders remembered more from their reading than did children who knew little or nothing about spiders. One inescapable fact drawn from this research on schema theory is the simple yet profound conclusion: Previous knowledge helps readers acquire new knowledge.

Notice how researchers have represented schemas.

Researchers have visually re-represented schemas as networks of associated meanings (A. M. Collins & Quillian, 1969; Lindsay & Norman, 1977). Each schema is connected to another related schema, forming an individual's vast interconnected network of composite knowledge and experiences. The size and content of each schema are influenced by past opportunities to learn. Thus, younger children generally possess fewer, less well-developed schemas than mature adults. For example, consider Figure 6.1, which represents a first grader's

Figure 6.1   First grader's bird schema network

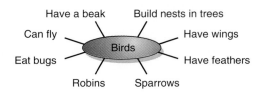

Figure 6.2   High school student's bird schema network

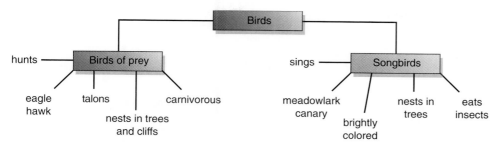

schema about birds; then in Figure 6.2, examine the bird schema of a high school student just completing a biology class.

Because individuals store personal meanings in memory, teachers must not assume that all children in a classroom possess identical or similar associations for a given concept or event. Although readers' schemas often have common features, as shown in Figures 6.1 and 6.2, the first grader's schema is less well elaborated than the high school student's. Thus, schemas are never complete; they simply provide a framework for storing new information. It is clear that the first grader's bird schema has great potential for growth, as evidenced by the many potential slots of information not yet filled in by experience, compared with the high school student's bird schema. A concept fundamental to schema theory is the idea of adding to a schema through a process called **slot filling.** In conclusion, a schema can be thought of as an abstract, flexible, and growing cognitive framework with slots that can be filled in by the personal and vicarious experiences of a reader.

Younger readers generally possess less well-developed schemata than older readers.

*Adding new information to an incomplete schema is called **slot filling.***

Understanding the Process of Comprehending Text

The act of comprehending a text is extremely complex. Thus, some simplification of this process is necessary when explaining reading comprehension. Based on schema theory, we describe the comprehension of text in four stages:

1. Searching for an appropriate schema by attending to minimal meaning clues taken from the situational context and the print.
2. Applying the selected schema to guide the interpretation of print.
3. Selecting and evaluating information to be retained or discarded by using the selected schema.
4. Composing a new text that is integrated into the existing schema or used to create a new schema. This process is illustrated in Figure 6.3.

***Comprehending** can be thought of as a four-step process: searching, applying, selecting and evaluating, and composing.*

Essentially, the process shows that when readers begin reading, they bring with them their collective set of schemas to help them construct meaning from the print. Expectations concerning the nature and content of print are influenced by two factors: (a) the function of the reading materials, such as labels, road signs, bus schedules, books, or newspapers, and (b) the situational context in which the act of reading takes place, such as a supermarket, a car, a bus terminal, a bookstore, or an easy chair at home. These contextual factors—function and situation—help readers efficiently select an initial or tentative schema for interpreting the print.

Figure 6.3   A schema-based explanation of processing text information

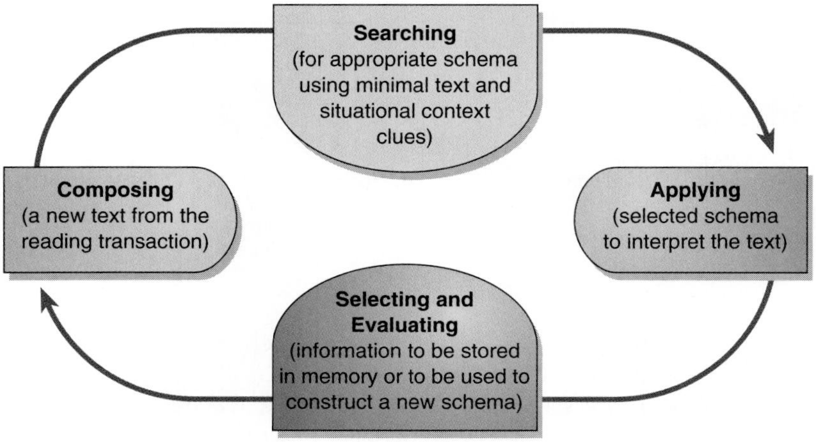

For example, imagine going to a local laundromat to wash your own clothes for the first time. As a novice, you will probably look around the laundromat for information to help you accomplish the task. On a nearby wall, you read the following sign posted above the washing machines:

> The procedure is actually quite simple. First you arrange the items into different groups. Of course one pile may be sufficient depending on how much there is to do. If you have to go somewhere else, due to lack of facilities that is the next step, otherwise you are pretty well set. It is important not to overdo things. That is it is better to do too few things at once than too many. In the short run this may not seem important but complications can easily arise. A mistake can be expensive as well. At first, the whole procedure will seem complicated. Soon, however, it will become just another facet of life. It is difficult to foresee any end to the necessity for this task in the immediate future, but then, one never can tell. After the procedure is complete one arranges the materials into different groups again. Then they can be put into their appropriate places. Eventually they will be used once more and the whole cycle will then have to be repeated. However, that is part of life. (J. D. Bransford & Franks, 1971, p. 719)

If you had not read these directions on a sign in the situational context of the laundromat, you may have had greater difficulty limiting your search for the correct schema to the act of washing clothes. Thus, the function of a sign and the situational context of reading (the laundromat) helped you limit your search to the most likely schema—washing clothes.

Once the most likely schema is selected, it is applied by the reader to interpret the text. In the laundromat scenario, the reader interprets the word *procedure* in the text to mean the act of, or steps involved in, washing clothes. If the reader had selected a postmaster schema by mistake, then the word *procedure* may have been interpreted as the act of, or steps in, sorting letters into post office boxes. Thus, the selected schema is used to guide the interpretation of each word in the text as well as the collective meaning of all the words in the text.

Schemas also provide a structure or framework for assimilating new information from text. The empty slots in a novice's laundry schema are filled in from the connections made between existing knowledge about laundry and the information conveyed in the sign. Thus, the empty slots in readers' schemas help them select and evaluate information. By referencing new information against existing schemas, readers can decide which information is important to add to the laundry schema for future use.

During this ongoing process, readers compose a new text, which represents the unique information retained from reading the laundry sign. In this sense, comprehending a text is very much like composing a text (Tierney & Pearson, 1983). The resulting text version of the sign as represented in the head of readers is not the same as the version posted on the wall. Instead, the text on the wall has been transformed into a new and personal re-representation of the meaning by using existing knowledge and the relevant information from the text. Thus, one change resulting from the reading transaction is that readers are changed. They now possess greater knowledge about doing the laundry than before reading the sign on the wall. The sign on the wall has changed, in a sense, because it has been transformed in the mind of the reader to re-represent personal meaning construction. Hence, the act of comprehending a text can be thought of in terms of a dialogue between reader and author that takes place in a specific situational context. The product of the reading transaction is best represented by the fact that the function of the text, the reader, and the situational context have combined, resulting in a new and personal text that replicates the original and intended meaning of the author's laundry text posted on the wall.

Schemas guide the construction of each word meaning as well as the meaning of the entire text.

Explaining Comprehension Difficulties

Rumelhart (1984) suggests that comprehension difficulties can be traced to four schema-related problems. Each of these problems is discussed with examples to help you gain an understanding by experiencing firsthand the difficulties students may encounter in comprehending.

- *Difficulty 1:* Students may not have the necessary schema to understand a specific topic. Without a schema for a particular event or concept, they simply cannot construct meaning for the text.

    For example, without the necessary schema, readers cannot appropriately interpret individual word meanings in the following passage, and they cannot construct a clear meaning for the overall text.

    > a—Machine-baste interfacing to WRONG side of one collar section ½″ from raw edges. Trim interfacing close to stitching. b—Clip dress neck edge to stay stitching. With RIGHT sides together, pin collar to dress, matching centers back and small dots. Baste. Stitch. Trim seam; clip curve. Press seam open. (Gibson & Levin, 1975, p. 7)

    Although those individuals who possess a sewing schema can readily interpret this passage, those without a sewing schema experience great difficulty in making any sense out of selected words (*baste, interfacing*) in the text or the text as a whole.

- *Difficulty 2:* Readers may have well-developed schemas for a topic, but authors may fail to provide enough information or clues for readers to locate or select a given schema.

    In some cases, readers know a great deal about the topic to be read. Some authors, however, may fail to provide enough clues that connect with the slots

Difficulty 1: Students may not have the necessary schema to understand a specific topic.

Difficulty 2: Readers may have well-developed schemas for a topic, but authors may fail to provide enough information or clues for readers to locate or select a given schema.

found in a reader's schema for a specific topic. For example, read the following text to see if you can locate your schema on this well-known topic.

> Our hero bravely defied all scornful laughter that tried to prevent his scheme. "Your *eyes deceive*," he had said, "An egg not a table correctly typifies this planet." Now three sturdy sisters sought proof, forging along sometimes through calm vastness. (J. C. Bransford & Johnson, 1972)

The authors, by failing to include relevant clues in the text such as explorer, ships, and America, make selecting the *Christopher Columbus* schema extremely difficult. Why? Because these key clues call up specific slots (*associations*) found in the Columbus schema. For the Columbus schema to be located and selected for interpreting this text, enough of these key clues must be found or instantiated by the text.

Difficulty 3: Readers may prematurely select a schema for interpreting a text, only to discover later that the text information does not fit the slots in the selected schema.

- *Difficulty 3:* Readers may prematurely select a schema for interpreting a text, only to discover later that the text information does not instantiate the slots in the selected schema.

  When this happens, readers may shift from using one schema to using another to interpret a text. You may recall the following example from chapter 3. Read this scenario again and think how your schema changes with new information.

  > John was on his way to school.
  >
  > He was terribly worried about the math lesson.
  >
  > He thought he might not be able to control the class again today.
  >
  > It was not a normal part of a janitor's duties. (Sanford & Garrod, 1981, p. 114)

  Did you experience several shifts to select the appropriate schema to interpret the text? Not only do schemas help readers interpret what they read, but text information influences the schemas selected.

Difficulty 4: The cultural experiences readers possess may affect their stance or perspective when selecting a schema to interpret a text. This leads to an "understanding" of the text but a misunderstanding of the author.

- *Difficulty 4:* The cultural experiences readers possess may affect their stance or perspective when selecting a schema to interpret a text. This leads to an "understanding" of the text but a misunderstanding of the author.

  To illustrate this point, Lipson (1983) conducted a study that found that Catholic and Jewish children comprehended texts better that were compatible with their own religious beliefs than those that conflicted with their religious schemas. Alvermann, Smith, and Readence (1985) found that schemas that conflicted with text information were strong enough to override text information. Reutzel and Hollingsworth (1991a) found that attitudes toward a particular schema were strong enough to influence comprehension of incompatible texts about a fictitious country called *Titubia*. S. J. Read and Rosson (1982) found that attitudes influenced recall of compatible and incompatible texts read about nuclear power. Thus, information represented in schemas can facilitate or inhibit assimilating new information from text. To illustrate this difficulty, R. C. Anderson, Reynolds, Schallert, and Goetz (1977) asked people to read the following paragraph:

  > Tony slowly got up from the mat, planning his escape. He hesitated a moment and thought. Things were not going well. What bothered him most

was being held, especially since the charge against him had been weak. He considered his present situation. The lock that held him was strong but he thought he could break it. He knew, however, that his timing would have to be perfect. Tony was aware that it was because of his early roughness that he had been penalized so severely—much too severely from his point of view. The situation was becoming frustrating; the pressure had been grinding on him for too long. He was being ridden unmercifully. Tony was getting angry now. He felt he was ready to make his move. He knew that his success or failure would depend on what he did in the next few seconds. (p. 372)

Most people in the study thought the passage described a convict planning his escape. There *is,* however, another possible interpretation. When physical education majors read the foregoing passage, they thought the passage was about wrestling. Thus, the cultural background of the readers influenced their perspectives by leading them to select entirely different schemas for interpreting the text.

Think of a time when your schemas inhibited or facilitated the process of assimilating new information from text. What were you aware of at that moment?

Instructional Implications of Schema Theory

Although schema theory has provided researchers with powerful explanations about how readers comprehend text, these discoveries can benefit children only when teachers clearly understand the instructional implications that arise from schema theory. Rumelhart (1980) discusses three types of learning that are possible in a schema-based learning system: accretion, tuning, and restructuring.

Accretion refers to learning new information that is added to existing information in a schema. Thus, accretion means that several of the potential slots in any given schema become filled, or instantiated. For the bird schema, perhaps children learn that the bones in a bird's body are hollow. This information is then added to the bird schema.

__Accretion__ involves adding new information to an existing schema.

Tuning involves major modification of an existing schema to fit new information. A schema may be tuned by making changes that allow the schema to become useful in interpreting a larger class or concepts or events; this is called *concept generalization.* For example, the bird schema is changed to include the idea that birds are not the only creatures whose young are hatched from eggs. Another schema change in connection with the concept of tuning relates to altering the schema structure to fit conflicting information. For example, not all birds have the ability to fly; penguins are one example.

__Tuning__ involves major modifications or changes to existing schemas to fit new understanding.

Restructuring relates to the idea of creating new schemas from old. For example, the bird schema may be used to create a schema for pterodactyl—a flying dinosaur. These three learning modes suggest several implications for the teacher of reading.

__Restructuring__ is the process by which new schemas are constructed from existing schemas.

When preparing students to read a text, the teacher must understand the critical role that schemas play in the comprehension process. Students may need the teacher's assistance to help them learn effectively from text. Teachers can provide this assistance in one of five ways. First, teachers will want to assess the background knowledge of their students to provide relevant and meaningful learning experiences. Second, the teacher may help students activate or select the appropriate schema for interpreting a text. Activation and selection of schemas may be accomplished in a variety of ways, discussed later in this chapter. Third, if teachers find that some students need to create a new schema for an unfamiliar concept, they should build the necessary background before asking students to read. Fourth, if teachers find that some

Students may need assistance to help them locate and use their schemas to comprehend text. For example, sometimes a picture can be very helpful.

students need to tune or modify their schemas to include other unfamiliar or incompatible concepts, they may provide examples and discussion to help them make the necessary changes. Finally, if teachers discover that students possess a fairly complete understanding of a concept or event, then reading may be assigned with relatively brief background-building discussions or lessons. One caution should be sounded at this point: Such a determination must emanate from *assessment* of prior knowledge—not from a teacher's *assumption*!

Generative Learning Theory

Generative learning theory suggests that readers need to actively construct relationships between the information in the text and their background knowledge.

Generative learning theory adds a noteworthy dimension to understanding schema theory and proposes significant implications for effective comprehension instruction, so we discuss it briefly here.

Generative learning theory (Doctorow, Wittrock, & Marks, 1978; Wittrock, 1974) grew out of the work of early cognitive researchers. This model of learning suggests that for reading comprehension to occur, readers must actively construct relationships between the information in the text and their background knowledge. The generative model of learning advances the idea that teachers can enhance reading comprehension by providing learning experiences that cause readers to actively make connections between their background knowledge and text information. Comprehension strategies such as summarizing, illustrating, writing headings, giving the main ideas of text, and retellings are just a few of the many strategies developed to generatively teach reading comprehension.

In the remainder of this chapter, we discuss practical applications of schema and generative learning theories as well as a model for providing effective and proactive reading comprehension instruction. The strategies selected for presentation integrate schema and generative learning theories into successful classroom practices that attend to the importance of background knowledge and to the active, generative involvement of students in making personal connections between text and their background knowledge.

A MODEL FOR EFFECTIVE COMPREHENSION INSTRUCTION

Gradual Release of Responsibility Instruction Model

The *Gradual Release of Responsibility model* depicts the idea that responsibility for comprehension tasks should be shifted gradually over time from the teacher to the student.

Growing out of Durkin's (1978) research findings showing that reading comprehension instruction was nearly nonexistent in the nation's schools, Pearson and Gallagher (1983) designed a model for providing effective comprehension instruction. These authors believe that the completion of any comprehension task requires some varying proportion of responsibility from teachers and students. In Figure 6.4, the diagonal line from the upper left-hand corner extending downward toward the lower right-hand corner represents the varying degrees of responsibility teachers and children share in accomplishing a comprehension task.

The upper left-hand corner in Figure 6.4 shows teachers carrying the major share of the responsibility for task completion, and the lower right-hand corner shows students carrying the major share of the responsibility. The model depicts the idea that responsibility for task completion should be shifted gradually over time from the teacher to the student. In this way, teachers transfer responsibility to the students, who then become capable and independent learners. In practice, the gradual release

Figure 6.4   The Gradual Release of Responsibility model of instruction

Proportion of responsibility
for task completion

All teacher   Joint responsibility   All student

Modeling

Guided practice

Gradual release of responsibility

Practice
or
application

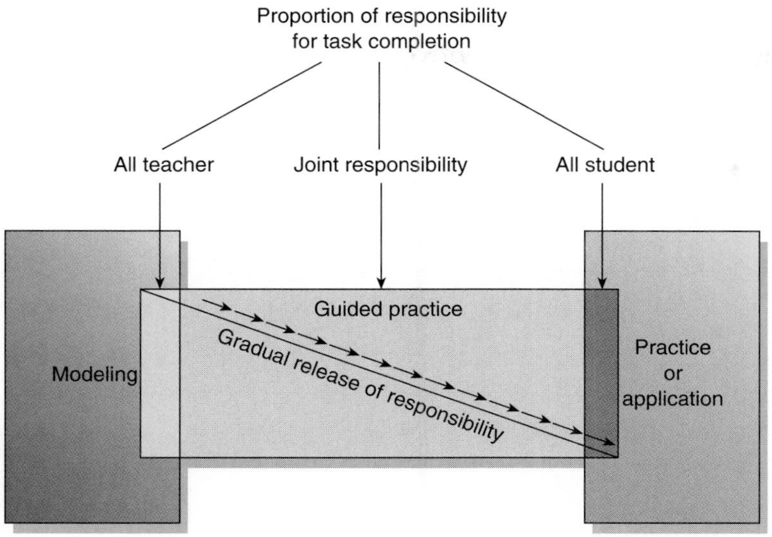

From "The Instruction of Reading Comprehension" by P. D. Pearson and M. C. Gallagher. 1983,
Contemporary Educational Psychology, 8(3), pp. 317–344. Copyright 1983 by Academic Press.
Reprinted by permission.

of responsibility is accomplished during the *guided practice* phase of comprehension
lessons under the teacher's supervision. Guided practice continues until the transfer
of responsibility from teacher to student is complete and success is ensured.

The concepts associated with this model of comprehension instruction can be
applied as a general framework to any of the comprehension strategy lessons presented in the remainder of this chapter. It is important at this point to recall again Vygotsky's (1962) zone of proximal development, which reminds us that children need
to be helped to do those things they cannot yet do independently. By releasing the
responsibility for task completion gradually to children, the Gradual Release of Responsibility model of instruction provides a useful framework for working into and out
of the zone of proximal development.

TEXT-BASED COMPREHENSION INSTRUCTION: FOCUS ON NARRATIVE STRUCTURE

Narrative Structure: Story Grammars

Perhaps one of the most important aspects of teaching reading comprehension is developing a schema for narrative text or stories (Vallecorsa & Bettencourt, 1997). A
story schema, or a sense of story structure, can be described by using the elements
of one of several published story grammars. By definition, a *grammar* describes principles or rules that govern the order of language. Thus, a **story grammar** describes
the order of language found in a story. Regardless of several slight differences among
story grammar descriptions, researchers generally agree on the following elements
for describing a story grammar: setting, problem, goal, events, and resolution.

Developing a sense of how stories are formed helps readers predict with greater
facility, store information more efficiently, and recall story elements with increased

*For more on the con-
cept of **story gram-
mar,** consult chapter 3
on developing a sense
of story.*

Figure 6.5   Story grammar map

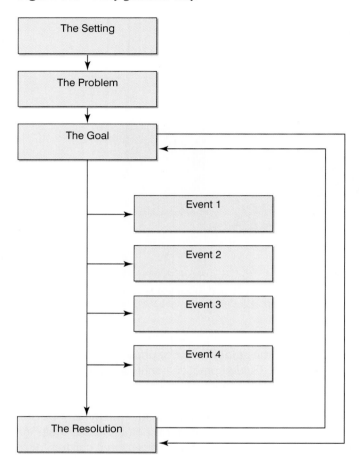

accuracy and completeness. In light of these findings, several researchers have described instructional procedures for developing readers' story structure awareness and knowledge. C. J. Gordon and Braun (1983) and Hagood (1997) recommend several guidelines for teaching story schema. We have adapted their recommendations as follows:

1. Instruction in story schema should use well-formed stories such as *Jack and the Beanstalk* (D. W. Johnson, 1976). A visual organizer can be used to guide the introduction of the concept of story schema (see Figure 6.5). For the first story used in story schema instruction, read the story aloud, stop at key points in the story, and discuss the information needed to fill in the diagram. For stories read after introducing the concept of story schema, use the visual organizer to introduce and elicit predictions about the story before reading. During and after reading, the visual organizer such as a story grammar map (shown later in this chapter) can be used to guide a discussion.
2. Set the purposes for reading by asking questions related to the structure of the story. Questioning designed to follow the story's structure will focus students' attention on major story elements.

3. After questioning and discussing story structure, specific questions about the story content can be asked.
4. For continued instruction, gradually introduce less well formed stories so that students will learn that not all stories are "ideal" in organization.
5. Extend this instruction by encouraging children to ask their own questions using story structure and to apply this understanding in writing their own stories.

Although instruction of story parts and story structure, as described by C. J. Gordon and Braun (1983), have been researched and found to be reasonably effective, the most effective route for helping children understand story structure is finding ways to encourage them to read great numbers of stories and to interact in cooperative learning groups (Mathes, 1997). In the following sections, we suggest two alternative approaches that have been shown to improve comprehension of narrative text.

Story Mapping

Story maps re-represent stories in a visual diagram to highlight specific story elements such as title, setting, plot, and the relationships among those constituent elements in a story such as simple sequencing, comparisons, and cause-and-effect chains. According to Reutzel (1985b, 1986c), story maps help teachers accomplish two major comprehension goals. First, by creating story maps, teachers become involved in thinking about the structure of stories and how story elements are related to one another, which presumably leads to increased planning and better organization of comprehension instruction. Second, when story mapping is used, students are led to understand the important parts of stories as well as how these parts relate to one another.

To design a story map, Reutzel (1985b) lists the following steps:

1. Read the story. Then, construct in sequence a summary list of the main ideas, major events, characters, and so on that make up the plot of the story.
2. Place the title or topic of the story in the center of the story map.
3. Draw enough ties projecting out symmetrically from the center of the map to accommodate the major elements of the story's plot and attach the elements from the summary list to these ties.
4. Draw enough ties projecting out symmetrically from each major element of the plot to accommodate the important details associated with these major plot elements and attach this information to the map from the summary list.

After the teacher creates the story map, children are introduced to the story by viewing a copy of the story map on an overhead projector or the chalkboard. Questions such as "What do you think the story we will read today is about?" are asked. Children focus their attention on the story map to guide their answers and predictions. Further discussion can be facilitated by asking about details represented in the story map such as "Who do you think the characters are in the story? Can we tell anything about this character from the information in the story map?"

In a lesson focusing on a story entitled *Haunted American History,* Reutzel (1985b) discussed the story map shown in Figure 6.6 with his students as described. Following the initial discussion, Reutzel asked the children if the story could be true, and they discussed their predictions and supporting reasons. He asked students to

Story schemas can be enhanced by teaching students the major structural elements of stories.

Story maps *help teachers and students think about the important elements of stories and visualize the story structure.*

Figure 6.6   Story map: Main idea—sequential detail

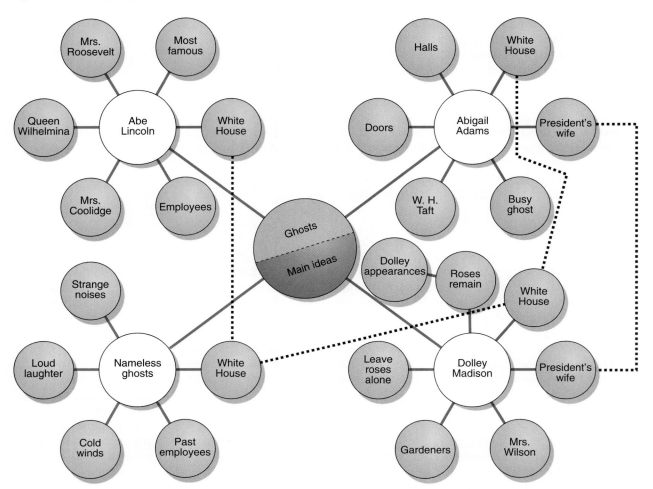

From "Story Maps Improve Comprehension" by D. R. Reutzel, 1985, *The Reading Teacher, 38*(4), pp. 400–411.
Copyright 1985 by International Reading Association. Reprinted by permission.

Story maps can be used before, during, and after reading to improve comprehension by helping children visualize the organization of a story.

read the story to see if their predictions based on the story map were accurate. During reading, children referenced the unfolding story against the information contained in the story map. In this way, the story map acted as a metacognitive aid to help students determine whether or not they were comprehending the elements and sequence of the story events as well as the relationship among these events. After reading, students were asked to write a summary of the story with the story map withdrawn, or they were asked to make their own recall and summary story map. Story maps can be adapted to focus on important elements of the story plot such as showing logical relationships like cause and effect and making comparisons among characters, as shown in Figures 6.7 and 6.8.

In summary, story maps can be used before, during, and after reading a story to visually represent the major elements of the story plot and the relationships among those elements. By using story maps, teachers plan and implement more purposeful, focused reading lessons, which lead to increased recall and comprehension.

Figure 6.7 Alternative story map: Cause–effect chain

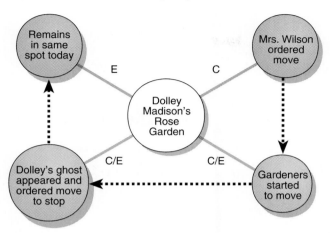

From "Story Maps Improve Comprehension" by D. R. Reutzel, 1985, *The Reading Teacher, 38*(4), pp. 400–411. Copyright 1985 by International Reading Association. Reprinted by permission.

Story Frames

Fowler (1982) and Nichols (1980) recommend using story frames and paragraph frames to develop comprehension among elementary and secondary students. Cudd and Roberts (1987) presented story frames as a means of helping first-grade children develop a sense of story structure. Thus, story frames can be used effectively with all ages of readers to improve text comprehension.

Because not all stories, especially those found in early basal primers, are well-formed stories (i.e., they do not contain all of the elements of a story in the proper order), teachers can design several types of story frames to improve students' comprehension. For most stories, the basic story frame is useful (Figure 6.9).

Story frames can be used with a variety of ages, text structures, and reading strategies to improve reading comprehension.

Figure 6.8 Alternative story map: Compare–contrast

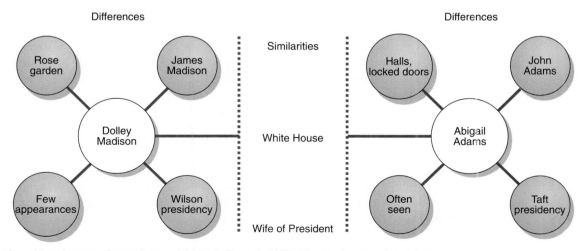

From "Story Maps Improve Comprehension" by D. R. Reutzel, 1985, *The Reading Teacher, 38*(4), pp. 400–411. Copyright 1985 by International Reading Association. Reprinted by permission.

Figure 6.9   Basic story frame

Title **The Best Birthday**

In this story the problem starts when **Maria gets sick and she can't have a birthday party**

After that, **her friends want to make her feel better.**

Next, **they go get a clown and ask him to help.**

Then, **the clown goes to Maria's house**

The problem is finally solved when **the clown makes Maria laugh**

The story ends **when Maria says this is the best Birthday ever.**

Figure 1 from "Using Story Frames to Develop Reading Comprehension in a 1st Grade Classroom" by Evelyn T. Cudd and Leslie L. Roberts, *The Reading Teacher*, October 1987, p. 75. Reprinted with permission of Evelyn T. Cudd and the International Reading Association.

Other types of story frames can be designed to facilitate comprehension of specific stories, short stories, or stories that contain no logical sequence of events such as those often found in early basal preprimers and primers. Other story frames can be designed to focus on the main idea or plot of the story or on the comparison and analysis of characters. Figures 6.10 through 6.12 illustrate different story frames that do not follow all of the elements of story structure in the proper order.

We have also found that story frames, especially the basic story frame, can be used to encourage children to make predictions about a story after it has been introduced by reading the title, looking at the illustrations, and having a brief discussion. When the story frame is displayed on large chart paper, predictions can be recorded for the group. Individual copies of the story frame can be distributed, and students can write in their own predictions before reading. We suggest that children write these predictions in pencil so that they can be changed during or after reading the story. Used in this way, story frames help children focus their thinking on important questions and information to be understood from reading a story.

After reading, we list the major story elements, such as setting, initiating events, and attempts, at the board. The predictions recorded on the group story frame displayed on the chart paper are discussed. Next, we cut parts of the story frame chart apart and scramble them up. Individual students or small groups are given one of the pieces of the story frame chart. They discuss which part of the story frames they have

Figure 6.10   Short summary frame

Title **Two cats**

A country cat came to the **city** to see **his brother**. But he didn't like **the cars**, and he didn't like **the noise**. Then the city cat went to **the country**. The city cat liked **the soft grass**, and he liked **the old barn**, but he didn't like **the big dogs**. He ran back to **the city** and stayed there.

Figure 4 from "Using Story Frames to Develop Reading Comprehension in a 1st Grade Classroom" Evelyn T. Cudd and Leslie L. Roberts, *The Reading Teacher,* October 1987, p. 77. Reprinted with permission of Evelyn T. Cudd and the International Reading Association.

in their hands. While pointing to a card at the board, such as *setting,* we ask children to raise their hands if they think they have this part of the story. We progress through the entire story structure until all of the parts of the story frame have been classified under one of the story structure headings at the board. A side benefit we have noticed from using story frames as a prediction and review discussion guide is that predictions and review discussions are sequenced in the typical order of story elements. This process seems to focus attention on and facilitate recall of major story parts. In this indirect way, we have been able to successfully alert children's attention to the structure of stories and thereby improve their comprehension.

Figure 6.11   Basic frame with no sequence of events

Title **The new pet**

The problem in this story is **Chen wanted a puppy**

This was a problem because **his apartment was too small for a dog**

The problem was finally solved when **his mother got him a kitten**

In the end, **Chen played with the kitten**

Figure 2 from "Using Story Frames to Develop Reading Comprehension in a 1st Grade Classroom" Evelyn T. Cudd and Leslie L. Roberts, *The Reading Teacher,* October 1987, p. 76. Reprinted with permission of Evelyn T. Cudd and the International Reading Association.

Figure 6.12   Main episode frame

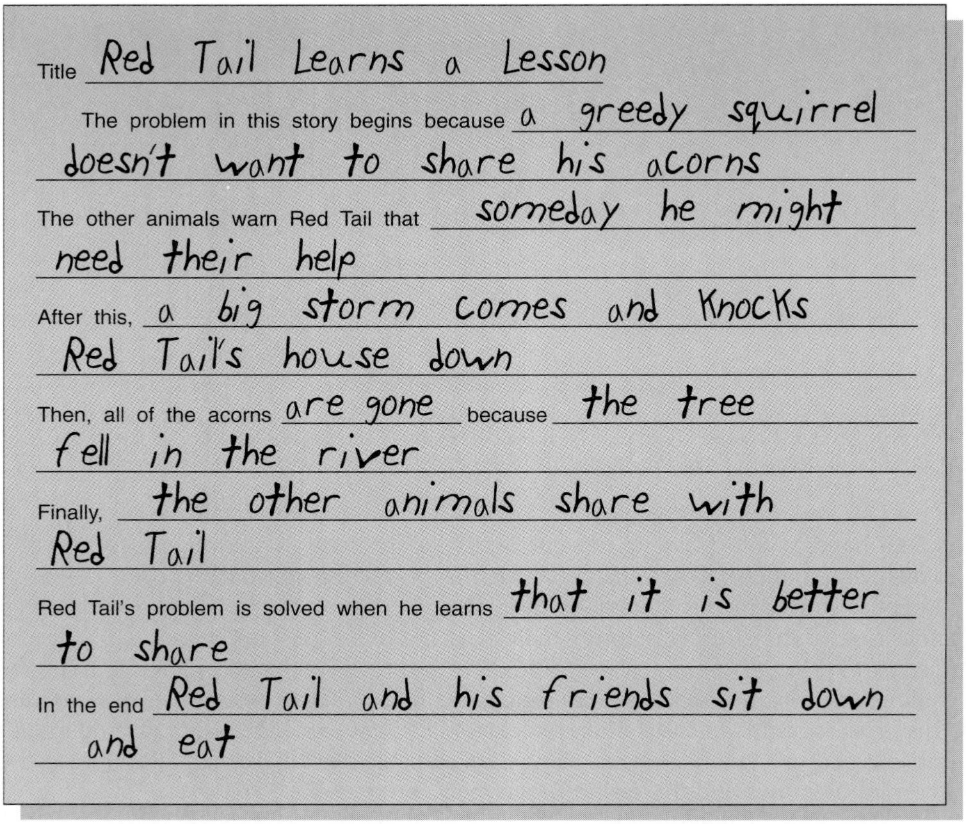

Title __Red Tail Learns a Lesson__

The problem in this story begins because a __greedy squirrel__ __doesn't want to share his acorns__

The other animals warn Red Tail that __someday he might__ __need their help__

After this, __a big storm comes and knocks__ __Red Tail's house down__

Then, all of the acorns __are gone__ because __the tree__ __fell in the river__

Finally, __the other animals share with__ __Red Tail__

Red Tail's problem is solved when he learns __that it is better__ __to share__

In the end __Red Tail and his friends sit down__ __and eat__

Figure 6 from "Using Story Frames to Develop Reading Comprehension in a 1st Grade Classroom"
Evelyn T. Cudd and Leslie L. Roberts, *The Reading Teacher*, October 1987, p. 79. Reprinted with
permission of Evelyn T. Cudd and the International Reading Association.

*Story frames also help
students develop a
sense of story structure
and story order.*

Cudd and Roberts (1987) have also found story frames helpful in focusing children's attention on specific text elements. For example, in Figure 6.13, a story frame is used to focus attention on key sequencing word clues embedded in the text.

Story frames can be adapted to many levels and elements found in narrative text. Benefits associated with using story frames include students' asking themselves and their peers questions based on their story structure knowledge. Students are also able to use their knowledge of story structure to help them predict, sample, and process narrative text more productively, resulting in increased recall and enjoyment of stories. Students seem to develop a sense for stories as whole and meaningful units of text to be enjoyed.

Perhaps the greatest benefit associated with using story frames is that students begin to read more like writers. They pay attention to structure, sequence, and sense in reading and expect text to be well formed and sensible. Further, their writing is improved because they begin to write stories that are more considerate of their readers. So, in this sense, students begin to write more like readers.

Figure 6.13   Story frame with key sequence words

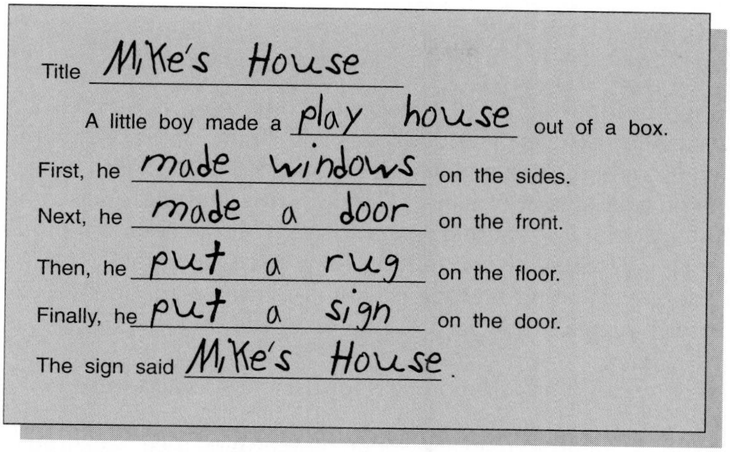

Title _Mike's House_

A little boy made a _play house_ out of a box.

First, he _made windows_ on the sides.

Next, he _made a door_ on the front.

Then, he _put a rug_ on the floor.

Finally, he _put a sign_ on the door.

The sign said _Mike's House_.

Figure 5 from "Using Story Frames to Develop Reading Comprehension in a 1st Grade Classroom" Evelyn T. Cudd and Leslie L. Roberts, *The Reading Teacher,* October 1987, p. 78. Reprinted with permission of Evelyn T. Cudd and the International Reading Association.

Schema Stories

Watson and Crowley (1988) suggest a strategy lesson for improving comprehension called *schema stories.* In this lesson, children use what they know about sentence and story structure to reconstruct a story. The key to this lesson is to select text that contains highly predictable structures such as "once upon a time" and "they lived happily ever after." The schema story strategy lesson can also be used with expository text such as science and social studies textbooks.

Schema stories are used to teach children to predict and confirm story predictions.

After selecting the text, prepare the lesson by physically cutting the story or text into sections, each of which is long enough to contain at least one main idea. Usually, one or two paragraphs will be sufficient in length to accomplish this purpose. To begin the lesson, each section of text is distributed to a small group of students (five to eight students). A student is selected in each group to read the text aloud to the group. The teacher invites the group that thinks it has the beginning of the story or text to come forward. The group must state why it believes it has the requested part of the story, and consensus must be reached by the class before proceeding to the next segment of text. If agreement cannot be reached, a group decision is made by a majority vote, and the dissenting opinion(s) noted by the teacher. This procedure continues as described until all of the segments of the text have been placed into order.

Schema story lessons make excellent small-group or individual comprehension lessons that can be placed into a center or station devoted to comprehension strategies. All of the segments of a text can be placed into an envelope and filed in the center. Small groups of children or individuals can come to the center and select an envelope and work individually or collectively on reconstructing the story. A key for self-checking can be included to reduce the amount of teacher supervision.

As children work through a schema story strategy lesson, they talk about how language works, the way in which authors construct texts, and how meaning is used to make sense of the scrambled elements of a text or story. In this way, children learn about the structure of language and text as well as the importance of attending to meaning as they read an unfamiliar text or story.

Discussion Webs

*Notice five steps for us-ing **discussion webs.***

Discussion plays an important part in guiding students' comprehension and inter-pretation of reading selections (Alvermann, Dillon, & O'Brien, 1987). Children are encouraged during discussions to examine more than one point of view as well as to refine their own comprehension of a text. **Discussion webs** are based on an adaptation of the cooperative teaming approach by McTighe and Lyman (1988) known as "Think–Pair–Share." The aim of using discussion webs is to en-courage children to adopt a listening attitude, to think individually and critically about ideas, and to involve typically less verbal children in the ongoing discussion of a reading selection.

Alvermann (1991) describes a five-step process for using discussion webs:

1. Begin by preparing students to read a selection by activating their background for the selection, introducing unfamiliar vocabulary terms and concepts, and setting a purpose for reading. An example may be based on the story *Tales of a Fourth Grade Nothing* (Blume, 1972), as shown in Figure 6.14.
2. After reading the selection, students are introduced to the discussion web. Students are placed in pairs and asked to discuss the pros and cons of the question in the center of the web, "Was Fudge really a bad kid?" Children take turns jotting down reasons for the yes and no continuum of the web.
3. Once children have had sufficient time to discuss the question in pairs and jot their ideas down on the web, one pair of students is placed with another pair of students. This group of four students discusses and shares its think-ing around the central question in the discussion web. Children are told to keep an open mind and to listen carefully during this part of the sharing. They are also reminded that it is appropriate to disagree with others in ap-propriate ways. The children work as a group toward a concluding statement that can be placed in the web.

Figure 6.14   Discussion web based on *Tales of a Fourth Grade Nothing* (Blume, 1972)

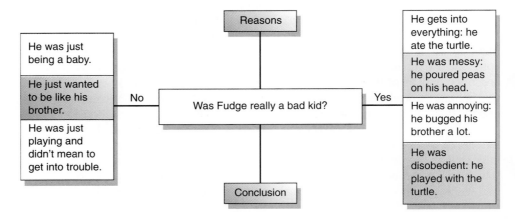

4. When each group of four has reached a conclusion, a spokesperson is selected to represent the conclusion during the general group discussion. Spokespeople are encouraged to represent dissenting points of view as well as the group's majority conclusion.
5. As a follow-up, children are asked to complete their own discussion webs by filling in their own ideas as well as those of the groups with whom they participated. These individual responses in the discussion webs should be prominently displayed in the classroom when completed.

Discussion webs help teachers lead students to deeper understandings of characters, story outcomes, how two sides of an issue may be considered, and using critical thinking strategies to make reasoned judgments.

TEXT-BASED COMPREHENSION INSTRUCTION: FOCUS ON EXPOSITORY STRUCTURE

Expository Structures

In expository text, authors use several predominant patterns for structuring the presentation of information. According to Armbruster and Anderson (1981) and Meyer (1979), the patterns most textbook authors use are time order (putting information into a temporal sequence); cause and effect (showing how something occurs because of another event); problem and solution (presenting a problem along with a solution to the problem); comparison (examining similarities and differences among concepts and events); and simple listing (registering in list form a group of facts, concepts, or events). Research has shown that readers who use an author's organizational pattern, a **pattern guide,** to structure their memory for reading are able to recall more than those who do not (Bartlett, 1978; Meyer, Brandt, & Bluth, 1980). Poor readers are less likely to use an author's organization of text to facilitate recall than are good readers. For students to comprehend expository text with ease and facility, teachers must help them understand and use the organizational patterns found there.

Expository text patterns include time order, cause and effect, problem and solution, comparison, and simple listing.

Pattern Guides

Olson and Longnion (1982) recommend several steps for using pattern guides to provide students practice in identifying the structure of expository texts. We have modified these recommendations as follows:

*Notice reasons why teachers would use **pattern guides.***

1. Identify a few important concepts in the text to be taught.
2. Determine the expository pattern used by the author.
3. Make a chart or a diagram for the students to complete that represents the text organization and the important concepts to be learned.
4. On an overhead projector, model for students how to use the guide with the first paragraph or two of the text.
5. Make sure the printed directions provided on the pattern guides are clear and understandable.
6. After modeling, distribute the pattern guides for independent use.

Figure 6.15 Pattern guide for time order

Time Order: "Religious Changes in Western Europe"

A time line is an excellent way to see the sequence of events. As you read about the religious leaders (p. 229–236), fill in the events on the time line below. Write what happened under the date.

1517 — p. 229

1521, 1526 — p. 230

1546, 1555 — p. 231

1558 — p. 234

Pattern guide created from *People and Our World: A Study of World History* (Kownslar, 1977).

Examples of pattern guides for science, health, and social studies texts are shown in Figures 6.15 through 6.20. Note that each example also uses a different type of text organization. Students' comprehension of expository text can be enhanced by helping them recognize and use the text organizational patterns found in their content area textbooks. Practice in identifying text organization as

Figure 6.16 Alternative pattern guide for time order

Time Order: "A Time of Conflict"

Religious factions caused by the Reformation triggered a number of religious wars in the 1500s and 1600s. Rewrite the events below in the order they occurred. Place the date of each event beside it (pp. 237–248).

1. The son of King Charles I was called back to England for the return of the monarchy.	1.
2. The Thirty Years War involved almost all major European countries.	2.
3. Most people in the northern half of the Spanish Netherlands became Protestant.	3.
4. In England, conflict between the king and Parliament led to Civil War.	4.
5. Sweden revolted against the Catholic king of Denmark and declared its independence.	5.
6. The Act of Succession was agreed to by William and Mary.	6.

Pattern guide created from *People and Our World: A Study of World History* (Kownslar, 1977). From "Pattern Guides: A Workable Alternative for Content Teachers" by M. W. Olson and B. Longnion, 1982, *Journal of Reading, 25*(8), pp. 736–741. Copyright by the International Reading Association. Reprinted by permission.

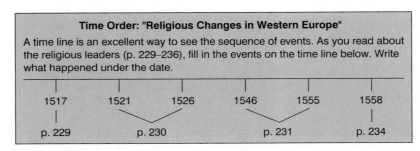

Figure 6.17 Pattern guide for cause and effect

> ### Cause–Effect: "Kinetic Theory"
>
> The kinetic theory explains the effects of heat and pressure on matter. Several ramifications of the theory are discussed in this chapter. Be alert to causal relationships as you read.
>
> 1. Gas exerts pressure on its container because
>   A. *p. 261, par. 1* _____
>   B. *p. 261, par. 1* _____
>
> 2. What causes pressure to be exerted in each arm of the manometer?
>   A. *pp. 261–262* _____
>   B. _____
>
> 3. The effects of colliding molecules that have unequal kinetic energy are *p. 266* _____
>
> 4. What causes the particles of a liquid to assume the shape of the container?
>   *p. 269, par. 1* _____
>   _____

Pattern guide created from *Chemistry, A Modern Course* (Smoot & Price, 1975).

well as important information related to text organization results in better recall of information in both good and poor readers.

Concept–Text–Application

Wong and Au (1985) developed concept–text–application (CTA) as a structure for lessons to improve comprehension of expository text. The CTA lesson organization is based on several assumptions of effective comprehension instruction. First, quality comprehension instruction should build on students' existing background knowledge. Second, expository text requires special instructional attention because it contains heavy concept and vocabulary loads, placing unusual demands on the reader. Third, expository text structure is less familiar for young readers than narrative text, prompting comprehension difficulties (Alvermann & Boothby, 1982).

A CTA lesson is composed of four stages: (a) planning, (b) concept assessment and development, (c) guided reading of the text, and (d) application, during which the teacher helps students draw relationships between the text information and their own background experiences. To clarify the CTA lesson structure, following is a lesson based on a book entitled *The Life of the Butterfly* (Drew, 1989).

Planning

To plan a CTA lesson, the teacher follows three steps. First, the teacher reads the book to determine the major concepts and main ideas in the text for which concepts will be developed in the concept assessment and development part of the lesson. Second, he or she rereads the text to look for major points to bring up during the discussion, formulate attention-focusing questions, and note important vocabulary

CTA is appropriately used with readers in second grade on up and is conceptually similar to the processes discussed in chapter 13 for analyzing content area reading materials and planning instruction for content area reading lessons.

A CTA lesson is composed of four stages: (a) planning, (b) concept assessment and development, (c) guided reading of the text, and (d) application.

Figure 6.18   Alternative pattern guide for cause and effect: Social studies lesson on *"Organizing the Forces of Labor"*

Cause–Effect	
In this section, look for cause-effect relationships in the situations mentioned below. Add the cause or effect in the proper column.	
1.	1. Saving money was difficult or impossible for unskilled labor (p. 400).
2. Owners felt it was necessary to keep labor costs as low as possible(p. 400).	2.
3.	3. Only the boldest workers dared to defy management and join labor organizations (p. 400).
4. By 1800s, wages of unskilled workers exceeded skilled artisans (p. 401).	4.
5.	5. The workingmen's parties supported Jackson after 1828 (pp. 402–403).

Pattern guide created from *The Adventure of the American People* (Craft & Krout, 1970). From "Pattern Guides: A Workable Alternative for Content Teachers" by M. W. Olson and B. Longnion, 1982, *Journal of Reading, 25*(8), pp. 736–741. Copyright by the International Reading Association. Reprinted by permission.

concepts that may need to be pretaught. When using CTA, many teachers find it useful to represent their planning by creating a visual organizer like that found in Figure 6.21. The final step in planning involves the teacher in thinking about ways the information learned from reading the text about the life of a butterfly can be shared, used, and extended into other related curriculum areas.

Concept Assessment and Development

Wong and Au (1985) tell teachers using CTA that capturing children's interest at the outset of the lesson is critical to success. This can be accomplished by asking questions that invite students to engage in dialogue about their own background experiences in interesting and imaginative ways. For example, while teaching the CTA using the book *The Life of the Butterfly* (Drew, 1989), the teacher began the lesson with the following introduction and question.

> *Teacher:*   (while holding the book up for the children to see) In this book, we will learn about how a caterpillar becomes a butterfly. Can you tell me what you know about caterpillars and butterflies?

After this initial discussion, subsequent questions could focus attention on critical or possibly unfamiliar concepts and vocabulary related to butterflies. For example, children may need to learn the vocabulary terms *spiracles, pupa, antennae,* and *proboscis.*

Figure 6.19   Pattern guide for compare and contrast: Social studies lesson on *"The United States Divided"*

Contrast and Compare

Using pages 264–265, you will contrast and compare the repercussions in the South and the North to the Supreme Court's decision in the Dred Scott Case.

The South	***The North***
1. (Hint: newspapers)	1.
2. (Hint: Democratic Party)	2.
3.	3.
4.	4.

Pattern guide created from *The Adventure of the American People* (Craft & Krout, 1970). From "Pattern Guides: A Workable Alternative for Content Teachers" by M. W. Olson and B. Longnion, 1982, *Journal of Reading, 25*(8), pp. 736–741. Copyright by the International Reading Association. Reprinted by permission.

Text

At this point in the lesson, the teacher moves into guided reading of predetermined parts of the text. Through questioning and discussion, teachers and children negotiate a purpose for reading each segment of the book. The lesson proceeds by alternating purpose setting, silent reading, and discussion for each segment of the text.

A visual organizer plays a central role in the alternating activities of purpose setting, reading, and discussion. By displaying an organizer, the teacher directs reading

Figure 6.20   Pattern guide for simple listing: Health lesson on *"Sleep, Fatigue, and Rest"*

Listing

This section of your textbook lists many causes of fatigue (pp. 96–97). Some of the causes are physical and some are mental. Fill in the causes under the appropriate heading.

I.   Physical causes of fatigue
    A.   short burst of intense effort
    B.   rapid growth
    C.   lack of important food
    D.   p. 96, par. 3
    E.
    F.
    G.
II.   Mental causes of fatigue
    A.   p. 96, par. 1
    B.

Pattern guide created from *Investigating Your Health* (Miller, Rosenberg, & Stackowski, 1971). From Pattern Guides: A Workable Alternative for Content Teachers" by M. W. Olson and B. Longnion, 1982, *Journal of Reading, 25*(8), pp. 736–741. Copyright by the International Reading Association. Reprinted by permission.

Figure 6.21   To structure a lesson based on the CTA strategy, a teacher might create a visual organizer such as this one for *The Life of the Butterfly* (Drew, 1989).

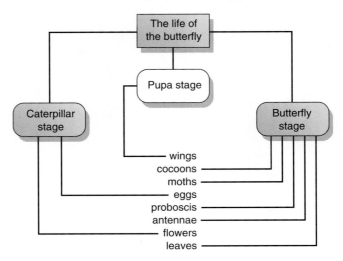

and discussion toward filling in the organizer. So, for each cycle of the lesson, the teacher fills in the organizer with additional information until it is complete. The lines are drawn in after the discussion to show which of the items previously discussed belonged with the phases of the life of a butterfly. In this way, the teacher represents the author's structure for conveying the information in the text. Thus, the text information is mapped onto the organizer, which visually depicts the organization and content of the information the author presented in the text.

Wong and Au (1985) advise teachers to look for opportunities to teach other useful concepts and vocabulary not presented in the text. They also recommend that teachers remain alert to opportunities to build or elaborate on children's existing butterfly schemas; for example, explaining that moths build cocoons and butterflies develop in a chrysalis is a topic with which the text deals only briefly.

Application

After the entire text has been read, the teacher helps students draw relationships between the text and their own background knowledge. By using the visual organizer, students are encouraged to synthesize and summarize the information discussed throughout the lesson.

Following the discussion or on another occasion, students may become involved in extension activities. These may range from something as simple as illustrating a selected butterfly to something as complex as building a three-dimensional diorama of collected and labeled butterflies. By following the steps in a CTA lesson, teachers offer students quality comprehension instruction in processing expository text at the whole-text level. Although we have offered many selected strategies for improving comprehension of narrative and expository text, these do not represent all of the possible strategies available. In the next section, we focus attention on microelements of the text that affect reading comprehension; these include sentence comprehension, cohesion elements, and typographical features in text.

TEACHING READING COMPREHENSION: FOCUS ON CONTEXT

The Cloze Procedure

As described in the Bullock Report (D.E.S., 1975), the **cloze** procedure is "the use of a piece of writing in which certain words have been deleted and the pupil has to make maximum possible use of context clues available in predicting the missing words" (p. 93). According to Rye (1982), the cloze procedure is a useful instructional strategy because "the human mind has a tendency to complete incomplete patterns or sequences" (p. 2). When cloze was first introduced by W. L. Taylor in 1953, it was proposed as a means of measuring reading ability. Since that time, a variety of instructional uses have been developed using cloze to improve children's reading comprehension and word identification. In the following paragraphs, we describe several instructional uses to improve children's reading comprehension.

The most familiar version of cloze involves an *every nth*-word deletion pattern. Typically, every 5th or 10th word in a passage of 250 words is deleted and left for students to complete using the context, or surrounding familiar words, in the sentence. Look at the following example, which uses an *every 5th-word* deletion pattern.

> Many scientists believe that there are other forms of intelligent life somewhere in space. These forms may not _____ the way we do. _____ often show life forms _____ space with silly-looking _____ . Movies often show them _____ frightening monsters. But have _____ ever wondered what those _____ life forms might think _____ us?

Primary-aged children experience greater success with the *every 10th-word* deletion pattern than with the *every 5th-word* deletion pattern because deleting *every 10th word* provides children with more context clues to use before encountering the next deletion.

Watson and Crowley (1988) describe another approach using the cloze procedure for instruction called *selected deletions*. This approach encourages children to use all the linguistic and experiential clues available to them to fill in deleted information. The advantage to this approach is that teachers can delete selected words depending on their instructional goals and the observed needs of their students. For example, to help students recognize comprehension clues embedded in text, teachers may delete structure words in sentences. A number of categories of words can be selected for deletion: words signaling the sequence of text (*first, second, next, before, after*), referring back to or ahead to other words in the text (*he, she, this, those, which*), showing location (*behind, on, under, next to*), signaling an explanation (*thus, because, so, therefore, as a result*), signaling comparisons (*but, yet, although, similarly*), and signaling an example (*such as, for example, that is, namely*). In addition, words or phrases that are easy for students to fill in using the meaning and sentence structure clues found in the text can be selected for deletion. By using selected deletions in this way, teachers can help students develop a sense for using language clues to fill in missing information. Examples of some of these selected deletions follow:

> Many scientists believe that there are other forms of intelligent _____ somewhere in space. These _____ may not look the way we do. Movies often show life _____ from space with silly-looking _____ . _____ often show them as frightening monsters. But have you ever wondered what those other _____ forms might think of us?

Use of cloze as an assessment procedure is also discussed in chapter 10.

With selected deletions, teachers delete selected words depending on their instructional goals and the observed needs of their students.

*The most familiar version of **cloze** involves an every nth-word deletion pattern.*

Zip Cloze Procedure

Zip cloze is used to help students use intrasentence and intersentence clues in text to construct meaning.

Blachowicz (1977) suggested using *zip cloze* to help students use intrasentence and intersentence clues (clues within and between sentences, respectively) in text to construct meaning. A zip cloze lesson is begun by making an overhead transparency of a section of a story or chapter in a textbook. Next, the teacher selects the words for deletion. By cutting masking tape into small, narrow strips, the teacher can cover the words selected for deletion with masking tape, peeling the edge of the masking tape back so that the tape can be easily removed. The teacher then places the overhead transparency onto the projector and has the class read the story as a group, either in unison or echo reading. At the covered words, the teacher has the children predict what the word might be and uncovers the word all at once or a letter at a time. When the children correctly predict the word using minimal text clues, the teacher zips the masking tape off and reveals the word. He or she continues this process until the text has been completely read. During this presentation, discussions may focus on how context was used to determine the appropriate word(s) for filling in the blanks.

Maze

When using maze, only nouns and verbs are deleted.

Maze is another cloze approach for improving readers' use of text clues to aid comprehension. Although many contexts will allow children to predict deleted content words successfully, some materials will not. This is particularly true for first-grade and second-grade reading instructional materials. The maze procedure proposed by Guthrie, Seifert, Burnham, and Caplan (1974) helps to compensate for this problem. When using maze, only nouns and verbs are deleted. However, instead of deleting these content words and leaving a blank to fill in, three choices are provided for each deletion. The three choices provided are carefully prescribed by the authors of this approach. First, one choice is the word deleted from the text. The second choice is a word that is the same part of speech as the word deleted. The third choice is a word that is a different part of speech than the word deleted. An example of a maze follows:

Chapter 8 discusses three more varieties of cloze that are particularly useful for helping children identify unfamiliar words: successive, regressive, and progressive cloze procedures.

	box
The boy in the forest lived in a log _____.	cabin
	run

Many more varieties of cloze are available for teaching children to attend to details in text for improving both reading comprehension, inferencing, and word identification (E. M. Carr, Dewitz, & Patberg, 1989).

Cohesive Ties

Words that link sentences together are called **cohesive ties.**

Another important research finding related to reading comprehension focuses on the relationship between cohesion and comprehension. Moe and Irwin (1986) describe cohesion as "a type of [language] redundancy that links one sentence or phrase with another" (p. 3). Research has found that the organization of text, or global coherence, is only one important means for rendering a text cohesive (Perfetti & Lesgold,

1977). Local coherence in text is established by using words that link sentences together, called **cohesive ties.** Some examples of cohesive ties follow:

Type of Cohesive Tie	Example
Reference Includes many pronoun types, location words, and time words.	Austin went to the park. *He* climbed the slide. "Mom, look at that car! Can we go over *there?*"
Substitution Replacing a word or phrase with another.	"My dress is old. I need a new *one.*" "Do you know him?" "No, *do* you?"
Ellipsis Omitting a word or phrase resulting in an implied repetition.	"Were you laughing?" "No, I wasn't." Ralph wears expensive sneakers. His look nicer.
Conjunction Connects phrases and sentences using additive, adversative, causal, and temporal ties	Jeremy went to the store *after* dinner. He didn't eat fish *because* he dislikes them.
Lexical Using synonymous or category terms to establish ties in text.	The bear went fishing. This large *mammal* likes to eat fish.

Teachers should be selective about which cohesive ties they teach. We suggest beginning with reference ties—especially common pronouns. A good rule of thumb for selection, however, is to observe the comprehension difficulties of your students. If children are experiencing difficulties with lexical cohesive ties, then instruction should focus on these.

We remind the reader that Durkin (1978) found very little reading comprehension instruction in classrooms—particularly explicit instruction that helped children work out the meaning of text larger than a single word. Cohesion is an area for comprehension instruction needing increased attention for many students. Reutzel and Morgan (1990) found that even prior knowledge did not compensate for the absence of (causal) cohesive ties in text.

Pulver (1986) and Baumann and Stevenson (1986) recommend several elements that should be included in lessons when teaching students about cohesive ties in text:

- Directly explain the cohesive link and how it works in text by providing examples.
- Orally model the cohesive link by describing your own thought processes as a reader.
- Ask questions of students to encourage discussion and description of their own thoughts about the cohesive tie.
- Spend time in group practice activities.
- Provide independent practice activities.

Typographic Features

As with cohesive ties, other text features affect the comprehensibility of text. When authors write, they use **typographic features.** Many of these include punctuation marks such as the period, comma, question mark, exclamation mark, capitalization, semicolon, and colon. Aside from these punctuation features, authors will sometimes use italics, boldfaced text, bullets, or boxes to highlight text features and make text more reader friendly. We suggest that teachers draw attention to these features during group readings to heighten students' awareness of their presence and functions in text. For example, we assign a unique vocal sound to mark the presence of each punctuation mark during oral reading (see "Verbal Punctuation" on p. 122 in chapter 4). Then, during a unison choral reading, we make each of the assigned sounds for the punctuation marks as we encounter them in the print. This approach is both fun and instructive for readers.

ACTIVATING BACKGROUND KNOWLEDGE
Prereading Plan

One way to activate prior knowledge of a topic for expository text or the message of narrative text is to use J. Langer's (1981) **prereading plan (PReP).** Begin a PReP lesson by examining the text to be read. Look for key words, phrases, and illustrations that relate to the topic or message of the text depending on the type of text to be read (narrative or expository). For example, you may be reading a passage about Mississippi river boats; words such as *steamers, barges,* and *dredging* may be selected along with illustrations for this lesson. Langer suggests that students' prior knowledge of a selection be assessed before beginning instruction. The key words from the selection can be listed on a handout and numbered. Students are asked to write down what they know about each of the selected words. Scoring can be accomplished by assigning each prior knowledge response a qualitative ranking ranging from 0 to 3.

> 0 = *Neither prior knowledge of nor response to the item.*
>
> 1 = *Little prior knowledge.* This is evidenced by responses that include words that sound like the stimulus word in the list, a short personal experience that is for the most part irrelevant, and supplying word parts, such as suffixes and prefixes.
>
>> dredge–ledge
>> I think my grandpa lived by a dredge.
>> Dredge, is that like dredging?
>
> 2 = *Some prior knowledge.* This level of prior knowledge is evidenced by responses containing examples, attributes, and definition of characteristics related to the stimulus term.
>
>> Isn't dredging like digging?
>> Don't you have to have a steam shovel or something like it to dredge?
>
> 3 = *Much prior knowledge.* This level of prior knowledge is evidenced by responses containing definitions, analogies, and category concept names (superordinate concept labels).

A dredge is like a shovel.
An apparatus for scooping up mud and debris.
A tool for digging.

After assessing the general status of prior knowledge among students in the classroom, teachers are better prepared to focus on students' prior knowledge needs to facilitate presenting the PReP lesson.

PReP is composed of three distinct phases: (a) association, (b) reflections on associations, and (c) organizing knowledge. The lesson is begun by asking students to free associate with a selected term or idea such as *steamboats*. This can be done by saying, "Tell me anything you think of when you hear the idea of the *steamboats*." These responses can be written at the board or recorded on chart paper for later reference. After jotting down the associations of the group, the teacher requests that students think about their associations. This may be done by saying, "What made you think of . . . ?" Following this phase of the lesson, students discuss any new ideas or knowledge they formulated during the previous phases of the lesson. These ideas should be recorded at the board or on chart paper as well. Before students read, tell them they should set some purposes for reading. This can be done by suggesting, "Write down several questions before beginning to read. These should be questions for which you want to find answers by reading the passage or story." After reading, students can summarize and organize their questions and answers. Both the questions and answers can be shared with the group.

PReP is a useful knowledge-based teaching strategy for helping students activate and elaborate what they know about a topic before reading to improve reading comprehension. PReP can also help students develop the ability to monitor the state of their own understanding. By engaging students in revealing their knowledge about a topic, concept, or event before reading, teachers help students become aware of how much or how little they know. Thus, PReP is helpful for assessment, activation, and elaboration of prior knowledge to improve readers' comprehension of text.

List two things PReP helps students do to succeed in reading expository text.

K-W-L

Another strategy that can be used to develop comprehension through activating prior knowledge is called K-W-L. Ogle (1986), the originator of K-W-L, asserts that this strategy is best suited for use with expository text, although we see no reason why it cannot be applied to stories with minor modifications.

Notice three steps for using K-W-L.

Step K: *What I Know*

K-W-L strategy lessons begin with step K, *what I know*. This step is composed of two levels of accessing prior knowledge: (a) brainstorming and (b) categorizing information. Begin by asking children to brainstorm about a particular topic (in the case of a narrative, brainstorm a particular theme or message). For instance, children may be asked what they know about bats. A list of associations is formed through brainstorming. When students make a contribution, Ogle (1986) suggests asking them where or how they got their information to challenge students into higher levels of thinking.

Next, teachers should help students look for ways in which the brainstorming list can be reorganized into categories of information. For example, teachers may notice that the brainstorming list shows three related pieces of information about how bats navigate; these can be reorganized into that category. Children are encouraged to look at the list and think about other categories represented in the brainstorming list.

Step W: *What Do I Want to Learn?*

During step W, students begin to recognize gaps, inaccuracies, and disagreements in their prior knowledge to decide what they want to learn. Teachers can play a central role in pointing out these problems and helping students frame questions for which they would like to have answers. Questions can be framed by having students use the question stem "I wonder." After the group generates a series of questions to be answered before reading, they are directed to write down personal questions for which they would like answers. Questions can be taken from those generated by the groups as well as others generated by individuals.

Step L: *What I Learned*

After students read, have them write down what they learned. They can write answers to specific questions they asked or a concise summary of their learning. These questions and answers can be discussed with the entire class or shared between pairs of students. In this way, other children benefit from the learning of their peers as well as from their own learning.

In summary, K-W-L has been shown to be effective in improving reading comprehension by causing students to activate, think about, and organize their prior knowledge as an aid to reading comprehension (DeWitz & Carr, 1987).

Generating Reciprocal Inferences Procedure (GRIP)

*Notice how teachers model the process of making an inference in the first stage of the **GRIP** strategy.*

P. M. Hollingsworth and Reutzel (1988) emphasize that one important part of reading comprehension involves the ability to make inferences. A two-stage approach is used to help students develop this ability in the Generating Reciprocal Inferences Procedure (GRIP). First, the teacher models explicitly how an inference is made by reading, and then the teacher highlights key or clue words in the text. For example, the teacher may read aloud the following passage, after which he or she highlights certain clue words in the text, as shown:

> The <u>elevator</u> <u>ride</u> was great fun. Now Kathy and Becky <u>looked</u> <u>down</u> through the wire fence as the wind whistled in their ears. The <u>people</u> and the <u>cars</u> <u>on</u> <u>the</u> <u>street</u> <u>looked</u> just like <u>tiny</u> toys. Although they were <u>very</u> <u>high</u> <u>up,</u> the girls were not frightened. It was exciting to <u>see</u> <u>the</u> <u>whole</u> <u>city</u> spread out before them.

Where were Kathy and Becky? This passage requires the reader to make a certain kind of slot-filling inference—a location inference. The teacher makes this inference after highlighting the clues in the text that led to that conclusion. After highlighting the relevant text clues and making the inference, the teacher justifies the inference by pointing out how each text clue, combined with prior knowledge, supported the inference that Kathy and Becky were on a high building overlooking a city—the location.

The GRIP lesson continues with four more paragraphs; these paragraphs are needed to gradually release the responsibility for inferencing from the teacher to the students. In the next paragraph, the teacher highlights the words, the children make

Figure 6.22 Generating Reciprocal Inferences Procedure (GRIP) game board

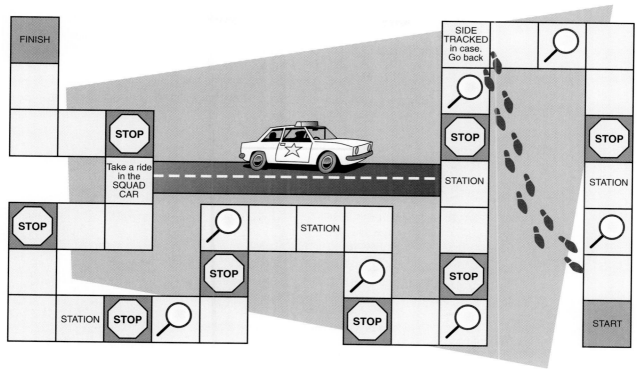

the inference, and the teacher justifies the inference the students made. The third paragraph is read, the children highlight the key words, the teacher makes the inference, and the students justify the inference. In the fourth and final passage, the students highlight the key words, make the inference, and justify the inference.

After children are able to assume full responsibility for finding key words, inferencing, and justifying the inference, they move into *generating* reciprocal inferences. Children are paired to write their own inference paragraphs. This is done by generating a list of five or more key words and writing the text, incorporating the clues without giving away the inference to be made. After writing, the students in each pair exchange paragraphs, mark key words, make the inference, and justify their inferences to the author. This process can continue as long as needed and as long as interest remains high. Variations of this approach include placing the paragraphs written by children on overhead transparencies and inviting children to locate the key words, make an inference, and justify their own inferences in writing. Another variation to this approach involves a game board activity (Figure 6.22) with directions for playing the game (Figure 6.23).

GRIP has been shown to increase children's abilities to make inferences across a wide variety of measures and under several conditions (Reutzel & Hollingsworth, 1988a). GRIP is a useful implementation of the Pearson and Gallagher (1983) model of gradual release in comprehension instruction, which improves inferential and global reading comprehension.

In the second stage of the GRIP strategy, students compose inferential text for peers to make inferences.

Figure 6.23   Directions for Generating Reciprocal Inferences Procedure (GRIP) game board

Children play the GRIP board game in pairs. Before the game begins, each child needs to understand the rules for playing the game and follow them carefully. We begin by discussing the game rules with the children:

1. Requires two players to play the game.
2. Write four sentences that go together to make a story. Underline the clue words in each sentence.
3. Select a marker.
4. Place marker on START.
5. Throw the die, letting the highest start the game.
6. Each player moves his/her marker the number of spaces shown on the die.
7. If you land on STATION, have the other player read a sentence.
8. If you land on MAGNIFYING GLASS, move to the nearest STATION, have the other player read a sentence.
9. A different sentence is read at each STATION.
10. You must be on STATION to guess, and you get only one guess.
11. If you land on STOP SIGN, go back to the space from which you started your turn.
12. You can be on the same space as the other player.
13. If you land on SIDETRACKED, follow the feet.
14. If you land on SQUAD CAR, follow the road.
15. Whoever guesses what the story is about is the winner, and the game is over.

When the GRIP board game is introduced, play the game with one child while the other children in the classroom watch. This makes the transition from discussing the rules to playing the game easier.

From "Get a GRIP on Comprehension" by P. M. Hollingsworth and D. R. Reutzel, 1988, *Reading Horizons, 29*(1), pp. 76–77. Copyright 1988 by Reading Horizons. Reprinted by permission.

MONITORING COMPREHENSION AND FIX-UP STRATEGIES

Metacognition in-volves readers in check-ing the status of their own understanding and taking steps to repair failing comprehension when necessary.

In addition to activating, elaborating, or modifying prior knowledge to improve comprehension, readers must learn to monitor the status of their own ongoing comprehension and know when comprehension breaks down. The act of monitoring one's unfolding comprehension of text is called **metacognition,** or sometimes *meta-comprehension.* The ability to plan, check, monitor, revise, and evaluate one's unfolding comprehension is of particular importance in reading. If a child fails to detect comprehension breakdowns, then he or she will take no action to correct misinterpretations of the text. However, if a child expects that text should make sense and has the ability to strategically self-correct comprehension problems, then reading can progress as it should.

To help students develop the ability to monitor their own comprehension processes, H. K. Carr (1986) suggested a strategy called *click or clunk.* This strategy urges readers to reflect at the end of each paragraph or section of reading by stopping and asking themselves if the meaning or message "clicks" for them or goes "clunk." If it clunks, what is wrong? What can be done to make sense of it?

Although the ability to detect when comprehension breaks down is important, it is equally important to know which strategies to select in repairing broken comprehension as well as when to use these strategies. Consequently, students may know that they need to take steps to repair comprehension but may not know which steps to take or when to take them. As a consequence, children should be introduced to the options available to them for repairing broken comprehension. A. Collins and Smith (1980) suggest the following **repair strategies** for use by readers who experience comprehension failure.

- Ignore the problem and continue reading.
- Suspend judgment for now and continue reading.
- Form a tentative hypothesis, using text information, and continue reading.
- Look back or reread the previous sentence.
- Stop and think about the previously read context, and reread if necessary.
- Seek help from the environment, reference materials, or other knowledgeable individuals.

To help students develop a sense for when to select these strategies for repairing failing comprehension, teachers may consider using a think-aloud modeling procedure. The teacher begins by reading part of a text aloud, and as he or she proceeds, comments on his or her thinking. By revealing this thinking to students, the hypotheses formed for the text, and anything that appears difficult or unclear, the teacher demonstrates for the students the processes successful readers use to comprehend a text. Next, the teacher reminds students of the click or clunk strategy. Gradually, the teacher releases the responsibility for modeling metacognitive strategies to the children during follow-up lessons on metacognitive monitoring. He or she displays the repair strategies shown previously in a prominent place in the classroom and draws students' attention to these strategies throughout the year.

For students needing additional help with metacognitive strategy development, we recommend Baumann, Jones, and Seifert-Kessell's (1993) **think-aloud lessons,** in which students are explicitly taught the strategies of metacognition through definition, description, and examples. Next, children are told why learning these strategies is important for helping them become better readers. Finally, students are taught how to use these strategies through a sequence of instruction using (a) verbal explanation, (b) teacher modeling, (c) guided practice, and (d) independent practice. The think-aloud lesson is centered on the following topics:

- Self-questioning (see self-questioning later in this chapter)
- Sources of information (see question–answer relationships, QARs, later in this chapter)
- Think-aloud modeling introduction (see GRIP, previously in this chapter)
- Think-aloud review and extension (see GRIP)
- Predicting, reading, and verifying
- Understanding unstated information
- Retelling a story (see next section and chapter 11)
- Rereading and reading on (see preceding discussion)
- Think-aloud/comprehension-monitoring application

We recommend this procedure because it brings together in an integrated fashion all of the elements of excellent, research-based metacognitive reading instruction, which has been shown to be very effective in helping students acquire a broad range of metacognitive strategies.

ASSESSING COMPREHENSION OF TEXT: STRATEGIES FOR EFFECTIVE QUESTIONING

Questions are an integral part of life both in and out of school. From birth, we learn about our world by asking questions and then by testing our answers against the confines of reality. In school, teachers ask questions to motivate children to become involved in learning. Because questions are so much a part of the schooling process and can affect the quality of children's comprehension, teachers must know how to use questioning effectively to deliver quality reading instruction.

Retellings as Comprehension Assessment

Focus on five steps for helping students retell successfully.

Gambrell, Pfeiffer, and Wilson (1985) found that using retellings following silent reading enhanced reading comprehension as measured by answers to literal and interpretive questions. Wilson and Gambrell (1988, pp. 53–54) speculate that retellings of text improve comprehension because students engage in rehearsing the structure and content of text. In the following list, we have modified Wilson and Gambrell's five tips for helping students retell text successfully:

1. Teachers can model retelling by taking a few minutes to retell a portion of a story, including the modeling of accurate sequencing.
2. Teachers can retell a portion of an event in a story and ask the students to finish retelling the story.
3. Students can be asked to tell about what they thought was the most important or interesting event or episode in a story.
4. Teachers can pair students off for retelling a story after reading. They can be instructed to tell their peer the story as if he or she had not read it.
5. During individual reading conferences, the teacher can ask students to retell what they have read as an assessment of reading comprehension. Retellings can be scored for major ideas or story grammar components, that is, setting, initiating event, attempts, resolution, and so on.

Retellings are an effective comprehension instructional strategy because they involve students in activating their prior knowledge for remembering stories and expositions. By requiring that readers select information from a text that is worth remembering, retellings help students focus selective attention on relevant information in text as well as increase sensitivity to a variety of text structures.

Questioning Taxonomies

For many years, the only means of teaching comprehension was through questioning students.

Questioning taxonomies played an integral role in early efforts to improve teacher questioning.

For many years, teachers thought they were teaching children to comprehend text by asking questions. Although it is true that questions may be used to teach, Durkin (1978, 1981a) found that the preponderance of teacher questions were used as comprehension evaluation and assessment rather than as comprehension instruction.

Figure 6.24   B. Bloom's (1956) taxonomy of the cognitive domain

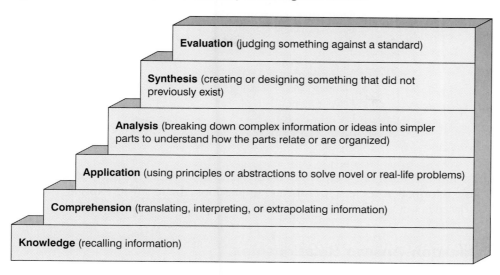

Herber (1978) asserted that the development of questioning taxonomies was an attempt to consolidate and simplify the task of teaching reading comprehension by reducing the long and elaborate lists of comprehension skills found in basal readers. During the past several decades, a variety of questioning taxonomies such as B. Bloom's (1956), T. Barrett's (1972), and Taba's (1975) taxonomies were published along with impassioned appeals for teachers to ask more higher level questions. Figure 6.24 illustrates Bloom's taxonomy.

In addition to simplifying the task of teaching reading comprehension to the act of asking questions at a few levels of thinking, taxonomies were thought to help teachers develop a sensitivity to the levels of questions they asked. Research of the day supported the proposition that teachers' questions and the questions in basal teacher's manuals were mostly lower level questions. By observing and classifying teacher questions, Guszak (1967) found that 70% of questions teachers asked during reading instruction were at a literal, recognition, or recall level. Such questions, he contended, did not foster higher level thought processes such as evaluation, application, generalization, or synthesis questions. In 1985, Shake and Allington found that the ratio of higher level to lower level questions had not changed markedly since 1967.

Others have challenged the idea that asking higher level questions leads to higher level thinking abilities (Gall et al., 1975). More recently, Farrar (1984) has objected to the concept that higher level questions are necessarily better at disposing students toward higher level thinking. Although much can be and will be argued about asking higher level questions for some time into the future, the fact is that students remain unaided in developing strategies for answering the host of questions they encounter on a daily basis in schools.

Asking higher level questions does not necessarily lead to higher level thinking abilities.

Pearson and Johnson (1978) devised a three-level questioning taxonomy (Figure 6.25) describing the sources of information available to students for answering questions rather than describing levels of thought processes. These authors contend that teachers should help students answer questions—not just ask questions. The Pearson

Asking questions is not enough; teachers must help students learn how to answer questions.

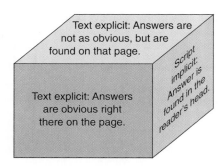

Figure 6.25   Pearson and Johnson (1978) questioning taxonomy

Text explicit: Answers are not as obvious, but are found on that page.

Text explicit: Answers are obvious right there on the page.

Script implicit: Answer is found in the reader's head.

and Johnson taxonomy helps students and teachers realize that they can draw on two basic information sources for answering questions: the text (text explicit), their own knowledge (script implicit), or a combination of both sources (text implicit).

Question–Answer Relationships

QARs help students learn to identify types of questions asked and where to get information necessary to answer questions.

A direct application of Pearson and Johnson's (1978) questioning taxonomy for training students to successfully navigate the obstacle course of questions encountered in school classrooms can be found in Raphael's **question–answer relationships (QARs)** (1982, 1986). The purpose of QARs is to teach children how to identify the types of questions asked of them as well as to determine the appropriate sources of information necessary to answer those questions. Raphael identified four QARs to help children identify the connection between the type of question asked and the information sources necessary and available for answering questions: (a) right there, (b) think and search (*putting it together*), (c) author and you, and (d) on my own. Figure 6.26 shows examples of each type of QAR.

Instruction using QARs begins by explaining to students that when they answer questions about reading, there are basically two places they can look to get information: *in the book* and *in my head.* This concept should be practiced with the students by reading aloud a text, asking questions, and having the students explain or show where they found their answers. Once students understand the two-category approach, expand the *in the book* category to include *right there* and *putting it together.* The distinction between these two categories should be practiced by reading several texts along with discussion. For older students, Raphael (1986) suggests that students be shown specific strategies for locating the answers to *right there* questions; these include looking in a single sentence or looking in two sentences connected by a pronoun. For *putting it together* questions, students can be asked to focus their attention on the structure of the text, such as cause–effect, problem–solution, listing–example, compare–contrast, and explanation.

Next, instruction should be directed toward two subcategories within the *in my head* category: (a) *author and me,* and (b) *on my own.* Here again, these categories can be practiced with the whole class by reading a text aloud, answering the questions, and discussing the sources of information. To expand this training, students can be asked to identify the types of questions asked in their basal readers, workbooks, content area texts, and tests as well as to determine the sources of information needed to answer these questions. Students may be informed that certain types of questions are asked before and after reading a text. For example, questions asked be-

Figure 6.26   Illustrations to explain question–answer relationships (QARs) to students

In the Book QARs

Right There
The answer is in the text, usually easy to find. The words used to make up the question and words used to answer the question are **Right There** in the same sentence.

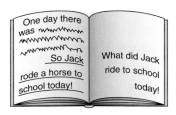

In My Head QARs

Author and You
The answer is *not* in the story. You need to think about what you already know, what the author tells you in the text, and how it fits together.

**Think and Search
(Putting It Together)**
The answer is in the story, but you need to put together different story parts to find it. Words for the question and words for the answer are not found in the same sentence. They come from different parts of the text.

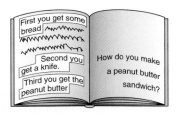

On My Own
The answer is *not* in the story. You can even answer the question without reading the story. You need to use your own experience.

Figure from "Teaching Question Answer Relationships, Revisited" by Taffy E. Raphael, *The Reading Teacher,* February 1986. Reprinted with permission of Taffy E. Raphael and the International Reading Association.

fore reading typically ask students to activate their own knowledge. Therefore, questions asked before reading will usually be *on my own* questions. However, questions asked after reading will make use of information found in the text. Therefore, questions asked after reading will typically focus on the *right there, putting it together,* and *author and me* types of questions.

Using the QAR question-answering training strategy is useful for at least two other purposes. First, it can help teachers examine their own questioning with respect to the types of questions and the information sources students need to use to answer their questions. Second, some teachers using QARs to monitor their own questioning behaviors may find that they are asking only *right there* types of questions. This discovery should lead teachers to ask questions that require the use of other information sources. Students can use QARs to initiate self-questioning before and after reading. Children may be asked to write questions for each of the QAR categories and then answer these questions. Finally, a poster displaying the information the class has gathered can heighten children's and teachers' awareness to the types of questions asked and the information sources available for answering those questions.

Raphael and Pearson (1982) provided evidence that training students to recognize these question–answer relationships resulted in improved comprehension and question-answering behavior. In addition, evidence also shows that teachers find the QAR strategies productive for improving their own questioning behaviors.

Asking Prereading Versus Postreading Questions

Prequestions focus the reader's attention on relevant items, whereas postquestions have a "reviewing" effect on students' recall.

The amount of attention a reader can give to remembering what has been read is limited. Requiring students to read to remember everything is simply not possible and interferes with memory (F. Smith, 1985). Tierney and Cunningham (1984) indicate that questions asked before reading can both restrict and facilitate readers' recall. When specific information is to be recalled from reading a selection, detail questions should be asked before reading. Prequestions focus the reader's attention on relevant items while screening out other less pertinent information. However, if extracting specific information from the text is not the objective, prequestions can restrict the reader's search to specifics in the text, thus leading to a fragmented understanding of the entirety of the text. If students are to read to get the gist or plot of a story, questions are best asked after reading. Postquestions have a "reviewing" effect on students' recall. Obviously, not all questions fall neatly into these two dichotomous categories. Rather, for questions to be used effectively for learning from text, teachers must make sure that the questioning practices employed are consistent with their instructional goals.

Reciprocal Questioning

*Refer to chapter 4 for an in-depth discussion of **ReQuest**.*

Students must at some point become responsible for their own learning (Manzo, 1969). A major goal of comprehension is to stimulate students to monitor their own comprehension (Baker & Brown, 1984). Teachers can serve as a much-needed model of questioning; but perhaps even more important, they can stimulate children to think about their own thinking and comprehension. One way to get students to think about their own comprehension is to help them to ask their own questions about reading (see the preceding discussion of metacognition). Singer (1978a) and Shanklin and Rhodes (1989) have declared that the goal of teacher questioning should be student-generated questions. Although this procedure was designed to be used one-on-one, reciprocal questioning (ReQuest) can be modified to involve whole groups by pairing students off for questioning. Carefully supervised by a caring teacher, ReQuest has been shown to improve reading comprehension (Dreher & Gambrell, 1985; Tierney, Readence, & Dishner, 1985).

Wait Time

Teachers can improve their questioning by waiting at least 3 seconds after asking a question before rephrasing, redirecting, or answering the question.

With the current emphasis on "pacing and content coverage" in the teacher-effectiveness literature, teachers may become tempted to embrace a "faster is better" teaching philosophy. Although these characteristics of "effective" teaching are important, we must not forget that not all children operate in the fast lane. Kagan (1966) coined the concept of *cognitive tempo,* which implies that one student might be an impulsive thinker, quick to respond, perhaps disregarding accuracy, whereas another student might be a more reflective thinker, slow to respond, but more concerned about accuracy. A fast-paced classroom environment, especially related to the pacing of questioning, may in fact lend itself to one cognitive tempo and not another, thus unintentionally impairing the thinker with a slower cognitive tempo.

In 1974, Rowe investigated the pacing of teacher questioning during science lessons. Her primary unit of observation centered on the length of the interval between the time a teacher asked a question and then expected a response, redirected the question to another student, or rephrased the original question; This interval was called **wait time.** Rowe found that the average teacher wait time was only 0.9 seconds. On the other hand, Rowe observed that when teachers allowed at least a 3-second wait time, both teacher questioning characteristics and student answering behavior improved appreciably. Improved teacher questioning characteristics included asking fewer but higher quality questions. Flexibility toward student responses considered acceptable increased, and the teachers' expectations for slower students changed. On the other hand, student responses were also affected positively by the increased wait time: Shy and slow students answered more questions, students' answers to questions were more elaborated, and greater confidence in their answers to questions was reflected in their vocal inflection. Knowing that a wait time of only 3 seconds holds the potential to improve both teacher questioning and student question-answering behavior, teachers should make concerted efforts to observe a 3-second wait time.

Questions Can Help Students Reconstruct a Model of the Text for Remembering

Beck and McKeown (1981) and Sadow (1982) suggested that teachers follow a rational model of the text for questioning. The rational model of text proposed to guide questioning was based on story grammars and was called *story grammar mapping* (Mandler & Johnson, 1977). Subsequent to their proposal, Beck, Omanson, and McKeown (1982) provided evidence that mapping the questioning of a story using a story grammar produced improved reading comprehension.

Teachers should ask questions about the major elements of a story and the order of the story.

At first glance, story grammars like that in Figure 6.27 look very similar to the major characteristics traditionally used to summarize a story's plot. According to Rumelhart's (1975) story grammar, the major elements of a story grammar are setting, problem, goal, events, and resolution. Questions about the setting generally request information about the time, locale, or props used in the story. Questions about the beginning of the story center around the problem that precipitated the initiation of an event in the story. Questions concerning the reaction to the problem examine the response of the protagonist in the story to the beginning event. A goal question asks the reader to provide information about the motives or objectives of the story characters. An event question asks that the reader provide information about what the story characters do to achieve the goal. To evaluate the success or failure of the characters' planned efforts to achieve a goal, readers can be asked questions regarding the outcome. A question about the ending can be asked to cause the reader to draw a conclusion or make a final judgment about the story episode(s).

Evidence from research on story grammars suggests that good readers have well-developed internal representations of story structure, whereas poor readers do not

Figure 6.27   Story grammar map of "Jack and the Beanstalk"

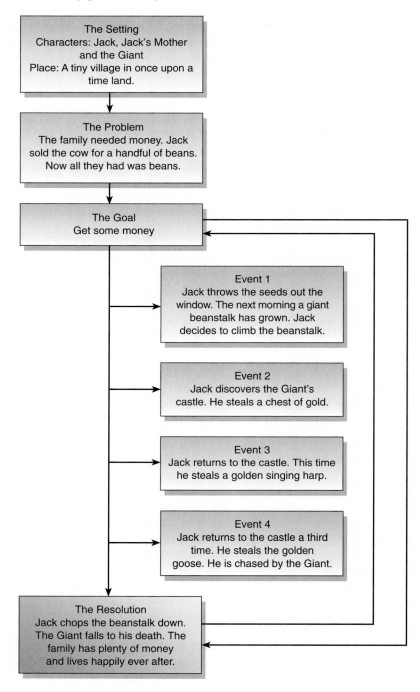

The Setting
Characters: Jack, Jack's Mother and the Giant
Place: A tiny village in once upon a time land.

The Problem
The family needed money. Jack sold the cow for a handful of beans. Now all they had was beans.

The Goal
Get some money

Event 1
Jack throws the seeds out the window. The next morning a giant beanstalk has grown. Jack decides to climb the beanstalk.

Event 2
Jack discovers the Giant's castle. He steals a chest of gold.

Event 3
Jack returns to the castle. This time he steals a golden singing harp.

Event 4
Jack returns to the castle a third time. He steals the golden goose. He is chased by the Giant.

The Resolution
Jack chops the beanstalk down. The Giant falls to his death. The family has plenty of money and lives happily ever after.

(Whaley, 1981). The motivation for using a story grammar in the design of questioning is to help increase readers' awareness of story structure and to provide a logical framework both for guiding teacher questioning and for students' remembering—all of which lead to improved comprehension.

Increasing Student Involvement

During the typical reading lesson, students respond one at a time to teacher questions. But what might happen to student question-answering behavior if *every* child could respond to *every* question? First, students could become more actively involved in answering questions. Second, teachers could observe the correctness of all student responses in lieu of sampling only a selected few. Third, shy students could answer questions without having to risk becoming the focus of attention. These few benefits alone should be enough to motivate teachers toward more frequent use of choral response methods in questioning.

Choral response to questions increases student involvement and allows for on-the-spot evaluation of all students' comprehension.

Hopkins (1979) recommended several ways teachers can make use of whole-group response methods. For word recognition, students could be given *yes/no* cards to respond to questions asked about words. *True/false* cards could be used to assess students' comprehension of the various aspects of stories. Stick figures could be used to answer questions about story characters.

Extensions of Hopkins's (1979) ideas for choral response to questions include the use of lap-sized chalkboards or magic slates that can be erased and reused to respond to questions. Another advantage to chalkboards and magic slates is that they need not be prepared before students use them, thus saving teacher time.

Teachers who use choral response methods soon recognize that students become more actively engaged in the reading lesson, and teachers receive more extensive feedback about the state of students' comprehension. In sum, both teacher and learner benefit from choral response techniques used during reading instruction.

HELPING STUDENTS WITH SPECIAL COMPREHENSION NEEDS

Reciprocal Teaching

Palincsar and Brown (1985) designed and evaluated an approach to improve the reading comprehension and comprehension monitoring of students who scored 2 years below grade level on standardized tests of reading ability and reading comprehension. Their results suggest a teaching strategy called **reciprocal teaching** that is useful for helping students who have difficulties with comprehension and comprehension monitoring. Essentially, this strategy involves teachers and students in exchanging roles, which increases student involvement in the lesson. The reciprocal teaching lesson is composed of the following four phases or steps:

Reciprocal teaching *is a useful strategy for helping students who have difficulties with comprehension and comprehension monitoring.*

1. *Prediction:* Students are asked to predict from the title and pictures the possible content of the text. The teacher records the predictions.
2. *Question generation:* Students generate purpose questions after reading a predetermined segment of the text, such as a paragraph or page.
3. *Summarizing:* Students write a brief summary for the text by starting with "This paragraph was about . . ." (p. 299). Summarizing helps students capture the gist of the text.

4. *Clarifying:* Students and teacher discuss a variety of reasons a text may be difficult or confusing, such as difficult vocabulary, poor text organization, unfamiliar content, or lack of cohesion. Students are then instructed in a variety of comprehension fix-up or repair strategies (as described earlier in this chapter).

Once the teacher has modeled this process with several segments of text, he or she assigns one of the students (preferably a good student) to assume the role of teacher for the next segment of text. While acting in the student role, the teacher can also provide appropriate prompts and feedback when necessary. When the next segment of text is completed, the student assigned as teacher asks another student to assume that role.

Teachers who use reciprocal teaching to help students with comprehension difficulties should follow four simple guidelines suggested by Palincsar and Brown (1985). First, assess student difficulties and provide reading materials appropriate to students' decoding abilities. Second, use reciprocal teaching for at least 30 minutes per day for 15 to 20 consecutive days. Third, model frequently and provide corrective feedback. Finally, monitor student progress regularly and individually to determine whether the instruction is having the intended effect. Palincsar and Brown (1985) have reported positive results for this intervention procedure by demonstrating dramatic changes in students' ineffective reading behaviors.

With minor changes, reciprocal teaching can be used with narrative as well as expository texts.

Although reciprocal teaching was originally intended for use with expository text, this intervention strategy can be used with narrative texts by focusing discussion and reading on the major elements of stories. By using reciprocal teaching with narrative texts, teachers can intervene earlier with those who are experiencing difficulties with comprehension and comprehension monitoring rather than delaying intervention until expository text is typically encountered in the intermediate years.

HELPING STUDENTS WITH SPECIAL CULTURAL AND LANGUAGE NEEDS

Contextual Diagrams

Contextual diagrams *allow LEP students to learn needed vocabulary before entering an unfamiliar societal setting.*

For many second language learners, pictures or diagrams of social or situational settings wherein objects and actions are labeled are of significant help for acquiring ability to speak, listen, read, and write in a largely unfamiliar language (Devillar, Faltis, & Cummins, 1994). The purpose of **contextual diagrams,** such as the one shown in Figure 6.28, is to allow students to learn language for settings outside the school classroom. Diagrams of the kitchen, bedroom, or bathroom at home can help students begin to learn to associate second language terms with familiar or even somewhat unfamiliar objects in another setting. Diagrams of stores, libraries, mechanic shops, or hospitals wherein objects and actions are labeled can move students' potential for language comprehension well beyond the physical and social confines of the school classroom. Hence, diagrams of whole, meaningful, and naturally occurring situations serve a purpose of expanding the language-learning contexts of English as second language (ESL) and limited English proficiency (LEP) students in schools.

Active Listening to First- and Second-Language Literature

Walters and Gunderson (1985) studied the effects on reading achievement of listening to stories read aloud in students' first and second languages. Results from the 16-week study showed that children benefited from listening to stories read

Figure 6.28 Situational context diagram

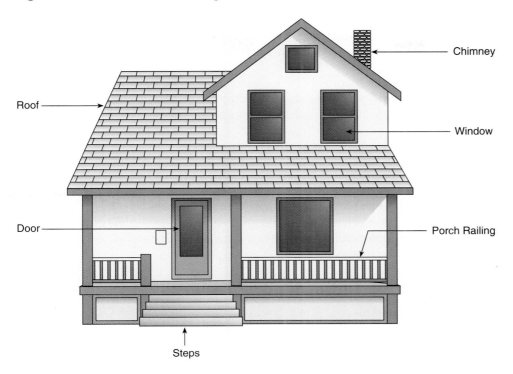

aloud in both the first and second languages. For students with limited first-language proficiency, listening to stories read in the first language helped them to understand that print represents spoken language (Gunderson, 1991). On the other hand, students with LEP who also had an ability to read in the first language learned how terms from the first and second languages correlate to one another (Heald-Taylor, 1991).

The most important part of active listening involves the selection of material that is interesting to the students. For some beginning students, wordless picture books are a good place to begin. Read the story or look at the book in small, pre-planned sections. If possible, read so that the students can see the print as it is read. In the case of using wordless picture books, students could dictate the print that tells a story to match the pictures. The print can then be recorded so that students can return to the book later and read their own dictated language, telling the story of the pictures. This may mean that the text will need to be enlarged for some groups. However, the active listening strategy can be used with individual students as well.

When using high-interest books selected for reading aloud, stop at strategic points and ask students, "What will happen next?" As a follow-up question, ask students to explain why they think a particular event will take place next in the story. It may even be appropriate when a story employs a repeated pattern, such as "Little Pig, Little Pig, Let me _____ _____," for the teacher to stop and invite the students to complete the pattern orally. In this way, students are drawn into careful and continuous active listening while hearing a text read aloud.

Active listening has been shown effective for both LEP and non-LEP students.

Summary

Teaching comprehension, unlike testing comprehension, involves teaching behaviors such as explaining, demonstrating, and defining. Teachers must not assume they are teaching children to comprehend text when they mention or assign comprehension skill practice sheets.

Schema theory, a theory about one's storehouse of prior knowledge and experience and how it influences the ability to comprehend text, is a simplified model of text comprehension involving searching, applying, selecting and evaluating, and composing.

The Gradual Release of Responsibility model of instruction provides a comprehensive framework for effective comprehension instruction. Other effective instructional strategies for improving comprehension of narrative text and expository text as well as focusing on comprehending text parts such as sentences, words, and typographic features were highlighted throughout the chapter.

Finally, several effective lesson strategies dealing with building background for reading, effective questioning strategies, and helping students with comprehension difficulties were discussed.

Concept Applications

In the Classroom

1. Examine a basal reader scope and sequence listing of comprehension skills. Choose two skills for "teaching" and provide a written description of how you will "teach" rather than "test" these skills.
2. Pick a favorite story. Describe the story grammar parts of your selection. Make a story map or a schema story lesson, or design a story grammar questioning map.
3. Select a chapter from an elementary science, health, math, or social studies text. Identify the organizational pattern used by the authors. Make a pattern guide.
4. Choose a literature or basal textbook selection. Design two metacognitive monitoring lessons of the 10 possible lessons described by Baumann et al. (1993) in this chapter. Be sure to include each of the lesson parts, that is, (a) verbal explanation, (b) teacher modeling, (c) guided practice, and (d) independent practice.
5. Choose a 250-word passage from a story or expository text. Show how you could use two cloze techniques on this passage by preparing two cloze lessons.
6. Make some group response cards or boards for use in your classroom to respond to questions.
7. Evaluate the recommendations for background building in a basal reader. If necessary, describe how you would alter the recommendations.

In the Field

1. Make arrangements to visit a public school classroom. Carefully observe and record the time devoted to teaching versus testing reading comprehension.

2. Visit with a classroom teacher about the skills he or she thinks are important for helping students become skilled readers. Summarize these views in a brief essay.

3. Devise a lesson to train children to use QARs, then try it out in an elementary school classroom. Reflect on this experience by making an entry in your professional journal.

4. Prepare a reciprocal teaching lesson. Make arrangements to visit a local resource or Title 1 classroom to teach your lesson.

5. Prepare a situational context diagram. Make arrangements to work with LEP or ESL students in an elementary school classroom. Use your diagram to teach a language lesson and report on your findings.

Recommended Readings

Alvermann, D. E., Dillon, D. R., & O'Brien, D. G. (1987). *Using discussion to promote reading comprehension.* Newark, DE: International Reading Association.

Bromley, K., DeVitis, L. I., & Modlo, M. (1995). *Graphic Organizers: Visual strategies for active learning.* New York: Scholastic.

Carr, E., Dewitz, P., & Patberg, J. (1989). Using cloze for inference training with expository text. *The Reading Teacher, 40,* 380–385.

Glazer, S. M. (1992). *Reading comprehension: Self-monitoring strategies to develop independent readers.* New York: Scholastic.

Irwin, J. W. (1986). *Teaching reading comprehension processes.* Upper Saddle River, NJ: Prentice Hall.

Johnston, P. H. (1983). *Reading comprehension assessment: A cognitive basis.* Newark, DE: International Reading Association.

McNeil, J. D. (1987). *Reading comprehension: New directions for classroom practice.* Glenview, IL: Scott, Foresman.

Pearson, P. D., & Johnson, D. D. (1978). *Teaching reading comprehension.* New York: Holt, Rinehart and Winston.

Robinson, H. A., Faroane, V., Hittleman, D. R., & Unruh, E. (1990). *Reading comprehension instruction 1783–1987: A review of trends and research.* Newark, DE: International Reading Association.

Wilson, R. M., & Gambrell, L. B. (1988). *Reading comprehension in the elementary school.* Reading, MA: Allyn & Bacon.

Acquiring Vocabulary:

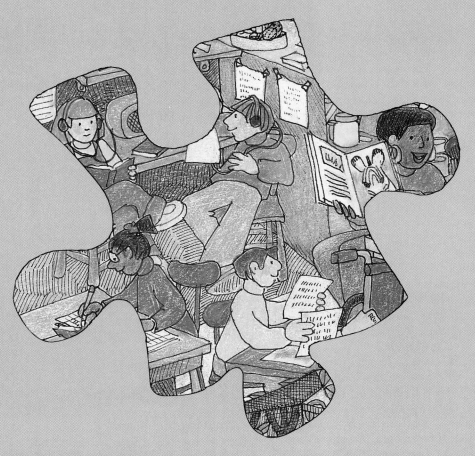

Focus Questions

When you are finished studying this chapter, you should be able to answer these questions:

1. What four hypotheses describe how vocabulary is learned?
2. What conclusions can be drawn from the research on vocabulary learning?
3. What four principles are identified in this chapter to make vocabulary instruction effective?
4. What are three strategies that teachers can use to assist students in building background knowledge and concepts?
5. What three strategies can students use to acquire new vocabulary on their own?
6. How does the study of various word functions (e.g., synonyms, euphemisms, onomatopoeia) enable students to better communicate and understand the messages of others?

Words for Reading and Writing

Key Concepts

Instrumental Hypothesis
Aptitude Hypothesis
Knowledge Hypothesis
Access Hypothesis
Principles for Effective Vocabulary
    Instruction
Sight Words
Word Banks
Cluing Technique
RIVET
Predict-O-Gram
Frayer Model
Opin
Word Cards

Structured Overview
Semantic Maps
Making Words
Semantic Feature Analysis
Exclusion Brainstorming
Concept Ladder
Free-Form Outlines
Capsule Vocabulary
Recasts
Word Map
Synonyms
Antonyms
Euphemisms
Village English Activity

Recognizing and understanding written vocabulary is essential to reading. Indeed, unless children are able to understand word meanings as they read, the process is reduced to mindless decoding (Fountas & Pinnell, 1996). Children who come to school with thousands of "words in their head"—words they can hear, understand, and use in their daily lives—are already on the path to learning success (Allington & Cunningham, 1996). Similarly, children who have small listening, speaking, and reading vocabularies—from what could be termed "language deprived backgrounds"—must receive immediate attention if they are to have any real chance at reading success (National Research Council, 1998).

HYPOTHESES ABOUT VOCABULARY LEARNING

For many years, linguists, psychologists, educational researchers, psycholinguists, and others have concerned themselves with the questions of how children learn new words. Frankly, this puzzle is yet to be fully pieced together. Several logical hypotheses have come forward in recent years, however, that may shed some light on this language learning phenomenon. Three views have been articulated by R. C. Anderson and Freebody (1981) and a fourth by Mezynski (1983), which we summarize in the following sections.

The Instrumental Hypothesis

Instrumentalists believe performance on vocabulary tests mirrors word knowledge.

It will probably not surprise you that some hypotheses concerning vocabulary learning are often linked to how well students do on standardized vocabulary tests; the **instrumental hypothesis** (R. C. Anderson & Freebody, 1981) is one such view. It suggests that children who do well on a vocabulary test are likely to know more words in school textbooks and other readings than children who do not do as well on these tests. The important assumption here is that knowing words directly assists students in reading comprehension.

The Aptitude Hypothesis

Aptitude *is the ability to learn words quickly.*

Another view drawn, at least in part, from how students perform on vocabulary tests is the **aptitude hypothesis.** Vocabulary aptitude is related to the ability of students to learn words quickly. The belief is that people with large vocabularies comprehend better and possess superior mental agility or quicker minds (R. C. Anderson & Freebody, 1981), possibly as a result of heredity. In the classroom, this means that with the same amount of exposure to information, students with high vocabulary aptitude will learn more new words than other students.

The Knowledge Hypothesis

Consider ways life experiences influence reading comprehension.

The **knowledge hypothesis** states that firsthand experience with the concept under study is directly related to reading comprehension (R. C. Anderson & Freebody, 1981). For instance, a child who grows up working in the family sporting goods business is likely to understand that the word *spinner* has something to do with fishing. This same kind of firsthand knowledge will probably help this child understand a fishing story in a favorite magazine that contains other fishing vocabulary such as *dry fly, tackle,* or *leader.* The knowledge hypothesis differs significantly from the instrumental hypothesis, even though they appear to be virtually the same at first glance. The instrumental hypothesis emphasizes individual word meanings, but the knowledge hypothesis is directly related to the development of knowledge structures, or schemas (see chapter 3 and chapter 6 for a discussion of schema theory). The knowledge hypothesis also provides us with some ideas on how vocabulary is learned.

The Access Hypothesis

The ability to think of correct word meanings is crucial to reading comprehension.

Mezynski (1983) describes the **access hypothesis,** which essentially states that aptitude is related to a blend of trainable subskills. In other words, children can be taught how to learn new vocabulary. Educators and researchers subscribing to this hypothesis have as their goal a kind of automatic behavior or *automaticity* (LaBerge & Samuels, 1985) in reading. According to Mezynski, the amount of practice we offer students is an important factor in word learning.

Which Hypothesis Is Correct?

We tend to favor the knowledge hypothesis, based on comprehension research during the 1980s. Truthfully, however, it is difficult to say that one, or any, of the preceding views is entirely correct. A review of contemporary vocabulary research can further inform teachers as to ways they can best help children expand their knowledge of words in print. In the next section, we continue this discussion and provide a brief review of the more important findings that can help you plan instruction.

The search for a workable hypothesis has led researchers to some interesting conclusions.

RESEARCH ON VOCABULARY LEARNING

As one reviews the most recent research on vocabulary learning and reading, one conclusion becomes crystal clear: Reading and writing, as meaning construction activities, are dependent on words. Indeed, all good readers have a large store of high-frequency words they can read and spell instantly and automatically (Allington & Cunningham, 1996). So what do we know about vocabulary learning? To partially answer this question, here are some key findings supported by recent research (Adams, 1990; Allington & Cunningham, 1996; Guthrie, 1982; Krashen, 1993; McKeown, Beck, Omanson, & Pople, 1985; Nagy, Herman, & Anderson, 1985; National Research Council [NRC], 1998; Stahl & Fairbanks, 1985; Stahl, Hare, Sinatra, & Gregory, 1991; Stahl & Jacobson, 1986; Templeton, 1997):

- Vocabulary instruction results in an increase in word knowledge and reading comprehension.
- Children from disadvantaged backgrounds where books and language-oriented games are less evident are at greater risk for reading failure.
- The most effective methods of vocabulary instruction include (a) information about word meanings, (b) showing vocabulary in a variety of contexts, and (c) multiple exposures of the new word.
- Explicit training on the strategic use of context for understanding word meanings is important.
- Adult–child shared book reading stimulates verbal interaction and contributes to language (especially vocabulary) development.
- Parents can do much to help their children succeed by taking them on vacations, answering their questions about new experiences, and encouraging regular pleasure reading time in the home.
- Repeated readings of familiar books and passages (e.g., songs and poetry) can help students in their vocabulary learning.
- Memorizing long lists of isolated words is a relatively ineffective way to teach new vocabulary. In fact, students learn new vocabulary some 10 times faster by reading than through intensive vocabulary instruction with word lists (Nagy, Herman, & Anderson, 1985; Krashen, 1993).

Quality vocabulary teaching results in improved reading comprehension.

Students learn new vocabulary much quicker through daily reading than by memorization of word lists.

PRINCIPLES FOR EFFECTIVE VOCABULARY INSTRUCTION

From results of the research cited previously, as well as that conducted by Stahl (1986) and Rasinski (1998), we have developed a list of principles for effective vocabulary instruction for teachers to consider.

Principle 1:   Vocabulary is learned best through *direct,* hands-on experience.

Context helps readers choose the correct meaning for multiple-meaning words.

The old adage that "experience is the best teacher" is certainly true in vocabulary learning. The next best way to learn new vocabulary is through indirect, vicarious experiences through daily reading in interesting and varied texts (Rasinski, 1998). Marilyn Jager Adams (1990) put it this way:

> The best way to build children's visual vocabulary is to have them read meaningful words in meaningful contexts. The more meaningful reading that children do, the larger will be their repertoires of meanings, the greater their sensitivity to orthographic structure, and the stronger, better refined, and more productive will be their associations between words and meanings. (p. 156)

Principle 2:   Teachers should offer both *definitions* and *context* during vocabulary instruction.

As children learn new words, they do so in two ways. First, students learn basic definitions or information that helps determine the connections of the new word to known words (i.e., elaboration). This step can be accomplished by simply providing the definition, building with students semantic maps linking the known with the new, and through other comparisons such as synonyms, antonyms, classification schemes, word roots, affixes.

Second, context information has to do with knowing the basic core definition of a word and how it varies, or is changed, in different texts. For example, the word *run* is generally thought of as a verb meaning "to move swiftly." When looking for this simple word in the dictionary, one quickly realizes that the word *run* has approximately 50 definitions! There is the word *run,* as in "running a race"; "a run of bad luck"; or the "run" women sometimes get in their hosiery. Context helps the reader know which definition is intended by the author. In fact, without context, it is impossible to say with certainty which meaning of the word *run* is intended. Thus, it is important for teachers to help students understand both the *definitional* and *contextual* relations of words. Vocabulary instruction should include both aspects if reading comprehension is to benefit.

Principle 3:   Effective vocabulary instruction must include a depth of learning component as well as a breadth of word knowledge.

Deep processing connects new vocabulary with students' background knowledge.

Depth of learning, or "deep processing" of vocabulary, has two potential meanings: relating the word to information the student already knows (elaboration), and spending time on the task of learning new words (expansion). Stahl (1986) defines three levels of processing for vocabulary instruction:

1. *Association processing:* Students learn simple associations through synonyms and word associations.

2. *Comprehension processing:* Students move beyond simple associations by doing something with the association, such as fitting the word into a sentence blank, classifying the word with other words, or finding antonyms.

3. *Generation processing:* Students use the comprehended association to generate a new or novel product (sometimes called *generative comprehension*). This process could involve a restatement of the definition in the student's own words, creating a novel sentence using the word correctly in a clear context, or comparing the definition to the student's personal experiences. One caution relates to the generation of sentences by students: Sometimes students generate sentences without really processing the information deeply, as with students who begin each sentence with "This is a . . ." (Pearson, 1985; Stahl, 1986).

Principle 4: Students need to have *multiple exposures* to new reading vocabulary words.

Vocabulary learning requires repetition. To learn words thoroughly, students need to see, hear, and use words many times in many contexts (Rasinski, 1998). Providing students with multiple exposures in varied contexts appears to significantly improve reading comprehension. The amount of time spent reading these new words also seems to be a relevant factor for improving comprehension.

Notice that multiple exposures to new vocabulary improve comprehension.

Which Words Should We Teach?

Where and how do students acquire new vocabulary? The truth is, there are many sources for learning new words and some of them may surprise you—at least, just a bit. To illustrate the point, here are some selected statistics revealing the sources of rare words found, and we presume learned by students, in various language and text forms (A. E. Cunningham & Stanovich, 1998; Rasinski, 1998):

Language or text source	Number of "rare" (uncommon) words per 1,000
Adult speech (expert testimony)	28.4
Adult speech (college graduates to friends)	17.3
Prime time adult television	22.7
Mister Rogers and *Sesame Street*	2.0
Children's books—Preschool	16.3
Children's book—Elementary	30.9
Comic books	53.5
Popular magazines	65.7
Newspapers	68.3
Adult books	52.7
Scientific article abstracts	128.0

Were you surprised by any of these findings? How about the number of rare words used by college graduates in their conversations with friends compared to the number commonly found in comic books!? Or, for that matter, the number of uncommon words found in comic books compared to elementary children's books? Perhaps there is a case to be made for daily reading for children in self-selected books—including comics and popular magazines!

M. McKeown and Beck (1988) have addressed an important issue in their research: *Which vocabulary should be taught in elementary classrooms?* They point out that one problem with traditional vocabulary instruction in basal readers has been the equal treatment of all categories of words. As an example, a mythology selection in a basal reader about Arachne, who loved to weave, gives the word *loom* as much attention as the word *agreement.* McKeown and Beck point out that although the word *loom* may be helpful in understanding more about spinning, it is a word of relatively low use compared to the word *agreement,* which is key to understanding the story and of much higher utility as students move into adult life.

Not all words are created equal, especially in elementary classrooms. As McKeown and Beck (1988) explained:

> The choice of which words to teach and what kind of attention to give them depends on a variety of factors, such as importance of the words for understanding the selection, relationship to specific domains of knowledge, general utility, and relationship to other lessons and classroom events. (p. 45)

In the end, the words you select for teaching should have high utility, facilitate concept development, as well as contribute to greater spelling and orthographic knowledge. A logical place to begin vocabulary instruction is the teaching of *sight words,* the subject of the next section.

When selecting new words to teach, consider the importance of the word to understanding the selection.

DEVELOPING SIGHT WORDS

Sight words occur frequently in most texts and account for a majority of written words.

Understanding text relies in part on the immediate recognition of often-used words, or **sight words.** Studies of print have found that just 109 words account for upwards of 50% of all words in student textbooks, and a total of only 5,000 words accounts for about 90% of the words in student texts (Adams 1990b; J. B. Carroll, Davies, & Richman, 1971). Knowledge of these high-frequency words logically can help the fluency of readers. Many of these words, such as *the, from, but, because, that,* and *this,* sometimes called *structure words,* carry little meaning but do affect the flow and coherence of the text being read. The actual meaning of the text depends on the ready knowledge of less frequent, or *lexical words,* such as *automobile, aristocrat, pulley, streetcar, Martin Luther King,* and *phantom.* Adams et al. (1991) state that

> while the cohesion and connectivity of English text is owed most to its frequent words (e.g., *it, that, this, and, because, when, while*), its meaning depends disproportionately on its less frequent words (e.g., *doctor, fever, infection, medicine, penicillin, Alexander, Fleming, melon, mold, poison, bacteria, antibiotic, protect, germs, disease*). (p. 394)

An important question for teachers is, how do we go about helping students acquire a large knowledge of words they can recognize immediately on sight? Word banks are a strategy and tool that we have had much success with in developing sight words.

Figure 7.1 A word bank

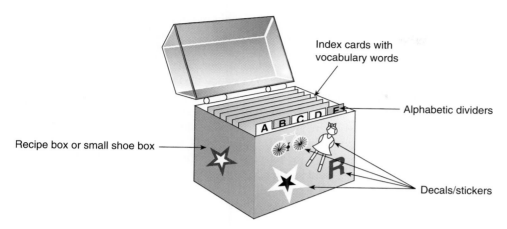

A word bank is a box in which children keep/file new words they
are learning. The words are usually written in isolation on one side
of the card, and in a sentence on the back of the card (usually
with a picture clue).

Example:

Word Banks

Word banks are used to help students collect and review sight words. They also
can be used as personal dictionaries. A word bank is simply a student-constructed
box, file, or notebook in which newly discovered words are stored and reviewed. In
the early grades, teachers often collect small shoe boxes from local stores for this
purpose. The children are asked at the beginning of the year to decorate the boxes
to make them their own. In the upper grades, more formal-looking word banks are
used to give an "adult" appearance; notebooks or recipe boxes are generally selected. Alphabetic dividers can also be used at all levels to facilitate the quick location of word bank words. Alphabetic dividers in the early grades also help students
rehearse and reinforce knowledge of alphabetical order. Figure 7.1 shows an example of a word bank.

Once students have word banks, the next problem for the teacher is helping students decide which words should be included and from what sources. At least four
sources can be considered for sight-word selection and inclusion in word banks. Each
is briefly discussed in the next section.

*Word banks help stu-
dents collect and use
new words for reading
and writing.*

Key Vocabulary

Silvia Ashton-Warner, in her popular book *Teacher* (1963), describes key vocabulary words as "organic," or words that come from within the child and his or her own experiences. Ashton-Warner states that key vocabulary words act as captions for important events in life that the child has experienced. The child comes to the teacher at an appointed time or during a group experience and indicates which words he or she would like to learn. For instance, the teacher may ask, "What word would you like to learn today?" The child responds with a word such as *police, ghost,* or *sing.* Ashton-Warner found that the most common categories of key vocabulary words for children were fear words (*dog, bull, kill, police*), sex (as she called them) or affection words (*love, kiss, sing, darling*), locomotion words (*bus, car, truck, jet*), and a *miscellaneous* category that generally reflects cultural and other considerations (*socks, frog, beer, Disneyland, Dallas Cowboys*).

Ashton-Warner (1963) calls key vocabulary "one-look words" because one look is usually all that is required for permanent learning to take place. The reason that these words seem so easy for children to learn is that they usually carry strong emotional significance for the children. Once the child has told the teacher a word he or she would like to learn, the teacher writes the word on an index card or a small piece of tag board using a dark marker. The student is then instructed to share the word with as many people as possible during the day. After the child has done so, the word is added to the word bank.

Basal Words

Many teachers are concerned that students will not learn high-frequency words if they do not use basal readers. Stories in basal readers tend to be written with high-frequency words, and publishers market their reading series describing that feature as a major selling point. Overreliance on high-frequency words, however, sometimes causes basal stories to seem stilted and unnatural. One remedy is for teachers to use randomly (or not use) adopted basals, trade books, or any language experience activities they please. Each week, they select several words from the high-frequency word lists offered by the basal to add to students' word banks. These words can then be used by children when needed in writing and other assignments. Basal words can be taught in a whole-group setting and reviewed periodically.

Figure 7.2 presents the Fry (1980) word list of the 300 most common words in print for teachers not having access to a basal series word list.

Basal Words for Bilingual Classrooms (Spanish)

Just as the most common words in print have been identified in English, high-frequency words have also been identified for Spanish (Cornejo, 1972). This popular word list is divided by grade and presented in Figure 7.3.

Discovery Words

During the course of a typical school day, students are exposed to many new words. These words are often discovered as a result of studies in the content areas. Words such as *experiment, algebra, social, enterprise, conquest, Bengal tiger, spider,* and *cocoon* find their way into students' listening and speaking vocabulary. Every effort

Figure 7.2 Fry New Instant Word List

The first 10 words make up about 24% of all written material, the first 100 words about 50% of all written material, and the first 300 about 65%.

1. the	44. each	87. who	130. through	173. home	216. never	259. walked
2. of	45. which	88. oil	131. much	174. us	217. started	260. white
3. and	46. she	89. its	132. before	175. move	218. city	261. sea
4. a	47. do	90. now	133. line	176. try	219. earth	262. began
5. to	48. how	91. find	134. right	177. kind	220. eyes	263. grow
6. in	49. their	92. long	135. too	178. hand	221. light	264. took
7. is	50. if	93. down	136. means	179. picture	222. thought	265. river
8. you	51. will	94. day	137. old	180. again	223. head	266. four
9. that	52. up	95. did	138. any	181. change	224. under	267. carry
10. it	53. other	96. get	139. same	182. off	225. story	268. state
11. he	54. about	97. come	140. tell	183. play	226. saw	269. once
12. was	55. out	98. made	141. boy	184. spell	227. left	270. book
13. for	56. many	99. may	142. following	185. air	228. don't	271. hear
14. on	57. then	100. part	143. came	186. away	229. few	272. stop
15. are	58. them	101. over	144. want	187. animals	230. while	273. without
16. as	59. these	102. new	145. show	188. house	231. along	274. second
17. with	60. so	103. sound	146. also	189. point	232. might	275. later
18. his	61. some	104. take	147. around	190. page	233. close	276. miss
19. they	62. her	105. only	148. form	191. letters	234. something	277. idea
20. I	63. would	106. little	149. three	192. mother	235. seemed	278. enough
21. at	64. make	107. work	150. small	193. answer	236. next	279. eat
22. be	65. like	108. know	151. set	194. found	237. hard	280. face
23. this	66. him	109. place	152. put	195. study	238. open	281. watch
24. have	67. into	110. years	153. end	196. still	239. example	282. far
25. from	68. time	111. live	154. does	197. learn	240. beginning	283. Indians
26. or	69. has	112. me	155. another	198. should	241. life	284. really
27. one	70. look	113. back	156. well	199. American	242. always	285. almost
28. had	71. two	114. give	157. large	200. world	243. those	286. let
29. by	72. more	115. most	158. must	201. high	244. both	287. above
30. words	73. write	116. very	159. big	202. every	245. paper	288. girl
31. but	74. go	117. after	160. even	203. near	246. together	289. some-
32. not	75. see	118. things	161. such	204. add	247. got	times
33. what	76. number	119. our	162. because	205. food	248. group	290. mountains
34. all	77. no	120. just	163. turned	206. between	249. often	291. cut
35. were	78. way	121. name	164. here	207. own	250. run	292. young
36. we	79. could	122. good	165. why	208. below	251. important	293. talk
37. when	80. people	123. sentence	166. asked	209. country	252. until	294. soon
38. your	81. my	124. man	167. went	210. plants	253. children	295. list
39. can	82. than	125. think	168. men	211. last	254. side	296. song
40. said	83. first	126. say	169. read	212. school	255. feet	297. being
41. there	84. water	127. great	170. need	213. father	256. car	298. leave
42. use	85. been	128. where	171. land	214. keep	257. miles	299. family
43. an	86. called	129. help	172. different	215. trees	258. night	300. it's

From "The New Instant Word List," by Edward Fry, *The Reading Teacher,* December 1980, pp. 284–289. Reprinted with permission of Edward Fry and the International Reading Association.

Figure 7.3   Cornejo's high-frequency word list for Spanish (graded)

Pre-Primer	Primer	1st	2nd	3rd	4th	5th
a	alto	bonita	ayer	amar	árbol	amistad
azul	flor	arriba	aqui	aquí	bandera	azucar
bajo	blusa	fruta	año	debajo	abeja	contento
mi	ella	globo	cerca	familia	escuela	corazón
mesa	ir	estar	desde	fiesta	fácil	compleaños
pan	leche	café	donde	grande	fuego	edad
mamá	más	letra	hacer	hermana	hacia	escribir
lado	niño	luna	hasta	jueves	idea	felicidad
la	padre	luz	hijo	lápiz	jardín	guitarra
papá	por	muy	hoy	miércoles	llegar	estrella
me	si	noche	leer	once	manzana	igual
no	tan	nombre	libro	quince	muñeca	invierno
esa	sobre	nosotros	martes	sábado	naranja	orquesta
el	sin	nunca	mejor	semana	saludar	primavera
en	tras	ojo	mucho	silla	sueño	recordar
cuna	color	pelota	oir	sobrino	señorita	respeto
dos	al	porque	papel	vivir	tierra	tijeras
mi	día	rojo	paz	zapato	traer	último
de	bien	té	quien	tarde	ventana	querer
los	chico	taza	usted	traje	queso	otoño

From Cornejo, R. (1972). *Spanish High Frequency Word List.* Austin, TX: Southwestern Educational Development Laboratory.

should be made to add these discovery words to the word bank as they are discussed in their natural context. Such words often appear in new student compositions.

Function ("Four-Letter") Words

Many words are very difficult for students to learn because they carry no definable meaning. Typical words in this category are *with, were, what,* and *want.* Referred to earlier in the chapter as structure words (also known as *functors, glue words,* and *four-letter words*), these words are most difficult to teach because they cannot be made concrete for children. Just imagine trying to define or draw a picture of the word *what!*

Patricia Cunningham (1980) developed the *drastic strategy* to help teachers solve this difficult instructional problem. The six-step process follows:

The drastic strategy is useful for teaching function words, those having little meaning; for example, what, with, and that.

Step 1:   Select a function word, and write it on a vocabulary card for each child. Locate a story for storytelling, or spontaneously create a story, in which you use the word many times. Before you begin your story, instruct the children to hold up their card every time they hear the word printed on their card. As you tell the story, pause briefly each time you come to the word in the text.

Developing vocabulary in content areas can help children discover words in their natural context.

Step 2: Ask children to volunteer to make up a story using the word on their card. Listeners should hold up their card each time they hear their classmate use the function word.

Step 3: Ask the children to study the word on their card. Next, go around to each child and cut the word into letters (or have the children do it for themselves). Have the children try to arrange the letters to make the word. Check each child's attempt for accuracy. They should mix up the letters and try to make the word again several times; each child should be able to do this before moving on to the next step. Put the letters into an envelope and write the word on the outside. Children should be encouraged to practice making the word during free times.

Step 4: Write the word on the chalkboard and ask children to pretend their eyes are like a camera and to take a picture of the word and put it in their mind. Have them close their eyes and try to see it in their mind. Next, they should open their eyes and check the board to see if they correctly imagined the word. They should do this three times. The last activity is for them to write the word from memory after the chalkboard has been erased, then check their spelling when it is rewritten on the chalkboard. This should be done three times.

Step 5: Write several sentences on the board containing a blank in the place of the word under study. As you come to the missing word in the sentences, invite a child to come to the board and write the word in the blank space provided.

Step 6: Give children real books or text in which the function word appears. Ask them to read through the story, and whenever they find the word being studied, they should lightly underline (in pencil) the new word. When they have done this, read the text to them, and pause each time you come to the word so the students can read it chorally.

We recommend one final step to the drastic strategy: Add the word under study to the child's word bank for future use in writing.

There is one drawback to the drastic strategy—*time*. Because this process can take quite a bit of time, it is not necessary to teach each and every step in the drastic strategy for all words. Teacher judgment should determine which steps are most needed.

STRATEGIES FOR BUILDING STUDENTS' BACKGROUND KNOWLEDGE

In chapters 3 and 6, we discussed the role of schema development in reading comprehension. It is important that children find ways to link new information to what they already know. These mental connections do not always happen through normal encounters with their environment, nor do they happen by accident. Therefore, an important task for teachers is the structuring of learning situations wherein new concept connections can be formed. This section describes several classroom-proven possibilities for teachers to consider. We suggest that this section be viewed as a small resource book of ideas for preservice and in-service teachers. A short list of activity books for teachers provided at the end of the chapter have additional teaching strategies appropriate for balanced literacy classrooms.

Gipe's Cluing Technique

Cluing uses teacher-made passages loaded with context clues related to the new word.

Research by Joan Gipe (1980, 1987) indicates that new word meanings are best taught by providing appropriate and familiar context. Gipe's **cluing technique** introduces new vocabulary through a series of sentences that rely heavily on context clues, or cluing. A four-phase procedure is recommended. Students are given a passage in which the first sentence uses the new word appropriately, thus providing valuable semantic and syntactic information (context clues). The second sentence of the passage describes some of the characteristics or attributes of the new word. With all of the sentences in the cluing technique, the context should be filled with familiar words and situations. The third sentence in the paragraph defines the new word, again with care being taken to use familiar concepts (Gipe, 1987, p. 152). The final sentence provides a generative thinking opportunity by asking students to relate the new word to their own lives. This step is achieved by having them write an answer to a question or complete an open-ended statement requiring application of the word meaning. Gipe provides the following example in her book *Corrective Reading Techniques for the Classroom Teacher* (1987):

> The boys who wanted to sing together formed a *quintet*. There were five boys singing in the quintet. Quintet means a group of five, and this group usually sings or plays music. If you were in a quintet, what instrument would you want to play? (p. 152)

After students complete this reading and writing exercise, responses can be shared in a group discussion. Answers to the final question or open-ended statement might be written on the chalkboard or on chart paper in much the same fashion as a language-experience chart. If students are keeping individual and/or a classroom word bank, these new words can be added, which will make the words readily available for future writing projects and thus provide natural repetition.

RIVET

RIVET is a vocabulary introduction activity created by Patricia M. Cunningham (1995) while she was observing a student teacher in a fourth-grade classroom. RIVET is designed to help students activate their prior knowledge about a topic and make predictions about what is to be read.

RIVET uses a kind of "Wheel of Fortune" approach to activate students' prior knowledge.

To plan for a RIVET lesson, read the selection you wish to use and choose six to eight words you want your students to learn. Cunningham recommends that they be multisyllable words or important names (i.e., concepts or proper nouns). Begin the RIVET activity by writing numbers and drawing lines on chart paper, a chalkboard, or a dry erase board to indicate how many letters are in each word. Have students copy this information on a piece of paper, or provide them with a photocopied version, if you want to save some time. Your board and their paper might look like this:

1. __ __ __ __ __ __
2. __ __ __ __ __ __ __
3. __ __ __ __ __ __ __   __ __ __ __ __
4. __ __ __ __ __ __ __ __ __
5. __ __ __ __ __ __ __ __ __
6. __ __ __ __ __ __ __ __ __

Begin your whole-group or whole-class lesson by filling in the letters of the first word slowly, one letter at a time. Have the students copy the letters as you write them and ask them to guess what the word might be as soon as they think they know. Explain that this is a bit like the game show *Wheel of Fortune*. So the first word might look initially like this when you begin the lesson:

1. M e x i __ __

then like this (after someone guesses and helps you to complete the spelling):

1. M e x i c o

Continue in this way so that, with the assistance of the students, you eventually complete your list much like the example shown:

1. M e x i c o
2. S p a n i s h
3. P a c i f i c O c e a n
4. n e i g h b o r s
5. c o n t i n e n t
6. p e n i n s u l a

The next step is to ask students to use these words to predict what the passage will be about, and perhaps write some questions about what they would like to know about the topic. This process of vocabulary development, prediction, and questioning helps boost concept learning, word knowledge, and higher order comprehension. And besides . . . it's also fun!

Predict-O-Gram

Story grammar elements are used to categorize vocabulary in the ***Predict-O-Grams*** *is strategy.*

The **Predict-O-Gram** (Blachowicz, 1986) is a charting process that asks students to organize vocabulary in relation to the structure of the selection. In the case of narrative text, this structure is the story grammar (setting, characters, problem, actions taken, resolution, etc.). To begin, teachers might write the new vocabulary and/or concepts on the chalkboard or an overhead transparency; note that this occurs before students have read the story. After a brief introductory discussion of the words, we recommend that teachers give students a copy of the story grammar elements and ask them to predict how the author might use the words and concepts in the story. As a final step before reading the selection, the class might discuss the predictions and why they were judged to be in their respective categories.

To illustrate the Predict-O-Gram procedure, let's say that important vocabulary for the book *Why Mosquitoes Buzz in People's Ears* (Aardema, 1975) includes *mosquito, iguana, farmer, reeds, burrow, feared, gathered, alarmed, council, killed, plotting, sticks,* and *whining.* After a quick run-through for definition purposes, the students, either independently or as a class, predict how each word might be used in the story. The results of the prediction might look something like what is presented in Figure 7.4.

After reading the selection, the teacher and class should return to the Predict-O-Gram to verify and/or modify the predictions based on new information from the selection. In our example in Figure 7.4, the words *killed* and *whining* are in incorrect categories and would be moved to the correct columns after reading the story.

Frayer Model

Examples and nonexamples are used to analyze new concepts in the ***Frayer model.***

The **Frayer model** was developed to provide students with a systematic means for analyzing and learning new concepts. The steps of the Frayer model, along with examples described by McNeil (1987, p. 116), follow:

1. Describe the necessary characteristics that are common to the concept in all situations. For example, a necessary characteristic for the concept *globe* is "spherical."

Figure 7.4 Predict-O-Gram for *Why Mosquitoes Buzz in People's Ears*

Directions: Predict how the author may use these words in our story.

The setting	**The characters**	**The problem/goal**
reeds	mosquito	feared
burrow	iguana	alarmed
	farmer	whining
Actions Taken	**Resolution**	**Other things**
gathered	killed	sticks
	plotting	council

2. Differentiate relevant from irrelevant characteristics concerning the concept. For example, size is an irrelevant characteristic for the concept *globe*.
3. Provide an example for the concept, such as showing students a classroom globe.
4. Provide a nonexample for the concept, such as a chart (because it is not spherical).
5. Compare the concept to a lesser or subordinate concept, such as a ball.
6. Relate the concept to a superordinate term, for instance *global*.
7. Compare the concept to a coordinate or related term, such as *map*.

To use the Frayer model, teachers begin by reviewing the reading selection to locate new vocabulary and concepts that are important to the topic. After a quick reading or discussion of the selection, teacher and students together try to write meanings for the new concepts, based on information presented by the author. Then, students try to think of nonexamples and examples for the concepts. The final step is to compare examples and nonexamples to discover necessary characteristics for the concepts. Be sure to choose examples that are best examples of the concepts to avoid confusion. For instance, *tomato* would probably not be the best example for *fruit* because it is often thought of as a vegetable.

Opin

Opin is a procedure that has children, working in small-group settings, come up with responses to cloze passages. Developed by Greene (1973), Opin is easy to implement and requires little preparation time. The following steps are suggested by Searfoss and Readence (1989):

Opin uses modified cloze passages to help students understand how context can be used to comprehend new words.

1. Begin by forming groups of three children each. Distribute several Opin sentences to the groups. For primary grades, it may be desirable to distribute the sentences one at a time. This is also true for all age groups when initially explaining or modeling this activity.
2. Each child should choose a word that makes sense and spend a minute or so trying to convince the other group members that their answer is correct. The group is to decide on one answer they think is best.
3. Then, the whole class/group assembles to hear the choice from each small group. The one rule is that the group must explain why their choice makes sense. This final step provides teachers with an excellent opportunity to point out how context can determine the choice of words.

Examples of Opin sentences and possible vocabulary words follow:

A fireman's _____ curves down in the back to allow water to drain off without getting his clothes wet. (helmet, hat, cap)

A person who is honest and truthful is said to have _____. (integrity, candid, fair, moral)

Many people feel _____ when moving to a new city or neighborhood. (anxious, sad, happy, scared)

Word Cards

E. Carr (1985) suggests the use of **word cards** to help students record and recall new vocabulary. The idea is to have students write the new word on an index card or word bank card. Then each student should record a word, phrase, name, and the like

Figure 7.5   Word card

> **vivacious**
>
> —Jennifer
>
> —lively, energetic, bouncy

that remind him or her of the new word's meanings. Finally, short definitional words should be added to clarify the correct usage of the word. The result looks something like a diagram (see Figure 7.5).

Structured Overview

*Chapter 13 describes how to construct **structured overviews** in more detail.*

A **structured overview** is a graphic organizer usually presented by the teacher before silent reading. It is then referred to by students during silent reading and reread as a guide to postreading discussions (Manzo & Manzo, 1990, p. 106). As a tool for building concept knowledge, the structured overview arranges both new and known concepts and vocabulary into a kind of diagram illustrating the relationships between the new word and known concepts and vocabulary. Structured overviews belong to a class of teacher-constructed instruments known as *graphic organizers,* which are usually applied to content area subjects (e.g., science, social studies). A graphic organizer is any pictorial representation of concepts, meanings, or vocabulary. The idea is to arrange synonyms, definitional words, examples, and other pertinent information into a kind of flowchart that moves from known information toward the new concept. Although the flow usually moves from the top down (known to new), a structured overview can actually be constructed in any form that makes sense. The procedure for constructing structured overviews along with an example is provided in chapter 13.

STRATEGIES FOR EXTENDING STUDENTS' VOCABULARY KNOWLEDGE

Semantic Mapping

***Semantic maps** illustrate relationships between concepts.*

Semantic maps are diagrams or graphic depictions of concepts that help children see how words relate to each other. An excellent activity for extending students' vocabulary knowledge, semantic mapping enables children to see known words in new contexts. The process for constructing semantic maps involves the following steps:

Step 1: Select a vocabulary word or concept important to the story, text, or book.

Step 2: Write the word or concept in the center of the chalkboard or an overhead transparency.

Step 3: Ask the class to help think of other words that have something to do with the word or concept at the center of the chalkboard or transparency.

Step 4: Group related words into categories and agree on labels for these categories (optional).

Figure 7.6   Semantic map

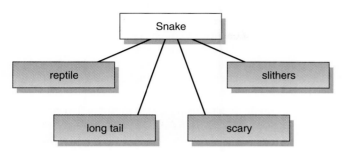

A discussion should follow in which the relationships of these words are examined. In essence, the teacher helps children to construct new schema structures for background knowledge enhancement. A completed semantic map is shown in Figure 7.6.

Making Words

Making Words (Cunningham & Cunningham, 1992) is an excellent word-learning strategy that helps children improve their phonetic understanding of words through invented or "temporary spellings" while also increasing their repertoire of vocabulary words they can recognize in print (Reutzel & Cooter, 1999). Making Words will be a familiar strategy for anyone who has ever played the popular crossword board game *Scrabble*.

Making Words begins when students are given a number of specific letters with which to make words. They begin by making two- or three-letter words using the letters during a set amount of time, then progress to words having more letters until they finally arrive at a specific word that uses all the letters. This final word is usually the main word to be taught for the day, but the other words discovered may be new for some students. By manipulating the letters to make words of two, three, four, and more letters using temporary or "transitional" spellings, students have an opportunity to practice their phonemic awareness skills. Making Words is recommended as a 15-minute activity when used with first- and second-graders. In Tables 7.1 and 7.2 we summarize and adapt the steps in planning and teaching a Making Words lesson suggested by Cunningham and Cunningham (1992).

Table 7.3 describes details necessary for creating two more Making Words lessons suggested by Cunningham and Cunningham (1992) that may be useful for helping students learn the procedure.

One way to help students apply their letter-sound knowledge is to use the **Making Words** *strategy.*

Store two sets of large single-letter cards in two envelopes—one for the teacher and one for children participating during the modeling activity.

Semantic Feature Analysis

D. D. Johnson and Pearson explain in their book *Teaching Reading Vocabulary* (1984) that concepts have certain relationships known as *class, example,* and *property*. First, a *class* is a group having common attributes; *fish* and *dogs* are considered classes. Next, *example relations* represent members of the class; *guppy* and *yellowtail* are examples of the class known as *fish,* and *cocker spaniel* and *golden retriever* are examples of the class known as *dogs*. Finally, *property relations* specify the properties or attributes associated with the class. For example, dogs bark, have fur, and often perform tricks; these are properties associated with the class *dogs*.

Class, example, and property are three relationships of vocabulary.

Table 7.1 Planning a Making Words lesson

1. Choose a word to be the final word or "big word" to be emphasized in the lesson. It should be a key word that is chosen from a selection to be read by the class, fiction or nonfiction, or it may be of interest to the group. Select a word that has enough vowels and/or one that fits letter-sound patterns useful for most children at their developmental stage in reading and writing. We will use the word *thunder* in these instructions, as suggested by Cunningham and Cunningham (1992).

2. Make a list of shorter words that can be spelled using letters from the "big word." Some words derived from *thunder* include: *red, Ted, Ned/den/end* (note: these all use the same letters), *her, hut, herd, turn, hunt, hurt, under, hunted, turned, thunder* (see Table 7.3).

   From the words you listed, select 12–15 words that include aspects of written language such as (a) words that emphasize a certain kind of pattern, (b) big and little words, (c) words made with the same letters in different positions (as with *Ned, end, den*), (d) a proper noun, if possible, to remind students when we use capital letters, and (e) words students have in their listening vocabularies.

3. Write all of these words on large index cards and order them from smallest to largest. Write the individual letters found in the key word for each day on large index cards (make two sets).

4. Reorder the words to group them according to letter patterns and/or to demonstrate how shifting around letters can form new words. Store the word stacks in envelopes and note on the outside the words/patterns emphasized during the lesson. Note clues you can use with children to help them discover the words you desire. For example, "See if you can make a three-letter word that is the name of the room in some people's homes where they like to watch television." (*den*)

Table 7.2 Teaching a Making Words lesson

1. Place the large single letters from the key word in a pocket chart or along the chalkboard ledge.

2. For modeling purposes the first time you use Making Words, select one student to be the "passer" and ask that child to pass the large single letters to other designated children.

3. Hold up and name each of the letter cards and have students selected to participate in the modeling exercise respond by holding up their matching card.

4. Write the numeral 2 (or 3, if there are no two-letter words in this lesson) on the board. Next, tell the student "volunteers" the clue you developed for the desired word. Then, tell the student volunteers to put together two (or three) of their letters to form the desired word.

5. Direct the students to make more words using the clues and the letter cards until you have helped them discover all but the final key word (the one using all the letters). Ask the volunteers if they can guess the key word. If not, ask the remainder of the class if they can guess. If no one can, offer them a meaning clue (e.g., "I am thinking of a word with __ letters that means . . . ").

6. Repeat these steps the next day with the whole group as a guided practice activity using a new word.

Table 7.3 Making Words: Additional examples

Sample Making Words Lessons (Cunningham & Cunningham, 1992)

Lesson using one vowel

Letter cards: u k n r s t

Words to make: us, nut, rut, sun, sunk, runs, ruts/rust, tusk, stun, stunk, trunk, *trunks* (the key word)

You can sort for . . . rhymes, "s" pairs (run, runs; rut, ruts; trunk, trunks)

Lesson using big words

Letter cards: a a a e i b c h l l p t

Words to make: itch, able, cable, table, batch, patch, pitch, petal, label, chapel, capital, capable, alphabet, *alphabetical* (the key word)

You can sort for . . . el, le, al, -itch, -atch

Through semantic mapping or feature analysis strategies, students can graphically illustrate these various relationships.

Semantic feature analysis builds on and expands the categories of concepts tucked away in students' memory banks (D. D. Johnson & Pearson, 1984). The object is to complete a grid or matrix that identifies common and unique traits of words classified into the same category. A classroom experience based on semantic feature analysis may proceed as follows:

1. Present to the class a list of words that have some common features. The category of *flying machines,* for example, might include words such as *jet, hovercraft, balloon, blimp,* and *rocket.* List these words in the vertical column at the far left of the grid on the chalkboard, chart paper, or overhead transparency.
2. Begin to list some features, with the assistance of the students, commonly associated with one or more of the flying machines. List these features across the top of the grid.
3. Children should complete the grid by putting either a "+" (meaning the example has that feature) or "−" beside each word under each feature.
4. Group discussion of the grid or matrix should follow, to lead the children to a better understanding of each word and to an understanding that no two words have exactly the same meaning.

An example of a semantic feature analysis matrix and grid is provided in Figure 7.7.

Figure 7.7 Semantic feature analysis for *flying machines*

	has wheels	passengers	has wings/fins	very fast
jet	+	+	+	+
Hovercraft	−	+	−	+
balloon	−	+	−	−
blimp	−	+	−	−
rocket	−	+/− (sometimes)	+	+

The Essential Vocabulary Words: Grades 4–6

Rasinski (1998) has identified high-utility words for grades 4–6.

The essential vocabulary words (Rasinski, 1998) listed in Figure 7.8 are words or derivations of words likely to show up in standardized tests of vocabulary. The words on these lists were taken from an analysis of two technical vocabulary lists and represent grade level and/or somewhat more challenging words according to the technical vocabularies consulted. Knowledge of and practice with these words can generalize to other words and concepts and will likely improve students' reading comprehension and general vocabulary. Here is the procedure:

1. Choose one or two words to teach per week. Make this a grade level or schoolwide project (try to be consistent across grade levels in the words chosen so that other teachers and school staff can reinforce the words throughout the week). The words chosen for "Words of the Week" do not necessarily need to come from these lists. Indeed, it may be wise to choose "Words of the Week" from current events, upcoming holidays, themes being studied by students. If no appropriate words are available, choose one or two words from these lists.

*"Unpacking words" means breaking words apart into their meaning units or **morphemes.***

2. Classroom teachers may introduce the essential words for the week; give definitions for the words and use the words in sentences on Monday; use the words in your instruction and conversation with students. Throughout the week, keep the words posted in your classroom and use them in your conversation and instruction with students. "Unpack the words" to show students how the words may have various meanings and how knowledge of certain parts of the words can help students understand related words (e.g., knowledge of the derivatives *cycle* and *bi* in *bicycle* may help students understand other words such as *binoculars, biped, unicycle,* and *tricycle*). On Friday, play word games that include the essential words for the week along with other words from previous weeks (e.g. scattergories, wordo).

3. Other teachers should post the Words for the Week in their classrooms, along with sentences that use the words in the context of the specific content area (e.g., acrophobia—a physical education teacher: "Basketball players need to be so tall, they better not suffer from acrophobia." Science: "People who are acrophobic can be trained to overcome this irrational fear.") All teachers can make it a point to define the essential word early in each class and to use it in instruction throughout the week.

Figure 7.8 Words of the Week Master List

Grade 4 words

Words	Notes
abandon	
agriculture	
boundary	
candidate	(*candid* means to be just, impartial, forthright)
climate	
deposit	
exhaust	
fatal	
frontier	
grief	
gulf	(note the figurative meaning of a "gulf" that can exist between people)
haste	
income	
jury	
knot	(note multiple meanings)
lecture	(*lect/lex* refers to *word*)
limp	(note multiple meanings)
magnificent	*magna/magni* means *large* or *great* (e.g., *Magna Carta*)
melody	(versus *lyrics*)
paradise	
parliament	(from French *parler—to speak; related word* is parlor)
pardon	
peer	
plantation	
professional	
prune	multiple meanings
recommend	base word is *commend*
retreat	
scorn	
severe	
shallow	
sober	
stable	multiple meanings
stern	
surrender	
survey	
telegraph	base words *tele* = from afar; *graph* = something in writing
telescope	base words *tele* = from afar; *scope* = to see

(Rasinski, 1998)

Figure 7.8 *continued*

Words	Notes
timber	
tradition	
transportation	base words *trans* = across; *port* = carry. Related words: porter, portage
unable	
unfortunate	
uniform	literally means *one style, one way of presentation*
vacant	from Latin *vac*, meaning *empty*. Related words: vacuum, vacation
victim	
wail	Wailing Wall in Jerusalem
width	related concept: breadth
weep	
yonder	

Grade 5 Words

Words	Notes
accurate	
admission	
anxiety	
bolt	multiple meanings
capital/capitol	*cap* is derivative for "head" (e.g., decapitate)
combat	*com* = with, *bat* is short for *battle*. Literally, in the battle.
dense	multiple meanings
distract	*tract* = pull, *dis* = from. Literally, to pull one's attention away from.
dome	
eliminate	
endure	
flourish	to grow well, as flowers do
furious	
genuine	
hearth	
hoist	
identical	
immense	
immortal	not mortal
impressive	
infinite	contrast with "finite"
jest	
leisure	

Figure 7.8 *continued*

Words	Notes
offense	contrast with a "defense"
parallel	
patriot	derives from *pater,* meaning *father;* devotion to one's fatherland
predict	*pre* = before; *dict* = to say. Literally, to say or state beforehand.
province	
rebel	
republic	government that is representative of the general public
residence	
rumor	
sample	multiple meanings
seam	
significant	an important sign of something
shudder	
solitary	
sphere	
spur	multiple meanings
stimulate	
superintendent	*super* = above
survive	*vive* is derived from *viva,* meaning *to live*
tariff	
tomb	
transform	*trans* = across; *form* = appearance or presentation. Change in appearance.
trench	
unconscious	
uneasy	
vault	multiple meanings
vital	
vivid	*viva* = to live; lifelike
warrant	

Grade 6 Words

Words	Notes
alien	
anticipate	
antisocial	not social
blunder	
circulate	base word: circle, which means *around.* Other word: circulation.
clutch	multiple meanings. Important situation.

245

Figure 7.8 *continued*

Words	Notes
complex	
contact	*con* = with; *tact* = touch; Literally in touch. Other word: tactile
contemporary	*con* = with; *temp* = time; Living with someone in the same time period.
crisis	
defect	
denounce	related words: announce, renounce
domestic	derived from *dom* = home
external	contrast with "internal"
fugitive	
hinder	
incredible	derived from *cred* = belief or believable; *in* = not
landlord	
massive	
martyr	
modify	
minority	contrast with majority
monopoly	*mono* = one; one who is in charge of all. Related word: oligopoly
originate	
pension	
peril	
perpetual	
philosophy	derived from *phil* = love of; *soph* = wisdom. Love of wisdom. Other words: philanthropy, Philadelphia, sophomore
preface	*pre* = before; *face* = the front. Part of a book before the front of the story.
prejudice	*pre* = before; *judice* = judge. Judge before all the facts are in.
prohibit	contrast with "inhibit"
psychology	*psych* = mind; *ology* = study of. Study of the mind.
radical	
random	
reliable	
scandal	
scope	
senior	contrast with "junior"
shroud	
spectator	*spec* = to view or see
submarine	*sub* = under; *marine* = having to do with water. Think of many related words.
subtle	
supervision	*super* = above; *vision* = to see or view; Literally, to oversee.

Figure 7.8 *continued*

Words	Notes
terrace	*terra* = having to do with the land. Related words: terrarium, Mediterranean, terrapin, terra cotta
text	
threshold	
throng	
toll	
torrent	
tropical	
trivial	
tributary	related words: contribute
tyrant	
utility	
valiant	
verdict	*ver* = truth; *dict* = to say; Literally, to say with truth.

4. Daily school announcements can include the "Words of the Week" along with their definitions and history. Each day a different aspect of the essential words can be presented. The words can also be posted in the school lobby along with descriptive sentences and other texts.
5. The "Words of the Week" can be sent home for further reinforcement by parents.
6. "Words of the Week" can be printed in the school publications along with brief stories on each word's meaning, history, or other interesting aspect.
7. The words can be highlighted/displayed in the school cafeteria and/or gymnasium and used to capture the students' interest.
8. Teachers can review the essential words and their derivatives periodically to help students maintain their knowledge of these key words.

Thorough knowledge of these essential vocabulary words should, at the very least, help students make substantial gains in the vocabulary subsection of any test they take in the future.

Exclusion Brainstorming

Blachowicz (1986) describes an activity called **exclusion brainstorming** in which students use their prior knowledge to anticipate new concepts. This activity is begun by creating an activity sheet or overhead transparency with the title or topic of the selection across the top. Beneath the title or topic, the teacher writes a few well-chosen words that come from the story and fit the topic, some words that clearly are

Notice that prior knowledge helps students select or reject word meanings.

Figure 7.9 Exclusion brainstorming

The Red Pony		
colt	tricycle	kids
currying	California	saddle

not consistent with the topic, and others that are ambiguous. An example for Steinbeck's (1937) *The Red Pony* is shown in Figure 7.9.

Students begin by deciding which words they think will not be found in the selection and underline those they think will appear. Students should be expected to explain their decisions, either orally or in writing. From this point in the discussion, the
teacher can highlight important words and concepts found in the passage. Exclusion
brainstorming offers teachers a wonderful blend of schema activation and vocabulary
analysis, and both are directly linked to the reading of a selection.

Concept Ladder

Teachers often need students to focus on single words that carry meaning for broader
concepts. An activity known as the **concept ladder** (Gillet & Temple, 1986) can
serve this purpose quite well. It provides a graphic depiction of how multiple concepts
are related to other words and concepts they already know. This procedure creates
a kind of semantic network for each term. Figure 7.10 displays a concept ladder for
ships. Note how the hierarchy can go up and down.

Free-Form Outline

*Name three types of
free-form outlines.*

Free-form outlines are postreading diagrams that include webs, maps, and radial
outlines. Like the structured overview discussed earlier, they provide a visual framework for new vocabulary and concepts (E. Carr & Wixson, 1986). Free-form outlines,
however, generally are not hierarchical and are generated by the students themselves
at the conclusion of a selection or unit of study.

Figure 7.11 shows a free-form outline based on the book *Charlotte's Web* (E. B.
White, 1952), in which the student has focused on characters and on events related
to the characters. In constructing free-form outlines, students select new vocabulary,
link the new words (in this case, the words were *egg sac, terrific,* and *radiant*) to
background knowledge gained from the text, and make associations between the important concepts.

Capsule Vocabulary

Capsule vocabulary (E. Carr & Wixson, 1986; Crist, 1975) encourages word
learning by involving the four language modes: listening, speaking, reading, and writing. Students are presented a list of words related to a topic under study. For example, if the class is studying computers, then the list of words might include *keyboard,
CRT, disk, hard copy, laser printer,* and *word processing.* Students work in pairs,
with one student discussing the topic for 5 minutes using the designated words; then
the partners switch roles. After the talk sessions, each student writes a summary of
the topic using the designated terms.

Figure 7.10   Concept ladder for *ships*

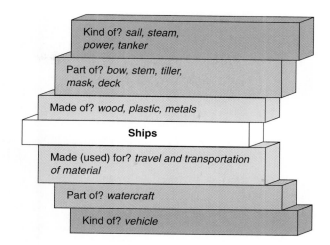

> Kind of? *sail, steam, power, tanker*
> Part of? *bow, stem, tiller, mask, deck*
> Made of? *wood, plastic, metals*
> **Ships**
> Made (used) for? *travel and transportation of material*
> Part of? *watercraft*
> Kind of? *vehicle*

STRATEGIES FOR HELPING STUDENTS ACQUIRE NEW VOCABULARY INDEPENDENTLY

The ultimate task for educators is to help students become independent learners. The continued learning of new vocabulary throughout life is unquestionably a key to continuing self-education. In this section, we feature ways students can help themselves become independent learners of new words they encounter while reading.

Encouraging Wide Reading

Reading is a cognitive skill that in some ways mirrors physical skill development. As with physical skills, the more one practices reading, the more one's ability increases. Over the years, in our work with at-risk students, we have come to realize that if we can simply get children to read every day for at least 15 to 20 minutes, their reading ability will increase quickly and exponentially. In one study, Reutzel and Hollingsworth (1991c) discovered that allowing children to read self-selected books

Wide reading is a powerful way to build vocabulary knowledge.

Figure 7.11   Free-form outline of *Charlotte's Web*

Charlotte
Spider
Friends with pig
Writes "messages" on her web
Produces an "egg sac" for her babies

Fern
The Arable's daughter
Saves Wilbur the pig from death
Is a true friend to Wilbur

Templeton
Rat
Befriends Charlotte and Wilbur
Saves Charlotte's "egg sac"
Wilbur promises a reward

Wilbur
Beloved pig
Charlotte's best friend
Feels "radiant" (p. 101) and "terrific"
Is allowed to live a long life

Encouraging children to read books that match their interests can motivate them to read independently and grow their vocabulary.

30 minutes every day resulted in significantly improved scores on reading comprehension tests. These children performed as well as students who had received 30 minutes of direct instruction on the tested reading comprehension skills. Their results suggest that regular daily reading is probably at least as effective as formal reading instruction, and the children can do it on their own!

Surveying student interests with an Individual Interest Sheet (IIS) helps teachers select free-reading materials. See chapter 13 for more information on choosing high-interest reading materials.

How can teachers encourage children to read independently on a regular basis? The answer probably lies in helping them recognize their interests and in finding books they can read. The interest issue can be resolved in two steps. First, the teacher should administer an interest inventory to the class at the beginning of the year (see Figure 10.2 on p. 360) to determine what types of books are indicated for classroom instruction. These results, however, could be taken a little further: As the second step, we suggest that the teacher start an individual interest sheet (IIS) for each child based on these results and present them to children during individual reading conferences (see chapter 12). The IIS sheet simply lists topics that appear to be of interest to the child and suggests books available in the school library. Over time, the children can list additional topics they discover to be of interest and can look for books in those areas. The principle is much the same as having children keep a list of topics they would like to write stories about, which is also discussed in chapter 12. Figure 7.12 shows a sample IIS, with new interests written in by the student.

What are some ways teachers can encourage wide reading?

A useful reference for teachers attempting to match children's interests with quality literature is Donna Norton's (1999) book *Through the Eyes of a Child: An Introduction to Children's Literature.* Most high-interest topic areas are discussed in this text and are matched to several possible book titles. Book suggestions include brief descriptions of the main story line to help in the decision-making process.

Figure 7.12   Sample individual interest sheet (IIS)

Individual Interest Sheet

Mrs. Harbor's Sixth Grade

Sunnydale School

Name: Holly Ambrose

Things I am interested in knowing more about, or topics that I like . . .

Topics	Books to consider from our library
horses	*The Red Pony* (J. Steinbeck)
getting along with friends	*Afternoon of the Elves* (J. Lisle)
romantic stories	*The Witch of Blackbird Pond* (E. Speare)
one-parent families	*The Moonlight Man* (P. Fox)

Shared Reading and Vocabulary Learning

M. Senechal and Cornell (1993) have studied ways vocabulary knowledge can be increased through shared reading experiences (those where adults and children read stories together). The methods investigated included reading the story verbatim (read alouds), asking questions, repeating sentences containing new vocabulary words, and what has been referred to as recasting new vocabulary introduced in the selection. **Recasts** build directly on sentences just read that contain a new word the teacher (or parent) may want to teach the child. Verbs, subjects, or objects are often changed to recast the word for further discussion and examination. Thus, if a child says or reads, "Look at the *snake*," the adult may recast the phrase by replying, "It is a large striped *snake*." In this example, the same meaning of the phrase was maintained, but adjectives were added to enhance understanding of the word *snake*.

List two ways teachers can enhance vocabulary learning.

Interestingly, Senechal and Cornell concluded that activities that involve requesting students' active participation, such as questioning and recasts, did not boost children's vocabulary learning (p. 369); reading a book verbatim to a child was just as effective. This does not mean that we should abandon these strategies; they are effective. Rather, we should understand that reading passages aloud to students can be just as potent as direct teaching strategies. We need to do both: read aloud regularly *and* discuss passages containing new vocabulary with students in challenging ways.

Computer-Assisted Vocabulary Learning

As computers become more accessible to students and teachers, the question arises: Can some of the new computer applications available help students learn new vocabulary? Reinking and Rickman (1990) studied the vocabulary growth of sixth-grade students who had computer-assisted programs available to them. They compared students who read passages on printed pages accompanied by either a standard dictionary or glossary (the traditional classroom situation) with students who read passages on a

Computer-assisted vocabulary instruction can be a motivational tool in a learning center.

computer screen. These computer-assisted programs provided either *optional assistance* (on command) for specific vocabulary words or *mandatory* (automatic) assistance. They learned two very interesting things from their research. First, students reading passages with computer assistance performed significantly better on vocabulary tests focusing on the words emphasized than did students in the traditional reading groups. Second, students receiving automatic computer assistance with the passages also outperformed the more traditional reading group on a passage comprehension test relating to information read in the experiment. These results strongly suggest that computer programs that offer students passages to read with vocabulary assistance can be helpful. Further, they suggest to us another possible advantage of the computer: teaching students to use what might be termed a *vocabulary enhancer,* such as a thesaurus program, with their writing, which could help students discover on their own new synonyms and antonyms for commonly used words. Most word processing programs, such as Microsoft Word, have a thesaurus program already installed for easy use.

Vocabulary Overview

Vocabulary overviews involve students in self-selecting the words they will learn.

In classroom settings, teachers can usually anticipate vocabulary that may be troublesome during reading and teach these words through brief mini-lessons. But when children read independently, they will need to compensate and find ways to learn new words on their own. An activity that serves this purpose is developing a vocabulary overview. Vocabulary overviews help students select unknown words in print and use their background knowledge and context clues from the passage to determine word meaning.

One way of helping students develop their own vocabulary overviews is Haggard's (1986) vocabulary self-selection strategy (VSS). Our version of the VSS begins with a small-group mini-lesson to learn the process. Students are asked to find at least one word they feel the class should learn. They are asked to define the word to the best of their ability, based on the context of the word in the text and any other information from their own background knowledge. On the day the words are presented, each child takes turns explaining (a) where each word was found, (b) his or her context-determined definition for the word, and (c) reasons why the class should learn the word.

As students practice the VSS, they become more cognizant of vocabulary that may require further investigation or extra thought. After practicing the VSS in small-group settings, the next step is to apply the strategy during self-selected reading (SSR) times. Words found in SSR books should be one of the topics of discussion during independent one-on-one reading conferences between the teacher and student. The heightened awareness that comes from student-generated vocabulary overviews eventually transfers and becomes an automatic reading strategy.

Word Maps

Word maps *help students tap schema connections to understand word meanings.*

A **word map** (Schwartz & Raphael, 1985) is a visual rendering of a word's definition. It answers three important questions about the word's meaning: *What is it? What is it like? What are some examples?* Answers to these questions are extremely valuable because they help children link the new word or concept to their prior knowledge and world experiences, a process known to have an *effect* on reading comprehension (Stahl et al., 1991). An example of a word map is shown in Figure 7.13.

Introducing this vocabulary-acquisition strategy to students is a relatively easy task. First, the teacher presents the idea of using picture strategies to understand new

Figure 7.13   Word map

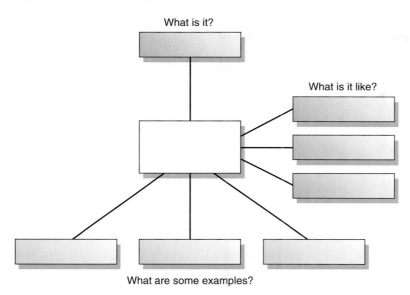

word meanings and explains that the word map is one example. Next, students should work with the teacher to organize familiar information in terms of the three questions used in the word map. In early practice exercises, simple concepts should be used, which will help students learn the map as a tool. For example, a practice map might be constructed using the word *car.* Answers for each of the story map questions that might be offered by elementary students follow:

Word: *car*

What is it? (transportation, movement)

What is it like? (four wheels, metal, glass, lights, moves, steering wheel)

What are some examples? (Corvette, station wagon, Firebird, convertible)

After working through several examples with the whole group or class, teachers should give students opportunities to practice using the word map. In the beginning, whole-class practice works best, followed by independent practice using narrative and expository texts of the students' or teacher's choosing.

Studying Word Functions and Changes

Synonyms

Synonyms are words that have similar, but not exactly the same, meanings (D. D. Johnson & Pearson, 1984). No two words carry exactly the same meaning in all situations. Thus, when teaching children about new words and their synonyms, teachers should provide numerous opportunities for students to see differences as well as similarities. As with all reading strategies, this is best done within the natural context of real books and authentic writing experiences.

One very productive way to get children interested in synonyms in the upper elementary grades is to teach the use of a thesaurus with their writing. Children can

Can you think of interesting reading materials that might be used to teach synonyms?

begin to see how using a thesaurus can "spice up" their writing projects. This tool is best used during revising and editing stages of the writing process (see chapter 12). For instance, children sometimes have a problem coming up with descriptive language in their writing. A character in a story may be tortured by hostile savages, and the child may write that the victim felt "bad." If this word is targeted for thesaurus research, then the child may come up with synonyms for *bad* such as *in pain, anguished, in misery, depressed,* or *desperate.*

Following are several common words that children overuse that could be researched using a thesaurus.

good	big	thing
pleasant	vast	object
glorious	grand	item
wonderful	enormous	like
delightful	huge	organism

One way to involve children with books and synonyms is to take text from old favorite books and revise selected words. Teachers might want to develop a modified cloze passage, deleting only certain kinds of words, and then let the children use synonyms to complete the blanks. Take, for example, the following excerpt from a book well suited for early to intermediate grade readers, *The Grouchy Ladybug* (Carle, 1986):

> "Good morning," said the friendly ladybug.
>
> "Go away!" shouted the grouchy ladybug. "I want those aphids."
>
> "We can share them," suggested the friendly ladybug.
>
> "No. They're mine, all mine," screamed the grouchy ladybug.
>
> "Or do you want to fight me for them?"*

One option is to delete words following a statement (e.g., *said, shouted, suggested, screamed*) and put them in a list on the chalkboard with possible synonyms, such as *hinted, greeted, growled, yelled, reminded, mentioned, pointed out,* and *offered.* The resulting rewrites may look something like the following:

> "Good morning," *greeted* the friendly ladybug.
>
> "Go away!" *growled* the grouchy ladybug. "I want those aphids."
>
> "We can share them," *hinted* the friendly ladybug.
>
> "No. They're mine, all mine," *yelled* the grouchy ladybug.
>
> "Or do you want to fight me for them?"

Class discussions might relate to how the use of different synonyms can alter meaning significantly, thus showing how synonyms have similar meanings, but not the exact same meanings. For example, if we took the sentence

> "Go away!" *shouted* the grouchy ladybug.

*From *The Grouchy Ladybug* by E. Carle, 1977, 1986. New York: HarperCollins. Reprinted by permission.

and changed it to read

"Go away!" *hinted* the grouchy ladybug.

it would be easy for children to understand how the author's message had been softened considerably. This cross-training with reading and writing experiences helps synonyms to take on new relevance as a literacy tool in the hands of children.

Antonyms

Antonyms are word opposites or near opposites. *Hard–soft, dark–light, big–small* are examples of antonym pairs. Like synonyms, antonyms help students gain insights into word meanings. When searching for ideal antonym examples, teachers should try to identify word sets that are mutually exclusive or that completely contradict each other.

> *Word opposites, or near opposites, are* ***antonyms.***

Several classes of antonyms have been identified (D. D. Johnson & Pearson, 1984) that may be useful in instruction. One class is called *relative pairs,* or *counterparts.* Examples include *mother–father, sister–brother, uncle–aunt, writer–reader,* because one term implies the other. Other antonyms reflect a complete opposite or reversal of meaning, such as *fast–slow, stop–go,* and *give–take.* Complimentary antonyms tend to lead from one to another such as *give–take, friend–foe,* and *hot–cold.*

Antonym activities, as with all language-learning activities, should be drawn from the context of familiar books and student writing samples. By using familiar text with clear meanings, it is easy for children to see the full impact and flavor of differing word meanings. Remember, in classroom instruction involving mini-lessons, teaching from whole text to parts (antonyms in this case) is the key. Thus, if the teacher decided to develop an antonym worksheet for students, then the worksheet should be drawn from a book that has already been shared (or will be shared) with the whole class or group. One example of a fun book for this exercise is *Weird Parents* by Audrey Wood (1990), which could yield sentences like the following (in the space provided, students write in antonyms for the underlined words):

1. There once was a boy who had <u>weird</u> (   ) parents.
2. In the <u>morning</u> (   ), the weird mother always walked the boy to his bus stop.
3. At 12 o'clock when the boy <u>opened</u> (   ) his lunch box, he'd always have a weird surprise.

Another possibility is to ask children to find words in their writing or reading for which they can think of antonyms. A student in sixth grade reading *A Wrinkle in Time* (L'Engle, 1962) might create the following list of book words and antonyms:

Wrinkle Words/Page No.	Antonyms
punishment/13	reward
hesitant/63	eager
frightening/111	pleasant

If a student in third grade had written a story about his new baby sister, he might select some of the following words and antonyms:

Baby Story Words	Opposites
asleep	awake
cry	laugh
wet	dry

One way to assess the ability to *recognize* antonyms is through multiple-choice and cloze exercises. The idea is to choose sentences from familiar text and let students select which word is the correct antonym from among three choices. The choices may include one synonym, the correct antonym, and a third choice that is a different part of speech. Following are two examples taken from the book *The Glorious Flight* (Provensen & Provensen, 1983):

1. Like a great swan, the *beautiful* (attractive, homely, shoots) glider rises into the air . . .
2. Papa is getting *lots* (limited, from, loads) of practice.

Of many possible classroom activities, the most profitable will probably be those in which students are required to generate their own responses. Simple recognition items, as with multiple-choice measures, do not cause children to look within themselves nearly as deeply to find and apply new knowledge.

Euphemisms

What is meant by the notion that **euphemisms** *"soften" our language?*

According to Tompkins and Hoskisson (1991, p. 122), **euphemisms** are words or phrases that are used to soften language to avoid harsh or distasteful realities (e.g., *passed away*), usually out of concern for people's feelings. Euphemisms are certainly worth some attention, because they not only help students improve their writing versatility but also aid in reading comprehension.

Two types of euphemisms include *inflated* and *deceptive* language. Inflated language euphemisms tend to make something sound greater or more sophisticated than it is. For example, *sanitation engineer* might be an inflated euphemism for *garbage collector.* Deceptive language euphemisms are words and phrases meant to intentionally misrepresent; for example in a cigarette ad saying "Tastes great . . . and they are mild!" the word "mild" implies that cigarettes will do no harm. Children should learn that this language often is used in advertisements to persuade an unknowing public.

Several examples of euphemisms based on the work of Lutz (cited in Tompkins & Hoskisson, 1991, p. 122) follow:

Euphemism	Real Meaning
dentures	false teeth
expecting	pregnant
funeral director	undertaker
passed away	died
previously owned	used
senior citizen	old person
terminal patient	dying

Onomatopoeia and Creative Words

Onomatopoeia are words that imitate sounds (*buzz, whir, vrrrrooom*). Some authors, such as Dr. Seuss, Shel Silverstein, and others, have made regular use of onomatopoeia and other creative words in their writing. One instance of onomatopoeia can be found in Dr. Seuss's book *Horton Hears a Who!* (1954) in the sentence "On clarinets, oom-pahs and boom-pahs and flutes." A wonderful example of creative language is found in Silverstein's (1974, p. 71) poem "Sarah Cynthia Sylvia Stout Would Not Take the Garbage Out" in the phrase "Rubbery blubbery macaroni . . ."

Children can be shown many interesting examples of onomatopoeia and creative words from the world of great children's literature. The natural extension to their own writing comes swiftly. Children may want to add a special section to their word banks for onomatopoeia and creative words to enhance their own written creations.

ASSISTING STUDENTS IN MULTICULTURAL SETTINGS WITH VOCABULARY DEVELOPMENT

Vocabulary development in spoken and written English is at the heart of literacy learning (Wheatley, Muller, & Miller, 1993). Because of the rich diversity found in American classrooms, teachers need to consider ways of adapting the curriculum so that all children can learn to recognize and use appropriate and descriptive vocabulary. In this section, we consider three possible avenues proven to be successful in multicultural settings.

List several ways to stimulate greater vocabulary learning in multicultural settings.

1. *Linking vocabulary studies to a broad topic or novel.* We know that there is a limit to the number of words that can be taught directly and in isolation. K. Au (1993) tells us that students in multicultural settings learn vocabulary best if the new words are related to a broader topic. Working on vocabulary development in connection with students' exploration of content area topics is a natural and connected way to learn new words and explore their various meanings. In chapter 13, we go into further detail about how vocabulary instruction can be conducted in content units, including the use of special computer-assisted programs.

2. *Wide reading as a vehicle for vocabulary development.* Reading for enjoyment on a daily basis helps students increase their vocabulary knowledge, not to mention improving myriad other reading abilities. Teachers can help students become regular readers by assessing their reading interests (see chapter 10), then locate books that "fit the reader." Matching books and students is a simple way of encouraging the kinds of reading behaviors that pay dividends. Teaching students how to choose books on their developmental level (see "Rule of Thumb" in chapter 12) is an important way to help them select books independently.

3. *The Village English activity.* L. Delpit (1988) writes about a method of teaching Native Alaskan students new vocabulary that works well in most multicultural settings. This **Village English activity** respects and encourages children's home languages while helping them see relationships between language use and power realities in the United States (Au, 1993, p. 133). The Village English activity begins with the teacher writing "Our Language Heritage" at the top of half a piece of poster board, and "Standard American English" at the top of the second half. The teacher explains to students that in America, people speak in many different ways, which makes our nation as colorful and interesting as a patchwork quilt. For elementary

students, we think this would be a good time to share *Elmer* by David McKee (1990), a book about an elephant of many colors (called a "patchwork elephant") who enriched the elephant culture. The teacher can explain that there are times when adults want to speak in the same way so they can be understood by people of all cultures, and that these times are usually formal situations. In formal situations, we speak Standard American English. When at home or with friends in our community, we usually speak the language of our heritage. It is like the difference between a picnic compared to a "dressed up" formal dinner. On the chart, then, phrases used in the native dialect can be written under the heading "Our Language Heritage," and comparative translations are noted and discussed on the side labeled "Standard American English." These comparisons can be noted in an ongoing way throughout the year as dialect or other forms of language are naturally encountered in the context of speech or reading activities. The Village English activity can be an interesting way to increase vocabulary knowledge while also valuing language differences.

Summary

Students' knowledge of words directly affects their success as readers. Hypotheses (e.g., instrumental, aptitude, knowledge, access) have been advanced to help explain how children learn new words. From these theories, we understand that parents can help their children succeed in expanding concept and vocabulary knowledge by exposing them to new experiences and helping them to read about and discuss new ideas in the home. Teachers can select learning activities that give students concrete opportunities to learn new vocabulary. These activities should help students internalize new words and concepts so that reading can become an automatic process. Learning experiences should help students acquire initial knowledge of new words and embellish or extend meanings of previously learned words or concepts. Ultimately, the task is to help students internalize strategies for the lifelong process of learning new words independently.

Concept Applications

In the Classroom

1. Design a mini-lesson introducing word maps to fifth-grade students. You should be certain that the lesson follows the "whole-to-parts" principle, as described in chapter 1.
2. Create a "Deceptive Language" bulletin board, either formal design or collage, that shows various uses of euphemisms in advertising aimed at children as consumers. Create a second board showing how these same tactics are used on adults through advertising (and perhaps by political leaders!).

In the Field

1. Do an interest inventory with five students in a local elementary school. Next, prepare an IIS that matches at least four of their interests to popular children's literature. Ideas for the books should come from the school librarian or from D. Norton's (1998) book *Through the Eyes of a Child: An Introduction to Children's Literature.* Finally, present the IIS forms to each child, and explain how they are to be used. Copies of both forms should be turned in to your college instructor, along with a journal entry explaining how each child reacted.

2. Prepare and teach a mini-lesson demonstrating the VSS. Develop a simple handout for the students with helpful hints about collecting new words for investigation.
3. Locate an elementary classroom in which the writing process (discussed in chapter 12) is practiced. Working with two child-volunteers, prepare a mini-lesson on synonyms and antonyms using samples they permit you to borrow from their writing folders.

Recommended Readings

Au, K. H. (1993). *Literacy instruction in multicultural settings.* Fort Worth, TX: Harcourt Brace.

Cunningham, P. M. (1995). *Phonics they use* (2nd ed.). New York: HarperCollins.

Johnson, D., & Pearson, P. D. (1984). *Teaching reading vocabulary.* New York: Holt, Rinehart and Winston.

McKee, D. (1990). *Elmer.* London: Red Fox.

Reutzel, D. R., and Cooter, R. B., Jr. (1999). *Balanced reading strategies and practices: Assessing and assisting readers with special needs.* Upper Saddle River, NJ: Merrill/Prentice Hall.

Focus Questions

When you are finished studying this chapter, you should be able to answer these questions:

1. What lessons can be drawn, positive as well as negative, concerning whole language practices?
2. What is the importance of *segmenting* and *blending* in reading and writing?
3. What are the differences among *phonemic awareness, alphabetic principle,* and *phonics?* When and how do each of these abilities develop in a balanced literacy classroom?
4. What are some of the pros and cons regarding the need for intensive phonics instruction?
5. What is the value of teaching onsets and rimes?
6. What is meant by *structural analysis?*
7. How can children in ESL (English as a second language) and bilingual classrooms be helped to develop phonemic awareness in beginning reading instruction?

Identifying Words in Print

Key Concepts

Blending
Segmenting
Alphabetic Principle
Phonemic Awareness
Phonemes
Onset and Rime
Alphabet Books

Phonics
Morphemes
Structural Analysis
Early Literacy Milestone Skills
Mini-Lessons
Whole to Parts to Whole
SOL Students

*R*eading education, as much as any other area in the teaching profession, is prone to pendulum swings in instructional practice. For the past several years, there has been a spirited, even bitter debate about *what* our children need to learn in beginning reading instruction, and *how* they should be taught. This latest controversy was triggered, at least in part, by a disastrous decline in the reading test scores of children in California (Lemann, 1997)—they slid from superiority levels to next to last place nationally, ahead of only Guam. Many California educators, balanced reading supporters, proponents of traditional skill and drill reading methods, and political leaders ultimately place the blame for this monumental educational debacle squarely on the American whole language movement.

RECENT RESEARCH CONCERNING BEGINNING READING INSTRUCTION

The latest "reading wars" debate has been a reprise of a century-old debate, this time between "phonics-first" advocates and American whole language promoters.

The current swing of the reading pendulum is but a reprise of a familiar argument. In the 19th century, the debate largely was between advocates of the *alphabetic approach* (the forerunner of phonics) and the *whole word* method for teaching reading. The much lampooned mid-twentieth-century *Dick and Jane* readers are based on a whole word methodology (Lemann, 1997): where children are familiarized with a limited set of simple words with which to begin reading instead of decoding words using phonics generalizations. The most recent rhetoric in the debate between whole language and phonics drill advocates portrays one side as a nurturing but skill-less environment in which children are expected to "naturally" blossom but rarely do (whole language), and the other side (phonics) as a kind of factory floor that will produce effective decoders who grow to hate reading in the process. As with most arguments, there is some truth, perhaps a great deal of it, evident in both criticisms.

Phonics drill advocates point to the research that says a whole language approach has failed to produce children who can read.

Whole language proponents worry that focusing on phonics will produce effective decoders who grow to hate learning to read.

What seemed to exacerbate "the reading wars" (Lemann, 1997) was the realization that literacy levels are indeed deteriorating in many locales, especially in urban centers. For example, in one Southwestern metropolis, only 45% of the children read on the expected grade level at the end of third grade. What makes matters worse is that the problem grows even more desperate over time, so that by ninth grade the average reading level in this major city is some 2 1/2 years below the expected level (Cooter, 1998). This description is just a microcosm of what is happening nationally; *we are losing ground in the struggle to achieve basic literacy levels in America.* Furthermore, it is clear from reviewing national trends over the past 2 decades (see National Assessment of Educational Progress [NAEP], 1994) that educational problems seen in urban settings today accurately foreshadow what will eventually come to suburbia tomorrow. Hence, the development of early reading *ability,* and the concomitant prevention of reading *disability,* are of major importance to our nation and world community.

> *With literacy levels declining in urban centers and elsewhere, it is clear that we have been losing the struggle to achieve basic literacy levels in America (Cooter, 1998).*

At about the same time as the California collapse, important research on beginning reading by Marilyn Jager Adams (1990a, 1990b) came onto the scene. Based on a review of nearly 100 years of reading research, Adams's findings concluded that the two best predictors of beginning reading success are *alphabet knowledge* and *phonemic awareness* (i.e., the understanding that spoken words are made up of individual speech sounds). The value of directly teaching children phonemic awareness, alphabetic principle, and phonics was further demonstrated in numerous other studies (e.g., Lyon, 1998), thus triggering a return swing of the reading pendulum toward explicit skill-drill or "phonics first" methods. Because so many teachers and researchers found the prior overemphasis on skill development to be so ineffective (i.e., mind-numbing word-identification drills taught within a context of contrived and boring "decodable" materials, such as texts like "the fat cat sat on the mat"), there has been considerable consternation that some of the positive lessons learned from the whole language era (i.e., the value of teaching reading with quality literature) might become the proverbial babies thrown out with the bath water.

> *Nearly 100 years of research indicates that alphabet knowledge and phonemic awareness are two predictors of beginning reading success (Adams, 1990a).*

So the friction point in reading education during the 1990s has largely been between traditional phonics-first advocates—refreshed by new supportive research—and American whole language proponents. Interestingly, both camps in the debate now seem to claim allegiance to a *balanced* approach (Lemann, 1997) involving some elements of whole language and phonics. Perhaps this situation is due, at least in part, to governmental leadership in many states, including California and Texas, mandating a "balanced approach" to reading instruction.

> *Paradoxically, the "reading wars" have been resolved with both sides of the debate in favor of balanced literacy approaches to word identification (Snow, 1999).*

One of the more ironic consequences of the current debate on what balanced reading methodology should look like is the further fragmentation of reading instruction itself. There appears to be a growing tendency with some teachers and researchers to try to merge whole language strategies with phonics, phonemic awareness worksheets, and related programs (what we refer to as "reading-in-a-box" programs)—all in an attempt to "balance" instruction. The confusion that often results can lead to children who are *instructionally* disabled: They fail to attain reading fluency because of poorly conceived teaching! How can we reverse this trend? The answer lies, as always, in knowledgeable teachers who have expertise in (a) systematically assessing where children are in their reading development, (b) thoughtfully planning instruction that attends to needed next steps within the child's zone of proximal development, and (c) offering best-teaching practices (see Snow, Burn, & Griffin, 1998 for supportive research).

Optimal word-identification instruction requires a knowledgeable teacher with expertise in assessment, grouping according to student needs, and discernment of best teaching strategies.

Decoding printed language involves, at least in part, the efficient use of phonics, word analysis, and other cueing systems.

*Reading entails **segmenting** and **blending** sound elements represented by alphabet letters and their combinations.*

In other words, the solution for meeting the literacy needs of all children is a knowledgeable and skilled classroom teacher. To that end, we review in this chapter the most potent research currently available for helping students acquire word-identification skills as well as ways of helping children acquire these important skills within a context of rich language and literature.

THE RELATIONSHIP OF DECODING INSTRUCTION WITH READING AND WRITING PROCESSES

It is a familiar truism in education that language arts instruction involves four primary areas: listening, speaking, reading, and writing. Listening and reading are considered "receptive" language arts because they involve *receiving* a message. In the case of reading, receiving a message partly involves translating or "decoding" printed language into speech using phonics and other skills. Speaking and writing are considered "productive" language arts because one is expected to *produce* a message for an audience to receive. In many ways, the receptive and productive language arts are mirror or reverse processes. The next two sections take a closer look at two of these processes, reading and writing, and the key skills they require.

Reading Uses "Segmenting" and "Blending"

Reading, as a receptive language process, depends heavily on the student's ability to break down (**segment**) unfamiliar words into individual sound units, **blend** them, then pronounce the word correctly. This is what people imply when they ask a child to "sound out" an unfamiliar word in print. This process must eventually become automatic for fluent reading and comprehension to develop. So the question becomes: How do we develop these skills in beginning readers?

A very logical sequence of development has been verified through a careful review of the research (R. Cooter, Reutzel, & K. Cooter, 1998). In Figure 8.1, we display the developmental sequence in which the decoding of words should be taught and learned.

Figure 8.1   Sequence of decoding skill instruction

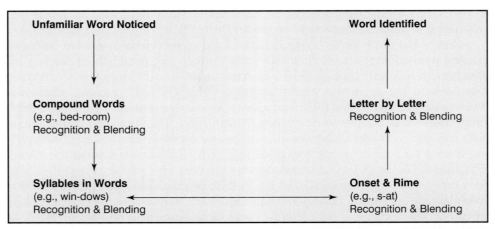

From *Sequence of Development and Instruction for Phonemic Awareness* by R. B. Cooter, Jr., D. R. Reutzel, and K. S. Cooter, 1998, unpublished paper.

Note that the sequence proceeds from breaking down the simplest sound and meaning units in words (compounds) to the most abstract skill (individual letter sounds). Students are first helped merely to attend to the fact that they have encountered a word in print that is unknown to them (we are assuming here that the student recognizes the word when it is spoken—completely unknown words must be attacked using dictionary skills and decoding to achieve true word recognition).

The first skill to be taught will be decoding compound words. This is the simplest strategy because the student can essentially attend to "little words within the big word" that are already known. Ideally, two-syllable words like *bathroom, sunshine, doghouse, bedroom, bookshelf,* and *toothbrush* can be used to introduce the skill, because each one-syllable word is familiar.

The next decoding skill to be taught is recognizing syllables. Simple two-syllable words like *window* and *table* are used to introduce this skill because they are phonetically regular, common words. Following the decoding of syllables, students are then led into breaking down single- and multisyllable words using onset and rime (the *rime* is the part of the syllable containing the vowel, and the *onset* is the letter or letters just before; discussed later in the chapter). This process would begin with one-syllable words like *sat* (s - at) and progress to more challenging multisyllable words like *kindergarten* (k-in/d-er/g-ar/t-en).

The final and most abstract phonics skill is letter-by-letter sounding. Again, instruction would begin with simple one-syllable words like *cat* (c-a-t) or *doll* (d-o-ll). Once the entire repertoire of decoding skills is learned and practiced through a great deal of sustained and pleasurable reading, children are much more able to select the simplest decoding strategy when needed and do it automatically. They have learned to move from the recognition of an unknown word in print ("*whole* word level") to decoding individual sound units ("*parts* level") to *blending* the individual letter sounds for the correct identification of the word ("*whole* word level"). This is why we say that reading uses blending, an important concept and skill for students in their trek toward fluent reading.

> *Instruction should begin with breaking down the simplest sound and meaning units in words and proceed gradually to the most abstract decoding skill (individual letter sounds).*

> *Skill instruction should proceed in a "whole-to-parts-to-whole" sequence (Reutzel & Cooter, 1992).*

Writing Uses "Segmenting" and "Blending"

Reading and writing are reciprocal processes that build on one another. They are also mirror image processes that rely on many of the same skills and abilities. As you help students become writers, they also mature as readers. Writing, at least in terms of the mechanical process of translating spoken words into print so that others can *receive* a message, relies on one's ability to segment words.

> *Writing also involves segmenting and blending skills.*

Segmenting in the writing process means breaking down spoken words into their individual sound units so that they can be represented by the accepted alphabet letter sequence. The process of matching the correct letter or letter combination to represent the speech sounds in a word is what we refer to as *mapping*. By *blending* what has been written, the writer verifies that he or she selected the correct letters to represent the sounds in each word.

Implications for Early and Emergent Reading Instruction

As we have demonstrated, reading and writing are heavily dependent on the student's ability to *segment* and *blend* words. In fact, there are elements of both segmenting and blending in each process. In reading, we must first break apart or segment unfamiliar words into sound-symbol (also called *phoneme-grapheme*) units, then blend them together to correctly "sound out" the word. In writing, using the reverse process, we must break apart or segment words in order to "map" letters (graphemes) to individual speech sounds (phonemes) correctly. We check our accuracy as writers when we "blend" the graphemes together and pronounce the word.

The implications for teaching emergent and early readers is clear. We must:

Describe four implications from the research for instructing early and emergent readers.

- help children understand that our spoken language is made up of individual words.
- help children understand that words have individual speech sounds.
- help children learn how to segment and blend spoken words as a precursor to doing those same skills in reading and writing.
- help children begin to understand that individual speech sounds can be represented by letters of the alphabet.

Research in the areas of phonemic awareness and alphabetic principle has addressed each of these requirements thoroughly. In the next sections, we take a closer look at each as well as at implications for teaching.

A DEVELOPMENTAL AND INSTRUCTIONAL SEQUENCE FOR PHONEMIC AWARENESS, ALPHABETIC PRINCIPLE, AND PHONICS

Phonemic awareness necessarily comes before alphabetic principle and phonics.

One of the continuing challenges for practicing teachers is how to unravel and apply myriad research findings in reading to their classroom teaching. This task has been especially challenging of late in the areas of phonemic awareness, alphabetic principle, and phonics. We are constantly asked to define each of these terms and answer questions like these: Aren't phonics and phonemic awareness basically the same? (Answer: No.) Does it matter when you offer instruction in these three areas? (Answer: Yes, indeed!) Is it appropriate to teach all children some of all three of these skill areas every day in grades K–2? (Answer: No, it is *not* appropriate.)

R. Cooter, Reutzel, and K. Cooter (1998) developed two instructional models to help teachers interpret the research on phonemic awareness, alphabetic principle, and phonics. Figure 8.2 shows the development of children from the emergent reading stage toward fluent reading, at least in terms of word identification.

Phonemic awareness activities are strictly oral in nature (i.e., no printed language or letters are used).

Notice that they have depicted the three developmental areas as a developmental staircase of sorts progressing from (a) the most basic level of **phonemic awareness** (an exclusively oral language activity), to (b) **alphabetic principle** development (matching elemental sounds and the letters that represent them), and ultimately to (c) **phonics** (decoding written symbols to speech sounds). This progression from exclusively speech/sound activities to eventually understanding how to decode symbols back to speech sounds is at the heart of recent breakthroughs in reading research.

Figure 8.3 on p. 268 breaks down the phonemic awareness step shown in Figure 8.2 to its constituent parts (R. Cooter, Reutzel, & K. Cooter, 1998).

The term "WHOLE" seen at the beginning of the flow with *Spoken Word* indicates that language instruction should begin with whole words and thoughts that make sense to the student. We discuss the concept of teaching skills from *whole to parts to whole* as described by Reutzel and Cooter (1992, 1996) later in this chapter. As you follow the arrows, you note that students will first become aware that spoken words have parts. For example, when we verbally stretch out the word *cat* in a

Figure 8.2 Phonemic awareness, alphabetic principle, and phonics: Developmental and instructional progression

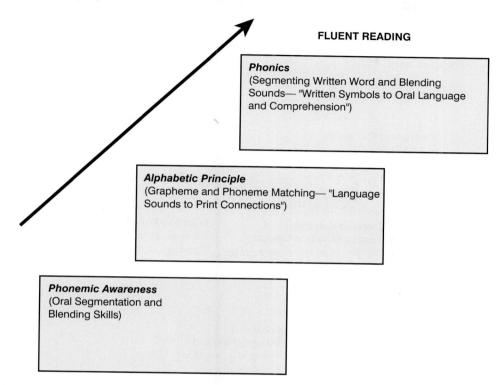

FLUENT READING

Phonics
(Segmenting Written Word and Blending Sounds— "Written Symbols to Oral Language and Comprehension")

Alphabetic Principle
(Grapheme and Phoneme Matching— "Language Sounds to Print Connections")

Phonemic Awareness
(Oral Segmentation and Blending Skills)

EMERGENT READING

From *Sequence of Development and Instruction for Phonemic Awareness* by R. B. Cooter, Jr., D. R. Reutzel, and K. S. Cooter, 1998, unpublished paper.

verbal exercise known as *word rubberbanding,* it is easy to notice that *cat* has three distinct speech sounds: the sound represented by "c," the sound represented by short "a," and the sound represented by "t." When the sounds are blended together, they give us the word we know as *cat* and the meaning that goes along with it.

The arrows in Figure 8.3 lead us through the developmental and teaching stages necessary to help children analyze words by their parts—hence, the word "PARTS" at the bottom of the model signifying our desire to help children break spoken words down into their individual sound elements. Finally, we bring students back to whole words as they are taught to blend the sound parts (thus, the word "WHOLE" at the top of the model). Once full phonemic awareness is attained, students are then ready to learn the alphabetic principle, followed by phonics.

PHONEMIC AWARENESS

An Anticipation Guide on Phonemic Awareness

In spite of the massive publicity surrounding the topic, there has been a good bit of confusion about phonemic awareness in recent years. To begin the study of this topic correctly, complete the anticipation guide (Figure 8.4 on p. 269) to discover the

Figure 8.2 provides an outline of the major topics for the next few sections of this chapter. Figure 8.3 is a rather detailed introduction for the first of these sections—phonemic awareness.

*Note that phonemic awareness teaching also moves from **whole to parts to whole.***

*Complete the phonemic awareness "anticipation guide" **before** reading further, then retake the quiz **after** reading to see if your prereading assumptions were accurate.*

Figure 8.3   Sequence of development and instruction for phonemic awareness

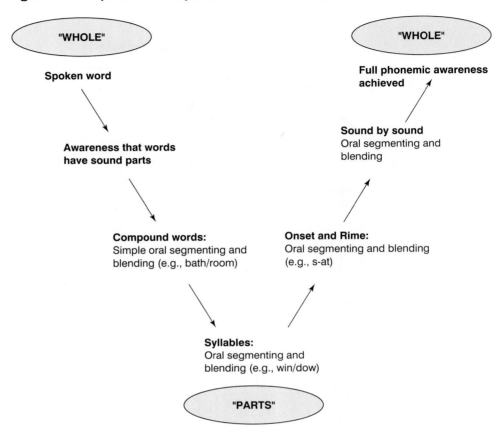

From *Sequence of Development and Instruction for Phonemic Awareness* by R. B. Cooter, Jr.,
D. R. Reutzel, and K. S. Cooter, 1998, unpublished paper.

depths of your own prior knowledge of phonemic awareness. After reading this section, you should complete the anticipation guide again to see if your opinions and understandings have changed. You may want to use this technique as a tool in future teaching situations as a kind of "action research" experiment.

Research on Phonemic Awareness

Much research in recent years has focused attention on two aspects of word identification: *phonemic awareness* and the *alphabetic principle. Phonemic awareness* refers to the understanding that spoken words are made up of individual sounds called **phonemes** (Pikulski & Templeton, 1997). The term *phonological awareness* is a more recent term appearing in professional writings that has an even broader meaning (referring to such oral language units as words, syllables, and individual speech sounds). For our purposes in this chapter, we use the much more common term *phonemic awareness* for all levels of oral language awareness.

When most children begin their schooling, they come equipped with a sizable vocabulary and a fairly well developed knowledge of syntax. However, many lack

Figure 8.4   Phonemic awareness

Anticipation Guide

Directions: Read each statement and decide if it is **TRUE** or **FALSE**. Write your response in column A. After reading this part of the chapter on Phonemic Awareness, reread the statements and respond in column B. Discuss the differences in your responses with a fellow student (or the instructor if you are taking a college course).

A   **B**

_____   1.   At least 80% of all children require instruction in phonemic awareness in order to be successful in learning to read.   _____

_____   2.   Phonemic awareness refers to a child's awareness of sounds that make up words.   _____

_____   3.   Measures of phonemic awareness have been found to predict success in early reading as well as measures of intelligence, general language development, and listening comprehension.   _____

_____   4.   Phonemic awareness has nothing to do with writing.   _____

_____   5.   Children who are low in reading performance rarely score low in phonemic awareness.   _____

_____   6.   Instruction in phonemic awareness alone is not enough to prevent and correct reading problems.   _____

_____   7.   If children have acquired phonemic awareness then they also understand the alphabetic principle.   _____

_____   8.   Individual sounds are easier to hear than syllables, so they should be taught first.   _____

_____   9.   Phonemic awareness is the same thing as phonics.   _____

_____   10.   Blending sounds to produce words is one of the easiest phonemic awareness skills.   _____

_____   11.   Research indicates a particular sequence for teaching phonemic awareness.   _____

_____   12.   Matching letters to the speech sounds they represent is an appropriate phonemic awareness activity.   _____

phonemic awareness. For instance, the word *dog* is known to many 4- and 5-year-olds only as a domestic animal that walks on four legs. They usually lack the awareness that *dog* is composed of three sound units or phonemes, /d/, /o/, and /g/.

Numerous studies have been conducted to determine whether phonemic awareness is necessary for children to become successful beginning readers. The answer seems to be that phonemic awareness is an important factor, but not sufficient in and of itself to ensure reading success (Lyon, 1997). Rather, instruction in phonemic awareness should be viewed as an important element of a balanced reading program in the early elementary grades. About 20% to 30% of students lack phonemic awareness, a problem that can be easily resolved with a few weeks of instruction for about 15 minutes each day.

Phonemic awareness is an important factor in beginning reading success (Lyon, 1997).

Five Basic Phonemic Awareness Tasks

Adams (1990) has identified five essential phonemic awareness tasks for students to acquire. Can you name them?

Marilyn Jager Adams (1990) has identified five basic tasks in phonemic awareness that can help children develop as readers. They have been described by Blevins (1997, p. 5) in this way:

Task 1:   **The ability to hear *rhymes* and *alliteration*.**

   Sample exercise: Listen to a nursery rhyme and ask the children to identify words that sound alike.

Task 2:   **The ability to do *oddity* tasks.**

   Sample exercise: Look at these pictures—*desk, dog, car.* Which word begins with a different sound? (*car*)

Task 3:   **The ability to *orally blend words* and *split syllables*.**

   Sample exercise: "I will say the first part of a word, then the rest of the word. Say the word as a whole. /m/ . . . ouse. What is the word?" (*mouse*).

Task 4:   **The ability to do *phonemic manipulation* tasks.**

   Sample exercise: "Replace the beginning sound in the word *book* with /l/. What is the new word?" (*look*)

Task 5:   **The ability to *orally segment words* (including counting sounds).**

   Sample exercise: "What sounds do you hear in the word *bat?*" (three—/b/ /a/ /t/)

The Instructional Sequence of Phonemic Awareness Tasks

Describe how "word rubberbanding" activities can help students learn to hear speech sounds.

Phonemic awareness instruction tackles the segmenting and blending of simple compound words first.

Another area of confusion has to do with the order of teaching and learning of the five primary phonemic awareness tasks. Figure 8.3 shows that the most basic starting point is helping students understand that spoken words are made up of individual speech sounds. Word stretching activities such as "word rubberbanding" can help students begin to hear these speech sounds. Once this most basic level of awareness begins to emerge, teachers should help students begin to develop simple segmenting and blending skills using compound words. For example, children are able to catch on quickly that simple compound words like *airport, bloodhound, clothespin,* and *rainbow* are just two smaller words "glued" together. They can hear and segment the two spoken words easily! If the compound words are chosen so that each word part is a one-syllable word that carries a meaning students easily understand, both the sound and meaning connections can be understood at once by most students. Learning simple segmenting and blending with compound words is the first major jump into phonemic awareness and partially accomplishes Blevins's (1997) Tasks 1 and 2.

   Syllables are the next speech sound unit for students to segment and blend. This step moves students from simply segmenting known word parts in compound words to dividing words by sound units that seem more abstract. Clapping sounds the student hears in words like *window* and *kindergarten* helps them to segment sound elements (i.e., win-dow, kin-der-gar-ten). Blending activities such as: "I will say the first part of a word, then the rest of the word. Say the word as a whole. /sha/ . . . dow. What is the word? (*shadow*)" help students further develop Task 1 and 2 level phonemic awareness skills.

The next phonemic awareness level calls for segmenting and blending **onset** and **rime.** An *onset* is the part of a syllable that comes before the vowel; the *rime* is the rest (Adams, 1990b, p. 55). This is the case in most one-syllable words. For example, in the word *sat,* "s" is the onset and "-at" is the rime. Similarly, in the first syllable of the word *turtle,* "t" is the onset and "-ur" is the rime. When this activity is done in the context of poetry (teaching rimes with *rhymes*), you are able to accomplish Blevins's (1997) Task 3.

We go into greater detail on onset and rime later in the chapter, and then show you how to do these oral/aural activities in chapter 11.

Segmenting spoken words sound by sound is the next and most abstract level of phonemic awareness, and is a necessary forerunner of letter-by-letter sounding out in phonics. The difference here is that we segment, then blend, individual *sounds* in spoken words.

The final stage of phonemic awareness development helps children use phonemic segmentation and blending in more sophisticated and fun ways (Tasks 4 and 5). As children are able to do oddity and manipulation tasks with ease, they are poised for the next big step: alphabetic principle. In chapter 11, we offer further ideas for teaching these five basic phonemic awareness tasks.

Some Tips for Planning Instruction in Phonemic Awareness

Blevins (1997, pp. 7–8) has summarized some useful points on phonemic awareness that are important for teachers in kindergarten through grade 2 to keep in mind as they plan for instruction.

What are some of the more important tips for planning phonemic awareness instruction offered by Blevins (1997)?

- *Phonemic awareness is not related to print.* Oral and aural (listening) activities are what phonemic awareness teaching and learning are all about. Once children can name and identify the letters of the alphabet, they are ready to move into learning the *alphabetic principle.*
- *Many, if not most, poor readers in the early grades have weak phonemic awareness skills.* Thus, phonemic awareness may be an important issue (on a limited basis) for teachers well beyond the K–2 years. Indeed, phonemic awareness training may well be indicated throughout K–12 education for students considered "remedial" readers.
- *Model, model, model!* Children need to see their teacher and other students actually doing the phonemic awareness activities you offer.

Several other recommendations have been suggested (National Association for the Education of Young Children, 1986; Yopp, 1992) for the selection of phonemic awareness activities.

- *Learning activities should help foster positive feelings toward learning through an atmosphere of playfulness and fun.* Drill activities in phonemic awareness should be avoided, as should rote memorization.
- *Interaction among children should be encouraged through group activities.* Language play seems to be most effective in group settings.
- *Curiosity about language and experimentation should be encouraged.* Teachers should react positively when students engage in language manipulation.

- *Teachers should be prepared for wide differences in the acquisition of phonemic awareness.* Some children will catch on quickly, whereas others will take much longer. Teachers should avoid making quick judgments about children based on how they perform in phonemic awareness activities.

REMINDER: Now that you have finished reading about phonemic awareness, go back and complete the anticipation guide in Figure 8.4.

ALPHABETIC PRINCIPLE

Alphabetic princi-ple is the knowledge that speech sounds can be represented by letters.

In chapter 11, we suggest a number of ways teachers can introduce the alphabetic princi-ple to young students.

Phonemic awareness combined with letter-sound knowledge is necessary for students to attain a new level of understanding called the *alphabetic principle* (Byrne & Fielding-Barnsley, 1989), which is the knowledge that speech sounds can be represented by a letter or letters and that when a given sound occurs anywhere in a word it can be represented by the same letter(s). Discovery of the alphabetic principle is thought to be necessary for students to fully master reading, although this is not all there is to reading; for instance, the ability to use context clues is essential. Therefore, teachers need to seek out activities that help students learn (a) the alphabet letters and the

How might the interaction among children develop their language skills?

Figure 8.5   An alphabet book for the letter *e*
Courtesy Carol Berrey and Ruth Marie Carter.

page 1:	Ed is an *egg* lover.
	For breakfast, he ate a . . .
page 2:	happy *egg.*
page 3:	Ed ate a boiled *egg.*
page 4:	Ed ate a fried *egg.*
page 5:	Ed ate a scrambled *egg.*
page 6:	For lunch, Ed ate an egg McMuffin (Don't
	forget to draw in the "Golden Arches!")
page 7:	Ed ate *egg* salad.
page 8:	Ed ate a deviled *egg.*
page 9:	And, Ed ate an *egg* sandwich.
page 10:	Ed went on an Easter *egg* hunt.
page 11:	Ed found a bird's *egg.*
page 12:	Ed found a chicken's *egg.*
page 13:	Ed found a duck's *egg.*
page 14:	Ed found a dozen *eggs.*
page 15:	Ed likes *eggs.* Don't you?

sounds they represent, (b) that speech is made up of individual sounds that can be represented by specific letters and letter combinations, and (c) that the spellings of words remain generally constant across the various books or texts children encounter. In the next section, we share one strategy with which we have had significant success.

An "Alphabet Books" Approach

Aside from the traditional way of teaching the alphabet (i.e., singing the alphabet to the tune of *Twinkle, Twinkle, Little Star*), teachers can construct highly predictable alphabet books to teach letter names and the sounds they represent (Cooter & Flynt, 1989). **Alphabet books** help students achieve two important goals in kindergarten and first-grade settings: develop (a) a sense from the first day of school that they can read and (b) a working knowledge of the alphabet and the sounds they represent.

These teacher-developed predictable books tend to follow one of several patterns. Some, for example, follow a "sentence that grows" pattern. These books begin with a kernel sentence, which is repeated, and added to, on each successive page. When the sentence becomes about as long as what a beginning reader can handle, a new kernel sentence is put into play.

Another alphabet book format uses a repeating word that simply changes the rest of the sentence each time. Carol Berrey and Ruth Marie Carter, two teachers from Chetopa, Kansas, developed such a book for the letter *e*. The last page of the book has a raised yellow center. Each preceding white page has the center cut out so the egg yolk appears on every page. The script for this book is in Figure 8.5.

In a third alphabet book format, the teacher rewrites lyrics of familiar songs such as "Eensy, Weensy Spider" or "Row, Row, Row Your Boat" to conform to a given

*This **alphabet books** approach has been proven effective in teaching students letters of the alphabet as well as many sight words.*

theme, such as *cats* for letter *c*. This alphabet book is made in the shape of a cat and should be sung to any familiar song's tune.

A Format for Using the Alphabet Books Approach

Once alphabet books have been written and produced for classroom use, several possibilities exist for their use. A format adapted from the first-grade study mentioned previously (Cooter & Flynt, 1989) is described in this section.

What is the progression of instruction with the alphabet books approach?

First, the teacher introduces a letter theme for the day with a collage bulletin board featuring many familiar objects in the children's environment that begin with the letter sound. For example, the letter *c* might feature pictures cut from magazines, such as a car, a cop, a calendar, a carpenter, and a cat. After identifying these objects, the teacher gathers the children into the shared reading experience area to listen to the alphabet book. The teacher holds the book up for the class to see as he or she reads the story aloud (the book is much easier to use if it has been made into a big book). After the teacher has read the alphabet book aloud once or twice and discussed its story, the children are invited to join in for choral rereading of the book several more times.

At this point in the lesson, the children return to their seats. In the Cooter and Flynt (1989) study, each child was then given a photocopy of the alphabet book made from the pattern of the teacher's copy (8 1/2 × 11-inch size). The story was read again chorally once or twice more, then the children were allowed a few minutes to color some of the pictures. The student copies were brought out again at the end of the day and reread chorally once or twice. Alphabet books went home in a large envelope with each child to read to as many people in the home as possible. A home reading response form (Figure 8.6) was attached to the envelope to be signed by each person who listened to the child read. This envelope was returned each day and checked by the teacher to confirm home support of the reading process.

Innovations With the Alphabet Books Approach

Reproduction and innovation books are wonderful activities for a writing center.

Children can combine reading and writing modes with alphabet books to increase emergent literacy opportunities. Typically, teachers establish a writing center in their classrooms in which students can create both reproductions and innovations of alphabet books already shared. A reproduction is a student-made copy of the original alphabet book: Children copy the text on each page exactly and draw their own illustrations. Innovations borrow the basic pattern of the alphabet book but change key words. For instance, one group of first-grade students took the book *Brown Bear, Brown Bear, What Do You See?* (Martin, 1983) and created an innovation based on Halloween characters. Part of the students' text read

Brown spider, brown spider,	Black cat, black cat,
What do you see?	What do you see?
I see a black cat looking at me!	I see a white skeleton looking at me.*

These reproductions and innovations help students take ownership of the text and encourage good-spirited risk taking in the classroom.

*Excerpts adapted from *Brown Bear, Brown Bear, What Do You See?*, copyright © 1970 by Harcourt, Inc. renewed 1998 by Bill Martin Jr., reprinted by permission of the publisher.

Figure 8.6   Home reading response form

Home Reading Response Form

Directions: Please indicate below that your child has read to you his/her book or that you have read it with him/her. Your child should then return the envelope and receive a new book tomorrow.

Thank you!

Name of the Book	Adult Partner	Date

Benefits of the Alphabet Books Approach

One of the great benefits of using alphabet books in either kindergarten or first grade is that no matter what the socioeconomic level of the children, every child ends up owning at least 26 readable books at the conclusion of the units. Children love these books and read them time and again.

Another benefit of this approach is the massive practice it gives children with high-frequency and high-interest words. In the Cooter and Flynt study (1989), the teacher carefully went through each of the alphabet books and verified which words were also found in the basal series adopted by the school district. All of the basal words were found in both the alphabet books and the first three preprimers of the first-grade basal series, with the exception of 10 words (e.g., *Buffy, Mack,* and other proper nouns).

Alphabet books can also be used as a springboard to other activities such as handwriting practice of each letter, word identification and phonics instruction through mini-lessons, and other lessons related to the reading and writing process. Cooter and Flynt (1989) reported:

> At the end of the [alphabet book units] each child has read 26 books . . . acquired basic handwriting skills including the formation of all letters (upper and lower case), developed a basic understanding of beginning, medial, and ending sounds in words, mastered most basic concepts about print, and [learned] something about authoring. (p. 278)

Commercial Alphabet Books

Many terrific alphabet books are available from commercial sources.

Teachers wanting to use alphabet books may not have the necessary time at first for making their own books. Many books already available in most school libraries could be used for much the same purpose. For instance, one could use Bill Martin's (1983) *Brown Bear, Brown Bear, What Do You See?* book for the letter *B* theme. The book entitled *What a Mess!* (Cowley, 1982), distributed by the Wright Group, could be used for the letter *M* theme. Teachers can introduce alphabet letter themes using a book like *Animalia* (Base, 1986), which features all of the alphabet letters with multiple pictures of animals whose name begins with that letter. The main thing to remember in selecting commercially produced alphabet books is that the objects or characters pictured should be easy to identify and should not have more than one commonly used name (D. Norton, 1995). Several commercially available alphabet books follow:

Baldwin, R. M. (1972). *One hundred nineteenth-century rhyming alphabets in English.* Carbondale, IL: Southern Illinois University.

Bayer, J. (1984). *My name is Alice* (Steven Kellogg, illustrator). New York: Dial Books.

Hague, K. (1984). *Alphabears: An ABC book* (Michael Hague, illustrator). New York: Holt, Rinehart and Winston.

MacDonald, S. (1986). *Alphabatics.* New York: Bradbury.

Martin, B., & Archambault, J. (1989). *Chicka chicka boom boom.* New York: Simon and Schuster.

Musgrove, M. (1976). *Ashanti to Zulu: African traditions.* New York: Dial.

PHONICS INSTRUCTION IN BALANCED LITERACY CLASSROOMS

A Phonics Prereading Quiz

Complete the phonics "quick test" before reading this section. This will help alert you to key points to remember!

Recent surveys conducted by the International Reading Association (IRA) indicate that "phonics" is one of the most talked about subjects in the field of reading education (second only to the topic of "balanced reading"). Reutzel and Cooter (1999) have developed a phonics "quick test" (Figure 8.7) so that you can see how much you already know about the subject. Complete the exercise *before* reading further (the results may surprise you!). As with the anticipation guide on phonemic awareness, you may benefit from retaking the phonics quick test *after* you have finished reading this section.

Phonics: What We Know from Research and Practice

According to Adams (1990b), the most effective word-identification approaches involve systematic code instruction along with the reading of meaningful connected text.

Marilyn Jager Adams (1990b), in her exhaustive review of **phonics** and other factors essential to word identification entitled *Beginning to Read: Thinking and Learning About Print,* found that prereaders' letter knowledge was the single best predictor of first-year reading achievement, with their ability to discriminate phonemes auditorily ranking a close second (p. 36). Approaches in which systematic code instruction is included along with the reading of meaningful connected text result in superior reading achievement overall, for both low-readiness and better prepared students (p. 125).

Figure 8.7   The phonics quick test*

1.   The word *sparkle* is divided between _____ and _____ . The *a* has an _____ controlled sound, and the *e* _____ .

2.   In the word *small, sm-* is known as the "onset" and *-all* is known as the

     _____ .

3.   *Ch* in the word *chair* is known as a _____ .

4.   The letter *c* in the word *city* is a _____ sound, and in the word *cow,* it is a

     _____ sound.

5.   The letters *bl* in the word *blue* are referred to as a consonant _____ .

6.   The underlined vowels in the words *author, spread, and blue* are known as

     vowel _____ .

7.   The words *tag, run, cot,* and *get* have which vowel pattern? _____

8.   The words *glide, take,* and *use* have the _____ vowel pattern.

9.   The single most powerful phonics skill we can teach to emergent readers

     for decoding unfamiliar words in print is _____ sounds in words.

     We introduce this skill using *consonant/vowel* (choose one) sounds because

     they are _____ .

10. The word part "work" in the word *working* is known as a _____ .

11. The word part "-ing" in the word *working* is known as a _____ .

12. Cues to the meaning and pronunciation of unfamiliar words in print are

     often found in the print surrounding the unfamiliar—which is to say, in the

     _____ .

*Answers to the phonics quick test are found at the end of this chapter.

Adams also noted that these conclusions seem to hold true regardless of the instructional approach used to teach reading. However, it should be noted that very few, if any, studies have been conducted comparing balanced literacy word identification teaching strategies with more traditional skills instructional models or basal readers. Thus, Adams's review of the research appears to have a decided bent in favor of decoding and skills-based instructional methods. At any rate, one cannot deny that there is a compelling need to include phonics as at least one part of a comprehensive reading program.

Those who support the use of intensive phonics instruction in beginning reading cite several benefits of this practice (Chall, 1967; Flesch, 1955, 1981). One argument is that English spelling patterns are relatively consistent; therefore, phonics rules can aid the reader in approximating the pronunciation of unfamiliar words. As a result, phonics rules can assist the reader in triggering meaning for unfamiliar words if they are in the reader's listening and speaking vocabulary. It is felt that when phonics rules are applied in conjunction with semantic (meaning) and syntactic (grammar) cues in the passage, the reader can positively identify unknown words in most elementary reading level materials.

Those opposing intensive phonics programs cite a number of justifications for their position as well. The chief complaint is that the English language is *not* all that regular and that phonics generalizations often have many exceptions (A. J. Harris & Sipay, 1990). Focusing on ambiguous details in words, to the exclusion of such comprehension-based strategies as context clues, can actually cause children to miss appropriate meaning and word clues.

Another problem with overreliance on phonics cues is the time factor for processing the author's message. When engaged in the act of reading, the reader stores the author's message—as represented by each word, sentence, and paragraph—in short-term memory. As thoughts are constructed from the text, they are then more fully processed and may become part of long-term memory. If a reader who encounters an unknown word spends too much time trying to decode the word, then he or she risks forgetting (or losing from short-term memory) that earlier part of the message already processed. That is why many teachers tell children to "skip" unknown words and let the context of the passage "do the work for them." When considering how many phonics rules and generalizations exist, it is easy to see why some teachers feel that overreliance on phonic analysis, to the exclusion of context, is not helpful to emerging readers.

Another criticism of heavy skill-and-drill phonics programs has to do with what are known as *decodable texts,* which offer children only those words that they have been taught the phonics skills to sound out. Richard Allington (1997), in an amusing but research-proven commentary, described his objections to decodable texts this way:

> The decodable texts displayed at the recent meeting of the International Reading Association reminded me of nothing so much as the 1960s' "Nan can fan Dan" and "Nat the rat" readers.
>
> I submit that there is not a single well-designed study that supports the exclusive use of decodable texts in beginning reading (or remedial instruction). . . . There *is* research support for providing children with "manageable" texts—texts they can read without too much difficulty. (p. 15)

The question in building phonics knowledge in a balanced literacy program is not whether one should teach phonics strategies. Rather, the appropriate questions concern *which phonics skills should we teach* and *how should we teach them.* The following section answers the "which phonics skills" question.

Seven Phonics Generalizations

The most important and efficient phonics rules to teach beginning and remedial readers pertain to *beginning consonant sounds in words.* When used in conjunction with context clues and the readers' background knowledge, beginning consonant sounds can help students identify up to 90% of words typically found in elementary reading materials through about grade 2 or 3. This is because consonant sounds tend to be the most constant or reliable, as compared to vowels, which account for much of the variance in English.

The chief complaint against intensive phonics approaches is that most phonics generalizations hold true less than 50% of the time.

What are Richard Allington's (1997) complaints against exclusive use of so-called "decodable texts"?

Phonics instruction is an essential part of balanced reading instruction in the early grades.

These seven phonics generalizations hold true much of the time and should be included with other word-identification strategies.

According to May and Elliot (1978), only a few other phonics generalizations have a fairly high degree of reliability for readers. When students use phonics generalizations in conjunction with a more comprehensive word-identification strategy discussed earlier in the chapter, they should be able to successfully identify most words found in elementary reading materials. (Note: explanations in some cases are adapted from Hull, 1989.)

1. The C Rule

The letter *c* is an irregular consonant letter that has no phoneme of its own. Instead, it assumes two other phonemes found in different words, *k* and *s*. In general, when the letter *c* is followed by *a, o,* or *u,* it will represent the sound associated with the letter *k,* also known as the "hard *c*" sound. Some examples are the words *cake, cosmic,* and *cute.*

On the other hand, the letter *c* can sometimes represent the sound associated with the letter *s;* this is referred to as the "soft *c*" sound. This sound is usually produced when *c* is followed by *e, i,* or *y.* Examples of the soft *c* sound are found in the words *celebrate, circus,* and *cycle.*

2. The G Rule

G is the key symbol for the phoneme we hear in the word *get* (Hull, 1989, p. 35). It also is irregular, having a soft and a hard *g* sound. The rules for the letter *c* apply to the letter *g:* When *g* is followed by *a, o,* or *u,* it usually represents the hard or regular sound as with the words *garden, go,* and *sugar;* when *g* is followed by *e, i,* or *y,* it represents a soft *g* or *j* sound, as with the words *gently, giraffe,* and *gym.*

The C and G rules are essentially the same. Can you explain why?

3. The CVC Generalization

When a vowel comes between two consonants, it usually has the short vowel sound. Examples of words following the CVC pattern are *sat, ran, let, pen, win, fit, hot, mop, sun,* and *cut.*

4. Vowel Digraphs

When two vowels come together in a word, the first vowel is usually long and the second is silent; this occurs especially often with the *oa, ee,* and *ay* combinations. Some examples are *toad, fleet,* and *day.* A common slogan used by teachers, which helps children remember this generalization, is "when two vowels go walking, the first one does the talking."

An old, familiar phonics rule: "When two vowels go walking, the first one does the talking!"

5. The VCE (Final E) Generalization

When two vowels appear in a word and one is an *e* at the end of the word, the first vowel is generally long and the final *e* is silent. Examples are *cape, rope,* and *kite.*

6. The CV Generalization

When a consonant is followed by a vowel, the vowel usually produces a long sound. This is especially easy to see in two-letter words such as *be, go,* and *so.*

7. R-Controlled Vowels

Vowels that appear before the letter *r* are usually neither long nor short but tend to be overpowered or "swallowed up" by the sound. Examples are *person, player, neighborhood,* and *herself.*

Other Important Phonics Terms and Skills

Even though the seven phonics generalizations offered here are the most useful, most basal reading programs focus attention on many others. In the interest of thoroughness, following are several terms, definitions, and examples of other phonics skills related to consonants and vowels not already discussed in this chapter.

- *Consonant digraphs*—Two consonants together in a word that produce only one speech sound (*th, sh, ng*).
- *Consonant blends or clusters*—Two or more consonants together in which the speech sounds of all the consonants can be heard (*bl, fr, sk, spl*).
- *Schwa*—Vowel letters that produce the *uh* sound (*a* in *America*). The schwa is represented by the upside-down *e* symbol: ə
- *Diphthongs*—Two vowels together in a word that produce a single, glided sound (*oi* in *oil, oy* in *boy*).

Onset and Rime

Onset **and** *rimes* **are a promising supplement to traditional word-identification instruction.**

An onset is the part of a syllable that comes before the vowel, the rime is the vowel and the rest (Adams, 1990b).

The next developmental step for students learning to identify words independently is the ability to recognize beginning and ending sounds in syllables and words. This can be a tricky proposition because many of these sounds are irregular in written English. However, Adams (1990b) has unearthed a promising alternative in the concept known as *onsets* and *rimes* (recall that the onset is the part of the syllable that comes before the vowel, and the rime is the rest) (p. 55). Although all syllables must have a rime, not all will have an onset. In the following list are a few examples of onsets and rimes in words:

Word	Onset	Rime
a	—	a
in	—	in
aft	—	aft
sat	s-	-at
trim	tr-	-im
spring	spr-	-ing

Rimes are far more consistent in their sounds than most traditional phonics rules.

There are numerous benefits to incorporating recognition of onsets and rimes into word-identification instruction. First, some evidence seems to indicate that children are more able to identify the spelling of whole rimes than of individual vowel sounds (Adams, 1990b; Barton, Miller, & Macken, 1980; Blevins, 1997; Treiman, 1985). Second, children as young as 5 and 6 years of age can transfer what they know about the pronunciation of one word to another that has the same rime, such as *call* and *ball* (Adams, 1990b). Third, although many traditional phonics generalizations with vowels are very unstable, even irregular phonics patterns seem to remain stable within rimes. For example, the *ea* vowel digraph is quite consistent within rimes, with the exception of *-ear* in *hear* compared to *bear*, and *-ead* in *bead* compared to *head* (Adams, 1990b). Finally, there appears to be some utility for children in the learning of rimes: Nearly 500 primary-level words can be derived through the following set of only 37 rimes (Adams, 1990b; Blachman, 1984):

-ack	-at	-ide	-ock
-ain	-ate	-ight	-oke
-ake	-aw	-ill	-op
-ale	-ay	-in	-or
-all	-eat	-ine	-ore
-ame	-ell	-ing	-uck
-an	-est	-ink	-ug
-ank	-ice	-ip	-ump
-ap	-ick	-ir	-unk
-ash			

The application of onset and rime to reading and word identification seems obvious. Students should find it easier to identify new words in print by locating familiar rimes and using the sound clue along with context to make accurate guesses about their pronunciations. Spelling efficiency may also increase as rimes are matched with onsets to construct "temporary" spellings.

One teacher recently remarked that the easiest way to teach rimes is through *rhymes!* She was quite right. Children learn many otherwise laborious tasks through rhymes, songs, chants, and raps. Any of these that use rhyming words can be very useful. For example, teachers may wish to use an excerpt like this one from the book *Taxi Dog* (1990) by Debra and Sal Barracca to emphasize the *-ide* and *-ill* rimes. The rimes are noted in bold type.

Rhymes, songs, and raps are fun ways to teach onsets and rimes.

It's just like a dream,
Me and Jim—we're a team!
I'm always there at his s**ide.**
We never stand st**ill,**
Every day's a new thr**ill**—
Come join us next time for a r**ide!** (p. 30)

Structural Analysis and Morphemic Clues

Words are made up of basic meaning units known as **morphemes.** Morphemes can be divided into two classes—*bound* and *free*. Bound morphemes must be attached to a root word (sometimes called a *base word*) to have meaning. Prefixes and suffixes are bound morphemes (e.g., *pre-, un-, dis-, en-, inter-, extra-, -ed, -ies, -er, -ing*). Free morphemes (base words or root words) are meaning units or words that can stand alone and have meaning. The word *retroactive* has both a bound and free morpheme: *retro-,* the bound morpheme (prefix) meaning "backward," and *active,* the free morpheme meaning "working." Sometimes two free morphemes combine to form a new word, such as *doghouse, outdoors, playground,* and *tonight.* Studying words in this way to identify familiar word elements is known as **structural analysis.**

Morphemes are the basic meaning units of words.

Comprehending prefixes, suffixes, and root words is a structural analysis skill.

As children become more proficient using word-identification strategies and context
clues, they become more confi-
dent in "attacking" unknown
words in print.

Teachers can help children begin to practice structural analysis in the same way as for onset and rime. The idea to get across to students is that whenever good readers come to a word they cannot identify through context alone they some-times look within the word for a recognizable base (root) word and its accompa-nying prefix, suffix, or endings (Durkin, 1989; Lass & Davis, 1985). In other words, they look for something they know within the word.

The following list of common root affixes is adapted from *The Reading Teacher's Book of Lists* (Fry, Polk, & Fountoukidis, 1993).

Prefixes

Prefix	Meaning	Example	Prefix	Meaning	Example
intro-	inside	introduce	ad-	to, toward	adhere
pro-	forward	project	para-	beside, by	paraphrase
post-	after	postdate	pre-	before	predate
sub-	under	submarine	per-	throughout	pervade
ultra-	beyond	ultramodern	ab-	from	abnormal
dis-	opposite	disagree	trans-	across	transatlantic

Suffixes

Suffix	Meaning	Example	Suffix	Meaning	Example
-ant	one who	servant	-ee	object of action	payee
-ist	one who practices	pianist	-ary	place for	library
-ence	state/quality of	violence	-ity	state/quality of	necessity
-ism	state/quality of	baptism	-ette	small	dinette
-s, -es	plural	cars	-ard	one who	coward
-kin	small	napkin	-ing	material	roofing

PUTTING IT ALL TOGETHER: A SEQUENCE OF WORD-IDENTIFICATION SKILLS

Based on the research summarized thus far in this chapter, it is now possible for us to suggest a general listing of early literacy skills that directly relate to word identification. This sequence of **early literacy milestone skills** (see Figure 8.8) proceeds from emergent levels of phonemic awareness through phonics and other decoding skills. Children who become proficient in these abilities and practice them regularly in pleasurable reading will attain a high degree of fluency.

Describe the sequence of word-identification skill instruction.

Figure 8.8 Early literacy milestone skills

Stage 1: Phonemic Awareness
Simple awareness that spoken words have individual sound parts
Compound words: simple oral segmenting and blending
Syllables: oral segmenting and blending
Onset and rime: oral segmenting and blending
Individual sound by sound: oral segmenting and blending
Advanced phonemic awareness skills: oddity tasks and sound manipulation

Stage 2: Alphabetic Principle
Alphabet learning
Sound/symbol associations (awareness of phoneme/grapheme relationships)

Stage 3: Reading: Phonics and Decoding Strategies Development*
Context clues (as a meaning-based word attack strategy)
Context clues plus the structural analysis skills
• compound words (segmenting and blending)
• syllabication (segmenting and blending)
• onset and rime (segmenting and blending)
Context clues plus letter-by-letter analysis (segmenting and blending)
• beginning sounds in words, plus . . .
• ending sounds in words, plus . . .
• medial sounds in words

*Note: Ways of assessing whether students have reached these and other literacy milestones are discussed in chapter 10: "Assessment: Determining Students' Progress in Literacy."

Teaching Skills Effectively Using Mini-lessons: Whole to Parts to Whole Instruction

Mini-lessons are the cornerstone of direct skill instruction.

Note: In chapter 9, we explore these three types of mini-lessons in greater detail.

Mini-lessons begin with a whole text example that makes sense.

One of the most useful procedures for teaching word-identification strategies is the mini-lesson. **Mini-lessons** are typically whole-class or group lessons that last approximately 5 to 10 minutes and can be used to teach strategies and skills, promote literary response, or teach a necessary procedure (Hagerty, 1992). Mini-lessons allow teachers to get to the point quickly and end the lesson before student attention fades. Thus, if a teacher wishes to teach a word-identification or comprehension strategy, such as context clues, then a mini-lesson can be offered once each day until students learn the strategy.

Another characteristic of mini-lessons is that they teach reading strategies from **whole to parts to whole** (Reutzel & Cooter, 1992, 1996; Strickland, 1998). Unlike basal readers and phonics drill programs that teach reading strategies from "parts to whole" (skill activities isolated from meaningful texts), mini-lessons begin with engaging stories or other texts and work down to the essential strategy or skill to be developed. This process allows students to see the relevance of the strategy being emphasized in real reading tasks. Following is a sample mini-lesson schedule for teaching context clues in the early elementary grades.

Mini-lesson Schedule (Whole to Parts to Whole)
Word-Identification Strategy: Context Clues*

Materials Needed: Big book version of *More Spaghetti, I Say!* (Gelman, 1977), overhead transparencies adapted from page 9 of the book, and teacher-made practice sheets in a modified cloze format.

Day 1 Activity: Shared Book Experience (WHOLE Text)

Using a big book version of *More Spaghetti, I Say!* read the book aloud with the class and discuss the class's favorite parts. This step provides a "whole" text example from which the new skill or "part" of language can be introduced.

Day 2 Activity: Teacher Modeling (PART of Language [reading skill] for our teaching focus)

Modeling involves "thinking aloud" and showing students how fluent readers use the new skill to be learned.

The mini-lesson continues by rereading portions of *More Spaghetti, I Say!* to remind students of the story line. Next, the teacher introduces this skill or "part" of reading to be learned (context clues) by explaining that "sometimes when reading, we come to words that we do not know. Good readers sometimes guess what the word might be and continue reading. As they read, the meaning of the story helps them to know whether their guess was correct or not."

The essence of modeling is the teacher thinking aloud for students so they can understand thought processes used to solve literacy problems. To illustrate context clues, the teacher may begin by showing a transparency copy of page 9 from the book on the overhead projector (Figure 8.9). The teacher and class reread the page

*Note: Context clues are often regarded by some reading researchers as a comprehension skill only, whereas others regard them as the first essential word-identification skill. In this example, we assume the latter position. There is agreement from most researchers, however, that all children should learn the utility of context clues.

Figure 8.9 Page 9 of *More Spaghetti, I Say!* intact text

No. I can **not**.
I can **not** jump and play.
Can't you see?
I need more.
More spaghetti, I say!

From *More Spaghetti, I Say!* by Rita Golden Gelman, illustrated by Jack Kent. Text copyright © 1977 by Rita Golden Gelman, illustration copyright © 1977 by Jack Kent. Reprinted by permission of Scholastic Inc.

chorally. Next, the teacher puts another copy of page 9 on the overhead projector, this time with selected words deleted and replaced with blanks in a modified cloze format (Figure 8.10). The teacher reads the passage aloud and "thinks" or "guesses" out loud what the missing word might be for each of the blanks. The emphasis should always be on "what makes sense" within the context of the passage. Notice that for the sentence "I _____ more," *need* and *want* would both make sense. This realization could easily lead into a later mini-lesson related to the word-identification strategy of beginning sounds in words. When beginning sounds are used in conjunction with context clues, children could easily determine that the unknown word is *need* because "it begins with the right sound." After this demonstration, the children are asked if they have any questions. They are now ready for the next mini-lesson.

Day 3 Activity: Guided and Independent Practice

Children at this point have seen the "part" of reading to be learned (context clues) demonstrated and have a growing understanding of the strategy. To make this strategy their own, they must practice it themselves. In order to begin shifting responsibility for using the skill from the teacher to the learners, another familiar page of text, page 24 for example, is selected from *More Spaghetti, I Say!* and a practice sheet is produced in the same format as the one demonstrated by the teacher before on Day 2 (Figure 8.11). Children are asked to complete the practice exercise with assistance from the teacher or in collaboration with other students. The teacher or parent volunteer then reviews the worksheet for accuracy. Remember, as long as the student response makes sense it should be accepted when developing context clues or when developing other comprehension strategies.

As mini-lessons proceed, the responsibility for using the skill gradually shifts from the teacher to the learner.

Figure 8.10   Page 9 of *More Spaghetti, I Say!* modified cloze for context clues lesson

No. I can **not**.
I can ____ jump and play.
Can't you ___?
I ____ more.
More _____, I say!

Adapted from *More Spaghetti, I Say!* by Rita Golden Gelman, illustrated by Jack Kent. Text copyright © 1977 by Rita Golden Gelman, illustration copyright © 1977 by Jack Kent. Reprinted by permission of Scholastic Inc.

The last activity at this stage is a final practice sheet drawn from the text origi- nally shared on Day 1, such as page 26 of *More Spaghetti, I Say!,* which the child completes without any assistance from others. If this exercise is completed without difficulty, the mini-lesson moves on to the next activity. If there are problems, how- ever, then reteaching should be done using a new text selection (i.e., repeat the same types of activities from Days 1 through 3).

Figure 8.11   Practice sheet developed from text on page 24 of *More Spaghetti, I Say!*

"Oh, Minnie,
that look on your ____!
You ____ bad.

____ look big.
You look green.
You look ____ .
You look sad."

Adapted from *More Spaghetti, I Say!* by Rita Golden Gelman, illustrated by Jack Kent. Text copyright © 1977 by Rita Golden Gelman, illustration copyright © 1977 by Jack Kent. Reprinted by permission of Scholastic Inc.

Day 4 Activity: Whole Text Reapplication (WHOLE)

The final stage of *whole to parts to whole* teaching involves helping students apply their new knowledge in new and complete (i.e., "whole") texts. This is accomplished by sharing an enlarged version of a new book, song, poem, or other text form with the class and inviting volunteers to use the new skill learned to solve a reading problem. In this example of the value of context clues to help identify an unknown word, the teacher might show an enlarged or big book version of *The Enormous Watermelon* (B. Parkes, 1986). As with previous examples, selected words should be covered by blank stick-on notes, and the student volunteers are invited to make their guesses as to what the unknown words might be. The teacher could then write the word predictions on the stick-on note over each unknown word and discuss with the group whether the guesses make sense with the author's message.

The key to success with this final "whole" text reapplication stage is to vividly demonstrate to students how this new skill they have learned can be used with virtually *any* text and thus is a valuable new tool in their literacy tool kit.

Show students through whole text reapplication how this new skill they have learned works with most any new text they'll encounter.

Day 5 Activity: Test-Wiseness Lesson (Optional)

To satisfy testing requirements, many teachers are required to give some sort of mastery test to children on the various reading strategies. These exercises may be end-of-basal tests, standardized achievement tests in reading, or state- or district-constructed tests. In the preceding whole to parts to whole example, one can be reasonably sure that all children have acquired the ability to use context clues, at least on a novice level, but one more step may be needed to help students apply the strategy on a mastery test. Recognizing that most districts rely on end-of-basal tests because of their easy access (they already own basal series), one or two of the basal reader "skill sheets," dealing with context clues in this case, can be duplicated for each student (Figure 8.12 is an example). By working through an example or two with the teacher and then

Teaching students "test-wiseness" skills for the new word-identification skill learned applies only to "tested skills" on state- or locally mandated assessments.

Figure 8.12   Skill sheet on context clues for test-wiseness lesson

Skill Lesson 22: Decoding Practice
Context Clues

Name _____

Sometimes the words in a sentence can help you figure out a word you don't know how to read yet. In the example below, the words _____ and _____ help you to know that the word _____ completes the sentence.
On a hot day, I like to go to the _____ pool.

| ice | swimming | day | up |

Directions: Complete the sentences below using a word from the box that makes sense.

| theater | gym | flavor | vacation |

Sean likes to play basketball in the _____ at school.
My favorite _____ of ice cream is chocolate.
Celeste and I went to the movie _____ to see the movie *Little Mermaid*.
Our family likes to go to Florida every summer on _____ .

Figure 8.13   Identification and matching

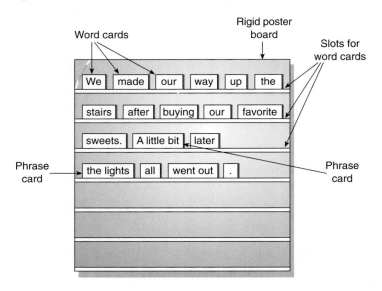

completing the remainder of the practice sheet themselves, students will become acquainted with the format of the test but not the actual test itself.

FOCUSING ATTENTION ON PRINT: BRIDGING FROM MEMORY TO TEXT

The bridging stage occurs when children learn to recognize known letters and words in familiar books.

One of the early stages in reading development is known as the bridging stage of literacy development (see chapter 3): when children can call out known words and letters in familiar books and contexts. At this stage, however, they cannot pick out the same words and letters in an unfamiliar book or context. In short, they have not generalized and transferred their budding word-identification abilities to other reading situations. For children to progress to the next stage of reading development, they need to begin to "bridge" word recognition from known books and contexts to new reading situations. In this section, we describe several classroom strategies teachers can use to help children who have memorized text, story, or books to be-

Figure 8.14   Progressive cloze

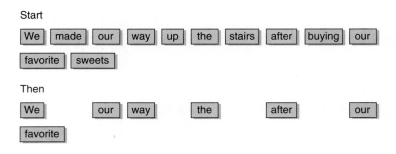

gin to focus their attention on the features of print rather than relying solely on meaningful and memorable features of familiar text. Many of these ideas are adapted for this purpose from the book *Literacy Through Literature* by T. D. Johnson and Louis (1987) and from Reutzel's (1995) *Learning About Print Strategies*. Once children move beyond this stage, they are ready for other aspects of the word identification process.

Recognition

To begin, students reread a text sample taken from a familiar and popular print source (a familiar book, big book, language experience chart, poem, chant, or song). Once completed, this text sample may be used to support the following print recognition transfer activities.

Identification and Matching

Begin by asking your students to listen and follow along as you read aloud related sentences, lines, phrases, words, or letters displayed in a pocket chart. Then, using text from a different familiar selection, have children find the same part of language in the pocket chart (see Figure 8.13). The idea is to transfer students' ability to recognize specific words in a familiar book or text to new books and text.

Pocket charts are a useful teaching tool for identification and matching skills.

Cloze Techniques

Three variations of the cloze techniques procedure may be used to help students bridge from memorized text: *progressive, regressive,* and *successive cloze*. With progressive cloze, teachers cut sentence strips into individual words and place them into a pocket chart. Next, children read the words after removing one or two words from the sentence at a time (Figure 8.14). Structure words, such as *the, but, and, a,* should not be removed. As a verbal placeholder, have children snap their fingers or say "blank" when they come to each missing word.

Regressive cloze is essentially the reverse of progressive cloze. Start with only the structure words from a sentence, line, or phrase. Replace one word at a time, and have children read what is in the pocket chart. Ask them to predict the full message of the sentence after each new word is added (Figure 8.15).

List and describe three cloze variations.

Figure 8.15　Regressive cloze

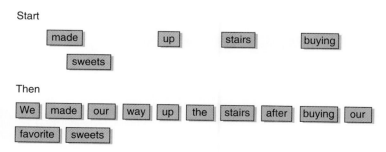

Figure 8.16   Successive cloze

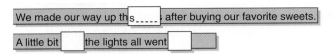

        Successive cloze is done by masking the beginning or ending letter of a word. Enough spaces for each missing letter are provided to help children use context and letter clues for solving words (Figure 8.16).

Substitution

Take a word from one sentence strip and substitute it for a word in another strip without telling students which word has been substituted. Tell the students what the strip said before the substitution was made. Ask them to locate the word that has been switched (Figure 8.17).

Error Detection

Students search for words that don't make sense in error detection.

Error detection is very similar to substitution: Take a sentence or phrase strip and substitute a word that does not make sense. Ask students to find the word that does not make sense.

Spoonerisms

Spoonerisms take the first letter(s) of two words and transpose them to alter their pronunciation. This results in humorous nonsense words that children enjoy immensely. Spoonerisms can be used to help children focus on initial letter sounds in words using self-stick memo notes in big books, overheads, or sentence strips in a pocket chart (Figure 8.18).

Vowel Substitution

Substitute initial, final, or medial vowel sounds from two or more words in a sentence, line, or phrase strip. Ask children to read the strip with the changes in place. For example, "Humpty Dumpty sat on a wall" becomes "Himpty Dimpty sit on a will."

Figure 8.17   Substitution

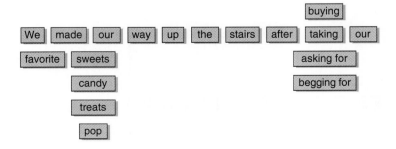

Figure 8.18   Spoonerisms

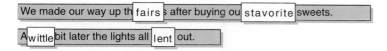

Word Rubberbanding

Word rubberbanding is a simple technique that can be used to help students pronounce unknown words in print and also as a strategy for invented spellings. In the classroom, the teacher may explain word rubberbanding by saying "Stretch (the word) like a rubber band . . . and listen to the sounds. . . . What sounds do you hear?" (Calkins, 1986, p. 174). Students should begin by using context as a word-identification strategy to think about which word might make sense in the text they are reading. By stretching the word out phoneme by phoneme, or perhaps by onset and rime, sound clues are provided to the students that help solve the word-identification puzzle.

One of the many uses of word rubberbanding is to help students with invented spellings.

As an invented spellings strategy, children are encouraged to stretch out the word they wish to spell vocally. Teacher modeling through mini-lessons is needed in the beginning to help children understand the process. For example, during the Christmas season, students may well want to write stories about Santa Claus. The teacher could offer the following model for the word *Scrooge* after explaining the concept of word rubberbanding:

Teacher:	Listen while I stretch out the name *Scrooge* as I say it out loud. Sssscccrrooooogggge. I sounded kind of like Marley's ghost when I said it like that, didn't I? Now, watch as I write the name Scrooge while saying it like Marley's ghost.
Observations:	As the teacher rubberbands the name Scrooge again orally, he or she writes the following letters that are easily heard. S-c-r-o-o-g.
Teacher:	Now that I have written the word *Scrooge,* I can begin to check it for accuracy, to see if I spelled it accurately. Where could I find the correct spelling of *Scrooge,* class?
Child Volunteer:	Maybe a dictionary. Maybe in the book *A Christmas Carol*?

From that point, the class and teacher can discover the correct spelling through some light research. The point is that once an invented spelling has been created, the word can be found using reference sources. Children have an opportunity to practice these skills in the context of real writing, and it all makes sense.

TEACHING SKILLS THROUGH RAPS, SONGS, AND CHANTS

Sometimes children are required to learn rather lengthy and abstract word-identification concepts, such as the alphabet, vowel generalizations, and various phonics rules. Teachers developing balanced reading programs have discovered that many of these concepts can be learned easily and quickly through songs and chants.

Figure 8.19   The vowel song

The Vowel Song

The vowels we know
And you will see,
That we can say each perfectly,
a as in *apple*
a as in *ate*
And don't you think that we are great!
e as in *egg*
e as in *eat*
And don't you think that we are neat!
i as in *it*
i as in *ice*
And don't you think that we are nice!
o as in *pot*
o as in *no*
And don't you think it's time to go!
u as in *cut*
u as in *cute*
Now it's time to light the fuse!
   Boom!!!

Raps, songs, and chants can transform rote learning into delightful experiences.

Songs and chants serve at least two purposes. First, they make rote learning tasks, such as the alphabet and vowel generalizations, easy to memorize and later transfer to real reading situations. Second, songs and chants provide a springboard into rich experiences with literature, song, drama, and other art activities.

Many songbooks are available for teachers that help children learn useful language and word-identification elements. The most obvious is the "Alphabet Song." It is probably a very safe bet that most American children learned the alphabet in this way. Students can also learn many fun and funny songs filled with rhyme with the help of Marsha and Jon Pankake's (1988) songbook entitled *A Prairie Home Companion Folk Song Book*. As noted earlier, the instruction of onsets and rimes can easily be facilitated through these wonderful songs.

The Vowel Song introduces basic long and short vowel sounds.

In one of the first studies of the effectiveness of holistic teaching as compared to basal readers (Reutzel & Cooter, 1990), Reutzel developed a song for teaching the long- and short-vowel generalizations. "The Vowel Song" was found to be easy enough for first graders to learn almost at once. The words are presented in Figure 8.19 ("The Vowel Song" can be sung to the tune of "Twinkle, Twinkle, Little Star"). Once children learned the vowel song, they began little by little to apply the words of the song to real reading and writing situations with occasional reminders from the teacher.

Two other vowel songs have been prepared by Reutzel, one for "silent *e*" and the other for "vowel pairs" (Figures 8.20 and 8.21).

Why do you think chants, raps, and songs are often effective ways of introducing word-identification skills?

Chants or "raps" can be equally effective with students as songs. With the popularity of rap music, students are naturally drawn to rhyming rhythms. Cooter, in the study mentioned (Reutzel & Cooter, 1990), used "The Vowel Song" strictly as a rap in his first-grade classroom. The first time he introduced "The Vowel Song," the children were instructed to snap their fingers in a moderately slow, steady rhythm with

Figure 8.20 Silent *e* song

Silent *e*

When you have an *e*
at the end of a word,
The *e* is silent so it's never heard.
The first vowel almost always
says its name,
Follow this rule below
you'll find it's the same . . .
c-a-m-e is *came*
P-e-t-e is *Pete*
l-i-k-e is *like*
h-o-m-e is *home*
c-u-t-e is *cute*

Remember this and be sure to use
The first vowel's name
in this reading game!

the teacher and to listen as he performed the rap. The rap was written in large letters on poster paper in a big-book fashion so the children could read along as it was performed. After the teacher went through the rap a few times, the children were invited to join in. Soon the rhythmic chant could be heard on the playground as children jumped rope. Within a week or so, every child in his first-grade class could recite

Figure 8.21 Vowel pairs song

Vowel Pairs

When you have two vowels
you have a pair.
The first vowel's name
is the name they share.
When you see two vowels
side by side,
The second vowel's name
will usually hide.

ee says *e* as in *meet*
ea says *e* as in *read*
ay says *a* as in *day*
oa says *o* as in *boat*
ai says *a* as in *paid*

If by chance you find
that this won't do,
Then try the second vowel's name
this might work, too!

"The Vowel Song" rap easily. They even developed hand gestures and dance movements to use while "performing" the rap.

It should be noted that songs and raps do not immediately transfer to application. Students are attracted to the aesthetic qualities of these art forms first; application and transfer occur gradually over a period of time.

Miss Mary Mack (J. Cole & Calmenson, 1990) is one book that might prove helpful to teachers interested in trying chants for the first time. Joanna Cole and Stephanie
Calmenson have put together various children's "street rhymes" categorized as *hand
clapping, ball bouncing, counting out, just-for-fun,* and *teases and comebacks.*
One example from *Miss Mary Mack* that works well as an introductory chant follows:

> Number one, touch your tongue.
> Number two, touch your shoe.
> Number three, touch your knee.
> Number four, touch the floor.
> Number five, learn to jive.
> Number six, pick up sticks.
> Number seven, go to heaven.
> Number eight, shut the gate.
> Number nine, touch your spine.
> Number ten, do it all again.

Many other books can provide fuel for chants and raps in the classroom. Shel
Silverstein's (1974) book of poetry entitled *Where the Sidewalk Ends* has several
poems especially well suited to teaching rhyme. The following poem is instructive
both in the areas of rhyme and words that are almost alike.

The Little Blue Engine*

The little blue engine looked up at the hill.
His light was weak, his whistle was shrill.
He was tired and small, and the hill was tall,
And his face blushed red as he softly said,
"I think I can, I think I can, I think I can."

So he started up with a chug and a strain,
And he puffed and pulled with might and main.
And slowly he climbed, a foot at a time,
And his engine coughed as he whispered soft,
"I think I can, I think I can, I think I can."

With a squeak and a creak and a toot and a sigh,
With an extra hop and an extra try,
He would not stop—now he neared the top—
And strong and proud he cried out loud,
"I think I can, I think I can, I think I can!"

He was almost there, when—CRASH! SMASH! BASH!
He slid down and mashed into engine hash
On the rocks below . . . which goes to show
If the track is tough and the hill is rough,
THINKING you can just ain't enough! (p. 158)

*"The Little Blue Engine" from *Where the Sidewalk Ends* by Shel Silverstein. Copyright © 1974 by
Evil Eye Music, Inc. Reprinted by permission of HarperCollins Publishers.

USING THE WRITING PROCESS TO FURTHER ENHANCE WORD-IDENTIFICATION SKILLS

Word-identification strategies have traditionally been taught in basal reading groups using bottom-up procedures, or parts to whole. One could argue that because most people have learned to read in such programs they must be effective. Perhaps they are to some degree, but many reading educators feel that such instructional processes do not produce individuals who enjoy reading or who want to continue reading into adulthood as a pastime. Therefore, the search has continued for more effective and interesting ways to help children acquire word-identification strategies.

In recent years, many teachers developing balanced literacy programs have decided to teach word-identification strategies as part of the Writing Workshop (discussed in detail in chapter 11). These teachers argue that literacy skills such as phonics knowledge, grammar, word identification, and basic writing mechanics can be taught effectively in the context of writing (Calkins, 1980; Varble, 1990). Regarding the teaching of phonics through the writing process, Jane Hansen (1987) writes, "Phonics is a servant. It serves the message. In our reading/writing program young children learn the purpose of phonics when they write" (p. 101).

Children apply phonics skills as they write through segmenting and blending.

In this section, several possibilities are reviewed for teaching word-identification strategies through the writing process. Because the superiority of these practices is only partially validated by research, readers may wish to set up their own classroom comparisons with traditional methods to judge their effectiveness.

"Temporary" Spellings

Children as young as preschoolers can use their knowledge of phonology to invent spellings of words (Bear, Invernizzi, Templeton, & Johnston, 1996; C. Read, 1971). Years ago, teachers thought that allowing children to use these invented spellings (we prefer the term *temporary spellings* because it conveys better to children and parents what is meant) might be detrimental because students would be learning an "incorrect" form of the word and would later have to *unlearn* it in favor of the correct spelling. More recently, educators have realized that some important benefits may be derived by learners when temporary spellings are encouraged.

Use of temporary spellings by students helps them to develop a deeper knowledge of phonics.

First of all, temporary spellings allow children to put into practice what they know about phonemes. In early grades, this means that children may spell favorite words with a single letter, such as *d* for *dinosaur, g* for *goat,* and *r* for *ring.* This early application of what is known helps students begin to transfer rote learning of such things as the "Alphabet Song" to actual literacy communications. Children also begin to feel that they are successful writers on a level they find rewarding.

Another benefit of temporary spellings is that students begin to apply simple phonics knowledge. As was pointed out earlier in the chapter, phonics strategies that seem to have the greatest utility when combined with context clues are beginning, ending, and medial sounds in words. As children progress in temporary spellings, they tend to mirror these very same strategies. Thus, for the word *dinosaur,* children will tend to progress in their early (semiphonetic) invented/temporary spellings from *d,* to *dr,* to *dinosr.* This kind of spelling and writing metamorphosis has direct benefits in reading: As the student becomes aware of the structure and functions of the written word and letters, word identification through sounding out or blending prominent letter sounds begins to make sense.

As alluded to, a third important benefit of temporary spellings is related to spelling development itself. After more than a century of formal spelling instruction, educators now know that attempting to teach words using spelling lists is not very effective. Children simply use short-term memory to temporarily conquer the spelling list and pass a test, then quickly forget the words through a lack of use. Richard Gentry (1987), in his book entitled *Spel . . . Is a Four-Letter Word,* mentions several important keys to encouraging spelling growth, which in turn affect invented spellings and transfer to word identification strategies:

- Kids learn to spell by inventing spelling. Inventing spellings allows children to engage in thinking about words and to demonstrate their acquired skills.
- Purposeful writing is the key to learning to spell.
- Spelling is a constructive developmental process.
- Allowing children to take risks in their own writing is the best technique. (Gentry, 1987, p. 28)

Editing Sessions

Editing sessions focus on making sense of print and on correct usage.

Editing sessions between writing "experts" and students can be most constructive for developing word identification strategies. The sessions are usually conducted in a one-on-one or small-group setting, and the primary focus is always on making sense. That is, the composition should use semantic and syntactic constructions that help the reader understand the author's message. Therefore, the focus of these sessions can be topics such as invented spellings and grammar. When we remind ourselves that reading and writing are reciprocal processes, it is easy to see how to help students with word identification through editing sessions. For example, let's say that a student named Shelley has been writing a story about motorcycle racing. The character in the story is leading in a big race, and the motorcycle on which she is riding begins to suffer some mechanical problems. When examining the story, the writing expert (teacher, parent volunteer, peer tutor from an upper grade) notices the following sentences:

> *As Laura made it through the curve she felt something hot down her leg. A quick down told her that she had a bad oil leak, probably from the new injection system Rob had installed just that morning.*

The editor first wants to commend Shelley for her idea and writing. They are certainly action packed and reveal some understanding of her topic. By beginning with positive comments, the editor is building a sense of acceptance and creating a safety net in the learning environment so that Shelley will be encouraged to continue to be a risk taker. Next on the agenda is to discuss possible ways the story could be improved, remembering that Shelley as author has the final say-so regarding changes. After discussing a few minor alterations, this portion of the story is revised. The new version appears with changes noted in bold type.

> *As Laura made it through the **tight hairpin** curve she felt something hot down her leg. A quick **glance** down told her that she had a bad oil leak, probably from the new injection system Rob, **the mechanic**, had installed just that morning.*

Several ideas come to mind that the editor might emphasize to help Shelley improve her word identification skills in reading. Some possible mini-lesson topics follow:

Correction: *tight hairpin*

Word identification strategy description: Context clues. Words immediately preceding a noun are typically descriptive words that help the reader create a clear mental picture of the setting. When coming to a word that is not known in this sort of context, descriptive word guesses will usually make sense.

Correction: *glance*

Word identification strategy description: Grammar. In this instance, a necessary word was missing. Through the use of simple context, an appropriate word could be chosen that made sense.

The strategy, then, for word identification in reading is: *When coming to an unknown word, use context and knowledge of sentence grammar to make an appropriate guess.*

HELPING STUDENTS WITH SPECIAL NEEDS DEVELOP WORD-IDENTIFICATION STRATEGIES

Students with special needs in reading often are derailed early in their learning of word-identification strategies. Learning to identify words in print is a complex process, enough so that many elementary students can lose sight of the main purpose of reading—understanding the author's message.

Special needs students frequently have not internalized strong word-identification strategies.

We have observed that many students having reading problems, in the early grades especially, essentially have not internalized the four aspects of the word-identification strategy described earlier in this chapter:.

1. Use of context clues
2. Beginning sounds and onsets in words
3. Ending sounds and rimes in words
4. Medial sounds and onsets and rimes in words

Where teachers' well-intentioned efforts to help special needs students sometimes break down is at the point of intervention: They frequently focus on sophisticated decoding strategies well ahead of the student's zone of proximal development (see chapter 3 for a review of this concept) instead of first making sure that the word-identification strategy has become automatic for the child. For example, it makes no sense to teach about the consonant-vowel-consonant (CVC) generalization when the student has not yet mastered beginning sounds and onsets as part of the word-identification strategy! S. McCormick (1995) explains that there are two levels of word identification or decoding development:

It is important to identify a student's zone of proximal development when teaching word-identification strategies.

Sequential decoding is learned first, followed by hierarchical decoding (Ehri, 1991). In sequential decoding, students learn simple one-to-one correspondences between letters and the sounds that the letters typically stand for—for example, that the sound

> typically associated with *f* usually is the sound heard at the beginning of *fat*. . . . In hierarchical decoding, more complicated understandings are developed, such as the concept that sometimes letters cue the sounds of other letters, as in certain common spelling patterns. (p. 303)

Thus, one must carefully assess where students are in their development of the word-identification strategy, which is essentially a sequential decoding act. In chapter 10, we discuss a number of authentic assessment methods teachers can use to assess word identification abilities. If the word-identification strategy is well internalized, then the teacher may wish to develop hierarchical decoding abilities. However, our experiences suggest that students who have internalized the word-identification strategy rarely have problems with decoding, especially in elementary grades.

Because many students with learning needs in reading have not yet internalized the word-identification strategy, it may be necessary to seek out alternative teaching strategies when the usual mini-lessons are not successful. Writing activities can be quite effective with special needs students because they involve both the encoding and decoding of written language. The more students write, the more they engage the elements of successful reading—use of context, sounds in words (invented/temporary spellings), and so on.

Writing activities involve both encoding and decoding.

Writing as a Tool to Develop Context Clue Awareness

Tompkins and Hoskisson (1995) describe pattern stories as those having a repetitive pattern or refrain. Numeroff's (1985) *If You Give a Mouse a Cookie* and Viorst's (1972) *Alexander and the Terrible Horrible No Good Very Bad Day* are cited as two very popular examples of this type of writing. In writing pattern stories, begin by sharing a pattern book, song, or poem so that students get a feel for the original text. Next, present students with a copy of the book, song, or poem with key elements deleted and ask them to re-create the story in their own way. This will require the use of context to determine the kind of word or phrase needed and also allow students to use their own background knowledge to complete the story. Have volunteers share their compositions in small groups or during author's chair (see chapter 11).

Some teachers prefer to share the original text last so that students can compare what they developed with that of the author.

One fun example uses the well-known song "I Know an Old Lady Who Swallowed a Fly," which is also available in book form. Figure 8.22 shows an excerpt of the original text (about midway through) with deletions/blanks that have been completed to create a pattern story/song.

Vowel and Consonant Sound Practice

S. McCormick (1995) suggests an interesting and sometimes challenging way for students to rehearse what they know about context clues, consonant sounds, consonant clues, and vowel sounds all at once. Provide students with one- and two-sentence passages that contain words with all vowels deleted; their task is to translate the sentence by filling in the missing vowels. Following is an example from Babette Cole's (1983) book *The Trouble With Mom* (she's a witch!):

Th__ tr__ble w__th m__m __s th__ h__ts sh__ w__rs . . .

Figure 8.22   Writing a pattern story to develop context clues awareness

I know an old _donkey_ who swallowed a _rat_ .

Imagine that, to swallow a _rat_ !

_He_ swallowed the _rat_ to catch the _goldfish_ ,

_He_ swallowed the _goldfish_ to catch the _worm_

That _squirmed_ and _turned_ and _churned_

inside _him_ ;

_He_ swallowed the _worm_ to catch the

apple ,

But I don't know why _he_ swallowed the _apple_ ,

I guess _he won't_ die!

Helping SOL (Speakers of Other Languages) Students Develop Phonemic Awareness

Yopp (1992) has stated that most children enter kindergarten with a rather sizable vocabulary and a serviceable knowledge of English syntax. This may not always be the case, however, for **"SOL" students** (Speakers of Other Languages). Some may be learning English as a second language (ESL) and may have to learn a second listening and speaking vocabulary before they can experience much reading success in English. Others may come to school with limited language ability because of linguistically deprived home environments.

SOL students often need assistance developing stronger listening and speaking vocabularies.

   In chapter 7, we suggested ways that teachers can develop vocabulary so that these challenges do not become obstacles. As SOL students build vocabulary knowledge, teachers must then help them acquire word-identification strategies. As discussed earlier in this chapter, an important precursor to students' developing alphabetic principle and phonics is phonemic awareness. Following are a few activities found to be quite effective and enjoyable for children in ESL/SOL classes, as well as students in general education (Yopp, 1992).

Sound Matching

In sound matching, students are asked to identify words that begin with a specified phoneme. This is a relatively easy task, which allows students to use words already in their listening and speaking vocabularies. The following simple lyric is used with the tune of "Jimmy Cracked Corn and I Don't Care." Note that the sound of the phoneme (in this case /m/), not the name of the letter, is used.

Who has an /m/ word to share with us?
Who has an /m/ word to share with us?
Who has an /m/ word to share with us?
It must start with the /m/ sound.

After a word is identified by a class volunteer, the whole group sings the following together:

Mask is a word that starts with /m/
Mask is a word that starts with /m/
Mask is a word that starts with /m/
Mask starts with the /m/ sound.

Sound Isolation

Sound isolation activities help students hear individual speech sounds.

A similar activity to sound matching is sound isolation, which uses lyrics sung to the tune of "Old MacDonald Had a Farm" and helps children to hear sounds at the beginning, middle (or medial position), or end of words. Following are examples for sounds in the medial position.

What's the sound in the middle of these words?
Creep and *deep* and *seat?*
(*wait for a response*)
/ee/ is the sound in the middle of these words:
Creep and *deep* and *seat.*
With an /ee/, /ee/ here, and an /ee/, /ee/ there,
Here an /ee/, there an /ee/, everywhere an /ee/, /ee/,
/ee/ is the sound in the middle of these words:
Creep and *deep* and *seat.*

Blending Activities

Blending activities help students pull sounds together to pronounce words.

Blending is a task that requires students to combine individual sounds to form a word. Yopp and Troyer (1992) developed an activity called "What am I thinking of?" wherein the teacher calls out the segmented sounds one at a time (e.g., /r/ - /a/ - /t/), then children try to blend them to guess the word (e.g., *rat*). As with the previous phonemic awareness tasks, blending can be sung using the following lyrics combined with the tune "If you're happy and you know it, clap your hands":

If you think you know this word, shout it out!
If you think you know this word, shout it out!
If you think you know this word,
Then tell me what you've heard,
If you think you know this word, shout it out!
(*Then say a segmented word, then children respond*)

Segmentation Activities

In segmentation activities, students must isolate individual sounds in a spoken word. This is a very difficult activity for many students, but one that can be important to developing an effective word-identification strategy. One activity suggested by Hallie Yopp (1992) is for students to sing favorite songs and repeat initial phonemes in key verses. For instance, in the old favorite (for kids) "I'm Looking Over, My Dead Dog Rover," the first verse might be sung "I'm l-l-l-looking over, m-m-m-my d-d-d-dead dog R-R-R-Rover. . . ." Another idea that Yopp suggests is a song that helps students with complete segmentations and can be sung to the tune "Twinkle, Twinkle, Little Star":

Listen, listen
To my word
Then tell me all the sounds you heard: *place*
(*say slowly*)
/pl/ is one sound
/a/ is two
/s/ is the last in *place*
It's true.
(*repeat verse with new words*)
Thanks for listening
To my words
And telling all the sounds you heard!

The Phonics Quick Test Answer Key

1. The word *sparkle* is divided between <u>r</u> and <u>k</u>. The *a* has an <u>r</u>-controlled sound, and the *e* <u>is silent</u>.
2. In the word *small,* sm- is known as the "onset" and *-all* is known as the <u>rime</u>. (See chapter 8 for a full explanation.)
3. *Ch* in the word *chair* is known as a <u>consonant digraph</u>.
4. The letter *c* in the word *city* is a <u>soft</u> sound, and in the word *cow* it is a <u>hard</u> sound.
5. The letters *bl* in the word *blue* are referred to as a consonant <u>blend</u>.
6. The underlined vowels in the words *<u>au</u>thor, spr<u>ea</u>d,* and *bl<u>ue</u>* are known as vowel <u>digraphs</u>.
7. The words *tag, run, cot,* and *get* have which vowel pattern? <u>Consonant – vowel – consonant (CVC)</u>
8. The words *glide, take,* and *use* have the <u>vowel – consonant – "e"</u> vowel pattern.
9. The single most powerful phonics skill we can teach to emergent readers for decoding unfamiliar words in print is <u>beginning</u> sounds in words. We introduce this skill using <u>consonant</u> sounds first because they are <u>the most constant (or "dependable" or "reliable")</u>.
10. The word part "work" in the word *working* is known as a <u>root (or "base" or "unbound morpheme") word</u>.
11. The word part "-ing" in the word *working* is known as a <u>suffix (or "bound morpheme")</u>.
12. Cues to the meaning and pronunciation of unfamiliar words in print are often found in the print surrounding the unfamiliar—which is to say, in the <u>context</u>.

Grading Key for Teachers

Number correct	Evaluation
12	Wow, you're good! (You must have had no social life in college.)
10–11	Not too bad, but you may need a brush-up (i.e., read this chapter).
7–9	Emergency! Take a refresher course, quick (i.e., read this chapter)!
0–6	Have you ever considered a career in tele-marketing?! (Just kidding, but read this chapter . . . right away!)

Summary

A long-standing debate was renewed during the 1990s regarding decoding instruction. Recent research studies have confirmed the necessity of teaching children phonemic awareness, alphabetic principle, and phonics skills explicitly. In this chapter, we have delineated a research-supported sequence for teaching phonemic awareness skills, moving from a simple understanding that spoken words are made up of sound parts to the most abstract level of sound by sound segmentation and blending. As competence in phonemic awareness is reached, students should be helped to gain an understanding that the sounds of spoken words can be symbolically represented by letters (alphabetic principle). This level of understanding brings students to the point of development where they are ready to acquire basic phonics skills. Thus, a great deal of this chapter presented a practical sequence of instruction leading to fluent level word identification.

We discussed how the most effective process for teaching word-identification skills is through *whole to parts to whole* instruction. We described in some detail how this can be achieved using *mini-lessons,* which are brief daily lessons wherein students learn strategic word-identification skills (as well as other needed reading skills). Mini-lessons begin by sharing an interesting text (a story, poem, song, rap, etc.) written at the students' independent reading level. The whole to parts to whole process then proceeds through (a) teacher modeling, (b) whole group practice, (c) independent practice, and (d) reapplication of the new skill in new texts. This comprehensive method has been proven effective in both urban and suburban classroom settings.

Finally, we discussed ways that students having special learning needs can be helped to learn word-identification skills. Ideas for assisting speakers of other languages (SOL) who are acquiring word-identification skills in English were also discussed in some length.

Concept Applications

In the Classroom

1. Construct a four-day mini-lesson plan teaching the use of beginning sounds in words as a decoding strategy for a first grade class. The lesson should use the *whole to parts to whole* process: Begin with whole text,

preferably using a children's book, and proceed to parts (beginning sounds in words), and conclude by reapplying the strategy in whole text.

2. Put together a collection of poems that can assist children in learning at least 10 of the rimes listed in this chapter that have high utility and frequency in words.

In the Field

1. Develop and teach to a small group of children several lessons for the following phonemic awareness skills:

   • simple oral segmenting and blending of compound words
   • oral segmenting and blending of syllables
   • oral segmenting and blending of onsets and rimes
   • sound-by-sound oral segmenting and blending

2. Prepare and teach a mini-lesson series on a skill that is developmentally appropriate for an SOL student in an urban school. Discuss any insights, problems, and successes with the bilingual teacher serving the student's class.

Classroom Resources for Teachers

Blevins, W. (1997). *Phonemic awareness activities for early reading success.* New York: Scholastic.

Flynt, E. S., & Cooter, R. B., Jr. (1999). *The English * Español Reading Inventory.* Upper Saddle River, NJ: Merrill/Prentice Hall.

Fry, E. B., Polk, J. K., & Fountoukidis, D. (1993). *The reading teacher's book of lists* (3rd ed.). Upper Saddle River, NJ: Merrill/Prentice Hall.

Reutzel, D. R., & Cooter, R. B., Jr. (1999). *Balanced reading strategies and practices: Assessing and assisting readers with special needs.* Upper Saddle River, NJ: Merrill/Prentice Hall.

Test of Phonological Awareness (TOPA). (1994). Austin, TX: Pro-Ed.

Recommended Readings

Adams, M. J. (1990). *Beginning to read: Thinking and learning about print.* Cambridge, MA: MIT Press.

Ashton-Warner, S. (1963). *Teacher.* New York: Touchstone.

Freeman, D. E., & Freeman, Y. S. (1994). *Between worlds: Access to second language acquisition.* Portsmouth, NH: Heinemann.

Strickland, D. S. (1998). *Teaching phonics today: A primer for educators.* Newark, DE: International Reading Association.

Yopp, H. K. (1992). Developing phonemic awareness in young children. *The Reading Teacher, 45*(9), 696–703.

Yopp, H. K. (1995). Read-aloud books for developing phonemic awareness: An annotated bibliography. *The Reading Teacher, 48*(6), 538–543.

chapter 9

Literacy Environments:

Focus Questions

When you are finished studying this chapter, you should be able to answer these questions:

1. What are four ways literacy props affect the environment–behavior relationships found in classrooms?
2. What are several areas into which classroom space can be subdivided for specific classroom activities?
3. What are five questions teachers should ask themselves when choosing computers and other information technologies for the classroom?
4. How are leveled books and decodable books similar and different?
5. How can teachers implement a classroom literacy volunteer project?
6. What are at least three alternative grouping plans to ability grouping?
7. What are at least three cooperative learning grouping plans?

Designing Classrooms that Promote Literacy

Key Concepts

Aggregation
Whole-Class Learning and Sharing Area
Writing Area
Collaborative Writing Area
Conference Area
Editing Area
Publishing Area
Silent Reading Area
Supported Reading Area

Reading Conference Area
Thematic Studies Area
Trade Books
Ability Grouping
Basal Reader Visiting Response Groups
Literature-Response Groups
Cooperative Learning
Mini-Lessons
Flexible Group

A *supportive and inviting classroom environment* is integral to achieving a balanced literacy program. Often, teachers become so involved in managing children, materials, time, and space that they forget that what goes on within the classroom environment will affect their students' development and interactions. The way teachers design the classroom environment will in large measure affect the value children attach to literacy and literacy instruction.

DESIGNING THE CLASSROOM ENVIRONMENT

> Schools too have atmosphere. . . . For a young child the school can have the feel of an alien and threatening place, or it can create an atmosphere which shelters the child and inspires him or her with security and confidence. (Van Manen, 1986, p. 32)

Describe two ways classroom environments are an important part of the total learning experience for elementary school-aged readers.

The environment of a balanced literacy classroom can contribute much to a child's sense of well-being. The climate, atmosphere, and environment in a classroom grow out of the teacher's beliefs, behaviors, and attitudes. Children are quick to pick up on their teacher's sensitivity to needs and interests as well as their personal enthusiasm for reading and writing. When teachers evidence sensitivity for children and enthusiasm for reading and writing, the classroom climate becomes a supportive and productive worklike atmosphere in which children are treated with respect and affection, the result of which is that the risks commonly associated with learning to read and write become minimized and the benefits maximized.

BALANCED LITERACY CLASSROOMS: UNDERSTANDING THE DYNAMICS OF CLASSROOM ENVIRONMENT

Recent research demonstrates a clear relationship between classroom environments and literacy-related behaviors and learning.

The physical environment of a balanced literacy classroom can be a powerful tool in support of literacy learning or an unrecognized and undirected influence on teaching and learning behaviors (Loughlin & Martin, 1987). Although the literacy environment of the classroom is generally accepted as an important part of literacy instruction, too little attention has been focused on what it brings to children and their learning. Research by Neuman and Roskos (1990, 1992) demonstrated a clear relationship between classroom environments and literacy-related behaviors and learning. Teacher decisions related to classroom literacy environments generally comprise two types: (a) what they *decide* about how to structure the environment and (b) what they *do* in the environment. Based on recent literacy environmental research, Reutzel and Wolfersberger (1996) have described a model similar to the one shown in Figure 9.1 to help teachers better comprehend the aspects of the environment–behavior relationships that condition and shape literacy learning in classrooms.

Providing Literacy Props Affects Children's Literacy-Learning Opportunities

Literacy behaviors increase with the number of literacy props provided in the classroom environment. For example, when children have a message board, they tend to write more often to their peers.

Research by Neuman and Roskos (1990, 1992) has shown that enriching play centers for young children with a variety of literacy props leads to marked increases in literacy learning. These researchers showed that play behaviors became more literacy focused; interactions occurred spontaneously and purposefully using reading and writing behaviors; and children more readily adopted roles appropriate to specific play areas, such as kitchen, post office, business office, or libraries.

When stocking classrooms, it is important that teachers consider their reasons for including specific literacy props. In Figure 9.2, we list several types of possible literacy props. Neuman and Roskos (1990) provided three guidelines for teachers as they make decisions about which literacy props will or will not be included in their classrooms. First, teachers should consider whether or not the props selected fit the criterion of *appropriateness*. To determine appropriateness, teachers might ask

Figure 9.1 Balanced literacy classrooms: Understanding environment-behavior relationships

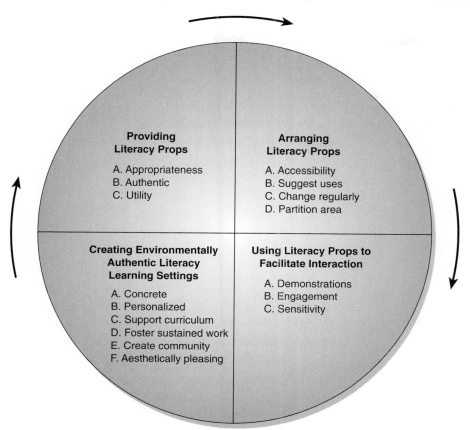

questions such as: Are the props age- and maturity-level appropriate? Can my children use this prop safely? Can my children use this prop in purposeful ways? Can my children use this prop in socially typical ways to communicate and interact? Second, teachers should decide if selected literacy props fit the criterion of *authenticity*. To determine whether or not a literacy prop fits this criterion, teachers may ask: Is this prop an item children would find that people typically use to engage in speaking, listening, reading, and writing? Finally, teachers should consider if a literacy prop fits the criterion of *utility*. In relation to this criterion, teachers might ask: Does this prop serve a literacy function that is familiar or that is found in *everyday* life? We have found these criteria to be very useful for deciding which literacy props to provide in classrooms.

The Arrangement of Literacy Props Affects the Quality and Quantity of Literacy Learning in Classrooms

Research by Morrow and Rand (1991) has shown that how literacy props are arranged in classroom play areas significantly increase children's literacy learning. Issues specifically related to arranging classroom literacy props for optimal effectiveness focus on three major points. First, literacy props should be kept in clearly

Notice three qualities associated with the arrangement of literacy props.

Figure 9.2   Possible literacy props to enrich literacy learning

Books, pamphlets, magazines	Posters of children's books	Appointment book
Ledger sheets	Small drawer trays	Signs (e.g., open/closed)
Cookbooks	Library book return cards	File folders
Labeled recipe boxes	A wide variety of children's books	In/out trays
Personal stationery		Business cards
Grocery store ads/fliers	Telephone books	Self-adhesive notes and address labels
Empty grocery containers	A sign-in/sign-out sheet	
Note cards	ABC index cards	Bookmarks
Pens, pencils, markers	Small plaques/decorative magnets	Post Office mailbox
Trays for holding items		Computer/address labels
Message pads	Assorted forms	Calendars of various types
Envelopes of various sizes	Blank recipe cards	
	Emergency number decals	Posters/signs about mailing
Racks for filing papers	Food coupons	Stamps for marking books
Index cards	Play money	
Clipboards	Small message board	Typewriter or computer keyboard
Stationery	Notepads of assorted sizes	
Stickers, stars, stamps, stamp pads		Telephone
A tote bag for mail	Large plastic clips	Paper of assorted sizes

marked or labeled containers that can be easily accessed and easily put away; children will not use literacy props as readily if they must ask teachers for them. Likewise, teachers will not want to allow children access to materials if they must take responsibility for their cleanup and storage. Second, teachers should suggest possible uses for literacy props. For example, a message board in the classroom might be used to post announcements, ask questions, or send personal communications. Used in a kitchen play center, a message board may be used to post a grocery list or take telephone messages. In an intermediate-grade science center, a message board may be used to list materials needed to conduct an experiment, record the steps of an experiment, or make a diagram for displaying the process. In any case, suggested uses for literacy props help children see the many potential uses for these objects as they learn and communicate. Third, teachers should change the availability of literacy props regularly. Just like adults, children grow weary of the same old thing. To add variety to learning, literacy props should be added to, deleted from, and rotated on a regular basis. Finally, areas where literacy props are located need to be partitioned off so that activities do not interfere with other events in the classroom. The points related to arranging literacy props in classrooms are summarized in Figure 9.1.

Literacy Props Help Focus Human Interaction Toward Acquiring Literacy Behaviors

F. Smith (1988) described three conditions that, when observed, optimize human literacy learning and communication: (a) demonstrations, (b) engagement, and (c) sensitivity. When teachers and children have access to literacy props, they use them to demonstrate how reading and writing are done. When children focus attention on the literacy demonstrations of others or engage on their own using available literacy props, they "learn by observation or by doing." Children do not engage in the literate behaviors of others without having first been sensitive to the presence and content of others' demonstrations of literate behavior.

When teachers share their favorite books such as *Poems for Laughing Out Loud* (Prelutsky, 1991) and chuckle or laugh, or read the *Bridge to Terabithia* (Paterson, 1977) and tears stream down their cheeks, children learn that books evoke an emotional response that teachers and children share, discuss, and ponder. When a child brings the teacher some cookies from home and finds a thank-you card the following morning, the child learns that cards communicate gratitude. In each of these examples, demonstrations using various literacy props help children see the value, utility, and purposes of becoming literate.

Having seen, experienced, and understood the value and power of reading and writing through demonstrations, children choose to engage in literacy by themselves or with others. They want to try to read and write just like the people they have seen around them. It is important to note that the decision to engage in reading and writing does not occur without a personal sensitivity to literacy demonstrations in the first place.

Children do not engage in literate acts without a belief or confidence that learning to read and write is possible. In fact, F. Smith (1985) maintains that the major precursor of reading and writing difficulties is a belief that learning to read and write is hard, painful, or impossible. Student beliefs, attitudes, and interests frame their motivation for engagement. Literacy props, particularly a variety of these tools, provide for a broad spectrum of beliefs, attitudes, and interests that spark desire and *press* children into engaging in literacy learning. For example, a typewriter in the corner of the room may be just what is needed for a child with illegible handwriting to move ahead with literacy. A telephone for talking and a notepad for taking down messages may be just the set of tools needed to influence a reluctant student to write. Literacy props influence the motivations or sensitivity of children to engage in literate behaviors in the first place. And conversely, children's engagement in literacy in the classroom affects the tone, the feel, and the available demonstrations of literate behavior for the other children in the classroom as well. Taken together, literacy props affect the dynamics of the classroom learning environment.

Describe the concept of press *as related to establishing literacy environments.*

Literacy Props Can Be Used to Create Authentic Literacy-Learning Settings

Designing the environment of classrooms has received considerable attention in recent years (Morrow, 1993; Neuman & Roskos, 1993; Rhodes & Shanklin, 1993). Recommendations regarding the way in which classrooms can be provisioned with literacy props fall into three broad categories, according to Neuman and Roskos (1993): (a) creating spatial boundaries, (b) displaying literacy props, and (c) using personal touches. At the core of each of these recommendations is the concept of organization—organizing the classroom to inform children in concrete and personal ways.

Classrooms, as research suggests, should be broken up into smaller, specific activity settings such as those shown on the cover of this book. Doing so encourages quieter classrooms, sustained engagement in literacy learning, more cooperative behaviors, and a sense of privacy to pursue personal projects. (The nuts and bolts of creating a variety of these spaces in the classroom is discussed later in this chapter.)

The arrangement of furnishings is one way of cordoning off specific activity areas in the classroom. Another way of designating activity areas is through the use of displays, labels, and signs. Each of these objects should attract attention, teach, and inform children as they roam the room.

Aggregation means that literacy props are collected into a related network of materials or objects for a particular purpose.

The key to displays and storing literacy props is the concept of **aggregation,** which means that props are collected into a related network of materials or objects for a particular purpose. For example, when designing a classroom library area, teachers aggregate or collect literacy props such as library books, cards, due date stamps, book marks, posters of favorite children's books, pictures of authors, and advertisements of new books for display and use in this area. There might be a card catalogue, a librarian's desk, a rotating wire book display rack, and a check out center. Bookshelves are labeled with section headers such as biographies, fiction, fables, folk tales, and fairy tales.

Other displays and areas in the classroom relate to themes taken from curriculum subject areas such as science or social studies. For instance, an area focusing on the Civil War where children make video news reports on the various issues, personalities, and events of the Civil War could be constructed. Each of these areas should enjoy a personal touch from home. Here again, furnishings and objects provide the key to this concept. Plants, beanbag chairs, pillows, children's portraits, mailboxes, message boards, galleries for artwork, and mobiles for displaying the main characters in books enhance the "personal" nature of the classroom. All combined, these elements of classroom design create a place for children to engage in literacy as an ongoing and enjoyable source of learning, creating, and growing.

In addition to these compelling reasons for using literacy props to create authentic settings for learning literacy, several other reasons are worthy of consideration. First, literacy props properly organized can be used to extend and enrich every other area of the curriculum. Second, because children enjoy using literacy props, they tend to remain on task for longer periods of time, sustaining children's attention and effort longer. As children work together in activity areas or centers using literacy props to learn, they develop a sense of independence as well as a strong network of interdependence with other classroom peers. And finally, when properly organized, authentic literacy-learning settings are aesthetically pleasing to children. A warm, comfortable, well-lit reading nook with the quiet bubbling sound of an aquarium has a calming and tranquilizing effect on children's behaviors. This is a place to go to think, experience quiet, and share a peaceful moment with print and others. Organizing literacy props into authentic literacy-learning settings provides not only an aesthetically pleasing learning environment but also one indispensable to children's language development.

PRACTICAL CONSIDERATIONS FOR ORGANIZING THE CLASSROOM ENVIRONMENT

Signs or labels set the standard for printed products in the classroom as well as provide children with an opportunity for environmental reading.

For both the novice and the experienced teacher, one of the immediate problems demanding attention is the physical arrangement of classroom space and supplying instructional resources to facilitate a collaborative, effective, and supportive learning environment. Faced in late summer or early fall with an empty classroom soon to be filled with lively and anxious children, teachers must somehow plan to make effective use of the space and other resources.

Classroom furnishings need to be arranged to allow easy movement between classroom areas and access to necessary materials, a clear view of chalkboards and

Storing big books for reading is easily accomplished with clothes hangers.

demonstration areas, as well as designated areas in the classroom for children to express their ideas. Areas for storing and reading books should be comfortable and well lit. Each area in the classroom should be clearly labeled with neatly printed or handwritten signs; neatness is important because these signs or labels set the standard for printed products in the classroom as well as provide children with an opportunity for environmental reading.

A major objective of the physical design of any literacy classroom is to encourage children to learn from the environment, each other, and the teacher. As teachers plan layouts and schedules for their classrooms, they often begin simply. Later, they may wish to subdivide the classroom into functional work areas. Much like homes—which are divided into smaller areas for performing specific tasks such as kitchens, recreation rooms, quiet areas, and sleeping rooms—classrooms can be divided into functional areas for accomplishing desired literacy tasks. Useful areas to have in a classroom include the following:

- Whole-class learning and sharing areas
- Writing and publishing areas
- Silent reading areas
- Supported reading areas
- Reading conference areas
- Display areas
- Storage areas

In the following sections, these areas are discussed in greater detail for teachers to consider as they carefully plan their classroom literacy-learning environments. It should be noted that these suggestions are to be viewed as potential classroom components that may be added to the typical classroom floor plan and schedule as teachers develop sufficient control and expertise to manage a more complex learning environment.

Figure 9.3   Whole-class learning and sharing area

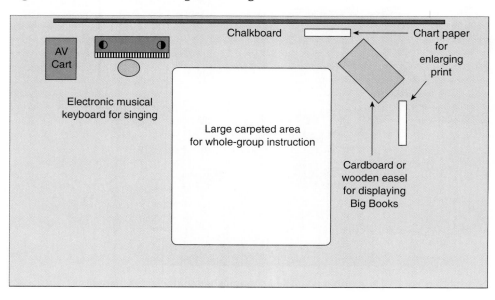

Whole-Class Learning and Sharing Area

*A **whole-class learning area** is useful for whole-class activities such as singing from a chart or performing a play.*

A **whole-class learning and sharing area** is logically located near chalkboards and well away from designated quiet areas in the classroom. A large piece of well-padded carpet can be used to comfortably seat the entire class of children in this area. Audiovisual equipment may include a wall-mounted television, video player, overhead projectors; tape players; easels for displaying enlarged print of stories, poems, riddles, songs, or group experience charts; electronic keyboards for music accompaniment; and display easels for reading commercial or child-produced big books. Audiovisual equipment needs to be located near the whole-class sharing area. This area should also be clear of obstructions and may occupy up to 25% of the total space in the classroom (see Figure 9.3).

Writing and Publishing Area

A **writing and publishing area** (see Figure 9.4) can be subdivided into three smaller working areas:

- Work area for collaborative writing projects, conferences, and editing
- Quiet area for silent sustained writing
- Publishing area with necessary supplies

The writing process is discussed in much greater detail in chapter 12.

The writing and publishing area is designed to be used with a process writing approach in the classroom. A **collaborative writing area** is designated for children to interact with teachers and peers about their writing projects—projects that may have been authored by individuals or groups or that may have been coauthored. Because of the nature of the activity in the collaborative writing area, it should be located away from the other quiet writing areas designated for silent sustained writing. A **conference area** with table and chairs can function as a location for conducting peer–student or teacher–student conferences about developing writing projects. An

Figure 9.4 Writing and publishing area

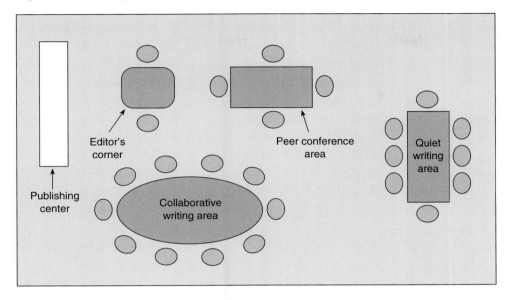

editing area can be located at a desk near the conference area. An older student, the teacher, or an adult volunteer can function as an editor for student-authored works in the classroom. An editor's visor, printer's apron, various writing and marking media, and a poster displaying editorial marks can be located here for the editor's use. The **publishing area** should be stocked with pencils, pens, markers, stapler, and various papers (colors and sizes) for covers. Binding materials also should be available for students to bind or publish their final writing products in a variety of ways. The location for each of the many supplies in this area can be indicated by a printed label or an outline of the object; doing so makes it easier for students to help in keeping the publishing area neat and tidy. Student works published in this area may take the form of big books, shape books, microbooks, accordion books, letters, notes, lists, posters, bulletin boards, murals, and so on.

Silent Reading Area

The **silent reading area** should be located well away from the mainstream activity of the classroom. Trade books can be organized into sections for easy reading, early reading, and advanced reading materials in the classroom library. Within each of these three categories of reading difficulty, books can be organized in alphabetical order by titles. When multiple copies of a single title are available, old cereal boxes cut in half, covered in contact paper, and displaying the title of the books on the side can be used to store these books as a group. Big books can be stored in shelves or on hooks, pants hangers, or easels near this area. This location can also be used to store the adopted basal readers. Whether a basal or multiple copies of trade books are used, this area is ideal for small-group or one-to-one story reading or literature response group meetings. It should be comfortable and well lit. Carpeting, beanbag chairs, a bathtub filled with pillows, pillow chairs, and the like can be used as a comfortable place for children to curl up with a favorite book. A large rocking chair can be located here for lap reading with younger children. Plants, aquariums, and so on

*A **silent reading area** needs to provide a comfortable, inviting environment for enjoying books.*

Figure 9.5   Book title and time log

Name of student _____

Monday—Date _____

Book Titles _____

_____Time in Minutes _____

Tuesday—Date _____

Book Titles _____

_____Time in Minutes _____

Wednesday—Date _____

Book Titles _____

_____Time in Minutes _____

Thursday—Date _____

Book Titles _____

_____Time in Minutes _____

Friday—Date _____

Book Titles _____

_____Time in Minutes _____

can do much to create a peaceful atmosphere for this part of the classroom. Record keeping for silent reading can be easily managed by using a book title and time log for each child, as found in Figure 9.5. The children record the amount of time in minutes spent reading silently and the titles they had sampled or finished that day.

If books or basals are to be checked out from this center for out-of-school reading, a librarian's center can be located near the silent reading area for check outs (see Figure 9.6 on p. 316). A storage container can be kept here for reading backpacks (Cooter, Mills-House, Marrin, Mathews, & Campbell, in press) so that take-home books can be protected. Children who serve as librarians keep records on books checked out and those overdue from the class library. All children are asked to be responsible for keeping the classroom library orderly.

Based on the book *Alexander and the Terrible Horrible No Good Very Bad Day* by Judith Viorst (1972), teachers might establish an Australia Escape Corner. When things in the classroom or a student's personal life are just too much to handle at the moment, they may retreat to Australia, just like Alexander, for 10 minutes,

A quiet, comfortable reading nook should invite children to read silently.

no questions asked, once a day. If they need to remain longer than 10 minutes, they should explain their reasons to the teacher privately. Teachers may also retreat on occasion to Australia. This action alone was found to be one of our best classroom discipline techniques!

Supported Reading Area

The **supported reading area** is a spot in the classroom where children can be helped by other competent readers in learning to read. As such, the supported reading area is typically found in kindergarten through grade 2 but may continue in upper grades on a more limited basis for children who experience unusual difficulties in learning to read and/or are second language learners.

Opportunities for collaborative reading activities between children, teachers, parent volunteers, older children, and senior citizen volunteers are made available in the supported reading area. One means of supporting emergent readers is to station a tape player for children to follow along with a prerecorded tape of the books or basal stories in this area. Another idea is to provide a computer equipped with a CD-ROM version of books to support students. Teachers can also display large charts containing poems, song lyrics, and riddles in this area for buddy reading or singing. A bank of word cards taken from children's language experience charts, big books, basals, and other shared reading materials can be located in this center. Children may also choose to work in pairs on word cards in the class word bank by reading them together or to each other, or by matching the word cards back into the books, stories, or charts from which they were taken. In terms of classroom space allocation, the whole-class sharing area can often double as the supported reading area because the two functions do not occur simultaneously in the classroom.

Younger readers need to be supported as they learn to read by the provision of read-along tapes, buddy readers, or "grandparent helpers" from the community.

Figure 9.6   Silent and supported reading area

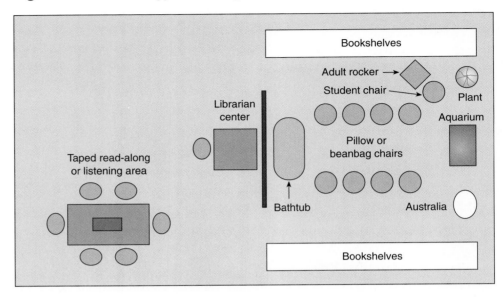

Reading Conference Area

The **reading conference area** is usually small and quiet (Figure 9.7). It is used for conducting individual reading conferences between teachers and individual students. Students make an appointment to meet with the teacher for an individual reading conference by signing up on the individual reading conference sign-up board, which is shown in Figure 9.8. The teacher and an individual student meet together briefly to read and discuss a selected trade book or a story taken from a basal reader. While the student reads, the teacher listens, encourages, records performance, and supports the child.

Thematic Studies or Inquiry-Based Study Area

The **thematic studies** or inquiry-based study area of the classroom is designated for in-depth study of a selected topic or theme. For example, children may express interest in the topic of magic as a result of having read the book *James and the Giant Peach* (Dahl, 1961). The teacher identifies resources available for investigating this topic. After brainstorming with the children, the teacher designs several activities to

Figure 9.7   Reading conference area

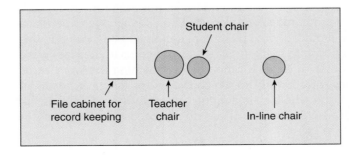

Figure 9.8 Individual reading conference sign-up board

Monday—Date _____

8:00 A.M.

Name _____ Book Title _____

_____ Page Numbers_____

8:10 A.M.

Name _____ Book Title _____

_____ Page Numbers_____

8:20 A.M.

Name _____ Book Title _____

_____ Page Numbers_____

Tuesday—Date _____

8:00 A.M.

Name _____ Book Title _____

_____ Page Numbers_____

8:10 A.M.

Name _____ Book Title _____

_____ Page Numbers_____

8:20 A.M.

Name _____ Book Title _____

_____ Page Numbers_____

focus the curriculum on the theme of magic. Children may listen to music about magic in this area, produce art that employs different media and that may seem magical, such as crayon-resist drawings or turpentine swirl painting. Geometric puzzles or math problems from *I Hate Mathematics* (M. Burns, 1987) provide several magical math problems and solutions.

The teacher must design a way to schedule opportunities for children to use the center and provide a means of record keeping. An example of a theme center activity log can be found in Figure 9.9. Children record in this log the activities they complete each day and write a short essay response to the activity.

Display Areas

The reason for having classroom displays is to immerse students in an environment of interesting and *functional* print. Display areas can be located almost anywhere in the classroom. Where possible, displays should be student produced rather than

Think of a classroom environment where children can use the walls, ceilings, windows, and floor to learn to read and to demonstrate their learning to read. What characteristics are you thinking of in such a classroom?

Figure 9.9   Theme center activity log

Name of Student _____	
Monday—Date_____	
Activity _____ Response _____	
_____	
_____	
Tuesday—Date _____	
Activity _____ Response _____	
_____	
_____	
Wednesday—Date _____	
Activity _____ Response _____	
_____	
_____	
Thursday—Date _____	
Activity _____ Response _____	
_____	
_____	
Friday—Date _____	
Activity _____ Response _____	
_____	
_____	

teacher produced. A message board for leaving notes is one means for teachers and students to communicate with each other. A sign-in board encourages even the very youngest children to write their names to begin the school day. Window writing using pens with water-soluble ink allows students to transcribe their stories, poems, jokes, riddles, and song lyrics onto the window glass. Windows are a fun and novel way to publish writing projects in classrooms. Many children are very intrigued by window-published writing projects.

A logo language wall or environmental print bulletin board can be devoted to print that children bring from home. Logo language is both fun and instructionally

Figure 9.10   Writing peer conference sign-up board

Monday—Date _____

8:00 A.M.

Name of Author _____ Names of Peers _____

_____

8:15 A.M.

Name of Author _____ Names of Peers _____

_____

8:30 A.M.

Name of Author _____ Names of Peers _____

_____

Tuesday—Date _____

8:00 A.M.

Name of Author _____ Names of Peers _____

_____

8:15 A.M.

Name of Author _____ Names of Peers _____

_____

8:30 A.M.

Name of Author _____ Names of Peers _____

_____

useful because it helps even the youngest children to know they can already read. Children bring labels from cans, cereal boxes, old packages, bumper stickers, newspaper ads, and so on to display on a logo language wall. This wall can be a resource for guided language lessons throughout the year. (Be sure to remind children that they must label the contents of a can if they remove the label before it is used!)

An informational display located in a prominent place in the classroom can be used for posting rules, calendars, lunch menus, TV guides, and posters. In addition, informational displays can be used to exhibit information about classroom routines, time schedules, hints on successful reading, the writing process, steps and media for publishing writing, lists of words the class knows, songs the class likes, favorite books, and so on. Scheduling displays can be used for making appointments with peers and teachers for reading and writing conferences as well as editing sessions. Figures 9.10 and 9.11 show examples of scheduling displays for these purposes.

Objects in the classroom can be labeled by the youngest children. Children may invent spellings for objects in the classroom and write these on cards. For example, we have

Figure 9.11   Editing session sign-up board

Monday—Date _____

8:00 A.M.

Name of Author _____ Name of Editor _____

_____

8:15 A.M.

Name of Author _____ Name of Editor _____

_____

8:30 A.M.

Name of Author _____ Name of Editor _____

_____

Tuesday—Date _____

8:00 A.M.

Name of Author _____ Name of Editor _____

_____

8:15 A.M.

Name of Author _____ Name of Editor _____

_____

8:30 A.M.

Name of Author _____ Name of Editor _____

_____

seen the following object labels written by young children: *seling (ceiling), klok (clock), weindos (windows), dr (door), fs (fish),* and *srk (shark).* During subsequent language lessons, children can be alerted to look for these words in their reading and to revise them. Many teachers find that within a matter of weeks, invented spellings used to label classroom objects will be revised to reflect conventional spellings (Calkins & Harwayne, 1987).

Other areas in the classroom can be used to display helpful reference information such as numbers, colors, alphabet letters, lunch time, and classroom helpers. Teachers should remember that displays should be neatly produced to set the standard for published works in the classroom.

Storage Areas

Selected areas in the classroom need to be devoted to storage of classroom and student materials. A writing storage area for children's emerging writing products is a must. Author's folders, response logs, and learning logs can be neatly filed in corrugated cardboard file boxes. Children's writing drafts can be stored in a three-ring binder in an accessible location such as a bookshelf. A small tablet for recording spelling words can be inserted in the pocket of this writing draft binder. Writing draft binders should have each child's name on them.

Personal storage areas using rubber tubs for each child in the classroom can serve dual purposes. First, these tubs can store children's personal writing materials, pencil boxes, and belongings. Second, storage tubs can double as post office boxes. Each tub can have a name and a P.O. box number written on the front. These tubs can be stored in specially constructed shelves or along coatracks and windowsills. Properly cleaned and covered with contact paper, two- to five-gallon ice cream buckets can be stacked along coatracks, cupboards, and windowsills for the same purposes without the expense of purchasing rubber tubs.

A publishing storage area houses materials such as staplers, paper punches, construction paper, and unlined paper. Publishing materials need to be arranged for easy accessibility. The proper location of each item in this area needs to be labeled to facilitate cleanup and maintenance. Properly labeled sorting baskets or bins can do much to ease the cleanup of this area and improve its appearance. The publishing storage area should also be located near other busy and potentially noisy areas in the classroom.

Book storage areas need to be properly located to facilitate retrieval, cleanup, and accessibility. A reading nook, loft, or corner should provide adequate shelf space for a classroom trade-book library. Books in this area can be organized and stored as discussed earlier. Word cards can be stored in old, labeled shoe boxes on the bookshelves in this area. Child-authored books should be afforded the same respect as commercially produced books. A library card pocket and a checkout card can be placed in each child-authored book. These books should have a section in the classroom library where they can be read, reread, and checked out. Child-authored big books and charts can be given a prominent display area and/or stored along with other commercially published big books. Plastic pants hangers can be used with clothespins to store or display big books and chart tablets effectively.

Storage for reference materials such as dictionaries, atlases, *The Guinness Book of World Records,* encyclopedias, almanacs, and spellers should be placed near the editing area in the classroom but accessible to students and the editors. Writing media should be placed near where they are needed in the classroom. Small rubber baskets, boxes, cut-down milk containers, and the like can be used for both storage and sorting of writing materials. Crayons, markers, pencils, pens, erasers, and chalk can be placed in individual containers for storage. In this way, children can easily sort and clean up writing materials scattered during busy writing output times. Other containers should be made available into which small quantities of writing media can be placed from large-capacity storage bins for transport to other classroom areas. These small transport containers can be taken to conference areas and collaborative project areas for use and returned and sorted for storage and cleanup.

INSTRUCTIONAL RESOURCES

The availability of classroom resources for instruction is another of the decisions facing teachers each year as they orchestrate their plans for providing effective and balanced literacy instruction. Schools often provide a wide array of possible instructional resources and supports for teaching reading. A discussion of the most common instructional resources available to teachers follows.

A balanced literacy classroom typically requires a minimum classroom library of 250 to 300 trade books.

Trade Books

Picture books and storybooks typically found in libraries or available for purchase in local bookstores are called **trade books.** Trade books should vary in content as well as length and difficulty. A variety of trade books should include wordless picture books, big books, books with limited print, and books with chapters.

The size and content of a trade-book library varies with the purpose it will serve in a classroom. For example, if the classroom library is to be used for self-selected, silent reading purposes or in an individualized reading program, Veatch (1968) suggests a minimum of 3 books for each student in the classroom. For the average-sized traditional or individualized classroom, this translates into about 75 to 90 books. On the other hand, if a balanced literacy program is contemplated, Stoodt (1989) recommends 10 books per student as a minimum. For the average-sized balanced literacy classroom, this translates into a minimum of 250 to 300 books. Some of these may be checked out of your central school library collection and temporarily housed in your classroom library.

The PTA can help acquire books by sponsoring bake sales and school stores where children buy books or other school supplies and by soliciting donations for books from local merchants. The school librarian can often be a source of trade books. Local thrift and secondhand stores are inexpensive sources for acquiring books. Garage and attic sales are also possible sources for acquiring trade books. Book auctions, where children bring their own trade books and auction them off to their peers for reading, are an exciting way to provide expanded trade-book access for children in schools.

Teachers and school administrators should make the acquisition of quality trade book literature a priority in school budget planning.

Teachers working in conjunction with their principals may decide to use funds allocated for consumable classroom supplies such as workbooks to purchase classroom trade-book libraries or multiple copies of paperback books. In addition, encouraging children to purchase their own paperback books through book clubs is a common way for teachers to acquire trade books to add to classroom collections: For every book purchased by an individual child in these book clubs, the teacher collects points toward free copies of books for the classroom library. Books for children in low-income communities can also be purchased in site-based managed schools using supplemental federal funds (e.g., Title I, RIF).

Some teachers solicit book donations from parents; used children's books donated from parents whose children have outgrown them are a valuable resource. The PTA can ask parents to donate a book in the name of their child to the classroom or school library rather than sending treats to school on the child's birthday. The possibilities for acquiring a vast supply of trade books for use in schools is limited only by the imagination and innovation of teachers and administrators.

However, it is important that teachers and school administrators not relegate the acquisition of trade books to the level of bake sale fund-raisers indefinitely. Rather, they must make acquiring quality trade books a regular line item in school budgets.

Chapter 4 provides a more in-depth discussion of the basal.

Basal Readers

Many recent basals have been organized around themed literature units.

Because basal readers are used in over 90% of schools today, teachers will not need to look very far to find a basal series for reading instruction. Recently published basals show concerted efforts to include a greater variety of children's literature selections. Newer basal teacher's manuals encourage the integration of the reading, writing, listening, and speaking modes of language. Some recently published basals are also thematically organized, allowing children to explore a topic thoroughly rather than flitting from one topic to the next with each subsequent story in the reader. T. D. Johnson and Louis (1987) suggest that basal stories can also be used in the early grades for extensive modeling and choral readings. We show in chapter 5 how basal readers can be used as a springboard into literature-based or balanced literacy programs. For many teachers, especially novice teachers, the basal becomes the departure point in making the instructional transition toward a more balanced literacy instructional program.

Workbooks, Worksheets, and Blackline Masters

Many teachers believe that workbook pages are an important component of the reading program. Unfortunately, however, they often use workbook pages unnecessarily or for classroom management purposes (Osborn, 1984); this is evidenced by the fact that children frequently spend as much time completing workbook pages, or pages from blackline masters, as they do interacting with teachers and real books.

The report *Becoming a Nation of Readers* (R. C. Anderson, Hiebert, Scott, & Wilkinson, 1985) states that children spend up to 70% of the time allocated in classrooms for reading instruction engaged in independent seat work, completing workbooks and worksheets. Durkin (1981a) informed the profession that workbook pages are typically used for assessment rather than for teaching reading. Suffice it to say at this point that teachers should carefully weigh the relative value of workbook activities as they plan reading instruction in their classrooms. From the currently available data, workbook and worksheet activities appear to dominate reading instruction in classrooms at the expense of reading and instructing with real stories and books (Osborn, 1984; Rupley & Blair, 1987; Tunnell & Jacobs, 1989).

The topic of workbooks and worksheets is treated in greater depth in chapter 4.

Workbook and worksheet activities appear to dominate reading instruction in classrooms at the expense of reading and instructing with real stories and books.

Leveled Books

In a balanced literacy classroom, leveled books are an indispensable classroom resource for providing guided reading instruction. Several leveling schemes have been recently developed and applied to books for emergent and early readers. Peterson's (1991) Reading Recovery® programs use a set of criteria that result in a range of leveled texts from levels 1–20, as shown in Figure 11.5 in chapter 11. The Reading Recovery® text grading scheme shows some of the aspects of texts that teachers should consider when creating a text gradient for the purposes of leveling books in the classroom. Guided reading materials also can be leveled using a scheme for grading texts found in the writings of Fountas and Pinnell (1996). Their leveling scheme, shown here, results in levels A–R. (Appendix A provides a list of leveled books)

A discussion of how leveled books are used for guided reading is offered in chapter 11.

> Levels A–B: Kindergarten/Early First Grade
>
> Levels C–I: First Grade
>
> Levels J–M: Second Grade
>
> Levels N–P: Third Grade
>
> Levels Q–R: Fourth Grade

Also, basal stories and tradebooks can be leveled using a complex statistical procedure resulting in Lexile® levels, which is related to earlier versions of readability formulas. The Lexile® system levels texts from preprimer levels (−200L to +200L) to graduate school levels of texts ranging from 1400L to 1800L (Stenner, 1996; Stenner & Burdick, 1997).

Regardless of the leveling scheme selected to grade texts, leveled books are used in connection with homogeneously created guided reading groups in the early grades to provide specific reading instruction in books that provide the optimal mix of familiarity and challenge. Fortunately, most publishing companies who market leveled books today have already provided leveling information using one or more of the leveling schemes discussed here for each book title. (A discussion of how leveled books are used for guided reading is offered in Chapter 11.)

Decodable Books

The use of decodable books to teach emergent or early readers has recently become popularized.

Many researchers advocate the use of decodable books to teach emergent or early readers (Adams, 1990a, 1990b; Foorman, et al., 1997; Lyons, 1998), although some question this recommendation (Allington, 1997). Decodable books contain text that is controlled to exemplify a particular phonics rule or pattern such as the one shown here, which you may recall from chapter 4:

The Big Hit*

Who hid? Pig.
Who had a mitt? Pig.
Who did not sit?
Who did hit?
Up. Up. Up.
Who had a big hit? Pig.
Who slid? Pig did!

Those who advocate the use of decodable texts insist that students must be given sufficient practice in phonically regular texts so that they will develop automatic decoding abilities before tackling the additional challenges associated with comprehending more complex written language. On the other hand, those who disagree with controlling texts along dimensions of phonics rules and patterns for early readers believe that such controls render books and stories dry and meaningless. Moreover, text controls are believed to force the use of or overreliance on the visual–sound cuing system in reading rather than encouraging the strategic use of multiple cuing systems by emergent readers. In any case, many national publishing companies are now producing decodable texts for teachers who wish to offer children phonically regular texts as a part of their classroom reading instruction.

Computers and Other Information Technologies (ITs) in the Classroom

The introduction of technology into classrooms has become a priority in school districts around the United States. Internet connections, personal computers (PCs), modems, T-1 (analog) and DS3 (digital) lines, laser printers, software programs, and, of course, technologists to train and maintain computers are absorbing more and more tax dollars. Yet, the benefit to children and learning thus far has been questionable at best. So what should be the role of computers in your classroom environment?

---

*From *Phonics Readers,* Scholastic Book 14, by Schreiber & Tuchman, pp. 2–7. Copyright 1997 by Scholastic, Inc. Reprinted by permission.

The renowned economist Peter Drucker (1998) has stated that when computers and other information technologies (or "ITs") came onto the scene in education, the emphasis was (and still is) on the "T" of *technology*. Massive amounts of resources thus have been channeled primarily into purchasing and updating technology hardware and software. Some have estimated that around two thirds or more of these resources have gone into the "T" in IT, and less than one third to training teachers how to use the technology effectively. That ratio is exactly backwards, by the way, from how expenditures should be allocated for IT. This wrongly skewed emphasis has led to a phenomenon we refer to as "invention becoming the mother of necessity"; that is, too much of our time and resources are spent trying to figure out how to use the computers and other ITs we want to purchase and use rather than focusing on what it is we want to accomplish with them in instruction.

Drucker went on to say that educators need to realize that the emphasis must be on the "I" in IT—*information*. Simply put, our job as teachers is to instill literacy skills to help our young charges seek and find information.

In choosing computers and other ITs for the classroom, teachers should ask themselves these questions:

1. Which literacy skills does this group of children need to learn?
2. Which activities and methods are the best practices for getting this information across to the students?
3. Which of the technologies available could assist me in teaching these skills in an efficient and cost-effective way?

Two other important questions should be considered before making IT selections.

4. Are there other nontechnological ways of accomplishing the same tasks just as well that are much less expensive?
5. If I am to use technology, is my choice the simplest and least expensive available?

Questions #3 and #5 are getting at an important principle: Choose technologies that are the simplest and cheapest available. For example, if a cassette player and book or "buddy reading" sessions will help students with fluency practice, then we shouldn't purchase expensive computers and CD software to do the same task. And if a cloze passage drawn from a popular shared reading activity will suffice, then we shouldn't purchase an expensive program to accomplish the same thing.

On the other hand, some technologies may well be "worth the bucks"! For instance, a program like IBM's *Writing to Read 2000* (see chapter 12) might be a good choice for some schools to help satisfy students' practice needs in writing. Or a middle school teacher or faculty may decide that the *Read 180* (New York: Scholastic) program may be an appropriate supplement for serving the needs of students having significant reading problems. The central point, as Drucker implies, is that technology should be selected only if it serves the needs of teachers as information and reading skills providers—and the simpler the better.

In chapters 12 and 13, we suggest computer and other information technologies that may be helpful to building a complete literacy-learning environment. Of course, to be wise consumers of ITs, teachers will need to consult with those who know—educational technologists within the school district or a reading specialist/professor at a local university who monitors emerging technologies.

Figure 9.12   Resources for reading program volunteers

- In-school personnel, e.g., principal, secretary, custodians
- Parents
- Grandparents
- Senior citizens
- Local rest homes
- Service clubs, e.g., Kiwanis, Lions, Rotary, Elks
- Government agencies
- Sponsoring businesses
- High school students
- Future Teachers of America
- Scout projects
- Older children in the school
- Church organizations
- News media organizations
- College students
- Student teachers
- Chamber of Commerce
- Reading Is Fundamental groups
- Retired teachers

Using Volunteers

Schools can and should make reading a community concern by implementing strong literacy volunteer programs that involve businesses, parents, retired teachers, service clubs, and the like.

Because children have a right to learn to read from people, helping children become readers ought to be a community concern. Volunteers can form the backbone of the reading program in schools. All sorts of people can be recruited as volunteers for helping with the classroom reading program. Ervin (1982) suggests using parents, retired teachers, college students, student teachers, high school students involved with Future Teachers of America Clubs, and community and government service organizations. Cassidy (1981) suggests using Grey Power or senior citizens in the classroom as volunteers for tutoring, instructional aides, and producers of instructional materials. More recently, Cooter, et al. (in press) have enlisted elderly volunteers in Texas via a group known as "Off Our Rockers"!

The Help America Read program is intended to help struggling young readers by providing tutors from the community in local public schools.

Recruitment of volunteers can be accomplished in various ways: Announcements made in PTA meetings, notices sent home to parents, pamphlets to community service organizations, and local radio, television, or newspaper advertisements are just a few ideas. Figures 9.12 and 9.13 show a listing of volunteer recruitment resources and sign-up forms for volunteers. Pinnell and Fountas (1997) offer a wonderful set of materials for training parent volunteers as a part of the U.S. Government's program *Help America Read.* In their handbook for volunteers, Pinnell and Fountas (1997) offer 10 ways that volunteers can help in school classrooms:

Talking with children

Reading TO children

Reading WITH children

Helping children read on their own

Writing FOR children

Writing WITH children

Helping children write on their own

Helping children understand phonics, letters, and words

Making books

Connecting with children's homes

Figure 9.13   Volunteer sign-up form

Volunteering for the School Reading Program

Children learn to read from other people who can read. Please help children learn to read by volunteering your time.

Name: _____Street Address: _____

City: _____Home Phone:_____

Business Phone: _____Occupation: _____

Grade Level Preference (if any): _____

Teacher Preference (if any): _____

Do you have a child in the school? Yes _____No _____

Name of child if applicable _____

When can you help? (Please check one)

Daily _____Weekly _____Monthly _____

How much time can you give on this basis? _____

Please list available times (e.g., Tuesday/Thursday 8–10 A.M.)

Where would you like to help? (Please check one or more)

_____Classrooms   _____Local library   _____In parents' home

_____Special classrooms   _____Day-care center   _____In your own home

_____Library   _____ Local businesses

How would you like to help?

(Please indicate your first three preferences with the numbers, 1, 2, & 3)

_____Read to students in a group   _____Give presentations on selected topics

_____Help children with reading   _____Solicit books for class library

_____Help with record keeping and   _____Write with small group of children
progress evaluation

_____Produce instructional materials   _____Make puppets

_____Conference with children about   _____Give book talks
their writing projects
                                         _____Help children make books
_____Help children edit writing projects
                                         _____Help children rehearse a play or
_____Tell stories   other dramatic production

_____Teach children songs   _____Take children's dictation and
                                         make little books from dictation
_____Share your own writing

_____Read with individual students

_____I have no particular preference; please place me where I am needed most.

Please list any special talents, abilities, experiences, or knowledge you would be willing to share: _____

All of these ideas for volunteer help are described in greater detail in chapter 11 of this book as a part of a balanced reading program (TO, WITH, and BY).

INSTRUCTIONAL ORGANIZATION: THE QUESTION OF GROUPING

Grouping decisions need to be based on benefits for both teachers and children.

Because teachers vary greatly in their experience and expertise in coping with the complexity of classrooms, the question of grouping in a classroom is of critical importance. The use of more groups and a greater variety of grouping plans adds to the complexity of coping with classroom management. Although the choice to use a particular grouping plan may reduce the administrative complexity of managing a classroom, the potential consequence of such a choice may be that individual students' needs are not being met. Thus, the decision to use a particular grouping plan should be made with full knowledge of the potential consequences. The ideal for most reading teachers is to begin with a simple and manageable grouping plan and gradually expand their efforts toward effectively using a wide range of grouping plans to provide for individual differences, allow for students' choices, foster collaboration, support individual readers as they develop, and encourage social interaction.

Placing students into smaller groups often fills a need for teachers who wish to bridge the gap between whole-class grouping and complete individualization of instruction. Perhaps one of the most controversial grouping plans is grouping children by ability for reading instruction.

Ability Grouping

Dividing children into reading groups on the basis of reading ability or achievement, called **ability grouping,** continues to be a popular practice in many classrooms. This practice has typically resulted in the formation of three levels of ability groups—above average, average, and below average. Groups are very often named to represent the levels of groups. Although teachers most often rely on standardized reading test performance scores as a means for assigning children to an ability group, other factors such as personality attributes, general academic competence, work habits, and home background are also weighed into the decision to assign children to ability groups (Haller & Waterman, 1985).

Ability grouping is often associated with the use of graded basal readers, workbooks, and skill lessons designed to follow a published scope and sequence of skill development. Many teachers use ability, achievement, or homogeneous grouping of children to accommodate individual student needs, and this practice is rooted in the idea of the capacity to profit from instruction. However, this decision is inconsistent with the desire to meet individuals' instructional needs: Teachers group children by ability to have children conform to the demands of instruction rather than modifying the instruction to conform to the needs of the students.

Low-ability group readers receive double the decoding instruction of high-ability group readers.

Numerous negative outcomes have been associated with the use of ability groups, despite their administrative ease and intuitive appeal.

- Children in low-ability groups spend more time in oral round-robin reading and reading workbook assignments than do their peers in high-ability groups (Allington, 1983; Leinhardt, Zigmond, & Cooley, 1981).
- Teachers tend to tolerate more outside interruptions in low-ability groups than in high-ability groups (Allington, 1980).

- In the spring of the school year, children assigned to low-ability groups for reading instruction exhibited three times the number of inattentive behaviors exhibited by their counterparts assigned to high-ability groups (Felmlee & Eder, 1983).
- Children in low-ability groups tend to have lowered academic expectations and self-concepts (Eder, 1983; Hiebert, 1983; Rosenbaum, 1980).
- Time devoted to decoding instruction and practice is fully double for low-ability group readers as compared to high-ability groups (Gambrell, Wilson, & Gnatt, 1981).
- Teachers tend to interrupt low readers more often when they miscue while reading than they do high readers (Allington, 1980).

Weinstein (1976) found that as much as 25% of the variation in reading achievement at the end of first grade could be attributed to group assignment. Kulik and Kulik (1982) analyzed the results of 52 studies and determined that (a) ability grouping *generally* has small effects on achievement, (b) high-ability readers profit more from ability grouping in terms of achievement, and (c) the effects of ability grouping on average- and low-ability children's achievement is only trivial. On the other hand, children's friendships tend to be increasingly influenced by continuing membership in an ability group (Hallinan & Sorensen, 1985). Eder (1983) showed that even one year in an ability group caused some children to begin to question the reasons underlying their group membership. Although reading achievement may be minimally affected by ability grouping, children's self-images and social circles appear to be profoundly affected (Oakes, 1992). Although ability or homogeneous grouping may be deemed necessary in some instances, it should be considered only on a temporary basis not to exceed one month in duration. Alternative grouping plans such as those suggested in the following discussion should be strongly considered.

Whole-Class Instruction

Whole-class grouping, if not overused, can be an effective means for safety-netting emerging readers as they develop more conventional and sophisticated reading strategies. Whole-class reading and sharing activities shield learners from the potentially harsh emotional and psychological consequences of individual risk taking by supporting readers who are learning to read. Whole-class reading activities can also reduce some of the negative effects associated with ability grouping or other labeling that occurs in schools, such as "slow learners," "resource rooms," and "learning disabled." Although some may contend that whole-class grouping fails to meet the needs of individual learners, we assert that whole-class reading activities put children in touch with the social nature of reading and learning to read while safety-netting the risks associated with this learning.

Whole-class reading activities provide a safety net for struggling and shy readers by shielding them from singular attention during reading.

Because learning to read is a social event, and because reading selections are meant to be shared, whole-class reading and sharing activities should be a regular and integral part of every reading classroom. Storytelling; dramatizations of stories; children reading books aloud and sharing their own authored stories, poems, songs; reading big books together; reading the enlarged text of songs, poems, raps, and jingles; sustained silent reading and writing; participating in an experiment or experience; and creating language experience charts are just a few examples of potentially appropriate activities for whole-class teaching.

Literature-response groups can work effectively for older and younger students. How might the tasks assigned to each vary?

Literature-Response Groups or Literature Circles

Teachers give "book talks" on selected trade books before organizing literature-response groups.

Literature-response groups or literature circles use trade books or literature books as the core for reading instruction. To form literature-response groups, the children first look through several selected titles of literature books available for small-group instruction. (This means that multiple copies of each title will be needed! We recommend that teachers purchase about 10 copies of each title rather than purchasing classroom sets for use with literature-response groups.) At the conclusion of this period, the teacher reads available book titles aloud and asks how many students would like to read these books. In this way, teachers can get a quick idea of which books seem to interest the students most and which engender no interest. The teacher selects from these high-interest trade books three to four titles, depending on how many groups he or she can reasonably manage. Next, the teacher prepares a "book talk" on each of the selected books to present to the students the next day. A book talk is a short, interesting introduction to the topic, setting, and problem of a book, followed by an oral reading of an excerpt from the book by the teacher. After presenting a book talk on each of the books selected, the teacher asks the children to identify their preferences; older children can write down the titles of their first two choices, and younger children can come to the chalkboard and sign their name under the titles of their two favorite books.

The teacher meets with only one literature-response group per day to discuss and respond to parts of the books.

Only one literature-response group meets with the teacher each day to discuss and respond to a chapter, or to read a predetermined number of pages in a trade book. It is best if the teacher meets with each literature-response group after children have indicated their choices to determine how long will be spent reading the book and how many pages per day need to be read to reach that goal.

Teachers and students set group goals for daily reading, arrange meeting dates, and decide how the group will respond to the literature.

The steps for organizing literature-response groups are summarized in the following list:

1. Select three or four titles you believe children will be interested in reading from the brief interest inventory of literature titles available in the school or classroom, as described.
2. Introduce each of the three book titles by giving a "book talk" on each.
3. Invite children to write down the titles of their two top choices.
4. Depending on the number of multiple copies of trade books available, fill each group with those children who indicated the book as their first choice. Once a group is filled, move the remaining children to their second choice until all children have been invited to attend the group of their first or second choice.
5. Decide how many days or weeks will be spent reading this series of book choices.
6. Meet with each of the literature-response groups and determine
   a. how many pages per day will need to be read to complete the book in the time allowed.
   b. when the first group meeting will be. (Meet with only one group per day.)
   c. how children will respond to their reading; this may involve writing in a reading response log, character report cards, or other possible responses. (See chapters 11 and 12 for response activities.)
7. Help children understand when the first or next meeting of their literature-response group will be, how many pages in the book will need to be read, and which type of response to the reading will need to be completed before the meeting of the group.
8. Near the completion of the book, the group may discuss possible extensions of the book to drama, music, art, and so on.

See chapter 12 for possible literature-response activities.

Peterson and Eeds (1990), in their book *Grand Conversations,* suggest a checklist form that teachers may use to track student preparation and participation in literature-response groups (Figure 9.14). Based on this concept, we have modified this form to be used with the literature-response groups as we have described their use in the Reading Workshop (Reutzel & Cooter, 1991), discussed in detail in chapter 12.

On completion of the trade book, literature-response groups are disbanded and new groups are formed for a new series of trade books. Thus, students' interests are engaged by encouraging choice, and the problem of static ability-grouping plans can be avoided. Further, children visit the group only for the length of time taken up in completing the trade book, and then new groups are formed.

Both basal reader visiting response groups and literature-response groups change regularly to prevent the stagnant nature of fixed ability groups.

Basal Reader Visiting Response Groups

Teachers in transition toward balanced literacy instruction can develop the ability to use literature-response groups by using their basal reader stories and beginning with **basal reader visiting response groups.** Students are invited to spend about 20 minutes browsing through the basal reader table of contents, looking at the pictures, and scanning the stories, as they might do in a library of literature. This requires that teachers and students think about the basal reader as an anthology of literature—a resource for reading material. Next, each title in the table of contents can be read aloud by the teacher. Students indicate their interest in each story by raising their hand, and the teacher records interest level information in the teacher's manual table of contents. This process provides a quick means of gauging interest for each story in the basal reader. Next, the teacher should look at story titles in the table

Using the basal as a literary anthology is discussed in chapter 5.

For some recently published basal readers with theme story selections, see chapter 4.

Figure 9.14   Checklist for teachers to track student preparation and participation

**Record of Goal Completion for
and Participation in Literature-Response Groups**

Name _____   Date _____
Author _____   Title _____

Preparation for Literature Study

Brought book to literature-response group.	Yes _____	No _____
Contributed to developing group reading goals.	Yes _____	No _____
Completed work according to group goals.	Yes _____	No _____
Read the assigned pages, chapters, etc.	Yes _____	No _____
Noted places to share (ones of interest, ones that were puzzling, etc.)	Yes _____	No _____
Completed group response assignments as they came to the day's discussion.	Yes _____	No _____

Participation in the Literature-Response Group

Participation in the discussion.	Weak _____	Good _____	Excellent _____
Quality of verbal responses.	Weak _____	Good _____	Excellent _____
Used text to support ideas.	Weak _____	Good _____	Excellent _____
Listened to others.	Weak _____	Good _____	Excellent _____

From *Grand Conversations* by R. Peterson and M. Eeds, 1990, New York: Scholastic. Copyright 1990 by Scholastic. Adapted by permission.

of contents for possible common themes or topics. Basal stories can then be grouped by themes, genre, or authors to provide several related basal story units for organizing basal reader visiting response groups. At a later time, the teacher will describe each basal story unit to the students. Then, students can select their first and second choices for group membership.

The remaining steps for forming basal reader visiting response groups are the same as those described for literature-response groups. Basal reader visiting response groups have been recommended by the Commission on Reading in the report *Becoming a Nation of Readers* (R. C. Anderson et al., 1985) and represent an effective transitional step toward teaching a balanced reading program. One final note: Basal reader visiting response groups can be used with the Reading Workshop as described in chapter 12 (Reutzel & Cooter, 1991).

Cooperative learning groups are heterogeneous groups ranging in size from two to five children working together to accomplish a team task.

Cooperative Learning Groups

One form of organizing for effective reading and writing instruction recently made popular is called **cooperative learning.** Cooperative learning groups are heterogeneous groups of from two to five children working together to accomplish a *team task*. Bill Harp (1989a) indicates four characteristics that identify cooperative learning groups.

1. Each lesson begins with teacher instruction and modeling.
2. The children in the group work together to accomplish a task assigned by the teacher.
3. Children work on individual assignments related to a group-assigned task. Each student must be willing to complete his or her part of the group shared assignment.
4. The team is recognized by averaging individual grades and assigning the group grade to each member of the group.

Research indicates that children in cooperative learning groups have consistently shown greater achievement than children who participate in traditional (ability or whole groups) grouping schemes (D. W. Johnson, Maruyama, Johnson, Nelson, & Skon, 1981; Jongsma, 1990; Slavin, 1995; Stevens, Madden, Slavin, & Farnish, 1987a, 1987b; Stevens & Slavin, 1995; Swafford, 1995; Topping, 1989; Webb & Schwartz, 1988; K. D. Wood, 1987). In a synthesis of research on cooperative learning, Slavin (1991) and Stevens and Slavin (1995) found that cooperative learning not only increased student achievement but also increased student self-concept and social skills. Manarino-Leggett and Saloman (1989), K. D. Wood (1987), and Swafford (1995) describe several grouping alternatives associated with the concept of cooperative learning. A number of these selected cooperative learning grouping alternatives are briefly described in Table 9.1.

> Cooperative learning groups have consistently shown greater achievement than children who participate in traditional grouping schemes.

Guided Reading Groups: Dynamic Homogeneous Grouping

Guided reading groups are dynamic groups composed of students who demonstrate similar abilities to independently read a leveled book, story, or text (Fountas & Pinnell, 1996; Mooney, 1990). There are three main assumptions underlying the use of guided reading groups. First, students evidence similar abilities to use a wide array of reading strategies. Second, guided reading groups are not static—they change on a continuous basis, at least monthly. Third, a variety of other grouping strategies are used during the reading instructional block in addition to guided reading groups.

> Guided reading groups are flexible and dynamic organizational structures intended to meet individual student needs and are an integral part of a balanced reading program.

Two processes combine to define a student's membership in a guided reading group. First, a group of books, stories, or texts are leveled along a standard gradient such as Reading Recovery's® levels 1–20, Fountas and Pinnell's A–R levels, or Lexiles®. Students are given books to read at their estimated level. For example, a student may be given a level C book, which is an early first grade level text. The student reads the book and a running record is taken (see chapter 10). If the running record shows that the student's percent of accuracy is roughly 90%, then the student may be placed in guided reading group at that level. If the book cannot be read with 90% accuracy, then lower level books are given to the child until one is found that can be read at approximately 90% accuracy. If the level of the book is too easy, higher level books are selected until a book can be found that the student reads at roughly the 90% accuracy level. All students placed into a guided reading group should be able to read that level of book, story, or text at about the 90% level.

Guided reading groups are best limited to five or six students and should meet at least every other day, with a daily meeting of 10 to 15 minutes preferred. The teacher carefully reads the leveled text selected for the day to be able to prepare the students for potential challenges or obstacles in the text. Once students are prepared to read the text through teacher-led discussion, they are asked to read the book independently (see lesson plan for guided reading in chapter 11). Students read aloud quietly at their

> Guided reading groups are flexible and dynamic organizational structures intended to meet individual student needs and are an integral part of a balanced reading instructional approach.

Table 9.1 Alternative grouping plans for encouraging cooperative learning

Book-Response Pairs

Students interview a peer or partner about a book they have read. After the interview, they write a report on their partner's book.

Cooperative Integrated Reading and Composition (CIRC)

CIRC is a programmatic approach to teaching reading and writing in the intermediate elementary grades (Stevens, Madden, Slavin, & Farnish, 1987a, 1987b). This program consists of three elements: (a) basal-related activities, (b) direct instruction in reading comprehension, and (c) integrated language arts writing.

Composition or Coauthoring Pairs

One of two students explains what he or she plans to write while the other student takes notes or outlines the discussion. Working together, the two students plan the lead-in, thesis, or opening statement. One student writes while the other student explains the outline or notes. They exchange roles as they write a single composition, or they can exchange roles to help each other write their own composition.

Computer Groups

Students work together on a computer to accomplish a given task. Students adopt specific roles such as keyboard operator, monitor, and checker throughout the process. Roles should be regularly rotated to allow each student to experience all three roles.

Drill Partners

Students pair off for drill activities such as working with words from personal or classroom word banks or rereading books to improve fluency.

Dyads

K. D. Wood (1987) assigns roles to each student in a dyad, or pair, of readers. Each student reads silently, or in some cases orally in unison, two pages of text. After reading these two pages, one student acts as recaller. This student verbally recounts what the two had read. The other student acts as listener and clarifier for the recaller. Dyad reading is an effective means for supporting young children's reading development, especially for at-risk readers (Eldredge & Quinn, 1988).

Focus Trios

Children may be randomly assigned or may form social groups of three students for the purposes of summarizing what they already know about a reading selection and developing questions to be answered during reading. After reading, the trio discusses answers to the questions, clarifies, and summarizes answers.

Group Reports

Students research a topic together as a group. Each person is responsible for contributing at least one resource to the report. Written or oral reports must involve all students in the final report.

Group Retellings

Students read different books or selections on the same topic. After reading, each student retells what he or she has read to the other group members. Group members may comment on or add to the retelling of any individual.

Groups of Four

Groups of four are randomly assigned task-completion groups. Each individual is given a responsibility to complete some phase of a larger task. For example, when writing a letter, one student could be the addresser, another the body writer, another the checker, and so on. In this way, all students contribute to the successful completion of the task. Roles should be exchanged regularly to allow students to experience all aspects of task completion.

Jigsaw

Students in a group are assigned to read a different part of the same selection. After reading, each student retells what he or she has read to the others in the group. A discussion usually ensues, during which students may interview or question the reteller to clarify any incomplete ideas or correct misunderstandings. After this discussion concludes, students can be invited to read the rest of the selection to confirm or correct the retellings of other group members.

Adapted from Manarino-Leggett and Saloman (1989) and K.D. Wood (1987).

Metacomprehension Pairs

Have students alternate reading and orally summarizing paragraphs or pages of a selection. One listens, follows along, and checks the accuracy of the other's comprehension of the selection.

Playwrights

Students select a piece of reading they wish to dramatize as a play. Students work together to develop a script, the set, and costumes, and then practice the play with individuals serving in various roles as director, characters, and other necessary functions. The culmination of the group is the performance of the play for a selected audience.

Problem-Solving and Project Groups

Having children work together cooperatively in pairs or small groups to solve reading or writing problems is another effective classroom practice involving the use of other children as a primary resource for enhancing classroom instruction. Problem-solving groups are small groups initiated by children who wish to work collaboratively on a self-selected reading or writing problem. In project groups, children are encouraged to explore a wide variety of possible reading and writing projects, such as plays, puppetry, reader's theater, research, authoring books, poetry, lyrics to songs, notes, invitations, and cards. The products resulting from project groups are to be of publishable quality. Thus, the culmination of a project group is sharing the project or product with an authentic audience.

Reading Buddies

In the lower grades, upper grade children can be selected as reading buddies to assist emergent readers. These buddies can be selected for a short period of time, say a week, then other children can be selected. This allows ample opportunities for upper grade readers to assist lower grade readers. In upper and lower grades, reading buddies can pair off and share a favorite book with a friend by reading exciting parts of the book or just discussing the book.

Strategy Teachers and Concept Clarifiers

Students work together in pairs on reading strategies, such as prediction, sequencing, making inferences, until both can do or explain these concepts or strategies easily.

Test Coaches

As students prepare for a test, a group of students can be given a prototype test. The group can divide the test items into even groups for each individual in the group. Each individual completes a part of the test. The group meets together to review the answers of each of the students, and check, confirm, or correct each answer.

Think-Pair-Share

Lyman (1988) recommends that students sit in pairs as the teacher presents a reading mini-lesson to the class. After the lesson, the teacher presents a problem to the group. The children individually think of an answer, then with their partners discuss and reach a consensus on the answer. A pair of students can be asked to share their agreed-on answer with the class.

Turn-to-Your-Neighbor

After listening to a student read a book aloud, share a book response, or share a piece of published writing, students can be asked to turn to a neighbor and tell one concept or idea they enjoyed about the presentation. They should also share one question they would like to ask the reader or author.

Worksheet and Homework Checkers

When teachers deem it necessary to use worksheets to provide practice for a concept or strategy taught during a reading mini-lesson, students can be organized into groups to check one another's work and provide feedback to each other.

Writing Response Groups

When a writer completes a publishable work or needs help with developing a draft, groups can be organized to listen to the author share his or her work. Afterward, group members can share ideas on how to improve the draft. If the piece is complete, group members should compliment the work and ask the author questions about the presentation.

In the lower grades, upper grade children can be selected as reading buddies to assist young readers.

own pace. The teacher listens in on each child as he or she reads aloud quietly; the purpose is to monitor student strategy application and provide individual guidance.

Needs Groups

Notice three possible opportunities for teachers to intervene using mini-lessons.

As teachers work with students in reading and writing instruction, they often note that some students are experiencing difficulties with a similar concept, skill, or procedure. When such shared difficulties are noted by the teacher, he or she may decide to form a temporary group to provide additional instruction related to a skill, strategy, concept, or procedure. This type of temporary grouping strategy is called *needs grouping.* The instructional vehicle chosen to provide needs group lessons is the **mini-lesson.**

Mini-lessons are an integral part of daily reading instruction for the whole group of students but may also arise as teachers and children work together collaboratively or individually on a selected story or text (Atwell, 1987; Calkins, 1986). Mini-lessons are presented to an entire class or to needs groups. They are *not* always meant to be lessons where outcomes are required; sometimes mini-lessons are simply invitations to engage in some literate behavior as part of immersing students in language.

Selected strategies for teaching mini-lessons in comprehension, vocabulary, and word identification are covered in chapters 6 to 8.

Hagerty (1992) describes three types of mini-lessons: procedural, literary, and strategy/skill. A listing of possible mini-lesson topics is found in Table 9.2. A procedural reading mini-lesson, for example, might involve the teacher and students in learning how to handle new books received for the classroom library as well as how to repair worn books in the classroom library. (The teacher may demonstrate how to break in a new book's binding by standing the book on its spine and opening a few pages on either side of the center of the book and carefully pressing them down. Cellophane tape and staplers can be used to demonstrate how to repair tears in a book's pages or covers. A heavy-duty stapler is used to reattach paperback book covers in another demonstration on caring for books.)

Procedural, literary, and skill/strategy are three types of potential mini-lessons.

Mini-lessons are a major vehicle in balanced literacy programs for providing children access to guided and, when needed, explicit demonstrations of skilled reading and writing behaviors, necessary procedural knowledge, and a greater understanding of literary and stylistic devices.

A literary mini-lesson for early readers might involve a child presenting the teacher with a small booklet written at home in the shape of a puppy that retells favorite parts from the book *Taxi Dog* (Barracca & Barracca, 1990), which may constitute an opportunity for the teacher to share the book with students as a demonstration of how another student shared his or her ideas using the writing process in the form of a shape book. After such sharing, a rash of shape books is likely to result. As a literary mini-lesson for the upper elementary level, a student may assemble a poster resembling the front page of a newspaper to show major events from a novel just read, such as Betsy Byars's (1970) *The Summer of the Swans.*

A strategy/skill mini-lesson for early readers might occur during the reading of a big book entitled *Cats and Mice* (Gelman, 1985), where the teacher notes that many of the words in the book end with the participle form of *-ing.* Noticing this regularity in the text, the teacher draws children's attention to the function of *-ing.* For example, while rereading the big book the next day, the teacher may cover each *-ing* ending with a small self-adhesive note. During the group rereading of the book, the teacher reveals the *-ing* ending at the end of the words covered. On subsequent readings, the teacher invites students to join in the reading while emphasizing the *-ing*

Table 9.2 Possible mini-lesson topics

Procedural Mini-lessons	Literary Mini-lessons	Strategy/Skills Mini-lessons
Where to sit during reading time	Differences between fiction and	How to choose a book
Giving a book talk	nonfiction books	Selecting literature log topics
How to be a good listener in a	Learning from dedications	Connecting reading material to
share session	Books that show emotion	your own life
What is an appropriate noise level	Books written in the first, second,	Tips for reading aloud
during reading time	or third person	Figuring out unknown words
What to do when you finish a	Author studies	Using context
book	How authors use quotations	Substituting
What kinds of questions to ask	How the story setting fits the story	Using picture clues
during a share session	Characteristics of different genres	Using the sounds of blends,
Running a small-group discussion	Development of characters, plot,	vowels, contractions, etc.
Self-evaluation	theme, mood	Using Post-its to mark interesting
Getting ready for a conference	How leads hook us	parts
How to have a peer conference	How authors use the problem/	Monitoring comprehension (Does
Where to sit during mini-lessons	event/solution pattern	this make sense and sound
Taking care of books	Differences between a picture	right?)
Keeping track of books read	book and a novel	Asking questions while reading
Rules of the workshop	Titles and their meanings	Making predictions
	Characters' points of view	Emergent strategies
	Examples of similes and	Concept of story
	metaphors	Concept that print carries
	Examples of foreshadowing	meaning
	How authors use dialogue	Making sense
	Predictable and surprise endings	Mapping a story
	Use of descriptive words and	How to retell a story orally
	phrases	Looking for relationships
	How illustrations enhance the	Looking for important ideas
	story	Making inferences
	Secrets in books	Drawing conclusions
		Summarizing a story
		Distinguishing fact from opinion
		Emergent reader skills:
		directionality, concept of "word,"
		sound/symbol relationships

From *Readers' Workshop: Real Reading* (pp. 113–115), by P. Hagerty, 1992, Ontario, Canada: Scholastic Canada Ltd. Copyright 1992 by Patricia Hagerty. Reprinted by permission.

sound at the end of words. Other words that children know are written at the board, and an *-ing* ending is added. Children take turns pronouncing these words with the *-ing* added. A mini-lesson for more advanced readers might pertain to patterns used by nonfiction writers to make abstract information better understood (e.g., cause–effect, description, problem–solution, and comparisons). This mini-lesson could involve (a) describing the patterns used; (b) searching for examples in science, mathematics, and social studies materials; then (c) students' writing/creating their examples of these patterns pertaining to a topic of choice.

Flexible Groups

Flexible grouping is another instructional grouping variation. Recall that in our discussion on transitions in chapter 5, we noted that the flexible grouping of children places them into temporary groups based on their level of independence as learners and their personal interests, which sustain independence. Because learning environments can be enhanced by the use of flexible groups, let's revisit the principles noted by Unsworth (1984, p. 300):

1. There are no permanent groups.
2. Groups are periodically created, modified, or disbanded, to meet new needs as they arise.
3. At times there is only one group consisting of all pupils.
4. Groups vary in size from 2 or 3 to 9 or 10, depending on the group's purpose.
5. Group membership is not fixed; it varies according to needs and purposes.
6. Student commitment is enhanced when students know how the group's work relates to the overall program or task.
7. Children should be able to evaluate the progress of the group and the teacher's assessment of the group's work.
8. There should be a clear strategy for supervising the group's work.

It is clear from these principles that flexible grouping strategies can be used to accommodate student interests, learning styles, and social needs such as friendship groups in addition to meeting instructional needs and goals. For flexible grouping to function effectively, the organization, purpose, and tasks must be clearly understood by students.

When the classroom has multiple centers or stations, the teacher can place children into temporary groups for managing rotation through center activities.

Concerns such as what is to be accomplished and how it is to be accomplished must be clearly stated and understood by students; the potential for unproductive chaos is high in flexible grouping arrangements if the teacher has not carefully prepared the learning tasks and the environment for success. For example, when children are grouped to perform specified tasks in learning centers or stations in a classroom, flexible grouping is ideal for managing children's rotations through center-based activities. Although the teacher may elect to encourage children to choose centers, this often leads to an overcrowding in one center and a dearth of participants in another. To help teachers manage the rotation of children through centers, flexible groups can be formed.

A group leader can be designated to oversee center cleanup, operation of cassette recorders, and other tasks.

Flexible groups are cohorts of six to eight children who are grouped together for the purpose of rotating or traveling through center activities in classrooms. These groups should include a mix of reading and writing ability levels, called heterogeneous grouping, to avoid the pitfalls associated with ability grouping. Flexible groups should exist for no longer than a month at a time; then the children should be regrouped. For example, a classroom in which flexible grouping is used to provide for participation in multiple centers or stations might operate something like this.

This hypothetical classroom has six literacy learning centers, established in various locations around the classroom. The first center is an alphabet and word-building station where children use magnetic letters and word pattern cards (rimes/word families) to build words, sort words, and store words in personalized word banks. A second center houses a listening station where students have multiple copies of a title to be read with a read-along cassette tape. A third center provides a quiet, comfortable area for reading self-selected books, magazines, comics, etc. A fourth center seats children around a horseshoe- or U-shaped table for guided reading and interactive writing sessions with the teacher. A fifth center provides a writing workshop where students can peer conference, get and give editing assistance, and prepare student-authored products from greeting cards, recipes, and calendars to newspaper ads, books, and story murals. Finally, there is a center for individual student conferences that are scheduled in advance with the teacher.

Flexible groups of children are formed to participate in these six designed center activities. These groups have assigned tasks to complete in each center. Behavioral and instructional guidelines and goals are clearly established and communicated to each group prior to center time. Most important, students are helped to know what they may do as follow-up work should they finish before the others. All of this requires extraordinary instructional planning and management skill on the part of the teacher, but the busy and productive activity and learning that come from the flexible grouping strategy makes it well worth the effort!

Think about three reasons why using flexible grouping is preferable to using ability or whole-class grouping.

Flexible Basal Reader Groups: Large-Group Lesson/Small-Group Follow-Up

Wiggins (1994) argues that basal reading instruction has for years resulted in teachers deciding to use three homogeneously formed reading groups or ability groups (like the *Eagles, Robins,* and *Buzzards* groups). Ability groups were typically formed on the basis of an achievement test score and resulted in teachers adjusting the materials for students rather than adjusting the nature and organization of the instruction. For many readers with special needs, grade-level reading materials are never a part of their instructional experience. In the flexible basal reader grouping approach, teachers are encouraged to adjust their instruction as well as the level of the materials.

Wiggins (1994, pp. 455–456) provides the following guidelines for using a flexible large group/small group follow-up organizational framework:

- Initial reading instruction (background building, vocabulary development, skill lessons, etc.) is given through a core lesson in a whole-class setting.
- The teacher meets daily with small groups to provide follow-up reinforcement of the core lesson.
- The makeup of the groups is determined by the needs of the students for that day's core lesson, the story; there is no standing assignment to a reading group.
- The makeup of the group changes depending on what is being reinforced, retaught, or enriched.
- The teacher differentiates follow-up activities based on the needs of the students to provide targeted instruction for low-level students and extra or extension activities for high-level students.

A typical classroom schedule for using large group/small group flexible grouping based on Wiggins (1994, p. 457) is shown in Figure 9.15.

Figure 9.15   Flexible grouping

Typical Classroom Day

9:00–9:20	Opening exercises
9:20–9:50	Whole-class teacher sharing and reading lesson
9:50–10:30	Special subject (music, art, or PE)
10:30–11:15	Whole-class math lesson
11:15–12:15	Seat work and centers

- small group 1 meets with teacher (20 min.)
- small group 2 meets with teacher (20 min.)
- small group 3 meets with teacher (20 min.)

Lunch

1:00–1:30	Whole-class teacher sharing and writing lesson
1:30–2:10	Science, social studies, or library
2:25–3:05	Seat work and centers

- small group 4 meets with teacher (20 min.)
- small group 5 meets with teacher (20 min.)

3:10	Dismissal

Based on Wiggins, R. A. (1994). Large group lesson/small group follow-up: Flexible grouping in a basal reading program. *The Reading Teacher 47*(6), 450–460.

ADAPTING THE ENVIRONMENT TO ASSIST CHILDREN WITH SPECIAL NEEDS

Focus on two ways to structure the classroom literacy-learning environment to help students with special needs.

For over 2 decades, teachers and schools have been under a legal mandate to provide the least restrictive learning environment possible for all children, especially those with handicapping conditions and other special needs. With the passage of Public Law 94-142, the Individuals with Disabilities Education Act, greater attention has been devoted to adapting typical classroom environments to accommodate children with special needs into the regular classroom. Teachers are searching for ways to be of greatest assistance to all children in their classrooms.

Concerning the physical environment, classrooms should be broken into smaller, functional areas for specific activities. According to Nordquist and Twardosz (1990), these should be bounded by low partitions or shelves. Literacy props for classroom activity areas should be selected based on "functionality" and "reactivity" to ensure maximal success, meaning that props should be appropriate for the mental or chronological age of the individual child. Also, literacy props that temporarily sustain motion or produce sensory feedback, such as read-along tapes, pop-up books, and typewriters, help to sustain appropriate classroom behaviors.

For children with attention deficit disorder, changing activity areas regularly, providing colorful props, inserting quiet, calming music, and furnishing activities that require engagement and an active response help these students maintain attention.

In some cases, children may need to be given medical treatment to help them focus their attention on learning.

It is important that students with special needs feel fully accepted as part of the classroom community—a sense of ownership and belonging. Voltz and Damiano-

Lantz (1993) have listed several strategies for helping children with special needs develop ownership of their classroom learning environment, which we have adapted as follows:

- Establish student-oriented bulletin boards that children can create, use, and maintain.
- Solicit student input on how to organize the physical environment of the classroom.
- Provide a "suggestion box" where children can put their ideas on how to make the classroom a better place.
- Invite student input on classroom rules and policies.
- Link subject matter studies to real-world concerns outside the classroom and school.
- Use a thematic approach to learning that provides in-depth learning and helps children make connections across disciplines.
- Provide a variety of ways to engage and respond to learning activities that make use of different modalities such as touching, moving, seeing, hearing, and tasting.
- Invite children to set their own learning goals.

ADAPTING THE ENVIRONMENT TO ASSIST LINGUISTICALLY AND CULTURALLY DIVERSE STUDENTS

Garcia and Malkin (1993) suggest three major considerations in creating supportive learning environments for linguistically and culturally diverse students. First, teachers should carefully select and evaluate instructional materials. Figure 9.16 is a checklist offered by Garcia and Malkin (1993).

Second, teachers should be sure to incorporate children's language and culture into the ongoing activities of the classroom. Activities such as family histories can invite children to explore their own roots and come to appreciate the unique characteristics of their religious, geographical, gender, ethnic, and language background.

Third, teachers should encourage involvement and participation of the parents and the community. These individuals can add richness to the learning environment by sharing backgrounds, talents, knowledge, and cultural understandings. In some cases, parents and community members can help teachers by acting as translators for a period of time to facilitate communication for ESL students.

Focus on how parent involvement adds richness and variety to the classroom environment for all students and helps to validate each child's culture, language, etc.

Summary

Research has led to the development of clear guidelines or principles for creating supportive literacy-learning environments. A four-part environmental model includes providing, arranging, and using literary props and creating authentic environments for learning. Next, the practical creation of learning spaces to include reading nooks, writing areas, library spaces, etc. were described. Similar to homes, classroom space can be subdivided into functional areas to support specific instructional goals and activities. Whole-class learning, collaborative writing, silent reading, supported reading, conferences, and thematic studies areas support reading, writing, and thematic studies in transitional and balanced literacy classrooms.

Figure 9.16   Checklist for selecting and evaluating materials for culturally and linguistically diverse learners

- Are the perspectives and contributions of people from diverse cultural and linguistic groups—both men and women, as well as people with disabilities—included in the curriculum?

- Are there curricula that will assist students in analyzing the various forms of the mass media for ethnocentrism, sexism, "handicapism," and stereotyping?

- Are men and women, diverse cultural/racial groups, and people with varying abilities shown in both active and passive roles?

- Are men and women, diverse cultural/racial groups, and people with disabilities shown in positions of power (i.e., the materials do not rely on the mainstream culture's character to achieve goals)?

- Do the materials identify strengths possessed by so-called "underachieving" diverse populations? Do they diminish the attention given to deficits, to reinforce positive behaviors that are desired and valued?

- Are members of diverse racial/cultural groups, men and women, and people with disabilities shown engaged in a broad range of social and professional activities?

- Are members of a particular culture or group depicted as having a range of physical features (e.g., hair color, hair texture, variations in facial characteristics and body build)?

- Do the materials represent historical events from the perspectives of the various groups involved or solely from the male, middle-class, and/or Western European perspective?

- Are the materials free from ethnocentric or sexist language patterns that may make implications about people or groups based solely on their culture, race, gender, or disability?

- Will students from different ethnic and cultural backgrounds find the materials personally meaningful to their life experiences?

- Are a wide variety of culturally different examples, situations, scenarios, and anecdotes used throughout the curriculum design to illustrate major intellectual concepts and principles?

- Are culturally diverse content, examples, and experiences comparable in kind, significance, magnitude, and function to those selected from mainstream culture?

From "Toward Defining Programs and Services for Culturally and Linguistically Diverse Learners in Special Education" by S. B. Garcia and D. H. Malkin, *Teaching Exceptional Children, 26*(1), 1993, pp. 52–58. Copyright 1993 by The Council for Exceptional Children. Reprinted with permission.

Basals, trade books, workbooks, leveled books, decodable books, volunteers, and computers are instructional resources available to the classroom teacher for supporting reading and writing instruction in the classroom. Examples of how computers can be used to support developing readers and writers include such recent developments as hypertext and hypermedia. Potential resources for implementing literacy volunteer programs include a volunteer sign-up form.

Evidence condemning the practice of ability grouping of students for reading instruction includes negative influences on teacher and student expectations, student self-concepts, and student friendship patterns. Literature-response groups, basal reader visiting response groups, whole-class groups, guided reading groups, needs groups, task or centers groups, and flexible basal reader groups are alternatives to ability grouping students for reading instruction. Cooperative learning groups, such as jigsaw groups, buddy reading, focus trios, are additional alternatives to the practice of ability grouping. Finally, unique considerations for assisting children with special needs and those with cultural or linguistic differences were presented.

Concept Applications

In the Classroom

1. Make a layout map of how you intend to divide up your classroom space during your 1st year of teaching. Give a supporting rationale for the design you choose. (Keep in mind the idea of transitions—beginning simple and moving to more complex classroom arrangements!)
2. Create a 5-year plan for building a classroom library of trade books. Include in your plan a target total number of trade books and relevant target dates for accomplishment of your goals.
3. Choose a topic for conducting a mini-lesson in reading or writing. Defend the authenticity of your choice in terms of whether or not real readers or writers would ever need to use this skill or strategy outside the school setting.
4. Pick the grade level at which you hope to teach your 1st year. Devise a story like those found in the latter part of chapter 5. In your story, detail your personal 5-year plan for making the transition in terms of your classroom design, curriculum, and lesson planning.
5. Analyze the cover of this text for qualities of design that are reflected in the research on creating literacy learning environments. What props are present? How are they arranged? Does this classroom provide for interaction and learning of literacy through demonstrations, engagement, and sensitivity? Is the classroom aesthetically pleasing? Does it inform children? Is it divided into functional areas? Has the teacher used personal touches? You might make an analysis grid or evaluation instrument based on the principles presented in this chapter to look at these questions for your own classroom.

In the Field

1. Visit at least two public or private school classrooms, and draw a layout map of the space in the classrooms and how it is used. Be sure to include bulletin boards and storage areas in your observations. Afterward, interview the teachers. Determine their reasons for the classroom arrangement and use.
2. Discuss with at least two parents the concept of volunteer work in schools. Determine whether or not parents would be willing to give their time to their local school. Invite them to fill out and discuss with you the volunteer sign-up form in Figure 9.13.

3. Visit two school classrooms, and note how teachers and children spend their time. On a separate paper, reflect in writing on your observations. Discuss relative advantages and disadvantages of teacher and student behaviors observed during reading instruction.

4. Interview at least two children in the above-average and below-average ability groups. Ask questions about how they like reading time, completing workbook and worksheet assignments, receiving books for presents, and reading aloud to their peers. Contrast your findings for the above-average and below-average readers.

Recommended Readings

Au, K. (1991). Organizing for instruction [Special issue]. *The Reading Teacher, 44*(8).

Butler, A., & Turbill, J. (1984). *Towards a reading-writing classroom.* Portsmouth, NH: Heinemann.

Cooter, R. B., Jr., Mills-House, E., Marrin, P., Mathews, B., & Campbell, S. (in press for Spring 1999). Family and community involvement: The bedrock of reading success. *The Reading Teacher.*

Hagerty, P. (1992). *Reader's workshop: Real reading.* New York: Scholastic.

McVitty, W. (1986). *Getting it together: Organizing the reading-writing classroom.* Portsmouth, NH: Heinemann.

Morrow, L. M., & Rand, M. K. (1991). Promoting literacy during play by designing early childhood classroom environments. *The Reading Teacher, 44*(6), 396–402.

Neuman, S. B., & Roskos, K. (1990). Play, print, and purpose: Enriching play environments for literacy development. *The Reading Teacher, 44*(3), 214–221.

Peterson, R., & Eeds, M. (1990). *Grand conversations: Literature groups in action.* New York: Scholastic.

Rasinski, T. (1989). Commentary: Reading the empowerment of parents. *The Reading Teacher, 43*(3), 226–231.

Reinking, D. (Ed.). (1987). *Computers and reading: Issues for theory and practice.* New York: Teachers College Press.

Slaughter, H. B. (1988). Indirect and direct teaching in a whole language program. *The Reading Teacher, 42*(1), 30–35.

Strickland, D. S., Feeley, J. T., & Wepner, S. B. (1987). *Using computers in the teaching of reading.* New York: Teachers College Press.

Van Manen, M. (1986). *The tone of teaching.* New York: Scholastic.

Whitaker, B. T., Schwartz, E., & Vockell, E. (1989). *The computer in the reading curriculum.* New York: McGraw-Hill.

Assessment:

Focus Questions

When you are finished studying this chapter, you should be able to answer these questions:
1. What are the basic principles of effective classroom literacy assessment?
2. How do traditional assessment procedures differ from balanced literacy assessment procedures?
3. What are some examples of the more common commercial reading tests available for classroom use?
4. What five balanced literacy assessment strategies can be used to inform instruction?
5. What is *profiling?* How is profiling used to form needs-based reading groups?
6. How can teachers derive grades from balanced literacy assessment strategies?
7. What are some of the current issues in reading assessment?

Determining Students' Progress in Literacy

Key Concepts

Balanced Literacy Assessment
Principles of Classroom Assessment
Portfolio Assessment
Kid Watching
Literacy-Learning Milestones
Reading Fluency
Running Records

Family Surveys
Rubrics
Profiling
Power and Timed Tests
Norm-Referenced Tests (NRT)
Authentic Grading
Affective and Conative Factors

eading assessment is intended to inform teaching. **Balanced literacy assessment** measures satisfy this purpose and are typically informal, analyze reading using real books, provide natural experiences with text, and are aimed at carefully analyzing overall student growth in the reading process.

Differences between traditional and balanced literacy assessment perspectives in reading can be likened to the differences between a black-and-white photograph and a color movie: Traditional assessment at best provides teachers and administrators with a limited view of readers (like a "snapshot" of a child), whereas balanced literacy assessment provides teachers with a much clearer and more comprehensive view of the learner (like a color movie).

In this chapter, we describe forms of traditional and balanced literacy assessment methods and examples of each. First, we explore some basic principles of classroom reading assessment.

PRINCIPLES OF CLASSROOM ASSESSMENT

The principles of classroom assessment help teachers select appropriate strategies.

The following **principles of classroom assessment** are intended to help teachers decide which assessment strategies should be adopted to improve classroom instruction. They are based on classroom experience, research in the field, and opinions expressed to us by teachers in the field.

Principle 1:   Assessment should inform and improve teaching.

When considering whether or not to perform any sort of reading assessment, the teacher should ask, "Will this procedure help me make educational decisions regarding this student's reading needs?" The procedure should yield rich insights as to approaches, materials, and ways of offering instruction (e.g., grouping based on student needs) that can positively affect students' literacy growth. The process begins with a careful survey of what is known about the student using information available (home surveys, cumulative records, informal assessments, student self-assessments, etc.). Next, the teacher begins to form hypotheses about where the student is in his or her reading development (Bintz, 1991). The next task is to select assessment procedures that will help the teacher better understand student abilities and confirm or reject earlier hypotheses. Armed with the information obtained from these processes, the teacher teaches lessons aimed at helping the student develop further. Figure 10.1 depicts this assessment-teaching process.

Principle 2:   Assessment procedures should help teachers discover what children can do, not what they cannot do.

Assessments should help teachers determine where students are in their literacy development.

Reading assessment in recent decades has usually followed what has been termed a *medical* or *clinical model*. The clinical model was used to cloak reading assessment in the robes of science and precision. A thinly veiled assumption was that children getting off to a rough beginning must have something organically wrong slowing their literacy development. The idea was that whenever a teacher discovered a student having difficulty with reading, a "diagnosis" of the child's problem areas would be developed using various reading tests. From this diagnosis of strengths and, more im-

Figure 10.1   Assessment-teaching process

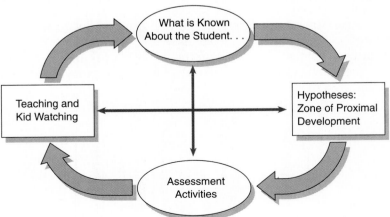

portant, weaknesses, a "prescription" or remediation program was developed. After several decades of following this medical model and the establishment of federally sponsored remedial programs to support them (Title 1 and Special Education), very little impact has been registered with students struggling in reading (Mullis, Campbell, & Farstrup, 1993). A new perspective in assessment seems warranted.

Rather than spending precious classroom time trying to identify what students *cannot* do, many teachers are finding that their time is much better spent finding out what students *can* do. Once teachers understand student abilities, it becomes much easier to decide which new learning experiences should be offered to help them develop further. Later in this chapter, we describe the literacy-learning milestones through which students progress to help you better judge where they are in their literacy development and what they may be able to learn next.

Principle 3: Every assessment procedure should have a specific purpose.

It is easy for teachers to fall into the habit of giving tests simply because of tradition within a school or school system. This frequently happens with some standardized tests routinely reserved for children who seem to be having significant reading problems. For example, at a school where one of the authors taught, it was common practice to give a "battery" of tests to all children having reading difficulties who were referred for assessment by a school psychologist. Such a battery today might include published tests such as the following:

Think of times in your life when you have done things needlessly simply because of past traditions.

- *Woodcock Reading Mastery Tests—Revised* (Woodcock, Mather, & Barnes, 1987)
- *Brigance® Comprehensive Inventory of Basic Skills—Revised* (Brigance, 1999)
- *Slosson Intelligence Test* (Slosson, 1971)
- *Test of Phonological Awareness* (TOPA). (1994). Austin, TX: Pro-Ed.
- Comprehensive Test of Nonverbal Intelligence

The problem with this sort of "shotgun" approach is that all children receive the same battery of tests without regard to known student abilities or anticipated needs (though these tests are quite helpful in certain situations).

"Shotgun" approaches to assessment waste valuable time and resources, and they are stressful to students.

Because reading assessment can be somewhat stressful to students, we should be careful to administer only those formal tests that are absolutely necessary; informal, less stressful procedures should be used when possible. This practice will most likely provide the necessary information to begin instruction, which will then lead to a better understanding of the student's ability.

Principle 4: Classroom assessment should provide insights into the *process* of reading.

Reading is a complex process that involves such important areas as skill development in decoding, vocabulary knowledge, interest-related factors, and command of oral language. Traditional testing, however, tends to view reading from a more limited skills perspective (see chapter 2 for a review of the various instructional models). Fortunately, there are assessment procedures available that view reading from a more balanced perspective. Clay (1985), for instance, developed an assessment procedure for primary level children known as the *Concepts About Print Test,* which assesses the print awareness of emerging readers and can be used to assess what they know about fundamental print concepts (Heathington, 1990). Clay has also suggested the use of running records for assessing reading ability more authentically. These and other balanced literacy assessment procedures are discussed later in this chapter.

Principle 5:   Assessment procedures should help identify zones of proximal development.

Balanced literacy assessment helps teachers understand which reading skills should be introduced next.

In chapter 3, we discussed Vygotsky's (1962, 1978) notion of a *zone of proximal development,* or the area of potential growth in reading that can occur with appropriate teacher and peer intervention. To identify students' zones of proximal development, teachers need to determine accurately what children can already do, and which new skills they may be ready to learn next. For example, in a kindergarten or first-grade classroom, children who can create story lines for wordless picture books, and who have been doing so for some time, should be ready for books containing simple and predictable text.

Teachers also need to watch for any problem areas students may have. Whether only one student or many students seem to have the same reading problem, the teacher should offer a mini-lesson to help them over the hurdle. In other words, the reading curriculum should be responsive and flexible according to students' demonstrated needs and patterns of ability.

Principle 6:   Assessment strategies should not supplant instruction.

Sometimes teachers can spend far too much time assessing in lieu of quality teaching-learning.

State- and locally mandated testing often seems to overpower the teacher and take over the classroom. If the teacher loses sight of the purpose of classroom assessment, namely, to inform and influence instruction, then he or she may well move into the role of *teacher as manager* rather than *teacher as teacher* (Pearson, 1985). The assessment program should complement the instructional program and grow naturally from it.

Principle 7:   The only truly valid and competent assessment is individual assessment.

Individual assessment is the best assessment.

Whole-group assessment tends to provide gross estimations of reading program effectiveness; neither individual student needs nor substantive conclusions concerning the reading program can be determined using such procedures. Teachers need to be able to watch, listen, and interact with individual students, one at a time, to develop clear understandings of their abilities.

In the remainder of this chapter, we survey assessment practices as they pertain to reading skills and processes. We begin with an analysis of traditional reading assessment practices that remain prevalent in American school districts. Later, we take a more in-depth look at balanced literacy assessment options and related issues.

TRADITIONAL READING ASSESSMENT

Traditional assessment typically fails to inform instruction adequately.

Traditional reading assessment in the United States typically provides district-wide and national comparisons of children using commercial reading tests. Though this information may provide only a general snapshot of student learning, these tests are widely used and should be understood by teachers.

In this section, two questions regarding traditional reading assessment are briefly addressed. First, what types of commercial reading tests are commonly available to teachers? Second, what problems are encountered by teachers who rely on these types of reading tests?

Informal Reading Inventories

An informal reading inventory (IRI) is typically individually administered (though some can be given to groups of children), and often have graded word lists and story passages. Emmett A. Betts is generally considered to be the first developer of the IRI; however, several other individuals contributed to its development as far back as the early 1900s (Johns & Lunn, 1983).

IRIs typically have passages more like authentic books than most other commercial tests.

The Teacher's Guide to Reading Tests (Cooter, 1990) cites several advantages and unique features of IRIs that help to explain why teachers continue to find them useful. One advantage is that IRIs provide for authentic assessments of the reading act: An IRI more closely resembles real reading. Students are better able to "put it all together" by reading whole stories or passages. Another advantage of IRIs is that they usually provide a systematic procedure for studying student miscues or errors (see the discussion of running records later in this chapter for examples of miscues).

IRIs are rather unusual when compared to other forms of reading assessment. First, because they are informal, no norms, reliability data, or validity information is usually available. This is often seen as a disadvantage by some public school educators, especially those in special education who need reliable figures for accountability purposes. Second, IRIs offer information that is often quite helpful to teachers in making curricular decisions, especially teachers who place students into needs-based or guided reading (Fountas & Pinnell, 1996) groups. IRIs provide an approximation of each child's ability in graded or "leveled" reading materials, such as basal readers and books used for guided reading. These approximations, or reading levels, are interpreted as independent level (easy or recreational), instructional level, or frustration level (failure or difficult). A third characteristic is that the various IRIs available tend to be quite different from each other. Beyond the usual graded word lists and passages, IRIs vary a great deal in the subtests offered (e.g., silent reading passages, phonics, interest inventories, concepts about print, phonemic awareness, auditory discrimination) and in the scoring criteria used to assess miscues. Finally, some argue that the best IRIs are those constructed by classroom teachers themselves using reading materials from their own classrooms (a form of content or curricular validity).

Reliability has to do with how consistently a test measures what it is designed to measure.

Several examples of IRIs now used in many school systems follow:

- *The Flynt/Cooter Reading Inventory for the Classroom, Third Edition* (Flynt & Cooter, 1998). The Flynt-Cooter Reading Inventory for the Classroom is a modern version of the traditional IRI concept. The authors incorporated current research on comprehension processes, running records, and miscue analysis into a more effective authentic reading assessment. They included such research-based procedures as unaided/aided recall and story grammar comprehension evaluation, high-interest selections, appropriate length passages, both expository and narrative passages, and a time-efficient miscue grid system for quick analyses of running records.

- *The English * Español Reading Inventory* (Flynt & Cooter, 1999). This newly released IRI features complete informal reading inventories for prekindergarten through grade 12 students in both Spanish and English. The Spanish passages were carefully developed and field tested with the aid of native Spanish-speaking teacher-researchers from the United States, Mexico,

*The English * Español Reading Inventory incorporates recent assessment research and high-interest passages in both Spanish and English.*

and Central and South America to avoid problems with dialect differences and to maximize their usefulness in United States classrooms.

- *Classroom Reading Inventory (CRI)* (Silvaroli, 1986). One of the oldest and most commonly used commercial IRIs, the "Silvaroli" (as it is commonly called) uses the classic graded word lists and passages combination. Unlike most of its competitors, the CRI also features illustrations that go along with each passage at the elementary levels. The test includes four forms (A, B, C, D), which cover elementary grades (1 to 6, on forms A and B), middle or junior high (form C), and high school students or adults (form D).

Group Reading Tests

Norm-referenced tests compare students to other students nationally.

Sometimes it is desirable to quickly assess the reading abilities of children in group settings and attain norm-referenced information. *Norm-referenced tests* compare student performance to a cross section of students in other areas of the country who were administered the same test. Group reading tests in this section feature norm-referenced data and also offer a few other benefits. For example, these tests are usually available in different forms, allowing school systems to measure learning by assessing children at the beginning of the school year or program and again at year's end. Group reading tests usually have several levels available, allowing learners to be matched to a test of appropriate difficulty.

The drawback to norm-referenced tests is that they provide very little information to help teachers plan instruction.

The major disadvantage of norm-referenced group reading tests is that they provide little or no usable information for modifying the classroom teacher's curriculum (i.e., informing instruction). Most information yielded by these tests tends to come in the form of stanines, percentile rankings, and grade equivalents. In more recent years, educators have begun to turn away from such statistics as grade equivalents in favor of the more meaningful normal curve equivalents or stanines. An example of a group reading test follows.

- *Gates-MacGinitie Reading Tests, Third Edition* (MacGinitie & MacGinitie, 1989). A most popular instrument with school systems and reading researchers, the Gates-MacGinitie assesses children ranging from prereading levels through grade 12. The prereading level, readiness level, and level one (kindergarten to 1.9 grade levels) have only one form available, but levels two through 10/12 (grades 1.5 to 12.9) have two forms each (Aaron & Gillespie, 1990). Levels two through 10/12 have essentially two measures of reading: vocabulary and comprehension.

Individual Diagnostic Reading Tests

Individual diagnostic tests can be helpful in assessing new students for whom prior assessments or permanent records are not yet available.

School districts sometimes feel it is necessary to assess an individual student's reading ability using norm-referenced measures. This often happens when new students move into a school district without their permanent records or when students are being considered for compensatory or extra assistance programs such as Title 1 or special education options. Following is an example of a commonly used test:

- *Woodcock Reading Mastery Tests—Revised* (Woodcock et al., 1987, 1997). The Woodcock Reading Mastery Tests—Revised (WRMT-R/NU) is a battery of six individually administered subtests intended to measure reading abilities from kindergarten through adult levels. Subtests cover visual-auditory learning, letter identification, word identification, word attack, word comprehen-

Standardized tests have traditionally been used to assess literacy progress.

sion, and passage comprehension. Its design reveals a skills perspective of reading, dividing the assessment into two sections appropriate to age and ability levels: readiness and reading achievement. The WRMT-R/NU reports norm-referenced data recalculated in 1997 for both of its forms, as well as insights into remediation oriented toward a skills perspective. Results may be calculated either manually or using the convenient scoring program developed for microcomputers. This test is frequently used by teachers in special education, Chapter 1 reading, and sometimes teachers assigned to regular classrooms.

Other Reading-Related Tests

Finally, many tests, though they may not all be reading tests per se, provide classroom teachers with some insights into children's reading behavior. Several examples follow:

- *Kaufman Test of Educational Achievement* (K-TEA/NU) (Kaufman & Kaufman, 1997). Sometimes teachers require norm-referenced data to determine how a child is progressing compared to other children nationally, such as when teachers are working with a population of students who are performing at atypically high or low levels. That is, working with these students over a long period of time may tend to give teachers a distorted view of what "normal" achievement looks like. The Kaufman Test of Educational Achievement (K-TEA/NU), available in both English and Spanish forms, can provide useful insights in these situations. The K-TEA/NU is a norm-referenced test yielding information in the areas of reading, mathematics, and spelling. Intended for students in grades 1 to 12, the K-TEA/NU is available in both a

The K-TEA/NU is an individually administered achievement test.

brief form for quick assessments (when only standardized data are needed) and a comprehensive form (provides both standardized data and insights into classroom remediation). Strictly speaking, alternate forms are not available, but the authors suggest that the two versions may be used as such for pretest–posttest measures.

- *Woodcock-Muñoz Language Survey* (WMLS), English and Spanish Forms (Woodcock & Muñoz-Sandoval, 1993). Teachers, particularly in urban centers, often have a large number of students who are learning English as a second language (ESL). The extent to which students have acquired a listening and speaking vocabulary in English is an important issue for reading instruction because (a) reading itself is a language skill, and (b) reading depends on learners having a fairly strong English vocabulary. The WMLS is a widely respected instrument used throughout the United States that takes about 20 minutes to administer. It features two subtests: Oral Language and Reading/Writing.

The PPVT-III can quickly assess a student's receptive vocabulary knowledge, which is an important predictor of reading success.

- *Peabody Picture Vocabulary Test, Third Edition* (PPVT-III) (Dunn & Dunn, 1997). Growth in reading ability is directly related to the student's vocabulary knowledge. In other words, one can read and understand only words that are already known. The PPVT-III is a quickly administered test (11–12 minutes) that indicates how strong a student's vocabulary knowledge is compared to other students of the same age nationally. Results can help the teacher better understand the needs of students in terms of formal and informal vocabulary instruction.

- *Test de Vocabulario en Imágenes Peabody* (TVIP), (Dunn, Lugo, Padilla, & Dunn, 1986). This test is an adaptation of an early version of the previously described *Peabody Picture Vocabulary Test* for native Spanish speakers. It takes about 10 to 15 minutes to administer and measures Spanish vocabulary knowledge.

Problems With Many Traditional Reading Tests

In this section, we have examined some of the traditional reading tests prevalent in many American schools. The primary strength of these instruments is their usefulness for documenting general reading performance. It has also been stated that compared to more *authentic* balanced literacy assessment methods, which are discussed in the next section, traditional assessments sometimes seem woefully inadequate. Following is a discussion of a few of the specific problems or shortcomings of traditional tests.

Traditional assessments are often based on outdated and incomplete views of the reading process.

- *Traditional tests often mirror outdated views of the reading process.* Although much reading research of recent decades has confirmed the balanced nature of the reading act, traditional reading assessment has remained in the relative dark ages of skills-only teaching. Traditional reading assessment stubbornly clings to the notion that reading can be conveniently divided into constituent pieces and discrete elements such as phonics knowledge, hierarchical comprehension elements, and reading and study skills. Although these factors are, of course, essential, they ignore other important factors such as the student's background knowledge, motivation to read, family support factors, the learning environment, and writing connections. In short, traditional reading assessment is frequently limited and simplistic in nature.

- *Traditional reading assessment fails to help teachers improve instruction.* Much traditional assessment yields information of little help from a classroom teaching point of view. Norm-referenced data (e.g., stanines, grade equivalents, percentiles) rarely identify specific skills or strategies a child is using while reading, because their purpose is to provide national comparisons for schools and school districts, not to chart the progress of students in literacy development. Many tests, such as group tests and skill sheets, fall short in helping the teacher plan instruction.

- *Traditional reading assessment fails to use authentic reading tasks.* Frequently, children are assessed in reading using only snippets of real reading passages, words and sounds in isolation, and multiple-choice formats. Reading assessment, if it is good classroom assessment (Valencia, 1990), will look like real reading. It should use different forms of text including stories (narrative), informational text, and environmental print. It should have students reading for different purposes and in different contexts.

- *Traditional reading tests provide incomplete assessments of reading ability.* Most traditional assessments are, in fact, paper-and-pencil tests that focus only on a few aspects of the reading act. Important parts of reading—such as interest, motivation, and ability to decode when reading self-selected books— are not usually investigated. Developing informed teaching opportunities for students is difficult with such limited information.

- *Traditional assessments, especially standardized tests, are frequently viewed negatively by classroom teachers for a number of important reasons.* Many teachers have found that standardized tests create a negative feeling in their classrooms and often hinder learning. Two classroom teachers (Nolan & Berry, 1993) spoke out on this point in a published interview:

[We] resented how the district's standardized tests intruded on class time, created an atmosphere of anxiety, and failed to reflect the complexity of [literacy] learning, the quality and presentation of the text, or the conditions of collaboration and discussion that are valued in [a thriving] classroom. (p. 606)

There are legitimate needs for traditional assessment in our schools, particularly for state and local accountability requirements. However, the needs of the classroom teacher go well beyond what traditional testing can satisfy. The day-to-day needs of classroom teachers—the need for data that inform instruction—are more effectively addressed in *balanced literacy assessment,* the subject of the next section.

BALANCED LITERACY ASSESSMENT

Traditional reading assessment, as described earlier, is often termed *formal* or *product assessment.* That is, most of the information yielded from these assessments is oriented toward bottom-line numerical comparisons of children and offers the classroom teacher very little that informs instruction (Cambourne & Turbill, 1990; Clay, 1990). On the other hand, balanced literacy assessment (sometimes called "authentic" assessment) is much more *informal* or *process oriented,* describing clearly what students do as they read. Balanced literacy assessments survey student development in reading and writing processes based on developmental theory and research, and are typically teacher initiated and teacher developed.

Traditional testing helps satisfy political and accountability needs, but little else.

Many teachers feel that excessive traditional testing common in most school districts creates stress and negative affect in students.

Balanced literacy assessments focus on "authentic" reading tasks to gauge literacy development in students.

Balanced literacy assessment tools, including *portfolios*, allow teachers to "see" the processes individual children use when they read and write.

The central purpose of balanced literacy assessment is to inform teaching decisions.

Teachers who develop high-quality balanced literacy assessment programs frequently have several purposes in mind. The central purpose is to inform their teaching decisions for improved student learning (Fountas & Pinnell, 1996). Teachers have a fundamental need to know where students are in terms of their literacy development and to create a record of their progress. Another need is to discover what students can do in reading.

Balanced literacy assessment assists teachers in another primary responsibility: reporting student progress to parents. Similarly, balanced literacy assessment assists in reporting the progress of students to administrators, school board members, and other stakeholders (Fountas & Pinnell, 1996). Finally, balanced literacy assessment helps teachers learn more about the reading process itself and how children can be assisted in becoming fluent readers.

Portfolio Assessment Schemes: An Approach for Collecting Information

Portfolio assessment is both a philosophy and a place for gathering student data.

Portfolio assessment schemes are a popular and extremely effective vehicle for authentically assessing reading development (Farr, 1991; Glazer & Brown, 1993; Tierney, Carter, & Desai, 1991; Valencia, McGinley, & Pearson, 1990). The reading portfolio is both a *philosophy,* or way of viewing assessment, and a *place* for gathering pieces of evidence indicating student growth and development in reading (Valencia, 1990). Cooter and Flynt (1996) explain that

List some of the process and product features of portfolio assessment.

the *philosophy* of portfolios suggests that we should consider all factors related to reading when assessing students. Portfolios are consistent with newer curriculum designs (Farr, 1991, p. 2) that emphasize the integration of the language arts (listening, speaking, reading and writing). They focus on the processes of constructing meaning, use of quality literature and other information aids, problem solving and application skills, and student collaborations. Therefore, portfolios are a means for dynamic and ongoing assessment (Tierney, 1992). (p. 42)

Portfolios also represent a *place* for collecting student work samples that provide "windows" on the strategies used by students when reading and writing (Farr, 1991; Farr & Tone, 1994; Jongsma, 1989; Tierney, 1992). File folders, storage boxes, hanging files, and notebooks are a few of the common portfolio containers used to hold daily samples or "evidence" of student learning.

Two sets of portfolios are often maintained in the classroom (Cooter & Flynt, 1996): *student portfolios* and *file portfolios*. Student portfolios are kept in the possession of students and may be added to by either the student or the teacher. File portfolios are year-long files kept by the teacher on each student that include representative samples of student development over time.

A portfolio assessment approach places the responsibility and control for (reading) assessment back into the hands of those most affected by it—teachers and students (Valencia, 1990), and provides the foundation for teacher/student conferences (Farr, 1991). Portfolio assessment schemes develop a vivid picture of how students are progressing from one reading developmental milestone to the next. They are certainly not the *only* way to conduct balanced literacy assessments, but they do represent an effective and popular mode for many teachers.

Kid Watching: Classroom Observations of Children and Reading

For many teachers, the most basic assessment strategy is systematic observations of children engaged in the reading act, or **kid watching.** Clay, in her book *The Early Detection of Reading Difficulties* (1985), explains her philosophy concerning observations:

> I am looking for movement in appropriate directions. . . . For if I do not watch what [the student] is doing, and if I do not capture what is happening in records of some kind, Johnny, who never gets under my feet and who never comes really into a situation where I can truly see what he is doing, may, in fact, for six months or even a year, practice behaviours that will handicap him in reading. (p. 49)

In kid watching, we are looking for positive "movement" in literacy learning (Clay, 1985).

Thus, observation is a critical tool at the teacher's disposal for early assessment of students and their abilities.

There appears to be some consensus among reading experts concerning critical features of observation (Clay, 1985; Holdaway, 1979; Rhodes & Dudley-Marling, 1988). A summary of these important points and additional points we recommend follows:

- *Begin with a knowledge of "literacy developmental milestones":* The teacher must fully understand the stages of literacy learning through which children develop in order to be an effective observer. These stages of learning or *literacy developmental milestones* are described in some detail in the next section of this chapter and should be thoroughly reviewed.
- *Adopt an attitude of researcher rather than teacher.* When making observations, it is important to step out of the usual directive role of teacher into a more participant-observer role. As teachers, we tend to interact, and then react. But to be an effective observer, we must resist the natural impulse to make

Teachers must have a thorough understanding of how reading develops for kid watching to be instructive.

Teachers as kid watchers are in a research mode.

midcourse corrections in the child's educational program. In other words, we need to observe, reflect on what we have seen, and then plan appropriate next steps in learning.

- *Make multiple observations over time (longitudinal).* Teachers should look at reading behaviors over time to detect patterns of ability and/or needs. One-shot observations tend to be unreliable indicators of where students are in their development and can lead to inaccurate conclusions. By making many observations over time, the teacher will be able to document growth and identify areas needing further development during group or individual mini-lessons. As a rule of thumb, the younger the child or the poorer the reader, the more time the teacher will need to spend both observing and pondering observations (Clay, 1985, p. 50).
- *Observe real reading in varied situations.* Most commercial reading tests require students to read in very artificial situations. The text may be boring, use stilted language, or be limited to narrative (story) compositions. Children should be observed reading self-selected materials as well as district-required reading materials. In addition, observing the student reading in varied settings (whole-class readings, teacher–student conferences, small reading group) is highly recommended.
- *Document observations with regularity and clarity.* Observations should be recorded promptly and regularly. All entries should be easy to read and tied to literacy developmental milestones agreed upon in the school or district. In fact, another teacher in the school should be able to read and interpret a student's reading portfolio or file without difficulty. In addition to written records, many teachers now include observation guides and videotape or audiotape recordings of student observations in their assessment portfolio.

Literacy Learning Milestones

One semester, a young student teacher was busily making notes on a clipboard as she watched second graders working in various centers. The students were engaged in activities such as reading, planning writing projects, working at a computer station, listening to books on tape while following along in small books, and several other literacy-learning tasks. When the student teacher was asked by the visiting college supervisor what she was working on, she said, "I'm noting what the children are doing as part of their reading portfolio." The supervisor responded, "That's great! How do you know what to watch for?" After a few moments of the student teacher appearing bewildered the supervisor said, "If you have time a little later, I'd like to share with you information about literacy-learning milestones. They are observable learning stages that can be noted as part of your assessment profiling system." She quickly accepted the offer and seemed to welcome the information enthusiastically.

To be an effective "kid watcher," the teacher must gain an understanding of the stages of literacy learning through which children grow. In the past few years, much has been added to our knowledge base about how literacy develops. In this section, we share basic information about the early developmental stages of reading according to the latest research. Knowing which of these skills students have and have not acquired helps the teacher construct a classroom profile and plan whole-class, small-group, and individualized instruction.

In the latter part of the 1990s, a major urban school district set out to identify what they called "end-of-year benchmark reading skills" for kindergarten through third grade (R. Cooter, 1998). With the benefit of a major grant, they established a

Numerous observations are necessary over time before valid conclusions can be drawn.

Think of ways that you could make kid watching a regular part of your teaching schedule.

Balanced literacy assessment is grounded in an understanding of literacy learning milestones.

The end-of-year benchmark reading skills resulted from research begun in a major urban school district.

team composed of notable reading researchers, master teachers, and distinguished school administrators to review the latest literacy research and develop a list of the reading skills that, if acquired by the end of third grade, would likely result in children reading fluently. R. Cooter and K. S. Cooter (1999) have adapted that list, adding the skills their own research indicates are essential for this range of students. They have also included reading skills required by most states as part of their accountability systems, thus giving this list a degree of national validity. Be sure to note that the use of grade level indicators for their **literacy learning milestones** (see Appendix C) is only an approximation, because children develop at differing rates. We recommend that you carefully consider these skills as you attempt to assess young or otherwise emerging readers.

Balanced literacy assessment begins with an understanding of these literacy learning milestones. It is essential that teachers come to know these observable behaviors and abilities well in order to describe where students are in their development, and to aid in planning future instruction fitted to the students' respective zones of proximal development.

METHODS FOR ASSESSING READING DEVELOPMENT

Once teachers have a clear understanding of literacy learning milestones they are ready to use this knowledge to selectively gather information on individual students. The goal: to plan instruction based on the needs of individual children. As this information is gathered and sorted, you will be able to plan instruction for large groups when most of the children have a demonstrated need for a particular reading skill, small-group instruction when only a few students need a given skill, or individualized instruction when only a single child needs a particular reading skill to continue his or her growth.

Classroom assessment methods should be easy to implement and reasonably quick to administer, and should reveal the needs of individual students.

In this section, we present a variety of effective ways to gather data on student literacy development. Of course, it is only a partial list, because of the limitations of a general reading textbook. However, these are arguably the most effective and commonly used strategies in use by master reading teachers. As you gain complete competence in each of these strategies, we encourage you to read further in a more specialized text (see Reutzel & Cooter, 1999, listed at the end of this chapter), and also to consider taking an advanced graduate course in reading assessment to increase your knowledge of assessment methods.

The Burke Reading Interview

The Burke Reading Interview (Burke, 1987) provides some initial insights into how students see themselves as readers and the reading task in general. The following questions have been adapted from the Burke procedure.

- When you are reading and come to a word you don't know, what do you do? What else can you do?
- Which of your friends is a good reader? What makes him/her a good reader?
- Do you think your teacher ever comes to a word she doesn't know when reading? What do you think she does when that happens?
- If you knew that one of your friends was having problems with his or her reading, what could you tell your friend that would help?

Figure 10.2   Interest inventory

Interest Inventory

Student's Name _____

Date _____

Instructions: Please answer the following questions on a separate sheet of paper.

1. If you could have three wishes, what would they be?
2. What would you do with $50,000?
3. What things in life bother you most?
4. What kind of person would you like to be when you are older?
5. What are your favorite classes at school, and why?
6. Who do you think is the greatest person? Why do you think so?
7. Who is your favorite person? Why?
8. What do you like to do with your free time?
9. Do you read any parts of the newspaper? Which parts?
10. How much TV do you watch each day? What are your favorite shows, and why?
11. What magazines do you like to read?
12. Name three of your favorite movies.
13. What do you like best about your home?
14. What books have you enjoyed reading?
15. What kind of books would you like to read in the future?

- How would a teacher help your friend with reading problems?
- How do you think you learned to read?
- Are you a good reader?
- What would you like to be able to do better as a reader?

Interest Inventory

Getting to know students is critical if the teacher is to have insights into background knowledge, oral language abilities, and for the selection of reading materials that will be of interest. An interest inventory that is administered either one-to-one or in small groups is a great tool for getting to know students, and we offer one example in Figure 10.2.

Concepts About Print

Teachers in the primary grades must understand in some detail what children know about print concepts. The _Concepts About Print_ (CAP) test was designed by Marie Clay (1985) to help teachers establish priorities in reading instruction for emergent and early readers. Clay's test assesses some 24 basic print awareness elements, in-

Print concepts are examined in some detail in chapter 3, "Emergent Literacy: Understanding the Literacy Development of Young Children."

Figure 10.3   Selected concepts about print surveyed on the CAP test (Clay, 1985)*

Selected Print Concepts

Front of the book
Knows that print contains the author's message
Knows where to start reading
Knows which way to go when reading
Return sweep to the left
Word by word matching
First and last concept
Bottom of the picture
Left page before right
Notices one change in word order
Notices one change in letter order
Knows the meaning of the question mark (?)
Knows the meaning of the period (.)
Knows the meaning of the comma (,)
Knows the meaning of quotation marks (" ")
Can identify the first and last letter of a word
Can identify one letter and two letters
Can identify capital letters

*Note: The learner is asked to identify each of the following within the context of a special book (e.g., *Sand* or *Stones*) developed for this purpose.

cluding: front of a book, print versus pictures, left-to-right progression, changes in word order, changes in letter order in words, meaning of a period, and location of a capital letter. The assessment is carried out using one of two available books called *Sand* and *Stones*. The procedure is for the teacher to read one of the books with the student and ask such questions as where to begin reading, which way to go, and where to go next (Fountas & Pinnell, 1996). Results of the CAP test can be especially helpful to kindergarten and first-grade teachers who want to establish an initial class profile of strengths and needs. A listing of the concepts about print assessed on the CAP test is shown in Figure 10.3.

Alphabet Knowledge (Early Readers)

Knowledge of the alphabet is essential in early reading instruction: it provides teachers and students with common language for discussing graphophonic relationships. Assessment of alphabet knowledge should occur in two contexts: letters in isolation, and letter recognition within words and sentences. We recommend that alphabet knowledge be assessed as part of the print awareness test discussed previously.

Alphabet knowledge is a critical stage of literacy development following phonemic awareness.

Additional Observation Checklists and Scales

Linda Lamme and Cecilia Hysmith (1991) recommend a scale that can be used to identify key developmental behaviors in emergent readers. It describes 11 levels often seen in the elementary school and could be used in tandem with the much more

Checklists are efficient tools that can address literacy developmental milestones.

comprehensive literacy learning milestones previously discussed. Following is a slight adaptation of that scale:

Level 11:   The student can read fluently from books and other reading materials.

Level 10:   The student seeks out new sources of information. He or she volunteers to share information from books with other children.

Level 9:   The student has developed the ability to independently use context clues, sentence structure, structural analysis, and phonic analysis to read new passages.

Level 8:   The student reads unfamiliar stories haltingly (not fluently), but requires little adult assistance.

Level 7:   The student reads familiar stories fluently.

Level 6:   The student reads word-by-word. He or she recognizes words in a new context.

Level 5:   The student memorizes text and can pretend to "read" a story.

Level 4:   The student participates in reading by doing such things as supplying words that rhyme and predictable text.

Level 3:   The student talks about or describes pictures. He or she pretends to read (storytelling). He or she makes up words that go along with pictures.

Level 2:   The student watches pictures as an adult reads a story.

Level 1:   The student listens to a story but does not look at the pictures.

Think of the elements of a checklist you would include to informally assess print concepts in a kindergarten or first-grade classroom.

Many teachers find that checklists that include a kind of Likert scale (a five-point scale) can be useful in student portfolios because many reading behaviors become more fluent over time. One example developed by Diffily (1994) is shown in Figure 10.4.

Fluency Evaluation

Fluency includes the ability to read at an appropriate rate.

Reading fluency, the ability of students to read at an appropriate speed and with proper phrasing, is an important ingredient in reading success. An informal assessment of fluency through teacher observations is not difficult, but more formal methods can consume a great deal of valuable classroom time. Two effective methods that streamline the process considerably are presented in this section.

Multidimensional Fluency Scale

Zutell and Rasinski (1991) have developed a *Multidimensional Fluency Scale* (MFS), which serves as a useful informal assessment of fluency. The MFS offers a practical measurement of students' oral reading fluency that provides clear and valid information. To administer an MFS, the teacher will collect a student self-selected passage of 200 to 300 words, the Multidimensional Fluency Scale document (see Figure 10.5), and a cassette tape player/recorder with blank tape.

Figure 10.4   Diffily's classroom observation checklist

Student's Name _____				Date

Literacy Development Checklist

	Seldom				Often
Chooses books for personal enjoyment	1	2	3	4	5
Knows print/picture difference	1	2	3	4	5
Knows print is read from left to right	1	2	3	4	5
Asks to be read to	1	2	3	4	5
Asks that story be read again	1	2	3	4	5
Listens attentively during story time	1	2	3	4	5
Knows what a title is	1	2	3	4	5
Knows what an author is	1	2	3	4	5
Knows what an illustrator is	1	2	3	4	5
In retellings, repeats 2+ details	1	2	3	4	5
Tells beginning, middle, end	1	2	3	4	5
Can read logos	1	2	3	4	5
Uses text in functional ways	1	2	3	4	5
"Reads" familiar books to self/others	1	2	3	4	5
Can read personal words	1	2	3	4	5
Can read sight words from books	1	2	3	4	5
Willing to "write"	1	2	3	4	5
Willing to "read" personal story	1	2	3	4	5
Willing to dictate story to adult	1	2	3	4	5

Gratefully used by the authors with the permission of Deborah Diffily, Ph.D., Alice Carlson Applied Learning Center, Ft. Worth, TX.

Reutzel and Cooter (1999) recommend that teachers have students rehearse a familiar self-selected word passage (200–300 words) at least three times prior to using the Multidimensional Fluency Scale. It may be informative for teachers also to observe the difference in a student's fluency with a practiced, self-selected, familiar text and with an unpracticed, teacher-selected, unfamiliar text chosen at the child's approximate grade level.

Rubric for Fluency Evaluation

The Rubric for Fluency Evaluation (Fountas & Pinnell, 1996) is recommended as a formal assessment technique. (A rubric is a tool for scoring student work; the concept is discussed in greater detail later in the chapter.) Children are asked to read aloud a selection they have read twice before and can read with at least 90% accuracy. The oral reading should be taped for analysis purposes (this part could

Cassette recordings of oral reading can help teachers verify the accuracy of their fluency assessments.

Figure 10.5   Multidimensional fluency scale

Multidimensional Fluency Scale (MFS)
(Zutell & Rasinski, 1991)

Use the following scales to rate reader fluency on the three dimensions of phrasing, smoothness, and pace.

A. **Phrasing**
   1. Monotonic with little sense of phrase boundaries, frequent word-by-word reading.
   2. Frequent two- and three-word phrases, giving the impression of choppy reading; improper stress and intonation that fail to mark ends of sentences and clauses.
   3. Mixture of run-ons, mid-sentence pauses for breath, and possibly some choppiness; reasonable stress/intonation.
   4. Generally well phrased, mostly in clause and sentence units, with adequate attention to expression.

B. **Smoothness**
   1. Frequent extended pauses, hesitations, false starts, sound-outs, repetitions, and/or multiple attempts.
   2. Several "rough spots" in text where extended pauses, hesitations, etc. are more frequent and disruptive.
   3. Occasional breaks in smoothness caused by difficulties with specific words and/or structures.
   4. Generally smooth reading with some breaks, but word and structure difficulties are resolved quickly, usually through self-correction.

C. **Pace** (during sections of minimal disruption)
   1. Slow and laborious.
   2. Moderately slow.
   3. Uneven mixture of fast and slow reading.
   4. Consistently conversational.

From "Training Teachers to Attend to Their Students' Oral Reading Fluency," by J. Zutell and T. Rasinski, 1991, *Theory Into Practice, 30*(3), pp. 211–217.

actually be done by students as a center activity or as an activity carried out by an adult volunteer). Listen to the tape and evaluate the oral reading using the Rubric for Fluency Evaluation shown in Figure 10.6, which we have adapted from Fountas and Pinnell (1996).

Reading Logs

Reading logs are daily records of student reading habits and interests, usually during sustained silent reading (SSR) periods (Cambourne & Turbill, 1990). Students keep these records for the teacher on simple forms kept in their student reading portfolio folder at their desks or another appropriate location. Reading logs list the date, book or text they have read, and page numbers.

Figure 10.6   Rubric for fluency evaluation

1. **Nonfluent Reading**
   - Word-by-word reading.
   - Frequent pauses between words (poor phrasing).
   - Little recognition of syntax.
   - Little response to punctuation.
   - Some awkward word groupings.
2. **Beginning Fluency**
   - Frequent word-by-word reading.
   - Some two- and three-word phrasing.
   - May reread for problem solving or to clarify (strategic reading).
   - Shows some awareness of syntax and punctuation.
3. **Transitional Fluency**
   - Combination of word-by-word reading and fluent phrase reading.
   - Some expressive phrasing.
   - Shows attention to punctuation and syntax.
4. **Fluent Reading**
   - Fluent reading with very few word-by-word interruptions.
   - Reads mostly in larger meaningful phrases.
   - Reads with expression.
   - Attends consistently to punctuation.
   - Rereads as necessary to clarify or problem-solve.

Adapted from Fountas, I. C., and Pinnell, G. S. (1996). *Guided Reading: Good First Reading for All Children*. Portsmouth, NH: Heinemann.

Running Records

Clay (1985) describes the **running record** as a reliable oral reading assessment strategy that can help inform teachers as to where students are in their reading development. The procedure is not difficult but requires practice; Clay (1985) estimates that it takes about 2 hours of practice for teachers to become relatively proficient. Clay recommends that three running records be obtained for each child on various levels of difficulty. The following criteria for judging oral reading are based on words correctly read aloud:

Running records are a preferred method for assessing oral reading.

Independent level (easy to read) text	95% to 100% correct
Instructional level text	90% to 94% correct
Frustration level (difficult) text	Less than 89% correct

Running records require about 10 minutes to transcribe. Guidelines for administration follow:

1. Choose samples from the books to be used that are 100 to 200 words in length. Passages will be needed from a variety of books and reading levels

Figure 10.7   Running record

Text	Record
If you give a mouse a cookie,	✓ ✓ ✓ ✓ ✓ ✓ ✓
he's going to ask for a glass of milk.	✓ ✓ ✓ ✓ ✓ ✓ *cup* ✓ ✓
When you give him the milk,	✓ ✓ ✓ ✓ ✓ ✓
he'll probably ask you for a straw.	✓ ⓈⒸ ✓ ✓ ✓ ✓ ✓ *premly*
When he's finished, he'll ask for a napkin.	✓ ✓ *through* ✓ ✓ ✓ ✓ ✓
Then he'll want to look in a mirror	✓ ✓ ✓ ✓ ✓ ✓ ✓ ✓
to make sure he doesn't	✓ ✓ ✓ ✓ ✓
have a milk mustache.	✓ ✓ ✓ ✓

From *If You Give a Mouse a Cookie* (pp. 1–6) by L. J. Numeroff, 1985, New York: HarperCollins. Copyright 1985 by HarperCollins. Reprinted by permission.

so that it will be possible to establish independent, instructional, and frustration levels for the student. For early readers, the passages can fall below 100 words.

2. Complete a running record for each passage selection used making "tick" marks (i.e., check marks) on a sheet of blank paper for each word said correctly. Errors should be described fully. Figure 10.7 shows an example of a running record taken from the early reading book *If You Give a Mouse a Cookie* (Numeroff, 1985, pp. 1–6).

Oral reading errors are known as **miscues.**

Examples of errors in oral reading, called *miscues,* and how to code them follow (adapted from Clay's guidelines):

1. *Word-call errors:* The student says a word that is different from the text in the book. The teacher writes the incorrect response(s) with the correct text under it.
   Student: *happen*
   Text: house
2. *Attempted decoding:* The student tries several times to say a word. The teacher records each attempt with the correct text under the trials.
   Student: *cake . . . c— . . . cook*
   Text: *cookie*
3. *Self-correction:* The student corrects an error him- or herself. Self-corrections are noted by writing "SC."
   Student: *mike money* SC
   Text: *monkey*
4. If no word is given, then the error is noted with a dash.
5. *Insertions:* A word that is not in the text is added. An insertion symbol (a caret) is recorded between the two appropriate words, and the inserted word is placed above the insertion symbol.
   Student: *have a*
   Text: *He'll want to^look in the mirror.*

6. *Teacher assistance:* The student is "stuck" on a word he or she cannot call, and the teacher pronounces the word for the student. The teacher records the incident as "TA" (teacher-assisted).

   Student: TA

   Text: *automobile*

7. *Repetition:* Sometimes children repeat words or phrases. These repetitions are not scored as an error but may be noted by drawing a line under the word that was repeated.

   Student: <u>He's</u> going to ask you for a glass of milk.

   Text: *He's going to ask you for a glass of milk.*

By noting the percentage of miscues or oral reading errors and by studying the errors for repeating patterns, the teacher can deduce how reading development is progressing for each child and which mini-lesson should be offered. In the next section, we show how running records can be used to inform teaching using a streamlined process.

Interpreting Running Records Using the Flynt/Cooter Scoring System

Flynt and Cooter (1998, 1999) have developed a method of scoring running records that makes the process both time efficient and useful to classroom teachers. Adopted in their informal reading inventories, *The Flynt/Cooter Reading Inventory for the Classroom* (1998) and *The English * Español Reading Inventory* (1999), this system involves the use of what they call a "miscue grid." This system can be extremely effective when used with text selections that are matched to student interests.

The miscue grid by Flynt and Cooter (1998, 1999) streamlines the process of interpreting running records.

In the following excerpt from *The Flynt/Cooter Reading Inventory* (Figure 10.8), you will notice how miscues can be noted on the left side of the grid over the text, then tallied after the student has finished reading in the appropriate columns to the right according to miscue type. This process makes the administration quicker and enables teachers to identify error patterns for each oral reading. We find that the "grid" idea can easily be adapted by teachers for use with excerpts from authentic literature samples.

It is recommended that teachers have students select the passage(s) to be read a day ahead of the actual reading so that the first 100 words can be transcribed onto the left-hand side of a blank grid patterned after the one shown in Figure 10.9. During the oral reading, tape-record the session so that the reading can later be reviewed for accuracy of transcription. Miscues should be noted in the left-hand column over the text facsimile using the symbols described earlier for miscues. After all miscues are noted, examine each miscue and make a final determination about its type (mispronunciation, substitution, insertion, etc.), then make a mark in the appropriate grid box on the right side of the form. Only one hash mark is made for each miscue. Once this process is completed, each column is tallied. In Figure 10.8, you will note that the reader had two mispronunciations, two insertions, and so on. When the student has read several passages for the teacher over a period of weeks and months, it becomes easy to identify "error patterns"—types of miscues that happen regularly—and to plan appropriate instruction for small-group or individual instruction.

For best results, allow students at least some choice in the books to be read for running records.

Note: We provide you with a blank miscue grid in Appendix D for your convenience.

Retellings

One of the best ways to find out if a student understands a story he or she has read is through retellings (Gambrell, Pfeiffer, & Wilson, 1985; Morrow, 1985). Retellings can be accomplished in many ways. First, the teacher may wish to use pictures from

*The first retelling (without teacher prompting) is known as **unaided recall.***

Figure 10.8   Flynt/Cooter running record scoring system

	Mispronounce	Substitute	Self-correct	Insertions	Teacher assist	Omissions	Other
Hot Shoes							
The guys at (the) I.B. Belcher						1	
Elementary School ~~loved~~ *lived* (SC) all the			1				
new sport shoes. Some ~~wore~~ *wib* the	1						
" Sky High" model by Nicky.							
Others who *really* couldn't afford *buy* ~~afford~~ Sky		1		1			
Highs would settle for ~~a lesser~~ *another*		1					
shoe. Some liked the "Street							
Smarts" by Concave, or (the)						1	
"Uptown-Downtown", by Beebop.				1			
The Belcher boys ~~got~~ *go* to the point		1					
with their shoes that they could							
~~identify~~ *impea* their friends just by	1						
looking at their ~~feet~~. *shoes* (SC) But the boy			1				
who was the ~~envy~~ *every* of all the fifth		1					
grade was Jamie Lee. He had a							
pair of "High Five Pump'em Ups"							
by Adeedee. The only thing Belcher							
boys loved as || much as their							
shoes was basketball.							
TOTALS	2	4	2	2	0	2	0

the story as a memory prompt. As the teacher flashes pictures sequentially from the book or story, the child retells the story from memory. A second option is *unaided recall,* or retelling without pictures or other prompts. We recommend a two-step process, in which the teacher begins by having the student retell everything he or she can remember about the passage. If it is a narrative passage, the teacher can use a record sheet like the one shown in Figure 10.9 to record critical elements of the story grammar the student has recalled. After the student stops retelling the first time, the teacher asks, "What else can you remember?" Usually the student will recall one or more bits of information. The teacher continues to ask the child, "What else do you

Figure 10.9 Story grammar retelling record sheet

Student's Name _____ Date _____

Story _____

Source/Book _____

Category	Prompt Questions (After Retelling)	Student's Retelling
Setting	Where did this story take place?	
	When did this story happen?	
Characters	Who were the characters in this story?	
	Who was the main character(s) in the story?	
	Describe _____ in the story.	
Challenge	What is the main challenge or problem in the story?	
	What were the characters trying to do?	
Events	What were the most important things that happened in the story?	
	What did _____ do in the story?	
Solution	How was the challenge/problem solved?	
	What did _____ do to solve the problem?	
	How did the other characters solve their problems?	
Theme	What was this author trying to tell us?	
	What did _____ learn at the end of the story?	

remember?" until he or she cannot remember anything more. Then the teacher refers to the story grammar record sheet for any categories (e.g., setting, characters) not addressed by the student and asks direct questions about the unaddressed areas. This is another form of aided recall.

Story Maps

Story maps (Beck & McKeown, 1981; Routman, 1988) can be used to determine whether a child understands the main parts of a narrative passage. Like the story grammar retelling record sheet previously mentioned in chapter 6, the same story grammar elements are used. The task is for students to complete a story map (Figure 10.10) after the completion of a story. A generic format, like the one shown, can be applied to almost any narrative text.

A story grammar retelling record sheet is helpful during unaided and aided recall assessments.

Figure 10.10   Story map form

> ### *Story Map*
>
> Name _____ Date_____
>
> Title _____ Author _____
>
> **Setting** (Where and when did this story take place?)
>
>
>
> **Characters** (Who were the main characters in this story?)
>
>
>
> **Challenge** (What is the main challenge or problem in the story?)
>
>
>
> **Events** (What were the events that happened in the story to solve the problem/challenge?)
>
>   Event 1.
>
>   Event 2.
>
>   Event 3.
>
> (List all the important events that happened.)
>
>
> **Solution** (How was the challenge/problem solved or not solved?)
>
>
>
> **Theme** (What was this author trying to tell us?)

Adapted from *Transitions: From Literature to Literacy* by R. Routman, 1988, Portsmouth, NH: Heinemann.

Teacher-Made Cloze Tests

Explain how cloze passages could be useful for both assessment and teaching sessions connected to context clue development.

A common assessment strategy is the use of teacher-made cloze tests. Cloze tests ("cloze" is derived from the word *closure*) cause students to use their knowledge of word order (syntax) and sentence meaning (semantics) to guess a missing word in print. A cloze passage is constructed as follows:

1. Select a narrative or expository passage.
2. Type or scan the passage onto a classroom computer. The first sentence should be typed exactly as it appears in the original text. Beginning with the

second sentence, one of the first five words is deleted and replaced with a blank. Then *every* fifth word is deleted and replaced with a blank.

3. Students then silently read the passage all the way through once before attempting to fill in the blanks.

4. Score the cloze passage using a one-third/one-half formula: If a student correctly guesses *more* than one-half of the deleted words, then the passage is on his independent reading level. If a student correctly guesses *less* than one-third of the missing words, then the passage is too difficult for classroom instruction at this time (the student's frustration level). Scores falling between the one-third to one-half criteria are within the student's instructional level range. With help from the teacher or peers, the student can succeed in this level passage, because it falls within his or her zone of proximal development (see sections in chapter 3 dealing with the teachings of L. Vygotsky for a review of this concept).

Questioning

Questioning is a most basic and effective means of assessing reading comprehension, and is dealt with at some length in chapter 6.

Family Surveys of Reading Habits

We recently observed a friend of ours who has a heart condition going through his normal daily activities with a small radiolike device attached to his belt. When asked what this gadget was, he indicated that it was a heart monitor. He went on to say that the device constantly measured his heart rate for an entire day to provide the doctor with a reliable account of his normal heart rhythms in the real world of daily activity. Traditional reading assessment has often failed to give teachers such a real world look at students' reading ability by restricting the assessment to school settings. So the question posed here is, "How do we acquire information about a student's reading habits and abilities away from the somewhat artificial environment of the school?" One way is to assess what is happening in the home using family surveys.

Reading behaviors noticed by family members can help illuminate a student's reading needs.

Family surveys are *brief* questionnaires (too long and they'll never be answered!) sent to adult family members periodically to provide teachers insights into reading behaviors at home. Taken into consideration with other assessment evidence from the classroom, family surveys enable teachers to develop a more accurate profile of the child's reading ability. An example of a family survey is provided in Figure 10.11.

Family surveys should be brief, simple, and available in the dominant language used at home.

Evaluating Your Program: Assessing the "Big Picture"

Balanced literacy assessment implies that teachers look at *all* relevant factors in the teaching and learning process. Teachers should develop a careful analysis of the classroom reading program to determine whether or not it meets the needs of all children. We suggest an analysis begin by considering the following:

- *Theoretical orientation:* What do you believe about how children learn to read? To which theoretical view of the reading process do you subscribe (see chapter 2)? To which instructional model do you subscribe (subskills, skills, balanced literacy, transitional)?

Figure 10.11   Family survey

September 6, 200____

Dear Adult Family Member:

   As we begin the new school year, I would like to know a little more about your child's reading habits at home. This information will help me provide the best possible learning plan for your child this year. Please take a few minutes to answer the questions below and return in the self-addressed stamped envelope provided. Should you have any questions, feel free to phone me at XXX–XXXX.

Cordially,

Mrs. Shelley

_____

1. My child likes to read the following at least once a week (check all that apply):

   Comic books _____   Sports page _____

   Magazines (example: *Highlights*) _____   Library books _____

   Cereal boxes _____   Cooking recipes _____

   T.V. Guide _____   Funny papers _____

   Others (please name):

2. Have you noticed your child having any reading problems? If so, please explain briefly.

3. What are some of your child's favorite books?

4. If you would like a conference to discuss your child's reading ability, please indicate which days and times (after school) would be most convenient.

Sometimes students having learning problems are fully capable, but "disabled" by an inappropriate curriculum or ineffective teaching.

- *Alignment of theory and practice:* How well does your program align with your theoretical beliefs? Are there any elements that do not seem to fit? If so, what can you do to make your beliefs and practices more consistent? Suggestion: Review the seven principles in chapter 1 and compare them to your usual teaching routines to determine which ones may not be consistent with balanced literacy ideals.

- *Resources:* What resources are available for your program that have not already been tapped (e.g., professional teaching materials at the school, family volunteers, Reading Is Fundamental [R.I.F.] books, support for purchasing learning materials from the PTA, adopt-a-school programs with corporate partners)?
- *Readers with special needs:* What is your procedure for readers with special needs? Do you have an intervention program established in your classroom for recovering readers having learning problems?

Evaluating the Classroom Environment

In chapter 5 and chapter 9, we discussed how a teacher making transitions toward balanced literacy may need to consider adjustments to the classroom environment. This is an important concern because the classroom environment affects student attitudes and, thus, reading performance. Ideally, the classroom environment should approach the comfort level of a home environment if one is to maximize learning potential. A careful description and mapping of the present classroom environment contrasted to those descriptions presented in chapters 5 and 9 will help teachers determine whether classroom modifications are needed.

The learning environment sets an emotional tone and provides the necessary milieu for learning.

Self-Rating Scales

No one knows better than the reader how he or she is doing in reading. A teacher carrying out an assessment agenda should never overlook the obvious: Ask kids how they're doing! Although this is best achieved in a one-on-one discussion setting, large class sizes frequently make it a prohibitive practice. A good alternative to one-to-one interviews for older elementary children is a student self-rating scale, in which students complete a questionnaire tailored to obtain specific information about the reader from the reader's point of view. One example is illustrated in Figure 10.12 for a teacher interested in reading and study strategies used with social studies readings. Whichever reading skills are to be surveyed, remember to keep self-rating scales focused and brief.

Don't forget the obvious: Ask students what they feel are their reading strengths and needs.

Additional Suggestions for Developing Reading Portfolios

Implementing a portfolio-style assessment program can be challenging. In our experience, attention to several details not previously mentioned can lead to a successful experience, including the development of an implementation plan, record-keeping systems, and the use of time management strategies. There are also a few pitfalls to avoid when constructing balanced literacy assessment programs. In this section, we discuss what we have learned about constructing reading portfolios, as well as other helpful ideas suggested in the professional literature.

Develop a Plan for Constructing Reading Portfolios

Implementation of reading portfolios can often seem overwhelming to many teachers just getting started. Success usually depends on having a simple logic to guide one's choices in this otherwise complex process. Margaret Puckett and Janet Black (1994) have described some key considerations for teachers as they begin to construct a portfolio system of assessment. They suggest that teachers (a) decide which basic components or framework will be used, (b) scrutinize information already at hand to decide what additional information may be needed to implement the assessment plan, and

For balanced literacy assessment to take root in a classroom, it must be included in your daily plans.

Figure 10.12   Self-rating scale: Reading social studies

Reading Social Studies

Name _____ Date _____

1. The first three things I usually do when I begin reading a chapter in social studies are (number 1, 2, 3):

   _____ Look at the pictures.

   _____ Read the chapter through one time silently.

   _____ Look at the new terms and definitions.

   _____ Read the questions at the end of the chapter.

   _____ Read the first paragraph or introduction.

   _____ Skip around and read the most interesting parts.

   _____ Skim the chapter.

   _____ Preview the chapter.

2. What is hardest for me about social studies is . . .

3. The easiest thing about social studies is . . .

4. The thing(s) I like best about reading social studies is (are) . . .

(c) outline the management process (how portfolios are used to inform teaching and to report progress to families).

Using Rubrics to Improve Reading Analyses

Rubrics are scoring guides that can make your evaluations more objective and consistent.

Rubrics are scoring guides or rating systems used in performance-based assessment (Farr & Tone, 1994; Webb & Willoughby, 1993). The intent of rubrics is to assist teachers in two ways: (a) make the analysis of student work samples simpler, and (b) make the rating process more reliable and objective. This is a tall order indeed because any assessment process is rarely objective, value free, or theoretically neutral (Bintz, 1991).

Webb and Willoughby (1993) explain that "the same rubric may be used for many tasks [once established] as long as the tasks require the same skills" (p. 14). Although a rubric may be set up in any number of ways, Farr and Tone (1994) have suggested a seven-step method that can be adapted to reading assessment. We have modified the process slightly to conform to reading assessment needs and shortened it to five relatively easy steps.

Anchor papers help teachers understand the range of development across a group of students.

Step 1: *Identify anchor papers.*

Begin by collecting and sorting student work samples into several stacks (e.g., reading response activities, student self-analysis papers, content reading responses) according to quality; these are known as *anchor papers*. Be sure to analyze why you feel some work samples represent more advanced development in reading than others and also why some work samples cannot be characterized as belonging in the more advanced categories. This will provide you with "range" papers.

Step 2: *Choose a scoring scale for the rubric: usually a three-, four-, or five-point scoring system is used.*

A three-point scale may be more reliable, meaning that if more than one teacher were to examine the same reading artifacts each would be likely to arrive at the same rubric score (1, 2, or 3). However, when multiple criteria are being considered, a five-point scale may be easier to use. A problem with reading rubrics is that they imply a hierarchy of skills that may not have been proven through reading research. (For example, in the upper grades, is the ability to *skim* text for information a higher or lower level skill than *scanning* text for information? Probably neither.) This brings us to Farr and Tone's (1994) next suggestion.

Step 3: *Choose scoring criteria that reflect what you believe about reading development.*

Two points relative to reading rubrics need to be considered in Step 3: scoring, and literacy learning milestones. First, a rubric is usually scored in a hierarchical fashion. That is, if on a five-point scale a student fulfills requirements for a 1, 2, and 3 score, but not the criteria for a 4, then even if he or she also fulfills the criteria for a 5, he or she would still be ranked as a 3. That system may work fairly well in areas such as mathematics where certain skills can be ranked hierarchically in a developmental sense. For example, for students to progress to the point of performing long division, they will need to be able to do the more basic skills of multiplying, carrying numbers, and subtraction. However, because many reading skills cannot be ranked that clearly, we recommend a slightly different procedure: If a five-point rubric is being used, the teacher should survey all five reading skills or strategies identified in the rubric when reviewing artifacts found in the portfolio. If the student has the ability to do four of them, the teacher ranks the student as a 4, regardless of where those skills are situated in the rubric. We hasten to add that this modification may not always be appropriate, especially with emergent readers, among whom clearer developmental milestones are evident.

> *Scoring criteria should reflect your beliefs about literacy learning milestones.*

Second, as already mentioned, teachers need to know well the major literacy learning milestones identified through classroom-based research. This knowledge can be applied as one constructs rubrics in collaboration with other teachers. Keeping literacy learning milestones in mind is the only way of ensuring validity in the process.

Step 4: *Select reading development work samples for each level of the rubric and write descriptive annotations.*

It is important for teachers to have samples of each performance criterion in mind when attempting to use a rubric. From the Stage 1 process, where range papers and anchor were identified, the teacher will have good examples of each reading skill or strategy being surveyed. After a careful review of these papers, it is possible to write short summary statements for each level in the rubric.

> *Model examples help teachers keep in mind what is possible for students to achieve.*

Figure 10.13 shows a sample rubric developed for a fifth-grade class wherein students are to describe (orally and through written response) cause–effect relationships based on in-class readings about water pollution.

Step 5: *Modify the rubric criteria as necessary.*

The teacher should feel free to modify a rubric's criteria as new information emerges. This is another way of maintaining validity in the process.

Figure 10.13   Sample rubric for a fifth-grade reading class

Cause-Effect Relationships: Scale for Oral and Written Response

Level 4:   Student clearly describes a cause and effect of water pollution, and provides concrete examples of each.

S/he can provide an example not found in the readings.

"We read about how sometimes toxic wastes are dumped into rivers by factories and most of the fish die. I remember hearing about how there was an oil spill in Alaska that did the same thing to fish and birds living in the area."

Level 3:   Student describes a cause and effect of water pollution found in the readings.

Student can define "pollution."

"I remember reading about how factories sometimes dump poisonous chemicals into rivers and all the fish die. Pollution means that someone makes a place so dirty that animals can't live there anymore."

Level 2:   Student can provide examples of water pollution or effects pollution had on the environment found in the readings.

"I remember reading that having enough clean water to drink is a problem in some places because of garbage being dumped into the rivers."

Level 1:   Student is not able to offer voluntarily information about the cause and effects of pollution found in the readings.

GETTING ORGANIZED: PROFILING YOUR CLASS

Profiling is a way of charting the individual and group learning needs of students.

The assessment ideas presented in this chapter provide the means for measuring the development of various reading skills—but that is only one part of the reading teacher's job. Collating and organizing the assessment data—first, for each child individually, then for the entire class—are extremely important next steps in instructional planning. Charting the literacy skills students have learned and still need to acquire, both individually and as a class, is what we mean by **profiling.**

Two Documents Needed for Profiling

Two profiling documents are needed: individual and group.

The profiling documents teachers use should directly parallel the reading skills scope and sequence chart used by the school district, or the literacy learning milestones we present in this chapter. Teachers generally need two profiling documents: a *student profile* document to record individual strengths and needs in some detail, and a *classroom profile* document to help organize the entire class's data for the formation of needs-based reading groups.

R. Cooter and K. S. Cooter (1999) have developed the *Balanced Literacy Assessment System & Training* (BLAST™) system, which typifies these two levels of profiling. Figure 10.14 is a prototype of their student profiling document, based on the literacy learning milestones for third grade (R. Cooter & K. S. Cooter, 1999) presented earlier in the chapter. A profiling system should be driven either by a similar

Figure 10.14　A partial student profiling instrument for third grade

Student Profile: THIRD GRADE LITERACY MILESTONES

Balanced Literacy Assessment System and Training

(BLAST™)

Student's Name _____

Teacher: Ms. K. M. Spencer

> *Instructions:* Record the date when each milestone skill was observed, and the degree of development (**E** = Emergent, **D** = Developing Skill, **P** = Proficient) in the blank to the left of each skill description.

Decoding and Word Recognition

_____ 3.D.1　　　　　Uses context clues, phonic knowledge, and structural analysis to decode words

Spelling and Writing

_____ 3.SW.1　　　Spells previously studied words and spelling patterns correctly in own writing

_____ 3.SW.2　　　Uses the dictionary to check and correct spelling

_____ 3.SW.3　　　Uses all aspects of the writing process in compositions and reports with assistance, including

　　　　　　_____ 3.SW.3.1　　Combines information from multiple sources in written reports

　　　　　　_____ 3.SW.3.2　　Revises and edits written work independently on a level appropriate for first semester of third grade

　　　　　　_____ 3.SW.3.3　　Produces a variety of written work (response to literature, reports, semantic maps)

　　　　　　_____ 3.SW.3.4　　Uses graphic organizational tools with a variety of texts

　　　　　　_____ 3.SW.3.5　　Incorporates elaborate descriptions and figurative language

　　　　　　_____ 3.SW.3.6　　Uses a variety of formal sentence structures in own writing

_____ 3.SW.S.1　　Writes proficiently using orthographic patterns and rules such as qu, use of n before v, m before b, m before p, and changing z to c when adding -es (Spanish only)

_____ 3.SW.S.2　　Spells words with three or more syllables using silent letters, dieresis marks, accents, verbs, r/rr, y/ll, s/c/z, q/c/k, g/j, j/x, b/v, ch, h, and i/y accurately (Spanish only)

Oral Reading

_____ 3.OR.1　　　Reads aloud with fluency any text that is appropriate for the first half of grade three

_____ 3.OR.2　　　Comprehends any text that is appropriate for the first half of grade three

Language Comprehension and Response to Text

_____ 3.C.1　　　Reads and comprehends both fiction and nonfiction that is appropriate for grade three

_____ 3.C.2　　　Reads chapter books independently

_____ 3.C.3　　　Identifies specific words or phrases that are causing comprehension difficulties (metacognition)

_____ 3.C.4　　　Summarizes major points from fiction and nonfiction text

_____ 3.C.5　　　Can discuss similarities in characters and events across stories

_____ 3.C.6　　　Can discuss underlying theme or message when interpreting fiction

_____ 3.C.7　　　Distinguishes between the following when interpreting nonfiction text:

　　　　　　_____ 3.C.7.1　　Cause and effect

　　　　　　_____ 3.C.7.2　　Fact and opinion

　　　　　　_____ 3.C.7.3　　Main idea and supporting details

_____	3.C.8	Uses information and reasoning to evaluate opinions
_____	3.C.9	Infers word meaning from roots, prefixes, and suffixes that have been taught
_____	3.C.10	Uses dictionary to determine meanings and usage of unknown words
_____	3.C.11	Uses new vocabulary in own speech and writing
_____	3.C.12	Uses basic grammar and parts of speech correctly in independent writing
_____	3.C.13	Shows familiarity with a number of read-aloud and independent reading selections, including nonfiction
_____	3.C.14	Uses multiple sources to locate information:
	_____ 3.C.14.1	Tables of contents
	_____ 3.C.14.2	Indexes
	_____ 3.C.14.3	Internet search engines
_____	3.C.15	Connects a variety of literary texts with life experiences

Reading Fluency

_____	3.F.1	Very few word-by-word interruptions
_____	3.F.2	Reads mostly in larger meaningful phrases
_____	3.F.3	Reads with expression
_____	3.F.4	Attends consistently to punctuation
_____	3.F.5	Rereads to clarify or problem-solve
_____	3.F.6	Sixty (60) words per minute reading rate (minimum)

listing of desired skills or the school district's scope and sequence skills list (these are usually provided in a curriculum guide to all teachers upon assignment to a school).

Student Profiling Document

Notice that the Cooter and Cooter (1999) profiling system includes a rubric for noting the extent to which a reading skill has been learned.

In the *BLAST*™ student profile (Figure 10.14), you will note that each skill has a blank space to the left; this is for the teacher to note (a) the date he or she observed the student performing that skill, and (b) the degree to which the student was able to execute the skill. For the latter, a three-point rubric is provided: "E" for students who are just emerging with an awareness of the skill, "D" for students who are in the midst of developing competency in the skill, and "P" for students who have attained proficiency (i.e., mastery) of the skill. These or other similar designations are important because they help the teacher to differentiate the needs of students in the class. The designations can also be useful for informing parents about how their child is developing as a reader. Note that in the example provided in Figure 10.15, the child has a number of skills at each level of development, as well as some with no designation at all (this means that the child has not yet reached that developmental stage for the skill(s) even at an emergent level). The student profile document should probably be the first contribution a teacher makes to the student's reading portfolio folder.

The complete student profiling instrument is included in Appendix C.

Name the major skill strands included in the BLAST™ system.

Classroom Profiling Document

Identify Rosa Maria's "emergent" reading skills from this example.

Necessarily accompanying the student profile is the classroom profile (*always* have both). This document lists the same literacy milestones as the student profile only in abbreviated form. In Figure 10.16 the reader again sees a *BLAST*™ prototype developed by R. Cooter & K. S. Cooter (1999). It is in the form of a classroom profile

Figure 10.15   Student profiling instrument (partial worksheet of 3rd Grade example)

Update 12 – 12
KMS

Student Profile: THIRD GRADE LITERACY MILESTONES
Balanced Literacy Assessment System and Training
(BLAST™) (R. Cooter & K. S. Cooter, 1999)

Student's Name   *Rosa Maria*

Teacher: Ms. K. M. Spencer

> **Instructions:** Record the date when each milestone skill was observed, and the degree of development (**E** = Emergent, **D** = Developing Skill, **P** = Proficient) in the blank to the left of each skill description.

Decoding and Word Recognition

$^{11}/_5$ D 3.D.1   Uses context clues, phonic knowledge, and structural analysis to decode words

Spelling and Writing

$^{11}/_{12}$ D 3.SW.1   Spells previously studied words and spelling patterns correctly in own writing

$^{11}/_{19}$ D 3.SW.2   Uses the dictionary to check and correct spelling

_____ 3.SW.3   Uses all aspects of the writing process in compositions and reports with assistance, including

      $^{10}/_{25}$ E 3.SW.3.1   Combines information from multiple sources in written reports

      $^{10}/_{18}$ E 3.SW.3.2   Revises and edits written work independently on a level appropriate for first semester of third grade

      $^9/_3$ D 3.SW.3.3   Produces a variety of written work (response to literature, reports, semantic maps)

      $^9/_3$ E 3.SW.3.4   Uses graphic organizational tools with a variety of texts

      $^9/_3$ E 3.SW.3.5   Incorporates elaborate descriptions and figurative language

      $^9/_{25}$ E 3.SW.3.6   Uses a variety of formal sentence structures in own writing

$^{11}/_{26}$ D 3.SW.S.1   Writes proficiently using orthographic patterns and rules such as qu, use of n before v, m before b, m before p, and changing z to c when adding -es (Spanish only)

$^9/_{14}$ P 3.SW.S.2   Spells words with three or more syllables using silent letters, dieresis marks, accents, verbs, r/rr, y/ll, s/c/z, q/c/k, g/j, j/x, b/v, ch, h, and i/y accurately (Spanish only)

Oral Reading

$^{11}/_{26}$ D 3.OR.1   Reads aloud with fluency any text that is appropriate for the first half of grade three

$^{11}/_{26}$ D 3.OR.2   Comprehends any text that is appropriate for the first half of grade three

Language Comprehension and Response to Text

$^9/_1$; $^{12}/_{10}$ $^P/_E$ 3.C.1   Reads and comprehends both fiction and nonfiction that is appropriate for grade three

$^{10}/_3$ P 3.C.2   Reads chapter books independently

$^{12}/_2$ E 3.C.3   Identifies specific words or phrases that are causing comprehension difficulties (metacognition)

$^{12}/_2$ D/E 3.C.4   Summarizes major points from fiction and nonfiction text

Figure 10.16 Partial classroom profiling instrument

CLASSROOM PROFILE (BLAST™): THIRD GRADE LITERACY MILESTONES

Teacher: _____   Date/Grading Period Completed: _____

Instructions: Record the degree to which each milestone skill has been achieved by each student (**E** = Emergent, **D** = Developing Skill, **P** = Proficient) in each box corresponding to the student and skill in the grid.

Decoding and Word Recognition

3.D.1   Context clues, phonic knowledge and structural analysis

Spelling and Writing

3.SW.1   Uses studied words and spelling patterns

3.SW.2   Uses the dictionary to check spelling

3.SW.3   Uses these aspects of the writing process:

    3.SW.3.1   Combines information/multiple sources

    3.SW.3.2   Revises and edits

    3.SW.3.3   Variety of written work

    3.SW.3.4   Graphic organizational tools

    3.SW.3.5   Descriptions and figurative language

    3.SW.3.6   Variety of formal sentence structures

3.SW.4.S.1   Orthographic patterns and rules (Spanish only)

3.SW.5.S.2   Spells words with three or more syllables using silent letters, dieresis marks, accents, verbs (Spanish only)

Oral Reading

3.OR.1   Reads aloud with fluency

Language Comprehension and Response to Text												
3.C.1	Comprehends both fiction and nonfiction on level											
3.C.2	Reads chapter books independently											
3.C.3	Identifies problem words or phrases											
3.C.4	Summarizes fiction and nonfiction text											
3.C.5	Similarities: characters/events across stories											
3.C.6	Theme or message: interpreting fiction											
3.C.7	Nonfiction:											
	3.C.7.1 Cause/effect											
	3.C.7.2 Fact/opinion											
	3.C.7.3 Main idea/details											
3.C.8	Evaluation: Uses information/reasoning											
3.C.9	Word meaning from roots and affixes											
3.C.10	Dictionary: Determine meanings/usage											
3.C.11	Uses new vocabulary in own speech and writing											
3.C.12	Writing: Basic grammar/parts of speech											
3.C.13	Familiar w/read-aloud, indep. reading, nonfiction											
3.C.14	Locates information using:											
	3.C.14.1 Tables of contents											
	3.C.14.2 Indexes											
	3.C.14.3 Internet search engines											
3.C.15	Connects literary texts with life experiences											
Reading Fluency												
3.F.1	Very few word-by-word interruptions											
3.F.2	Reads mostly in larger meaningful phrases											
3.F.3	Reads with expression											
3.F.4	Attends consistently to punctuation											
3.F.5	Rereads to clarify or problem-solve											
3.F.6	Reads sixty (60) words per minute (minimum)											

for third grade matching the previous student profile. Notice that each skill listed uses the same skill code (i.e., 3D.1, 3RF.1). This simple coding system breaks down as follows: For "3D.1," 3 = third grade, D = the DECODING skill strand, and 1 = the first skill in the DECODING strand. Students' names are written in the blank spaces across the top and the matching designation for how competent the student is with each skill (i.e., the codes E, D, or P) are transcribed from their individual student profile forms.

It is easy to see from Figure 10.17 how the teacher can begin forming reading groups based on student needs. For instance, the teacher not only might form a group of students who need to develop skill "3.SW.3.2—Revises and edits," but also recognize that actually two groups are needed—one for those who are emerging in this ability (E-level students), and another for those who are a little further along or "developing" (D-level students). To demonstrate how individual student data can be collated into a class profile and help the teacher form reading groups based on needed skills, we provide an example in Figure 10.17. This example is for both Decoding and Word Recognition, as well as Spelling and Writing skills assessment.

REPORTING PROGRESS TO FAMILIES: WHAT ABOUT GRADES?

In this section on balanced literacy assessment, we have listed several ways that children's growth in reading can be measured. Frequently, however, teachers become a little perplexed about how to report progress to families and convert assessment information into grades. Some say that although balanced literacy assessments are more valid than traditional procedures, they are also more difficult to quantify or translate into grades as required by many school districts. We believe the solution to this problem is to adopt a new perspective for reporting and grading and to learn how to derive traditional grades from these rather nontraditional assessment schemes.

Some elements of balanced literacy assessment should not be reported as grades to families—for example, alphabet knowledge and self-rating scales.

First, it may be helpful to distinguish between *graded* assessment measures, which relate to gradable tasks, and *ungraded* measures, which provide developmental information about the student that would be inappropriate to grade. Both ungraded and graded assessment options are included in the umbrella term *portfolio assessment* because the teacher uses all of this information to inform and improve instruction. Most of the assessment procedures discussed in this chapter are categorized in the following lists:

Identify the small group of children who are at the "emergent" level for skill 3.SW.3.4, graphic organizational tools, in Figure 10.17. This is a way of forming needs-based groups.

Graded Assessment Measures	Ungraded Assessment Measures
Reading logs	Print-awareness tests (CAP, etc.)
Running records	Alphabet knowledge tests
Retellings (unaided and aided recall)	Family surveys
Literature-response projects	Self-rating scales
Cloze passages	Story maps
Questioning	
Evaluation forms	
Fluency assessments	

Ungraded assessment measures provide teachers with background information to help begin instruction during the first few weeks of school. Ungraded assessment measures cannot and should not be viewed as a source for grades. For instance, it

Figure 10.17 Needs-based groups

CLASSROOM PROFILE (BLAST™): THIRD GRADE LITERACY MILESTONES

Teacher: K. Spencer **Date/Grading Period Completed:** 12 – 14

Instructions: Record the degree to which each milestone skill has been achieved by each student (**E** = Emergent, **D** = Developing Skill, **P** = Proficient) in each box corresponding to the student and skill in the grid.

		Anna	Johnny	Alicia	Syporia	Dirk	James	Harry	Rosa Maria	Jason	Ameenah	Paula	Dora
Decoding and Word Recognition													
3.D.1	Context clues, phonic knowledge and structural analysis	P	P	D	P	D	P	P	D	P	P	P	P
Spelling and Writing													
3.SW.1	Uses studied words and spelling patterns	P	E	E	P	D	E	D	D	E	E	D	D
3.SW.2	Uses the dictionary to check spelling	P	E	D	D	D	P	D	D	D	D	D	D
3.SW.3	Uses these aspects of the writing process:												
3.SW.3.1	Combines information/multiple sources	E	E	E	E	E	E	E	E	E	E	E	E
3.SW.3.2	Revises and edits		E	E	D	D	E	E	E	E	D	E	D
3.SW.3.3	Variety of written work		E	E	E	E	E	P	D	E	P	D	E
3.SW.3.4	Graphic organizational tools		E	E	E	P	D	E	E	D	E	D	E
3.SW.3.5	Descriptions and figurative language	D	E	D	D	P	D	E	E	P	E	E	E
3.SW.3.6	Variety of formal sentence structures	P	E	E	E	D	D	D	E	D	D	D	D
3.SW.4.S.1	Orthographic patterns and rules (Spanish only)						D		D	D		P	D
3.SW.5.S.2	Spells words with three or more syllables using silent letters, dieresis marks, accents, verbs (Spanish only)						D		P			P	P

383

would be absurd to "grade" a family survey form and use such information to score a child's performance at school! Teachers, therefore, use ungraded assessment measures to gain insights into what students already know or have been exposed to in the past.

Grades usually can be derived from the graded assessment measures listed. In the remainder of this section, we discuss ways each of these assessment procedures can yield quantitative scores or grades. As with other examples throughout this book, we offer this information as merely one way of getting the job done, not the only way or even necessarily the best way. An alternative system for reporting called *authentic grading* is also suggested later in the chapter.

Graded assessment measures are reported to satisfy accountability requirements.

Reading Logs

Although some would say that reading logs should be ungraded, it is possible to add a retelling component (see p. 385) and thus derive grades. Following is one example usable in a fourth-or fifth-grade classroom.

A = 4 or more books read along with a reading conference with the teacher
B = 3 books read along with a reading conference with the teacher
C = 2 books read along with a reading conference with the teacher
D = 1 book read along with a reading conference with the teacher

Running Records

Running records can be used in grading some aspects of reading growth.

Running records should be done with each student about three times per quarter, or about once every 3 weeks. They are especially helpful through about second or third grade. If running records are to be used as a grading source, grades may be derived from (a) the number of oral reading miscues, and (b) combining the running record information with retellings (discussed next).

To use the running record for grading purposes, it is necessary to do an initial ungraded reading to be used as a baseline. After several rereadings of the text about 3 weeks apart, the student's performance can be compared to the baseline performance, then contrasted to a predetermined criterion to establish a grade. For example, earlier in the chapter, we provided a sample passage and analysis taken from *If You Give a Mouse a Cookie* (Numeroff, 1985). Let us assume that, after an initial baseline reading and several subsequent individual reading conferences in a first-grade classroom, the student Annie had the results shown in Table 10.1 as she read this popular children's book.

A Sample Criterion for Running Records

If You Give a Mouse a Cookie, approximately 289 words

A = (98% correct oral reading) 6 miscues or fewer

B = (95% to 97%) 9 to 13 miscues

C = (90% to 94%) 17 to 29 miscues

Annie's grade could be computed easily at each of the rereading intervals using the preceding criteria. The criteria in this example are arbitrary and should be adjusted to suit the teacher's belief system. Annie's first reading would place her at the top of the "C" range, her second rereading at the top of the "B" range, and the third

Table 10.1   Annie's running record summary

Miscue Category Student: Annie	Baseline (9/12/01)	1st Rereading (10/3/01)	2nd Rereading (10/25/01)	3rd Rereading (11/10/01)
Book: *If You Give a Mouse . . .*				
1. Word call errors	3	1	0	0
2. Attempted decoding	6	4	3	1
3. Self-correction	2	1	1	1
4. Insertions	4	2	1	1
5. Teacher assistance	6	4	2	2
6. Repetition	4	5	2	1
Totals	25	17	9	6

rereading at the "A" level. After two or three rereadings for grading purposes, a new book thought to be more challenging would be selected for a new baseline measurement. To assess comprehension, retellings would be used in other books on her instructional reading level.

Retellings

Retellings, as mentioned earlier, are a two-step proposition involving both unaided and aided recall. For grading purposes, we recommend that teachers construct a checklist of important elements from the selection. For narrative selections, the checklist can be generic like the one previously shown in Figure 10.9. As the student retells the story (unaided recall), the teacher records elements remembered relating to setting, characters, challenge, and so on. After the retelling is complete, the teacher then asks questions from those story grammar categories not addressed during the student's retelling (aided recall). At the conclusion of the retelling process, criteria such as the following (or others established by the teacher) could be used to convert the comprehension performance (combined unaided and aided recall) into a letter grade:

A retellings record sheet can be constructed in such a way as to be useful in grading.

A = 95% recall or better
B = 88% recall
C = 80% recall
D = 75% recall

For students in the upper grades who are reading longer passages or books, we recommend that only a portion of the text be selected for this retelling exercise.

Literature-Response Projects

The literature-response category is perhaps the most subjective for grading. Also, just how much weight literature-response project grades should carry in the overall portfolio will vary according to how much effort and detail were involved. Two very different projects presented here carry different values in the overall portfolio because

Figure 10.18   Criteria for "wall of fame" poster

> **Criteria for *Fast Sam, Cool Clyde, and Stuff* (Myers, 1975)**
>
> **"Wall of Fame Poster"**
>
> **Ms. Holden's Sixth Grade**
>
> *Directions:* To qualify for the grade you want, you must not only have the total number of ideas required but also *have at least one idea from each of the story grammar categories* (setting, characters, challenge, events, solution, theme).
>
> | Grade Desired | Requirement |
> |---|---|
> | A | 12 or more ideas recalled |
> | B | 9–11 ideas recalled |
> | C | 7–8 ideas recalled |
> | D | 6 ideas recalled (one idea from each of the story grammar categories) |

Literary posters are created around a specific aspect of the story line as a response activity.

of levels of difficulty: a literary poster (T. D. Johnson & Louis, 1987) and a group-developed "radio play."

A literary poster has students create a poster around some aspect of a reading selection. The essence of the poster is recalling several important bits of information from the text. Some of the poster types suggested by T. D. Johnson and Louis (1987) are "missing persons," "greatest hero," and "wall of fame." This literature-response activity is done by students as seat work and does not require collaboration with peers. Typically, literary posters require about 20 minutes to complete. To grade such a project, or any other literature-response project for that matter, the teacher must once again decide what is to be measured by naming the criteria. Figure 10.18 shows one possible set of criteria for the upper elementary level book *Fast Sam, Cool Clyde, and Stuff* (Myers, 1975).

Three-way grading is used with radio plays.

A radio play is a drama written by a small group of students (three to five) drawn from a key incident in a book they have all read. The drama, once written, is then read aloud into a tape recorder by the student-actors, complete with sound effects. Radio plays in finished form are usually played for the entire class over the public address system in the school, giving the impression of an actual radio production. Grading for this kind of literature-response activity is often *triangulated,* or three-way. A description of the three grade sources follows:

- *Within-group grade:* Students in the radio play group grade each other. This tends to prevent one or more students from "goofing off" and still getting full credit for the project.
- *Class evaluation:* All members of the class not associated with the project grade the radio play according to criteria outlined by the teacher. Each of the criteria grades is tabulated by the teacher, and an average or mean grade is calculated based on the overall class evaluation.
- *Teacher grade:* Naturally, the teacher has veto power over any portion of the process if he or she feels the children were not just in their assessment. Additionally, the teacher grades the performance and factors in his or her grade

as one third of the overall group grade. Based on the within-group grade, the teacher then decides if all students in the group get the same grade, or not, based on their contribution.

Cloze Tests

Cloze tests can serve a dual function: as a teaching activity for such reading strategies as using context clues or inferential comprehension development, or for use as an assessment procedure. Typically, most teachers using cloze modify the passage so that specific elements are deleted, such as character names, facts related to setting, and key events in the story. Grading is simply a matter of applying the classroom criteria to the percentage of correct responses (94% to 100% = A, 85% to 93% = B, etc.).

Classroom-based criteria can be used to grade cloze tests.

Questioning

Questioning is explained in some depth in chapter 6. For grading purposes, we suggest (a) establishing basic minimum criteria, such as the child must correctly identify at least one element from each of the story grammar criteria during questioning, and (b) applying the overall percentage correct to the classroom grading criteria, just as was explained for cloze texts.

Evaluation Forms

Valencia (1990) suggests that good evaluation begins with a knowledge of what is to be assessed and how to interpret the performance. Evaluation forms have many different formats reflecting the needs of teachers making transitions. For example, some teachers in early-to-intermediate transitions may elect to use some of the skill sheets supplied by the basal reader as evaluation forms for grading. Why? Because skill sheets tend to focus on discrete, definable reading strategies and easily lend themselves to grading (e.g., 5 of 5 correct = A, 4 of 5 correct = B). For advanced transition teachers, skill sheets may not be an acceptable alternative, because they divorce the reader from more authentic reading activities. These teachers may prefer an evaluation form that is based on teacher observations while the child is reading whole text. Figure 10.19 is one example of an evaluation form that might be used to grade content reading strategies (based in part on Kemp, 1987).

Evaluation forms are often useful in grading content reading tasks.

Fluency Measures

Fluency is one of the most noticeable indicators of how well students are progressing in their reading development. Parents are usually quite aware in some general sense of how fluent their child is becoming in reading and care very much about the teacher's assessment of the child's progress. The literacy learning milestones (R. B. Cooter & K. S. Cooter, 1999) presented earlier describe minimum fluency indicators for grades 1 to 3. At grade 3, the point at which we hope for a high degree of fluency by year's end, the milestones read as follows:

Fluency can be graded using a modified rubric.

3.F.1	Very few word-by-word interruptions
3.F.2	Reads mostly in larger meaningful phrases
3.F.3	Reads with expression
3.F.4	Attends consistently to punctuation
3.F.5	Rereads to clarify or problem-solve
3.F.6	60 words per minute reading rate (minimum)

Figure 10.19   Content reading evaluation form
Based in part on Kemp, 1987.

Name _____   Date _____

Text _____   Pages _____

Content Reading Strategies Practiced After Whole Group Mini-lessons

1.   Follows class instructions given orally
2.   Follows written instructions
3.   Uses previewing strategy
4.   Scans for important information on request
5.   Surveys text before reading
6.   Completes task on time
7.   Can justify inferences drawn from text
8.   Distinguishes between relevant and irrelevant facts
9.   Other observations

Criteria:

A =   Observed competence in this area and was used at appropriate times

B =   Observed ability, but missed an opportunity to correctly apply the strategy

C =   Used the strategy only once and/or missed obvious opportunities to apply

D =   Appears not to fully understand the strategy or when to apply it

Of these milestones, there are two that would not necessarily be accounted for in a regular running record assessment regime: *reading with expression,* and *reading rate* (words per minute/wpm). Reading with expression is very difficult to measure objectively, but reading rate is not. Once again, using a fairly contrived set of criteria, we suggest a grading scale based on the percent of attainment of a predetermined end-of-grade criterion for reading rate. In Figure 10.20 we translate the percentage for third grade using the end-of-grade criterion of 60 words per minute (wpm). Note that the criteria are fairly rigorous and increase in the second semester grading scale.

POTENTIAL PITFALLS IN USING PORTFOLIOS

In working with teachers experimenting with literacy portfolios in their classrooms, we have been struck by certain commonalities when they encounter problems. They are in some cases the same problems we have encountered ourselves when trying out new ideas in the classroom. In this section we alert readers to some of these rather predictable difficulties.

Overcommitment (by Teachers) to Daily Entries

Teachers must be careful to establish realistic assessment goals.

When teachers discover just how informative reading conferences with students can be, it is natural to want to conduct these conferences more and more often. We frequently encounter teachers who want to have daily reading conferences with every child. Even though strategies like running records, story retellings, and other assess-

Figure 10.20   Third grade criteria for assessing reading fluency

Fluency: First Semester Scale

A = 95% or better of the reading rate goal (57–60 wpm*)

B = 90–94% of the reading rate goal (54–56 wpm*)

C = 85–89% of the reading rate goal (51–53 wpm*)

Fluency: Second Semester Scale

A = 98% or better (59–60 wpm*)

B = 95–97% (57–58 wpm*)

C = 90–94% (54–56 wpm*)

*Based on the third grade end-of-year criterion of 60 wpm.

ment ideas we have presented are indeed powerful, attempting such regular conferences is not a very reasonable goal to set for oneself. Most teachers find that weekly or bi-weekly reading conferences are quite sufficient.

Spending Too Much Time Managing Portfolios

Trying to manage portfolio assessment systems can become an almost crushing burden when added to the myriad other responsibilities of classroom teachers. Frankly, there is no easy solution to this problem. Many teachers find that using some of the various checklists available by publishers can help organize their observations.

Too Many Contributions by Students

Although we want students to make contributions to their reading and writing portfolios, sometimes they have trouble knowing "how much is too much!?" Teachers sometimes notice students putting nearly everything they can think of into their portfolios, making it difficult for teachers to sort and manage them. Whole-group instruction sessions where the teacher shares the contents of an exemplary portfolio from a previous year or from a student volunteer can usually help students develop perspective.

Ask a master reading teacher what he or she feels are reasonable weekly expectations for student contributions to their reading portfolios.

OTHER ISSUES IN READING ASSESSMENT

Reading assessment in American education has essentially followed a skills-based medical model since the 1930s, in which assessment is viewed as the act of diagnosing strengths and weaknesses and defining which skills are known, to be learned, or to be remediated. After decades of following this model, many educators, public officials, and adult family members feel that gains in literacy have been modest. Results of the National Assessment of Educational Progress (NAEP) after more than two decades verify that only modest gains have been registered. Many people concerned with literacy development are calling for new approaches to both reading assessment and instruction. In this section, we briefly describe a few issues that are presently being debated in reading assessment.

The Notion of Skill Mastery

For decades, educators have discussed the notion of *skill mastery:* the level at which students can automatically and independently perform a given reading skill. In recent years, as reading skills and assessment have become much more politically

Reading skill acquisition happens by degrees: from emergent, to developing, and finally to proficient.

charged issues (Cantrell, 1999), how teachers go about defining whether or not a skill has been fully learned has become increasingly important. As seen in our earlier discussion on student profiling documents, we favor a rubric system that represents skill attainment as a continuum ranging from *emergent* (E) to *developing* (D) and then on to *proficient* (P). This approach would also seem consistent with the teachings of Lev Vygotsky concerning the zone of proximal development (see chapter 3).

The Need for a Variety of Contexts and Literary Forms

Reading is often viewed by test makers as a singular skill. In other words, if a student is given a norm-referenced reading test in seventh grade as part of an overall achievement test, he or she will receive a single reading grade equivalent score or a single percentile ranking. In assessment terms, this is called "reductionist" thinking because it reduces reading, a complex process involving many different skills, to a single number.

Assessments should include the variety of text types students encounter.

This kind of reductionist thinking as applied to reading is an erroneous notion indeed. Here's why: Different types of texts that one might read (e.g., a mystery, poem, song, histories, scientific journal article, religious texts) all use unique writing styles and require different skills from the reader. Additionally, a student may be inherently more interested in some text forms and topics than others, which will certainly have an effect on reading performance. Thus, there is a need for a variety of literary forms and contexts in reading assessment to provide an accurate picture of the student's development.

Power Tests Versus Timed Tests

Power and *timed tests* yield different results and serve differing purposes.

A **power test** is one in which the test items are arranged in order of increasing difficulty. There is no time limit on a power test; rather, the student continues until he or she has missed a prescribed number of items or completed the test. A **timed test,** as the name implies, is given for a specific amount of time, and students continue working at the test until the time limit has been reached. Items on a timed test are not usually arranged in any particular order of difficulty.

Each of these tests has its own values and problems. In the best circumstances, a power test, such as the *Peabody Picture Vocabulary Test—Third Edition* (PPVT-III) (Dunn & Dunn, 1997) allows students to reach their own ability level or "ceiling." The same thing is true of an informal reading inventory such as *The Flynt/Cooter Reading Inventory for the Classroom* (Flynt & Cooter, 1998), which is also a kind of power test.

Timed tests can yield particularly inaccurate results for students who "fatigue out" or who have fluency problems.

There are some inherent problems with these test types. For example, a student who has a slow reading rate may either run out of time (a problem with timed tests, of course), or run out of mental energy and "fatigue out" on a power test. The problem with running out of time on a timed test is that it causes students to appear particularly weak on skill categories covered in the last part of the test. We have seen this happen on the *Iowa Test of Basic Skills,* for example, where at the third grade level the final portion of the reading test measures predominantly higher-order comprehension skills. Thus, a student who only gets to item 15 out of a 21-item subtest may falsely appear weak in higher-order comprehension simply because he or she ran out of time on the test.

Norm-Referenced Tests Versus State-Developed Tests

Many states have now developed their own competency tests for reading and other academic areas (e.g., Texas, Kentucky, Tennessee, and Florida). The intent of state leaders is to establish minimum levels of skill knowledge for students so that school districts have a degree of uniformity. In addition to the state-developed tests, most school districts also administer **norm-referenced tests** (NRTs) assessing the major academic areas. NRT data allow districts to compare the performance of their students to other students nationally of the same age and grade placement. Valencia and Pearson (1987) note that norm-referenced tests are the most commonly used measures in U.S. schools.

Norm-referenced tests are helpful for making national and program comparisons.

In recent years, some school administrators and state officials have argued that NRTs are no longer necessary because they can get all the data they need from state-developed competency tests. NRT advocates counter that simply "passing" a state reading test, for example, is not the same as actually reading on grade level (something an NRT can reliably indicate). The high mobility of American families, NRT proponents argue, also figures into the need for reliable measures of reading ability. Because maintaining credibility with families, the business community, private foundations, and other stakeholders is an important concern for school administrators seeking bond elections and so forth, this issue will continue to be an important one.

State-developed tests are usually "minimum competency" measures useful for within-state comparisons.

"Authentic Grading"

Teachers and researchers advocating the use of portfolio assessment in reading are sometimes opposed to grading students. They feel it is inappropriate to grade an area of language development that is so student-specific and that is contradictory to developmental learning theories. Nevertheless, most, if not all, school districts require grades for elementary school reading instruction.

Cooter and Flynt (1996) have proposed a compromise system for reporting grades to families called **authentic grading.** This procedure offers the possibility of satisfying the accountability requirements of many school districts and appeases teachers who seek more valid reporting methods for student reading development. Such a reporting system might contain the following information:

- A letter grade reflecting how well the student has progressed during the grading period (comparing the student to him- or herself).
- A summary paragraph explaining in some detail what the student has achieved during this grading period and what he or she might accomplish next (relates to Vygotsky's zone of proximal development). This information can be derived from a literacy learning milestones checklist for each student kept by the teacher as well as other data from the students' portfolios.
- A grade or rating coupled with an explanation that reflects how the student compares to others at his or her level.

These three components would constitute full reporting of student progress and most likely satisfy the requirement to inform parents, students, and school administrators. In Figure 10.21 we offer one conceptualization of an authentic grading report form.

Figure 10.21   Authentic grading report form

Reading Report Form
Oxford Elementary School

Student's Name_____Grade _____

Teacher _____School _____

Grading Period _____

Part I: **How your child has progressed in reading this grading period.**

   a.   Grade _____

   b.   What your child has learned about reading this grading period . . .

   c.   What we hope your child will be able to do next in reading . . .

   d.   Things you can do at home to help his/her growth in reading . . .

Part II: **How your child compares to other children his/her age or grade level in reading.**

   a.   How your child compares to other students at this grade level:

   _____

   Early in   Usual   Advanced
   Development   Development   Development

   b.   Comments:

Authentic grading includes the informative benefits of portfolio assessment and is useful for reporting to families.

Some balanced literacy educators may object to a system like the one proposed, but the issue of reporting to families in a way that makes use of portfolio learning artifacts is certainly needed. We encourage teachers and school administrators to continue searching for acceptable reporting solutions.

Assessing Affective and Conative Factors in Reading

Consider ways that interest, attitude, and motivation can have powerful effects on reading performance.

One of the most important (and elusive) aspects of reading assessment is the affective domain, which deals with feelings about the reading act (Mathewson, 1985). Attitude, motivation, interest, beliefs, and values are all aspects of affect that have profound effects on reading development. In the past, affect has been discussed very little in reading assessment and has largely been limited to the administration of interest inventories, observation checklists, and attitude surveys (Walker, 1991). Teachers building balanced literacy programs require information in student portfolios that provides insights into positive affective aspects that drive the reading process.

Two steps are generally required for teachers to assess **affective factors.** First, teachers must become knowledgeable about affective aspects of reading. Second, teachers need to carefully review each assessment strategy to be used for its potential to probe affective aspects of reading in students. Further discussion and examples of these two points may help the reader begin to discover new ways of focusing on affective dimensions.

What Are the Affective Variables for Reading?

Mathewson (1985) identified four affective variables that drive the reading process: *attitude, motives, feelings,* and *physical sensation.* These variables may affect one's reading by influencing one's decision to read, attention, comprehension, recall, and other factors. In addition, Mathewson identified eight motives that also appear to affect students' decision to read and reading behavior. With a basic awareness of these affective motivations in reading, one can subjectively analyze various portfolio assessment strategies for their potential to yield insights into students' motivations to read. We have compared Mathewson's eight motives affecting the decision to read with nine reading activities frequently used as balanced literacy assessment strategies. Although our specific conclusions (represented in Table 10.2) may be debatable to some, they demonstrate that it may be possible to learn valuable affective reading behavior information through procedures already known and practiced.

What Are Conative Factors for Reading?

A related area of research pertains to **conative factors** (Berlak, 1992; Raven, 1992). Conative factors include such aspects of human behavior as determination, persistence, and will. As Berlak (1992) stated in summarizing Raven's work in this area:

*Persistence and determination are **conative factors.***

> [Students] can enjoy doing something without being determined to see it through, and he or she can hate doing something, but still be determined . . . taking initiative (which would be categorized as an "affective" outcome in Bloom's Taxonomy) is inseparable from intellectual or cognitive functioning, and from action. (p. 17)

These researchers believed that conative factors have been falsely subsumed under the affective label and actually constitute a separate domain of human behavior.

Cooter (1994) interpreted Raven's (1992) conative research relative to balanced literacy assessment applications in reading. In so doing, he raised a few questions for further classroom-based research:

> If it is true that [when] teachers and students [are] moving in positive affective/conative directions [it] can result in learning success, what happens when the teacher and student(s) are moving in opposite directions? For example, will a highly motivated student who is determined to learn to read mathematics materials more effectively but who encounters a teacher disinterested in her students still be able to learn? What about the reverse—where a student is disinterested in an academic task, but who

Table 10.2   Motives affecting decision to read that may be discernible through authentic assessment measures

	Belong/ Love	Curiosity	Compe- tence	Achieve- ment	Esteem	Self-actu- alization	Desire to know	Aesthetic
Reading Logs	X	X	O	X	X	X	X	X
Running Records	O	O	X	X	O	O	O	O
Retellings	X	X	X	O	X	X	X	X
Radio Play	X	X	X	O	O	X	X	X
Wanted Poster	O	X	X	X	O	O	X	X
Burgess Summary	O	O	X	X	O	O	X	O
Diorama	X	X	X	X	O	X	X	X
Schema Map	X	X	X	X	O	O	X	X
Comic Strip	X	X	X	X	X	X	X	X

encounters a highly motivated and inspiring teacher? It is difficult to predict in either case whether students will learn. It may be that the answer lies with how strong the affective and conative drives are for students and teachers alike.

Another assessment question combines the role of affective and conative factors when students read expository versus narrative texts. Classroom experience suggests that interest, motivation, determination, and persistence tend to diminish when students read many expository materials, especially textbooks. Is this less true when using expository trade books? Can these feelings be reversed if enticing text response activities are used? (Cooter, 1994, p. 89)

Although answers to these and other questions concerning affective and conative factors are yet to be resolved, they are essential to the effectiveness of any balanced literacy assessment program. To ignore such factors as interest, motivation, and determination is to have an incomplete assessment. As Cooter (1994) summarizes, it would be "somewhat akin to a mechanic claiming to have done a complete assessment of an automobile after only checking tire pressures!" (p. 86).

Summary

In this chapter, we explored basic principles of classroom reading assessment and described ways of profiling students according to their acquisition of literacy learning milestones, key strategies for measuring student growth, and valid ways that teachers can award grades. We saw that balanced literacy assessment carefully analyzes over-all student growth in the reading process and helps teachers plan effective instruction.

Differences between traditional and balanced literacy assessment perspectives were likened to the differences between a black-and-white photograph and a color movie. With traditional models of assessment, the learner's literacy abilities are usually estimated using simplistic procedures, such as paper and pencil tests, work-book pages, or norm-referenced tests, and look at only a few forms for reading behavior. Balanced literacy assessment procedures, on the other hand, provide teachers with the clearest and most comprehensive view of the learner. Many as-pects of reading are studied in a holistic way using genuine reading situations whenever possible to reveal insights into the learner's zones of proximal develop-ment. Running records, home surveys, story retellings, fluency measures, affective surveys, and self assessment are just a few of the tools available in balanced liter-acy assessment.

Current issues in reading assessment seem to be focusing on

- what is meant by "skill mastery,"
- the need for a variety of text forms and contexts in reading assessment,
- the proper place of *timed* versus *power* tests in reading,
- a growing competition between makers of standardized reading tests and state education agencies developing their own measures of reading,
- problems with reporting progress to families and grading.

Other equally perplexing problems in reading assessment relate to the affective do-main and conative factors.

Concept Applications

In the Classroom

1. As a review, develop a comparison grid or chart analyzing the differ-ences and similarities between traditional and balanced assessment per-spectives.
2. Develop a schedule for your classroom (name the grade level) that in-cludes time for the daily assessment of at least four students. What will be the typical assessment "tools" you will probably use during this time period? (Name at least four.) Explain and justify why you have selected these particular tools.
3. Develop three evaluation checklist forms that could be used in your class-room or a grade level you specify for reading comprehension, word identification, and content reading strategies. Include a possible rubric.

In the Field

Arrange through your college instructor, or through a neighborhood school, to work with an elementary-age student who is reportedly having difficulty in reading. The fol-lowing two major assignments can be completed with your assigned student.

Part 1: Complete the following informal assessment procedures:

- A running record and analysis of the miscues using the Flynt/Cooter scoring system and text from a book chosen by the student
- A commercial informal reading inventory of your choice
- An oral retelling of a book read by the student

- Three classroom observations of the student in various classroom settings, such as reading group, content area materials, and free reading
- An interest inventory, which you have constructed or adapted from the one in this chapter

Part 2: After compiling and summarizing the preceding information, construct a reading profile of the student that includes the following:

- Approximate reading level (instructional)
- Reading milestone skills that appear to be strengths for the child
- Reading milestone skills that need to be developed

Recommended Readings and Assessment Instruments

Dunn, L., & Dunn, L. M. (1997). *Peabody Picture Vocabulary Test—Third Edition* (PPVT-III). Circle Pines, MN: American Guidance Service.

Dunn, L., Lugo, D. E., Padilla, E. R., & Dunn, L. M. (1986). *Test de Vocabulario en Imágenes Peabody* (TVIP). Circle Pines, MN: American Guidance Service.

Flynt, E. S., & Cooter, R. B., Jr. (1999). *The Flynt/Cooter English * Español Reading Inventory.* Upper Saddle River, NJ: Merrill/Prentice Hall.

Reutzel, D. R., & Cooter, R. B., Jr. (1999). *Balanced reading strategies and practices: Assessing and assisting readers with special needs.* Upper Saddle River, NJ: Merrill/Prentice Hall.

mammals   biome   endangered
birds   desert   habitat
fish   ocean
insects   woodland forest
reptiles   tundra
characteristic   rainforest
           prairie

Galapagos Islands

Frigate Bird

Bats

Brown Pelican

Iguana

Hawk

Sea Lion

JANUARY

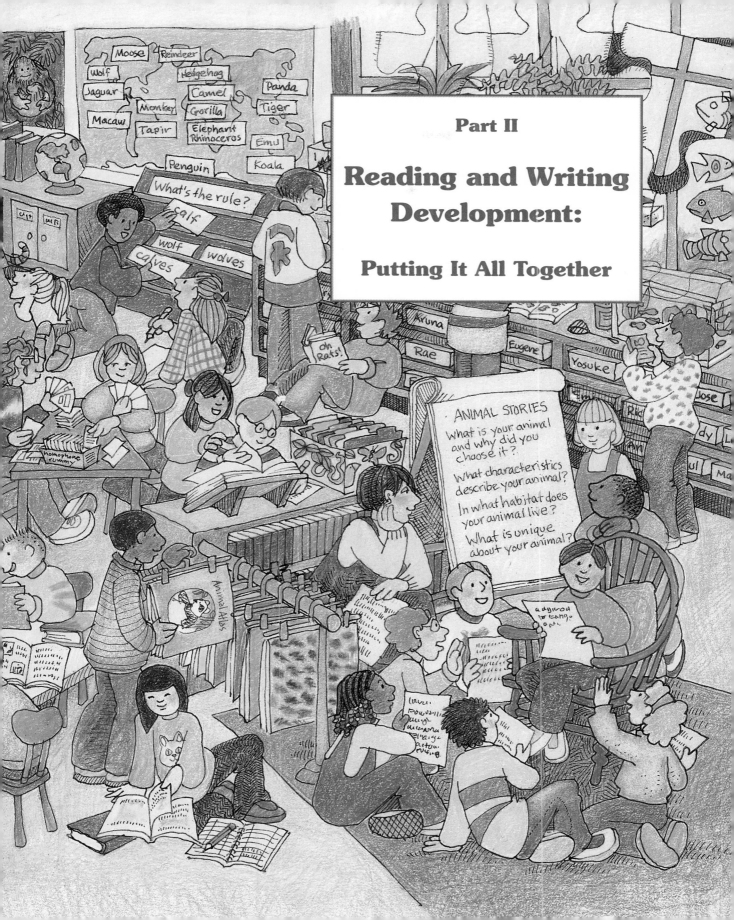

Part II

Reading and Writing Development:

Putting It All Together

The Early Years:

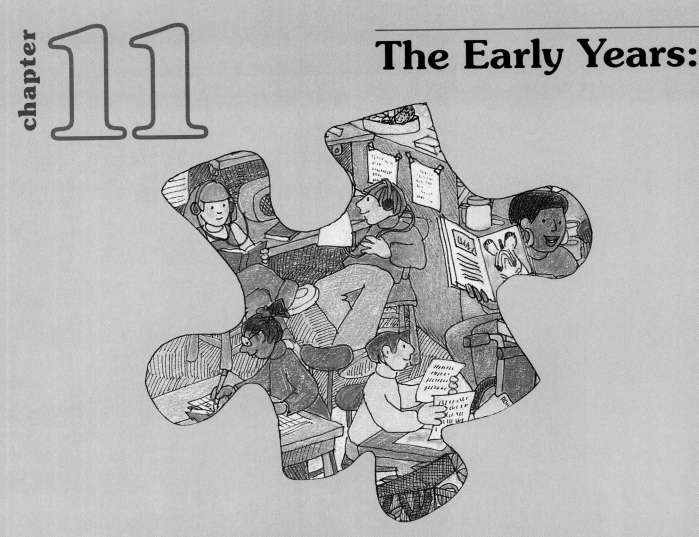

Focus Questions

When you are finished studying this chapter, you should be able to answer these questions:

1. What are the major elements of a balanced literacy program as outlined in this chapter?
2. What are six language routines that can be used to structure daily reading and writing experiences for young children?
3. How can young children learn to make sense of printed language by learning phonemic awareness, the alphabetic principle, and phonics?
4. How can young children learn to develop an understanding of the function and structure of books and stories?
5. What are some strategies for helping young children respond to their reading through drawing and art?
6. How can any special needs or cultural and linguistic needs of young readers be met?

Reading and Writing in Grades K–2

Key Concepts

Balanced Literacy Program
Shared Book Experience
Predictable Books
Big Books
Supported Reading
Guided Reading
Language Experience Approach
Language Routines
Tune-In Routine
Old-Favorite Language Routine

Learning about Language
New-Story Routine
Independent Output Activities
Sharing Time
Print-Rich Environment
Directed Listening Thinking Activity
   (DLTA)
Story Retellings
Transmediation
Themed Studies

Thirty-four bright-eyed and curious first-grade children gather around a kidney-bean-shaped table at the back of the room on the first day of school. The teacher places a soda bottle half-filled with white vinegar on the table. She says, "I am going to blow this balloon up with a soda bottle." The children giggle and watch intently as the teacher places a limp red balloon over the lip of the bottle. She pulls the balloon tight over the lip and shakes the balloon back and forth a couple of times. A puff of white powder falls into the vinegar. The liquid inside the bottle begins to foam; at the same time, the balloon begins to fill with air. It grows bigger and bigger. The children move away from the bottle expecting the balloon to burst at any moment. Just as suddenly as it began, the liquid stops foaming and the balloon stops growing. "How did the bottle blow up the balloon?" asked the teacher. "Let's go over to the carpet for a minute, and I'll write down your ideas on this chart paper." For a few minutes, the teacher writes down the children's ideas as they dictate them. Then, the teacher rereads the ideas and asks the children to join in rereading the ideas with her. As this teacher records her students' ideas, she evidences a concern and respect for children's thoughts and language.

A BALANCED LITERACY PROGRAM: READING TO, WITH, AND BY YOUNG CHILDREN

Teachers play a critical role in creating the conditions that support the learning of young children. The way in which teachers interact with children every day is a living demonstration from which children may choose to learn. Albert Schweitzer once said, "Example isn't the best teacher, it is the only teacher!" When teachers listen carefully to children, they demonstrate sensitivity and value for children and their ideas. By surrounding children with books and other printed media and by encouraging them to engage in reading and writing collectively and individually, the teacher creates an environment in which children begin to view themselves as skilled readers and writers. Children learn to read and write with the help of their teachers. They act like skilled language users and doing the things that readers and writers do, namely, reading, writing, talking, playing, thinking, listening, and drawing. The information presented in this chapter is designed to assist teachers to design and implement balanced literacy programs and practices to help young children become joyful readers and writers.

Deciding on the program elements necessary to provide children with successful and enriching literacy learning experiences is typically a teacher's first order of business. The elements of **balanced literacy programs** have been well defined for over 3 decades by literacy scholars and practitioners working in New Zealand and Australia (Holdaway, 1979; Mooney, 1990; Reutzel, 1996a, 1996b, 1998; Weaver, 1998; Wellington, NZ Department of Education, 1985). *When used in combination,* these elements of a balanced literacy program ensure that children receive well-rounded experiences with reading and writing. Recent research has strongly suggested that balanced reading and literacy programs will provide a comprehensive solution to the extremist philosophical positions and practices of past decades that vacillated between skill-and-drill phonics and whole language approaches (Every Child a Reader, 1995; Snow, Burns, & Griffin, 1998; Wharton-McDonald et al., 1997).

In the succeeding sections of this chapter, we describe the elements of balanced literacy programs. Even though literacy programs always integrate reading and writing (because they are inseparable language processes), for purposes of clarity, we focus on the elements of balanced reading and balanced writing programs separately. We begin by examining the major elements of balanced reading programs shown in Figure 11.1. Note that beneath each major element specific instructional practices are listed.

READING TO CHILDREN

Reading Aloud

Sometimes, teachers are asked why they spend valuable instructional time during a school day reading aloud to children. Although reading aloud to children can be taken to extremes, robbing children of the opportunity to read, there are several good reasons to read aloud to children for 10 to 15 minutes daily. Trelease (1995) states,

> [The] reasons are the same reasons you talk to a child: to reassure, to entertain, to inform or explain, to arouse curiosity, and to inspire—and to do it all personally, not impersonally with a machine. All those experiences create or strengthen a positive attitude about reading (p. 2)

Research by Durkin (1966) revealed that children who learned to read early often came from homes where parents read to them regularly. Other researchers have asserted that read-aloud activities help young children develop a sense of how stories

Figure 11.1 Major elements of balanced reading programs

> ### *Reading TO Children*
> - Teacher Read Alouds
> - Small-Group or One-to-One Reading
>
> ### *Reading WITH Children*
> - Shared Book Experience
> - Shared Rhythm and Singing Experience
> - Supported Reading
> - Language Experience
> - Guided Reading
>
> ### *Reading BY Children*
> - Readers' Theater
> - Sustained Silent Reading (SSR) / Drop Everything and Read (DEAR)
> - School and Class Libraries

are constructed (Morrow, 1993; Morrow & Roskos, 1993). An understanding of how stories are organized or structured has been closely linked with readers' ability to comprehend text (McGee, Ratliff, Sinex, Head, & LaCroix, 1984). During read alouds, children see teachers and others as models of the reading process and witness first-hand the enjoyment of reading as well as the breadth of available reading genres and materials (Mooney, 1990; Reutzel, 1996a, 1996b). Reading aloud provides children with an ever expanding exposure to the world of oral and printed language.

Read alouds expand children's cognitive understanding of the world around them. By listening to texts read aloud, children learn about ideas, concepts, and events that are within their ability to comprehend but beyond the boundaries of their immediate spatial context. However, books read aloud to children should challenge their intellectual development but not exceed their emotional maturity, because they will not enjoy the experience. For example, children who are read poetry about romance or the symbolic beauties of nature at young ages typically do not enjoy poetry, or even worse, develop a contempt for poetry. Instead, wise teachers and parents recognize that 5- and 6-year-olds are not yet emotionally ready for romantic relationships in life or in poetry, so instead they read children humorous poetry by Silverstein or Prelutsky. Young children are emotionally prepared to identify with humorous topics and events. When teachers observe this simple truth, the read-aloud experience becomes far more enjoyable and comprehensible for young children.

Name three do's and don'ts related to reading aloud to children.

Another caution focuses on the difficulty level of the books chosen for read alouds: Teachers should read aloud books that students cannot yet handle independently or with teacher support and guidance. Read-aloud books should be those that exceed the students' reading abilities. Based on Trelease's (1995) *The New Read-Aloud Handbook*, several other "do's" and "don'ts" of read alouds for teachers are listed in Figure 11.2.

Small-Group and One-to-One Reading

Although most reading aloud in school takes place with the entire class, Morrow (1988b) reminds teachers to take advantage of the benefits associated with reading aloud to smaller groups of young children and individuals. One of the benefits associated with reading to children at home is the interaction between parent and child. This same

List two reasons why teachers should read aloud in small groups or one-to-one settings.

Figure 11.2   The do's and don'ts of read alouds

Do's

- Begin reading to children as soon as possible. The younger you start them, the better.
- Use Mother Goose rhymes and songs to stimulate children's language and listening.
- Read as often as you and the child (or class) have time for.
- Try to set aside at least one traditional time each day for a story.
- Picture books can be read easily to a family of children widely separated in age.
- Start with picture books, and build to storybooks and novels.
- Vary the length and subject matter of your readings.
- Follow through with your reading.
- Occasionally read above the children's intellectual level and challenge their minds.
- Remember that even sixth-grade students love a good picture book now and then.
- Allow time for class discussion after reading a story.
- Use plenty of expression when reading.
- The most common mistake in reading aloud is reading too fast. Read slowly enough for the child to build mental pictures.
- Bring the author to life, as well as his or her book.
- Add a third dimension to the book whenever possible.
- Follow the suggestion of Dr. Caroline Bauer and post a reminder sign by your door: "Don't Forget Your *Flood* Book."
- Fathers should make an extra effort to read to their children.
- Lead by example.

Don'ts

- Don't read stories that you don't enjoy yourself.
- Don't continue reading a book once it is obvious that it was a poor choice. Admit the mistake and choose another.
- If you are a teacher, don't feel you have to tie every book to classwork.
- Don't read above a child's emotional level.
- Don't impose interpretations of a story on your audience.
- Don't confuse quantity with quality.
- Don't use the book as a threat, "If you don't pick up your room, no story tonight!"

Based on Trelease (1989).

benefit can be replicated in the school setting. Children whose reading development lags behind that of their peers can be helped a great deal by teachers, volunteers, or older peers who take time to read to them in small-group or individual settings. In this setting, young children can stop the reader to ask questions, make comments, or respond to the story; this seldom happens when teachers read aloud to the whole class. Morrow (1989) also suggests that individual readings be recorded and analyzed to provide diagnostic information to inform future instruction. (The coding sheet in Figure 11.29 (see p. 456) can be used to perform such analyses.)

READING WITH CHILDREN
Shared Book Experience

Many children have learned to read by having books read with them. These books were usually shared by parents or siblings during bedtime reading or lap reading. Although learning to read by being read with has been shown to be successful and meaningful for one-to-one reading events, what seemed to be missing was a way to replicate in a classroom all of the important characteristics of the bedtime or lap-reading event. The **shared book experience** was the suggested solution to this problem (Holdaway, 1979, 1981).

A critical part of the shared book experience involves the selection of good, **predictable books** to be shared. Several criteria need to be observed. For example, books and stories chosen for shared book experiences need to have been proven to be loved by children. Any book or story (including those selections in basal readers) to be shared should have literary merit and engaging content. The pictures should match the text and tell or support the telling of the story in proper sequence. The text should be characterized by repetition, cumulative sequence, rhyme, and rhythm to entice the children into the melody of the language and "hook" them on the visual and auditory patterns. Books should be chosen that put reasonable demands on the reader. Put another way, the amount of unfamiliar print should not overburden the reader. Thus, in the earliest books selected for shared book experiences, the pictures should carry the story, with the print amounting to little more than a caption, such as in *Brown Bear, Brown Bear* or *Polar Bear, Polar Bear* by Martin (1990, 1991). As children develop increasing skill and familiarity with the reading process, books in which the print and the picture carry a more equal share of the story can be selected. Once children have had practice and increased independence in reading, books can be selected in which the print carries the story and the illustrations simply augment the text. Finally, and perhaps most important, the books chosen for shared book experiences need to have a visual impact on 20 to 25 children similar to the impact that a standard-sized book would have on the knee of a child or in the lap of a parent. This requirement associated with books to be used in the shared book experience has led to the development, marketing, and use of **big books** for teaching young children to read (Figure 11.3). When all of these conditions for book selection are met, children and teachers truly share the reading experience. They share the discovery of good books, an awareness of how print works, and the power of language. What is more, children gain a growing confidence in their ability to read (F. L. Barrett, 1982).

A shared book experience is begun with the teacher's introducing the book. The intent of the introduction is to heighten children's desire to read the story and help them draw on their own experiences to enjoy and interpret it. If the big book *The Gingerbread Man* (1985) is selected for sharing, the introduction may begin with children looking at the book cover and the teacher reading the title aloud. The teacher may talk about the front and back of the book and may demonstrate certain features of the book, such as author and illustrator names, publisher, copyright, and title page. Next, the teacher may say, "Look at the pictures. What do you think the words will tell you?"

After looking at the cover and reading the title aloud, children may want to relate personal anecdotes or make predictions about the relationship between the print and the pictures. The sensitive teacher will encourage and praise these contributions to the discussion and attempts to read the big book by the children.

Next, the teacher reads the story with "full dramatic punch, perhaps overdoing a little some of the best parts" (F. L. Barrett, 1982, p. 16). If the story possesses the

Predictable books *should have literary merit and engaging content and pictures that match the text, and the text should be characterized by repetition.*

"After discussion, the teacher should read the story with full dramatic punch, perhaps overdoing a little some of the best parts" (F. L. Barrett, 1982, p. 16).

Figure 11.3   Big book and standard-sized version

Book cover from *Caps, Hats, Socks, and Mittens* by Louise Borden. Jacket illustration copyright © 1988 by Lillian Hoban. Reprinted by permission of Scholastic Inc.

previously outlined characteristics that make the text predictable, soon after the teacher begins reading, the children will begin chiming in on the repetitive and predictable parts. In the story of *The Gingerbread Man* (1985), the children may join in on the phrase, "Run, run as fast as you can. You can't catch me; I'm the Gingerbread man!" At key points, the teacher may pause during reading to encourage children to predict what is coming next in the book.

Increasing involvement on a second reading can be accomplished by adding hand movements or rhythm instruments.

After the first reading, a discussion ensues. Children often want to talk about their favorite parts, share their feelings and experiences, and discuss how well they were able to predict and participate. The book can be reread on subsequent days and will eventually become a part of the stock of favorite stories to be requested for rereading. One means for increasing involvement on a second reading is to use hand movements or rhythm instruments (see the old-favorites routine described later).

Research by Ribowsky (1985) compared the shared book experience approach to a phonics-emphasis approach, the J. B. Lippincott basal, and found that the shared book experience resulted in higher end-of-year achievement scores and phonic analysis subtest scores than did the direct-instruction phonics approach used in the Lippincott basal. In recent studies, Reutzel, Hollingsworth, and Eldredge (1994) and Eldredge, Reutzel, and Hollingsworth (1996) showed that the shared book experience resulted in substantial reading progress for second-grade children across measures of word recognition, vocabulary, comprehension, and fluency when compared to other forms of oral reading practice. More recently, Koskinen, Blum, Bisson, Phillips, Creamer, and Baker (1999) have shown that shared book reading has a positive affect on the reading development of diverse students in school and at home.

Figure 11.4 Song lyrics enlarged on a chart

Oh, Shen-an-doah, I long to hear you, Way, - hey, you rolling riv-er! Oh, Shen-an-doah, I long to hear you, Way, hey, we're bound a-way, 'Cross the wide Mis-sour-i.

Shared Musical Reading Experience

Music is a great motivator for reading! According to O'Bruba (1987), music broadens reading into a multisensory experience, heightens interest and involvement, brings variety and pleasure to reading, and reduces the tedium of repetition and drill. Gardner (1993) has shown that musical intelligence is one of several types of intelligence that can help students learn a variety of subjects well—including sharpening language intelligence.

One variation on the shared book experience is the shared musical reading experience. Bill Harp (1988), Blacher and Jaffee (1998), and Blackburn (1997) suggest that teachers fill the classroom with lively songs. In addition, we suggest filling the classroom with exciting chants, poems, and raps. Whether song, poem, chant, or rap, the text selected for the shared musical reading experience should have the potential to be enjoyed by children. (Selected resources for songs, poems, chants, and raps to be used in the shared rhythm and singing experience are listed in Appendix B.)

Selected songs and texts should place reasonable demands on the readers and should contain lyrics and text that emphasize repetition, cumulative sequence, rhyme, and rhythm. Next, the text of selected songs, poems, chants, and raps must be enlarged, as in Figure 11.4.

The criteria for selecting songs, chants, poems, and raps are similar to those for choosing books to be shared in the shared book experience. Favorite songs such as "BINGO," "Oh My Aunt Came Back," and "On Top of Spaghetti" will be sung joyfully again and again by children. New words and lyrics can be substituted or invented by the children for the standard song lyrics and recorded on large charts or at the chalkboard. For example, the lyrics to the song "BINGO" can be replaced with new lyrics, such as "TEDDY," "MOMMY," or "DADDY." The lyrics to the song "Everybody Hates Me, Nobody Likes Me, Think I'll Go Eat Worms" can be changed by substituting in other miserable things to eat, such as grasshoppers or flies. Beating out the rhythm of a favorite song, poem, rap, or chant by clapping or using rhythm instruments will make a joyful sound in every classroom. Poems such as "Warning" or "Sick" in Shel Silverstein's *Falling Up* (1996) or *A Pizza the Size of the Sun* by Jack Prelutsky (1996) are

Texts selected for the shared rhythm and singing experience should have the potential to be loved by children.

Favorite songs such as "BINGO," "Oh My Aunt Came Back," and "On Top of Spaghetti" will be sung joyfully again and again by children.

just a few popular poems children may wish to put to rhythm. Chants such as "Squid Sauce" in Sonja Dunn's (1990) *Butterscotch Dreams* performed with actions and rhythm will elicit calls on a daily basis for more chants. Using dance, hand movements, and actions along with music and rhythm captures and sustains children's interest. Children delight in using rhythm instruments to accompany their singing and choral readings, although using these devices can be a very noisy enterprise!

After several readings, children can be invited up to the chart to point out words pronounced by the teacher. Words can be copied onto a word card the same size as the words on the chart. These word cards can then be shuffled, and children match the words on the cards back into the text of the song, poem, chant, or rap. The text of the songs, poems, raps, and chants on the charts can be copied to produce small personal booklets of the text on the charts. These copied individual booklets of songs, chants, poems, and raps can then be taken home to be read, shared, and sung with parents and siblings.

Research has demonstrated the positive effects of music on learning language, both oral and written. G. C. Taylor (1981) determined that music-centered language arts instruction resulted in enhanced listening, language awareness, and reading readiness skills. Eastlund (1980) found that music as a medium of language made learning and language acquisition easier for young children. McGuire (1984) reported that children taught music on a daily basis had significantly higher reading growth scores than did children who were not taught music. In short, the shared musical reading experience is an entertaining and beneficial extension of the shared book experience, which enlivens and integrates learning to read with music and diverse types of rhythmic texts.

Supported Reading: Read-Along Cassettes and Take-Home Books

Children taught music on a daily basis had significantly higher reading growth scores than did children who were not taught music.

Just as parents support their children when they are learning to ride a bicycle with training wheels by holding onto the back of the seat, teachers need to support the emergent reader through the process of learning to read. **Supported reading** strategies include the use of adult and child volunteers as well as mechanical support devices such as computers and read-along cassette tapes. Read-along cassettes can be used to support readers effectively through the reading of new or relatively unfamiliar books at all levels. This practice, however, seems to make best sense in the emergent or initial stages of learning to read. Read-along cassettes and CD-ROM programs are commercially available for a wide variety of predictable books. When tapes are not available, teachers can record their own read-along cassettes or involve parent volunteers in the production of cassettes. These carefully paced, prerecorded readings support children through the reading of a book when the teacher is needed elsewhere in the classroom. Tapes or CD-ROM programs can, for example, be color coded for varying text levels (e.g., green for emergent, yellow for easy reading, and blue for independent reading) and stored in specially designed storage cases.

Supported reading strategies include the use of adult and child volunteers as well as mechanical support devices such as computers and read-along cassette tapes.

See chapter 9 for ideas on recruiting volunteers.

Take-home books are a means for involving parents in supporting their children's reading.

Take-home books are a means for parents to support their children's reading growth. To construct take-home books for students, we suggest the use of published, predictable books as patterns. For example, the classic book *On Market Street* (Lobel, 1981) uses an alphabet pattern with words and pictures for each alphabet letter. This book can be rewritten with different words and illustrations for each alphabet letter (e.g., alligators, beds). This revised version of the original is copied for each child. To make these copied take-home books more visually attractive, children may wish to color the illustrations. The remaining step is to take the books home to parents. Teachers can produce multiple copies of read-along cassette tapes to accompany these take-home books for additional home practice opportunities when parents are unable to assist.

Guided Reading

Guided reading is an essential part of a balanced reading program (Fountas & Pinnell, 1996; Mooney, 1990). Unlike basal readers that claim to engage children and teachers in "guided reading" activities, the notion of guided reading in a balanced reading program focuses on reading leveled books with children that would present too many challenges for them if they were to take full responsibility for the first reading. Thus, the major purposes of guided reading are (a) to develop reading strategies, and (b) to move children toward independent reading.

Children are grouped by developmental levels that reflect a range of competencies, experiences, and interests (Fountas & Pinnell, 1996; Mooney, 1990). The most important consideration centers on the child's ability to successfully manipulate and process the text with limited teacher guidance and interaction. Guided reading groups typically include four levels of children's reading development: (a) early emergent, (b) emergent, (c) early fluency, and (d) fluency. Guided reading groups are composed of six to eight children who will work together for a period of time under the direct guidance of the teacher. One caution: *Guided reading groups change as children progress during the year.* This is a crucial point in using guided reading groups, because failure to modify group composition can result in static ability groups like the "Eagles, Bluebirds, and Buzzards," as seen and practiced in previous decades. The static nature of these ability groups— particularly those children in the "lower" developmental groups—caused children to suffer documented self-esteem damage and lowered academic expectations.

Before a guided reading group is begun, the teacher must take great care to match the levels of text with the identified needs of a group of children to ensure that the group can enjoy and control the story throughout the first reading. Texts chosen for each leveled group should present children with a reasonable challenge but also with a high degree of potential success. Typically, children should be able to read approximately 90% of the words in a book selected for a guided reading group. Books used in early emergent guided reading should demonstrate a close match of text and pictures, gradual introduction of unfamiliar concepts and words, as well as sufficient repetition of predictable elements to provide support for novice readers. Peterson (1991, p. 135) has constructed a very helpful text gradient summary for selecting and leveling guided reading books, shown in Figure 11.5.

In Figure 11.5, levels 1 to 4 are linked to emergent guided reading. Early reading is linked to levels 5 to 8. Levels 9 to 12 function as a bridge between the lower levels and upper levels, capturing elements of emergent and fluent reading. For early fluent readers, levels 13 to 15 seem most appropriate, and levels 16 to 20 are aimed at fluent reader levels.

Levels 1–4—Preprimer

Levels 5–8—Primer

Levels 9–12—Early 1st Grade

Levels 13–15—Mid 1st Grade

Levels 16–20—End 1st Grade

Children should *not* be introduced to guided reading until they have had ample opportunities to listen to stories, poems, songs, and so forth and to participate in

*During **guided reading,** children are grouped homogeneously by developmental levels and by the ability to handle specific reading materials.*

Books selected for guided reading should provide a reasonable challenge and potential for high success: 90% to 95% of the words should be easily read by students.

Guided reading should be introduced after children have enjoyed ample opportunities to participate in shared reading experiences.

Figure 11.5   Aid for selecting guided reading books: Sources of predictability in groups of levels

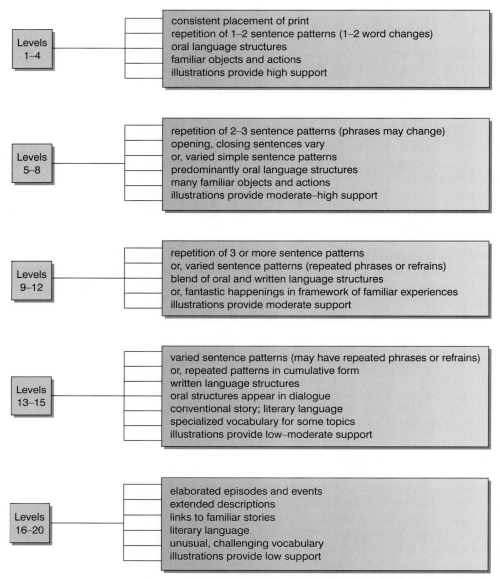

Levels 1–4
- consistent placement of print
- repetition of 1–2 sentence patterns (1–2 word changes)
- oral language structures
- familiar objects and actions
- illustrations provide high support

Levels 5–8
- repetition of 2–3 sentence patterns (phrases may change)
- opening, closing sentences vary
- or, varied simple sentence patterns
- predominantly oral language structures
- many familiar objects and actions
- illustrations provide moderate–high support

Levels 9–12
- repetition of 3 or more sentence patterns
- or, varied sentence patterns (repeated phrases or refrains)
- blend of oral and written language structures
- or, fantastic happenings in framework of familiar experiences
- illustrations provide moderate support

Levels 13–15
- varied sentence patterns (may have repeated phrases or refrains)
- or, repeated patterns in cumulative form
- written language structures
- oral structures appear in dialogue
- conventional story; literary language
- specialized vocabulary for some topics
- illustrations provide low–moderate support

Levels 16–20
- elaborated episodes and events
- extended descriptions
- links to familiar stories
- literary language
- unusual, challenging vocabulary
- illustrations provide low support

From "Selecting Books for Beginning Readers" by B. Peterson, in *Bridges to Literacy: Learning From Reading Recovery* (p. 135) edited by D. E. DeFord, C. A. Lyons, and G. S. Pinnell, 1991, Portsmouth, NH: Heinemann. Copyright 1991 by Heinemann Educational Books, Inc. Reprinted by permission.

shared reading experiences. The basic lesson pattern employed in guided reading lessons consists of seven phases, which are listed in Figure 11.6.

As teachers work with children in guided reading, they lead children to understand that there are three important cueing systems that good readers use to unlock unfamiliar text (Mooney, 1990): meaning, organization or order, and the visual–sound system, as shown in Figure 11.7.

Figure 11.6   Guided reading lesson overview

Picture Talk •Walk through a new book by looking at the pictures. Ask children, "What do you see?"

First Reading •Depending on the students' developmental levels, the first reading is initially done by the teacher with children following the lead. Later, the teacher gradually releases responsibility for the first reading to the children by sharing the reading role and then fading into one who encourages children to try it on their own.

Language Play • In this phase of the guided reading lesson, the teacher carefully analyzes the text to find specific elements associated with written language to teach children how language works. For early emergent readers, this may mean letter identification, punctuation, or directionality. In the fluency stage, children might identify text genre or compound words.

Rereading • Children read the text again with the assistance of the teacher, a peer, or a mechanical device such as a computer or tape. Novice readers are encouraged to point to the text as they read, whereas fluent readers are encouraged to "read the text with your eyes" or silently.

Retelling • Children retell what they have read to their teacher or to their peers. Typically we say, "Can you tell me what you've read?" Sometimes we probe children's retellings with other questions to prompt recall.

Follow-up • The most effective follow-up activity to a guided reading lesson is to invite children to take guided reading books home for demonstrating their ability to parents and siblings. This provides needed practice time and promotes increased confidence and self-esteem among young readers.

Extensions • Extending books through performances, murals, artwork, and even music helps children deepen their understandings and increase their interpretations of text.

To help young children access the cueing systems for fluent reading, teachers usually model the application of these systems by asking questions and making comments that direct children to select and apply one or more of the four major reading cueing strategies: predicting, sampling, confirming, and cross-checking to self-correct. Examples of questions and comments teachers use to direct or guide children to use the four reading cueing strategies are listed in Figure 11.8.

As children progress along the continuum of reading development in guided reading, teachers begin by taking responsibility for the first reading of the text with students. Thus, early guided reading looks in practice much like the shared reading

Name four reading strategies to be developed during guided reading.

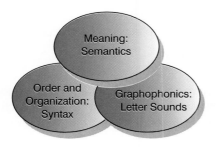

Figure 11.7   Three cueing systems for reading

Figure 11.8   Teacher questions and comments to guide children to use the four reading cueing strategies

> **Predicting** *Look at the pictures. What do you think the words will tell you?*
> **Sampling** *Look at the print. What do you see? Read it with your (fingers) eyes.*
> **Confirming** *How do you know? Can you show me by pointing and reading it to me?*
> **Cross-Checking and Self-Correcting** *Does it make sense? Does it sound right? Does it look right?*

experience; the main difference is the size of the group. Over time and with development, children assume more of the responsibility for the first reading of the text, with the teacher taking a supporting role through echoing, coaching, and helping where needed. The gradual release of responsibility for the first reading of a guided reading book generally occurs as teachers observe that children understand basic print concepts and have acquired a basic sight word vocabulary.

During the earliest stages and ages of reading development, children use their fingers to finger-point read.

During these earliest stages and ages of reading development, children use their fingers to finger-point read (Ehri & Sweet, 1991). Finger-point reading involves children in voice pointing or indicating the one-to-one correspondence of spoken words with written words (Reutzel, 1995). During early emergent guided reading, teachers focus children's attention on *predictions* by *sampling* text features such as picture clues and known words. In addition, teachers focus early emergent readers' attention on print concepts such as directionality (left to right, top to bottom, etc.).

During emergent guided reading, teachers focus children's attention on processing text with the use of multiple strategies such as confirming, cross-checking, and self-correcting. In addition, emergent guided reading groups are led by the teacher to summarize and/or retell the text as well as engage in the beginnings of silent reading. As children enter early fluency, teachers broaden guidance to include an understanding of story structure, characterization, and silent reading. In the final developmental stage, *fluency,* intermediate, upper elementary, and middle school teachers expand children's strategies and understandings of text to include studies of genre, reading like a writer (stylistic examinations), literary devices, and dialogue.

Reading WITH children in guided reading has been typically lacking in many early reading experiences associated with so-called whole language approaches. Teachers who understand the reading process also know that children learn to read from people, not from programs, materials, or even books, although each of these is important in its own place. Learning to read is a social process motivated primarily by a need to understand and be understood. Consequently, guided reading experiences, when coupled with individual reading conferences (described in chapter 9) and assessed by the use of running records (described in chapter 10), ensure that young children will receive the experiences and personal guidance necessary to develop into successful, fluent readers.

Language Experience

The LEA uses children's oral language and personal experiences as the basis for creating personalized reading materials.

The **language experience approach** (LEA) is intended to develop and support children's reading and writing abilities. The essence of this approach is to use children's talk about personal or vicarious experiences as the basis for creating personalized reading materials.

Lamoreaux and Lee (1943) trace the beginnings of the LEA approach to reading and writing instruction of the late 1930s and early 1940s. An early contributor to the LEA approach was Ashton-Warner (1963), who worked with Maori children in New Zealand. Her approach to LEA, called *organic reading,* used children's personal words or key vocabulary to teach reading.

LEA is recommended as a part of a balanced reading program because the most predictable text for children to begin reading is a text transcribed from their oral dictation of a personally meaningful event or experience. Children's LEA dictated stories can be recorded for use by teachers and children in at least three ways:

1. The group experience chart
2. The individual language experience story
3. The key vocabulary word bank

The most predictable text for a child to begin reading is a text transcribed from her oral dictation of a personally meaningful event or experience.

Creating the Group Experience Chart

The group experience chart is a means of recording the firsthand or vicarious experiences of an entire group of children. This means, of course, that the entire group of children would have shared an experience such as a field trip, a new book read aloud, or the visit of an outside expert. Although entire classrooms of children are often involved in the creation of group experience charts, it is also advisable to involve smaller groups of children periodically to maximize the involvement of individual children. The typical course of events associated with the creation of a group experience chart follows:

1. The children participate in a common experience.
2. Teachers and children discuss the common experience.
3. Children dictate the chart, while the teacher transcribes the dictation.
4. Teachers and children share in reading the chart.
5. The chart is used to learn about words and other important language concepts such as punctuation, left-to-right, and sight words.

The selection of an interesting and stimulating experience or topic for children can determine the success or failure of any LEA activity. Topics and experiences simply must capture the interest of children to provide the motivation necessary for learning. The following activities, like the science experiment that began this chapter, are a few examples of ideas for beginning a group experience chart:

Focus on why selecting an interesting and stimulating experience or topic for children can spell the success or failure of any LEA activity.

- Our mother hamster had babies last night.
- Writing a new version of *The Napping House* (A. Wood, 1984).
- What mountain men did in the old days.
- What we want for our birthdays.
- Planning our Valentine's Day party.
- What did Martin Luther King, Jr., do?
- Sometimes I have scary dreams. Once . . .
- Once I got into trouble for . . .
- A classmate is ill; make a get-well card from the class.

Discussing the experience or topic carefully can help children assess what they have learned about the topic, help them make personal connections, and motivate them to share with others their knowledge, experiences, and personal connections. Of course, the teacher should be careful not to dominate the discussion; asking too many focused questions can turn an otherwise open and exciting discussion into a dull exercise in knowledge interrogation. The teacher's questions should invite children to engage in dialogue rather than to give short, unelaborated responses. Also, many teachers make the mistake of beginning dictation too early in the discussion. If this is done, the results will reflect a dull, even robotic, recounting of the experience or topic.

Imagine a teacher who has read aloud the book *The Polar Express* by Chris Van Allsburg (1985). After inviting children to respond to the book, the teacher asks, "If you had been chosen by Santa to receive the first gift of Christmas, what would you have said?" The teacher calls on individual children to give their responses to the book. After plenty of discussion, the teacher calls on children to respond to the book by dictating aloud their best ideas for responding to this question. The teacher records each child's dictation on the chart. With emergent readers, the teacher may record each child's dictation with different colored markers; the colors help children identify their own dictation more easily in the future. Later, the teacher may write the children's names by their dictation. When the chart is complete, the teacher typically reads the chart aloud to the children while pointing to each word. After the teacher has read the chart aloud, he or she invites the children to read along a second time. Next, the teacher may ask individual children to read their own responses aloud or invite volunteers to read aloud the responses of other children.

The teacher may read aloud a certain line from the chart and ask for a child to come up to the chart and point to the line the teacher just read aloud. He or she may copy the lines of the chart on sentence strips and have children pick a sentence strip and match it to the line in the chart. Favorite words in the chart story can be copied onto word cards for matching activities as well. Thus, the text generated by the children for the chart story can be used in subsequent large- and small-group meetings to build the students' sight vocabulary of words in the chart, demonstrate word-recognition strategies, and even help children learn about letter sounds for decoding purposes. The chart also can be copied and sent home with each child for individual practice.

Creating the Individual Language Experience Story

All children in the classroom have their own set of experiences and as a result a unique story to tell. Whereas group experience charts serve a purpose for the entire group, the individual language experience story provides an opportunity for children to talk about their experiences and to have these experiences recorded. Just as with writing, a steady diet of teacher-initiated topics and experiences used to produce group experience charts ignores the fact that children should be given opportunities to compose for their own purposes. Motivation for topic choices comes from many different sources in the child's life, both in and out of the classroom. Graves (1983) is adamant about the need for children to choose their own topics for writing. Harwayne (1992) describes composing as an inside-out process that adds justification for encouraging children to choose their own topic for the individual language experience story.

We have found that it is helpful to have parent volunteers available when recording individual language experience stories. In our classrooms, we referred to this process as the make-a-book approach. An example appears in Figure 11.9.

We like to give recognition to individual language experience stories, as we do all child-authored books, by placing a card pocket and a library card in each child's book. These books can then be placed in the classroom library for other children to read.

Think of three questions that could be asked during a discussion of an LEA group chart that would invite children to engage in dialogue rather than to give short, unelaborated responses.

The individual experience story provides an opportunity for children to tell their own story and have these experiences recorded.

Figure 11.9   An example of an individual language experience story: Make a book

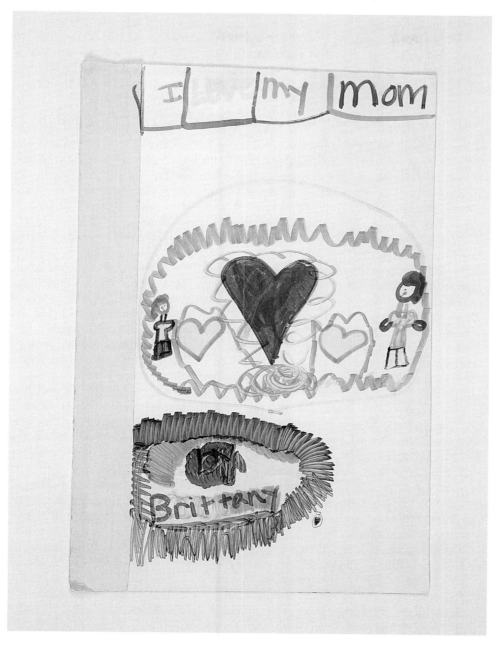

A story reader's chair or chairs can be designated for encouraging children to read their individual language experience stories aloud to peers in their own classroom and in other classrooms in the school.

    A variation of individual language experience stories we particularly like is shape stories (Figure 11.10). The cover and pages of the dictated individual language experience story are drawn and cut into the shape of the book topic. For example, if a child has just returned from Disneyland, the book might be cut into the shape of Mickey Mouse's head; a trip to Texas might be recorded in a book cut into the shape of the state of Texas.

For most young children, no single individual is more important and exciting to talk or read about than they are. This fact alone explains why individual language experience stories always provide meaningful, predictable stories for children to read: The stories are drawn from each child's own language and personal experiences.

Teaching Vocabulary and Word Recognition Using LEA: The Word Bank

Key vocabulary words can be stored in a box called a word bank.

Ashton-Warner (1963), in a book entitled *Teacher,* described how she taught young Maori children to read in New Zealand. With little more than a chalkboard, chalk, black crayons, and a few pieces of paper for word cards, this amazing teacher taught children to read. She believed that learning to read was essentially very personal: Children needed to have a desire and reason to learn to read. Ashton-Warner also believed that learning to read should be a natural or organic process. Thus, when children had difficulty learning to read the high-frequency sight words typically found in primary basal readers, Ashton-Warner turned to asking children which words they wanted to learn to read instead! She found that although children had difficulty learning to recognize words like *come* and *look,* they had little difficulty recognizing their own words, such as *knife* and *tigers.* Each day children were asked to come to school with a word they wanted to learn to read. Ashton-Warner listened to the word and wrote it on a card for each child. These key vocabulary words were stored in a box called a *word bank.* Children used these words to compose sentences and stories. They copied these words onto the chalkboard, practiced them with peers, and played games with word cards drawn from their word banks.

Two types of word banks can be used with students: personalized or class word banks.

In our first-grade classrooms, we used two types of word banks with our students. First, we created a personalized word bank for each child. Similar to Ashton-Warner (1963), we asked children on a daily basis to tell us a word they wanted to have in their own word bank. These words were written on cards and stored in alphabetical order in a small shoe, cigar, or index box. Often, two or three children combined their word banks by dumping the word cards on the floor and mixing them together. The object of the game was to sort through the pile of words and find their own word cards again and place them back into their word banks. Children combined the words from their own word banks with those of another child to write coauthored or collaborative sentences and stories.

Thus, the use of personalized word banks serves several important functions for developing children's reading ability.

- Personalized word banks allow children to integrate words from outside the classroom into their learning about reading and writing.
- These words provide repeated, meaningful exposures to a core of highly personal or one-look words.
- These words are used for word games, sentence-building activities, matching, and skill instruction.
- These words provide a reference for children to use during their own writing and spelling.

Activities using the group word bank are described in chapter 7.

A second type of word bank we found useful is a class or group word bank. When group experience charts, big books, enlarged text of poems, songs, and the like were

Figure 11.10   Examples of shape books

read by large or small groups of children, we asked our students to choose several favorite or useful words from these sources to place into a group word bank. We placed a piece of oak tag card stock beneath each word selected in the chart or book. While children watched, we copied the word onto the word card and placed it into the group word bank. These cards were used later for matching and word-substitution activities, as well as for word-recognition and decoding instruction.

Additional Viewpoints

Research for many years now has substantiated the fact that the LEA is as effective as basal reader instruction (Bond & Dykstra, 1967; M. A. Hall, 1981). In fact, in a review of studies comparing basal reader instruction and LEA whole-language instruction, Stahl and Miller (1989) found a 0.6 standard deviation advantage for LEA whole language approaches over basal reading instruction for kindergarten readers.

One oft-cited criticism of LEA is that students will not gain as much vocabulary knowledge as they would using other approaches. M. A. Hall (1978) refutes this criticism in her review of the literature, showing the LEA children acquire vocabulary as well as, if not better than, students taught with other methods. C. Chomsky (1971) also showed that LEA students usually became better spellers than students taught with basal readers. Although LEA is certainly not a panacea, it presents certain advantages that other approaches to reading instruction cannot claim. Typical advantages and disadvantages of LEA are summarized in Figure 11.11.

LEA can be adapted and used successfully with basal reader stories. In fact, many current basal reader programs advocate supplementing the basal reader with language experience activities (Jones & Nessel, 1985; Reimer, 1983).

Research has shown LEA to be as effective as or more effective than basal reader instruction.

Using LEA with basal reader instruction is discussed in chapter 4.

Figure 11.11   Advantages and limitations of the language experience approach

---

Advantages

1.   It enables children to conceptualize reading as "talk written down."
2.   It ensures that children will have a background of experiences to bring to reading material.
3.   It enables children to read their own language patterns.
4.   It has a beneficial motivating effect when used with older disabled readers.
5.   It stresses the interrelationships among the four language arts of listening, speaking, reading, and writing.
6.   It stresses reading comprehension.
7.   It enhances creativity of children.
8.   It creates an interest in and love of reading.

Limitations

1.   It lacks sequential skill development.
2.   It offers little direct guidance for teachers.
3.   It lacks vocabulary control.
4.   It demands much teacher time (for transcribing stories and individual help).
5.   It presupposes a well-equipped room and a rich and motivating classroom environment.
6.   It cannot be used as a major method of teaching reading beyond the primary grades.

READING BY CHILDREN

Sustained Silent Reading, or Drop Everything and Read

If children are going to improve as readers, they must have daily time to read as is provided in SSR or DEAR.

An important part of a balanced reading program is the inclusion of reading BY children. Children must be given opportunities to enjoy reading self-selected materials on a regular basis. Sustained silent reading (SSR), or drop everything and read (DEAR), is a structured approach that provides needed reading events for young children. Hunt (1970) explained that SSR is a structured activity in which children are given regular, fixed time periods for silently reading self-selected materials. Put differently, SSR is an activity where everyone in the classroom—students, teachers, parents, volunteers—reads silently something he or she has personally selected for a designated period of time.

The purposes of SSR are grounded in the belief that anyone—children or adults—gets better at anything they practice regularly. We believe that the more children read, the more they will learn about the process of becoming a successful reader. R. Allington (1977) once raised the question, "If they don't read much, how they ever gonna get good?" Other purposes for engaging in SSR include encouraging children to read voluntarily material they have selected for enjoyment or information. To help children derive greater purpose and understanding from SSR, display a chart much like the following (D. Spiegel, 1981).

> We will learn to enjoy reading more and try a variety of reading materials.
>
> We will learn about new places, new faces, and new ideas.
>
> We will get better at reading and learn to concentrate while reading.

McCracken and McCracken (1978) describe several positive reasons for implementing an SSR or DEAR classroom reading-by-children program:

Notice at least four reasons for implementing a daily reading time.

- Reading books is important. Children come to understand what teachers value by taking note of what they are asked to do.
- Anyone can read a book. Readers with special needs do not feel singled out for attention when they engage in reading or looking at a book during SSR.
- Children learn that reading is interacting with an author through sustained engagement with a self-selected text.
- Children develop the ability to remain on task for an extended period of time during SSR.
- Books were meant to be read in large chunks for extended periods of time. Children may get the wrong idea that reading is done during small segments of time and focus on short texts such as those often found in basal readers.
- Comprehension is improved through SSR activities (Reutzel & Hollingsworth, 1991c).
- Finally, children learn to judge the appropriateness of the materials they select for reading during SSR. Reutzel and Gali (1998) found that for most children the hardest part of learning to read was choosing the right book.

Implementing an SSR program is a relatively straightforward process:

List the steps for implementing an effective SSR or DEAR classroom program.

1. *Designate a specific daily time for reading.* Teachers have found that three time slots work well for SSR: The first is as children enter the classroom first thing in the morning; the second is following lunch or recess; and the third is right before children go home for the day. Typically, teachers allocate about 15 to 20 minutes per day for SSR. For younger children, teachers might begin with a 10-minute SSR time and lengthen this time throughout the year as children indicate a desire for more time. We have found that a cooking timer with a bell is a welcome addition for younger children so they do not become worried about watching the clock.

2. *Hold a procedural mini-lesson to describe the rules of SSR.* To set the stage for successful experiences with SSR, we suggest that teachers conduct a brief lesson on the rules and expectations associated with SSR time. Begin by stating the purposes of SSR shown previously. Second, review with children the rules for participation in SSR. We have found that enlarging these rules and placing them on a chart for the class helps students take responsibility for their own behavior. Finally, explain how students can ready themselves for this time each day. The rules for SSR are shown in Figure 11.12.

3. *Extend the experience through sharing.* Children can be asked to share their books with other students at the conclusion of SSR through a "say something" or "turn to your neighbor" activity. In addition to these informal share sessions, groups of children may organize a response to a book through art, drama, writing, or musical performances to be shared with others.

In any case, beginning an SSR program with young children, even in kindergarten, convinces children of the value of reading and gives them important practice

Figure 11.12   The rules for sustained silent reading (SSR)

- Children must select their own books or reading materials.
- Changing books during sustained silent reading (SSR) is discouraged to avoid interruptions.
- Each individual in the classroom is expected to read silently without interruption during the fixed period of time for SSR.
- The teacher and other visitors in the classroom are expected to read silently materials of their own choosing as well.
- Children are not expected to make reports or answer teacher questions about the books they have been reading during SSR.

time. Clearly, SSR has the potential to help children develop life-long reading enjoyment and habits.

Reader's Theater and Dramatizations

In reader's theater, emphasis is placed on presenting an interpretation of literature read in dramatic style for an audience who imagines setting and actions.

Reader's theater is an effective and enjoyable strategy for developing oral reading fluency among young children. In reader's theater, children practice reading from a script and then share their oral interpretations with classmates and selected audiences (Hill, 1990b; Sloyer, 1982). Unlike a play, where students memorize lines, practice actions, and use elaborate stage sets to make their presentation, emphasis in reader's theater is placed on presenting an interpretation of literature read in a dramatic style for an audience who imagines setting and actions.

List three criteria for selecting texts to be read in reader's theater productions.

Easy texts are selected for reader's theater with students and should be drawn from tales originating from the oral tradition, poetry, or quality picture books designed to be read aloud. In some cases, information texts such as *The Popcorn Book* (dePaola, 1978) and *The Magic School Bus Lost in the Solar System* (Cole, 1990) can be used as reader's theater practice scripts (Young & Vardell, 1993). Selections should be packed with action, have an element of suspense, and comprise an entire meaningful story or episode. Also, texts selected for use in reader's theater should contain sufficient dialogue to make reading and preparing the text challenging and to involve several students as characters. A few examples of such texts are Martin and Archambault's *Knots on a Counting Rope* (1987), Viorst's *Alexander and the Terrible Horrible No Good Very Bad Day* (1972), and Barbara Robinson's *The Best Christmas Pageant Ever* (1972).

Minimal props are used in reader's theater; masks, hats, or simple costumes can be used. If a story is selected for reading, students are assigned to read a character's part. If poems are selected for reader's theater, students may read alternating lines or groups of lines. *Reader's theater in-the-round,* where readers stand around the perimeter of the room and the audience is in the center surrounded by the readers, is a fun and interesting variation for both performers and audience.

Young or inexperienced readers will often benefit from a discussion before the first reading of a reader's theater script. This discussion is designed to help them make connections between their own background experiences and the text to be read. Also, young children benefit from listening to a previously recorded performance of the text as an oral language model before the initial reading of the script.

Hennings (1974) described a simplified procedure for preparing reader's theater scripts for classroom performance. First, the text to be performed is read silently by the individual students. Second, the text is read again orally, sometimes using choral reading in a group. After the second reading, children either choose their parts, or the teacher assigns parts to the children. (We suggest that students be allowed to select their three most desired parts, write these choices on a slip of paper, and submit them to the teacher, and that teachers do everything possible to assign one of these three choices.) The third reading is also an oral reading with students reading their parts with scripts in hand. Students may have several rehearsal readings as they prepare for the final reading or performance in front of the class or a special audience.

The School Library

Media specialists and librarians always seemed to have a magical way with children. Their secret was their knowledge of books children loved! When it was announced that it was time to visit the library, our students snapped to attention. They were always anxious to hear the new story our librarian, Mrs. Harmer, would read. But better yet, they were anxious to spend uninterrupted time browsing through the shelves of books that captured their imagination and interest.

The school library and the librarian should be a focal point for teachers, parents, and early readers. For example, in cooperation with the school librarian, a monthly newsletter could be sent home announcing new library acquisitions to parents and children while inviting both parents and children to make better use of the school library. In this newsletter, two or three of the new books could be highlighted for parents and children. For special occasions such as holidays, the newsletter may feature books about Halloween, Kwanzaa, Thanksgiving, Hanukkah, or Christmas.

The school library and the librarian should be a focal point for teachers, parents, and early readers.

Because teachers are often too busy to keep up on the newest myriad of children's books published, school librarians may be asked to present selected books at school faculty meetings. A children's choices book list from the school library could be published annually and made available to teachers and parents. By keeping teachers and parents better informed, librarians open the world of books to their patrons.

Parents and teachers should make sure each child uses the school library regularly. Beyond this, parents should be encouraged to take their children to the community library and acquire a library card for each of them. A letter home from teachers and the school librarian to parents encouraging library visits as a family activity will contribute much to helping young children develop lifelong library habits.

Library visits also provide a setting for children to learn about book-selection strategies. Teachers, parents, and librarians can assist children in selecting books by brainstorming interests with them and by teaching children fundamental library skills such as using the card catalogue system. It is important to remember that children learn to use the library by using the library—frequently! In spite of busy school-day schedules, regular visits to the library should not be crowded out. Children should visit the school library at least twice weekly, and more often if possible. Libraries, if properly integrated into the school reading program, will become busy hubs of activity where children read for enjoyment and pleasure and places where librarians, parents, and teachers share a love of books with their children and students.

BALANCED LITERACY PROGRAMS: WRITING TO AND FOR, WITH, AND BY YOUNG CHILDREN

The major elements of balanced writing programs include those listed in Figure 11.13. Beneath each major element heading, specific instructional practices are listed.

Figure 11.13 The major elements of balanced writing programs

> ### *Writing TO Children*
> - Dialogue Journals
> - Message Boards
>
> ### *Writing WITH Children*
> - Shared Writing Experience
> - Language Experience Approach
> - Traveling Tales
>
> ### *Writing BY Children*
> - Journals
> - Post Office Letter Writing
> - Pocketbooks
> - Reading Logs

WRITING TO AND FOR CHILDREN

Dialogue Journals

Writing TO and FOR children motivates both reading and writing development. Young children enjoy receiving written notes, letters, invitations, and so on from peers, but they particularly value receiving written communication from their teachers. In this spirit, we have found *dialogue journals* to be useful in sparking a written conversation between teachers and children in the early grades. Gambrell (1985) describes the use of dialogue journals as a number of steps, as outlined in Figure 11.14.

Dialogue journals form a perfect link between reading and writing while offering a direct and natural way for teachers to write TO their children.

Dialogue journals form a perfect link between reading and writing while offering a direct and natural way for teachers to write TO their children. Teachers who have used dialogue journals have found them to be effective but also time-consuming. Gambrell (1985) suggests that teachers not try to write to the entire class but rather to select a smaller group of children with whom they can communicate. In our experience, we have found that children are willing to write daily in their dialogue journals and also seem to be willing to accept an occasional but regular response from the teacher. For instance, we have responded to 20% to 25% of the children's daily journal entries each day to ameliorate the problem of having to respond to the entire class.

Message Board

Children like to receive notes from their teachers. One means for communicating with a classroom of children is to display a message board that is set aside for writing notes to children. The notes left on the message center are compliments, comments, directions, and the like. These notes are often brief, and many children consult these notes at the beginning or throughout the school day. Our students enjoyed writing and reading responses to books posted in the book message center.

Language Experience Approach

For young writers, the process of composing is much less taxing than the process of transcribing thoughts into the written code. By the time they enter school, young children are fairly adept at expressing thoughts using oral language. The LEA en-

Figure 11.14   Steps in implementing dialogue journals with young children

1. Each day, children write something about an interest, concern, or experience.
2. Each day, the teacher responds to the child's journal entry by commenting, asking questions, and encouraging the children to continue their journal writing.
3. Use a bound composition book or other similarly bound writing book.
4. To start children writing, talk about how people write letters to one another. Describe how they write to you, and you write to them.
5. If children have a difficult time getting started, you may want to suggest some topics such as favorite foods, after-school activities, etc. You may also want to provide stimulus sentence leads such as, "My favorite thing to do after school is. . . ."
6. Set aside about 10 to 15 minutes daily time for writing and reading in the dialogue journals.
7. Do not correct children's mechanical or grammatical errors, because dialogue journals are intended to encourage open communication. If children use incorrect mechanics or grammar, model the correct uses in your response.
8. Use comments in your responses that encourage children to write, such as, "Tell me more about when . . ." or "you didn't answer my question last time about. . . ."
9. Children should be told that the information in the dialogue journal is private, just between the two of you.
10. If you or the children want to share information with others, each should ask the other for permission to share.

Adapted from "Dialogue Journals: Reading-Writing Instruction" by L. B. Gambrell, 1985, *The Reading Teacher, 38*(6), pp. 512–515. Copyright 1985 by the International Reading Association.

courages teachers to capitalize on children's strengths by tapping into their ability to manipulate and compose using oral language. As described earlier, children use oral language and the assistance of others to orally collect interesting words in a word bank and to compose both group charts and individual stories. Using oral composition as a springboard, teachers write for children so that they learn that printed language is much like *talk written down.* As children dictate experiences, they may watch for words they want to add to their word banks. Blank cards can be made available for children to copy these words from environmental displays and from books and other texts. Children can form authoring teams to work on producing a group experience chart to be shared with other children in the classroom using their own word cards or the assistance of the teacher as scribe. They can work together to make signs, captions, labels, or directions for objects and events that transpire in their classroom. Many children will choose to write for themselves when they see their dictation recorded and their art work come together in a book or story. In short, LEA exposes children to printed language in relevant, functional ways to promote curiosity about print that leads to selecting writing as an appealing, independent activity. Examples of LEA stories produced by first-graders are shown in Figure 11.15.

Figure 11.15   Examples of LEA stories produced by first-graders

WRITING WITH CHILDREN

Interactive Writing

Interactive writing is an important part of a balanced literacy program. At first, the practice of interactive writing was known as *shared writing* and was developed by Moira McKenzie, Warden of the Inner London Education Authority. McKenzie's interactive writing approach was largely influenced by Holdaway's (1979) writings on *shared reading* and *language experience* (Fountas & Pinnell, 1996). An interactive writing session focuses on the teacher writing WITH children:

- To connect reading and writing by using literature as a takeoff point for writing reproductions, innovations, and new texts
- To develop increasingly sophisticated writing strategies
- To demonstrate saying words slowly and connecting sounds in words to letters and letter combinations
- To expand children's repertoire of writing genres and forms
- To learn how the spelling process works

Interactive writing was known at first as **shared writing** *or* **sharing the pen.**

List in your mind the five stages of an interactive writing session.

The subject and form of interactive writing may vary greatly, depending on the developmental levels of the children and the context of experiences in the classroom. As children learn more about the writing process and different types of writing forms and genres, the teacher makes different decisions about how to *share the pen* during interactive writing. There is no one correct way to teach an interactive writing lesson, but based on the writings of Fountas and Pinnell (1996), we recommend the following:

1. In the early stages of writing, the teacher helps children compose a simple message drawn from literature or from the group's experiences that is re-

peated several times. For example consider this line from *The Very Hungry Caterpillar* (1981), <u>On Monday he ate through one apple.</u> If the teacher asked children to innovate on what the caterpillar ate on Monday, a child could offer the following: On Monday he ate through one <u>tomato.</u> When the teacher asks children to add new words to a line, as was done in the preceding example, the entire message is reread from the beginning to help children remember how composing proceeds.

2. The teacher and children *share the pen* as a message is written word by word. When new words are added to a line of text, the children reread the line up to the new or added word. In the earliest stages of writing development, the teacher may write the word for children. With time and development, the teacher shares the pen, inviting children to contribute a letter, several letters, or an entire word.

3. Where appropriate, the teacher encourages the child to stretch the word and say it slowly to predict the letters by analyzing the sounds (see word rubberbanding in chapter 8). Children may attempt any letter in the word in any order. Working within the child's zone of proximal development à la Vygotsky (1962), the teacher fills in those letters that children are unable to analyze on their own.

4. A word wall, like those recommended by Cunningham (1995), can be used as a writing resource for children in the classroom. Words can be listed on the wall as *words we know and can write, words we almost know,* and *words we need to analyze and write with help.*

5. As teachers and children write interactively, the teacher helps children learn directionality, punctuation, spaces, features of print, and capitalization. In this fashion, children learn the mechanics and the authoring processes necessary to eventually produce high-quality writing products.

Interactive writing sessions typically last from 5 to 30 minutes, depending on the nature of the text to be negotiated and the levels of student writing development. The goal of interactive writing is a neat, legible text; not (at least in the beginning) a totally accurate text. Some days the writing project will need to be stopped and continued the next day, which teaches children the value of persisting with a piece of writing. The rereadings and discussion of the text on subsequent days also help children learn to value the processes of conversation and rethinking that always attend the production of quality writing.

In our former first-grade classrooms, we focused interactive writing on the reproduction, innovations, and original production of big books. Because children loved reading big books, it was not long before they wanted to write their own (Figure 11.16). We began our interactive writing of big books by innovating on the big book as a class. During group discussions following the reading of a big book, we invited children to invent a different story line or problem based on the story in the big book. For example, after finishing reading the big book *Hubert Hunts His Hum* (Lock, 1980), we rewrote it as *Hubert Hunts His Hair.* Children contributed ideas for rewriting the big book as a group. We wrote part of the ideas on blank pages of an empty big book while inviting children to come and help write the ideas by *sharing the pen.* Later during the day, children illustrated the pages of the big book.

Think of at least five writing projects that could be used in an interactive writing session.

Figure 11.16   Child-authored big book

Later during the year, children, often in pairs, rewrote or condensed stories they had heard or read on their own into a big book to be shared with others by sharing the pen between or among several peer aged writers. Older children (grades 2 and 3) were often invited to read their big books to younger children in kindergarten and first grade. These coauthored big books were a popular way for our young students to share in the writing of big books while learning about the

Figure 11.17   Writing activities across the grades

Personal		*Public*
1. Notes	34. Couplets	1. Maps
2. Friendly Letters	35. Triplets	2. Business Letters
3. Lists	36. Quatrain	3. Teachers to Administrators
4. Tasks	37. Cinquain	4. Notes from Teachers to Parents
5. Goals	38. Haiku	5. Resumes
6. Shopping Lists	39. Sonnets	6. Orders
7. Christmas	40. Limericks	7. Contracts
8. Wish Lists	41. Free Verse	8. Collection Notices
9. Labels	42. Tanka	9. Bills
10. Boxes	43. Septolet	10. Recommendations
11. Objects	44. Lantern	11. Promotional Letters
12. Clothing	45. Diamante	12. Instructional Letters
13. Treasure Hunt Clues	46. Messages	13. Birth Announcements
14. Assignments	47. Phone	14. Research Reports
15. Cards	48. Warning	15. Public Notices
16. Get Well	49. Information	16. Obituaries
17. Greeting	50. Family Management–Budgets	17. Newspapers
18. Holiday	51. Scrapbooks	18. Magazines
19. Sympathy	52. Baby Books	19. Books
20. Thank You	53. Travel Itineraries	20. Scripts
21. Romance	54. Applications	21. Musical Lyrics
22. Change of Address	55. Credit Cards	22. Critiques
23. Want Ads	56. Job	23. Evaluations
24. Interviews	57. Social Security	24. Tax Forms
25. Instructions	58. College Scholarships	25. Eulogies
26. Newsletters	59. Pagent	26. Court Orders
27. Postcards	60. Loan	27. Summons
28. Journals	61. Grants	28. Speeches
29. Dialogue Journal	62. Checks	29. Pamphlets
30. Graffiti		30. Wanted Posters
31. Diaries		31. Posters
32. Job Charts		32. Lesson Plans
33. Poems		33. Informational

conventions, mechanics, and stylistic devices of writing. In Figure 11.17, we list various types of writing projects that teachers and children may want to consider together during interactive writing.

Traveling Tales

The traveling tales backpack activity (Figure 11.18) can be used to involve parents with their children in collaborative writing projects (Reutzel & Fawson, 1990; Reutzel & Fawson, 1998; Richgels & Wold, 1998; Yellin & Blake, 1994). A traveling tales backpack is filled with writing media and guidelines for parents in working with their

A traveling tales backpack is used to involve parents with their children in writing together by including a short description of the writing process as well as a host of writing media.

Figure 11.18   Traveling tales backpack

children at home to produce a self-selected writing project. The contents of the traveling tales backpack include:

Plain unlined paper

Scissors

Lined paper

Small stapler

Staples

Construction paper—multiple colors

Letter stencils

Brass fasteners

Drawing paper

Card stock

Poster paper

Hole punch

Crayons

Yarn

Watercolors

Wallpaper for book covers

Water-based markers

Glue stick

Colored pencils

Pencils

Tape

Paper clips

Felt-tip pens

Ruler

Felt-tip calligraphy pens

The backpack is sent home with a child for two nights. Parents are contacted by phone or note before the backpack is sent home to maximize involvement and success. Parents and children can choose a variety of ways to respond to their favorite book: They can write shape stories, pocketbooks, accordion books, or cards. Included in the traveling tales backpack is a letter (Figure 11.19) to the parents with guidelines on how to engage their child in the writing process.

After completing the project, parent and child are invited to share their work with the entire group of children in the author's chair at school. After sharing, the written product is placed on display for the other children to read and enjoy.

WRITING BY CHILDREN

One effective application of the writing process is found in responding to literature. Readers deepen and extend their interpretation and understanding of stories when they respond through writing. Although writing should never be thought of as the only way to respond to a story, it certainly should be considered an effective and enjoyable alternative to oral discussion. In fact, discussions are often more productive when students have already responded to their reading through writing. Writing encourages students to reflect on their insights and interpretations gained from reading as well as to reflect on the processes they used during reading to arrive at their interpretations. Also, writing about reading helps students become better readers. Calkins (1994) has said that writing helps children become insiders on the reading process. By constructing their own texts, children develop insights into how authors write. They begin to read other texts through the eyes of an author, noticing structure, sequence, and style. In this way, children become better readers because they are writers. Although the list of possible ways to respond to reading in writing is almost endless, we have selected several techniques that we have found to be successful when used with younger children (chapter 12 also provides several literature-response writing activities).

Classroom Post Office for Letter Writing

A variation of the book message center described previously in this chapter is a classroom post office. Children like to write letters to each other, the teacher, and the principal. We encouraged our students to write letters to their peers, the teacher, or a principal when they had read a particularly interesting book and wanted to share it with others. We set up a post office station with slots for "in-class" and "out-of-class" mail. Children were invited to send letters about books they have read to students, faculty, and staff in the school.

A classroom post office can be set up for students to write letters to their peers, the teacher, or a principal when they read a particularly interesting book and want to share it with others.

To implement a post office for letter writing in the classroom, one student is selected to serve as postmaster and another as mail carrier. These responsibilities are rotated on a weekly basis to allow all children to participate in these roles. The postmaster sorts mail by classroom and fills the mail carrier's bag. The mail carrier takes letters to the classrooms of other teachers and children as well as to the librarian and the principal. Teachers, staff members, students, and the principal enjoy reading the information about books, poems, and stories shared with them through the classroom post offices.

Wordless Picture Books

Wordless picture books are a relatively new arrival in the world of picture books (D. Norton, 1999). In these books, the illustrations tell the entire story. Wordless picture books offer teachers and children opportunities to compose their own print to accompany the pictures.

In wordless picture books, the illustrations tell the entire story.

Figure 11.19 Traveling tales parent letter

Dear Parent(s):

Writing activities provided at home can have a great influence on your child's reading and writing development. Traveling Tales is a backpack that includes a variety of writing materials for use by you and your child. As per our conversation, we encourage you to work together cooperatively with your child to create a story that will be shared at school. *Please avoid competition or trying to outdo others.*

Your child has been given this backpack for two nights. If you need more time, please call us at XXX–XXXX. Otherwise, we will be looking forward to you and your child returning the Traveling Tales backpack in two days.

We would like to suggest some guidelines that may help you have a successful and enjoyable Traveling Tales experience with your child.

1.   Help your child brainstorm a list of ideas or topics by asking questions that will invite him or her to express ideas, interests, feelings, etc., about which he or she may wish to write. Stories about personal experiences (factual or fictional), information stories that tell of an area that your child finds interesting, biographies of family members or others, and stories of science or history are possible topics.

2.   After selecting a topic, help your child decide which of the writing materials included in the Traveling Tales backpack he or she will need to use to create his or her story. Suggest that the story may take several different forms. Some ideas include (1) poetry, (2) fold-out books, (3) puppet plays, (4) pocket books, (5) backward books, and (6) shape books.

3.   Help your child think through or rehearse the story before beginning writing. You may wish to write down some of the ideas your child expresses for him or her to use in writing the first draft.

4.   Remember, your child's first draft is a rough draft. It may contain misspellings, poor handwriting, and incomplete ideas. This should be expected. Be available to answer questions as your child works on the first draft. Be careful to encourage him or her to keep writing and not worry about spelling, punctuation, etc. Tell him or her to just do his or her best and both of you can work on correctness later. *This is the idea development stage of writing.*

5.   Once the first draft is completed, try to involve others in the household by asking them to listen to the first draft read aloud. Reading one's writing aloud helps writ-

ers determine the sensibleness of the message. Be sure to tell those who are invited to listen to be encouraging rather than critical. Ask questions about ideas that were unclear or were poorly developed. Questions help a writer think about his or her writing without feeling defensive.

6.   Write down the questions and suggestions made by the home audience. Talk with your child about how a second draft could use these suggestions to make the story easier to understand or more exciting. Remember to be supportive and encouraging! Offer your help, but encourage your child to make his or her best efforts first.

7.   After the second draft is completed, your child may wish to read his or her writing to the family group again. If so, encourage it. If not, it is time to edit the writing. Now is the time to correct spellings, punctuation, etc. Praise your child for his or her attempts and tell him or her you want to help make his or her writing the best it can be. Show your child which words are misspelled and why. Do the same with punctuation and capitalization.

8.   With the editing complete, the writing is ready to be revised for the final time. When your child writes the final draft, encourage him or her to use neat handwriting as a courtesy to the reader. Feel free to help your child at any point as he or she makes final revisions.

9.   Once finished, encourage the members of your family or household to listen to the final story. This practice will instill confidence in your child as he or she shares his or her writing at school.

10.   We cordially invite you to come to school with your child, if possible, to share the writing you have done together. Your child will appreciate the support, and we would like to talk with you.

Thank you for your help. We appreciate your involvement. If you have an interesting or special experience and are unable to come to school with your child, we would appreciate hearing about these. Please call us or send a note with your child. We will be glad to call back or visit with you. Thanks again for your support. We hope you enjoyed your experiences!

Figure 11.20   Artist's drawing of a story frame board

Using wordless picture books is much like using the Language Experience Approach. Norton (1995, p. 220) offers several hints for selecting wordless picture books for sharing and instruction.

- Do the pictures follow a sequentially organized plot?
- Is the depth of detail appropriate for the children's age levels?
- Do the children have enough experiential background to interpret the illustrations?
- Is the size of the book appropriate for group sharing?
- Is the subject one that will appeal to children?

Wordless picture books are ideal for involving children in oral composing and dictating stories. For example, the teacher may select the Caldecott Award-winning wordless picture book *Noah's Ark* (Spier, 1977) or *Just in Passing* (Bonners, 1989), physically cut it apart, and temporarily mount the pages on separate pieces of chart paper or place them inside an acetate story frame board (Figure 11.20). (One disadvantage of the story frame board is that two copies of the book are needed to display both sides of the pages. However, this disadvantage is offset by the advantage of providing protection for the pictures in the book as well as the ease of cleanup and use.) A water-based pen can be used to record children's dictation on the acetate sheets of the story frame board and can be cleaned off with water and a dry rag. Chart paper is a little less easy to use and provides less protection for the original pages of the book.

When a wordless picture book like *Noah's Ark* (Spier, 1977) is introduced, children and teachers can begin by looking carefully at each picture in the book. They can discuss what they think is happening in each of the pictures. After this initial discussion, individual children can be called on to describe the events in a particular pic-

Descriptions dictated by the children can be written beneath wordless picture book pages on the chart or on the story frame board.

Figure 11.21   Children's pocketbooks

ture. The descriptions dictated by the children can be written beneath the wordless picture book pages on the chart or on the story frame board. The text of these dictated wordless picture book stories can be used for instruction in many of the same ways as the LEA group experience charts and big books.

Pocketbooks

For many years now, we have known that young children prefer small, soft-bound paperback books. Lowery and Grafft (1967) speculated that the improved attitudes of children who were given paperback books to read may be attributed to the size— thin books that could be read in a single sitting—and the coverings, which made books soft and easy to handle. Thus, we shared with our students another written response to books or stories they had read—the pocketbook. These books are 3 1/2 inches wide and 4 inches long, with condensed reproductions of a story or book that has been read aloud with a whole group or in a small group. In spite of the small size, children enjoy making illustrations for these books. Pocketbooks are small enough to fit in students' and teachers' pockets. Children often swapped their pocketbooks with each other, which acquainted them with a wide variety of books available for reading in the school and classroom libraries.

Teachers can use pocketbooks as rewards for outstanding individual achievements: Rather than giving out stickers or candy, teachers can reward children with a pocketbook from their pocket. Children enjoy pocketbooks as a means of responding in writing to their reading. An unexpected outcome of writing, sharing, and swapping pocketbooks among our students was an increased desire to read and write. Examples appear in Figure 11.21.

Reading Response Logs and Journals

One of many ways to invite children to respond to their reading of books is to use a reading log or journal. No particular format is required for these journals. For young children, we suggest that reading logs and journals be very open-ended by including

Pocketbooks are small books about 3 1/2 inches wide by 4 inches long with condensed reproductions of a story or book.

Reading response logs or journals are open-ended invitations to register one's feelings about a book in drawing, writing, or both.

Figure 11.22   A language routine lesson guide for reading instruction

Tune-In

(10% of allocated reading time or about 10 min.)

Enjoyment of favorite poems, songs, and jingles, displayed on enlarged text and chosen by request. There is likely to be a new piece for the day or a new activity, such as actions, for an old familiar piece.

Practices: Singing songs, poems, jingles, riddles, movement stories, puppetry, stories, chants, choral readings, naming, word rubberbanding, playing with words and letters, dictations, etc.

Old Favorites

(10% of allocated reading time or about 10 min.)

The children choose an old favorite story, chart, poem, etc., which they have enjoyed in the enlarged format. Cloze and masking can be used to encourage predictions. Words and letters can also be discussed.

Practices: Shared book experience, group language experience approach (LEA) charts, overhead transparencies of poems or stories, and readers' theater scripts.

Learning About Language

(15% of allocated reading time or about 15 min.)

During this very brief period, something useful in decoding the new story today will be taught or something previously taught will be reviewed.

Practices: Mini-lessons on decoding, strategy instructions, drastic strategy, word rubberbanding, predicting, brainstorming, mapping, webbing, organizing, zip cloze, etc.

Adapted from *Stability and Change in Literary Learning* (pp. 44–46) by D. Holdaway, 1984, Portsmouth, NH: Heinemann Educational Books, Copyright 1984 by Heinemann Educational Books.

unlined paper, so that children can register their meanings for their reading through both drawing and writing. Reading logs and journals should be bound and the date for each entry should be registered; if each morning is begun by reviewing the calendar, day, and date, children can copy this information from a display in the classroom. As a counting activity, children can number the pages in their journals/logs from 1 to 10 and beyond. Early in the year, journal entries should be regular, but not necessarily daily.

Language routines provide an alternative organizational framework to the basal readers' Directed Reading Activity.

ESTABLISHING DAILY READING AND WRITING ROUTINES FOR YOUNG CHILDREN

Children develop a sense of security when the school day revolves around an established daily routine. Many teachers rely heavily on basal readers for providing reading instruction. The reading lessons found in most U.S. classrooms usually followed the six-step format of the Directed Reading Activity (DRA) authored by E. Betts

New Story

(10% to 15% of allocated reading time or about 10 to 15 min.)

Introducing a new story, generally in an enlarged format, or composing a new story from an old favorite.

Practices: Shared book experience, group LEA charts, and overheads of new books, poems, songs, etc.

Independent Reading and Writing

(50% of allocated reading and writing time, or about 50 min.)

This is the reason for all of the previous activity: Children and the environment are now ready for independent involvement and output activities. This period can be subdivided into two periods of reading and writing, for ease of administration.

Practices: Logo language, reading nook sustained silent reading (SSR), read-along tapes, older with younger, word banks (key vocabulary), paired reading, reading conferences, the writing workshop, drama center.

Reading Period: Logo language, reading nook, SSR, read-along tapes, older children reading with younger, word banks (key vocabulary), assisted reading, individual reading conferences, story corners, performances, and small-group strategy lessons.

Writing Period: Writing workshop, mini-lessons, peer conferences, editing, revising, publishing, authors' chairs, sustained silent writing (SSW) projects.

Closing Sharing Time

(5% of allocated reading time or about 5 min.)

Students share books they have read or writing projects published.

(1946) or the format of the Directed Reading Thinking Activity of Stauffer (1969). Although the DRA and DRTA are two ways of designing reading instruction, an alternative and effective scaffolding for structuring early reading instruction is called **language routines** (LRs). Language routines have been used extensively and successfully in New Zealand, Australia, and Canada.

Language routines are specific, short, teacher-organized language learning opportunities. In balanced literacy classrooms, teachers who use language routines establish a variety of subroutines for sharing language and literature with children. Although basal reader instruction often focuses on skill instruction, balanced reading instruction focuses on processing (strategy selection and application) and responding to connected, meaningful language (comprehension and fluency development) that naturally engages the interests of children.

Don Holdaway (1984) describes LRs for working with young children that have undergone years of extensive field testing by teachers in Australia, New Zealand, the United States, and Canada. An outline of adapted routines is found in Figure 11.22.

Tune-In

Each school day is begun by warming children up or tuning them in to language. The **tune-in routine** is a time for teachers to help children focus on language and acquaint them with a variety of language learning opportunities. Young children and teachers participate in reading poems, jingles, chants, and word games, or in singing songs. Often, teachers select songs and chants to support specific reading instructional goals, such as learning the alphabet, recognizing words, understanding decoding strategies, or predicting. Playing with language is also common during the tune-in routine. For example, *Sniglets* (R. Hall, 1984) can be an intriguing way to help children to tune in to language. Sniglets are words that are not found in the dictionary but should be. For example, the Sniglet for the burnt, black piece of cereal in the box of puffed rice is a *rice roach*.

Pundles (Nash & Nash, 1980) can help children find enjoyment in exploring and playing with language. Can you tell what this Pundle means: iriigihiti? Look carefully. Can you see it represents the common phrase "right between the eyes"? Riddles and jokes are also very useful resources for sharing during the tune-in routine.

The teacher should enlarge any printed material selected for tune-in (poems, chants, songs, etc.) so that the entire group of children can read the print. Enlarging a text can be accomplished in any number of ways. If the text of a poem, song, or joke is to be used only a few times, the chalkboard may be used. If a text is to be used again and again, however, we suggest using a large chart or tablet displayed on an easel. With frequent use, these charts may become torn and frayed around the edges; to prevent this, 2-inch-wide library cellophane tape can be placed around the edges of each page on the tablet or charts. To provide easy access on later occasions, we also suggest that the first page or two of the chart or tablet be used as a table of contents. Tablets and charts can be read again and again by individuals or small groups of children during another LR called *independent output activities* (see p. 439).

Another means for enlarging the text of books, poems, or songs is to transcribe the text on color overhead transparencies. Short books can be photocopied on color overhead transparencies. From teacher experiences, children do not seem to enjoy the use of black and white transparency texts and books as much as teacher-produced charts, big books, or books copied onto color transparencies.

When using the tune-in routine to introduce new songs, poems, or chants on a daily basis, teachers conscientiously provide time for expanding children's literary horizons while fanning the fires of language enjoyment. Because tune-in activities take place with the whole class, we have also found that the risks associated with learning to read become minimized while children are simultaneously rewarded with highly successful, motivating, and supportive language learning opportunities.

Old Favorites

The **old-favorite language routine** provides daily time to return to and reread favorite enlarged texts of songs, poems, chants, and books for enjoyment or to deepen understanding. In this way, the old-favorite routine provides children with massive and regular practice of familiar texts.

Because old-favorite books have been read for enjoyment on previous occasions, Holdaway (1981) suggests that this may be an appropriate time for deepening understanding of the reading process and for teaching the skills and strategies associated with reading in the context of a familiar book. When focusing on skills, caution should be exercised not to isolate skill instruction from a meaningful context if at all possible. We remind ourselves constantly that skills and strategies are best taught in a whole-to-part-to-whole manner, which means that skills and strategies are taught in context, isolated if necessary, and returned to context. In the Wellington, New Zealand, handbook for teachers entitled *Reading in Junior Classes* (Department of Education, 1985), teachers are told:

> Children, learning to read, have to pay particular attention to print. It is sometimes necessary, then, to have them focus on detail. They may temporarily isolate, for example, a letter, and identify the sound usually associated with it. But any learning of separate items needs to be combined with other items of information, both in the text and in the reader, before its use is truly understood and applied. Separate items of learning need to be *taken back into reading,* i.e., teachers should ensure that any item which has been isolated for attention should be looked at again in its original context, and what has been learned applied later in other contexts. (p. 32)

Helping children learn about the parts of a book and the way in which print functions can be explored within the pages of an old-favorite big book. (As previously mentioned, a big book is an enlargement of a standard-sized trade book.) Teachers may begin book and print concept instruction by pointing out the front and back of a big book. Also, when the teacher points to the print during reading, children learn how the print moves in a linear direction from left to right and from top to bottom on a page. Research has shown that children learn as much about the concepts of printed language, such as directionality or line movement, from this type of contextualized and natural demonstration in a big book as they do from isolated, direct instruction lessons on book parts and print directions (Reutzel, Oda, & Moore, 1989).

A big book is an enlarged standard-sized trade book.

Using self-adhesive notes to cover up or mask selected words in a big book can encourage children to give careful attention to using context clues. Interesting words in big books can be copied from the book on cards and stored in a class word bank for later practice by children.

Children's understanding of books can be deepened through dramatization. A favorite book may be dramatized as a play. Puppet plays are particularly exciting for young children. Children can role-play parts of a story or certain characters. In the story "The Little Red Hen," a group of children might be given a stick puppet for each character—the dog, the cat, the goose, and the little red hen. When repetitive parts of a story are read, such as, " 'Not I,' said the . . . ," the group of children given stick puppets for that character are prompted to hold them up and join in a unison or choral reading of that part of the book. Also, favorite stories can be turned into reader's theater scripts for dramatizing a story with minimum props. Rehearsing for a dramatization provides additional opportunities for reading practice.

Techniques for helping children develop word-recognition and phonic skills are described in detail in chapter 8.

The old-favorites routine provides a time and a context for massive practice of favorite books and texts as well as time for teaching reading strategies and skills in the familiar context of a favorite book or text.

Learning About Language

Holdaway (1984) describes the **learning about language routine** as a time for teaching a "very brief skill lesson" (p. 36). Such a skill lesson should not be an isolated skill-and-drill lesson; rather, it should be a short lesson provided in a meaningful situational and language context. Calkin's (1986) idea of a mini-lesson seems to have been created with a similar purpose in mind. For example, a teacher who wishes

*The **learning about language** routine is a time for teaching a very brief skill lesson.*

to teach his or her children about the alphabet, or linguistic units called *rimes* (see chapter 8), can involve them in chants, games, rhymes, and songs emphasizing certain letter names and letter or letter combination sounds. Children can be asked to bring environmental print to school, such as soda can logos, cereal boxes, and candy wrappers. These materials can be put into letter categories using beginning letter sounds. For example a group of *S* environmental print logos could be bound together on 5 by 7-inch index cards to help children learn about the *S* letter name and sound.

Other learning about language lessons may center on pointing out and discussing the role of punctuation marks in enlarged print. Favorite words selected from familiar books can be placed on cards to be stored in a class word bank to teach word-recognition skills. The learning about language routine may also be an appropriate time to share and discuss various forms and genres of writing with children, such as notes, letters, books, cards, posters, fairy tales, and folktales, as well as to provide brief mini-lessons on handwriting, writing conventions, and mechanics (e.g., punctuation, capitalization, and spelling). The learning about language routine can be used to present and review the process approach to writing including drafting, conferencing, editing, and publishing. Most important, teachers should remember that when skill lessons for reading and writing are provided, four criteria should be considered and met, if at all possible:

See chapter 12 for a discussion of the writing process.

- The lesson should grow out of an observed student need or desire to enrich children's literacy horizons and not just to teach the next skill on the basal or district skill list.
- A mini-lesson is not a maxi-lesson, and as such should be brief—5 to 10 minutes maximum.
- The skill selected for instruction should be one that helps young children read better and with greater enjoyment. Lessons focusing on the syllabication, diacritical marks, the schwa, finding the accent, and so on do little to meet this criterion.
- Finally, any skill selected for instruction should be demonstrated with real texts and/or books the children have been reading or writing, thus providing a meaningful language context for instruction.

New Story

*The **new-story routine** is a time for children to experience a brand-new story.*

The **new-story routine** is often the highlight of the day and is a time for children to discover a brand-new story. Before introducing the new story, the teacher should select a book that contains interesting illustrations and language. Books such as *On Market Street* (Lobel, 1981), *The Carrot Seed* (Krauss, 1945), and *The Napping House* (A. Wood, 1984) are ideal because the illustrations match the text and the language is predictable, playful, and interesting. Because of increasing availability, many teachers are selecting information books more often, such as *Frogs* (Henwood, 1988), *A Checkup With the Doctor* (K. A. Smith, 1989), *Spiders* (N. S. Barrett, 1984), and *Trucks* (N. S. Barrett, 1989) for sharing during the new-story routine.

When introducing a new story, teachers may choose a big book and involve the entire group of children in a shared book experience, or they may choose to use several traditional-sized copies of a story in a basal with a small group of children. Teachers often begin the new story by talking about it. They may draw children's attention to the front and back covers of the book, the title page, the names of the author(s) and illustrator(s), the illustrations, and any interesting print displays. A question such as, "Have we read other books by this author or illustrator?" may be discussed. During the introduction of each new story, children may be asked to make predictions about the story by looking carefully at the book cover and illustrations. (Prediction and other reading preparatory activities for younger readers are described in detail later in this chapter.)

After introducing the new book or story, the teacher should read the story aloud straight through in a dramatic and enthusiastic fashion. After this reading, children and teacher discuss the book, confirm or correct their predictions, elaborate on favorite parts, talk about any surprises, and relate the story to their own experiences. Following a discussion, time permitting, the book may be read a second time using hand actions or rhythm instruments to increase student involvement. Subsequent readings may be used to induce word-solving strategies in context and to focus on unfamiliar vocabulary words.

Independent Output Activities

The **independent output activities** routine is aimed at involving individual children in reading, writing, and other language-output activities. Providing independent reading and writing opportunities selected from a wide range of possibilities is the ideal. Teachers often create stations or centers around the room to involve children in a variety of reading and writing activities. During this time, the teacher may be occupied in a single center with a group of children conducting a mini-lesson or a reading response group. When not occupied with a single group of children, the teacher is free to move about the classroom during independent output activities time to engage in conferences with individual students, to offer help and suggestions, or to conduct informal evaluations of individual progress.

*The **independent output activities** routine is aimed at involving individual children in reading, writing, and other language-output activities.*

Several classroom centers can be arranged to require a minimum of teacher supervision. In fact, centers that require minimum teacher supervision are ideal and provide the teacher freedom and flexibility to meet individual student needs. A reading nook; a read-along table with cassette tapes of books, charts, and logo language collections; a logo language wall; message boards; a post office; big books; a publishing area; and many other stations can be created to provide for children's varied output. Initially, some teachers may choose to place students in flexible traveling groups to rotate through certain stations on a time schedule. Rotation times can be determined by the school schedule or by a classroom-imposed time schedule, and can be signaled by the ringing of a cooking timer bell, a school bell, or playing the first five notes of Beethoven's *Fifth Symphony* on a piano or electronic keyboard, as Ashton-Warner (1963) described in her book *Teacher.* The order of rotation through classroom stations can be prescribed by using a rotating wheel like the one shown in Figure 11.23.

These stations are described in chapter 9.

Flexible traveling groups are described in detail in chapter 9.

With time, experience, and effort, teachers and children may feel comfortable enough with each other to relax time and rotation schedules to encourage greater flexibility and spontaneity during the independent output activities routine.

Sharing Time

As a concluding language routine, during **sharing time** children can be gathered together in a whole group or in several smaller groups to share the things they have been reading or writing during the day. Several types of language sharing strategies have been developed and used successfully in elementary classrooms. First is the author's chair. A chair in the classroom can be designated, even decorated, as the author's chair. Children who have published their writing in one form or another can

***Sharing time** is a time when children gather together in a whole group or several smaller groups to share the things they have been reading or writing during the day.*

Figure 11.23 Rotation wheel
(SSR, sustained silent reading;
SSW, sustained silent writing)

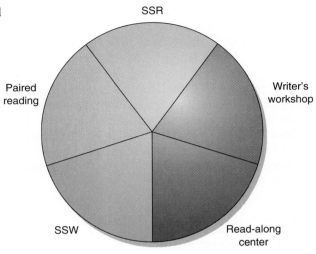

be given an opportunity to share their work with the class. Although a single author's chair is useful, we found that, as more and more children began writing and publishing in our own classrooms, a single author's chair was insufficient. Thus, our students proposed authors' corners.

Authors' corners provide more students with the opportunity to share their work with a smaller audience. Each author is invited by the teacher to stand in an assigned corner in the classroom. Authors are asked to share a bit of their writing project with the group to capture the interest of their peers. Each student shares his or her project briefly. The remaining students in the classroom audience can select which of the authors' corners they want to attend that day.

Authors' chairs and corners provide children with multiple opportunities to share their written or published works.

A similar means of providing time for children to read their favorite book aloud to an audience is the reader's chair or readers' corners. These reading and sharing opportunities are important for those children who have read a particularly interesting book that day or who want to demonstrate to their peers their emerging ability to read.

Readers' chairs and corners provide younger students with opportunities to demonstrate their emerging abilities.

A whole-group sharing approach called the *sharing circle* allows children time to share in abbreviated form how they have spent their time in the independent output activities time that day. Children briefly share the title of the book they have read or written, the play they have been working on, or even on occasion perform a play for the entire group when scheduled with the teacher. Typically, individual sharing progresses rapidly around the entire circle and class of participants. The only difficulty often experienced with sharing time is the children's apparent enjoyment. Stopping is always difficult!

If the right conditions can be created in classrooms, children can learn to read and write as naturally as they learn to speak. No child should be led to believe that learning to read and write is something they cannot do.

INSTRUCTIONAL STRATEGIES FOR TEACHING YOUNG CHILDREN TO READ AND WRITE

Helping emergent readers and writers succeed requires that teachers know and be able to use a wide variety of instructional strategies effectively. Emergent readers require instructional support that is balanced in representing the major cueing systems found in written language, semantics or meaning, syntax or grammar and order, and visual–sound relations. Emergent and early readers need help in gaining an understanding of how to look at and process the visual details of print, how to decode an alphabetic language by putting sound values with visual symbols, and how to develop and apply comprehension and literature-response strategies to the comprehension and enjoyment of printed texts. In the final section of this chapter, instructional strategies are presented to help teachers work with emergent and early readers to successfully develop concepts of print, decoding, reading comprehension skills, and literature-response strategies toward the goal of developing independent, silent, fluent readers.

LEARNING ABOUT WORDS

Environmental Print

Old cereal boxes, signs, bumper stickers, and candy wrappers can be used in interesting ways to give children confidence in reading as well as to help them come to understand how print works. A display area, bulletin board, or wall can be designated as a logo language wall. Children can be asked to bring environmental print or product logos from home to put on the wall. Some teachers request that children bring environmental print that begins with a particular letter sound. Other teachers simply fill the wall with print children bring from home and can read.

Reading environmental print such as product labels, signs, or bumper stickers can give children an early sense of success in learning to read.

Another way environmental print can be used is to make I-can-read books. Children select from a group of collected logos to make these books. I-can-read books are often dictated to the teacher or some other adult, and the product logos are used in place of specific dictated words. These books are easily read by every child and become a source of confidence building and enjoyment.

Teachers can ask children to bring environmental print to school for a specific letter name and sound. These items can then be used for specific lessons on letter names and sounds while maintaining an authentic language context for learning the alphabetic principle. After discussing and displaying letter-specific environmental print, teachers and children can cut and paste environmental print items onto 5 by 7-inch plain index cards. These specific letter-name and letter-sound environmental print collections can be bound together with a clip or ring to be practiced in small groups or by individuals in center or station activities. Phonic generalizations such as the final silent *e* can also be taught from known environmental print. Teachers can collect product logos and bind these items together, similar to the alphabet letter collections.

Children can use environmental print to produce classroom signs using logos to substitute for written word(s). They can also cut up environmental print to send notes to each other or to make word collages for an art activity.

We have field tested these strategies with young children and have experienced exciting results. Hiebert and Ham (1981) documented that children who were taught with environmental print learned significantly more letter names and sounds than did children who learned alphabet letters without using environmental print. McGee, Lomax, and Head (1988) have also found that young children attend to print in environmental displays and are not just reading the entire context.

Children who were taught with environmental print learned significantly more letter names and sounds than did children who learned alphabet letters without using environmental print.

Learning the Alphabetic Principle

Research has shown that children learn to read without being able to identify every letter of the alphabet (Teale, 1987). In fact, children are constantly learning how to read. They pick up sight words off bathroom doors, cereal boxes, and billboards.

Children need to learn the alphabetic principle to become fluent and independent readers.

Most children can write and recognize their own name without mastering the identification of *every* alphabet letter name and sound. Conversely, no sensible individual will argue against the fact that children need to learn the alphabetic principle to become fluent and independent readers. As stated in chapter 8, alphabetic principle is the knowledge that speech sounds can be represented by certain letter(s). How does one learn the alphabetic principle, and what does this fact imply for teachers and parents? Learning letter names and sounds is most effectively done when it is enjoyable and meaningful for young children. Put another way, it must have a purpose and make sense to a 5-year-old!

According to the reports *Becoming a Nation of Readers* (R. C. Anderson et al., 1985), *Beginning to Read* (Adams, 1990b), and *Preventing Reading Difficulties in Young Children* (Snow, Burns, & Griffin, 1998), the purpose of phonics instruction is to apply the alphabetic principle, the concept that written letters roughly represent certain sounds used in spoken language. Phonics instruction should focus on only the most important letter–sound relationships. Learning the alphabetic principle does not necessarily imply that all letter–sound combinations, rules, and exceptions need to be explicitly taught one at a time for years on end. The fact is that young children do not need this amount of instructional overkill to induce the alphabetic principle.

There are many ways children can be made aware of letter names and sounds. One way to help children learn about the letters and sounds of the alphabet is to make use of environmental print. Labeling the classroom, using a child's name, and constructing personal word collections or word banks arranged in alphabetical order provide personally interesting and meaningful takeoff points for young children in learning the alphabet. A wall can be designated to display uppercase and lowercase alphabet letters. Children who bring environmental print items from home can place each logo underneath the appropriate alphabet letter display. This helps children become aware of the alphabet letters and alphabetical order in a natural way, one that extends beyond school boundaries. (Other suggestions for using environmental print are outlined in the previous section.)

An alphabet station or center that is stocked with alphabet puzzles, magnetic letters, sandpaper letters, alphabet games, stencils, flashcards, and alphabet charts should be part of every kindergarten or first-grade classroom.

An alphabet station or center stocked with alphabet puzzles, magnetic letters, sandpaper letters, alphabet games, stencils, flashcards, and alphabet charts should be a part of *every* kindergarten or first-grade classroom. In this station or center, children have an opportunity to explore the alphabet in a gaming and essentially risk-free setting. Inviting children to write, trace, copy, and experiment with letters in these centers can be accomplished without drill by furnishing the alphabet center with individual-sized chalkboards, dry-erase boards, clay trays, tracing paper, and painting easels. More tasty approaches can be added to this rich alphabet menu: Periodic eating of alphabet soup, animal crackers, and cereal, and sorting the letters or animals into letter categories increase children's awareness of letters, sounds, and alphabetical order.

Morrow (1993) specifically advises against the practice of teaching a letter a week.

Teachers should acquire or have on hand in the school collections of quality alphabet trade books. Books like *On Market Street* (Lobel, 1981), *Animalia* (Base, 1986), and *The Z Was Zapped* (Van Allsburg, 1987) are just a few of the many delightful alphabet books that can be used to teach children the alphabet as a whole rather than a letter a week, or one at a time (Reutzel, 1992). Morrow (1993) specifically advises against the practice of teaching a letter a week: "Systematic teaching of the alphabet, one letter per week, is not as successful as teaching children letters that are meaningful to them" (p. 214). By reading and rereading favorite alphabet books over a period of weeks and months, children naturally learn the names of all the alphabet letters and begin to associate the letters with many of their related sounds.

Weaver (1994) says that many teachers who teach the alphabet select specific songs, poetry, raps, and chants to emphasize a selected letter of the alphabet. For example, if a teacher wanted to emphasize the letter *S* for a day or so, he or she might select and enlarge on a chart to be read by the group the text of "Sally Go Round the Sun" or "Squid Sauce" (S. Dunn, 1987), or "Miss Mary Mac, Mac, Mac" (Hill, 1990a). Songs such as "See Saw, Margery Daw" (Dallin & Dallin, 1980) or "Sandy Land" (Dallin & Dallin, 1980) could be selected and enlarged on charts for practice and group singing. Shel Silverstein's (1974) "Sister for Sale" or Jack Prelutsky's (1984) "Sneaky Sue" poems could be likewise enlarged and used to emphasize the name and sound of the letter *S*. Sensory experiences can be integrated into this lesson as well. A sip of Sprite, a bite of a Snickers candy bar, a long spaghetti noodle to munch on, and a handful of Skittles to taste can successfully emphasize *S*. Art experiences, with children creating pictures using an *S,* can be used as the beginning point. Collages of things that begin with *S,* such as a sack, screw, safety pin, salt, silver, or sand, can be created and displayed. In this **print-rich environment** and through teacher-planned experiences with the alphabet, children learn the alphabet in natural, enjoyable, and meaningful ways. (See Appendix A, "Resources for Teachers," for poetry, songs, chants, and other sources useful for conveying the alphabetic principle to emergent readers.)

A listing of poetry, song, and chant titles, and sources useful for conveying the alphabetic principle to emergent readers are found in Appendix A.

Acquiring Phonemic Awareness

In recent years, a number of researchers have emphasized the importance of developing phonemic awareness among emergent readers (Adams, 1990a; Bear, Templeton, Invernizzi, & Johnston, 1996; Blevins, 1997, 1998; Cunningham, 1995; Ericson & Juliebo, 1998; Fox, 1996; Goswami & Bryant, 1990; Lyons, 1998; Moustafa, 1997; National Science Academy, 1998; Strickland, 1998; Wilde, 1997). It is estimated that roughly 20% of young children lack phonemic awareness (Blevins, 1997). Phonemic awareness is defined both conceptually and in terms of performance. Conceptually, phonemic awareness is defined as an understanding that spoken words are made up of sounds. In terms of performance, phonemic awareness is defined as the ability to pick out and manipulate sounds in spoken words. So, when speaking of phonemic awareness, awareness is not enough. Children must be able to perform specified tasks—they must be able to manipulate spoken sounds.

Phonemic awareness is defined as an understanding that spoken words are made up of sounds.

Adams (1990a, 1990b), in her landmark research review on beginning reading, asserted that the two best predictors of early reading success are alphabet recognition and phonemic awareness. According to Adams, there are several basic performance-related phonemic awareness tasks:

Think about the types of performance tasks Adams recommended for young readers.

- Hearing rhymes (rime)
- Hearing alliteration (onset)
- Hearing assonance (vowel or vowel combination sounds)
- Hearing and recognizing the nonmatching sound or word (oddity)
- Hearing and blending syllables in words
- Splitting syllables and oral blending (onset-rime-whole word)
- Analyzing words into syllables and sounds (segmenting)
- Manipulating sounds in words (substitutions and deletions)
- Connecting sounds with letters for spelling

It is important to note here that phonemic awareness training focuses only on the auditory modality—hearing. No written words are being presented or analyzed in combination with the sound values during phonemic awareness training. Phonemic awareness training is a prerequisite to phonics instruction because phonics instruction presupposes the ability to hear and manipulate sound values in decoding unfamiliar words. Many researchers have indicated that as little as 11 to 15 hours of intensive phonemic awareness training spread over an appropriate time frame (no more than 10 minutes daily in kindergarten) can achieve the desired result. Matched with the tasks just shown, we provide several examples in Figure 11.24 of tasks appropriate for training phonemic awareness.

Take the tasks that Adams recommends and put them into a scope and sequence of instruction as Blevins recommends.

Phonemic awareness instruction should be intentional and logically sequenced from the whole to the parts—working from the known to the new. This means, generally, that we begin with words, move to syllables, then to syllable parts such as onset and rime, and then to individual sounds or phonemes (Blevins, 1997; Fox, 1996; Moustafa, 1997; Strickland, 1998a, 1998b). Blevins (1997) recommends a 20-week scope and sequence for teaching phonemic awareness as follows:

Rhyme/alliteration/assonance:	Weeks 1–10
Oddity tasks:	Weeks 2–12
Oral blending:	Weeks 3–20
Analyzing words into sounds:	Weeks 9–20
Manipulating sounds in words:	Weeks 16–20
Connecting sounds to letters for spelling:	Weeks 19–20

Research has clearly shown that once children acquire a basic level of phonemic awareness, phonics instruction can then be effective. Too many teachers do not take the time to develop their students' hearing of the sounds of language before introducing them to the unfamiliar world of connecting printed symbols with the sounds of spoken language.

Developmental Phonics for Early or Emergent Readers

Several key issues surround the teaching of phonics in a TO, WITH, and BY balanced literacy program. These issues clearly relate to which phonics skills are taught, how phonics is taught, and how much phonics is taught to make decoding ability *automatic*. Major issues for teaching phonics to young children include:

- Whole-to-Part-to-Whole Skill Instruction vs. Parts to Whole
- Utility vs. Totality
- Intentional vs. Accidental
- Contextual vs. Isolated
- Processes vs. Products

Whole to Part to Whole

Most researchers and practitioners realize that phonics should be taught from whole to parts to whole.

First, the concept of teaching phonics from whole to part to whole has long been recommended by Reutzel and Cooter (1992). D. Strickland (1998, p. 43) in her recent book, *Teaching Phonics Today: A Primer for Educators,* and Moustafa and Maldonado-Colon (1999) advocate the teaching of phonics to emergent and early readers using a whole-to-part-to-whole approach. The *whole* typically includes

Figure 11.24 Tasks for training phonemic awareness

From *Where the Sidewalk Ends* by Shel Silverstein. Copyright © 1974 by Evil Eye Music, Inc. From *Butterscotch Dreams* by Sonja Dunn. Portsmouth NH: Heinemann.

- Hearing rhymes
  Jimmie Jet and His TV Set
  I'll tell you the story of Jimmy Jet—
  And you know what I tell you is true.
  He loved to watch his TV set
  Almost as much as you.
  (Silverstein, 1974, pp. 28–29)

- Hearing alliteration (beginning sounds)
  Squid sauce good for supper
  Squid sauce good for lunch
  Squid sauce good for breakfast.
  (Dunn, 1987, p. 26)

- Oddity task—onset (sounds before the vowel in a syllable or word)
  Which word begins with a different sound: *run, fit, rat*?

- Oddity task—rime
  Which word does not rhyme: *sat, hit, mat*?

- Oddity task—short vowel
  Which word does not have the same sound in the middle: *mat, man, fin*?

- Oddity task—long vowel
  Which word does not have the same sound in the middle: *snake, meat, bait*?

- Syllable blending
  Listen to these word parts: *win . . . dow*. Say the word: *window*.

- Spliting syllables into onset and rime—oral blending
  Listen to these word parts: */s/ . . . at* Say the word: *sat*.

- Analyzing words into syllables
  Listen to this word: pilot. Say each syllable: pi/ lot.

- Analyzing words into onsets and rimes
  Listen to this word: sun. Say the first sound in the word, and then the rest of the word like this: (/s/ . . . un).

- Analyzing words into sounds
  Listen to this word as I stretch it: rrr . . . aaa . . . nnn. Now, say the word sound by sound with me: rrr . . . aaa . . . nnn. How many sounds do you hear? Let's count them: rrr (1) aaa (2) nnn (3).

- Manipulating sounds—substitution (initial, final, or vowel)
  Replace the first (last /m/ or vowel /a/) sound in the word *run* with /s/. (*sun, rum, ran*).

- Manipulating sounds—deletions
  Say the word *sun* without the /s/. (un)
  Say the word *sun* without the /n/. (su)
  Say the word *table* without the *ta*. (ble)

- Connecting sounds to letters for spelling
  Say the word *mat* slowly with me. Let's count the number of letters. Now, let's write the letter for each sound we hear as we stretch the word again. mmmmm . . . . . (m) . . . . . aaaaa . . . . . (a) . . . . . t (t). Now let's say the word we have written together—mat. (See prior section on interactive writing practices in this chapter.)

shared and guided reading participation (i.e., sharing "whole" stories and texts). The *part* typically refers to teaching mini-lessons on phonemic awareness, onsets and rimes, structural analysis, blending, segmenting, spelling, and so forth. Instructed phonic elements are usually drawn from the stories read in the "whole" context of shared or guided reading. A return to the *whole* in phonics instruction involves applying phonics skills in new or similar texts, in writing innovative texts, and in rereading stories or texts. Often during rereadings of the same text, teachers use masking, word and sentence strips, pocket charts, and sliding print windows to draw attention to instructed phonics elements in the whole of the text or story.

Utility Versus Totality

Second, the issue of *utility* versus *totality* centers on how much phonics instruction is needed and what type. Some educators advocate that all letters and sounds be learned as a prerequisite to reading stories and other texts. More recently, research indicates that children learn to use phonics elements by analogy—meaning the more words children know, the more they learn about how letters and letter groups and sounds or sound patterns connect. In short, a few powerful examples usually provide students with generalizable understandings about how sounds are put with letter map in language (Moustafa, 1997).

Learning a few sound-to-letter correspondence patterns leads students to learn others without the necessity of direct teaching of every sound-to-letter correspondence.

Children do not need to learn all of the letter names, all of the letter sounds (vowels and consonants), all of the letter positions (initial, medial, and final), and all of the letter combinations (blends, digraphs, and diphthongs) to begin to use phonics knowledge in reading and writing; they only need to learn a few connections to begin useful application. For example, most onsets are consonants. The easiest to blend consonants are continuous—those consonants that can be voiced so long as the individual has breath support to sustain sound, such as /s/ /m/ /f/ /n/ /l/ /r/. Continuous consonants and rimes such as *an, at,* and *ick* are easy to blend together to get pronounceable words that lie within a child's oral vocabulary. The point here is that with only a few consonants (onsets) and a few letter patterns (rimes), children can begin to form words in reading or writing. Immediate application of a few phonics exemplars motivates emergent and early readers to look carefully for patterns and letter–sound connections that facilitate further development in learning to read and write.

Intentional Versus Accidental

Phonics instruction must be intentional rather than accidental. This means teachers plan to teach specific phonics elements.

The third issue centers on teaching phonics intentionally rather than accidentally. This means that teachers have a plan for how they will proceed with phonics instruction instead of relying totally on incidental occurrences of phonics elements in texts or stories.

Contextual Versus Isolated

To teach phonics from the whole to parts to whole, instruction must begin with the context of connected language.

The fourth issue focuses on whether phonics elements should be taught in isolation or in conjunction with the language students are reading in their books or are writing in their stories. Recent research suggests that an in-out-in approach to teaching phonics is appropriate (Dept. of Education, Wellington, NZ, 1985; Fox, 1996; Moustafa & Maldonado-Colon, 1999; Strickland, 1998). Phonics needs to be taught in context, then isolated for brief attention, and then returned to the context of the same, similar, or related texts. For example, the book entitled *Who's in the Shed?* (Parkes, 1986) is filled with words that begin with the initial consonant digraph /sh/. It also contains a number of words that rhyme with *shed*, making the teaching of the rime *ed* appropriate. After making note of this regularity in the text, phonics lessons can focus children's attention on the /sh/ words in the text by using self-sticking notes to mask this letter combination. To focus on the rime *ed*, the teacher can write the rime on the board and ask children to combine various onsets (letters or letter combinations such as r, l, b, w, sl, sh) with it to make new words. These words can be written on cards as an interactive writing session where the teacher shares the pen with children. Word cards can be placed on the Word Wall under the heading of "ed" words. On the next rereading of the same text or of a different or similar text, children can be instructed to look carefully for words that contain the *ed* rime to add to the word cards on the Word Wall. Or, children could innovate on the text of *Who's in the Shed* by changing the story to *Who's in the bed.*

Processes Versus Products

The final issue is centered on the teaching of phonics processes as opposed to products. Many teachers feel that they should teach children the consonant blends, vowel diphthongs, and so on, one at a time rather than teaching children the processes of *blending* and *segmenting*. It is clear to anyone who thinks about this issue that *knowing how* to blend (or segment) will give children access to all of the "blends" in language. It is important that teachers teach children that "sounding out" words in reading and writing are reverse processes. In reading, to sound out means to blend letter sounds together to form words. In writing, to sound out means to take a word and segment it into its individual sounds and letters.

In summary, high-quality phonics instruction for emergent or early readers consists of:

Teaching students how to blend sounds rather than teaching them "the blends" is a more useful instructional process.

- A whole-to-part-to-whole lesson design
- A focus on early application of phonics knowledge to form words
- A sequence of phonics instruction as suggested here—
    Teach 4 to 5 onsets
    Teach 3 to 4 rimes
    Teach blending of onsets and rimes
    Continue teaching onsets (consonants and digraphs)
    Continue teaching rimes (37)
    Continue blending of onsets and rimes
    Teach vowel digraphs and diphthongs
    Segment words into syllables
    Segment syllables into onsets and rimes
    Segment rimes into single letter sounds and connect to letters
    Teach single compound words (*bathroom*) before other syllables, affixes,
        base words, prefixes, and suffixes
- A presentation of phonic elements to be learned in-context-out-of-context-in-context (in-out-in)
- An emphasis on developing process skills such as blending and segmenting rather than on instructing isolated phonic elements such as blends and diphthongs

Think about how the recommended sequence of phonics instruction can be put into a classroom time frame spanning 20 or more weeks of instruction.

Research on children's reading and writing acquisition (Adams, 1990a; Temple & Gillet, 1996) indicate that emergent and early readers' phonics knowledge is acquired developmentally. Application of developmental patterns that respect and align with how young children develop as readers, writers, and spellers is likely to achieve optimal results for both teachers and children.

HELPING YOUNG CHILDREN DEVELOP A SENSE OF STORY

Picture Schema Stories

Picture schema stories help students construct the order of a text based on meaning and comprehension of text.

Watson and Crowley (1988) describe schema stories as a reading strategy designed to require readers to "reconstruct the order of a text based on meaning and story grammar" (p. 263). A prelude to this strategy, appropriate for emergent readers, is a modification developed by Reutzel and Fawson (1987) known as *picture schema stories*. This approach uses wordless picture books or pictures copied from emergent-reader trade books. The pictures from the books are displayed in random order on a flannel board. Each picture is discussed. Questions about who is in the picture, what the character is doing, and so on may be asked. A picture from the display is handed to selected children. The teacher asks, "Who has the first picture in the story?" The child who thinks he or she has the first picture indicates this and explains why. The teacher places the pictures in linear order from top to bottom or left to right in the display. The teacher then reads the story aloud while the children watch their picture predictions at the board or on the chart. Much like the literature web (see p. 449), the picture schema story activity can be extended to include a dictation of responses to the story and possible language extensions. The picture schema story can be mounted on the top of chart paper for recording the children's responses (oral dictation) about the story. These responses can be read later.

DEVELOPING COMPREHENSION WITH YOUNG CHILDREN

Picture Story Frames

Fowler (1982) described a strategy for developing a sense of story called *story frames.* Reutzel and Fawson (1987) adapted this strategy to be used with emergent readers. Several paperback picture books and emergent-level trade books are purchased and physically cut apart. Old basal stories can also be used. If text accompanies the pictures, and it often does, the text is cut away. The pictures are placed in a story frame board covered with acetate sheets, as shown in Figure 11.20 on p. 432.

Pictures that portray the major story elements (i.e., setting, problems, attempts, etc.) are selected to be used in the story frame board (Reutzel & Fawson, 1987). These selected pictures are then placed in each frame of the story frame board in the proper story sequence. Each picture is placed near the top of the story frame, leaving room at the bottom of the frame to record children's descriptions of what the picture is about.

Picture story frame activities are ideally used with small groups for composing a story based on story structure knowledge.

The picture story frame activity is ideally used with smaller groups of children, ranging from five to eight. Before taking down any ideas on the acetate sheets of the story frame board, the teacher invites children to look at each picture of the story in order. He or she may direct the children to "think about what the author may have

Figure 11.25 Artist's drawing of random order literature web

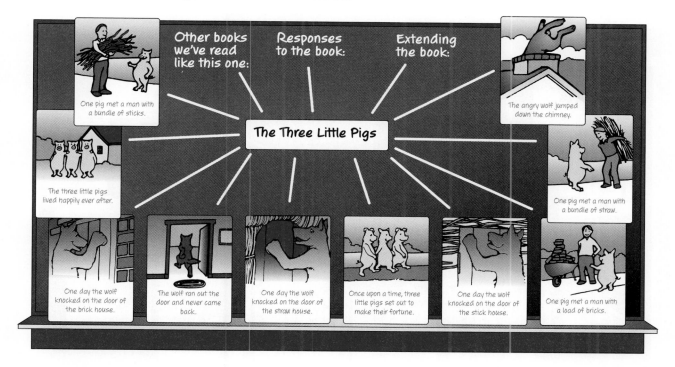

written to tell this story as you look at the pictures." Next, the teacher invites one child to describe what he or she thought the author might have written about the first picture. This idea can be written with water-based felt-tipped markers, which can be cleaned off with a wet sponge. The teacher invites each child to build on the previous student's story line as well as to think about the author's point of view as shown in the picture. Once the children have composed the story from the pictures, the teacher reads the actual book aloud to the children. The two versions provide interesting discussions about point of view and other stylistic devices. Children seem to like reading their own version of the story as well as the author's!

Literature Webbing With Predictable Books

Bromley (1991) describes a successful strategy lesson designed by Reutzel and Fawson in 1989 to be used with predictable books for building children's understanding of story structure: a literature web is constructed from the major elements of a predictable book. This is accomplished by selecting sentences from the book that tell about each major element of the story, that is, setting, characters, problems, attempts, and solution. These sentences are placed around the title of the book in random order on a chalkboard or a large bulletin board, as shown in Figure 11.25. Before reading the story, the children read the sentences aloud with the teacher. In the early part of the school year, the sentences selected for the web sentence strips are usually heavily augmented with hand-drawn or copied pictures from the book.

Children are divided into small groups, and each group is given a picture and sentence card from the board. The children are asked which group thinks they have

Literature webs can be used to help improve students' story structure knowledge and comprehension of text.

Figure 11.26   Artist's drawing of predicted literature web

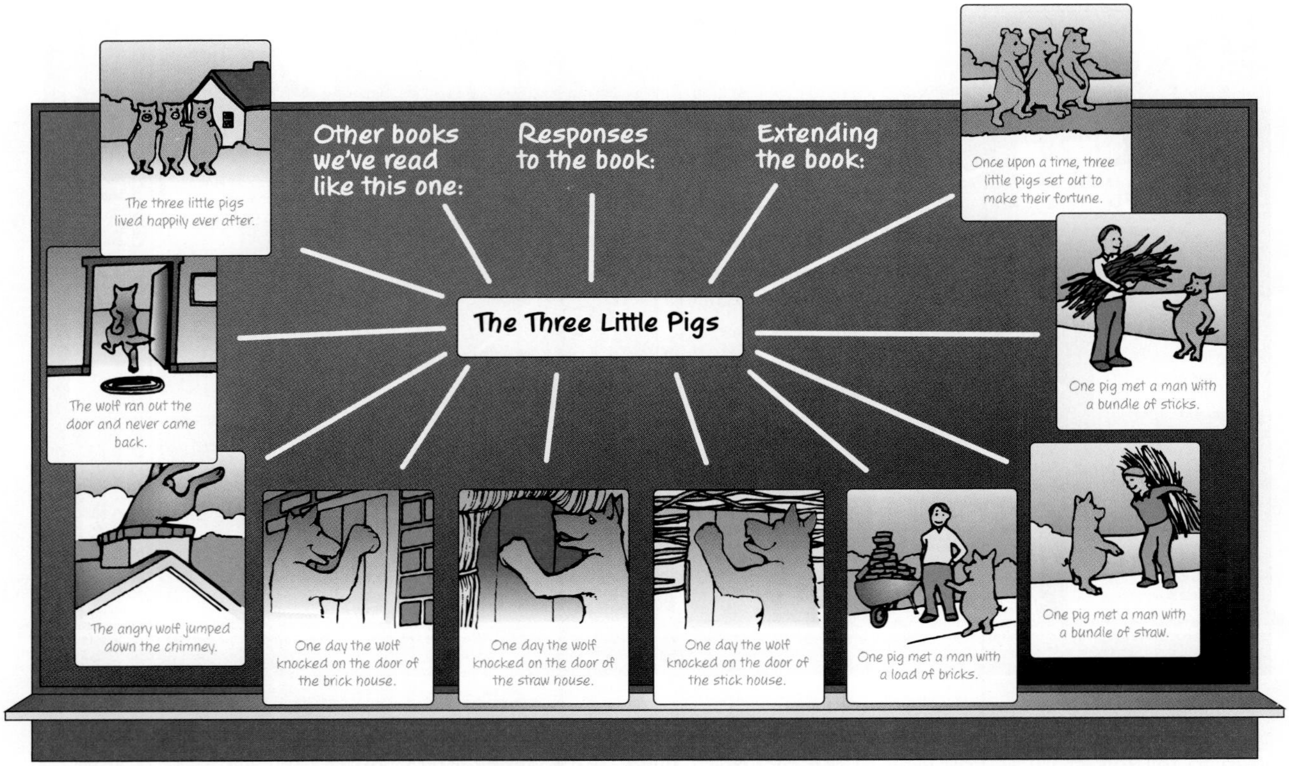

the first part of the story. After discussion and group agreement is reached, the first sentence and picture card are placed at the one-o'clock position on the literature web. The remainder of the groups are asked which sentence and picture card comes next, and the cards are placed around the literature web in clockwise order, as in Figure 11.26. (Literature webs can also be designed to be linear rather than circular. Teachers should decide which way is best.)

Next, the story is read from a traditional-sized trade book or big book. Children listen attentively to confirm or correct their literature web predictions. After the reading, corrections are made to the predictions in the literature web if necessary. Children respond to the story, and these responses are recorded near the end of the literature web. Other books similar to the one read may be discussed and recorded on the web. Finally, the children and teacher brainstorm together to produce some ideas about how to extend the reading of the book into the other language arts while recording these ideas on the web. A completed web appears in Figure 11.27.

Reutzel and Fawson (1989, 1991) and Reutzel and Hollingsworth (1991d) demonstrated that first-grade children, especially low-achieving first-grade children, who participate in the literature webbing of a predictable book learn to read these books with fewer reading miscues, fewer miscues that distort comprehension, and greater recall. They attribute this performance to the fact that children must impose an organization on their predictions when using literature webs, rather than simply making random predictions from story titles and pictures.

Figure 11.27   Artist's drawing of completed literature web

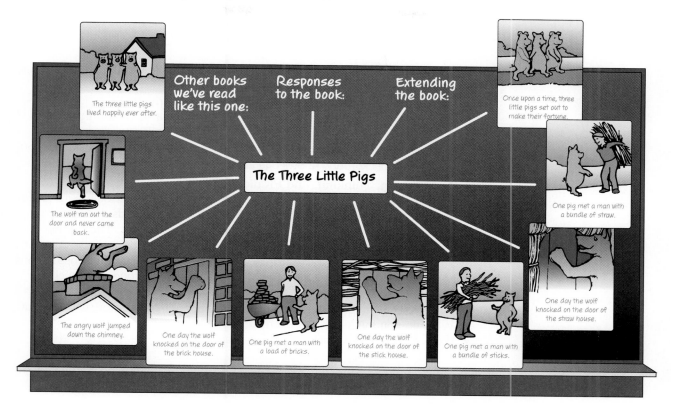

Directed Listening Thinking Activity

The **Directed Listening Thinking Activity** (DLTA) is an adaptation of Russell Stauffer's (1975) Directed Reading Thinking Activity (DRTA). During DRTA, students read, made predictions about a story, and read on to confirm or correct their predictions. During DLTA, emergent readers listen to a story read aloud, predict, and continue to listen to confirm or correct their predictions. The DLTA has become a popular strategy to help emergent readers develop a sense of story (Morrow, 1984; Slaughter, 1988). The following steps illustrate the DLTA strategy:

Step 1: Introducing the Story and Predicting

Teachers can introduce a story like *The Three Billy Goats Gruff* by showing students the cover of the book and reading the title. After discussing the title, the cover, and some of the pictures, the teacher may ask students to make a prediction about the story. This is usually accomplished by asking a series of questions such as:

- What do you think this story may be about?
- What do you think might happen in this story?
- Do the pictures give you any clues about what might happen?

Directed Reading Thinking Activity is presented in chapter 4.

During DLTA, students listen, make predictions about a story, and listen again to confirm or correct their predictions.

Sometimes the teacher may read the first few paragraphs of the story to provide students with enough information to make reasonable predictions. Following an initial discussion, students decide which of the predictions they wish to accept. This process can be facilitated by asking questions such as:

- Which of the ideas about how the story will turn out do you think is most likely correct?
- Have you ever wished that you could live somewhere else?
- Have you ever thought some of your friends have a better life than you do?

Relating questions to the real-life experiences of the children helps them make vital connections with their background knowledge and experience to guide their predictions.

Step 2: Listening, Thinking, and Predicting
Once students commit to a prediction, they have in effect set their own purpose for listening as the teacher reads the story aloud. As the story unfolds during the reading, students begin to confirm, reject, or modify their predictions. The teacher usually stops at key points in the story and asks students more questions; these questions are meant to involve children in confirming, rejecting, or modifying their predictions using the new information they have heard. Teachers may ask questions such as:

- Have you changed your original predictions about how the story will turn out?
- What do you think will happen next?
- If . . . happens, how will that change your ideas?

The teacher continues to read the story aloud, stopping at key points in the story to repeat this procedure until the end of the story is reached.

Step 3: Supporting With Evidence
During the final part of the DLTA, the teacher asks students to remember information from the story to support their predictions. He or she may also ask students to recall which information in the story caused students to change their predictions. Again, the teacher uses questioning to invite students to respond to the story:

- Can you remember how many times your predictions changed?
- What happened in the story that caused you to change your predictions?

The DLTA provides teachers with a structure for introducing and discussing stories read aloud to children while supplying the children with a generalizable framework for listening to these stories.

The DLTA provides teachers with a structure for introducing and discussing stories read aloud to children while supplying the children with a generalizable framework for listening to these stories. Research has shown that using a DLTA significantly increases children's listening comprehension of a story (Morrow, 1984). With frequent use of the DLTA, young children can internalize the procedure and transfer its use to new stories read aloud (R. C. Anderson, Mason, & Shirey, 1984).

Story Retellings

Story retellings ask children to retell a story orally. These can be recorded and examined for purposes of assessing comprehension.

In most elementary school classrooms, children are asked to answer a series of questions after completing the reading of a selection to assess reading comprehension. In many cases, these questions require students to recall bits and pieces of the story in a rather piecemeal or incoherent fashion. On the other hand, asking children to retell a story involves them in reconstruction of the entire story. **Story retellings** require that students sequence the story, recall important elements of the plot, make inferences, and notice relevant details. Thus, retellings assess story comprehension in a holistic, sequenced, and organized manner when compared to typical questioning practices.

Children can quickly learn to retell stories with the help of demonstrations and practice, although retelling is not easy for young children (Morrow, 1985). The teacher may begin by demonstrating the retelling of a favorite story for children. A pre- and postreading discussion of the story also can be helpful in preparing students for retelling. Morrow (1989) suggests that students be told before reading that they will be asked to retell a story. In addition, we suggest that individual children be given at least three reading rehearsals before they are to retell the story from their own reading. Teachers can ask children to pay attention to the sequence of the story or empathize with the main characters' feelings to focus student attention on particular aspects of the story. In this way, retellings become much more than assessment.

Morrow (1985) suggests that teachers prompt children to begin story retellings with a statement such as, "A little while ago, we read a story called [*name the story*]. Would you retell the story as if you were telling it to a friend who has never heard it before?" (p. 659). Other prompts during the recall can be framed as questions:

- How does the story begin? [or] Once upon a time . . .
- What happens next?
- What happened to [the main character] when . . . ?
- Where did the story take place?
- When did the story take place?
- How did [the main character] solve the problem in the story?
- How did the story end?

Morrow (1989) is explicit in her advice that teachers offer only general prompts like those listed here rather than prompting specific details, ideas, or sequence of events in the story.

Assessment of children's story retellings can reveal much about their understanding of story structure, story sequence, and the major elements of the story plot. Evaluating a story retelling is accomplished by first parsing a story into four categories: setting, theme, events, and resolution, as shown in Figure 11.28.

Second, a guide sheet for analyzing the story retellings can be constructed, much like the one illustrated in Figure 11.29 on p. 456, to accompany the parsed story outline. Children should be given credit for partial recall or recalling the gist of the story in the retelling. The guide sheet in Figure 11.30 on p. 457 also provides for analyzing a student's retelling for proper ordering of events. Thus, items included or omitted in recall as well as event order in the retelling are assessed. The information gleaned from the retelling can be used to help teachers focus their instruction in the future. The information may also indicate the nature of the information to be focused on in future retellings or the nature of the prompts to be given during retellings.

Evaluating a story retelling is accomplished by parsing a story into four categories: setting, theme, events, and resolution.

Figure 11.28   Story grammar parsing of the story *The Little Red Hen*

The Setting

Once upon a time there was a little red hen who shared her cottage with a goose, a cat, and a dog.

The goose was a gossip. She chatted with the neighbors all day long.

The cat was very vain. She brushed her fur, straightened her whiskers, and polished her claws all day long.

The dog was always sleepy. He napped on the front porch swing all day long.

The Theme

The Little Red Hen ended up doing all the work around the house. She cooked. She cleaned. She washed the clothes and took out the trash. She mowed the lawn and raked the leaves. She even did all of the shopping.

The Events

One morning on her way to market, the Little Red Hen found a few grains of wheat. She put them in the pocket of her apron. When she got home she asked her friends, "Who will plant these grains of wheat?"

"Not I," said the goose.
"Not I," said the cat.
"Not I," said the dog.
"Then I will plant them myself," said the Little Red Hen.
And she did.

When the grains of wheat began to sprout, the Little Red Hen cried, "Look, the wheat I planted is coming up! Who will help me take care of it this summer?"

"Not I," said the goose.
"Not I," said the cat.
"Not I," said the dog.
"Then I will take care of it myself," said the Little Red Hen.
And she did.

All summer long she cared for the growing wheat. She made sure that it got enough water, and she hoed the weeds out carefully between each row. By the end of the summer the wheat had grown tall. And when it turned from green to gold, she asked her friends, "Who will help me cut and thresh this wheat?"

"Not I," said the goose.
"Not I," said the cat.
"Not I," said the dog.
"Then I will cut and thresh it myself," said the Little Red Hen.

And she did.

When all of the wheat had been cut and threshed the Little Red Hen scooped the wheat into a wheel barrow and said, "This wheat must be ground into flour. Who will help me take it to the mill?"

"Not I," said the goose.
"Not I," said the cat.
"Not I," said the dog.
"Then I will take it myself," said the Little Red Hen.
And she did.

The miller ground the wheat into flour and put it into a bag for the Little Red Hen. Then, all by herself, she pushed the bag home in the wheel barrow. One cool fall morning not many days later, the Little Red Hen got up early and said, "Today would be a perfect day to bake some bread. Who will help me bake a loaf of bread with the flour I brought home from the mill?"

"Not I," said the goose.
"Not I," said the cat.
"Not I," said the dog.
"Then I will bake the bread myself," said the Little Red Hen.
And she did.

She mixed the flour with milk and eggs and butter and salt. She kneaded the dough and shaped it into a nice plump loaf. Then she put the loaf in the oven and watched it as it baked.

The Resolution

The smell of baking bread soon filled the air. It smelled so delicious that the goose stopped chatting . . . The cat stopped brushing . . . The dog stopped napping. One by one they came into the kitchen. When the Little Red Hen took the freshly baked loaf of bread out of the oven, she said, "Who will help me eat this bread?"

"Oh, I will!" said the goose.
"And I will!" said the cat.
"And I will!" said the dog.
"You will?" said the Little Red Hen.

"Who planted the wheat and took care of it? I did. Who cut the wheat? Who threshed it and took it to the mill? I did. Who brought the flour home and baked this loaf of bread? I did. I did it all by myself. Now, I am going to eat it all by myself."

And that is exactly what she did.

Figure 11.29 Coding children's responses during story readings

Child's name _____ Date _____ Story _____

(Read one story to the child or a small group of children. Encourage the children to respond with questions and comments. Tape-record the session. Transcribe or listen to the tape, noting each child's responses by placing checks in the appropriate categories. A category may receive more than one check, and a single response may be credited to more than one category. Total the number of checks in each category.)

1. Focus on Story Structure
   a. Setting (time, place)   _____
   b. Characters   _____
   c. Theme (problem or goal)   _____
   d. Plot episodes (events leading toward problem solution   _____
      or goal attainment)
   e. Resolution   _____

2. Focus on Meaning
   a. Labeling   _____
   b. Detail   _____
   c. Interpreting (associations, elaborations)   _____
   d. Predicting   _____
   e. Drawing from one's experience   _____
   f. Seeking definitions of words   _____
   g. Using narrational behavior (reciting parts of the book   _____
      along with the teacher)

3. Focus on Print
   a. Questions or comments about letters   _____
   b. Questions or comments about sounds   _____
   c. Questions or comments about words   _____
   d. Reads words   _____
   e. Reads sentences   _____

4. Focus on Illustrations
   a. Responses and questions that are related to illustrations   _____

From *Literacy Development in the Early Years: Helping Children Read and Write* (p. 109) by L. M. Morrow, 1989, Boston: Allyn & Bacon. Copyright © by Allyn & Bacon. Reprinted by permission.

YOUNG CHILDREN RESPONDING TO LITERATURE

Drawing is typically used as one of the first symbol systems intended to carry a message.

Teachers often invite children to respond to books and stories through discussion and other oral language activities, and increasing numbers of teachers of young children are beginning to appreciate the role of writing in responding to stories and books.

Figure 11.30   Story retelling evaluation guide sheet

Child's Name _____   Age _____

Title of Story _____   Date _____

General directions: Give 1 point for each element included as well as for "gist." Give 1 point for each character named as well as for such words as *boy, girl,* or *dog.* Credit plurals (friends, for instance) with 2 points under characters.

Sense of Story Structure

Setting
a.   Begins story with an introduction
b.   Names main character   _____
c.   Number of other characters named
d.   Actual number of other characters   _____
e.   Score for "other characters" (c/d)   _____
f.   Includes statement about time or place   _____

Theme
Refers to main character's primary goal or problem to be solved   _____

Plot Episodes
a.   Number of episodes recalled   _____
b.   Number of episodes in story   _____
Score for "plot episodes" (a/b)   _____

Resolution
a.   Names problem solution/goal attainment   _____
b.   Ends story   _____

Sequence
Retells story in structural order: setting, theme, plot episodes, resolution. (Score 2 for proper, 1 for partial, 0 for no sequence evident.)   _____

Highest score possible: _____   Child's score   _____

Checks can be used instead of numbers to get a general sense of elements children include and progress over time. A quantitative analysis as shown above is optional. Retellings can be evaluated for interpretive critical comments as well.

Adapted from *Literacy Development in the Early Years: Helping Children to Read and Write* by L. M. Morrow, 1989, Needham Heights, MA: Allyn & Bacon. Copyright © by Allyn & Bacon. Reprinted by permission.

When children are first given a pencil, pen, or crayon to write with, they seem to approach the paper with an intent to explore what will happen. These first encounters with writing generally result in what adults call *scribbling*. Scribble writing, however, usually gives way quickly to discovering lines, curves, circles, and other forms that may be used to represent objects and events in drawings. In the writing of very young children, drawing is typically used as one of the first symbol systems intended to carry a message (Clay, 1987; Ferreiro & Teberosky, 1982). Drawings represent the fact that children have come to understand the difference between the object or event itself and culturally recognized symbols that can be used to signify the object or event.

During kindergarten and first grade, children use drawing a great deal. Research into the uses of drawing and its effect on writing development has shown that drawing seems to inform and enhance writing development initially but that writing also acts to embellish drawings later (Bissex, 1980; Calkins, 1994). Calkins (1986) relates an incident when she was visiting a first-grade classroom. She asked Chris, a first-grade boy, what he was going to write about. Chris looked at Calkins with astonishment and responded, "How should I know; I haven't drawed it yet!" (pp. 47, 50). Thus, drawing can help children rehearse for writing by providing a scaffolding from which a piece of writing can be constructed. Drawings can also be used to help children hold the world still for a moment—long enough to select a topic for writing. This may explain why drawing pictures often precedes the use of letters or words in children's writing. Drawings give children something to guide the selection of words for writing. In a sense, drawing appears to be a primordial form of representing the world to assist writing. Therefore, Calkins (1994) recommends, particularly for kindergarten and first-grade children, that drawing be used liberally to enhance children's development of writing.

Most important, drawing helps children to understand that many symbol systems are available for communicating a message, that is, music, art, drama, writing, movement, and so on. Siegel (1983) claims that by taking what we have come to know from one communication or symbol system and recasting into another, new knowledge is generated. This process of recasting knowledge in alternative symbol systems is called **transmediation.** For example, inviting children to recast into drawings a story read aloud causes children to develop new insights for the story. Thus, drawing not only can help children become more proficient and expressive writers, it can help children respond to reading in a way that deepens their knowledge and leads to new insights and interpretations.

Sketch to Stretch

"Sketch to stretch" (Short, Harste, & Burke, 1996; Siegel, 1983) offers a wonderful opportunity for students to draw pictures illustrating "what this story meant to me or my favorite part of the story." The procedure for using "sketch to stretch" follows:

1. Place children in groups of about four or five with multiple copies of the same story (either a basal story or a trade book).
2. After the children have read the story, each child independently reflects on the meaning of the story. Then, they draw their own interpretations of the story. Plenty of time should be given for students to complete their sketches. Remember that the emphasis is on meaning, not artistic ability.
3. Next, each student shares his or her sketch (without comment) and then allows the other group members to speculate on its meaning as related to the book. Once the questions and comments of the other children are concluded, the artist has the final word.
4. After each child in the group has shared a sketch, the group may wish to pick one sketch to share with the class. The sketch chosen by the group usually offers a good synopsis of the book or story.

Taking what we have come to know from one communication or symbol system and recasting it into another is called ***transmediation.***

Inviting children to draw about what they've read improves students' understanding and enjoyment of the story by allowing them many opportunities to plan and rehearse their writing ideas.

"Sketch to stretch" offers teachers an opportunity to discuss with students why each reader may have different interpretations of a story even though the gist is recognized by all. "Sketch to stretch" also helps encourage a spirit of risk taking among students because they see that there is no single "correct" response to stories and books but that interpretations depend on a reader's background knowledge and interests.

"Sketch to stretch" has many follow-up possibilities. For example, sketches can be collected as part of the teacher's ongoing assessment portfolio, bound together into a group or class book, displayed on bulletin boards, or used as a metacognitive strategy to help students monitor their own comprehension of a story. Another possibility is that sketches can be collected and combined to create a kind of story map to depict major events in a story. Thus, "sketch to stretch" can:

- Aid students' story comprehension.
- Serve as an entree into the writing process.
- Provide documentation of students' reading comprehension and progress.

"Sketch to stretch" allows children the opportunity to represent the interpretation of a story in another symbolic system.

See chapter 10 for a discussion of assessment portfolios.

MURALS

In Ms. Bonnell's kindergarten class, the children had just finished reading the story Why Can't I Fly? *(Gelman, 1976). Ms. Bonnell wanted to extend the reading of the book into a class art project. Instinctively, she knew that inviting children to draw about what they had read about would improve her students' understanding and enjoyment of the story. A mural was decided on as the class art project. Children busily worked in small groups and pairs, drawing and painting the characters from the story: a ladybug, a duck, and a monkey. A 30-foot-long light-blue roll of butcher paper was spread out in the hall of the school. The children and the teacher reviewed the sequence of the story before pasting the characters in sequence on the mural. Bubbles were added above the heads of the characters with the text copied from the story.*

Ms. Bonnell noted that the children had internalized this story to the point of endearment and could read and write many of the words found in the story.

As shown in Figure 11.31, murals can capture the sequence, the episodes, and the warmth of the original story. Moreover, murals display the added warmth of the children's hand-drawn characters or carefully selected excerpts of text copied from the original book.

Murals provide a wonderful means for groups of children to register their response to literature.

Posters

Advertising a favorite book or character in the form of a poster is a simple yet popular idea for inviting children to respond to a book through drawing. Several varieties of posters can be suggested for children: "wanted" posters, missing person poster, favorite character poster, and best book posters. At a local elementary school, for example, the teachers and librarians invited children to make a poster about their favorite book. A display case in the library was used to display the posters during the year. Each time a book on display in the library display case was checked out that week, the librarian made note of it. At the end of the year, the authors of the five

A poster is a simple yet popular idea for inviting children to respond to a book through drawing.

Figure 11.31   An example of a class-made mural, which can assist children's writing and reading development

This mural was based on *Appelemando's Dreams* by P. Polacco, 1991. New York: Philomel Books. Copyright 1991 by Patricia Polacco.

posters that had sparked the largest number of check outs from the library were each given a book certificate from a local bookstore.

"Wanted" or missing person posters (T. D. Johnson & Louis, 1987) are also a popular drawing or art-related response to a book or story. To begin, the teacher may display a poster in a prominent place in the classroom of a book the children have already read, one that will naturally foster curiosity and questions. A discussion may focus on the information contained in the poster, and a list could be made at the board. Before reading a story aloud, the teacher tells students to listen carefully for information that may be used in making a poster like the one displayed and discussed. After reading, information for a "wanted" or missing person poster could be discussed and listed at the board. Children could then be sent to work in pairs or individually on their own poster for the book or story. Johnson and Louis (1987) point out that poster making involves the use of a number of important reading skills: "reading for a purpose as well as gathering, organizing, and synthesizing information and selecting main ideas and significant details" (p. 84).

Figure 11.32   Art and drawing literature response list

- Make character puppets.

- Draw an illustration of the setting of the story.

- Construct a shoe box diorama of the story setting.

- Prepare a comic strip version of the story events.

- Design a book jacket for a favorite book or chapter.

- Make a transparency story for use on the overhead.

- Trace a friend and illustrate her as a character from a book.

- Draw a picture from your favorite book or story. Cut it into a jigsaw puzzle for a friend to put together.

- Produce illustrated bookmarks.

- Model book's characters from soap, clay, or salt dough.

- Make place mats advertising your favorite book. Cover with clear contact paper and place in school cafeteria.

- Design character masks to be worn during a dramatization of a story or book.

Character Mobiles

A favorite among young children for using drawing and art to respond to books and stories is the creation of character mobiles. Children illustrate the characters from the book or story and cut these drawings out and hang them on pieces of string. The character strings can be hung on coat hangers or pipe cleaners, which are hung from the ceiling of the classroom. Usually, the title of the book or story is also written on the mobile. Each mobile represents a child's representation of the characters in the book or story. By drawing these characters, children review the story, deepen their understanding, and expand on interpretations.

To make character mobiles, children illustrate the characters from the book or story and cut these drawings out and hang them on a piece of string.

The ideas described here for responding to books through art and drawing are just a few of many possibilities. Figure 11.32 lists several more suggestions for using drawing and art as a medium for responding to books and stories with young children.

DEVELOPING FLUENCY: YOUNG CHILDREN REREADING

Radio Reading

Radio reading (Searfoss, 1975) is a procedure for developing oral reading fluency in a group setting, a process that shields neophyte readers from the sometimes harsh emotional consequences from peers in response to their developing reading abilities. In radio reading, each student is given a "script" to read aloud. Selections can be drawn from any print media such as newspapers, magazines, or any print source that

Radio reading is a procedure for developing oral reading fluency in a group setting.

can be converted into a news story. The student acts as a news broadcaster, and other students act as listeners. Only the reader and the teacher have copies of the script. Because other students have no script to follow, minor word-recognition errors will go unnoticed if the text is well presented. At-risk readers have enjoyed radio reading from *Know Your World:* this publication is well suited for use in radio reading activities because the content and level of difficulty make it possible for younger readers to read with ease and enjoyment.

Before reading aloud to the group, students should rehearse the story silently to themselves or aloud to the teacher until they have gained confidence. Emphasis is first placed on the meaning of the story so that the students can paraphrase any difficult portions of the text. Students are encouraged to keep the ideas flowing in the same way a broadcaster would. In contrast to the typical "round-robin" reading method, in which all mistakes are apparent to anyone following along in the text, radio reading allows students to deviate from the text without embarrassment by stressing the idea that their reading should make sense.

Repeated Readings

The basic purpose of repeated readings is to enhance students' oral reading fluency.

Repeated readings simply engage students in reading interesting passages orally over and over again. The basic purpose is to enhance students' reading fluency (Dowhower, 1987; J. Samuels, 1979). Although it might seem that reading a text again and again would lead to boredom, it actually has just the opposite effect. Because in this exercise each reading is timed and then recorded on a chart or graph, students compete with themselves trying to better their reading rate and cut down on errors in each successive attempt. Also, with each attempt, students' comprehension and vocal inflections improve (Dowhower, 1987; Reutzel & Hollingsworth, 1993). Young readers find it reinforcing to see visible evidence of their improvement, such as a personal (and private) graph of their fluency progress in repeated readings.

Repeated readings help students by expanding the total number of words they can recognize instantaneously and, as previously mentioned, help improve students' comprehension and oral elocution with each succeeding attempt. This quickly leads students to improved confidence regarding reading aloud and positive attitudes toward the act of reading. Additionally, because high-frequency words (*the, and, but, was,* etc.) occur in literally all reading situations, the increase in automatic sight word knowledge developed through repeated readings transfers far beyond the practiced texts.

In the beginning, texts selected for repeated readings should be short, predictable, and easy. Examples of poetry we recommend for repeated readings with young readers include those authored by Shel Silverstein and Jack Prelutsky. Stories by Bill Martin such as *Brown Bear, Brown Bear, What Do You See?* or Eric Carle's *The Very Hungry Caterpillar* are also wonderful places to start this activity. When students attain adequate speed and accuracy with easy texts, the length and difficulty of the stories and poems can gradually be increased.

Students can tape-record their oral reading performances as a source of immediate feedback. If two cassette tape player/recorders are available, students can listen and read along with the taped version of the text using headphones, while at the same time, the second recorder records the student's oral reading. The child can then either replay his or her version simultaneously with the teacher-recorded version to compare, or else simply listen to his or her own rendition alone. Either way, the feedback can be both instant and effective (Cooter, 1993).

Teachers can use the tape recording of repeated readings for further analysis of each young reader's improvement in fluency and comprehension. Using a tape recorder also frees the teacher to work with other students, thereby conserving precious instructional time and leaving behind an audit trail of student readings for later assessment and documentation. On occasion, teachers should listen to the tape with the reader present so that effective ways of reducing word-recognition errors and increasing reading rate can be modeled by the teacher.

THEMED, PROJECT, OR INQUIRY-BASED INSTRUCTION WITH YOUNG CHILDREN

Themed and project studies, also known as *topical studies,* are undertaken with young children for a purpose, which relates to the content to be studied and a personal or societal need to know (Weaver, Chaston, & Peterson, 1993). For example, one may choose to study about the development of aviation as a theme because it is important to know. **Themed study** is not just a thinly disguised excuse for learning to recognize certain words, to spell a list of 20 words, or to punctuate a sentence from a textbook. Because the processes for developing both literature-based and thematic studies units are described fully in chapters 12 and 13, we will mention here only a few considerations crucial to the success of using themed studies with very young students.

Planning a themed studies unit begins with understanding what makes for a quality theme for study. Gamberg, Kwak, Hutchings, and Altheim (1988) describe 10 criteria that characterize a quality theme.

List 10 criteria that characterize the selection and development of a quality theme for thematic studies.

1. A theme is the focus of attention, not a curriculum goal or skill such as reading and math.
2. A themed studies unit involves in-depth study.
3. A theme must be of interest to the children.
4. A theme must be broad enough to be subdivided into smaller subtopics also of interest to the children.
5. A theme and its relation to the subtopics must remain clear.
6. A theme must not be geographically or historically limiting.
7. A theme must lend itself to comparing and contrasting of ideas.
8. A theme must permit extensive investigation of concrete situations, materials, and resources.
9. A theme must be conducive to breaking down the wall of curriculum barriers in the school.
10. A theme must assist in breaking down the walls between the school and society.

To begin a themed studies unit, teachers select a theme from the universe of worthy and interesting themes such as oceanography, aviation, bones and bodies, transportation, weather, feelings, or magic. Because themed or project studies grow out of a need to know, Short, Harste, and Burke (1996) describe an approach called *inquiry-based* instruction. This process begins with planning-to-plan (Watson, Burke, & Harste, 1990), which uses a webbing approach to planning the aspects of a topic to be investigated. To begin, teachers brainstorm resources such as print materials, hands-on materials, community resources, audiovisual resources, and human

Figure 11.33   Second-grade students' "I know–I wonder" web

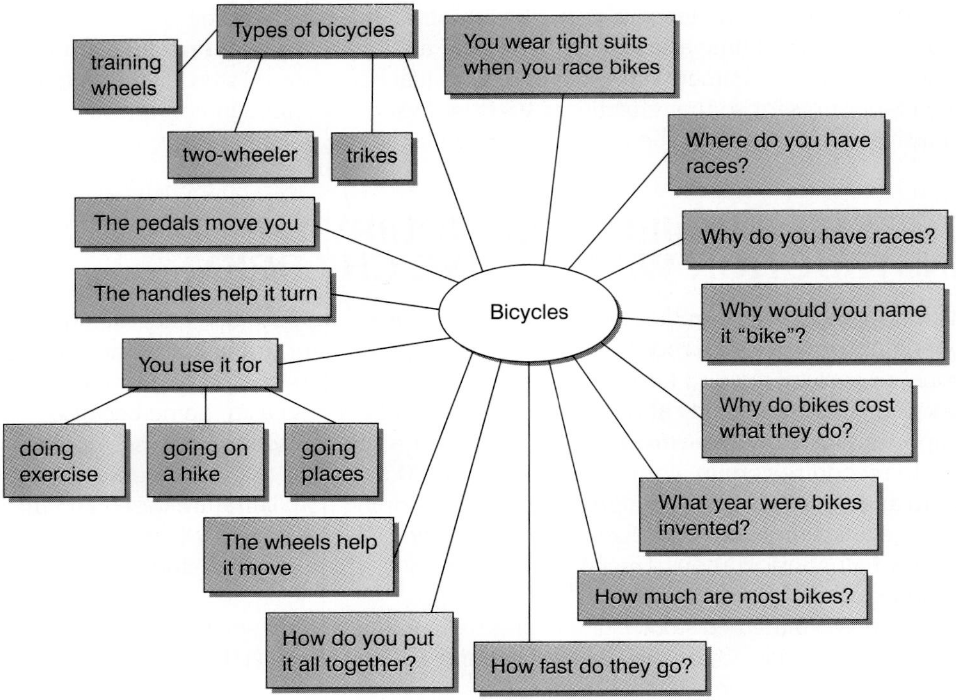

Types of bicycles

training wheels

You wear tight suits when you race bikes

two-wheeler   trikes

Where do you have races?

The pedals move you

Why do you have races?

The handles help it turn

Bicycles

Why would you name it "bike"?

You use it for

Why do bikes cost what they do?

doing exercise   going on a hike   going places

What year were bikes invented?

The wheels help it move

How much are most bikes?

How do you put it all together?   How fast do they go?

resources to support the theme. Next, they brainstorm strategies that should be used in the inquiry project or theme.

Very often, teachers use an "I know" and "I wonder" webbing approach to invite children into the themed studies unit. They ask children to brainstorm everything they know about the theme and record this information on an "I know" web. Next, children are invited to brainstorm "I wonder" statements to be attached to the web to guide the exploration of the theme. For some teachers, a large "I wonder" wall chart organized into columns of "I wonder," "I found out," and "How I found out" works very well for children to organize and record information learned about the theme, as shown in Figure 11.33.

Teachers organize children into smaller groups to pursue specific subtopics of the theme or answer specific "I wonder" questions. The products of thematic study units include written documents, murals, charts, and graphs, as well as displays, fairs, speeches, demonstrations, plays, dioramas, and tours.

Two "Yes—But" issues loom large over teachers who question their ability to engage in thematic studies with young children. First, what about managing the classroom? And second, what about assessment? Organization, clear objectives, and flexibility are the keys to the first concern. Well-organized classroom centers with clear tasks and expectations make the classroom a much easier place to manage during themed studies. When problems occur, class meetings provide a democratic and useful forum for discussing and solving problems related to conduct and management in a classroom. The second concern, that of evaluating themed studies, is directly addressed by the use of authentic assessment. This approach to evaluation is fully described in chapter 10.

ASSISTING YOUNG READERS WITH SPECIAL NEEDS

When students in the early elementary grades have trouble with beginning literacy experiences, the effect can be far reaching: The child's self-esteem is usually damaged, life at home is affected, and a cycle of failure may develop. School systems spend many thousands of dollars trying to help readers with special needs close the gap between them and their peers and get back on track with their education. Unfortunately, many students are never able to close the gap between their performance and their potential. In this section, we summarize innovative practices for assisting early readers.

Reading Recovery

In recent years, many reading researchers have called for direct and focused attention on beginning literacy problems in our schools. The idea is to "recover" early those children who are having problems in beginning reading. This can potentially spare children a lifetime of emotional and economic damage related to literacy problems, and schools can preserve valuable resources otherwise spent on remedial education.

One of the most successful early-intervention programs is Reading Recovery. Developed by Marie Clay (1993), an educator from New Zealand, Reading Recovery identifies at-risk children during their 1st year of reading instruction and provides them with individualized tutoring for 30 minutes each day. Reading Recovery has experienced success not only in New Zealand but in the United States as well (Pinnell, Fried, & Estice, 1990). In a recent study, Pinnell, Lyons, DeFord, Bryk, and Seltzer (1994) showed that Chapter 1 students assigned to Reading Recovery produced the only statistically significant gains on all reading measures used in the study as compared with three other treatment groups and a control group. Other researchers have called into question the effectiveness of Reading Recovery, but up to this point have offered no well-documented alternatives (Shannahan & Barr, 1995).

Reading Recovery is one of the most successful early-intervention reading programs.

A typical tutoring session (Clay, 1993) includes each of the following activities:

- Rereading of two or more familiar books
- Rereading of yesterday's new book and taking a running record
- Letter identification (plastic letters on a magnetic board)
- Writing a story (including hearing sounds in words)
- Cut-up story to be rearranged
- New book introduced
- New book attempted

See chapter 10 for a complete description of running records.

The Reading Recovery approach is effective with readers with special needs for several reasons. First, Reading Recovery provides young children with a great deal of individual attention, which can be very beneficial for readers with special needs who feel insecure in a classroom setting. Also, Reading Recovery immerses children in pleasurable reading and writing opportunities. It promotes risk taking, attachment to favorite literature, self-selection of books, and creative writing production. Finally, teachers are better able to adjust the learning program and respond to student needs because of the one-on-one tutorial setup.

In essence, Reading Recovery offers readers with special needs a daily, individualized, balanced literacy teaching program with heavy emphasis on writing and reading in children's trade books. Teachers who enjoy adequate support from their school system should be able to achieve similar results as they construct transition programs of their own.

HELPING STUDENTS WITH SPECIAL CULTURAL AND LANGUAGE NEEDS SUCCEED IN THE EARLY YEARS

"The major advantage of captioned television is the multi-sensory stimulation of viewing the drama, hearing the sound, and seeing the captions." (Koskinen et al., 1985, p. 6)

Several researchers (Koskinen, Wilson, & Jensema, 1985; Neuman & Koskinen, 1992) have found that closed caption television is a particularly effective tool for motivating reluctant language-minority students to learn to read and to improve fluency and comprehension. Closed caption television, which uses written subtitles, provides students with meaningful and motivating reading material set in the evolving context of a TV program. The following materials are necessary for using closed caption TV: (a) a video recorder/player, (b) a video monitor, (c) close captioning reader, and (d) videotapes.

The teacher begins by carefully selecting high-interest television programs, recording and previewing programs before making final selections, and then introducing the program(s) to students with attention to vocabulary and prior knowledge factors (Koskinen et al., 1985). Three elements should be considered in a successful closed caption lesson.

1. The group watches a part of the captioned TV program together (5 to 10 minutes). The teacher stops the tape and asks students to predict what will happen next in the program. Then the teacher continues showing the program so that students can check their predictions.
2. Students watch a segment of the program that has examples of certain kinds of phonic patterns, word uses, or punctuation. For example, students can be alerted to the use of quotation marks and the fact that these marks signal dialogue. Students can then watch the remainder of the tape to identify the dialogue using their knowledge of quotation marks.
3. After watching a closed caption TV program, students can practice reading aloud along with the captions. If necessary, both the auditory portion and the closed captioning can be played simultaneously to provide at-risk readers support through their initial attempts to read. At some later point, students can be allowed to practice reading the captioning without the auditory portion of the program. Koskinen et al. (1985) add that they "do not recommend that the sound be turned off if this, in effect, turns off the children. The major advantage of captioned television is the multi-sensory stimulation of viewing the drama, hearing the sound, and seeing the captions" (p. 6).

Summary

Language routines and strategies for structuring classroom reading and writing events involve children and teachers in, for example, sharing literacy, as during the tune-in routine. Repeated reading of favorite stories and text is provided during the old-favorites routine. The learning about language routine provides time for teachers to teach mini-lessons on strategies and skills that they have designated as useful for their students. Predictable books and literature are shared daily during the new-story routine. And finally, children engage in a variety of independent reading and writing activities to deepen and extend their growing understanding and control of the reading and writing processes during the independent output activities routine.

Strategies for helping younger readers behave like skilled readers to the fullest extent possible from the very beginning of their experiences with reading and writing include using environmental print that children encounter daily in their lives. Teaching phonemic awareness, alphabetic principle, and phonics through regular encounters with whole books, poems, songs, and chants helps young children grasp the relationship between sounds, symbols, spoken words, and written words in a way that parallels their natural learning processes. A sense of story can be developed through using strategies that keep stories whole, connected, and meaningful for younger children. As young children encounter stories with the help of sensitive teachers, they internalize the structure of stories as well as the structures of various other literary genres. They can then use their understanding of story structure to make sense of unfamiliar stories and print.

Children need to respond to their reading to deepen and extend their understanding and interpretations. For emergent readers, response to a story can be elicited effectively and enjoyably by using drawing and art; younger children are familiar with representing their meanings on paper through the symbol system of shapes and figures. With time and exposure to printed language, their drawing responses to reading gradually give way to using the symbol system of printed language. Ashton-Warner (1963) once said, "First words are different from first drawings only in medium" (p. 28).

Concept Applications

In the Classroom

1. Start an alphabetized collection of environmental print. Arrange to meet with a child and make an I-can-read book.
2. Start a collection of favorite songs, poems, riddles, language games, and puzzles for use during the tune-in routine.
3. Make a committee of peers to level the stories in your basal readers for guided reading groups.
4. Design phonemic awareness lessons to follow the scope and sequence recommended in this chapter.
5. Design phonics lessons for emergent readers to follow the scope and sequence recommended in this chapter.

In the Field

1. Buy a wordless picture book. Make arrangements to meet with a small group of kindergarten children. Take down their dictation for the pictures. Help them to read their dictated story for the pictures.

2. Choose a predictable book and make a literature web for it. Arrange to meet with a group of first-grade children to use the literature web and read the predictable book.

3. Arrange to meet with a child in first grade to read a book. Ask the child to retell the book, and record his or her retelling. Analyze the book and the retelling using Morrow's (1989) guides.

4. Read a predictable book to a group of kindergartners or first-grade children. Have them respond to the book by using the sketch-to-stretch activity. Write a brief summary of your observations from the experience.

5. Locate a teacher who uses Reading Recovery and interview him or her. You may wish to ask how the teacher became acquainted with Reading Recovery, where he or she received training, and if he or she is experiencing success.

Recommended Readings

Barrett, F. L. (1982). *A teacher's guide to shared reading.* Ontario, Canada: Scholastic-TAB Publications.

Bear, D. R., Templeton, S., Invernizzi, M., & Johnston, F. (1996). *Words their way: Word study for phonics, vocabulary, and spelling instruction.* Columbus, OH: Prentice Hall/Merrill.

Blackburn, L. (1997). *Whole music: A whole language approach to teaching music.* Westport, CT: Heinemann.

Blecher, S., & Jaffee, K. (1998). *Weaving in the arts: Widening the learning circle.* Westport, CT: Heinemann.

Blevins, W. (1997). *Phonemic awareness activities for early reading success.* New York: Scholastic.

Blevins, W. (1998). *Phonics from A to Z.* New York: Scholastic.

Brown, H., & Cambourne, B. (1987). *Read and retell.* Portsmouth, NH: Heinemann.

Clay, M. (1985). *The early detection of reading difficulties* (3rd ed). Portsmouth, NH: Heinemann.

Fountas, I. C., & Pinnell, G. S. (1996). *Guided reading instruction: Good first teaching for all children.* Portsmouth, NH: Heinemann.

Gambrell, L. (1985). Dialogue journals: Reading-writing instruction. *The Reading Teacher, 38*(6), 512–515.

Harwayne, S. (1992). *Lasting impressions.* Portsmouth, NH: Heinemann.

Hill, S. (1989). *Books alive! Using literature in the classroom.* Portsmouth, NH: Heinemann.

Hill, S. (1990). *Raps and rhymes.* Portsmouth, NH: Heinemann.

Johnson, T. D., & Louis, D. R. (1990). *Bringing it all together: A program for literacy.* Portsmouth, NH: Heinemann.

Koskinen, P. S., Blum, I. H., Bisson, S. A., Phillips, S. M., Creamer, T. S., & Baker, T. K. (1999). Shared reading, books, and audiotapes: Supporting diverse students in school and at home. *The Reading Teacher, 52*(5), 430–444.

Langer, J. A. (1995). *Envisioning literature.* New York: Teachers College Press.

Lynch, P. (1986). *Using big books and predictable books.* New York: Scholastic.

Mathes, P. G. (1997). Cooperative story mapping. *Remedial and Special Education, 18*(1), 20–27.

Moustafa, M., & Maldonado-Colon, E. (1999). Whole-to-parts phonics instruction: Building on what children know to help them know more. *The Reading Teacher, 52*(5), 448–458.

Nathan, R., Temple, F., Juntunen, K., & Temple, C. (1989). *Classroom strategies that work: An elementary teacher's guide to process writing.* Portsmouth, NH: Heinemann.

Parsons, L. (1990). *Response journals.* Portsmouth, NH: Heinemann.

Pinnell, G. S., Fried, M. D., & Estice, R. M. (1990). Reading recovery: Learning how to make a difference. *The Reading Teacher, 43*(3), 282–295.

Raskinski, T. V. (1995). *Parents and teachers: Helping children learn to read and write.* New York: Harcourt Brace.

Reutzel, D. R. (1996). A balanced reading approach. In J. Baltas & S. Shafer (Eds.), *Scholastic guide to balanced reading: Grade 3–6* (pp. 7–11). New York: Scholastic.

Reutzel, D. R. (1996). A balanced reading approach. In J. Baltas & S. Shafer (Eds.), *Scholastic guide to balanced reading: K–2* (pp. 6–12). New York: Scholastic.

Reutzel, D. R. (1999). On balanced reading. *The Reading Teacher, 52*(4), 2–4.

Reutzel, D. R., & Fawson, P. C. (1998). Global literacy connections: Stepping into the future. *Think, 8*(2), 32–34.

Richgels, D. J., & Wold, L. S. (1998). Literacy on the road: Backpacking partnerships between school and home. *The Reading Teacher, 52*(1), 18–29.

Routman, R. (1996). *Literacy at the crossroads: Crucial talk about reading, writing, and other teaching dilemmas.* Portsmouth, NH: Heinemann.

Weaver, C. (1998). *Reconsidering a balanced approach to reading.* Urbana, IL: National Council of Teachers of English.

chapter

12

The Elementary Years:

Focus Questions

When you are finished studying this chapter, you should be able to answer these questions:

1. What are the differences between core book units and themed literature units? In what ways are they similar?
2. What happens during individual reading conferences that helps teachers assess reading development and plan for instruction?
3. What is the purpose of a writing process approach to composition instruction?
4. In what ways are the Reading and Writing Workshops similar?
5. What is meant by "publishing"?
6. What is meant by "integration of the curriculum"?
7. Are literature-based reading programs and Writing Workshops helpful to readers with learning problems? Is substantial modification necessary? If so, why?

Reading and Writing in Grades 3–5

Key Concepts

To, With, and By
Core Books
Individualized Reading
Themed Literature Units
Reading Workshop

Fluency
Writing Process
Writing Workshop
Limited English Proficient Students (LEP)

The years of learning at this level have rightly been referred to as the "transitional grades" because children exhibit a wide range of literacy development. At one end of the continuum are some students struggling to conquer early reading and writing skills; at the other end are students who have gained fluency in narrative texts, stories and the like, and are now transitioning into "reading to learn" strategies with informational texts. Master teachers in grades 3 through 5 necessarily have a deep understanding of the literacy-learning milestones (see chapter 10) ranging from the earliest stages through fluency. They also have a significant arsenal of strategies for teaching a wide range of literacy skills. Finally, they are able to establish effective and flexible classroom routines involving small- and large-group instruction, learning centers, and independent learning activities.

From our own experiences as third- and fourth-grade teachers, we can assure you that teaching at this level is as exciting as it is rewarding. We begin this chapter with a few points to remember in establishing rich and effective intermediate-level classrooms.

BALANCED LITERACY INSTRUCTION IN GRADES 3 THROUGH 5

Keeping Our "Balance"

Grade 3 has become an important benchmark year in many states in terms of reading achievement.

There can be a great deal of pressure at this level to show significant literacy gains on state-mandated and norm-referenced tests. Grade 3 has especially become a pressure point. President Clinton's national goal established in 1997 calls for all students to be reading on grade level by the end of third grade. This goal in various forms has been adopted in many, if not most, of the states as of this writing.

Other curriculum-oriented pressure points commonly occur during the intermediate years. We all remember as children being introduced during intermediate years to cursive writing, long division, and more in-depth studies of science, social studies, and the arts. If we are not careful as teachers, we can lose our balance in continuing to develop literacy skills in our students. Teachers must continue to place reading and writing instruction at the core of each learning day and spend at least half their time in literacy-related learning activities. Because these skills can easily be developed within the context of other subject areas, continuing to maintain a balanced literacy program is not as problematic as it may seem. Indeed, it is a necessity!

Literacy "To, With, and By"

What do we mean by reading TO, WITH, and BY?

The glue that holds a comprehensive balanced literacy program together is the **To, With, and By** philosophy (Mooney, 1990) described earlier in our book. "To, With, and By" learning elements—which apply to the speaking, reading, and writing language arts activities—must be in clear evidence in (a) the plan books of teachers, (b) the learning activities they employ each day with students, and (c) the ongoing assessment strategies chosen. This easy-to-remember slogan of To, With, and By can help you to conduct regular, quick assessments of what you are doing each day. For example, in Figure 12.1, we present an actual daily schedule used by one of the authors when teaching fourth grade. We have added the words "To," "With," and "By" (whichever applies) by each activity to determine whether we are being true to the philosophy. You are encouraged to do similar self-assessments with your own teaching.

The Role of Basal Readers

Basal readers can have a valuable place in balanced reading programs. Name three examples.

In chapter 4, we discussed how basal readers could be used effectively and creatively. Basal readers have improved greatly in the past decade, especially when it comes to using high-quality children's literature. Basals are particularly useful for teachers in their first 3 years of teaching, but can also be quite helpful to experienced teachers. We encourage you to use basal readers as a part of your instructional program. For experienced teachers, it may be helpful to think in terms of using basal readers for about one week in every four to five weeks of the literature-based reading instruction activities described in this chapter.

What role specifically should basal readers play in intermediate classrooms? Certainly this is a choice to be made by each teacher based on the needs of his or her children, but we invite you to think about using basal selections for the following purposes:

- Guided reading activities (Fountas & Pinnell, 1996)
- Mini-lessons to teach the selected literacy learning milestone skills to small groups
- Construction of assessment activities (running records, cloze passages, etc.)

Figure 12.1   TO, WITH, and BY schedule analysis

8:00–8:10	**Morning business**
8:10–8:25	**"Author's Chair" and special writing assignments** (developmental writing) (Reading "BY" students)
8:25–8:35	**"Old Favorites and New Friends"** (oral reading) (Reading "TO" and "WITH" students)
8:35–8:55	**"Learning About Language"** (skills instruction and practice) Based on whole-group needs in such areas as vocabulary, development, decoding, and higher-order comprehension. (Reading "WITH" students)
8:55–9:10	**Restroom break**
9:10–10:20	*Small-group instruction* (3 group rotation, 20 minutes each) **Group 1:** **Instructional level reading** (20 minutes) (guided reading; basal work; themed units; skill instruction and practice; assessment) ("TO," "WITH," *or* "BY," depending on lesson) **Group 2:** **Developmental writing** (20 minutes) (New Jersey Writing Project; PDK Writing; Bay Area Writing; etc.) (Writing "BY" students) **Group 3:** **Learning centers** (20 minutes) (spelling; computer; phonics, etc.; library; writing; listening; math; science)
10:20–10:40	**D.E.A.R. time (Drop Everything and Read)** (independent reading) (Reading "BY" students)

- Learning activities associated with themed literature units (discussed later in this chapter)
- Small-group reading instruction

The Reading–Writing Connection

Reading and writing are reflections of the same language processes (Squire, 1983). For example, one aspect of the reading act is concerned with *decoding* graphic symbols into words, whereas writing is concerned with *encoding* meaning into graphic symbols. Similarly, writers create meaning in text, and readers interpret meaning from text.

Reading and writing are reciprocal processes.

From a language learning perspective, teachers understand that reading and writing are reciprocal processes (Shanahan, 1984). As children become authors, they also become better readers, because "writers must read and reread during writing" (K. S. Goodman & Goodman, 1983, p. 591). Indeed, it does not seem possible to positively affect one without improving the other. Reading quality text that is stimulating and writing for authentic purposes are crucial elements of a balanced reading program.

In chapter 11, we saw how emerging reading and writing abilities are facilitated by literacy-learning events in the classroom. As children move into the intermediate years, their teachers seek ways of facilitating and advancing their literacy development to inspire lifelong reading and writing activities. Because of the complementary benefits of reading and writing instruction, teachers frequently seek ways of involving the two simultaneously. An integrated curriculum is a powerful vehicle for merging reading and writing instruction, problem-solving skills, cooperative learning, and other desirable curriculum elements in authentic learning situations.

Integrated curriculums move from fragmented teaching to a more unified model.

Integrated curriculums are usually accomplished in two stages. At the first level of integration, the language arts curriculum (reading, writing, listening, speaking) makes the transition from a fragmented schedule to a more unified model; this is often accomplished through *literature-based reading units*. At the second level of curriculum integration, the language arts are integrated across the curriculum; this is often accomplished through *interdisciplinary thematic units*.

In this chapter, we mainly concern ourselves with the first level of curriculum integration: how literature-based reading programs are constructed and how the writing process can be used effectively in the intermediate grades. Later in the chapter, we offer some fascinating ideas for how integrated language arts programs can be used as a catalyst for substantive study of diverse cultures and to benefit readers with learning needs.

LITERATURE-BASED READING INSTRUCTION

Teachers appreciate the inherently motivational value of quality literature.

Several years ago, while visiting a publishers' exhibit at an annual conference of the International Reading Association (IRA), we found that the "hot" topic that year seemed to be the rediscovery of children's books as a vehicle for teaching reading. As this mammoth exhibit opened in the New Orleans convention center, thousands of teachers grabbed virtually every trade book in sight. They seemed motivated to update their classrooms with the latest materials and to feel a part of the literature-based reading movement. Teachers clearly understand the inherent motivational value of quality literature.

More recently, some have questioned whether literature-based reading instruction is a vestige of the whole language movement that has been so roundly criticized. In a recent survey of reading experts in the United States, Commeyras and DeGroff (1998) determined that most (82%) feel that the best instruction includes both literature-based and skills instruction. Thus, teachers who want to use literature for reading instruction need to understand clearly how to use children's books in effective and coherent ways *and* how to teach important literacy skills to truly balance their instruction (Freppon & Dahl, 1998).

There are a number of viable literature-based strategies for teachers to choose (see, for instance, Cooter & Griffith, 1989; Cox & Zarillo, 1993; Hiebert & Colt, 1989; Reutzel & Cooter, 1990; Zarillo, 1989). We find that there are four effective program designs: (a) core books, (b) individualized or self-selected and self-pacing units, (c) themed literature units, and (d) the Reading Workshop. It is important for the reader to note that these options are basically organizational structures for the classroom using mostly the same components.

In this section, we begin with a brief review of student reading interests and resources for selecting quality books for literature-based reading instruction. Next, we review the essential elements of core books and the individualized reading approach. In the final part of this discussion of literature-based reading instruction, we present details of themed literature units and the Reading Workshop.

Name three successful approaches to literature-based reading instruction.

What Kinds of Books Do Students *Enjoy* Reading?

There are at least two good reasons for knowing the reading preferences of intermediate-age students (Harkrader & Moore, 1997; Huck & Kuhn, 1968). First, matching students with books of high interest causes them to read for longer periods and, thus, strengthen their reading abilities. Second, knowing student interests can help the teacher to build on that base by leading students into new genres.

Mary Ann Harkrader and Richard Moore (1997) conducted a recent study of reading interests for students in the middle years. Several valuable insights can be learned from their work.

Boys as well as girls tend to prefer fiction to nonfiction, though both should be included in the reading curriculum.

- There are some gender differences in the reading preferences of boys and girls, though they both prefer fiction to nonfiction.
- Favored topics of interest for girls in fiction include mystery, friendship, adventure, fairy tales, and animal stories. Their favored nonfiction topics include art and hobbies.
- Favored topics of interest for boys in fiction include science fiction, mystery, and adventure. Nonfiction categories include earth science, how-to science experiments, and sometimes the arts and hobbies.
- Topics of interest in fiction to both boys and girls include mystery, adventure, and perhaps science fiction. Nonfiction interests that overlap somewhat include earth science and how-to science experiments, and perhaps arts and hobbies.
- Girls tend to prefer fiction books having female main characters and, similarly, boys usually prefer male main characters in fiction texts. However, there are some books where the main character is of the opposite gender that will interest boys and girls.

Core Book Units

Core books are defined as "those [literary] selections that are to be taught in the classroom, are given close reading and intensive consideration, and are likely to be an important stimulus for writing and discussion" (California State Department of Education, 1980, p. ix). With core book units, a single trade-book title is selected and enough copies are acquired so each student has one to use. When used in conjunction with free reading and writing activities, core books offer teachers and students many enjoyable literacy experiences.

Successful teachers of core book units have several things in common (Cox & Zarillo, 1993; Zarillo, 1989). First, they usually do not restrict students to a short list of "approved" books but allow them to select books of their own choosing or from an extensive list of popular literature. Teachers may find it helpful each year to consult such lists as the "Children's Choices" and "Teachers' Choices" for the best new books being released; these lists are published annually by the IRA in its journal, *The Reading Teacher.* Second, successful core book unit teachers present the selection

Core book units use enough copies of a single selection for an entire class or group.

Figure 12.2   A template for planning core book units

Background Preparations

- Confer with authoritative sources (other teachers, media specialists/librarians, lists of popular children's and adolescent books) concerning possible core books, then make your selection.
- Read the selected core book.
- Obtain background information about the book, author, and general theme of the book.
- Order multiple copies of the core book so that each student will have a copy. For bilingual classrooms and students early in their learning of English, obtain, if available, translated editions of the core book.
- Obtain a book jacket, pictures and other props to use in "selling" the book.
- Obtain extension materials related to the general theme of the book (these will be part of a temporary classroom library and/or reference center).
- Make a list of literature-reponse projects that may be suggested to students (numerous examples are suggested later in this chapter).

Part 1: Book and Author Introduction

The primary purpose is to introduce the core book and other books by the same author and/or suggest related books that might be enticing to students. Teachers should also describe in a general way choices that will be available to students pertaining to literature response, written reponses, and group collaborations. Following are typical activities that transpire in Phase 1:

- **Book introduction** using book jacket and other displays or props.
- **Sharing information** about the author and why he or she wrote the book (Note: for a great example, see Jerry Spinelli's 1991 article "Catching Maniac Magee" in which he explains his motives in writing this Newberry Award winning book.)
- **Book talk** — the teacher dramatically reads an interesting portion of the book leading up to a thrilling point, then leaves the class hanging.
- **Distribution of the book**
- **Sustained Silent Reading (SSR)** to permit students to begin reading the core book and, hopefully, get hooked.
- **Description of initial choices for literature reponse,** which usually are of an individual nature (i.e., reading response journals, reading logs, story mapping, etc.).

Core books can be used as a springboard for other reading and writing activities.

to the class with enthusiasm and drama. Sometimes selected students are involved in introducing a book or book chapter through reader's theater. Teacher book talks and shared book experiences are also effective means of developing enthusiasm for the book. Most important, successful teachers use the core book as a springboard for independent reading and writing activities.

Perhaps the greatest concern related to using core books is the idea of requiring *all* children to read the same book. Although there are many books that educators hope children will not miss, there are probably none that should be required of *every* child (Huck, Helper, & Hickman, 1987; Zarillo, 1989). Whenever the element of choice is removed from students, teachers run the risk of alienating them from books. Further, the use of core books as the only method of instruction in a literature-based program ignores the importance of allowing children to match books to their individual interests.

- **Introduction of the library and resource centers,** which house additional free-reading materials for self-selected reading and research into related topics.
- **Assignment of goal pages** so that students are aware of minimal reading expecttions for coming days.

Part 2: Reading and Reponse

In this phase, students read and discuss events in the book with the teacher and peers. Literature-reponse activities, including written response, commence. Phase 2 activities may include

- **Discussion of responses** noted in reading journals pertaining to the goal pages.
- **Read alouds/choral rereadings** by the teacher or students who have rehearsed with a partner(s). Choral readings are intended to assist students in developing fluency.
- **Group response sessions** wherein students develop a project to demonstrate their comprehension of the book (e.g., discussion webs, "Novels in the News," dramatic portrayals).
- **Student-teacher conferences,** which permit one-on-one interaction for the purpose of ongoing assessment
- **SSR time** to allow students time to read portions of the core book during school hours and subtly remind students that "reading is a priority" in our education.
- **Literacy skill/strategy activities** in which teacher-led mini-lessons are presented to help students continue their development in such areas as vocabulary knowledge, comprehension strategies, study skills, decoding abilities, writing/composition, and fluency.

Part 3: Conclusion and Presentations

In the final phase, students complete the reading and analysis of the core book. Group and individual reponse projects are presented to the class. Phase 3 often involves

- **Class discussions** about the book and other related books read by class members.
- **Presentations of literature-response activities,** such as murals, posters, mobiles, dramatizations, and panel discussions.
- **Closure activities** led by the teacher to help bring about a sense of completion and inspire a continuing desire to read other books by the same author or by other authors in the same genre.

Another concern relates to allowing children to read the core book independently: Students should be allowed to read the book at their own pace. Sometimes children become so absorbed by a book that they want to read it quickly. Let them! There are plenty of other related books of high quality they can read while their classmates are still reading. On the other hand, some children may not get very far into the book without some direction. To solve this problem, many teachers assign "goal pages" each night to keep the class moving and to let readers know which part of the book will be discussed next in class.

Core book units usually have several fundamental parts and follow a common sequence. Offered next is a kind of template we have used in constructing core book units. As with all teaching suggestions, these should be tried out in the classroom and adapted to suit the teacher's needs.

Individualized Reading

Individualized reading (Veatch, 1978), also known as self-selected or self-paced reading, is at virtually the other end of the continuum of literature-based reading instruction from core books (Hiebert & Colt, 1989). Instead of reading a book chosen by the teacher, students are permitted to select for themselves from a library of trade books. Virtually all reading instruction springs from these books that students have self-selected.

Individualized reading begins with students learning how to self-select books of interest. A procedure known as "rule of thumb" (also called the "sticky palm" and "greasy fingers" method) is taught to the class, enabling students to efficiently choose books that are "just right." First, the child finds a book that looks appealing. Second, he or she opens the book to any page with a lot of words and begins to read. Each time the child comes to a new word, he or she puts a finger down. If, by the time the child comes to the end of the page, all fingers on one hand have been used, then the book is probably too hard, and the child should put it back and find another he or she likes just as well. This procedure can be taught easily to students from primary grades on up.

Once a book has been selected, students engage in many activities, both independently and as a class. These include self-selected reading (SSR), whole-class language experience approach (LEA), Writing Workshop, and literature-response projects (skits, dioramas, writing new endings to stories). Teachers conduct conferences with each child to monitor and assess comprehension, to develop reading strategies, and to teach related literacy skills. Groups are formed on the basis of mutual need for learning specific reading skills or strategies. Individualized reading culminates with an opportunity for students to read aloud a favorite part of their book to the teacher or class.

Zarillo (1989) cites five common concerns educators often have regarding individualized reading programs:

1. They lack administrative support.
2. They face a shortage of books in classroom libraries.
3. They fear that individualized reading will lead to a chaotic environment.
4. They believe students will not fare as well on standardized reading tests.
5. They feel uninformed about how to implement individualized reading programs.

Themed literature units and the Reading Workshop are two additional organizational schemes that have been used with great success. As with core book and individualized reading units, themed literature units and the Reading Workshop have a common purpose: teaching reading using children's or adolescent literature. The components found in themed literature units and the Reading Workshop are quite interchangeable. Because of their comprehensive nature, they are presented in some detail in the following two sections.

Using a Themed Literature Units Approach

Themed literature units (Cooter & Griffith, 1989) organize reading and writing activities around a central concept or theme. They differ from a themed studies or thematic approach (discussed fully in chapter 13) in the sense that themed studies integrate content areas (e.g., science, mathematics, literature, and social studies),

Figure 12.3 Journeys theme web

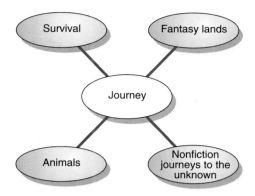

whereas themed literature units pertain mainly to reading. With themed literature units, students are permitted to choose a book from a short list of book options. After reading the book, reader response groups (also called literature-response groups) are formed to develop a project that demonstrates their comprehension of the book.

The professional literature concerning themed literature units suggests certain common elements. A brief description follows:

Themes are linked to quality literature or expository text. Themes help teachers select from the vast numbers of quality children's literature and nonfiction books available. A good theme is broad enough to allow for the selection of books that accommodate the wide range of reading interests and abilities in every classroom, yet narrow enough to be manageable. Themes are not limited to fictional stories or narrative text but often involve content themes as well (in science, social studies, health, etc.). Several examples may help to clarify this point.

"Journeys" and "courage" are two popular themes often selected by teachers.

One of the more successful themed literature units developed for intermediate grades is called "journeys." In planning a unit using the journeys theme, teachers first brainstorm as many interpretations as possible for the theme and diagram them on paper in the form of a web (Figure 12.3). After subtopics have been identified, teachers search for popular children's books that might go along with each subtheme.

For instance, in children's literature, characters are often seen going on long journeys into "fantasy lands" full of mystery and danger. Such books as *The Lion, the Witch, and the Wardrobe* (Lewis, 1961), *The Phantom Tollbooth* (Juster, 1961), *Charlie and the Chocolate Factory* (Dahl, 1964), or the old favorite book by Frank Baum (1972), *The Wizard of Oz,* all fit nicely into this interpretation of journeys. Figure 12.4 shows a completed web for the journeys theme with subtopics and possible book titles.

Think of the various forms of courage depicted in quality books.

Another popular theme is "courage." Courage is a superb theme because it can be interpreted in many ways, yet allows teachers to choose books from a manageable body of literature. Again, teachers wishing to develop a themed literature unit using courage as the theme should begin by "webbing out" several interpretations or subtopics. For instance, there is the kind of courage demonstrated on a battlefield that might be called "bravery in battle." Another interpretation involves the kind of courage exhibited by people having to cope with problems of the human condition; this subtopic might be called "overcoming adversity." Many times, young people have to develop courage when dealing with "peer relationships." These are only a few interpretations that could be used in a themed literature unit titled "Courage."

Figure 12.4   Completed journeys web

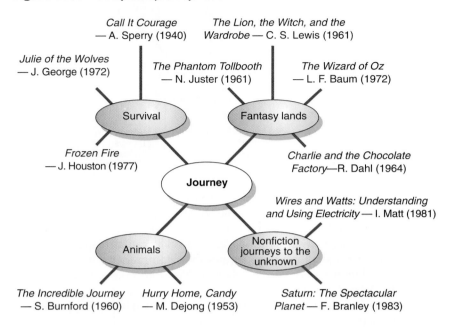

Figure 12.5 shows a fully developed web with book possibilities for a courage theme for upper elementary students.

A good theme can be interpreted in many ways and linked to quality reading selections.

To review, a good theme is broadly interpretable and can be linked to quality children's books. When these criteria are met, planning a successful themed literature unit is possible. A number of viable themes have been collected from several school systems using themed literature units and are included in the list in Table 12.1. In-service teachers have classified them into specific grade levels.

Students have the freedom to choose which books they wish to read. When possible, students should be permitted to select themes so as to enhance interest (Jacobs & Borland, 1986). Each theme should include a variety of choices that reflect the diversity of interests and ability levels in the classroom. This view of reading instruction is in sharp contrast to the overstructured "teacher as dictator" forms of teaching. After previewing each of the book choices through teacher book talks, students are then able to make their selection.

Literature response allows students to demonstrate what they have learned. In addition to answering teacher-generated comprehension questions, students complete special projects pertaining to the book's content. These projects may take the form of student dramas, creative writing projects, or other creative responses.

Notice that teachers creating themed literature units prefer to work on them collaboratively.

Team planning and collaboration help teachers efficiently develop themed literature units. In themed literature units, the teacher guides students toward new and exciting discoveries in a seemingly effortless fashion. The secret to a good themed literature unit, however, is adequate planning. Themed literature units are usually developed through team planning involving reading and language arts teachers at each grade level. Team planning allows teachers to develop units quicker and with greater depth. The old adage "two heads are better than one" definitely holds true here.

Figure 12.5   Completed courage theme web

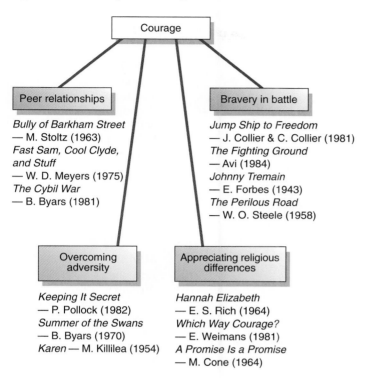

Sometimes teachers from various academic disciplines join in to help plan interdisciplinary units.

An important consideration for the success of themed literature units is school system support. Developing effective themed literature units is a major undertaking requiring a great deal of teacher planning time, financial resources (primarily for the purchase of paperback books), and administrative approval. This means that school systems should provide teachers with some form of compensated planning time after school hours or release time during the school day. It may be most desirable for school districts to address this need during the summer season when schools are usually not in session. Additionally, school districts should carefully select in-service leaders to assist teachers planning themed literature units for the first time. Leaders should be up to date on the professional literature concerning themed literature units and should have classroom experience using these procedures.

Teaching Themed Literature Units: The Nuts and Bolts

Once themes have been chosen, teachers are ready to gather learning resources and plan for instruction. The next two sections describe which resources are needed for successful implementation of themed literature units and how required reading skills and strategies can be documented. In the last part of this section, a 5-week sample plan is presented.

Table 12.1   Selected themes by grade level: Prekindergarten through sixth grade

Prekindergarten and Kindergarten	Giants	Tales–Tails
ABC	Grandparents*	Wheels*
Color	Native Americans*	
Community Helpers*	Sea*	**Fifth Grade**
Dinosaurs*	Space*	Cultures*
Fairy tales	Tall Tales	Fantasy–Fairy tales
Families*	Weather*	Friends
Friends		Journeys
Holidays*	**Third Grade**	Little People–Giants
Monsters	Adventure	Monsters
Pets*	Beasts/Creatures	Occupations*
School*	Biographies*	Prejudices*
Seasons*	Culture*	Seasons of Life*
	Folktales	Survival
First Grade	Legends	The Future*
Animals*	Magic	Transportation*
Famous People*	Mystery	
Feelings	Pioneers*	**Sixth Grade**
Food*	Sports*	Adventure
Growing Up*	War*	Animals*
Insects*	Western Stories	Cars and Motorcycles*
Numbers	Witches	Conflict*
Poems		Family*
Travel*	**Fourth Grade**	Ghosts
	Changes in Life*	Heroes*
Second Grade	Explorers*	Humor
Author (specific)*	Geographical Regions*	Music*
Birthdays	Heroes*	Overcoming Adversity
Deserts*	Mysteries	Seasonal
Fable	Myths*	Sports*
Fairy Tales	Night Frights	Survival
	Space*	

Note: Many of the themes could be used at different grade levels
*Nonfiction and/or expository text.

Gathering Learning Resources

Themed literature units can be started on a relatively small budget.

Once the teacher has selected a theme, resources must be assembled. Although large amounts of capital are not required, a substantial commitment of time and other assets is needed for full implementation. One school system using our approach began piloting themed literature units for about $1,500 per school, most of which was spent on multiple copies of paperback books.

Following is a short "shopping list" of items needed for themed literature units:

- Multiple copies of books selected ("perma-bound" books are preferred)
- Classroom library related to theme (textbooks, trade books from the school library, filmstrips, recordings, etc.)

- Art supplies for literature-response projects (e.g., markers, scissors, tag board, rulers)
- Classroom computers
- Reference books (e.g., dictionaries, encyclopedia, thesaurus)

Maintaining Balance: Documenting Progress with Literacy-Learning Milestones

As mentioned in previous chapters, most school systems have mandated performance objectives for students that tend to be based on, or correlate highly with, basal reader scope and sequence charts and state curriculum requirements. In chapter 10, we outlined our own literacy-learning milestones for learning to read that are quite similar. A common concern among administrators when themed literature units or other literature-based reading programs are used relates to documentation of student performance objectives. This is one of the political realities to which teachers must give some attention.

Student learning must be carefully documented to inform instruction and for accountability purposes.

These student performance objectives can easily be addressed in the early planning stages of a themed literature unit. Observing the following considerations will help teachers account for performance objectives (or literacy-learning milestones) and avoid difficulties in justifying the themed literature program.

Ways of assessing student learning are discussed thoroughly in chapter 10.

1. Secure a copy of the state and local curriculum guides and identify all required objectives for the grade level(s) involved.
2. Study the objectives thoroughly, and identify possible learning experiences that could satisfy the requirements. Be sure to consider alternative grouping patterns and materials for each learning experience.
3. As plans for the themed literature unit are drawn up, all objectives should be clearly stated and plans for assessing each objective described.

It is not unusual for teachers to discover that some objectives cannot be easily accommodated in themed literature units. These objectives can be addressed through short-term, whole-group mini-lessons.

Themed Literature Unit Time Line: An Example

Themed literature units can be as short as 1 day or as long as 6 weeks. Factors such as grade or developmental level, the nature of the theme itself, and curriculum requirements usually help teachers decide what sort of time frame might be best. For illustrative purposes, a 5-week time line for upper elementary or middle school students has been selected. Figure 12.6 presents the time line and is followed by descriptions of each element.

Week 1: Introducing the Theme

Many teachers like to begin themed literature units with introductory activities of some sort. The purposes are to activate students' prior knowledge and generate motivational feelings about the theme to be studied. Introductory activities might include a collage bulletin board depicting many interpretations of the new theme, role-playing, a guest speaker, or group participation activities.

Figure 12.6   Themed literature unit time line for fifth- or sixth-grade students

WEEK 1:	Class introduction to the theme.
	Book talks and book selection.
	Self-selected reading (SSR).
WEEK 2:	Reading response groups are formed.
	Response projects approved by the teacher.
	Groups begin work on projects.
WEEKS 3 to 4:	Response project work continues.
	Teacher conducts mini-lessons (student performance objectives).
WEEK 5:	Students present response projects to class.
	Closure activities by the teacher and class.

One classroom about to begin work using the courage theme reviewed a teacher-made collage bulletin board. The teacher had clipped pictures from magazines depicting several interpretations of the word *courage.* These pictures included two police officers on patrol in their squad car, a young woman in a wheelchair, a young student making a speech, and a soldier on a battlefield. The teacher and class had a most productive discussion about the theme, and the stage was set for the introduction of the books.

Another very similar bulletin board could be constructed using jackets from the books to be introduced. For the courage theme, a teacher might simply display the word *courage* in bold letters at the center of the bulletin board. Lines could spiral out from the theme word in a web format and connect to each of the book jackets. With this type of bulletin board, the teacher can introduce the theme and book choices at once.

Get together with a colleague and brainstorm ways students could be introduced to a theme of your choice.

Many other theme introductions are possible. A guest speaker might come and talk to the class. For instance, before beginning a theme entitled "animals," the teacher could invite a local veterinarian to visit the class and speak about specific animals portrayed in the books selected for the unit. In one instance we observed, the presenter brought along some of the instruments used for administering medicine to animals, talked about some of the myths and facts about the animals under study, and answered questions from the class. This experience produced a strong interest in the theme and resulted in a great deal of recreational reading in the library and student writing (in the form of language experience stories).

Other introductory activities may involve drama. Role-playing, reader's theater, and even an occasional video production can be used for theme introduction. Once a mental mind-set has been created for the theme, the teacher is ready to introduce the books.

Book talks call on teachers to use their drama skills to entice students into choosing a book of interest.

Book Talks.   One of the most enjoyable parts of a themed literature unit, for both teacher and students, is book talks (Fader, 1976). The object is to draw the children into the books and interest them deeply, so they will want to read. When the book talk is well executed, all children want to read several of the books mentioned. In fact, a little frustration may result as each student tries to choose the one book he or she most wants to read.

The book talk activity is very easy to do. First, the teacher finds a most enticing section in each of the books to be used (about six titles for a class of 25, with five copies of each title available). We recommend that the section of the book to be emphasized take about 5 to 10 minutes to read and come from the first third of the book. Second, the teacher enthusiastically tells the class about each book, perhaps adding some background information about the author, then reads a juicy part of the book to the class. Naturally, the more drama and excitement a teacher puts into the book talk, the easier it will be to get the class hooked on each book. Third, the teacher should conclude the reading without giving away the plot. In other words, the book talk should be a cliffhanger. In fact, the suspense of not knowing what will happen to the characters in the story should create an almost overpowering urge to read the book. After each book has been introduced, the children are ready to make their selection.

Student Self-Selection.   An important element for the success of any holistic reading program is for students to feel that they have choices. In themed literature units, students are allowed to choose which of the books they will read. As mentioned, about six titles (five copies of each title) usually are selected for a class of 25 children.

In helping children choose which book to read, a good way to avoid peer pressure among students is to have them select their books by secret ballot. Ask the children to write their names on a blank piece of paper, then list in order their first, second, and third choices. Inform them that they will be given one of their choices and, if at all possible, their first choice.

During the teacher's planning period, he or she simply lists on a sheet of paper the title for each book and writes the numbers from one to five under each title (this corresponds to the multiple copies acquired for each title). Next, the teacher opens the ballots and gives each child his or her first choice. Should the teacher run out of a given title, he or she simply gives the child the second choice. Even if the teacher has to give children their second choice, the children still feel they were given a book of their own choosing instead of one chosen by the teacher. Figure 12.7 illustrates a typical class assignment chart. Sometimes only one child chooses a given title. In this event, the student simply works through the project alone. In fact, during the course of a school year, all children should have an opportunity to work alone at least once.

Self-Selected Reading.   Once the book assignments have been announced, the children are ready to begin reading. It is recommended that the unit begin in earnest by allowing students uninterrupted time to read their books. We call this reading period *self-selected reading* (SSR), rather than the usual label *sustained silent reading,* simply because readers may want to share an exciting reading discovery with a friend during the period. These positive encounters with books should be encouraged as long as class disruption does not become a factor.

The purpose of SSR in this situation is threefold. First, children are given time to read, an activity that improves reading ability over time. Second, the children are allowed to get involved with their books, which creates a strong motivation to continue reading. A third purpose is to allow children who may have selected a book that is too difficult time to change their minds and trade their book in for one of the remaining titles. Usually, a 24-hour grace period is allowed for exchanging books. The equivalent of two reading class periods on consecutive days is a good start for SSR.

A question teachers frequently ask relates to how long students should be expected to take to complete their books. Some teachers feel that when students are given a great deal of time to finish reading their books, say 3 to 4 weeks, students simply procrastinate until 1 or 2 days before the deadline. The result is a not-so-pleasurable reading experience for the student, opposite of our intended purpose. To

Students primarily choose their book based on interest.

Children spend at least two reading periods reading their new book selections.

Time limits are usually set for students to finish reading their books.

Figure 12.7   Themed literature unit assignment chart example

---

Themed Unit Title: "Courage"

Book: *Fast Sam, Cool Clyde and Stuff*
1. Jason B.
2. Jina M.
3. Melanie C.
4. Bill J.
5. Mark S.

Book: *Summer of the Swans*
1. Austin K.
2. Sutton E.
3. Jill E.
4. Emilio C.
5. Bruce W.

Book: *Johnny Tremain*
1. Shelley P.
2. Jackson B.
3. Deb F.
4.
5.

Book: *The Perilous Road*
1. Christen M.
2. Ramesh B.
3. Michelle L.
4. Jason L.
5.

Book: *Which Way Courage?*
1. Skip C.
2. Margarette S.
3. Julian G.
4. Jason U.
5.

Book: *The Cybil War*
1. Toni G.
2. Marion H.
3. Luis J.
4. Jillian Y.
5. Charesse D.

---

counteract this problem, some teachers prefer to use a shortened timetable for reading the book, say 5 to 7 days for books of about 120 pages. With this timetable comes a mild sense of urgency or feeling on the part of the student that "I better get busy reading or I won't be finished in time."

Some books naturally require more time than others for reading because of length or complexity. Usually, the teacher can work out a formula to determine how many days should be allowed for the reading of each book. For instance, if the teacher feels that the average child can read 20 pages of a given book per night, then a 300-page book will require at least 15 days to read. Teachers should also consider such factors as print size, number of words per page, and the author's writing style when developing these formulas. Whatever the formula used, teachers should try to come up with reasonable limits that help students stay on task and enjoy the book.

Week 2: Beginning Literature-Response Projects

Literature-response groups begin work during the second week.

As teachers well know, sometimes students can be very reluctant readers. Literature-response activities can be a wonderful vehicle for spurring interest in books and can create writing opportunities. During the second week, students begin work with their literature-response groups (LRGs). Children are grouped based on mutual interest, namely, which book they chose. For example, all students (up to four or five) who choose to read *Henry and Beezus* (Cleary, 1952) as part of a friendship theme become the Henry and Beezus Group. All children reading *The Lion, the Witch, and the Wardrobe* (Lewis, 1961) as part of the journeys theme become The Lion, the Witch, and the Wardrobe Group. This type of grouping capitalizes on students' intrinsic interests, needs, and motivations.

Students working in LRGs are required to conceive of a project that demonstrates their comprehension of their book. All project ideas are subject to approval by the teacher because refinement of some ideas will be required. We observed one group who read Lewis's *The Lion, the Witch, and the Wardrobe* and decided to create a "Narnia game" that was constructed in the image of popular trivia games. Contestants landing on certain spaces on the gameboard were required to answer questions related to the book. Because students in the LRG were required to write all questions and answers for the game (on a variety of cognitive levels), comprehension of the book seemed to be deeper than one might typically expect from, for example, workbook exercises.

Think about some of the advantages of LRG projects over traditional reading follow-up activities.

Next, we discuss several popular LRG project ideas that have been successful with themed literature units. Some are rather extensive and take considerable preparation, whereas others may be accomplished in just one or two sessions.

Student Dramas.   Reenactment of major events in a book is a particularly popular LRG activity for students in elementary through middle school grades. These student dramas foster deeper understanding of story structures and narrative competence (Martinez, 1993), facilitate content mastery, and provide a marvelous forum in which to display oral fluency skills. Only minimal props and costumes are needed to help students participate.

Students sometimes choose to create dramas based on their reading selection.

Students begin by choosing a favorite part of the book to retell through drama. Next, they develop a script based on a combination of actual dialogue in the book and narration. Usually the narration is delivered by a reader or narrator, who explains such story elements as setting, problem, and other pertinent information. Typically, the drama is presented as a one-act play and concludes in the same way as a book talk—it leaves the audience in suspense. This often makes the audience (other students in the class) want to select the book themselves for recreational reading.

Martinez (1993) points out that modeling can be especially helpful in encouraging students to choose this option for literature response. Inviting a professional or amateur actor to explain to students some of the rudiments of performance is a good way to stimulate interest.

The accompanying box shows a script developed by students for the novel *Fast Sam, Cool Clyde, and Stuff* (Myers, 1975). This script includes dialogue excerpts from the book along with narration developed by the students.

Dialogue Retellings.   Cudd and Roberts (1993) suggest another drama form using fables to help students better understand the importance of dialogue. First, the teacher selects a short fable having two characters and reads it to the class; Cudd and Roberts suggest Arnold Lobel's (1983) *Fables*. Second, the teacher chooses two students to retell the fable orally, each assuming the part of one character. The other students listen for story sequence and help supply any missing parts. The whole class has a discussion about how dialogue is important to story and character development. Third, the teacher provides each student with a copy of the fable for rereading and analysis of the dialogue mechanics in writing. Fourth, students working in pairs write a retelling of the fable from memory with each student assuming one of the character roles. As they write/retell the dialogue and their character speaks, the paper used to create the draft should be physically handed to the appropriate person so that they are constantly reminded to indent. In the final stages of this activity, students can share their dialogues with the class, then create their own original fables individually, in pairs, or in groups.

Figure 12.8   Script for *Fast Sam, Cool Clyde, and Stuff*

Stuff:	Sam and Clyde were going to enter the contest. Only, one of them was going to get decked out like a girl.
Sam:	You can be the woman, and I'll be the man, and we can win this contest. Ain't nobody around going to beat us. And that's a f-a-c-t fact.
Clyde:	How come I have to be the woman? You can be the woman, and I can be the guy.
Sam:	I got to be the guy. Because I can't be no woman.
Clyde:	Why not?
Sam:	Because it messes with my image.
Clyde:	And it messes with my image, too.
Sam:	Anyway, I'm so manly that anybody looking at me could tell I was a man.
Stuff:	We told Angel and Maria and it was decided that me, Angel, and Maria would decide who would be the girl and who would be the guy. Me and Angel figured the guy who was the more manly would be the guy and the other person would be the girl. Maria, Angel's sister, said the guy who was the most manly would be the girl "cause it wouldn't bother him as much being the girl." Which made sense in a funny kind of way. Anyway, we had a manly contest to see who was the most manly between Clyde and Sam.
	The contest was simple. Whoever did the manliest thing was going to be the woman, and the other guy would be the man. We figured we had three votes, and it couldn't be a tie. But that was before we considered Maria.

Adapted from the text by R. Cooter, 1990.

Radio plays involve both reading and writing activities.

Radio Play.   Developing a radio play involves virtually the same process as any other student drama, except that it involves a purely oral–aural (i.e., speaking–listening) delivery. Students first write a one-act play based on their book as described in the preceding section. Next, materials are gathered for the purpose of creating needed sound effects (police whistles, recorded train sound effects, door opening/closing, etc.), and different human sounds are practiced (such as a girl's or boy's scream, tongue clicking noise, and throat clearing). After thorough rehearsal of the script with sound effects, the radio play is taped on a cassette recorder and played over the school's public address system into the classroom.

Teachers may want to obtain recordings of old radio shows, such as "The Shadow," to help students better understand the concept. Another source is Garrison Keillor's radio program, "A Prairie Home Companion," which airs every Saturday night on National Public Radio stations and usually has several radio dramas each week.

Think of ways parent volunteers could assist students with LRG projects.

Evening Newscast.   Students enjoy acting out book summaries in the form of a nightly newscast, often titled something like the "10 O'clock Eyewitness Action News." Each student prepares a news story script (using the Writing Workshop method described later in this chapter) that retells an important event or piece of

> Sam and Clyde, me, Angel, and Maria all met at Clyde's house. Sam was supposed to do his manly thing first.
>
> *Sam:*   I am going to do 50 push-ups. Every time I go down I'll go all the way down until my *mustache* touches the floor.
>
> *Stuff:* When he said "mustache" he gave Clyde a look because Sam was the only one in the whole bunch who had even a little bit of a mustache.
>
> *Clyde:* He got his mustache by having a transplant from under his arms.
>
> *Sam:*   Yeah, baby, but match these 50.
>
> *Stuff:* Sam then did 50 push-ups. I think he could have done more if he wanted to, too. Then it was Clyde's turn. Clyde announced that he was going to take any *torture* that Sam could dish out. Torture!!!
>
> *Angel:* You're going to let him torture you?
>
> *Clyde:* Right, and I'm going to take it without giving up.
>
> *Sam:*   You got to be jiving, man. I'll put you through so many changes that you won't even remember your name. I'll put bamboo splinters under your eyelids and tap dance over your forehead. You might as well give it up, turkey, because you're going to be crying for mercy in the worse kind of way.
>
> *Stuff:* Clyde laid down on the floor and crossed his arms over his chest.
>
> *Clyde:* Sock it to me, and see what a real man can take.
>
> *Stuff:* Now, man. If you dudes want to know what came down next, you gotta read the book. You know man, if you wanna see the show you gotta pay the toll!

information in the book. After LRG members have helped each other refine their scripts, they dress up and rehearse as news reporters until the performance is ready for presentation to the class. The evening newscast can either be acted out before the class or recorded using a video camera, then replayed to the class on television.

Novels in the News.   Rice (1991) describes an activity called *novels in the news,* which has students learn to combine the journalistic style found in newspaper headlines with the story structure of novels. The idea is to reduce major events in the novel or nonfiction book to simplest terms, then display these mock headlines on a bulletin board. Thus, one might see such headlines as LOCAL SCARECROW SEEKS BRAIN IMPLANT for *The Wizard of Oz* (Baum, 1972), COB STEALS TRUMPET FROM LOCAL MUSIC STORE for *The Trumpet of the Swan* (White, 1970), or LOCAL BOY BECOMES FOOTBALL HERO for *Forrest Gump* (Groom, 1986).

In a more advanced version of *novels in the news,* a mock newspaper front page is created. News stories are created with each LRG member acting as a writer/reporter in much the same way as explained in the evening newscast activity. Stories are typed at the computer, printed out, then pasted onto a large piece of poster board using a newspaper front-page style. The front page is then displayed in a prominent place and presented to the class. *Hint:* Show the class a copy of the book *The True Story of the 3 Little Pigs, by A. Wolf* (Scieszka, 1989) which has an excellent example on the front cover.

Many popular writers are formula writers.

Formula Retelling.   Many popular authors are *formula* writers; they have discovered a successful basic story line, which is altered in each book in terms of setting, characters, and problem. In *formula retelling* (Cooter, 1994), students in LRGs read two or three stories or books by the same author, chart the basic story line, then respond through group writing to create their own short story using the author's formula.

For example, Donald Sobol, author of the popular *Encyclopedia Brown* series, appears to have used a formula in creating these detective stories. These titles are also excellent choices for a themed literature unit with young readers because of their high-interest content, easy readability, and avoidance of profanity and adult situations that might cause some parents to object. Group members (usually a group of five) begin by reading at least one story in an *Encyclopedia Brown* book, with all the chapters read by someone in the group. As the stories are read and the plots unfold, students begin a comparison grid detailing major points in the story. Eventually the stories are completed, as is the comparison grid. After carefully examining the comparison grid and discussing similarities, the final step is for students to create their own short story using common elements from the author's formula.

Design your own comparison grid for three children's book authors who are formula writers.

In Figure 12.9, a completed formula retelling comparison grid is shown depicting Sobol's formula for three stories in *Encyclopedia Brown Solves Them All.* The students' short story can be presented to the class using either a dramatic reading format, printed copies of the short story, radio play, or dramatic production.

Teachers in middle elementary grades may want to consider some of the works of such authors as E. B. White, C. S. Lewis, Beverly Cleary, and Betsy Byars for formula-retelling activities.

List some popular TV shows of the past and present that could serve as a template for this kind of project.

A Meeting of Minds.   In the early days of television, Steve Allen hosted a program called "A Meeting of Minds." Famous people of the past were played by actors who held high-level discussions about issues of their time and problems they were trying to solve. Peggy Lathlaen (1993) has adapted "Meeting of Minds" in her classroom and found it especially useful with biographies.

Students begin by thoroughly researching their famous person from the past so that they can later "become" this person before the class. This work involves careful reading of one or more books, construction of a time line for this person's life (which is then compared to a general time line recording significant inventions and world events at the time), research into costumes of the era, developing Venn diagrams comparing their person to others being researched in the LRGs, and searching Bartlett's *Familiar Quotations* for memorable quotes made by the individual. Reenactments of famous events and question–answer sessions are typical presentations made by students. Famous figures portrayed in Lathlaen's classroom include Thomas Jefferson, Queen Elizabeth I, Barbara Jordan, and George Bush.

Dioramas.   A diorama is an important scene from the chosen book that is re-created for presentation. Students, usually working in pairs, often re-create the scene on a small scale using art materials. The diorama is presented to the class along

Figure 12.9 Formula retelling comparison grid (plot similarities noted in bold)
Stories from *Encyclopedia Brown Solves Them All* by Donald Sobol

	The Case of the Missing Clues	*The Case of Sir Biscuit-Shooter*	*The Case of the Muscle Maker*	*Our Story*
The hero	**Encyclopedia Brown**	**Encyclopedia Brown**	**Encyclopedia Brown**	
Problem to solve	Is Bugs threatening Abner?	Who robbed Princess Marta?	Is the Hercules's Strength Tonic fake?	
How Encyclopedia gets involved	Abner **hires** him	Sally **asks him to help**	Cadmus **hires** him	
Villian	Bugs Meany	Kitty, the bareback rider	Wilford Wiggins	
What Encyclopedia does	**Listens** to Abner, examines clubhouse, **finds inconsistencies**	**Listens** to accusations against Barney, **finds inconsistencies**	**Listens** to Wilford's claims, **finds inconsistencies**	
Clues	Cherries	Noise of pots and pans	Suit coat	
In the end	**Encyclopedia proves Bugs lied**	**Encyclopedia proves Kitty lied**	**Encyclopedia proves Wilford lied**	
Results	Bugs repaid Abner	Kitty confessed	Wilford repaid Cadmus	

with a prepared explanation of why this scene was deemed important to the book. Multiple dioramas can be presented to portray a visual sequence retelling key scenes in the book.

Big Book or Predictable Book with Captions.   A great response activity that can be constructed by either individuals or groups is a big book or predictable book version of the novel or nonfiction book. The idea is for students to create a simplified

Rewriting books or chapters for first graders requires deep comprehension and skillful writing.

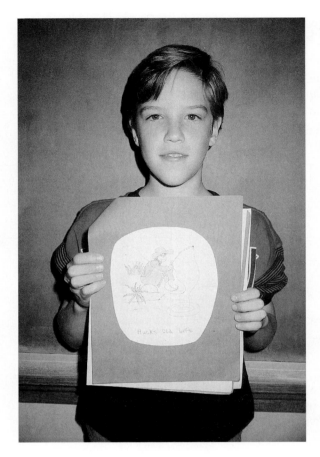

Figure 12.10   Student holding book he made in class

version of the book, which can be shared with kindergarten or first-grade audiences. One middle school student at a school adopting our themed literature units model decided to construct a multiple-page predictable book retelling the story line of *Huckleberry Finn* (Figure 12.10).

After completion of his project, he shared his predictable book with first-grade classes at the neighboring elementary school—a treat for the young children and the author alike!

Discussion Webs.   Discussion webs are a kind of graphic aid for teaching students to look at both sides of an issue before making final judgments (Alvermann, 1991). They may be useful with novels and other narrative selections, but we feel they can be particularly useful with nonfiction materials. Adapted from the work of social studies teacher James Duthie (1986), there are basically five steps in using discussion webs. The first step is much like traditional reading activities in that a discussion is held to activate background knowledge, discuss new or challenging vocabulary, and provide a purpose for reading. Students then read, or begin reading, the selection. The second step is to state the central question to be considered and introduce the discussion web. Students complete both the *yes* and *no* columns individually, usually recording key thoughts as opposed to complete sentences. The third step is for stu-

Figure 12.11   Students' discussion web: TV cameras in courtrooms?

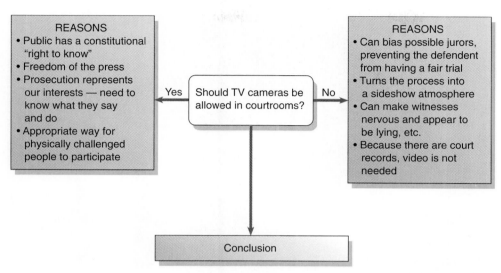

dents to be paired for comparing responses and beginning to work toward consensus. Later, two pairs work together for the purpose of further consensus building. In the fourth step, a group spokesperson reports to the whole class which of the reasons best reflects the consensus of the group; usually, a 3-minute period is allotted for reporting. The final step suggested is that students individually write a follow-up position paper about their judgment on the matter. In Figure 12.11, we present a discussion web completed by students researching whether television cameras should be permitted in courtrooms.

Homemade Filmstrip.   Homemade filmstrips are an interesting way for students to retell the sequence of a story. Pictures are made with captions that retell important parts of the book. The pictures are then taped together in sequence and viewed with the aid of an opaque projector (if available). This activity is in some ways similar in purpose to the creation of big books or predictable books described earlier.

David Letterman or Oprah Talk Show.   In a combination of drama, action news, and "A Meeting of Minds," students write a script for a TV talk show. One of the students is cast as a TV host or interviewer ("Dave" or "Oprah"), and the other team members represent characters from their chosen book being interviewed. The talk show can either be acted out in front of the class, followed by questions and answers, or videotaped and shown over television to the class using VCR/TV equipment.

For schools not having video equipment, teachers can check with the high school football coach; coaches have such equipment and may be willing to make it available at convenient times.

Giant Comic Strips.   Similar to a mural in size, giant comic strips are made by students to re-create and retell the main story line of a book they've read. First, the group sketches out a comic strip having, typically, six to eight panels that retell an important part of a narrative story or facts explained in a nonfiction book. Next, the comic strip sketch is reviewed by the teacher for accuracy and approved for final stages. The group then reproduces the comic strip on a large sheet of butcher paper and displays

Figure 12.12   Student-made giant comic strip

it on a wall in the classroom. Giant comic strips are helpful in assessing understanding of sequence. Figure 12.12 shows a giant comic strip created by an intermediate-level group.

Students must be helped to learn appropriate group behavior; it doesn't occur naturally.

Group Etiquette for Successful Literature-Response Groups.   Finally, note that students do not work in groups harmoniously by accident; some careful training must occur. Through role-playing experiences, children can be helped to understand appropriate kinds of behavior expected while working in LRGs. One group of teachers in Kenton, Ohio, came up with a wonderful idea for teaching "group etiquette." One day after school, teachers at each grade level met to dramatize both positive and negative group behavior. They dressed in the clothing styles of young adolescents and role-played negative group behavior, then positive group behavior. These performances were recorded on videocassette tape and shown to their classes during the introduction to themed literature units. Students enjoyed the production and were able to identify "do's and don'ts" for their LRGs. Figure 12.13 shows some typical rules that might emerge from a discussion of group etiquette.

Weeks 3 and 4: LRG Projects and Skill Mini-lessons

Mini-lessons are taught using examples drawn from the selected books, or other readings consistent with the overall theme.

Work continues on LRG projects in weeks 3 and 4, but the teacher claims part of the time for mini-lessons. Mini-lessons, as applied to themed literature units, allow teachers to (a) help students develop reading and study strategies within the context of the theme and (b) satisfy local or state mandates regarding student performance objectives. For example, if the class is reading books related to the theme "animal stories," then the teacher may prepare a related mini-lesson about using the card catalog in the library to locate other books on animals.

Figure 12.13   Group etiquette rules (student generated)

1. Remember that we are taking part in a discussion to learn and help others to learn.
2. We need to bring a paper and pencil to each meeting.
3. Listen to people without interrupting when they talk. Let everyone have their say.
4. Don't show off in a discussion.
5. Everyone has to take part in the discussion.
6. It's OK to change your mind when you have been proven wrong.
7. If someone is having trouble saying what they mean and you understand, help them say it in another way.
8. Always have one member of the group write down important ideas.

In weeks 3 and 4 of the unit, students should be allowed approximately one half to two thirds of the time for working on LRG projects and SSR. Students who feel they require more time to work on their LRG projects should do so out of class as homework.

Week 5: Project Presentations and Closure Activities

The final week of themed literature units is set aside for students to present their projects to the class. These presentations serve two important functions. First, they are a sharing time that provides LRGs with an opportunity to make public their efforts. Second, students in the class are reintroduced to the books they did not read, a process that often stimulates further recreational reading.

Themes should be concluded with some sort of closure activity that brings about a positive sense that the work is now complete and the class is ready to move on to something new. Closure activities might include a guest speaker, a field trip, or perhaps a film presentation related to the theme.

Evaluating Themed Literature Units

Teachers can accumulate evidence of student growth in themed literature units in many ways. Generally, a typical themed literature unit presents 5 to 10 assessment opportunities. The following list includes some of the potential sources for student assessments:

Themed literature units provide many assessment opportunities.

- *Book Tests:* Teachers often give a brief paper-and-pencil test for the middle and end of each book.
- *Literature-Response Projects:* Teachers quickly realize that a few students will sometimes attempt to let their fellow group members do all of the work, then claim their share of the credit. This attitude is rarely successful for very long, mainly as a result of peer pressure. Using the following evaluation scheme tends to produce fair and defensible grades:
    1. *Class Evaluations:* Each student in the class viewing the project presentations completes an evaluation form (teacher designed) for

Figure 12.14   The Reading Workshop

Reading Workshop (70 min)		
Sharing Time (5–10 min) Mini-lesson (5–10 min) State of the Class (5 min)		
Self-Selected Reading (SSR) and Response (35–45 min)		

SSR
1. Self-selected book
2. Reading their goal pages for literature-response group
3. Responding to literature
4. Record keeping
   a. Book time and title logs
   b. Updating state of class
   c. Signing up for individual reading conference
 	
10 min
	Literature response
	1. Group meeting for response
	2. New meeting
	3. Determine new response mode
	
	15–20 min
		Individual reading conferences
		1. Two a day
		2. Running record
		   a. Taped
		   b. Retellings
		
		10–15 min

Sharing time (children) (5–10 min)		

From "Organizing for Effective Instruction: The Reading Workshop" by D. R. Reutzel and R. B. Cooter, Jr., 1991, *The Reading Teacher,* 44(8), pp. 548–555. Copyright 1991 by International Reading Association. Reprinted by permission.

each group. Criteria for evaluating each group should be negotiated with the LRG at the beginning of week 2, then used by the class members as evaluation criteria during the class presentation.

2. *Intragroup Evaluation:* Each member in the LRG should rate the productivity and contribution of each of the other group members.

3. *Teacher's Evaluation:* Based on the preceding criteria, the teacher awards each individual group member an LRG grade.

- *Mini-lesson Grades:* Summative grades and evaluations accumulated during mini-lessons become part of the overall assessment.
- *Student–Teacher Conferences:* These generally take the form described in the following section on the Reading Workshop.

Student–teacher conferences are a convenient assessment forum.

In chapter 10, we discuss many other authentic assessment methods that can be applied to themed literature units.

The Reading Workshop: Organizing for Instruction

*The **Reading Workshop** is another organizational framework for literature-based reading instruction.*

The **Reading Workshop** (Reutzel & Cooter, 1991) is an organizational scheme providing for the full integration of children's literature or basal stories into the classroom reading program. It is not intended to be prescriptive but rather to offer a functional and flexible instructional scaffolding for reading. The five main components are sharing time, mini-lesson, state of the class, Reading Workshop, and sharing time. Each of these components is explained in the following paragraphs and outlined in Figure 12.14.

Phase 1: Sharing Time (5 to 10 Minutes)

During sharing time, teachers share new discoveries they have made in children's literature (e.g., folktales, short stories, nonfiction, poetry). For example, the teacher may have been looking for spooky stories for the Halloween season and just discovered Jack Prelutsky's (1976) collection of poetry called *Nightmares: Poems to Trouble Your Sleep.* With permission from the publisher, the teacher might make overhead transparencies of a few of the spooky pen-and-ink sketches from a few of the poems in the book and display them on the overhead screen while reading aloud the selections on vampires and ghouls. The idea is to spark interest in various literary genres for free reading. (Note: Good judgment on the teacher's part will dictate which selections should be used. Thus, certain poems may not be appropriate for some audiences.) Sometimes, the sharing time activity can serve as a catalyst for Writing Workshop projects (explained later in this chapter) or as an introduction for the Reading Workshop mini-lesson.

Sharing time is a teacher-conducted read-aloud period.

Phase 2: Mini-lesson (5 to 10 Minutes)

Mini-lessons (Reutzel & Cooter, 1999) are small- and whole-group instructional sessions whose purpose is the teaching of reading skills and strategies. (In chapter 8, we discuss the step-by-step process for teaching effective mini-lessons.) Mini-lesson topics are chosen according to

Mini-lessons should be developed based on the demonstrated needs of the students and the nonnegotiable skills that must be learned.

- demonstrated needs of students discovered during individual reading conferences (discussed more fully later in this section),
- the list of nonnegotiable skills at each grade level, and
- literature preparation (prereading) activities to assist students with new books they are to begin reading.

Mini-lessons are certainly a powerful tool for teaching literacy skills. Another potential use of the mini-lesson is for *prereading* activities. Specifically, the following activities are intended to assist students in drawing on past experiences or schemas before reading to enhance comprehension. Literature-preparation activities should also help create a stronger affective climate for students before reading (e.g., interest, positive attitude, motivation). These activities should be studied and earmarked for future classroom use.

Story Frames.   Story frames (Fowler, 1982) are series of blanks hooked together by important "language elements" reflecting a specific line of thought. Examples of story frames are presented in chapter 6.

Story Sequence Clothesline.   Many teachers have found that having children predict what might happen in a story before reading boosts overall comprehension. Typically, the teacher has an introductory discussion to tap students' relevant prior experiences, then predictions are made by students and recorded on the chalkboard. After reading, the story predictions are checked and revised for accuracy. However, a weakness of this procedure is that students generally attend to random story events without regard to sequence.

A story sequence clothesline can help students see the relationship of events in a story.

One literature-preparation activity that helps students develop sequence comprehension strategies is the story sequence clothesline (Reutzel & Cooter, 1987).

Figure 12.15   Clothesline predictions for *The Polar Express* (Van Allsburg, 1985)

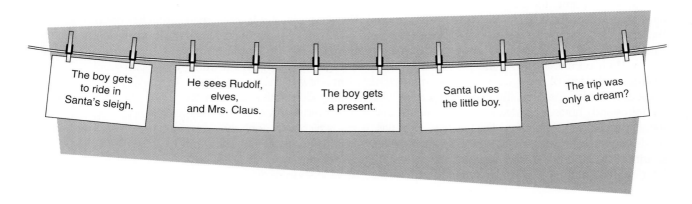

This activity requires a clothesline strung across the front of the classroom, clothespins, tag board cut into large strips or rectangles, and a dark marker. The procedure follows:

1. The teacher conducts an activity intended to bring to the students' minds past experiences relevant to the story (discussion, role-playing activity, guest speaker, demonstration, etc.).
2. The teacher then introduces the selection, discusses troublesome new vocabulary with students, and asks students to predict what might happen in the story.
3. The teacher records predictions on the pieces of tag board and places them in front of the class, such as on the chalkboard chalk tray, and asks students to predict the order in which events will occur.
4. As the class makes predictions about what will happen first, second, and so on, the teacher pins the predictions written on tag board in order on the clothesline.
5. Students read the selection, revise and clarify predictions, and make corrections regarding the sequence of events as needed.

*Books like **The Polar Express** (Van Allsburg, 1985) can be very useful in teaching sequence.*

Figures 12.15 and 12.16 depict both a predicted sequence of events and the revised sequence for the wonderful Christmas book *The Polar Express* by Chris Van Allsburg (1985).

Schema Stories.   Schema stories (Harste, Short, & Burke, 1988) challenge students to construct or reconstruct stories using meaning and story grammar. An explanation of schema stories is presented in chapter 6.

Phase 3: State of the Class (3 to 5 Minutes)

State of the class

helps teachers monitor student learning and helps students stay on task.

One of the concerns for teachers trying out the Reading Workshop is monitoring what youngsters do during independent work periods. *State of the class* is a wonderful classroom management tool that informs teachers of student activities each day *and* reminds students of their responsibilities during the workshop period. Each day, students

Figure 12.16   *Revised predictions for* The Polar Express *(Van Allsburg, 1985)*

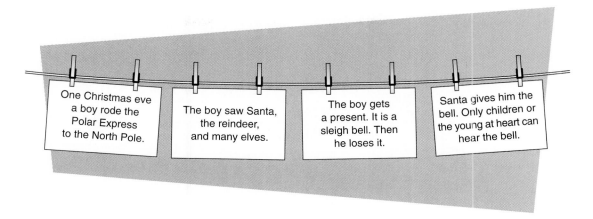

fill in a state of the class chart like the one shown in Figure 12.17, explaining their major activities for the next day. Just before the SSR and response period begins (see next section), the teacher reviews the chart with the students to help them remember what they are supposed to be doing and assign deadlines. Some teachers, like Nancy Atwell (1987), prefer to complete the chart themselves with the whole class. Atwell describes state of the class as a brief (3 to 5 minutes) and effective way of "eavesdropping" on students' plans and activities during independent activity periods.

When problems are observed, such as a student's spending several days on one task with no apparent progress, then a "house call" or teacher–student conference is scheduled (see individual reading conferences in Figure 12.14). This simple process ensures that students having difficulty do not "fall through the cracks" and provides teachers with a daily audit trail of each student's work that can be referred to during conferences with parents and for planning minilessons.

Teachers make frequent "house calls" to monitor and extend student learning on an individual basis.

Phase 4: Self-Selected Reading and Response (40 Minutes)

The heart of the reading period is called *self-selected reading and response* (SSR&R). It involves three student activities: SSR, literature response (LR), and individual reading conferences (IRC).

Self-Selected Reading.   During SSR, students may become involved in one or more activities. To begin the workshop period, students and teachers engage in free reading of a book they have chosen for 10 minutes of SSR. Another option is for students to read goal pages established by their LRG. *Goal pages* are daily reading goals established by students themselves to accomplish the reading of a book within a given time frame.

Students who continue in SSR during the LRG meeting (discussed in the next section) engage in four priority choices. First, they must complete their LRG goal pages. Next, they complete LR projects. Literature-response logs are regular records, usually daily, that children keep as running diaries of their reading. Third, they update their reading records—filling in book time and title logs, updating their activities on the state of the class chart, or signing up for an IRC with the teacher. When these three activities are completed, students can self-select a book for recreational reading as a fourth choice.

SSR activities ensure that students get massive amounts of practice using their reading skills.

Figure 12.17   State of the class chart

State of the Class Chart					
Student Name	M	T	W	TH	F
John	LR-GM	LR-GM			
Maria	LR-NM	IRC			
Jalissa	LR-NM	LR-GM			
Sue	IRC	LR-NM			
Miguel	SSR-LRG	SSR-LRG			
Yumiko	IRC	SSR-LRG			
Jamie Lee	LR-NM	LR-GM			
Seth	SSR-SSB	SSR-SSB			
Andrea	SSR-SSB	SSR-RL			
Martin	IRC	SSR-SSB			
Heather	SSR-SSB	SSR-SSB			
April	LR-NM	LR-GM			
Jason	ABSENT	SSR-SSB			
Malik	LR-GM	IRC			
Juanita	SSR-LRG	SSR-LRG			
J.T.	SSR-LRG	SSR-LRG			
Francesca	ABSENT	IRC			
Shelley	LR-NM	LR-GP			
Melanie	SSR-SSB	SSR-LRG			

Key

SSR:	Self-selected reading	RK:	Record keeping
SSB:	Self-selected book	LR:	Literature-response group
LRG:	Literature-response group goal pages	GM:	Group meeting for response
		NM:	New meeting
		RM:	Determining new response
RL:	Responding to literature	IRC:	Individual reading conference

From "Organizing for Effective Instruction: The Reading Workshop" by D. R. Reutzel and R. B. Cooter, Jr., 1991, *The Reading Teacher, 44*(8), pp. 548–555. Copyright 1991 by the International Reading Association. Reprinted by permission.

Think about some of the reasons adults value collaboration in the workplace. How are those motivations similar to those of students in LRGs?

Literature-Response Groups.   After the initial 10 minutes of SSR&R, one or more groups of children per day move into an LRG by appointment while the remainder of the class continues working in SSR. As described earlier, literature-response groups are made up of students who come together by choice, not assignment, to read and respond to a chosen piece of literature and develop related projects. Teachers meet with one LRG each day to participate in and facilitate response activities. Some teach-

Figure 12.18 Burgess summary for *The Trumpet of the Swan* (E. B. White, 1970)

> Lewis was a trumpeter swan born without a <u>blurber</u>. Lewis' father, the cob, decided that something must be done. If Lewis <u>ciz</u> ever to have a chance for a normal life he <u>wrost</u> need a trumpet, the kind humans play in a band. The cob flew into the nearest town, Billings, in <u>dweeb</u> of the needed trumpet. Then he saw it, a <u>renzee</u> store with a shiny, new trumpet with a dangling red cord hanging in <u>sas</u> window. Now was his chance to risk everything on one bold move.

ers like to act in the role of recorder for the group, whereas others wait in silence; this allows them to be quiet participants in the group's activities. Other LRGs may wish to meet at this same time without the teacher present to continue work on projects.

Harste et al. (1988) encourage using written conversations to talk about books of interest. This format provides for regular feedback to students and establishes an audit trail for student progress. Many authorities in the field recommend that children avoid simply summarizing their daily readings but rather react to what they have read (Parsons, 1990). At the conclusion of the LRG meeting, goals for continued reading in the book (goal pages) and the next group meeting date are arranged. Some examples of LR alternatives follow.

Burgess Summary. A kind of cloze passage, Burgess summaries (T. D. Johnson & Louis, 1987) are teacher constructed, using a summary of a selected story. Instead of blanks representing selected missing words from the story, nonsense words replace the missing words. The ratio suggested for replacement words to regular text is about 1:12. Burgess summaries may need to be simplified greatly when used with younger children in the early stages of reading development. Figure 12.18 is a brief example of a passage developed from E. B. White's (1970) *The Trumpet of the Swan.*

A Burgess summary is essentially a modified cloze activity.

Character and Author Report Cards. Although children often have a great deal of anxiety concerning their own report cards, they enjoy giving grades to others. In this activity, students have the opportunity to grade the author or character(s) in the book they have been reading. Character and author report cards (T. D. Johnson & Louis, 1987) are developed by the teacher with appropriate categories for grading included. Students grade each aspect called for, then write a justification for the grade based on evidence from the book. Both explicit (factual) and implicit (inferred) justifications should be identified. Figure 12.19 offers a simple example of a character report card.

Clue Cards. Clue cards (T. D. Johnson & Louis, 1987) are a relatively simple idea useful in developing vocabulary knowledge. The child draws cards from a deck specially prepared for that book. On the front of the card is a sentence summarizing or defining the target word using context from the story. The word being emphasized is printed on the back so that children can self-monitor their prediction. Figure 12.20 offers several examples drawn from *The Red Pony* by John Steinbeck (1937).

The Unknown Character The Unknown Character is an activity patterned after the old familiar game of 20 Questions. The teacher assumes the role of one of the characters from a book or story. Students ask questions that can be answered with a simple "yes" or "no." Teachers find in this activity a natural vehicle for teaching

Figure 12.19   Character report card

Clemmons School Ms. Robert's Third Grade Character Report Card		
Name: _____		
Date: _____		
Character: Lewis's Father		
Book: *The Trumpet of the Swan*		

Subject	Grade	Comments
Honesty		
Commitment		
Courage		
Love of family		

children about characterization and inferential comprehension. (Teaching hint: A greater sense of drama can be created if the teacher puts on some sort of "Unknown Character" mask while in this role.)

Yakity-Yak involves both oral reading and retelling activities.

Yakity-Yak.   Yakity-Yak is a reciprocal retelling procedure involving groups of two students each. After the initial reading of the whole story, each pair of students sits together with copies of the same story. Students then take turns rereading sections, usually paragraphs, then stop to retell their partner what they have just read. Then the process is repeated by the other student using the next section of text. Yakity-Yak can be combined with Manzo's (1969) ReQuest procedure in upper elementary grades for comprehensive student analysis of the passage.

Figure 12.20   Clue cards for *The Red Pony* (Steinbeck, 1937)

Front of the card	*Back of the card*
Sometimes I had to talk to Jody as though I was his father.	**Billy Buck**
Sounded the triangle in the morning and said irritably, "Don't you go out until you get a good breakfast in you."	**Jody's mother**

ReQuest   ReQuest (Manzo, 1969) is very similar to Yakity-Yak in that it is also a reciprocal response procedure that follows an initial reading of the whole text. Typically, students working together in a one-to-one setting take turns silently rereading a portion of text. Next, one team member asks the other as many questions as possible about the portion of text just read. After the questioning is complete, the students continue reading the next unit of text and the second partner assumes the role of questioner. In Manzo's (1969) scheme, the story is reread sentence by sentence, but larger units of text are often preferred. Manzo also presents ReQuest as a procedure to be practiced between the teacher and one student, usually in a tutorial setting. However, questioning could easily be addressed in a whole-class mini-lesson, thus allowing students to work together.

Yakity-Yak and ReQuest could easily be combined in the following format:

1. Students read the entire selection or chapter independently.
2. Student groups of two each are created.
3. The children begin by rereading portions of the text. Then, one partner (called the "listener") says "Yakity-Yak!" indicating that the teller should retell the passage just read. After the retelling is complete, the "listener" asks his or her partner (the "teller") as many questions as possible related to story elements not mentioned.
4. The process is repeated over and over with the children switching roles each time.

Newspaper Reports.   Using various newspaper reporting styles offers motivating ways to help students develop many important comprehension abilities. Some of the formats that newspaper reports can follow are listed here:

Newspaper reports have students summarize main ideas using brief and precise language.

- *Ads*

  Wanted—Time Traveler!

  Have mutant VCR capable of zapping people back in time. Need partner to help stop robbery and shooting of relative. No pay, just thrills. Phone Kelly at 293-4321. (Pfeffer, 1989)

- *Headlines*

  CHILDREN DISCOVER WORLD THROUGH OLD WARDROBE
  TRACK COACH RESNICK SAYS "TAKE A LONG JUMP"!
  JOHN HENRY BEATS STEAM HAMMER, WINS RACE!

- *Crossword:* Can be developed for *Henry and Beezus* (Cleary, 1952) using a Minnesota Educational Computing Consortium (MECC) computer program.
- Other stimulating literature-response projects using the newspaper motif include Letters to the Editor, Dear Gabby, editorials, sports, and cooking.

Literature-Response Logs.   Literature-response logs are regular records, usually daily, that children keep as running diaries of their readings. As mentioned previously, many authorities in the field recommend that children avoid simply summarizing their daily readings but rather react to what they have read (Parsons, 1990).

Develop some literature-response log entries using popular children's books to use as modeling activities during mini-lessons.

Individual Reading Conferences   During the last 10 to 15 minutes of each Reading Workshop, the teacher usually meets with two children for individual reading conferences (IRCs). Students make appointments on a sign-up board at least one day in advance, usually at the teacher's request during the state of the class period; the advance notice gives the teacher enough lead time to review the student's reading portfolio (see chapter 10) and decide how to spend IRC time. We recommend (as a goal) that three individual conferences per quarter be conducted with each student. If students forget or avoid conferences, the teacher should inform them of their next appointment. During IRC time, students not involved return to the previously described activities to continue SSR&R. Assessment activities described earlier for themed literature units work just as well for IRC time in the Reading Workshop. In chapter 10, we also discuss in great detail additional assessment activities that might be selected for IRC time.

Phase 5: Student Sharing Time (5 to 10 Minutes)

As a daily closing activity in the Reading Workshop, we recommend a sharing time for teachers and children to come together for a few minutes to share with the group activities, books, poetry, and projects with which they have been working. Student groups might share progress reports on their literature-response projects, such as play practices, murals, or reader's theater scripts. Some children may wish to share books they have been reading during SSR in the form of book talks. Others can share their responses to books discussed in their LRG. Teachers may comment in IRCs and celebrate the accomplishments of individual children or share a part of a book they themselves were reading during SSR. The only problem associated with this second block of sharing time is sticking to the 10-minute time limit because children sincerely enjoy this time for sharing their ideas, work, and discoveries.

Atwell (1987), in her book for middle school teachers, suggests that students write letters to the teacher about what they have read. Teachers write back to the students, sometimes asking questions or making clarifying remarks. This format provides for regular feedback to students and establishes an audit trail for student progress.

One of the seven principles for encouraging literacy development discussed in chapter 1 relates to the connection between reading and writing instruction. The writing process and ways of encouraging authorship are described in some detail in the second half of this chapter.

DEVELOPING READING FLUENCY AS PART OF LITERATURE-BASED READING INSTRUCTION

Fluency has to do with the ability to read accurately and at an appropriate rate. Reutzel and Cooter (1999) describe the main parts of reading fluency as comprising (a) accuracy of decoding, (b) appropriate use of pitch, juncture, and stress (prosodic features) in one's voice, (c) appropriate text phrasing or "chunking," and (d) reading speed or rate. Thus, a fluent reader can read accurately, naturally, and with relative ease.

Research conducted in recent years indicates that students who can read fluently are better able to focus on the meaning of the passage and comprehend better (Homan, Klesius, & Hite, 1993; Rasinski, 1990; Walley, 1993). The opposite also seems to be true, which is to say that students having difficulty with reading often show evidence of slow, hesitant, and effortful reading (Mathes, Simmons, & Davis, 1992).

Several theories have been suggested about the role fluency plays in reading success and the ability to comprehend the author's message. Perhaps most prominent is the "automaticity theory" described by LaBerge and Samuels (1974). This theory suggests that some readers have difficulty comprehending because too much time and attention are consumed decoding words in print, whereas more fluent readers can identify words automatically without devoting conscious attention to the process. Fluent readers are therefore better able to process meaning at the same time words are being decoded. For a reader to comprehend what is being read, word recognition must be automatic so that thinking resources can be devoted to comprehension (Homan et al., 1993). To the degree teachers help their students become fluent readers, they increase the likelihood of their students' success. In this section, we summarize ways of promoting reading fluency within the context of literature-based reading programs.

Strategies for Improving Fluency

A number of strategies have been shown to improve reading fluency. There are at least three main considerations to remember when selecting fluency activities.

1. The activity must include an "expert reader" to serve as a *fluent model* of reading. The fluent model could be the teacher, but might just as well be a fluent peer, a student from a higher grade, an adult volunteer, or an instructional aid (e.g., tape recordings).
2. There should be *repeated readings* of text. This is for practice or rehearsal, as with radio plays and other student dramas.
3. *Choice* should be involved. For example, students should have some say in the text or book to be used, as well as what portion of the chosen book will be practiced and read.

When adhered to, these three factors—fluent model of reading, repeated readings, and choice—establish an environment for improved fluency.

Repeated Readings and Oral Previewing

The strategy called *repeated readings* (S. J. Samuels, 1979) has the ability to improve fluency, comprehension, and motivation with students having reading problems. The repeated readings strategy usually involves the following steps:

Repeated readings of text are a powerful fluency-development activity.

Step 1: The student reads a passage aloud while the teacher records any miscues (errors) to assess student needs.

Step 2: The student practices rereading the passage orally or silently several times.

Step 3: The student rereads the passage for the teacher, who records the amount of time required for reading and any miscues.

Step 4: The teacher and student prepare a graph together showing the student's growth between readings.

A variation of repeated readings is *oral previewing,* which begins by having the student preview the passage by first listening to an expert reader reading the passage. After listening to the fluent reader several times and feeling more comfortable with the passage, the student reads the passage independently. Rasinski (1990) has found that oral previewing and repeated readings are equally effective in improving fluency.

Oral previewing begins with monitoring a fluent reader reading the targeted passage.

Teacher-Assisted Nonrepetitive Oral Reading Strategies

Recent research has revealed a third class of strategies, known as *teacher-assisted nonrepetitive oral reading strategies,* that seem to be effective in improving reading fluency. They are considered "nonrepetitive" because students are not asked to repeat the text. Nonrepetitive oral reading strategies appear to be about as effective as repeated readings and offer several advantages over repeated readings (Homan et al., 1993). Here are the reasons:

- Because students read a passage only once, they are able to read a wider range of literature in the same amount of time as repeated readings.
- Because students tend to acquire most new vocabulary through wide reading and because this approach increases student encounters with books, greater vocabulary learning results.
- The exposure to a wider range of reading materials in this approach can improve such affective factors as interest, attitudes about reading, and motivation.

Maintaining interest and motivation while improving fluency is an important goal.

Echo reading and *unison reading* are two forms of nonrepetitive oral reading that have been thoroughly researched. In echo reading, the teacher or other fluent reader reads part of a passage, then students read the same part back. In unison reading, the teacher and students read a passage together with the teacher assuming the lead role, that is, reading loud enough to be heard above the group. Both echo and unison reading are considered forms of choral reading because students usually read together as a group rather than individually.

Student Dramas

Student dramas are a frequent choice of students for practicing fluent reading.

Stayter and Allington (1991) tell about a reader's theater activity for which a group of heterogeneously grouped seventh graders spent 5 days reading, rehearsing, and performing short dramas. After a first reading, students began to negotiate about which role they would read. More hesitant students were permitted to opt for smaller parts, but everyone was required to participate. As time passed, the students critiqued each others' readings and made suggestions as to how they should sound (e.g., "You should sound like a snob"). The most common response in this experience related to how the repeated readings through drama helped them better understand the text. One student said,

> The first time I read to know what the words are. Then I read to know what the words say and later as I read I thought about how to say the words. . . . As I got to know the character better, I put more feeling in my voice. (Stayter & Allington, 1991, p. 145)

Dialogue Retellings

Fluency activities that involve both reading and writing activities are most effective.

We recommend that students adapt dialogue retellings, previously described, by first writing retellings of either fables or other narratives using as much actual dialogue as possible from the book, then prepare a puppet show for younger students. Participants should rehearse their parts until they are perfectly fluent, and should solicit suggestions from other LRGs before the day of performance. A book like *The Lion, the Witch, and the Wardrobe* by C. S. Lewis (1961) makes a great example for teachers to use in explaining this option. Walley (1993) recommends the use of cumulative stories, those having a minimum of plot and a maximum of rhythm and rhyme, in early elementary grades. Jane Yolen's (1976) *An Invitation to a Butterfly Ball* is one such example.

Evening Newscast

The evening newscast activity offers maximum opportunity for students to practice their roles using the kind of intonation characteristic of newscasters. Teachers may want to encourage students to adopt and adapt the particular style of a favorite personality, such as "Katie Curtsy" or "Bryant Gummball."

The Unknown Character

In the Unknown Character activity, the student rehearses a number of key passages from the selected text. He or she reads them one by one until classmates guess the character or mystery book.

THE WRITING PROCESS: MAKING AUTHORS OF READERS

Understanding the Writing Process

Teaching students the **writing process** helps them learn how to become authors. Goals of writing instruction include helping students understand the kinds of thinking processes skilled writers use in producing different forms of text and how to become authors themselves. As authors, children are better able to read books in order to learn how skillful writers paint pictures with words in the reader's mind, discover words that convey just the right meaning for a given thought, and phrases that grab the attention of readers. Through writing process instruction, children become "wordsmiths" and begin to enjoy the works of other authors on new and higher levels.

Teaching the writing process helps students appreciate the power of words and ideas.

Writing instruction has changed significantly in recent years. Teachers of the past typically assigned students such tasks as preparing research papers or reports as the primary mode of instruction. In this "one-draft mentality" (Calkins, 1986) students handed in their report, the reports were graded by the teacher, returned, and most likely forgotten. In recent years, researcher-practitioners such as Donald Graves (1983, 1994) and his protégé Lucy Calkins (1994) have helped teachers (and students) understand that writing is a process instead of a one-time "quick and dirty" project. Children are taught to understand and use the phases of authorship.

Child-authors begin to feel like insiders in the world of books.

Writers do not move rigidly from one stage to another. Rather, they sometimes move back and forth from one phase to another, or even quit in the middle of a writing project to start another. But for emergent writers in the elementary school, it is very instructive to examine the various modes or stages that writers go through in producing text: *prewriting, drafting, revising and editing,* and *publishing.*

The Prewriting Stage

Prewriting is the getting-ready-to-write stage (Tompkins, 1994). Writing begins with an idea or message. Many teachers help students begin the writing process by asking them to brainstorm a list of topics they might be interested in writing about at some point in the future. They should be topics that generate a certain amount of emotion for the student. Donald Graves, in his classic book *Writing: Teachers and Children at Work* (1983), suggests that teachers model each of the stages in the

Prewriting *is the getting-ready stage.*

Figure 12.21   Sample outline format

> ***My Birthday Trip to Universal Studios (by Jina)***
>
> I.   Arrival at Universal Studios
>   a.   Came with Mom, Dad, Melanie, Michelle, and Rob, and Uncle Dan
>   b.   Arrived in our new van
>   c.   It was a hot day in August
>   d.   We all rode the shuttle to the front gate
>   e.   It was my birthday
> II.   Sights of Special Interest
>   a.   We saw the car from the movie *Back to the Future*
>   b.   We saw the special effects studio for "Battlestar Galactica"
>   c.   They have a special street on the back lot with houses from "Leave It to Beaver," "The Addams Family," and *Psycho*
>   d.   King Kong jumps out at you at one point on the shuttle ride
>   e.   We saw an action scene from "Miami Vice"
> III.   Special Events That Happened on My Birthday Trip
>   a.   I was chosen to ride on a bicycle on the set of *E.T.* The camera made it look like I was flying in mid-air.
>   b.   Next, I was chosen to be in a film sequence in a boat. I got all wet!

writing process to help children see adult examples. For this first step of brainstorming, the teacher might list at the overhead projector or chalkboard several topics that he or she is interested in writing about, such as sailing, collecting antiques, attending wrestling matches, traveling to South Pacific islands, or whatever else is stimulating to the teacher. It is important that teachers explain to the class why each topic is appealing to them. A brainstorming session sometimes helps children who are having difficulty discovering topics of interest. The key to success is helping students find topics that generate emotion, which helps "drive" the entire writing process through to completion.

After students have selected an interesting topic, they gather information—conduct their "research." Depending on the nature of the topic, students may need to make a trip to the library to gather background information, "surf the Internet" for the latest news on their subject, interview people in their family or community, or write to local, state, or federal agencies.

Opening sentences should grab and hold the reader.

Once the student-writer has settled on a topic and collected useful support information, he or she is ready to begin organizing ideas for presentation; in short, to develop an outline of some kind. The outline's form is not really important, but the writer should have some kind of organizational scheme for the composition. This step helps make the piece clear, concise, and thorough. Several outline formats depicting the story theme "Our Family's Trip to Universal Studios" written by an intermediate student named Jina are presented as examples in Figures 12.21 through 12.23.

Once the outline of ideas has been completed, it is often helpful for the writer to create several opening sentences for the story, or alternative leads. Having an interesting beginning, one that grabs the reader, helps create a successful composition.

Figure 12.22   Semantic web

For example, in the story entitled "My Birthday Trip to Universal Studios," Jina may have begun her story thus:

> *On my birthday my family and I went to Universal Studios. It was a very fun day that I will never forget.*

On the other hand, if Jina wrote several alternative leads, then picked the most exciting one to begin her story, perhaps she would come up with a beginning more like this:

> *Imagine a birthday party with* King Kong, *E.T., and the stars from* Miami Vice *as your guests! That's exactly what happened to me on my 13th birthday. If you think that's something, hold on to your seat while I tell you the rest of my story.*

Figure 12.23   Structured overview

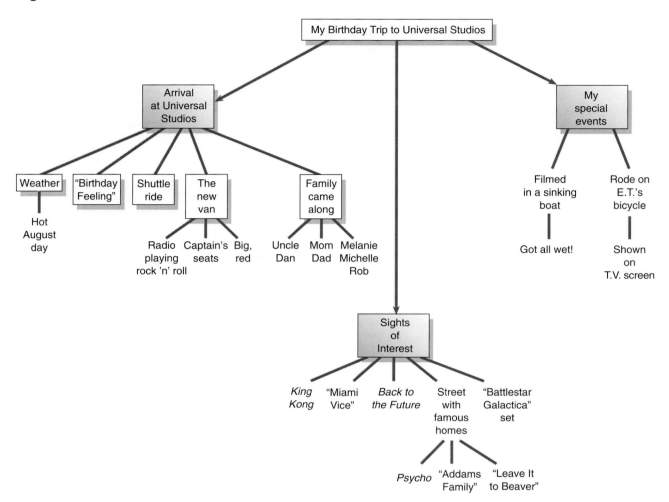

Free writing is a simple strategy for helping students come up with ideas for their compositions.

Sometimes children have a difficult time getting started with their composition, or even coming up with an idea compelling enough to commit to paper. In this situation, it is usually helpful to engage in free writing. *Free writing* simply means that students sit down for a sustained period of time and write down anything at all that comes to mind. What often emerges is a rather rambling narrative with many idea fragments. Lucy Calkins (1986, 1994) has suggested that children might begin by simply listing things in their immediate environment until they come to an idea they wish to write about. After students have an organized set of ideas about which to write and have constructed alternative leads, they are ready for the drafting stage.

The Drafting Stage

First drafts are often referred to as "sloppy copies."

The drafting stage represents an author's first attempt to get ideas down on paper. Teachers should emphasize that the most important part of drafting is simply getting thoughts down, not mechanical correctness. The first draft is sometimes referred to as creating a "sloppy version" of the composition. Such fine points as verb-tense agreement or spelling correctness are *not* important at this stage; *ideas* are the most important consideration.

The following ideas may be useful reminders for students as they are drafting. Some modification may be needed for clarity and to fit the maturity of the writer(s).

- Write as though you were telling a story to an interested friend.
- Use your own "voice" instead of trying to sound like your favorite author.
- Try to use words that create a picture in the reader's mind. Your words should be descriptive and clear.
- Be sure to describe sights, sounds, smells, and other sensory images that are important parts of the story you want to tell.
- Say what you want to say directly ("more" is not necessarily "better;" sometimes *less* is *more* if one's words are chosen well).

Some students may have difficulty getting ideas down on paper the first time they attempt drafting. Frequently their handwriting ability is slower than the flow of ideas coming from their minds. One solution is to have students dictate their story into a tape recorder, then transcribe the story on paper later. This solution helps keep the students from becoming frustrated and also helps them improve those same skills as they transcribe the story on paper. Another possibility is to allow students to dictate their story to an older student or a peer tutor. The advantage here is that the storyteller can get valuable and immediate feedback from the peer tutor, aiding in the clarity of the composition.

Revising and Editing

Once the draft has been completed, the author is ready to begin the final production stage of editing and revising. *Revising,* or "re-visioning" (taking a second look), is the act of changing the manuscript to include any new ideas the author has discovered for improving the manuscript. *Editing* has to do with the process of reading and rereading the manuscript to find errors and omissions of one kind or another. Editing is often a joint effort between the author and peer readers who offer constructive criticism.

The revision process can begin in many ways, each offering advantages for the student and teacher. Perhaps the most traditional method is the student–teacher writing conference, in which students meet with the teacher after the teacher has read the composition. The teacher asks questions about the manuscript and offers suggestions for revising the manuscript. Some teachers like to use a form for recording their comments for the student as an aid in the revision process. Figure 12.24 offers one such form for this purpose.

Another option for helping students improve their compositions is *peer editing*. Many students prefer to get suggestions from their peers for improving their compositions before "publishing." Peer editing allows them to get suggestions in a collaborative and risk-free environment. Although some students may be able to work successfully one on one with their peers, peer editing is often more effective in small groups known as *teacherless writing teams* or *peer editing conferences*. These teams comprise three to four students who work together to develop the best compositions possible. At each stage of the writing process, students share their work with the team, then team members ask questions of the author and offer suggestions for improving the composition.

Revising is a second look at one's composition and its message.

Editing often involves checking the correctness of spellings, grammar, subject–verb agreement, and so forth.

Students should work collaboratively in peer editing conferences to help make initial "repairs" to the manuscript.

Figure 12.24   Writing evaluation form

> ### Writing Evaluation Form
>
> Student Name _____   Date _____
> Title of Composition _____
>
> Overall Evaluation of the Composition:
>
> ──▶
> Underdeveloped   Partially Ready   Advanced   Excellent
>
> #### Areas Needing Further Development
>
> _____ Character development   _____ Spelling
> _____ Setting   _____ Grammar
> _____ Conflict description   _____ Punctuation
> _____ Conflict resolution   _____ Capitalization
> _____ Story closure

Editing involves careful review of the composition to check for such things as correct spellings, usage errors (verb tense, etc.), sentence constructions, topic sentences, awkward language, and whether the composition makes sense. Many teachers encourage children to use word banks or key word lists pertaining to the subject, a thesaurus, and dictionaries or spelling and grammar checking features on word processing programs. Although some have advocated the use of reference tools during the drafting stage, Calkins (1986, 1994) recommends reserving them for these final stages of the writing process.

Teach students how to use proofreaders' marks to make the process work more efficiently and painlessly.

During the editing stage, it is often useful for writers to use proofreaders' marks; these are notations that an author uses on manuscripts to add, delete, or rearrange information. Figure 12.25 depicts a few examples teachers might consider demonstrating to young writers.

As just alluded to, many schools provide students with word processing/computer equipment for writing projects. Hardware like the Apple Macintosh, IBM-PCs,

Figure 12.25   Proofreaders' marks

> | *Text With Proofreader Markings* | *Explanation* |
> |---|---|
> | injured
Jamie carried the puppy home. | $\wedge$ is for inserting missing words |
> | Let's go to Mark's house over. | $\cup$ for moving text |
> | Let's go to Mark's house over. | for marking out text |

and their "clones" make the editing process both quick and relatively painless for young writers, although students must first learn keyboarding skills. Word processing programs enable classroom computers to become word processing systems. Selected computer applications for assisting writing development are discussed in greater detail later in this chapter.

Publishing

A natural desire for most authors, young or seasoned, is that their composition be shared with an audience. For children, publishing can take many exciting forms. One publishing experience common in elementary classrooms is called *author's chair.* Each day at a designated time, young authors who have completed a composition can sign up to share their most recent compositions in the author's chair. When the appointed time arrives, children take turns reading their creations to the class, answering questions about their story, and reaping generous applause. Other forms of publishing include letter writing to pen pals, school officials, favorite authors, and media stars, or making stories into classroom books, newspapers, and yearbooks. Information concerning publishing centers, which assist child-authors in preparing compositions for sharing, is presented in chapter 9.

Publishing is an opportunity for students to share their creations.

The key to success in publishing is that students feel their writing projects have a purpose and an audience beyond a teacher with a red grading pencil.

Using the Writing Workshop: Organizing for Instruction

Once teachers understand the essential elements of the writing process, they are ready to begin planning for instruction. The **Writing Workshop** is an organizational structure for teaching—facilitating writing development. It is one model for instruction that can be modified as needed. Classroom periods could be organized to include five phases: teacher sharing time, mini-lesson, state of the class, workshop activities, and student sharing time. Figure 12.26 depicts the organizational scheme for the Writing Workshop. A description of each of the five phases follows.

*The **Writing Workshop** is an organizational scheme for planning instruction.*

Phase 1: Teacher Sharing Time (5 to 10 Minutes)

The purpose of teacher sharing time is to present children with language and experiences through writing that stimulate the natural energies of thinking (Holdaway, 1984). The substance of these teacher-led presentations is usually an assortment of such writing products as brain-enticing poems, songs, stories, and exposition that have been written by the teacher. The goal is to inspire students to have an urge to strike out on new adventures in writing. This phase of instruction should be brief, perhaps 5 to 10 minutes, and serves as a stimulating introduction to the rest of the writing period.

Teachers share some of their own creations during sharing time.

Phase 2: The Mini-lesson (5 to 10 Minutes)

The mini-lesson (Calkins, 1986, 1994) is a brief period of time set aside for offering student-writers tips from the teacher about good writing. Class discussions about topics such as selecting good ideas to write about, focusing topics, clustering information (webbing), gathering reference materials, conducting interviews, publishing, and

Mini-lessons focus on all aspects of the writing process, such as webbing, creating lists of needed words, and proofreaders' marks.

Figure 12.26   The Writing Workshop

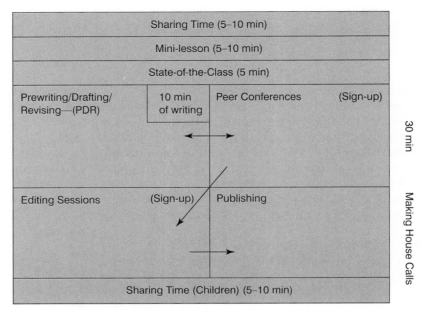

Teachers usually use some of their own writing samples, and those volunteered by students, in teaching these brief mini-lessons. The main focus of the mini-lesson at all grade levels is helping students write with quality at their stage of development.

many more writing-related ideas are all viable. A few examples of common mini-lesson topics suggested by Atwell (1987) follow:

Illustrations	Narrative leads
Essay writing	Spelling
Form	Writing good fiction
Mythology	The dictionary
Resume writing	Genre
Writing conferences with yourself	Job applications
Correspondence	Punctuation
Focus	Style
Greek mythology	Writing short stories

Teachers usually use some of their own writing samples, and those volunteered by students, in teaching these brief mini-lessons. The main focus of the mini-lesson at all grade levels is helping students write with quality at their stage of development.

Phase 3: State of the Class (5 Minutes)

The state of the class phase for the Writing Workshop takes the same form as in the Reading Workshop: The teacher simply lists each child's name on the left of the chart, and students fill in the blanks for each day, indicating what they will be doing (e.g., drafting, peer conferences, editing session, or publishing). Sometimes teachers, like Atwell (1987), prefer to complete the state of the class chart themselves in a whole-class setting and find the experience quite useful.

> I think the [state of the class] conference is worth three minutes of the whole class's time. I can't begin to know all the ways my students find ideas for writing, but I do know that eavesdropping is right up there. When they make their plans publicly, writers naturally teach each other about new options for topic and genre. (Atwell, 1987, p. 90)

By recording students' plans for writing and saving them over the weeks of the school year, teachers can see almost at a glance which students are failing to progress (Atwell, 1987). State of the class helps teachers negotiate deadlines for key stages of the writing process with individual students, hold students accountable, and determine when house calls may be needed.

Phase 4: Workshop Activities (30 Minutes)

Four activities operate concurrently during the workshop activities phase: (a) prewriting, drafting, and revising; (b) peer editing conferences; (c) editing sessions (with the teacher or peers); and (d) preparing for publishing. Students sign up for one of these activities each day and work accordingly during the workshop period. For descriptive purposes, it may be useful to distinguish between activities the teacher is engaged in versus those of the students.

For the teacher, several activities take place during this time frame. In the first 10 minutes or so of the Writing Workshop, teachers themselves engage in sustained silent writing (SSW). While working on a written product of his or her choice, the teacher provides children with (a) a model of positive writing behavior, and (b) needed examples for the teacher sharing time period previously described. After the teacher's SSW period, he or she is ready to move on to making individual "house calls" and working with students in private editing sessions.

Note that teachers have specific tasks to complete throughout the Writing Workshop period.

Children are allowed to move at their own pace during the workshop activities and select from four alternatives. In the *prewriting, drafting, and revising* option, children may choose topics for narratives, gather resources and references, conduct interviews, or create an outline for organizing their stories, and eventually produce a draft.

Once children finish their first drafts, they are ready to sign up for a *peer conference*. Peer conferences are small groups of children, usually three or four, who sign up to read each other's first drafts and make recommendations to their peer authors for revisions. Peer conferences are sometimes known as *teacherless writing groups* because the teacher is not involved during this analysis phase unless invited by the group for consulting purposes.

Peer conferences are a means for helping students learn to help each other instead of having total dependence on the teacher.

Teachers have told us that some students beginning to learn the Writing Workshop system seem to want to peer conference almost all the time. This can be problematic because a goal of balanced teaching is to promote peer collaboration and cooperation. One solution might be to establish guidelines differentiating peer conferences from what might be termed "1-minute conferences." When children need a quick opinion on their composition, they can usually arrange a 1-minute conference with a peer. Students should not require more than three 1-minute conferences during a workshop activity period.

Group etiquette rules should be established early in the school year to ensure maximum productivity and to minimize conflicts. Role-playing is one way to form

Role-playing is a great way to help students write group etiquette rules.

group-developed rules. As mentioned previously, in one school, teachers made a videotape acting out positive and negative group behavior. Students have no problem coming up with a list of their own group etiquette rules, which function well in all group experiences. (Group etiquette rules were discussed earlier in this chapter in the Reading Workshop section.)

A word regarding classroom noise levels seems warranted: Whenever teachers begin to experiment with modes of learning that allow children to work on their own or in small groups, the noise level will invariably go up. This may be a little distressing at first for some teachers, but this issue can be addressed. If the class becomes unruly, then appropriate steps must be taken to maintain class control. More often than not, however, the increase in classroom noise should be viewed as the sound of learning and creative interaction. Silvia Ashton-Warner (1963) refers to this kind of classroom hubbub as "peaceful noise."

Once the peer conference group meets and considers each child's manuscript, suggestions are made for improving the writing project. Of course, each child is free to accept or reject the suggestions according to the principle of choice and independence, as discussed in chapter 1. Thus, manuscript revisions follow the peer conference in preparation for the editing session with the teacher.

Editing sessions are times for students to receive "coaching" from their teacher.

Editing sessions are special times for students to meet with teachers to discuss their writing projects and receive skill instruction. To take part in the editing session, children should sign up the day before the conference and submit a copy of their writing project; this allows teachers time to read the project and make notes for the student. Teachers should avoid writing directly on the paper or project. Instead, remarks should be made on a separate sheet of paper or a stick-on note to prevent defacing the project. The teacher may wish to review a story grammar outline for narrative compositions to decide whether all important elements have been included. Semantic and syntactic considerations should also be discussed during this time.

After the editing session, students frequently need to edit or revise further before publishing. It may be desirable for the student and teacher to have an additional editing session before publishing to go over modifications.

A visit in the publishing center is the final option for the workshop activities period. The purpose is to prepare the writing project for publication. One final point: Publishing does not necessarily happen with every writing project. Sometimes students will say to the teacher, "I'm running out of interest for this story. May I work on another one?" Most writers occasionally run out of gas during a writing project and start a new one. Some may have several projects in process. It is not the number of publications a child produces during a given time period that is important, but the process itself. Although it is desirable for the child to reach closure on a regular basis with writing projects, it does not have to happen every time.

Phase 5: Sharing Time (5 to 10 Minutes)

The Writing Workshop concludes with student sharing time. This period is for sharing and publishing completed writing projects. Children proceed to sharing time only with the approval of the teacher during the editing session.

Student sharing time is an initial publishing experience before their peers.

Even students who may be publishing their writing project outside of class (e.g., putting their book in the school library or submitting their story to a children's magazine) should take part in sharing time. This allows other children to see their finished product and enjoy the story. The most common format for sharing time for students is the author's chair experience, previously described in this chapter.

Classroom Computers and Writing Development

When teachers think of computers, word processing often comes to mind. *Word processing* is a general term for software programs that permit someone to write, edit, store, and print text (Strickland, Feeley, & Wepner, 1987, p. 13). Word processing software programs enable the computer to be used much like a typewriter but with all the added advantages a computer offers. In addition to standard word processing packages for elementary and middle school-age students, other related computer software programs are available that help students develop as writers.

> *Word processing programs permit students to use the computer somewhat like a typewriter.*

Because computer software programs come and go so rapidly, it is very difficult for us to make specific recommendations. Professional publications in the literacy field, such as *The Reading Teacher, Reading Research and Instruction,* and *Language Arts,* and product journals like *MacWorld,* frequently have product reviews that can help guide your decisions. In order to give you a brief sampling, however, of the kind of products that have come along in recent years, we offer some brief summaries in this section of writing programs.

IBM's *Writing to Read 2000*

Writing to Read 2000 is the next generation of the landmark product from IBM—*Writing to Read.* It is a beginning reading–writing program based on a modified alphabet idea (one symbol for each of 42 language sounds) for kindergarten and first grade. Developed by John Henry Martin, a retired teacher and school administrator, the original *Writing to Read* program was marketed by IBM, which makes the computers used in the program. The typical routine, usually lasting 30 to 40 minutes per day, takes children through a five-station rotation in a special computer lab away from the regular classroom. Students begin with the computer station, where they are taught to type 42 phonemes (representing the English language sounds) using color images and synthesized speech. These lessons are repeated in a work journal, then students listen to a tape-recorded story while following along in a book in the listening library. These activities are followed by a typing–writing center, in which students can write compositions of their own choosing. The final center is called "make words," where other reinforcement activities are practiced.

> *Writing to Read 2000 is a beginning reading–writing program.*

Writing to Read 2000 includes a component called the Computer Center, where "cycle words" teach young children sound/letter relationships. Four other centers support and encourage children to practice these associations using a variety of activities, including work journals, manipulatives, books, and writing. Other components in the new program follow:

- a writing/typing center program called *Write Along*
- graphical menus, audio support, and mouse, enabling easy and independent navigation for young students
- context rhymes that introduce "cycle words"
- teacher options, which include bookmarking, partner support, student management, and reporting information
- a *Writing to Read 2000 Game Board* and assortment of games, puzzles, and manipulatives
- a collection of 23 age-appropriate children's literature books, 16 of the books accompanied by natural, expressive voice cassette recordings
- a Teacher's Guide that provides cross-curricular connections, curriculum integration, and thematic unit suggestions

Word Processing Software

There are many word processing software programs coming onto the market almost weekly that can be quite helpful in your classroom.

Word processing software has been a major focal point for developers in recent years. These efforts have resulted in many affordable programs that help students develop and extend their authoring abilities. Listed here are a few programs that represent some of the technologies that have been available.

Bank Street Writer: One of the pioneering efforts in this field, *Bank Street Writer* is both easy to use and affordable. It is suggested for grades 3 and up.

MacWrite 4.6:   *MacWrite* is the oldest text processing program for the Macintosh computer, and remains a format that all applications running on the Mac can open. Therefore, the format of the version 4.6 (or even 5), which was freely bundled with all Macintosh computers up to the model SE, remains a very useful format, even with the size limit (*MacWrite 4.6* files can't exceed 64 KB).

ASSISTING LIMITED ENGLISH PROFICIENT (LEP) STUDENTS

The needs of LEP students are a growing concern in many intermediate-level classrooms.

Larger and larger numbers of students in U.S. and Canadian school districts speak English as a second language (Reutzel & Cooter, 1999). The needs of these **Limited English Proficient** (LEP) learners are certainly a factor for some intermediate-level learners in our schools because English is the dominant language of learning and instruction. Until recently, few books on teaching and learning have attended to the English as a Second Language (ESL) risk factor (Fitzgerald, 1995; Gunderson, 1991). Many teachers find themselves seeking guidance to promote literacy success for LEP students (Boyle & Peregoy, 1990; Fitzgerald, 1993, 1994, 1995).

There is a major shortage of qualified bilingual teachers to work with LEP populations.

In an ideal world, students would become fluent speakers, readers, writers, and listeners in their first language and *then* acquire those same skills in English. Although there are attempts to do just that in many places, the reality is that there are simply not enough bilingual teachers to go around. For instance, Dallas (Texas) Public Schools estimate that some 600 additional bilingual teachers are needed to adequately staff all classrooms with significant LEP populations (Cooter, 1999). The same is true in major urban districts in the West and Southwest regions of the United States. Thus, we must find ways to help LEP students succeed with the tools at our disposal.

It is important to remember that LEP students acquire receptive (listening, reading) and expressive (writing, speaking) skills in the same basic ways as monolingual students. These methods of learning include

- developing basic classification systems from the most basic to the very complex.
- increasing the length of utterances in both spoken and written forms, beginning with short and simple and gradually growing to the more complex.
- learning "language labels" for concrete objects and experiences they have had.
- the inclusion of immersion (i.e., modeling) and learning-by-doing (i.e., guided and independent practice) activities as the primary methods of language development.

Strategies for helping LEP students can also help monolingual students develop listening and speaking vocabularies.

Following are some suggestions for helping LEP students succeed. It happens that these ideas are also quite useful for assisting monolingual students who may have underdeveloped language skills. These suggestions are adapted from a chapter found in our activities book for teachers entitled *Balanced Reading Strategies and Practices: Assessing and Assisting Readers with Special Needs* (Reutzel & Cooter, 1999).

Environmental Print

Using printed matter from the world outside the school enables second language learners to view their own lives, circumstances, and cultural contexts as places for learning and applying their evolving knowledge of English as a second language. Signs, billboards, storefronts, bus schedules, displays, and so on in the everyday lives of LEP students can provide personally relevant bridges from learning English in the school classroom into learning and using English beyond the classroom. The use of environmental print has proven worthwhile for developing both first and second language oral and written skills among younger learners (Hiebert & Ham, 1981).

Students can make collections of environmental print they can read by storing these items in scrapbooks, files, or envelopes. Students can use these easily recognizable print items to compose books, sentences, or other written texts. Bulletin boards can be filled with environmental print items. Some teachers organize environmental print items into alphabetical categories to practice alphabet knowledge. Environmental print items are inexpensive and provide wide access to print beyond the boundaries of school classrooms.

Sentence Strips

Dictated sentences recorded on sentence strips can be used to further develop awareness of English sentence patterns (Gunderson, 1991). Sentence strips are especially useful for teaching second language learners because the length of the text is limited and they provide basic examples of the most rudimentary meaningful units in language. You will need colored marking pens, masking tape for hanging the strips on the wall, and pre-cut sentence strips (these can be purchased in a variety of colors from a teacher supply store). Another useful tool is a wall sentence strip hanger as shown in Figure 12.27. Storing and displaying sentence strips can present some opportunities for classroom teachers to encourage incidental language

Notice how sentence strips can be used to increase awareness of common English sentence patterns.

Figure 12.27   Sentence strip wall hanger

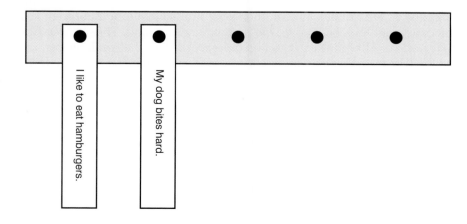

learning. For example, constructing a wall hanger for sentence strips provides just such an opportunity.

When composing sentence strips, teachers initially dictate the sentences, but students should be invited to dictate their own as soon as they seem willing. Using words drawn from student word banks (discussed in chapter 7) can serve as a rich resource for building sentences from known and familiar language. In addition, using words from a word bank allows students to manipulate words and sentences and provides a record of language development.

Sentence strips can be copied and then stored by punching a hole in the upper right-hand corner of each strip and hanging them on a cup hook, hanger, or peg on the wall. At some later point, sentence strips can be copied from stories and literature the children are reading. Students can be invited to trace over these sentence strips or copy the sentences in a space on the strips directly beneath the original sentence.

An example of using sentence strips with LEP students is as follows. The teacher begins by telling students that they will practice reading in English today. The teacher then writes the sentence onto a sentence strip as students watch: "I like to eat hamburgers!" Then the teacher says while pointing to the sentence, "This says, I like to eat hamburgers!" Next, the teacher points to the sentence strip and asks, "What does this say?" The student then responds with the text written on the sentence strip. Students are then encouraged to share their sentence strips with others by reading them or inviting others to read their sentence strips.

Active Listening

LEP students must be helped to become active listeners.

Reading researchers (Blum, 1995; Walters & Gunderson, 1985) have discovered reading achievement benefits for LEP students listening to stories read aloud in their first and second languages. In some studies, the stories were simply read aloud by volunteers, whereas in others they were prerecorded on cassette tapes. One of the many benefits cited was that students with Limited English Proficiency and an ability to read in the first language learned how terms from the first and second languages translate. Stories, poems, jokes, riddles, or other enticing texts to be read aloud, as always, are the starting point. Adult language models for the read-aloud experiences can be accomplished either through a volunteer program and/or by using prerecorded audiotapes.

For some beginning students, wordless picture books are a good place to begin, as long as the content is not too "young" for the students. Read the story or share the book in small, preplanned sections. Students could be asked later on to dictate a story to match the pictures. The dictation could then be typed on the computer by the teacher or a volunteer, then laser printed in a font that resembles type commonly found in a book (e.g., we recommend the fonts *Times, New Roman,* or *Helvetica*). The print can then be taperecorded so that students can return to the book later and read their own dictated language retelling the story from the pictures.

When using books selected for read aloud, stop reading aloud at strategic points and ask students, "What do you think might happen next?" As a follow-up question, ask students to explain why they think a particular event will take place next in the story.

Audiotaped books can be used effectively to extend language learning into the home environment.

A slightly different version of "Active Listening" was employed in a study by Blum et al. (1995), where LEP students were provided audiotaped books to extend their classroom literacy instruction into the home context. Books were recorded onto audiotapes by English-speaking adults at a pace that would allow beginning readers to follow along. For turning pages, 3 seconds were allowed after hearing a sound signaling the need to turn the page. Tape recorders and an electric cord were furnished by the school. Each night, ESL students were allowed to check out a backpack into which they would place the tape recorder, cord, book(s) and accompanying audiotape(s). Active listening procedures such as those just outlined were followed in listening to the audiotaped books at home. Blum et al. (1995) found that all ESL learners received substantial benefit from active listening to audiotaped books at home.

Personal Dictionaries

For more proficient second language users and for older students, a personal dictionary can be developed to record spellings of words and/or word meanings in English. When younger students demonstrate limited fluency and proficiency in the second language, or when younger or older students begin to ask questions about how English words are spelled or about specific word meanings, they are ready to construct a personal dictionary (Gunderson, 1991). Personal dictionaries can be simple or elaborate in construction. They can be fixed in terms of numbers of pages, or flexible, allowing for more pages to be added with increased language acquisition. But one thing is certain: Personal dictionaries are well worth the effort!

> *Personal dictionaries are helpful for increasing the reading and writing vocabularies of both LEP and monolingual students.*

To construct personal dictionaries, students will need a spiral or loose-leaf bound notebook, various drawing media such as crayons, markers, and colored pencils, tabs for marking alphabetic divisions, and (possibly) laminating material for flimsy covers. In the beginning, students will need help setting up their dictionaries and learning how to make entries. Later, when students approach the teacher about how to spell a word or to find out what it means, the teacher can help students become more independent learners by encouraging the use of their personal dictionary.

Hints about how words begin and listening to the order of the sounds in words can help students figure out the potential spelling of words as well as where to record words in their personal dictionaries. When a student learns a new word he or she wants to remember from others in reading or in everyday life, he or she can be invited to write the new word in the dictionary with a picture and a sentence explaining its meaning. Then, when a student asks how to spell a word or what a word means, teachers can often simply say "It's in your personal dictionary!" Making and using a personal dictionary helps students assume more control over their own learning and develop a real spirit of independence in accessing language for their use in reading and writing.

Helping LEP Students With Content Area Texts

LEP students can be severely challenged by nonfiction or "content area" texts. In this section, we very briefly describe ways you can help LEP students meet the challenge these informational texts can pose.

Linguistic Variables You Can Modify

Limited knowledge of a second language can prevent learners from making full use of semantic, syntactic, and other clues in content reading materials. Kang (1994) suggests the following tactics to help LEP students with content demands:

- Reduce the vocabulary load.
- Preteach key vocabulary concepts before students read an assigned passage.

- Use prereading questions, highlighting text, notes, or questions in the margins, and graphic organizers to help students attend to important information.
- Use postreading discussion groups to expose LEP learners to more complex language input.

Knowledge Variables You Can Modify

How does a lack of background knowledge impede content learning? (Hint: Think about schema structures.)

A second variable affecting an LEP student's ability to learn from reading content area texts is background knowledge. In some cases, a text may presuppose culture-specific background knowledge that is not part of an LEP student's experiences. Likewise, some LEP readers may focus their reading too heavily on the print (decoding), thus failing to activate their prior knowledge to assist in understanding content area text. In either of these scenarios, Kang (1994) suggests strategies for *before, during,* and *after reading* that may help LEP learners succeed in reading content area texts. (Note: Many of these ideas are discussed more fully in other chapters.)

Before Reading

- semantic mapping
- structured overviews
- discussion that draws attention to:
  - contradictions
  - opposing examples
  - exceptions
  - categorization
  - comparisons
  - relating to concepts in the native language

During Reading

- Pattern guides
- Marginal glosses

After Reading

- Semantic feature analysis
- Small-group discussion

Literacy Variables

Think of ways instruction can be modified before, during, and after reading content materials to help LEP students comprehend more effectively.

In some cases, LEP students may have limited first language literacy skills. Other LEP students may have insufficient second language proficiency to use well-developed first language literacy skills. In either case, specific *prereading, during reading,* and *postreading* strategies can optimize LEP students' opportunities to read content texts effectively.

Before Reading

- Preview the text by showing students how to use headings, subheadings, bold text, marginal glosses or notes, illustrations, or end-of-chapter questions.
- Help students set a purpose for reading by teaching self-questioning strategies.

During Reading

- Provide directions, signals, and questions to focus students' reading on an interaction with the text and their own knowledge.
- Suggest a study strategy and model its use with the text.
- Help students adjust their reading rate to the text difficulty.
- Help students develop skimming and scanning skills.
- Help students predict outcomes, make and confirm inferences, and solve problems.
- Help students use metacognitive monitoring skills.
- Remind students of when and how to use "fix up" or "repair" strategies when comprehension breaks down.

After Reading

- Writing text summaries or completing text pattern guides will help students get more experience with the organization of various text patterns in content area reading.

Summary

Reading and writing are closely related processes that have a reciprocal developmental influence. Balanced literacy programs depend heavily on these processes for overall language development. Four organizational schemes for literature-based reading instruction may be used: core books, individualized reading instruction, themed literature units, and the Reading Workshop. Core book units involve using a single book as the reading curriculum, and as a springboard for other reading and writing experiences. Individualized reading instruction allows each child to choose the book he or she will read, then groups children based on need for reading skill instruction. Themed literature units combine the teaching convenience of core book units with the student self-selection of books from individualized reading units for an appealing third alternative. The Reading Workshop is a fourth alternative for teachers moving into advanced transitions that can be used with either basal readers or trade books.

The writing process approach helps students learn composition skills similar to those of professional writers. Children learn and progress through a series of writing process stages with each composition: prewriting, drafting, revising, editing, and publishing. The Writing Workshop is an organizational scheme offered to preservice and in-service teachers for implementing process writing in the elementary school.

As teachers become knowledgeable in reading and language arts integration and progress toward advanced transitions, they often adopt the themed studies approach.

This organizational scheme leads to full curriculum integration, the ultimate goal of balanced literacy programs.

Readers with learning needs benefit from both literature-based reading programs and the writing process approach. Although many readers with learning needs respond well to these program models, as presented, some may require additional intervention strategies.

Concept Applications

In the Classroom

1. Identify an interested colleague and develop a themed literature unit using one of the following themes: courage, relationships, discovering new worlds, changes, or animals. Your plans should include a web of the unit, a list of books chosen from popular children's literature, possible reading strategies to be taught in teacher-directed sessions, and suggested ideas for literature-response activities.
2. Develop plans for your own Writing Workshop. Sketch out how you will manage the program within the constraints of a typical classroom environment. What physical facilities (furniture, space, etc.) will you need? Draw up a series of lesson plans for demonstrating or modeling to your class how the Writing Workshop will work.
3. Using the section in this chapter on Reading Workshops, map out plans and materials needed to get started. Identify children's literature to be used, sources of ideas for prereading activities and literature-response projects, and materials to be used in literature-response groups.
4. Prepare an annotated bibliography of software available for either the Apple Macintosh or PC computers, or other computer of your choice that could be helpful in reading and writing instruction. You should first develop a list of criteria by which each program can be judged, then evaluate the programs accordingly. Use the Internet to locate the latest product information.

In the Field

Develop a writing and publishing center for your classroom. It should have a variety of writing instruments, different kinds of paper, an assortment of envelopes, and materials useful for binding stories into books. Solicit parent volunteers to help staff the station on selected days to assist students.

Recommended Readings

Atwell, N. (1987). *In the middle: Writing, reading, and learning with adolescents.* Portsmouth, NH: Heinemann.

Calkins, L. M. (1994). *The art of teaching writing* (new ed.). Portsmouth, NH: Heinemann.

Calkins, L. M., & Harwayne, S. (1987). *The writing workshop: A world of difference.* Portsmouth, NH: Heinemann. (Note: An excellent videotape by the same name is available from the publisher for teacher education purposes.)

Fader, D. N. (1976). *The new hooked on books.* New York: Berkley.

Lathlaen, P. (1993). A meeting of minds: Teaching using biographies. *The Reading Teacher, 46*(6), 529–531.

Martinez, M. (1993). Motivating dramatic story reenactments. *The Reading Teacher, 46*(8), 682–688.

Moore, M. A. (1991). Electronic dialoguing: An avenue to literacy. *The Reading Teacher, 45*(4), 280–286.

Tompkins, G. E. (1994). *Teaching writing: Balancing process and product* (2nd ed.). Upper Saddle River, NJ: Merrill/Prentice Hall.

Veatch, J. (1978). *Reading in the elementary school* (2nd ed.). New York: Owen.

Focus Questions

When you are finished studying this chapter, you should be able to answer these questions:

1. How do narrative texts and expository texts differ in purpose?
2. What effect does concept load have on the readability of content reading assignments?
3. What are the different expository text patterns used in textbook chapters or units of study?
4. How does one analyze a unit of study in terms of essential information to be conveyed to students?
5. What is an anticipation guide? Why might you choose to use one in a content class?
6. What are some specific efficient reading and study strategies that can be taught within the context of content instruction?
7. What accommodations can be made for readers with learning needs to help them succeed in content area classrooms?

Reading and Writing in Grades 6–8

Key Concepts

Expository Text
Content Area Reading
Concept Load
Readability
Content Analysis
Graphic Organizer
Study Guide

Three-Level Guide
Anticipation Guide
Prereading Plan (PReP)
Skimming, Scanning, and Previewing
Metacognition
Themed Studies

As students make the move from elementary school to middle school, they enter a very challenging phase of literacy learning. In the best case scenario, students have become reasonably fluent in reading and are ready to explore in greater detail the myriad subjects offered in their content classes (i.e., the sciences, social studies, mathematics, the arts). As is often said of typical middle schoolers, they have *learned to read* and now *read to learn*.

HELPING STUDENTS SUCCEED WITH CONTENT READING MATERIALS

For students who are still learning basic reading abilities, content classes can be a formidable hurdle. As one writer has remarked, reading problems in the middle school become *viral,* attacking the ability of students to continue their academic progress (K. S. Cooter, 1999). The job of teaching reading at this level also becomes more rigorous because the stakes are higher. Concerning those students struggling with reading skills, the well-known reading researcher Jeanne S. Chall, of Harvard University, has written:

> The public has become more conscious about the importance of literacy, for students and for adults. . . . The reading achievement of too many children, young people, and adults, is not up to what it should be . . . The students of low-income families and students of all social levels who are predisposed to having reading difficulty—are not doing as well as they can. . . . They need excellent teachers. (1998, pp. 20, 22)

In this chapter, we take a careful look at ways teachers can help students succeed with content reading materials commonly found in the middle school, and understand the unique ways subject area texts are written and the reading demands placed on this group of youngsters. Before closing this final chapter of our book, we also consider ways of helping students who are still learning to read. It is our goal that this chapter will help you better understand how we can help all students read to learn while in middle school and on into adulthood.

WHY CONTENT READING IS SO CHALLENGING FOR SOME STUDENTS: THE NATURE OF EXPOSITORY TEXTS

Content area reading is the field of study that deals with applying reading skills in expository texts (Cooter & Flynt, 1996).

There are at least four forms of informational text commonly found in the middle school: *argumentation, description, exposition,* and *narration.* The majority of readings middle schoolers are asked to learn are informational or **expository texts.** For the middle school teacher, formal reading instruction focuses on successful strategies for reading and comprehending expository texts, study skills, and efficient reading or "speed reading" strategies. The field of study in our profession that deals with applying reading skills in expository texts is known as **content area reading** (Cooter & Flynt, 1996).

Unlike the stories or *narrative texts* commonly used in beginning reading instruction, expository texts have unique organizational patterns. Explaining new ideas to others is a different form of language than storytelling, so different styles must be used to get important points across to the learner. Hence, different writing and reading techniques are employed in content area reading materials.

In this section, we begin with a brief review of the writing patterns or structures commonly used in expository texts. Also included is a discussion of the text demands that tend to make reading these kinds of materials challenging to the adolescent reader, such as increased concept load and readability considerations.

Specialized Vocabulary and Concepts

There are four levels of vocabulary knowledge: listening, speaking, reading, and writing.

A formidable task for every middle school teacher is helping students learn previously unknown concepts and vocabulary. Vocabulary knowledge is developmental and is based on background experiences (Heilman, Blair, & Rupley, 1990). Teachers need

Middle school students benefit from learning a variety of skills to help them comprehend the diversity of content they will encounter in expository texts.

to lead their students through four levels of vocabulary knowledge—*listening, speaking, reading,* and *writing*—if new content or "specialized" vocabulary are to become part of their permanent memory. *Listening vocabulary,* the largest of the four vocabularies, is made up of all words people can hear and understand, which includes not only the words we use in our everyday speech but also those words we can understand only when used in context. For instance, while listening to an evening news report, a child in sixth grade may hear about the latest breakthrough in cancer research. Although the youngster may be able to hear and understand the news report, he or she probably would not be able to reproduce the specialized medical terms used (e.g., carcinomas, metastasis, chemotherapy). Some have speculated that students entering first grade may have a listening vocabulary of around 20,000 words! The second level of vocabulary knowledge is called the *speaking vocabulary,* consisting of words we not only can hear and understand but also can use in our everyday speech. The third level of vocabulary knowledge is called *reading vocabulary:* These are words we can hear and understand, use as part of our speech communications, and recognize in print. The final level, *writing vocabulary,* is made up of words we can understand on all these levels, listening, speaking, and reading, and likewise use in our written communications. In teaching new technical vocabulary like that found in typical content readings, a primary goal is to bring students through each of these levels of vocabulary knowledge.

The best way to teach students about new ideas is through concrete, or "hands-on," experience. For example, if one wanted to teach students from rural Wyoming about life in New York City, then the most effective way to do so would be to take them there for a visit. Similarly, the very best way one could teach students about the space shuttle would be to put them through astronaut training and then send them into space on a future mission! Obviously, neither of these experiences is feasible in today's schools, so we must seek the best concrete experiences within our reach as teachers.

The best way to teach new ideas and vocabulary is through "hands-on" experience.

Figure 13.1   Pyramid of classroom experiences

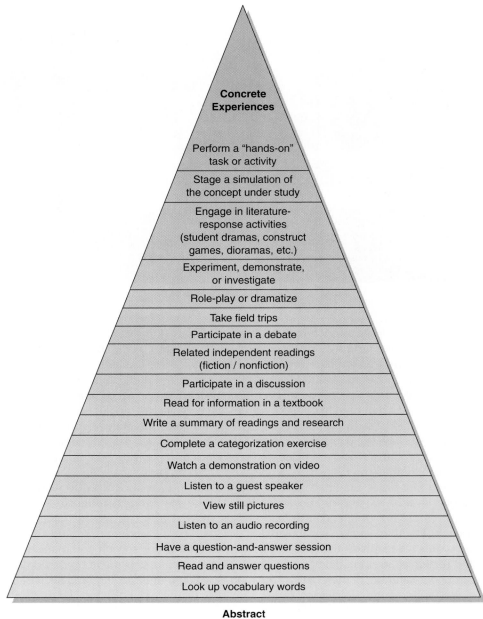

Some educators (Dale, 1969; Estes & Vaughan, 1978) have suggested hierarchies for typical classroom activities, ranging from concrete to abstract experiences. Such hierarchies help prospective teachers select concept and vocabulary development activities of a more concrete nature, and they help practicing teachers review their past practices for evaluative and curriculum redesign purposes. We have developed a composite version of these hierarchies, which is presented in Figure 13.1.

Notice that as one ascends toward the top of the *classroom experiences pyramid,* activities become more concrete and thus easier for students to assimilate.

Studies indicate that effective vocabulary development (Nagy, 1988) in content classes seems to have three important properties in common: (a) integration of new words with known experiences and concepts, (b) sufficient repetition so that students will recognize words as they read, and (c) meaningful use of new words brought about through stimulating practice experiences. In light of these requirements, we offer several examples of vocabulary development activities for whole-group and individual teaching situations later in this chapter.

Think of ways you could integrate Nagy's (1988) vocabulary development suggestions into a lesson on a science topic of your choice.

Increased Concept Load

Concept load (also called *concept density*) has to do with the number of new ideas and amount of technical vocabulary introduced by an author (Singer & Donlan, 1989); sentences of equal length may, in fact, require very different comprehension skills from a reader. Expository reading materials found in content classrooms are often much more difficult to understand than narrative/story readings because of greater concept load (Harris & Sipay, 1990), because story writers usually present information gradually and build to a conclusion or climax. Elements such as setting, plot, and characterization are laced with information quite familiar to most readers. Expository writers, however, usually present new and abstract information unfamiliar to the reader, which requires the building of new schemas or memory structures in the brain. Authors who introduce several new concepts in a single sentence (high concept load) create a situation that is extremely difficult for all but the best readers.

Concept load is the number of new ideas introduced by an author.

Teachers should obviously consider concept load when they think about ordering or adopting new learning materials. High concept load reading materials will create a major obstacle for readers lacking in fluency. One alternative to selecting conceptually dense textbooks is to select several smaller books that concentrate on just a few topics and cover them in some depth. If this option is not possible, the teacher can have students read through materials in dyads (groups of two) and write summaries of key points using good paragraph structure to flesh things out: a topic sentence, which tells the key idea; supporting sentences, which explain the key idea in greater detail; several examples; and a closing summarizing sentence.

Readability Considerations

Another concern of teachers preparing content material for instruction is text difficulty or **readability.** Text difficulty is most often measured using a *readability formula.* The purpose of a readability formula is to assign a grade-level equivalent, or approximate difficulty level, to narrative or expository reading material used to teach children. Sentence length and complexity of vocabulary used are two elements often measured in readability formulas.

Readability formulas help teachers judge the difficulty of reading materials.

A number of readability formulas are available for classroom use. The Fry (1977) readability formula (Figure 13.2) is one of the more popular formulas available and bases its estimates on sentence and word length. Another formula that is significantly quicker and easier to use (Baldwin & Kaufman, 1979) is the Raygor (1977) readability graph (Figure 13.3); instead of having to count the number of syllables contained in a 100-word passage, teachers merely count the number of words having six or more letters.

The problem with readability formulas in general is that they are too narrow in scope and too simplistic; many factors determine whether or not students can read

Figure 13.2 The Fry readability formula

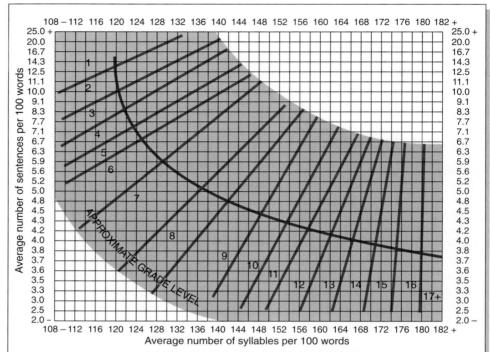

Expanded Directions for Working Readability Graph

1. Randomly select (3) three sample passages and count out exactly 100 words each, beginning with the beginning of a sentence. Do count proper nouns, initializations, and numerals.
2. Count the number of sentences in the 100 words, estimating length of the fraction of the last sentence to the nearest one-tenth.
3. Count the total number of syllables in the 100 word passage. If you don't have a hand counter available, an easy way is to simply put a mark above every syllable over one in each word: then when you get to the end of the passage, count the number of marks and add 100. Small calculators can also be used as counters by pushing numeral 1, then push the + sign for each word or syllable when counting.
4. Enter graph with *average* sentence length and *average* number of syllables: plot dot where the two lines intersect. Area where dot is plotted will give you the approximate grade level.
5. If a great deal of variability is found in syllable count or sentence count, putting more samples into the average is desirable.
6. A word is defined as a group of symbols with a space on either side: thus, *Joe, IRA, 1945*, and *&* are each one word.
7. A syllable is defined as a phonic syllable. Generally, there are as many syllables as vowel sounds. For example, *stopped* is one syllable and *wanted* is two syllables. When counting syllables for numerals and initializations, count one syllable for each symbol. For example, *1945* is four syllables, *IRA* is three syllables, and *&* is one syllable.

From "Fry's Readability Graph: Clarifications, Validity, and Extension to Level 17" by Edward Fry, 1977, *Journal of Reading, 21*, pp. 242–252.

Figure 13.3   The Raygor readability formula

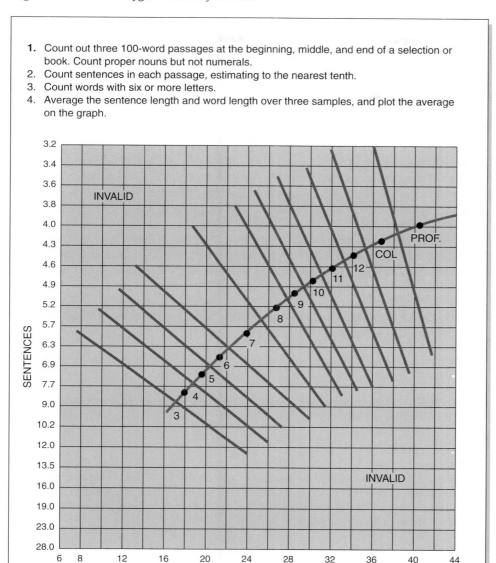

1. Count out three 100-word passages at the beginning, middle, and end of a selection or book. Count proper nouns but not numerals.
2. Count sentences in each passage, estimating to the nearest tenth.
3. Count words with six or more letters.
4. Average the sentence length and word length over three samples, and plot the average on the graph.

From "The Raygor Readability Estimate: A Quick and Easy Way to Determine Difficulty" by A. L. Raygor, in *Reading: Theory, Research and Practice, Twenty-Sixth Yearbook of the National Reading Conference* (pp. 259–263) edited by P. D. Pearson, 1977, Clemson, SC: National Reading Conference.

a given passage effectively. Klare (1963) concluded that some 289 factors influence readability, 20 of which were found to be significant. Typical readability formulas, such as the Fry (1977) and Raygor (1977), account for only two factors. An important factor affecting both readability and comprehension is interest (Cooter, 1994). If a student is highly interested in a subject, say cooking, then words such as *cuisine, parfait, pastry, pasta,* and *guacamole* likely will be immediately recognizable, even if the text is found to be several years above the student's so-called reading level. Another student at the same point of reading development who is not interested in cooking may find the same words incomprehensible. This is so because interest in a subject usually corresponds directly to a student's background and vocabulary knowledge in that subject area. In summary, readability formulas may be helpful in determining a very general difficulty level, but they should not be considered anything more than a gross estimate.

Unique Writing Patterns

Just as narrative (story) passages use distinct writing patterns, expository texts have five distinct patterns that are commonly used.

Narrative text has been described using a story grammar scheme, which includes such common elements as setting, theme, characterization, plot, and resolution. Expository text, however, is quite different: Its structure tends to be much more compact, detailed, and explanatory (Heilman et al., 1990). Similar to the story grammar research for narrative text, five common expository text structures have been described by Meyer and Freedle (1984): *description, collection, causation, problem/solution,* and *comparison.* When preparing to teach units in the content areas, teachers need to establish which expository text structures are used and organize for instruction accordingly. Next, Meyer and Freedle's (1984) five expository text patterns are described along with examples taken from content textbooks:

Description: **Explains something about a topic or presents a characteristic or setting for a topic.**

Decimals are another way to write fractions when the denominators are 10, 100, and so on. (From *Merrill Mathematics* [Grade 5], 1985, p. 247)

Collection: **A number of descriptions (specifics, characteristics, or settings) presented together.**

Water Habitats
Freshwater habitats are found in ponds, bogs, swamps, lakes, and rivers. Each freshwater habitat has special kinds of plants and animals that live there. Some plants and animals live in waters that are very cold. Others live in waters that are warm. Some plants and animals adapt to waters that flow fast. Others adapt to still water. (From *Merrill Science* [Grade 3], 1989, p. 226)

Causation *includes a time sequence.*

Causation: **Elements grouped according to time sequence with a cause— effect relationship specified.**

America Enters the War
On Sunday, December 7, 1941, World War II came to the United States. At 7:55 A.M. Japanese warplanes swooped through the clouds above <u>Pearl Harbor.</u> Pearl Harbor was the American naval base in the Hawaiian Islands. A deadly load of bombs was dropped on the American ships and airfield. It was a day, Roosevelt said, that would "live in infamy." *Infamy* (IN·fuh·mee) means remembered for being evil.

The United States had been attacked. That meant war. (From The *United States: Its History and Neighbors* [Grade 5], Harcourt Brace Jovanovich, 1985, p. 493)

Problem/Solution: **Includes a relationship (between a problem and its possible causes[s]) and a set of solution possibilities, one of which can break the link between the problem and its cause.**

Agreement by Compromise (Events That Led to the Civil War)
For a while there was an equal number of Southern and Northern states. That meant that there were just as many Senators in Congress from slave states as from free states. Neither had more votes in the Senate, so they usually reached agreement on new laws by compromise. (From *The United States and the Other Americas* [Grade 5], Macmillan, 1980, p. 190)

Comparison: **Organizes factors on the basis of differences and similarities. Comparison does not contain elements of sequence or causality.**

Comparison *deals with areas of similarity and difference.*

Segregation
Segregation laws said that blacks had to live separate, or apart, from whites. Like whites, during segregation blacks had their own parks, hospitals, and swimming pools. Theaters, buses, and trains were segregated.

Students often have difficulty with comparisons. Why do you think this is so?

Many people said that the segregation laws were unfair. But in 1896, the Supreme Court ruled segregation legal if the separate facilities for blacks were equal to those for whites. "Separate but equal" became the law in many parts of the country.

But separate was not equal. . . . One of the most serious problems was education. Black parents felt that their students were not receiving an equal education in segregated schools. Sometimes the segregated schools had teachers who were not as well educated as teachers in the white schools. Textbooks were often very old and out-of-date, if they had any books at all. But in many of the white schools the books were the newest ones. Without a good education, the blacks argued, their students would not be able to get good jobs as adults.

Finally in 1954, the Supreme Court changed the law. (Adapted from *The American People* [Grade 6], American Book Company, 1982, p. 364)

PREPARING TO TEACH: ANALYZING READINGS AND CREATING STUDY AIDS

Performing a Content Analysis

One of the best ways of planning strategies for content area instruction is to perform a content analysis. The purpose of a **content analysis** is to help teachers identify the important *facts, concepts,* and *generalizations* presented in a given unit of study. This is an essential process for establishing curriculum objectives and learning activities for students (Martorella, 1985). By carefully analyzing new information to be presented, the teacher is able to locate important information, disregard useless trivia, and determine which areas of the unit require deeper development for students. As a result of this process, teachers will be able to develop a cohesive unit of study that gives new knowledge to their students and builds new cognitive structures. In explaining the significance of analyzing informational text prior to teaching, Martorella (1985) remarked:

A **content analysis** *helps teachers determine important facts, concepts, generalizations, and vocabulary that must be taught.*

> What we regard as an individual's knowledge consists of a complex network of the elements of reflection. The fact of our date of birth, for example, is linked in some way to our concept of *birthday*. As further reflection occurs, we incorporate the new information into our network and it becomes related with the old knowledge. (pp. 69–70) [*Author's note:* This is the stage at which a new generalization is created.]

Facts are individual bits of information, or details, presented in a unit under study. In a science unit dealing with our solar system, some of the facts to be learned might include *atmosphere, satellite,* and *Saturn.* For a history unit pertaining to events surrounding the life of Dr. Martin Luther King, Jr., possible facts found in the readings might relate to the March on Washington, sit-ins, and Civil Rights legislation.

Concepts are categories into which we group all facts or phenomena known through our experiences (Martorella, 1985). In the previous example of a unit about the solar system, *satellite* and *Saturn* could be grouped into a single concept called "objects orbiting the sun." Concepts are usually stated in a simple word, phrase, or sentence that captures the main idea.

A *generalization* is a principle or conclusion that applies to the entire class or sample being examined (T. L. Harris & Hodges, 1981). A generalization is teacher generated, written in the language of the students, and usually expressed in complete sentences. Generalizations organize and summarize a large amount of information, sometimes an entire unit. Two examples of generalizations follow:

> There are many reasons why Harry Truman, perhaps an unlikely president, chose public life.
>
> Our solar system is made up of many "satellites."

Once facts, concepts, and generalizations have been identified, the teacher should organize them into some form of graphic representation: a traditional outline, semantic web, structured overview, or another preferred form. Arranging information structurally allows the teacher to analyze the unit and begin making decisions about organizing for instruction. One typical query follows:

Question: What should a teacher do if the adopted textbook contains information that is not relevant to any of the major concepts?

Answer: If the information helps build background understandings for the students that are important to the facts, concepts, and generalizations taught, then the teacher should keep and use that information. If the information serves no real purpose, however, it should not be included in unit activities or discussion.

Figures 13.4 and 13.5 are examples of partially finished content analysis graphic representations by two middle school teachers. Notice that they are essentially schema maps.

Constructing Learning Tools

Interesting and informative content area units do not come together by accident; they require deliberate planning and certain key ingredients, which can be drawn from the content analysis you have constructed. Tools you can develop directly from the content analysis are *graphic organizers, vocabulary-* and *concept-learning activities, study guides,* and *expository text response activities.*

Using Graphic Organizers to Draw on Background Experiences and Build Concept Knowledge

A **graphic organizer** is essentially a map or graph that summarizes information to be learned and the relationship between ideas (Alvermann & Phelps, 1994; Barron, 1969). It provides a means for presenting new vocabulary and its relationship to

Concepts are clusters of related facts.

Generalizations are principles or conclusions that relate to an entire unit of study.

Teacher-made "learning tools" are developed based on student needs and data gained from the content analysis.

How are graphic organizers and schema maps alike?

Figure 13.4 Partial content analysis of *matter*

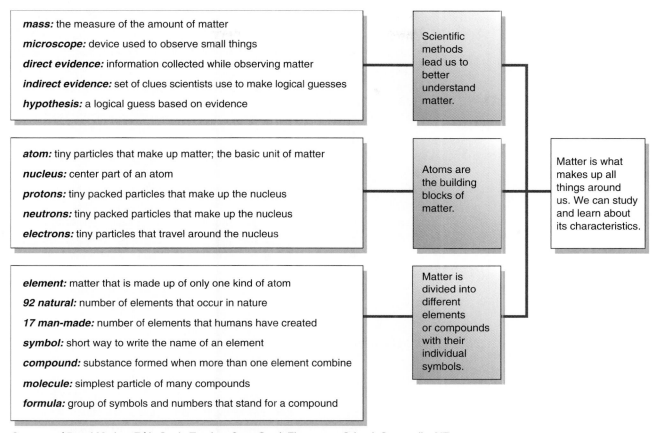

mass: the measure of the amount of matter

microscope: device used to observe small things

direct evidence: information collected while observing matter

indirect evidence: set of clues scientists use to make logical guesses

hypothesis: a logical guess based on evidence

Scientific methods lead us to better understand matter.

atom: tiny particles that make up matter; the basic unit of matter

nucleus: center part of an atom

protons: tiny packed particles that make up the nucleus

neutrons: tiny packed particles that make up the nucleus

electrons: tiny particles that travel around the nucleus

Atoms are the building blocks of matter.

Matter is what makes up all things around us. We can study and learn about its characteristics.

element: matter that is made up of only one kind of atom

92 natural: number of elements that occur in nature

17 man-made: number of elements that humans have created

symbol: short way to write the name of an element

compound: substance formed when more than one element combine

molecule: simplest particle of many compounds

formula: group of symbols and numbers that stand for a compound

Matter is divided into different elements or compounds with their individual symbols.

Courtesy of David Harlan, Fifth-Grade Teacher, Sage Creek Elementary School, Springville, UT.

larger concepts and generalizations (Tierney, Readence, & Dishner, 1990). Graphic organizers are generally used as an introductory instrument to begin a unit of study, are referred to regularly during the course of the unit, and are used as a review instrument near the end of a unit of study.

Constructing a graphic organizer is a simple matter once a content analysis has been completed: Simplify or condense the facts, concepts, and generalizations in the unit by reducing each to a single word or phrase, then arrange them graphically in the same hierarchical pattern as the content analysis. If a thorough content analysis is not possible, however, the following steps can be used to develop a graphic organizer (adapted from Barron, 1969):

1. The teacher should identify all facts and vocabulary he or she feels are essential to understanding the unit under study; thus forming the bottom layer of information, or subordinate concepts (Thelen, 1984). For the sake of consistency with the content analysis idea discussed earlier in the chapter, we refer to these subordinate concepts as *facts*.
2. Next, group related facts into clusters. These clusters form a second layer of understanding in the unit we refer to as *concepts*.

Figure 13.5 Partial content analysis of events leading to the Civil War

---

Generalization

Differences between states in the North and South led to the Civil War.

Concept

The northern economy was based on industry; the southern economy was based on agriculture.

Facts

Samuel Slater built many factories in the North.

In these factories, Slater discovered that machines could be used instead of people to make things more quickly and cheaply.

Soon, things made in northern factories were being sold to people living in southern states.

Farmers discovered that cotton could be processed more quickly and easily with the cotton gin than by hand.

Many southern farmers grew cotton and sold it to people living in northern states.

Many immigrants became factory workers; many slaves were forced to work in cotton fields.

Concept

Both the North and the South fought for control of the government.

Facts

The North wanted laws favoring business and industry; the South wanted laws favoring farming and slavery.

Northerners wanted any new states entering the Union to be free states.

Southerners wanted any new states entering the Union to be slave states.

In 1820, when Missouri asked to become a state, there were 11 free and 11 slave states in the Union.

Northerners wanted Missouri to be a free state; Southerners wanted Missouri to be a slave state.

Courtesy of Laurie McNeal, Fifth-Grade Unit, Brigham Young University.

3. Finally, concepts that relate to each other should be grouped under the major heading for the unit we refer to as a *generalization*. Most often, the unit will have only a single generalization, but occasionally, two or more generalizations may be needed, especially for large or complex units.

A variety of graphic formats can be used to depict key information from the unit of study.

Teachers may wish to use a variety of graphic formats to depict the different units covered each year. One style is not particularly better than another, but using a different style for each unit may help hold students' attention. Several popular formats for graphic organizers are shown in Figures 13.6 through 13.9 for a unit pertaining to the structure of American government.

Figure 13.6 Traditional outline

> ### *Structure of American Government*
>
> 1. Constitution provides for three branches
>   - A. Executive Branch
>   1. President
>   - B. Legislative Branch
>   1. House of Representatives
>   2. Senate
>   - C. Judicial Branch
>   1. Supreme Court

Study Guides

Study guides, also known as *reading guides* (Manzo & Manzo, 1990; R. T. Vacca & Vacca, 1989), are teacher-made activities intended to help students move successfully through a unit of study. They can be used before, during, and/or after reading the unit materials (Manzo & Manzo, 1990). Frequently, study guides consist of a series of key questions or problems for students to work through, followed by page references to text materials used in the unit. Students use the references to seek out answers and become familiar with the content. Tutolo (1977) described two types of study guides: interlocking and noninterlocking. An *interlocking* study guide groups questions according to three comprehension levels: literal, interpretative, and applied. A *noninterlocking* study guide does not use a hierarchical relationship for questions. Tutolo (1977) feels that with some text selections, the reader may need to move from the literal level to the application level and back to the literal level. Thus, grouping of study questions in this situation might be inappropriate.

Study guides are teacher-made activities that help students progress successfully through a unit of study.

Figure 13.7 Structured overview

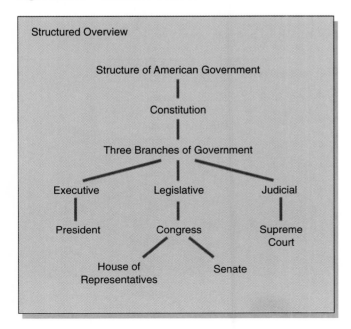

Structured Overview

Structure of American Government

Constitution

Three Branches of Government

Executive — Legislative — Judicial

President — Congress — Supreme Court

House of Representatives — Senate

Figure 13.8 Pyramid outline

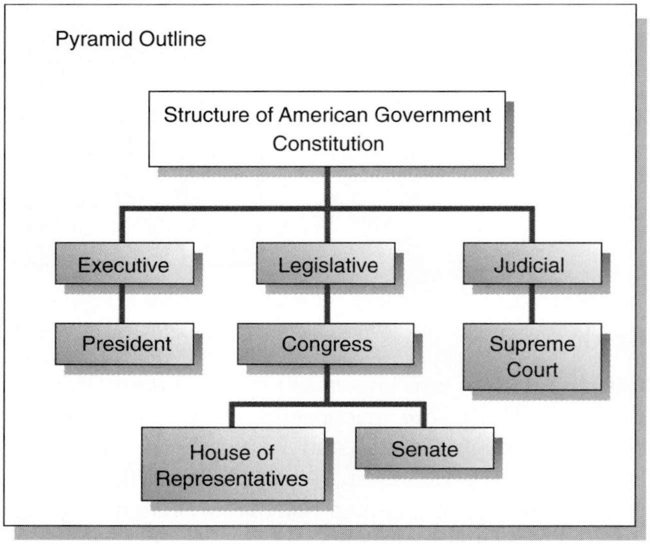

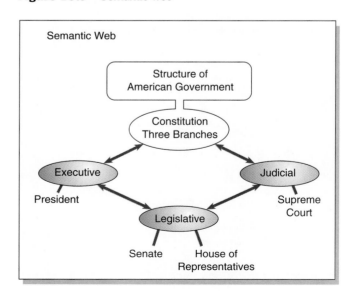

Many useful study guide formats are appropriate for middle school classrooms. We recommend that teachers use a combination of (a) interlocking or noninterlocking guides for students to use independently along with (b) whole-group activities such as the anticipation guide or prereading plan (PReP). Descriptions of a few examples follow.

*A **three-level guide** helps students move through basic to advanced comprehension levels.*

Three-Level Guide.   A **three-level guide** (Herber, 1978) is a classic interlocking guide in that it leads students from basic levels of comprehension to more advanced levels (Manzo & Manzo, 1990). The first level (literal comprehension level) of the guide helps students understand what the author said, the second level (interpretative

Figure 13.9 Semantic web

comprehension level) helps students understand what the author means, and the third level (applied comprehension level) helps students understand how text information can be applied (Manzo & Manzo, 1990). Although three-level guides have traditionally been constructed using declarative statements, we feel that it is just as appropriate to use a question or problem-solving format.

In constructing a three-level guide, we suggest the following guidelines, which have been adapted from R. T. Vacca and Vacca (1989):

1. Begin by constructing the study guide at the interpretative comprehension level by determining what the author means. Write inferences that make sense and that fit the content objectives. Revise your statements so that they are simple and clear. Part 2 of the guide is now completed.
2. Next, search the text for explicit pieces of information (details, facts, and propositions) that support inferences chosen for the second part of the guide. Put these into statement, question, or problem form. Part 1 of the guide is now completed.
3. Next, develop statements, questions, or problems for the applied comprehension level of the guide (Part 3); they should represent additional insights or principles that may be drawn when analyzing parts 1 and 2 of the guide. Part 3 should help students connect what they already know with what they have learned from the study of the unit.

Teachers should be flexible when using a three-level guide. The format should be varied from unit to unit to help hold students' attention. It may also be a good idea to occasionally put in *distracter* or "foil" items (i.e., false items); distracters sometimes prevent students from indiscriminately focusing on every item and cause them to focus on the information search more carefully (R. T. Vacca & Vacca, 1989).

The format of three-level guides should vary so as to hold student interest.

Finally, we recommend that teachers include page numbers in parentheses following each question, problem, or statement where answers can be found in the reading assignment. This alerts students to key ideas found on each page and enables them to screen out irrelevant information.

Anticipation Guides. **Anticipation guides** are prereading activities used to survey students' prior knowledge and attitudes about a given subject or topic. They usually consist of three to five teacher-prepared declarative statements that students read and react to before reading the text selection. Statements can be either true or false. The important factor is for students to respond to the statements based on their own experiences (Wiesendanger, 1986). Figure 13.10 shows a sample anticipation guide for "Our Picture of the Universe" (Hawking, 1988).

Anticipation guides survey students' prior knowledge of the topic to be studied.

Prereading Plan. The **prereading plan (PReP)** was developed by Judith Langer (1981) and provides both instructional and assessment benefits (see chapter 6, p. 339). In this three-step process, the teacher first identifies key concepts in the reading selection for the students. Next, the teacher asks students to discuss their associations with each of these terms or concepts. Their associations might be displayed on the chalkboard using a web or structured overview format. Once the group has discussed the different student associations, the teacher "reforms" the associations by asking students if they have any new interpretations to suggest about the major concepts and terms before reading the selection.

PReP has both instructional and assessment benefits.

Figure 13.10   Anticipation guide based on "Our Picture of the Universe" from Stephen W. Hawking's *A Brief History of Time* (1988)

Our Picture of the Universe

Directions: Read each statement below and decide whether you agree or disagree with the statement. If you agree with a statement, put an "X" in the ***Before I Read*** blank before that statement. If you disagree, put an "O" in the blank. After you have finished reading "Our Picture of the Universe," complete the blanks labeled ***Hawking's Views,*** indicating how you think the author would answer those same questions.

Before I Read   ***Hawking's Views***

_____   Many of the early scientists, like Aristotle (340 B.C.),   _____
                 believed the Earth was round instead of flat.

_____   The universe was created at some point in time in   _____
                 the past more or less as we observe it today.

_____   An expanding universe theory (big bang) does not   _____
                 preclude a creator.

_____   Knowing how the universe came about millions of   _____
                 years ago can help mankind to survive in the future.

PReP helps teachers assess what students already know about the topic before reading and helps students who may have inadequate knowledge about the topic under study to acquire more background knowledge from their peers and teacher before reading.

Vocabulary Development Activities

Thelen cited an idea in her book *Improving Reading in Science* (1984) that helps "students relate newly learned verbal associations to familiar and emphasized relationships" (p. 36). The format for this categorizing activity is shown in Figure 13.11.

Whole-Group Vocabulary Instruction

Whole-group instruction can be an effective mode of teaching vocabulary if not overused.

When teaching in large- or small-group situations, the teacher's primary vehicle for integrating new vocabulary with known experiences, which was discussed earlier in this chapter, is the graphic organizer. Graphic organizers (semantic web, pyramid, etc.) can be used to introduce and review new words throughout the unit. Because of their schemalike nature, they are ideal for this type of learning situation.

Another way to approach vocabulary instruction is through whole-group vocabulary mini-lessons that involve the entire class in activities demonstrating the meaning of new vocabulary. Whole-group vocabulary mini-lessons will not work with all new vocabulary but may be helpful on an occasional basis. The idea is to provide concrete understanding for abstract ideas. Following is an example for fifth graders learning about the basic components of an atom.

Figure 13.11   Vocabulary reinforcement: Functions of cells

```
                Functions of Cells: Vocabulary Review*

    Name    _____

    1.  _____        3.  _____

            neutrons                        diffusion osmosis
            protons                         active transport
            electrons                       pinocytosis

    2.  _____        4.  _____

            light reaction                  metabolism
            chlorophyll                     respiration
            nutrients from soil             homeostasis
```

*Answers: 1. atoms, 2. photosynthesis, 3. transport, 4. cell functions

Atomic Kid Power!

Step 1:   The teacher introduces key information about atomic structure (e.g., nucleus made up of protons and neutrons, electrons orbiting the nucleus).

Step 2:   The teacher takes the class out to the play area and assigns students to a role-playing situation wherein they take turns being subatomic particles (e.g., protons, neutrons, electrons). Protons could wear a special hat, colored purple; neutrons wear a white hat; and electrons wear a bright orange hat.

Step 3:   A circle large enough for approximately six students to stand within is drawn with chalk on the playground surface. Several students are assigned to play the part of the nucleus, and the appropriate number of child(ren) will be the electron(s).

Step 4:   Finally, the nucleus students stand together in the circle, hopping up and down simulating a live atomic nucleus. The electron child(ren) run around the nucleus, keeping about a 20-foot distance at all times. For extra instructional benefit, a parent helper could stand on a ladder (or perhaps the roof of the building), film the simulation using a video camcorder, and replay the film to the class at a later time for review purposes.

Individual Vocabulary Instruction

Nist and Simpson (1993) argue convincingly that we must help students get to know words and concepts on four distinct levels. The first level is the word's basic definition. Level two concerns understanding of synonyms, antonyms, examples, and nonexamples. Level three involves an understanding of connotations and characteristics of the word. The fourth level of understanding involves applying the word to personal and new situations apart from the original encounter in the content area classroom. Nist and Simpson liken these levels of understanding to an iceberg: The top level that we see first is the dictionary definition, but the bigger picture by far is composed of the three other levels of conceptual word knowledge lying beneath the surface. In this section, we offer two teacher-tested ideas that help achieve these goals.

Figure 13.12   Concept thinking matrix: Lesson on African-American art

Concepts/ Vocabulary	Dictionary Definition	Synonyms, Antonyms, Examples, Nonexamples	Connotations, Characteristics	Other Uses of the Word(s)
race consciousness		Syn.: Ant.: Ex./nonex.:	Connot.: Char.:	
African-American "art idiom"		Syn.: Ant.: Ex./nonex.:	Connot.: Char.:	
images		Syn.: Ant.: Ex./nonex.:	Connot.: Char.:	
flattened space		Syn.: Ant.: Ex./nonex.:	Connot.: Char.:	
compressed gestures		Syn.: Ant.: Ex./nonex.:	Connot.: Char.:	
controlled palette		Syn.: Ant.: Ex./nonex.:	Connot.: Char.:	

Some feel the thinking matrix activity helps students anticipate new information and construct schemas. Consider reasons why.

Thinking Matrix   The *thinking matrix* is designed to help students generate their own questions as an end-of-unit review, or to help student groups lead class discussions (Alvermann & Phelps, 1994; McTighe & Lyman, 1988). A concept thinking matrix is easily adapted to vocabulary learning by simply listing key concepts and words to be learned down one axis and the four levels of understanding across the top columns. In Figure 13.12, we illustrate a concept thinking matrix using terms from a lesson on African-American art. Completion of the matrix necessitates higher order analysis of each concept or term and is a perfect opportunity for student collaboration.

*Students essentially create their own dictionaries with **content-specific vocabulary cards.***

Content-Specific Vocabulary Cards   Another idea suggested by Nist and Simpson (1993) is *content-specific vocabulary cards*. The cards are like personal dictionaries developed by students kept on 3 × 5 index cards in plastic recipe boxes or bound together using steel rings. Nist and Simpson tell us that students typically keep two types of vocabulary cards: general and content specific. General vocabulary cards are for common everyday language, whereas content-specific vocabulary cards, as the name implies, are to assist with learning specialized content area terms (scientific terms, mathematical concepts, etc.). The procedure is simple: On one side, the student writes the term or concept to be learned. On the back side, the student writes pertinent in-

Figure 13.13 Content-specific vocabulary card

contaminant

def. something that soils or corrupts by contact.

syn. – taint, pollute, defile

ex. – acid rain, industrial chemicals dumped into a river, an open cesspool.

formation about its meaning, such as a definition, synonyms, antonyms, and examples. Figure 13.13 presents an example of a content-specific vocabulary card for the word *contaminant* from a unit on air pollution.

Choosing High-Interest Reading Materials

It has been well established through research that middle school students are much more inclined to read when they are offered interesting reading materials (Alexander & Filler, 1976; Dewey, 1913; Krashen, 1992; Worthy, Moorman, & Turner, 1999). With the absolute wealth of materials available on most every subject, there is no reason to limit content information to the district-adopted textbook. For example, here is a short list of resources available in most schools now to supplement content studies:

As interest in a topic increases, so does student learning.

- trade books (fiction and nonfiction books found in the library),
- journal-magazines (e.g., *National Geographic, The Smithsonian*),
- magazines and other popular press publications, and
- Internet resources such as World Wide Web "tours," search engines, "Bookmark" files in the classroom, and educational web sites (Cafolla, Kauffman, & Knee, 1997).

What Do Middle School Students Enjoy Reading?

There have been many studies of student reading habits over the years. In the most recent study of the reading preferences of middle school students that we could find (Worthy, Moorman, & Turner, 1999), some very interesting conclusions were reached. First, this team of researchers identified specific reading interests, which are shown in Table 13.1.

Worthy and her colleagues also posed the following question to the students: "If you could read anything at all, what would it be?" The students' responses were analyzed and are summarized in Table 13.2.

The second conclusion of the researchers was somewhat frustrating. Namely, in the schools studied by the researchers, not many of the preferred materials could be found. Obviously, many of the appropriate reading preferences and materials reported in this study should be considered, and obtained, when preparing content units.

Students indicate a profound lack of interest in information books about math and science (Worthy, Moorman, & Turner, 1999). What could you do to reverse this trend?

Table 13.1   Reading preferences* of sixth-grade students

Rank	Type of Material	Percentage of who would read often
1	Scary books or story collections	66%
2	Cartoons and comics	65%
3	*Popular magazines*	*38%*
4	*Sports*	*33%*
5	*Drawing books*	*29%*
6	Cars and trucks	22%
7	Animals	21%
8	Series	21%
9	Funny novels	20%
10	Books written mostly for adults	17%
11	Novels about people	17%
12	Science fiction or fantasy	17%
13	Picture books	16%
14	Almanacs or record books	14%
15	Poetry	12%
16	Biography	10%
17	Adventure novels	9%
18	Information books about history	6%
19	Encyclopedias	6%
20	Information books about science or math	2%

*Note that after #1 and #2 on the list, there is a sharp drop for #3–5, and an even sharper drop after that for the other preferences.

Using Trade Books as Supplements to Textbooks

Trade books (library books) can breathe life into content investigations while also providing needed background information for best comprehension and schema building (Wepner & Feeley, 1993). The key to success in weaving good literature into the content curriculum is remembering that books can be read aesthetically for enjoyment or to learn new information (Cox & Zarillo, 1993). Both purposes are important to encourage the synergy that is possible between good books and content learning.

Content teachers should read aloud to their students almost daily from interesting books pertaining to the subject under study.

A good beginning is for the teacher to read a relevant trade book daily to students for about 15 to 20 minutes (Brozo & Simpson, 1995). For example, if a unit on Japan is under way and the teacher decides that some knowledge of feudal times is important, he or she may choose to read aloud *The Coming of the Bear* by Lensey Namioka (1992). In a science class focusing on robotics and mechanization, the teacher could select such traditional favorites as *Jed's Junior Space Patrol* (Marzollo

Table 13.2 Summary of responses to the question: *If you could read anything at all, what would it be?*

Materials or topics named 10 or more times*	Number of responses
Scary	*124*
Sports magazines/books	**41**
Comics and cartoons	28
Teen magazines	26
Mystery	16
Car magazines	14
Science fiction/fantasy	13
Romance	12
Novels written for adults	11
Other fiction	47
Other magazines (e.g., music, ethnic, video games)	24
Other information books	20

*Note the great preference for scary books, followed by a steep drop to partical interest in sports materials, then another steep drop to the other categories.

& Marzollo, 1982), *The White Mountain* (Christopher, 1967), or Simon Watson's (1976) *No Man's Land*. Reading aloud great books such as these sparks interest in the subject matter and makes complex ideas more accessible to students.

It is equally important that students be encouraged to read trade books pertaining to the subject under study themselves. Three literature-based reading methods described in chapter 12—core books, themed literature units, and individualized reading instruction—have been recommended for adaptation in content classes (Brozo & Simpson, 1995; Cox & Zarillo, 1993). Regardless of the format used to incorporate trade books in content classes, we favor the second-sweep (i.e., second reading) method so that students can enjoy books as literature before seeking needed information.

Teachers can use several resources to locate appropriate trade books for content classes. Here are just a few that we have found helpful.

- *Journal of Adolescent & Adult Literacy*. International Reading Association. A periodical for middle school and secondary teachers that features a "Books for Adolescents" column and reviews of classroom materials. Substantial summaries presented in these issues are most helpful in planning units.
- Lima, C., & Lima, J. (1993). *A to Zoo: Subject Access to Children's Picture Books*. New York: Bowker. A reference tool useful in locating books for specific topics and themes.
- Norton, D. E. (1998). *Through the Eyes of a Child: An Introduction to Children's Literature* (5th ed.). Upper Saddle River, NJ: Merrill/Prentice Hall. An

The Journal of Adolescent & Adult Literacy *is the premier publication for content area reading.*

up-to-date textbook that offers brief descriptions of trade books and their uses for read alouds, themed studies, and so on.

- *The Newbery and Caldecott Awards: A Guide to Medal and Honor Books.* American Library Association. Provides helpful information regarding some of the most celebrated trade books available.
- *The Reading Teacher.* International Reading Association. A periodical for elementary and upper elementary/middle school teachers that publishes lists of popular books each year called "Children's Choices" (October issue) and "Teachers' Choices" (November issue). Summaries presented in these issues are helpful in planning units.

PROVEN STUDY STRATEGIES: HELPING STUDENTS HELP THEMSELVES

Efficient ("Speed Reading") Study Strategies

Efficient reading strategies help students make economical use of their study time and generally improve self-esteem and comprehension.

One of the characteristics of successful mature readers is that they read *selectively* instead of word by word. Mature reading has been characterized as a "psycholinguistic guessing game" (K. S. Goodman, 1967). This means that efficient reading strategies are a conscious or unconscious search for meaning in the text, not a word-by-word, laborious process.

Even though much of efficient reading is an unconscious process carried out automatically by the brain (LaBerge & Samuels, 1974), it is desirable for teachers to show students several efficient reading strategies that, when practiced, become internalized in the student over time, resulting in improved reading fluency and comprehension. A discussion of several of these strategies follows.

Skimming and Scanning

Think of times when you find yourself skimming materials. How is your purpose for reading different from times when you read for pleasure?

Skimming is an easy strategy to learn and can be useful with a variety of reading materials. It is very helpful with periodicals, popular press materials, and with most science and social studies textbooks. Skimming can be used to preview materials or for review purposes. The object of skimming is quite simple: Students practice forcing their eyes to move quickly across each line of print. As they do so, they try to attend to a few key words from each line. Sometimes it is helpful for students to move their finger rapidly under each line of text, following the text with their eyes (this is called *pacing*). At first, comprehension will drop off dramatically, because students are concentrating more on the physical movement of their eyes than on the meaning of the text. But over time and with practice, students are able to perform the skimming operation with as much or more comprehension than usual.

The teacher should lead the class through some practice exercises. Emphasis should be on the fact that the key words on each line will tend to be nouns, verbs, and adjectives—in other words, the meaning-carrying words. Articles, conjunctions, and other function words in the sentence add little to the comprehension process and can essentially be ignored.

Scanning is a rapid search for a particular type of information, such as a date or a name.

Scanning, on the other hand, is a much simpler strategy to teach and learn. The idea is to have students visually sweep or scan a page of text to locate information, such as an important date, key words, or answers to a specific question. Instead of attempting to comprehend all information on the page, the reader is simply trying to locate an information bit. Teachers should be able to demonstrate this strategy through simple modeling.

Previewing

Previewing is especially useful for getting a general idea of heavy reading, such as nonfiction books. Previewing allows readers to cover nonfiction material in a fraction of the usual time with up to 50% comprehension. The procedure is simple to teach and learn but may take quite a bit of practice to achieve useful and practical comprehension levels. The first step is to read the first two paragraphs of the chapter or selection. Most authors provide the reader with an overview of the chapter in the first couple of paragraphs, so reading every word of the first two paragraphs is essential. The second step is for students to read only the first sentence of each paragraph thereafter; most professional writers of textbooks and nonfiction texts begin paragraphs with a topic sentence, which summarizes the main idea of each paragraph. Thus, reading the first sentence in each paragraph will provide crucial information to the reader, but remember that some of the important details that follow will be missed. Finally, the student reads the final two paragraphs of the chapter or selection, which provide the reader with a summary of major points covered. If the final section is labeled "Summary," "Conclusions," or something similar, then the student should read the entire section.

Adjusting Reading Rate to Match the Text Type

Another important efficient reading lesson is varying reading rate. Reading rate is the speed at which readers attempt to process text. Different types of content usually require a different reading speed for best comprehension to occur. For example, some students may be able to read a *Hardy Boys* mystery at a very fast reading rate. After all, not every word is crucial to understanding the author's message in a book of this kind, and a previewing or skimming strategy may be sufficient for good comprehension. On the other hand, when students read a story problem in mathematics, it is important to read each word carefully at a reading rate much slower than for a mystery story. Therefore, students need to be made aware of the need to consciously vary their reading rate to match the style and purpose of the text they are reading.

Students should have practice in varying their reading rate (speed) according to purpose and type of text.

Our Recommended Efficient Reading Strategy

After working with many students in the middle school, we have arrived at an efficient reading strategy that appears to be comprehensive and helpful with most expository and narrative materials. The one exception is mathematics, which requires more specialized strategies. The procedure is a combination of previewing and skimming, as previously described. Here are the steps to follow:

This efficient reading strategy combines elements of previewing and skimming strategies.

1. Read the first two paragraphs of the selection to get an overview of the piece.
2. Next, read the first sentence of each successive paragraph. Then skim the remainder of the paragraph to get important supporting details for each topic sentence.
3. Read the final two paragraphs of the selection to review main ideas.

This procedure has yielded comprehension rates of up to 80% with mature readers but requires only about one third the time of normal reading.

In addition to the efficient reading strategies just introduced in this chapter, educational research has supported the use of many other tactics helpful to students in their content area pursuits. It seems that when students understand *what* to study, *how* to study quickly and efficiently, and *why* the information is pertinent to their world, classroom performance is improved. We have chosen some of the more popular study strategies for brief discussion in this section.

SQ3R

SQ3R is a widely taught study strategy that has met with some success.

Perhaps the most widely used study system is *SQ3R* (Robinson, 1946), which is an acronym for *survey, question, read, recite, review*. Especially effective with expository text, SQ3R provides students with a step-by-step study method that ensures multiple exposures to the new material to be learned. Many students also find that they can trim their study time using SQ3R and still earn better grades.

SQ3R is best taught through teacher modeling followed by a whole-class walk-through. Each step of SQ3R is explained in the following list:

- *Survey:* To survey a chapter in a textbook, students read and think about the title, headings and subheadings, captions under any pictures, vocabulary in bold print, side entries on each page (if there are any), and the summary.
- *Question:* Next, students use the survey information, particularly headings and subheadings, to write prediction questions about what they are about to read. Students frequently need teacher assistance the first few times they use SQ3R in developing questions that will alert them to important concepts in the unit.
- *Read:* The third step is for students to read actively (Manzo & Manzo, 1990), looking for answers to their questions. They should also attend to boldface type, graphs, charts, and any other comprehension aid provided.
- *Recite:* Once the material has been read and the questions answered fully, the students should test themselves on the material. Anything difficult to remember should be rehearsed aloud or recited. This multisensory experience helps the difficult material to move into short-term, and with practice, long-term, memory.
- *Review:* The final step is to review the information learned periodically. This can be done orally with a peer, through rewriting notes from memory and comparing to the students' master set of notes, or with mock quizzes developed by a peer or the teacher.

SQRQCQ

What adaptations does the SQRQCQ strategy employ to suit the special needs of mathematics texts?

Although the SQ3R method can be very effective with most expository texts, it is difficult to apply to mathematics. A similar plan developed especially for mathematics story problems (Fay, 1965) is known as *SQRQCQ: survey, question, read, question, compute, question*. As with SQ3R, the teacher should model SQRQCQ with the class and conduct whole-class practice before expecting students to attempt the procedure on their own (P. C. Burns, Roe, & Ross, 1988). The steps of this procedure follow:

- *Survey:* Students read through the story problem quickly to get a general feel for what the problem is about.
- *Question:* Next, students should ask themselves general questions related to problem solving, such as, "What is the problem to be solved?" "What do I need to find out?" and "What important information is provided in the story problem?"

- *Read:* Students read the problem again carefully, giving close attention to details and relationships that will assist in the problem-solving process.
- *Question:* Students answer the question, "What mathematical operation is needed to solve this problem?"
- *Compute:* Students do the computation associated with the operation decided on in the previous step.
- *Question:* Students answer the question, "Does this answer make sense?" If it does not, then the students may need to repeat some or all of the process.

Comprehension Monitoring (Metacognition)

Metacognition, or comprehension monitoring, has to do with helping students recognize what they know or need to know about what they are learning. Research suggests that good readers can describe their methods for reading and getting meaning, but poor readers seem virtually unaware of strategies that can be employed (A. Brown, 1982). F. Smith (1967) found that poor readers fail to adjust their reading behavior when reading for different purposes, such as reading for specific details or general impressions. A crucial role for the content area reading teacher is to help students (a) become aware of their own reading comprehension abilities and needs (called *metacognitive awareness*), and (b) learn specific strategies that can be used to fit their own comprehension needs at any given time.

Metacognition has to do with self-monitoring of thinking and learning processes.

A. Brown (1982) makes an eloquent case for why we need to include metacognitive instruction as a fundamental part of study skill instruction:

> I emphasize the need for "cognitive training with awareness" because the whole history of attempts to instill study strategies in ineffectual learners attests to the futility of having students execute some strategy in the absence of a concomitant understanding of why or how that activity works. [For example] . . . we see that outlining itself is not a desired end product, and merely telling students it would be a good idea to outline, underline, or take notes is not going to help them become more effective studiers (A. Brown & Smiley, 1978). Detailed, *informed* instruction of the purposes of outlining and methods of using the strategy intelligently are needed before sizable benefits accrue. (pp. 46–47)

A. Brown (1982) has developed a four-step model for teaching students metacognitive processes:

1. *Determine the nature of the material to be learned:* Students should review the text—for example, using the previewing method described earlier in this chapter (see SQ3R)—to learn what kind of material it is (narrative, expository, etc.). Most content area texts and materials in each of the subject areas follow a fairly well-defined pattern. Understanding the pattern involved at the outset helps the reader to anticipate reading demands and expectations.

2. *Consider the essential task involved:* Students need to understand what they are looking for in the text. What is the critical information that will likely appear on tests and other assessment activities? T. H. Anderson and Armbruster (1980) indicate that when students modify their study plans accordingly, they tend to learn more than if the criterion task remains vague.

Students should keep in mind what they need to know from the text.

3. *Consider your own strengths and weaknesses:* As A. Brown (1982) points out, some students are good at numbers or have a good rote memory,

whereas others may have trouble remembering details or learning new languages (foreign, computer, scientific, etc.). In general, the task is to make new, abstract ideas familiar and memorable. Learners need to assess their own strengths and weaknesses in each of the content fields they study in preparation for the final phase of the four-step sequence.

4. *Employ appropriate strategies to overcome learning weaknesses:* Once students understand where they have specific learning difficulties, remedial action to overcome these weaknesses is essential. Strategies such as look-backs (going back over text to find key information via scanning), rereading, reading ahead, highlighting, note taking, summary writing, webbing, and outlining suddenly become of great interest to students when they are taught in connection with their new metacognitive self-awareness.

Writing to Deepen Learning: Having Students Create Their Own Expository Texts

Of the many ways to help readers succeed with content materials, teaching them to become authors of expository texts may be the most powerful. There is something about creating our own texts that clarifies and embeds permanently the new concepts, facts, and vocabulary in our minds. It also appears that our interest frequently increases in content information as we gain mastery over it in writing. In this section, we suggest a few ways students create expository texts and, by doing so, become more competent and fluent readers.

Paraphrase Writing

Writing helps clarify what we have learned.

Shelley M. Gahn (1989), an eighth-grade language arts teacher in Ohio, recommends paraphrase writing as one way students can re-create content information found in textbooks. The basic idea is that students restate information in their own words, which tends to keep the vocabulary simple and the resulting material brief. This strategy helps students to clarify their personal understanding of what has been studied. Gahn suggests three types of paraphrase writing: *rephrasing, summarizing,* and *elaborating.* Rephrasing involves rewording relatively short paragraphs from content textbook chapters. Summarizing calls on students to identify the text's major points. Elaborating requires students to compare information in the new text to previous knowledge, sometimes using graphs, charts, or comparison grids. Paraphrase writing is often most effective when students write in small groups or pairs. It is also crucial that teachers model each type of writing for students, showing examples of acceptable paraphrases and those that are flawed.

Using Text Structures

This strategy applies Meyer and Freedle's (1984) theories in a practical way.

Earlier in this chapter, we discussed expository text patterns (Meyer & Freedle, 1984) frequently found in textbooks. Because these patterns can be difficult for many readers to comprehend, teaching students to write using expository text patterns can often lead to wonderful breakthroughs in understanding. We advocate a four-step process for teaching students how to become authors of these forms of expository writing.

Responding to expository text content can be accomplished through writing activities that ask students to compare information they read.

Step 1:   The teacher describes the five expository text patterns. The teacher explains the differences between description, collection, causation, problem/solution, and comparison. The teacher presents examples of each using the overhead projector or chalkboard.

Step 2:   The teacher identifies these patterns in content textbooks. Using previously researched materials, the teacher asks students to help locate examples of each expository text pattern on photocopies supplied to them for this purpose.

Step 3:   The teacher models the writing of one of the expository text patterns. Beginning with description, the teacher creates an example of a description passage at the overhead projector or chalkboard based on text materials that the class has been reading. The teacher encourages students to coach him or her through premeditated mistakes in the example. The teacher should be sure to think aloud while creating the example, because this is the key element of modeling.

Step 4:   The teacher asks students to create their own example. Step 3 is repeated, but this time, the teacher asks students to do the work. As with many writing and reading tasks, it may be profitable for students to work in pairs. Volunteers should be asked to share their examples with the class.

As students become comfortable creating simple expository text structures, they should be encouraged to combine structures in creating more lengthy compositions and projects. Using multiple structures in lengthy pieces is an essential tool for writers. This fact can easily be examined in the adopted textbook.

Cubes

Cubes *is an activity that helps students review ideas from six perspectives.*

G. Tompkins (1994) recommends *cubes* as an expository writing activity. She explains that a cube has six sides, and in this activity, students review what they are learning about a topic from six sides, or perspectives, using the following tasks:

- Describe it.
- Compare it to other things you know about.
- Associate it to things it makes you think of.
- Analyze it as to what it is composed of.
- Apply it by explaining what you can do with it.
- Argue for or against it using reasons you have discovered through your investigation.

READING *ACROSS* THE CURRICULUM: THEMED STUDIES

Themed studies are a popular vehicle for applying literacy skills across the curriculum.

The teaching of reading and writing using a balanced reading perspective has been the focus of this book. Although reading and writing have sometimes been presented as separate entities for the sake of clarity, teachers establishing balanced literacy classrooms typically do not use these literacy skills separately. Rather, they are integrated *across* the curriculum (Savage, 1994) so that these boundaries virtually cease to exist. In a full curriculum integration, reading and writing become integral parts of subject area investigations, and vice versa via expanded interdisciplinary **themed studies.** A theme such as "changes" can become an exciting classroom experience involving social studies, the sciences, mathematics, literature, art history, and other important areas of the curriculum. This themed studies approach is what balanced literacy teaching is all about in its purest form.

The advantages of curriculum integration are numerous. Reading and writing abilities are acquired and refined within a rich context of real world significance, which in turn inspires students to want to know more. Skills are no longer taught in isolation as rote drill but are learned as welcomed tools for communicating ideas. Holistic integration of the curriculum results in a blend of instruction in literacy communication skills and content as well as the planting of seeds for future searches for new knowledge.

In one description of successful themed studies in Canada, Gamberg, Kwak, Hutchings, and Altheim (1988) identified a number of important characteristics. First, themed studies are in-depth investigations of a topic, concept, or theme. Second, they are high-interest topics that are broad enough to be divided into smaller subtopics. Third, themed studies are not geographically or historically limiting, and they help in breaking down artificial curriculum barriers. For middle school students, "The History of Buildings" and "Around the World in 60 Days" are examples of themes that facilitate themed investigations.

Guidelines for Conducting Themed Studies

Themed studies are very similar to the themed literature units discussed in chapter 12, differing mainly at the level of curricular integration (language arts integration vs. total curriculum integration); thus, an exhaustive discussion of the key elements is not

Figure 13.14 Teacher brainstorming web for theme studies

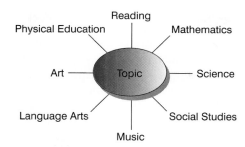

necessary. A brief summary of essential components of theme studies—as identified from the work of Paradis (1984) and Gamberg et al. (1988)—follows:

- *Theme selection:* Themes that meet the criteria previously described should be chosen.
- *Identifying resources:* Teaching and learning materials should be identified and collected by the teacher before beginning the unit. Examples include non-fiction books; other pertinent print media (e.g., documents, travel brochures, and government publications); hands-on materials from the real world that pertain to the topic; community experts; nonprint media (videotapes, films, radio recordings); parent volunteers; relevant basal stories; and identification of possible field trips.
- *Brainstorming:* Themed studies involve brainstorming for both the teacher and students. Teachers brainstorm as part of the planning process to anticipate ways that curriculums can be integrated into the unit and to assist in the selection of materials. Paradis (1984) offers a brainstorming web (Figure 13.14) to assist teachers in this process. Students are also encouraged to brainstorm as a way of becoming involved initially with the topic. Brainstorming helps students focus their thinking and value each of their peers' ideas, encourages collaboration, and reveals student interests and background knowledge.
- *Learning demonstrations:* Students complete projects and tasks that demonstrate their newly acquired knowledge. Projects like those cited for themed literature units generally apply here. In addition, students may complete other products such as displays, speeches, demonstration fairs, and guided tours.

Think of creative sources for materials to be used in themed studies.

Teachers building themed studies search for ways to incorporate reading and other basic literacy skills into content subjects because they know that these processes help students deepen their knowledge of the real world. The dynamic created in these cross-curricular units is quite powerful and spawns many positive outcomes in the classroom, including heightened interest in the subject matter and a sense of empowerment (Cox & Zarillo, 1993; Wepner & Feeley, 1993).

After many years of helping school districts around the nation build thematic units, we have made a few important discoveries that tend to speed the process of curricular integration. The most efficient way to begin is by first constructing a themed literature unit using the process described in chapter 12; this achieves full integration of the language arts within the context of great literature. Themed literature units also contain all the essential elements for a balanced literacy program, such as daily reading and writing, the teaching of nonnegotiable skills, literature response,

Themed studies include all the elements of a balanced literacy program.

cooperative groups, opportunities to practice fluency, and student self-evaluation. Once teachers build themed literature units as the curriculum core, it becomes a relatively simple matter to interlace the content areas. Finally, we have learned that once teachers go through the process we will describe in building thematic units, they better understand all the essential elements and can re-create the process in the future in their own way—keeping some elements, deleting others, to create a balanced learning system that meets the needs of their students.

Planning thematic units involves five major phases, which can be applied equally well in grades 6 through 8. These phases are *theme selection, setting goals and objectives, webbing, choosing major activities and materials,* and *unit scaffolding.*

Theme Selection

The success of thematic units often depends on the selection of interesting and flexible themes.

In many ways, the success of thematic units depends on the concept chosen to be the theme. It must be broad enough to accomplish linkage between the various content subjects, to address local and state requirements listed in curriculum guides (Pappas, Kiefer, & Levstik, 1990), include quality nonfiction and fictional literature, and still be interesting to youngsters. Topics like "state history" or "nutrition" can be far too confining for the kinds of engaging learning experiences we hope to craft. In chapter 12, we suggest a large number of possible topics by grade level, which might give the reader a good starting point; these include "legends," "survival," "heroes," "changes," "seasons," and "journeys." If the theme selected is broad enough, teachers will discover creative and enticing ways to weave the various content subjects into the unit. To demonstrate more clearly ways thematic units can be constructed, we build on the themed literature unit called "journeys."

Setting Goals and Objectives

Notice that the skills to be taught are selected after the theme is chosen.

Once the theme has been selected, teachers should consult the district curriculum guide and other available resources to determine possible goals and objectives. Some teachers prefer to do this step first because themes occasionally grow logically out of the required curriculum. Whether done as a first or second step, establishing goals and objectives must come early so that appropriate learning activities and materials can be chosen.

Webbing

The next step in planning thematic units is *webbing,* which is essentially the process of creating a schematic or schema map of the linkage between each aspect of the unit. By creating a web of the major aspects of the proposed unit, the teacher can gain a global view—the "big picture." Webs can also be revised and adapted later to use as an advance organizer for students at the beginning of the thematic unit. In Figure 13.15, we see an initial (not fully developed) thematic unit web for the journeys theme. The journeys theme now spans three additional content areas: social studies, science, and mathematics. Major activities have also been suggested, which is the next topic we explore.

Choosing Major Activities and Materials

Introducing new themes is a very creative process for teachers.

One of the joys of thematic units is that they infuse the curriculum with great ideas, activities, and materials that energize learners. What a great alternative this is for teachers ready for modest yet powerful change. Activities chosen for thematic units

Figure 13.15   Initial thematic unit web: Journeys

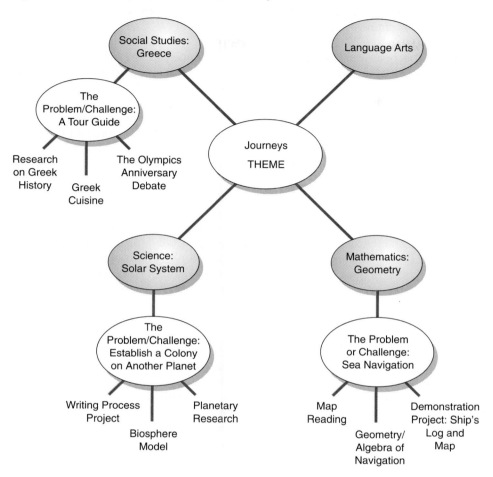

provide students with opportunities to apply literacy skills within a real-world context. Sometimes students complete these activities independently, other times as part of a problem-solving team. Occasions for personal exploration and reflection are also seen as valuable aspects of thematic unit activities.

In Figure 13.15, we include several interesting activities that fit the journeys theme nicely and allow the teacher great flexibility. Although it may not be obvious at first glance, various state and district curriculum requirements can be built into the journeys theme. These include studies of Greece, investigations into the solar system, and rudiments of geometry and algebra. A "problem/challenge" scheme has been selected as the means for discovering each curriculum objective within a real world context.

Social Studies   In the social studies component, the problem/challenge activity is for students working in groups of four to assume the role of travel agents charged with the responsibility of developing a "tour guide" for clients traveling to Greece. Required parts of the tour guide involve information about ancient Greece, Greek cui-

Brainstorm a list of possible problems/challenges for social studies.

sine, and the founding of the Olympics in ancient Greece. Students in each group present what they have learned to the class, or other classes, in the form of an enlarged travel brochure.

Science   The problem/challenge activity for science has student groups assume the role of astronauts aboard a space shuttle. Their mission is to travel to a planet of their choosing and establish a colony. This activity involves scientific research into such things as what humans need to sustain life, surface conditions on the selected planet, as well as useful natural resources (if any), and information about the building of life-supporting human environments (biospheres). To present their findings, students in each group will draft a report in the form of a book using the writing process, and construct a model of the biosphere they propose to build on the planet surface.

Mathematics   The problem/challenge activity for mathematics is for students to assume the role of sea voyagers who must navigate their ship to Greece from the United States. This is an individual project, or it can be conducted in pairs. Skills involved include basics in map reading, geometry as related to navigation, translation of miles per hour to knots, and journal writing. The product is a ship's log, which details daily destinations, map coordinates, travel times, and (if desired) some brief information about what students see at each port.

Thematic Unit Materials

". . . as with chocolate, you never have enough books" (Pappas et al., 1990)

The preceding examples clearly alert us that many and diverse materials are needed. Both fiction and nonfiction materials are needed to plan rich and interesting activities. The core materials are books, lots of books of every kind. Pappas et al. (1990) got it just right when they said, "as with chocolate, you never have enough books!" Essential are reference materials, fictional books to read aloud that awaken imaginations, and nonfiction books to read aloud. Teachers will also need to locate what are known by historians as "primary source materials"—factual, original sources of information. Later in this chapter, we mention a number of time-saving resources for locating specialty books and other media.

Unit Scaffolding

*Assembling the basic daily plans of thematic units is the process known as **scaffolding**.*

The final stage of planning is what we term *unit scaffolding*. At this point, the teacher determines just how long the unit should run and makes final decisions about which activities to include. Typically, thematic units last 1 to 2 weeks in the lower grades (Wiseman, 1992) and up to 4 or 5 weeks in the upper grades. The teacher should resist the temptation to run units for months at a time, because this usually becomes too much of a good thing and turns high student interest into boredom.

Seamless integration *depends heavily on schedule flexibility.*

One of the decisions to make is whether the unit is to be fully integrated and presented as a seamless curriculum. Some teachers choose to operate in a non-departmentalized fashion. In this case, our journeys unit may operate for a few days or a week, strictly focusing on the social studies problem/challenge. When the social studies portion is concluded, the class may move on to the science problem/challenge, focusing on that aspect for whole days at a time. The mathematics problem/challenge may come next. The value of seamless integration is that students pursue problems in much the same way as adults in the professional

Figure 13.16   Segmented integration for journeys theme

8:30–9:30	**Language Arts:** Themed Literature Unit on Journeys
9:30–10:45	**Social Studies:** Greece/Tour Guide
10:55–11:30	Computer Lab
11:30–12:30	**Science:** Solar System/Biosphere Model
12:30–1:00	Lunch
1:00–2:15	Specials: Library, P.E.
2:30–3:25	**Mathematics:** Sea Navigation

world, incorporating literacy skills throughout the day. Another benefit is that students can move from one problem/challenge to another every few days, thus maintaining a higher level of interest. Unfortunately, seamless integration cannot be achieved very easily in departmentalized schools—self-contained classrooms are generally necessary.

Another option for organizing thematic units that can be used either in self-contained or departmentalized situations is called segmented integration. In segmented integration, each content area portion is developed concurrently by either the self-contained teacher or content specialists. A sample daily schedule depicting how this integration might occur in a departmentalized middle school setting is shown in Figure 13.16. Segmented integration permits teachers in fully departmentalized schools to develop thematic units collaboratively as faculty teams. Sometimes all teachers in a departmentalized team will choose to take part in the thematic unit; on other occasions, one or two teachers may feel a need to do something different to satisfy district or state mandates. Participation should be a matter of choice. Further, one teacher may decide to run a thematic unit in his or her classroom for 3 weeks, whereas other teachers may have the unit run for 4 or 5 weeks. Whenever possible, however, it is usually a good thing to begin and end the unit at the same time to achieve proper closure.

Segmented integration of the curriculum works best in departmentalized and "pod system" schools.

We have found that planning daily activities is greatly facilitated by webbing each content component separately. Teachers should include in the web such information as key reference books, computer software, important questions to be answered, special activities, and demonstrations that teachers may wish to perform. In Figure 13.17, we share a web used in the science portion of the journeys theme.

TACTICS FOR MIDDLE SCHOOLERS HAVING LEARNING PROBLEMS

Readers with learning problems often face feelings of discouragement and bewilderment in content area classes. Reflecting on our own past experiences as classroom teachers, we have observed many similarities among readers having learning problems that sometimes compound their learning difficulties. First, and probably most

The first barrier to overcome for students having learning problems is a negative self-image.

Figure 13.17   Science web for journeys theme

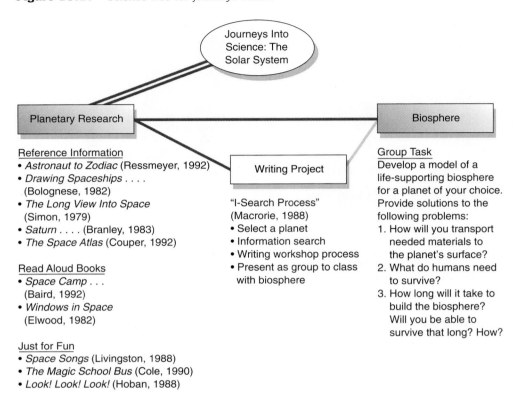

Reference Information
- *Astronaut to Zodiac* (Ressmeyer, 1992)
- *Drawing Spaceships . . . .*
  (Bolognese, 1982)
- *The Long View Into Space*
  (Simon, 1979)
- *Saturn . . . .* (Branley, 1983)
- *The Space Atlas* (Couper, 1992)

Read Aloud Books
- *Space Camp . . .*
  (Baird, 1992)
- *Windows in Space*
  (Elwood, 1982)

Just for Fun
- *Space Songs* (Livingston, 1988)
- *The Magic School Bus* (Cole, 1990)
- *Look! Look! Look!* (Hoban, 1988)

troubling, is a student attitude that says "I'm dumb and can't do the work . . ." This feeling has usually developed over a period of years and is usually due to unsuccessful experiences in the classroom. For these students, the "classroom safety net" may not have been established or maintained by previous teachers, and risk taking on the students' part (trying new learning tasks) is not as likely to occur. Second, middle school students who struggle with content area subjects are usually poorly organized. When students are helped to become systematic in their reading and thinking strategies, positive results follow. Third, readers with learning problems tend to have weak overall reading ability, often characterized by one or more of the following: poor reading comprehension, a slow reading rate, underdeveloped study skills, and limited reading vocabulary. Fortunately, these problems can be repaired, sometimes easily, within the middle school classroom.

Comprehension "Strategy Families"

Note the similarities and differences in these comprehension strategies.

Dana (1989) has grouped several effective reading comprehension strategies for readers with learning problems into what she refers to as *strategy families.* They can be used with relative ease, in minimal time, and they have similar or complementary functions in aiding comprehension. The first strategy family mentioned here, *SIP (summarize, imaging, predict)* helps students focus on content, and the second strategy, called *EEEZ (take it easy, explain, explore, expand),* is a set of elaborative strategies that can be used as a postreading experience to "help anchor the content in memory" (Dana, 1989, p. 32). In each of these strategy families, the acronym reminds students of important steps they are to follow.

SIP: The SIP set of strategies is reportedly consistent with R. C. Anderson's (1970) findings indicating that students benefit from learning task activities that require attention to content and active engagement in processing. The steps for SIP follow.

> **S** reminds students to *summarize* the content of each page or naturally divided section of the text. This summarization of text invites students to reflect on and interact with the content in producing a summarized version.

> **I** represents the notion of *imaging.* This is a reminder that students should form an internal visual display of the content while reading, which provides a second imprint of the text's content.

> **P** reminds students to *predict* while reading. As each page or naturally divided section is read, students should pause to predict what they may learn next. While reading the section predicted, students verify, revise, or modify predictions according to what they learned. This process of predicting and verifying can carry students through entire selections and help hold their interest.

EEEZ: The second strategy gets students to elaborate mentally on new content information to facilitate long-term retention. In her introduction to this strategy, Dana (1989) explains

> After reading, it is recommended that students review what they have read in light of the purpose that was set for the reading assignment. Students are told that after reading they should "take it easy" (EEEZ) and make an attempt to *explain* (E) the content in a manner commensurate with the purpose set for reading. They might have to answer questions, generate questions, define a concept, or provide a summary. (p. 33)

The other ideas represented by the EEEZ acronym are

> **E:** *Explore* the same content material as it has been described by other authors of different texts. These comparisons often help students to clarify important ideas.

> **E:** *Expand* the subject matter by reading other texts that go beyond the content covered by the original text.

After expanding, students should respond to the original purpose for reading the assignment given by the teacher and should embellish their responses with additional content discovered during the EEEZ process.

Fluency Strategies: Improving Reading Speed

All students, and especially those with reading problems, should spend significant amounts of time—20 to 30 minutes per day—in the act of reading if they are to grow and progress. Krashen's (1992) research demonstrates that 20 minutes of daily sustained reading in materials of high interest and appropriate difficulty can help students grow by as much as six months per year in overall reading fluency. Daily

All students should read books they enjoy at least 20–30 minutes each day to build fluency (Krashen, 1992).

sustained reading builds vocabulary knowledge and sharpens students' reading skills. Following is one idea that can help you build reading fluency with middle schoolers.

Group-Assisted Reading

Dyad reading is one of the most powerful reading improvement tools.

The term *group-assisted reading* (Eldredge, 1990) refers to teachers helping a group of students read text material in unison—emphasizing correct phrasing, intonation, and pitch. In group-assisted reading, teachers read each book many times with students until students can read it fluently with expression. In a variation of group-assisted reading called *dyad* reading groups, the teacher's role is filled with a peer "lead reader." Both group-assisted and dyad reading groups have been shown to be more effective in classroom settings with at-risk readers than more traditional methods (Eldredge, 1990; Eldredge & Quinn, 1988).

It is also crucial that a Writing Workshop program be established as part of the balanced literacy program. Although not empirically tested, we believe a writing-dyad system should be used with students having learning problems. Because of the reciprocal nature of reading and writing, the natural development of word-spelling knowledge and phonic awareness fostered in students through the writing process, as well as the accompanying interest in books and authors that springs from writing experiences, make writing a mainstay in any literacy program for students having reading problems.

Commercial Programs for Low-Performing Readers

Drop-out rates are often directly related to poor reading ability.

There seem to be new reading programs springing up regularly to assist unsuccessful middle school students. Their relative financial success is not surprising, especially when considering the growing numbers of students who are struggling in middle school and eventually dropping out as soon as they are old enough to do so. In some large urban centers, for example, drop-out rates have reached 40% or more, with a majority of all students in these locales reading well below expected levels!

We believe the long-term solution to illiteracy problems lies in improving teacher expertise, providing sufficient learning materials, appropriate and safe classroom environments, and proper support from family and community members. In the end, it really does take a village to properly raise a child.

The Boys Town Reading Program *and* Read 180 *are two very promising intervention programs with substantial research support.*

Nevertheless, some research-proven commercial reading programs can be helpful as supplemental tools in balanced literacy classrooms. Here are a few examples of programs that appear to be useful with certain populations of students (be sure to study the research on each program to determine the kinds of students with whom they seem to be most effective—avoid the "one-size-fits-all" mentality).

Boys Town Reading Program (Omaha, NE: *Boys Town*)—A four-course reading program developed at the world famous Father Flanagan's *Boys Town* in Omaha for problem readers. It features a diagnostic component for student placement into one of the four reading courses. The courses progress in difficulty from the first level, which is appropriate for students still learning basic reading skills, to a rather sophisticated level for advanced readers. The intent is for all middle schoolers to have an appropriate reading development course in which they can enroll.

Read 180 (New York: Scholastic)—This is a new computer-supported program developed at Peabody College for Teachers at Vanderbilt University, then field tested in Orlando (Florida) schools. It appears to be quite motivating and effective with students in grades 5 to 8.

Summary

In this final chapter of our book, we have discussed how middle school students can be helped to use *reading to learn* strategies in their content area classes. Expository or informative texts in various forms now make up the daily reading diet of these students. The reading challenges they face include complicated vocabulary, increased concept load, and less readable texts.

Teachers are able to help students attack these new challenges successfully in many ways. A content analysis helps teachers identify important facts, concepts, and generalizations students must learn. Armed with this knowledge, teachers can construct an array of student-support learning aids, including graphic organizers, study guides, and vocabulary development activities. Students can also be taught various efficient study strategies such as skimming and scanning techniques. Another important skill middle school students acquire is the ability to monitor and adjust their own reading comprehension, or metacognition.

Students who are struggling with basic reading tasks in the middle school can be helped to close the gap in a number of ways. Improving reading fluency through sustained reading periods, vocabulary development, and research-proven commercial programs can be instrumental in helping these students succeed.

Finally, it is our responsibility as teachers to make sure that all of our students become as literate as their innate talents and abilities permit them. Literacy is the key that opens the door to opportunity. We accomplish that, at least in part, by continuing to learn ourselves about the science and art form of teaching and learning.

Concept Applications

In the Classroom

1. Select a chapter from a middle school social studies book on a level of your choice. Using the descriptors for expository text patterns discussed in this chapter, identify as many patterns (e.g., description, comparison) as possible in the unit and answer the following questions: Which patterns do you find? How often do they occur in the unit? Are any patterns missing? If so, what could you do as the classroom teacher to compensate for these omissions? Is it possible that omission of some patterns could lead to learning difficulties for some children? If so, why?

2. Developing a thorough content analysis is the foundation for the successful teaching of content area subjects. To practice and refine this ability, try the following: Form a group with two or three of your colleagues. Select several lengthy magazine articles having to do with various topics relevant to middle school subjects. You may want to consider such magazines as *Air & Space* or *National Geographic* for these articles. After reading these articles, each person should develop a content analysis to present to the rest of the group. By comparing analyses, it will be possible to detect whether important bits of information (or for that matter, superfluous information) have been included.

In the Field

Computer applications in education account for one of the fastest growing industries in the world. Perform a library search and compile a list of the latest software and Internet web sites available for the teaching of content area vocabulary and concepts for two topics (Mount Everest, the field of Quantum Physics, research on automobile safety, etc.). Perhaps a media specialist at a local middle school will assist you in this effort. After your list has been compiled, write to the various sources requesting more detailed information. This process will help you to determine which programs are most beneficial, and it may be possible to order new software and other resources for your school's library/media center in the future.

Recommended Readings

Cafolla, R., Kauffman, D., & Knee, R. (1997). *World Wide Web for teachers: An interactive guide.* Boston: Allyn & Bacon.

Cooter, R. B., Jr., & Flynt, E. S. (1996). *Teaching reading in the content areas: Developing content literacy for all students.* Upper Saddle River, NJ: Merrill/Prentice Hall.

Gahn, S. M. (1989). A practical guide for teaching writing in the content areas. *Journal of Reading, 33,* 525–531.

Worthy, J., Moorman, M., & Turner, M. (1999). What Johnny likes to read is hard to find in school. *Reading Research Quarterly, 34*(1), 12–27.

Balanced Literacy

A message to our literacy education colleagues . . . The purpose of Appendix A is to offer our readers a selection of resources useful in constructing Reading Resource Rooms and/or classroom libraries that facilitate Balanced Literacy Instruction. These materials and ideas are meant as only a starting point, and we hope that readers will consider helping us to continue building this "data base" by contacting us individually or through our publisher.

HOW TO CREATE A READING RESOURCE ROOM: RECOMMENDATIONS FROM THE DALLAS READING PLAN

What Is a Reading Resource Room?

Many schools are finding that they can make their dollars go farther by setting up a room in which to place all of the books that are suitable for Guided Reading. Many of these books have been purchased with Title 1 money and other district resources (in other words, books NOT purchased with the teacher's own personal funds), then distributed to various classrooms. As a result, no one teacher has a large enough range of books (i.e., multiple copies of single titles, topics, etc.) for the students in her/his room. When all of the books in the school have been gathered, sorted by level using Reading Recovery or other similar formulae, and cataloged in one place teachers can then check out the books they need by choosing the appropriate level and the number of books.

What If I Don't Have a Room?

Some schools have been able to find space in the media center; others have used an office once used by a teaching assistant, etc. A central location works best.

What Grade Levels Would Find a Reading Resource Room Useful, and When?

Kindergarten teachers begin to use the books sometime after the winter holidays, grades 1–3 use the room anytime during the school year, and grades 4–6 use the room if they have students struggling in reading. As the room grows in content, most schools add chapter books for the upper grades.

How Much Does a Reading Resource Room Cost?

If you had to start from scratch, close to $25,000. However, most schools have many books that have been purchased previously by district or federal funds.

Resources for Teachers

How Do I Begin?

1. Locate a space.
2. Locate all of the suitable books already in the school.
3. Involve *all* teachers in the planning, especially in grades K–3.

What's the Bottom Line for What I Need?

- When you have located the **books** you now have you will need to order some books to fill in the gaps so that you have enough titles for each level. You will need:
  - 20 to 25 titles (per Reading Recovery or Guided Reading levels)
  - 12-15 copies of each title

Again, remember to start with what you have and gradually build from there.

- After the space has been determined, you'll need to locate some **shelving.** The shelving does not have to be fancy. Home Depot, Lowes, and other warehouse stores have plastic shelves for about $40, but you may be able to find some cheaper. (You can get 70 magazine boxes on the shelves if you use both sides.)
- You will need some **magazine boxes** to contain the books. These can be ordered locally. The number needed will be determined by how many books you have or plan to order. Plastic boxes are also available, but are more expensive.
- **Labels** can be purchased at any office supply. We suggest Avery #5165. This is a single sheet of self-stick labels—100 sheets per box.
- **Clothespins** to use in checking out books can be purchased at Wal-Mart or Target. Each teacher using the room will need 20-30 clothespins which can be stored in a resealable plastic bag. The teacher places a clothespin with his/her name on it to the front of the box of the books being borrowed.
- You will need some **rubber stamps with the school name** to stamp each book.
- If you include Big Books for Shared Reading in your room, you will need six big **plastic tubs.** These can be found at Target, Wal-Mart, etc., for about $5 each.

Can the Room Be Used for Anything Else Besides Guided Reading Books?

Some schools have added Big Books, read-alouds, and so on to the room.

GUIDED READING LEVELING COMPARISONS

Following is a handy guide for helping you to translate books that are listed from publishers using Guided Reading ratings to leveling systems commonly in one-to-one tutorial programs (i.e., Reading Recovery, Cooter & Cooter's *BLAST* program, etc.)

Grade Level (Basal)	Guided Reading Level (Fountas-Pinnell)	One-to-One Tutoring Level (Cooter & Cooter, 1999); RR;	Stages of Reading
Kindergarten	A B	A 1 2	Emergent
Pre-Primer	C D E	3 4 6–8	
Primer	F G	10 12	Early
1st Grade	H I	14 16	
2nd Grade	J–K L–M	18–20 24–28	Transitional
3rd Grade	N O–P	30 34–38	Fluent/Extending
4th Grade	Q–R	40	
5th Grade	—	44	
6th Grade	—	—	

GENERAL EXPLANATION OF CRITERIA FOR DETERMINING THE READING LEVELS OF TEXTS: LEVELS 1–20 (A–K)

Levels 1–4 (A–D)

- Repeating language patterns
- Illustrations that match and explain most of the text. Actions are clearly presented without much in the way of extraneous detail that might confuse the reader.
- Whole meaning or story that is likely to match the experiences and conceptual knowledge common to most beginning readers.
- The language of the text developmentally matches syntax and organization of most young children's speech for whom the text is intended.
- Sentences and books themselves are comparatively short (e.g., 10–60 words).
- Print is carefully laid out so that it consistently appears on the same place on the page throughout each book.

Assumption at this level: That when students encounter an unknown word in print they can easily use context from known words and illustrations along with language pattern cues and early word analysis skills for successful decoding.

Levels 5–8 (D–E)

- One often sees predictable, repetitive language patterns, but without allowing the same pattern to dominate the entire text.
- There is now more variation of language patterns, as opposed to one or two word changes, for example.
- Words and phrases may appear to express different meanings through varying sentence structures.
- By the end of these stages, the syntax is more typical of written or "book" language. Illustrations provide minimal support for readers determining exact language.

Levels 9–12 (E–G)

- Variation in sentence patterns is now the norm.
- Longer sentences with less predictable text.
- Written language styles and genre become more prominent including the use of some verb forms not often used by young children in oral settings.
- The average sentence length in texts increases (double that found in levels 5–8).
- Events in a story may continue over several pages.
- Illustrations provide only moderate support to the meaning of the stories.

Levels 13–15* (G–H)

(*Consider these characteristics as enhancements to the description for levels 9–12.)
- There is a greater variety of words and the inclusion of more specialized vocabulary.
- Pictures provide some support for the overall meaning of the story, but cannot be used by the reader to interpret the precise message.

Levels 16–20 (I–K)

- Now there are longer stories or sequences of events.
- Story events are developed more fully than texts at lower levels.
- Vocabulary is progressively more rich and varied.
- Illustrations are used to help to create the atmosphere and setting, rather than to specifically depict the content of the text.
- It is now common to have full pages of print.

SELECTED GUIDED READING BOOKS (ENGLISH)

Title	GR Level	RR Tutoring Level	Publisher	Author/Series
After the Flood	G	12	Rigby	PM Green/Exten Add-to
Airplane, The	B	2	Wright Group	Sunshine
All Fall Down	C	3	Oxford	Wildsmith, Brian
Amanda's Bear	G	12	Dominie Press	Reading Corners
Amazing Popple Seed, The	F	11	Rigby	Read-Alongs/Stg. 1
Animal Habitats	C	3	Sundance	Little Red Readers
Animal Homes	B	2	Sundance	Little Red Readers
Are You a Ladybug?	E	7	Wright Group	Sunshine
Arguments	J-K	18	Wright Group	Sunshine
Ask Nicely	F	10	Rigby	Literacy 2000
At School	B	2	Wright Group	Sunshine
At the Farm	B	2	Sundance	Little Red Readers
At the Library	C	3	Rigby	PM Starters 2
Baby Elephant's New Bike	F	10	Wright Group	Foundations
Baby Monkey	I	16	Scott-Foresman	Reading Unlimited
Babysitter, The	G	13	Rigby	PM Green/Exten Add-to
Banana Shake	D	4	Wright Group	Book Bank
Barrel of Gold, A	J-K	18	Wright Group	Storybox
Basketball	A	1	Wright Group	Wonder World
Bath for a Beagle, A	D	5	Troll	First Start
Bears in the Night	D	4	Random House	Berenstain
Bee, The	C	3	Wright Group	Storybox
Ben's Tooth	G	13	Rigby	PM/Green Level
Bicycle, The	C	3	Wright Group	Storybox
Big Kick, The	D	4	Rigby	PM/Red Level
Big Toe, The	E	7	Wright Group	Storybox Read-Togethers

Title	GR Level	RR Tutoring Level	Publisher	Author/Series
Biggest Cake in the World, The	E	9	Richard Owen	Ready to Read
Birthday Cake	D	5	Rigby	Guided Reading/Stg. 1
Blackbird's Nest	G	12	Richard Owen	Ready to Read
Blue Jay, The	H	14	D. C. Heath	Little Readers
Boggywooga	I	16	Wright Group	Sunshine
Boy Who Cried Wolf, The	I	16	Wright Group	Aesop
Brave Triceratops	G	12	Rigby	PM/Green Level
Brown Bear, Brown Bear	D	4	Holt	Martin, Bill
Bus Ride, The	D	4	Scott-Foresman	Reading Unlimited
Camping	E	7	Wright Group	Sunshine Ext.
Carrot Seed, The	G	12	Harper & Collins	Kraus, Ruth
Cat and Mouse	B	2	Rigby	PM Starters 2
Cat on the Mat	B	2	Oxford	Wildsmith, Brian
Chew Chew Chew	D	5	Rigby	Guided Reading/Stg. 2
Chicken Pox	H	14	D. C. Heath	Little Readers
Choosing a Puppy	E	7	Rigby	PM Yellow/Exten Add-to
Christmas Tree, The	F	10	Rigby	PM/Blue Level
Clifford, the Big Red Dog	J-K	18	Scholastic	Bridwell, Norman
Clothes	C	3	Rigby	Interaction
Coyote Plants a Peach Tree	I	16	Richard Owen	Young Learners
Creepy Caterpillar	E	7	D. C. Heath	Little Readers
Dad's Headache	F	10	Wright Group	Sunshine
Dad's New Path	F	10	Wright Group	Foundations
Danger	D	4	Wright Group	Storybox
Dear Santa	B	2	Rigby	Guided Reading/Stg. 2
Dizzy Lizzy	E	8	Rigby	Guided Reading/Stg. 2
Don't Forget the Bacon	J–K	20	Greenwillow	Hutchins, Pat
Don't Wake the Baby	B	2	Rigby	Guided Reading/Stg. 1
Dr. Green	G	12	D. C. Heath	Little Readers
Dressing Up	A	1	Rigby	PM Starters 1
Earthquake	J–K	20	Wright Group	Wonder World
Exploding Frog	I	16	Modern Curriculum	Language Works
Families	B	2	Rigby	Interaction
Farm Concert, The	D	5	Wright Group	Storybox Read-Togethers
Farm, The	A	1	Rigby	Guided Reading/Stg. 1
Father Bear Goes Fishing	D	5	Rigby	PM/Red Level
Feet	D	5	Wright Group	Storybox
First Day at School	D	5	Dominie Press	Carousel Readers
Five Little Monkeys Jumping on..Bed	E	8	Clarion	Christelow, Eileen
Flying Fish, The	H	14	Rigby	PM Green/Exten Add-to
Four Ice Creams	D	4	Rigby	PM Starters 2
Fox and the Little Red Hen, The	J–K	19	Rigby	Traditional Tales 1
Friends are Forever	J–K	18	Rigby	Literacy 2000 Satellites
Frog and Toad Are Friends	J–K	19	Harper & Collins	Lobel, Arnold
Getting Dressed	A	1	Wright Group	Sunshine
Gingerbread Boy, The (story)	F	10	Stech-Vaughn	New Way (red)

Title	GR Level	RR Tutoring Level	Publisher	Author/Series
Gingerbread Man, The	E	9	D. C. Heath	Little Readers
Goldilocks and the Three Bears	G	13	Rigby	Traditional Tales 1
Goodnight Moon	H	14	Harper & Row	Brown
Grandpa Snored	E	9	Rigby	Guided Reading/Stg. 2
Great Big Enormous Turnip	G	13	Scott-Foresman	Reading Unlimited
Hand-Me-Downs, The	G	12	D. C. Heath	Little Readers
Happy Birthday!	D	4	Rigby	Guided Reading/Stg. 1
Haunted House, The	E	7	Wright Group	Storybox
Have You Seen the Crocodile?	E	9	Harper & Row	West, Colin
Henny Penny	I	16	Clarion	Galdone
Henry's Choice	J–K	20	Scott-Foresman	Reading Unlimited
Hole in Harry's Pocket, The	H	15	D. C. Heath	Little Readers
Horrible Thing with Hairy Feet	H	14	Rigby	Read-Alongs/Stg. 2
How Do I Put It On	H	14	Penguin	Watanabe, Shigeo
How Grandmother Spider Got the Sun	I	17	D. C. Heath	Little Readers
How to Ride a Giraffe	I	16	D. C. Heath	Little Readers
Hungry Giant, The	F	10	Wright Group	Storybox Read-Togethers
I am a Dentist	C	3	Dominie Press	Read More Books
I am a Fireman	E	6	Dominie Press	Read More Books
I am a Photographer	E	7	Dominie Press	Read More Books
I Can Make Music	A	1	Sundance	Little Red Readers
I Can Read	B	2	Richard Owen	Ready to Read
I Like to Eat	A	1	Dominie Press	Reading Corners
I Like to Paint	A	1	Dominie Press	Reading Corners
I Live in a House	E	6	Dominie Press	Read More Books
I Live in an Apartment	E	6	Dominie Press	Read More Books
I Want Ice Cream	C	3	Wright Group	Storybox
I'm the King of the Mountain	G	12	Richard Owen	Ready to Read
In a Dark, Dark Wood	E	7	Wright Group	Storybox Read-Togethers
Invisible	I	16	Rigby	Read-Alongs/Stg. 2
It Looked Like Spilt Milk	E	7	Harper & Row	Shaw, Charles
Jack and the Beanstalk	H	15	Rigby	Traditional Tales 2
Jack-O-Lantern	A	1	Wright Group	Twig Books
Jackson's Monster	I	16	D. C. Heath	Little Readers
Joe and the Mouse	F	10	Oxford Univ. Press	Reading Tree
Joe's Father	E	7	Wright Group	Book Bank
Jungle Parade: A Singing Game	D	5	Scott-Foresman	Little Celebrations
Just Like Daddy	E	9	Simon & Schuster	Asch, Frank
Just Like Grandpa	E	8	Rigby	Guided Reading/Stg. 3
Just Like Me	E	7	Children's Press	Rookie Readers
Kangaroo	D	4	Dominie Press	Reading Corners
Kites	B	2	Scott-Foresman	Special Practice Books
Late for Football	F	11	Rigby	PM/Blue Level
Lion and the Mouse, The	G	12	Rigby	Traditional Tales 1
Little Gorilla	I	17	Clarion	Bornstein, Ruth
Little Red Hen, The	J-K	18	Viking	Galdone, Paul
Lizard Loses His Tail	D	5	Rigby	PM/Red Level

Title	GR Level	RR Tutoring Level	Publisher	Author/Series
Lizards and Salamanders	J-K	20	Scott-Foresman	Reading Unlimited
Look at Me	B	2	Rigby	PM Starters 1
Looking for Halloween	D	4	Kaeden Corp.	Urmston, K.
Lots of Cats	E	6	Scott-Foresman	Special Practice Books
Lunch Time	D	5	Dominie Press	Carousel Readers
Making Oatmeal	E	7	Rigby	Interaction
Matthew Likes to Read	I	17	Richard Owen	Ready to Read
Me	C	3	Dominie Press	Reading Corners
Michael in the Hospital	E	8	Oxford Univ. Press	Reading Tree
Mike's New Bike	E	9	Troll	First Start Easy
Miss Nelson Is Missing	J–K	20	Houghton Mifflin	Allard, Harry
Mom	A	1	Rigby	PM Starters 1
Moms and Dads	A	1	Rigby	PM Starters 1
Monkeys	G	12	Scott-Foresman	Special Practice Books
Monster	H	15	Rigby	Read-Alongs/Stg. 3
Monster Party, The	D	4	Wright Group	Storybox Read-Togethers
More Spaghetti I Say	F	11	Scholastic	Gilman, Rita
Mosquito Buzzed, A	E	8	D. C. Heath	Little Readers
Mouse and the Elephant, The	I	17	D. C. Heath	Little Readers
Moving	B	2	Sundance	Little Red Readers
Mrs. Wishy Washy	E	8	Wright Group	Storybox Read-Togethers
Mud Pie	D	4	Rigby	Guided Reading/Stg. 1
Mumps	E	6	Rigby	PM/Yellow Level
My Bike	E	8	Richard Owen	Ready to Read
My Birthday Party	A	1	D. C. Heath	Little Readers
My Book	A	1	Penguin	Maris, Ron
My Computer	F	11	Wright Group	Wonder World
My Holiday Diary	F	10	Around the World	Hall, N., & Robinson, A.
My Shadow	C	3	Wright Group	Sunshine
New Baby, The	E	7	Rigby	PM/Yellow Level
Night the Lights Went Out, The	H	14	D. C. Heath	Little Readers
Noisy Nora	I	16	Dial	Wells, Rosemary
On a Cold, Cold Day	C	3	Rigby	Tadpoles
On Top of Spaghetti	F	11	Scott-Foresman	Little Celebrations
One Sock, Two Socks	G	12	Dominie Press	Reading Corners
Our Teacher, Miss Pool	E	6	Richard Owen	Ready to Read
Pancakes	F	11	Wright Group	Foundations
Peaches the Pig	—-	—-	D. C. Heath	Little Readers
Pet Hamster	E	6	Scott-Foresman	Special Practice Books
Pip and the Little Monkey	F	10	Oxford Univ. Press	Reading Tree
Pip at the Zoo	E	9	Oxford Univ. Press	Reading Tree
Popcorn Book, The	J–K	18	Scott-Foresman	Reading Unlimited
Rabbits	F	11	Scott-Foresman	Special Practice Books
Rain	B	2	Dominie Press	Reading Corners
Rain, Rain	D	5	Richard Owen	Ready to Read
Reading Is Everywhere	D	5	Wright Group	Sunshine-Social Studies
Red and Blue Mittens	J–K	20	Scott-Foresman	Reading Unlimited

Title	GR Level	RR Tutoring Level	Publisher	Author/Series
Rescue, The	J–K	19	Richard Owen	Ready to Read
Ride, Ride, Ride	E	8	Macmillan	Series R
Roll Over: A Counting People Song	D	4	Clarion	Peek
Rosie's Walk	E	9	Macmillan	Hutchins, Pat
Rumpelstiltskin	J–K	20	Wright Group	Once Upon a Time
Safe Place, The	H	14	Richard Owen	Ready to Read
Sam's Ball	E	6	Morrow	Lindgren, Barbro
Sausages	D	4	Rigby	PM/Red Level
Shoe Grabber, The	I	16	Rigby	Read-Alongs/Stg. 2
Shopping	C	3	Sundance	Little Red Readers
Shopping at the Mall	G	12	Kaeden Corp.	Urmston, K., & Evans, K.
Smarty Pants	E	8	Wright Group	Storybox Read-Togethers
Snake Slithers, A	H	14	Scott-Foresman	Special Practice Books
Snow Walk	D	5	Dominie Press	Reading Corners
Soccer at the Park	E	8	Rigby	PM Yellow/Exten Add-to
Space Journey	A	1	Wright Group	Sunshine
Space Race	I	17	Wright Group	Sunshine
Splish Splash	E	6	Scott-Foresman	Little Celebrations
Sticky Stanley	F	10	Troll	First Start Easy
Sun/Wind/Rain	H	15	Scott-Foresman	Special Practice Books
Surprise for Mom, A	E	9	Kaeden Corp.	Urmston, K., & Evans, K.
Susie Goes Shopping	F	10	Troll	First Start Easy
T-Shirts	E	9	Richard Owen	Ready to Read
Tee-Ball	C	3	Scott-Foresman	Little Celebrations
Teeny, Tiny Woman, The	I	16	Scholastic	Seuling, Barbara
Ten Little Bears	F	11	Scott-Foresman	Reading Unlimited
Tents	H	15	Scott-Foresman	Reading Unlimited
Thank You	I	17	Richard Owen	Ready to Read
There's a Nightmare in My Closet	I	16	Dial	Mayer, Mercer
Things I Like	D	5	Knopf	Browne, Anthony
Three Billy Goats Gruff	G	12	D. C. Heath	Little Readers
Three Little Pigs	G	13	Scott-Foresman	Reading Unlimited
Three Little Pigs, The	G	13	Dominie Press	Reading Corners
Tidy Titch	I	16	Greenwillow	Hutchins, Pat
To the Beach	E	6	Kaeden Corp.	Urmston, K., & Evans, K.
Too Fast	A	1	Dominie Press	Reading Corners
Toot, Toot	C	3	Oxford	Wildsmith, Brian
Tracks	E	7	Scott-Foresman	Special Practice Books
Tree House, The	B	2	Wright Group	Storybox
Try It	D	5	Dominie Press	Reading Corners
Ugly Duckling, The	J-K	18	Rigby	Traditional Tales 2
Underwater	F	11	Wright Group	Twig Books
Very Hungry Caterpillar, The	J-K	18	Putnam	Carle, Eric
Wagon, The	G	13	Scott-Foresman	Special Practice Books
Wait Skates	F	11	Children's Press	Rookie Readers
Walk, The	G	12	Scott-Foresman	Special Practice Books
Watching TV	B	2	Wright Group	Sunshine Extensions

Title	GR Level	RR Tutoring Level	Publisher	Author/Series
What a Dog	E	9	Troll	First Start Easy
What Am I	G	12	Wright Group	Sunshine
What Animals Do You See	D	4	Dominie Press	Read More Books
What Are Purple Elephants Good For?	G	13	Dominie Press	Reading Corners
What Can I Do?	D	4	Dominie Press	Read More Books
What Comes Out at Night	B	2	Sundance	Little Red Readers
What Do You Like to Wear?	D	5	Dominie Press	Read More Books
What Goes in the Bathtub?	C	3	Rigby	Guided Reading/Stg. 1
What I Like at School	B	2	Sundance	Little Red Readers
What Is It Called?	D	5	Scott-Foresman	Special Practice Books
What's for Dinner?	E	7	Seedling	Salem, L., & Stewart, J.
Wheels on the Bus	E	9	Random House	Ziefert
When Dad Came Home	E	9	Rigby	Guided Reading/Stg. 2
When the Circus Comes to Town	A	1	Sundance	Little Red Readers
Where Are My Socks?	E	6	Richard Owen	Ready to Read
Where Is Miss Pool?	E	6	Richard Owen	Ready to Read
Where Is the Cat?	D	4	Dominie Press	Read More Books
Who Ate the Broccoli	E	7	D. C. Heath	Little Readers
Who Likes Ice Cream	A	1	Rigby	Guided Reading/Stg. 1
Who Took the Farmer's Hat?	H	15	Scholastic	Nodset, Joan
Wiggly, Jiggly, Joggly, Tooth, A	E	7	Scott-Foresman	Little Celebrations
Willy the Helper	E	6	D. C. Heath	Little Readers
Wind, The	E	8	Richard Owen	Ready to Read
Winter Sleeps	E	9	Dominie Press	Reading Corners
Witch's Haircut, The	G	12	Wright Group	Windmill
Worms for Breakfast	I	16	D. C. Heath	Little Readers
Zoo Food	D	4	Dominie Press	Reading Corners

SELECTED GUIDED READING BOOKS (SPANISH)

Title	GR Level	RR Tutoring Level	Publisher	Author/Series
El caldo	A	1	Celebration Press	Más Piñata - Stage 1
La charreada	A	1	Celebration Press	Más Piñata - Stage 1
Mi muñeco de nieve	C	3	Celebration Press	Más Piñata - Stage 1
Un pajarito	E	5	Celebration Press	Más Piñata - Stage 1
¡Yo bailo!	B	2	Celebration Press	Más Piñata - Stage 1
¡A tocar?	E	6	Celebration Press	Más Piñata - Stage 2
Insectos, insectos	D	4	Celebration Press	Más Piñata - Stage 2
¿Qué puedo comprar?	E	8	Celebration Press	Más Piñata - Stage 2
Compartiendo a un papá	E	9	Celebration Press	Pequeñitas Cel
Las gallinas de Señora Sato	E	6	Celebration Press	Pequeñitas Cel
Los cinco dinosaurios	E	7	Celebration Press	Pequeñitas Cel
El renacuajo	F	10	Celebration Press	Piñata Series 2
¿Qué dia es hoy?	F	10	Celebration Press	Piñata Series 2
¿Qué viene en grupos de tres?	E	5/6	Creative Teaching Press	Marlene Beierle/Anne Sylvan

Title	GR Level	RR Tutoring Level	Publisher	Author/Series
A través de la semana con Gato y Perro	E	8	Creative Teaching Press	Rozanne Lancazk Williams
Cuidemos a la Tierra	E	6	Creative Teaching Press	Science Series
¿Qué hay en mi bolsillo?	D	5	Creative Teaching Press	Science Series
¿Quién vive aqui?	E	6	Creative Teaching Press	Science Series
Primer dia de escuela	G	12	Dominie Press	Carrusel A
Algo para compartir	F	11	Dominie Press	Carrusel D
Una amiga especial	F	11	Dominie Press	Carrusel E
Los Payasos	C	3	Dominie Press	Col. Cándida
A mi Tambien	C	3	Dominie Press	Series 1/Col. para el maestro
Felices fiestas	B	2	Dominie Press	Series 1/Col. para el maestro
Pasatiempo invernal	C	3	Dominie Press	Series 1/Col. para el maestro
Acerca de los dino saurios	C	3	Dominie Press	Series 2/Col. para el maestro
La amistad	E	9	Dominie Press	Fiesta de los Libros
De compras	E	7	Dominie Press	Leamos Más
Mi casa	E	7	Dominie Press	Leamos Más
Un dia en mi apartamento	E	6	Dominie Press	Leamos Más
Cinco de mayo	H	14	Dominie Press	Librios Dias Festivos
El cuatro de Julio	I	16	Dominie Press	Librios Dias Festivos
El Dia de las Madres	H	15	Dominie Press	Librios Dias Festivos
La Navidad	G	12	Dominie Press	Librios Dias Festivos
¿Dónde estará el Chango Feliz?	C	3	Dominie Press	Librios Alegria A
La luna	E	6	Dominie Press	Librios Alegria C
Cuenta con la familia	A	1	Hampton-Brown	Pan y Canela - A
El chivo comilón	B	2	Hampton-Brown	Pan y Canela - A
La feria	B	2	Hampton-Brown	Pan y Canela - A
Mi caballito	D	4	Hampton-Brown	Pan y Canela - A
Chiles	E	8	Hampton-Brown	Pan y Canela - B
Papi y yo	C	3	Hampton-Brown	Pan y Canela - B
Uno, dos, tres, y cuatro	E	6	Hampton-Brown	Pan y Canela - B
¿Cuál es el mío	E	8	Hampton-Brown	Pan y Canela - B
Pedrito el exagerado	G	13	Hampton-Brown	
El jardin de Gregorio	F	11	Oxford Press	William Stobbs
El perro de Gregorio	E	6	Oxford Press	
Tomás y su tractor	E	8	Oxford Press	
Tuu tuu	C	3	Oxford Press	
¡Pum! ¡Pum! ¡Pum!	D	5	Oxford Press	
Los edificios de Nueva York	F	9/10	Richard C. Owen	Ann Mace
El Zorro	C	3	Richard C. Owen	Janice Boland
Pájaro, pajaro (AIS*)	D	5	Richard C. Owen	Margaret Mahy
¡Los cerdos espían!	D	5	Richard C. Owen	Rhonda Cox
Colas		RATK	Rigby	Arbol de Lit/Animal Antics
El pirata y el perico	E	8	Rigby	Arbol de Lit/Animal Antics
Mi abuelito roncaba	E	8	Rigby	Arbol de Lit/Animal Antics
Soy un gato	E	8	Rigby	Arbol de Lit/Animal Antics
¿Qué viste?	E	7	Rigby	Arbol de Lit/Animal Antics
El sombrero mágico	B	2	Rigby	Arbol de Lit/Food & Fun

Title	GR Level	RR Tutoring Level	Publisher	Author/Series
La fiesta sorpresa	C	3	Rigby	Arbol de Lit/Food & Fun
Los koalas	D	4	Rigby	Arbol de Lit/Food & Fun
Manos, manos, manos	C	3	Rigby	Arbol de Lit/Food & Fun
Me gusta pintar	B	2	Rigby	Arbol de Lit/Food & Fun
Picos	E	5	Rigby	Arbol de Lit/Food & Fun
¿Quién se comió la lechuga?	C	3	Rigby	Arbol de Lit/Food & Fun
Ana va a la escuela	F	9	Rigby	Arbol de Lit/Let's Get Togt.
Camiones	E	7	Rigby	Arbol de Lit/Let's Get Togt.
En la noche	E	6	Rigby	Arbol de Lit/Let's Get Togt.
La semilla de Sara	G	12	Rigby	Arbol de Lit/Let's Get Togt.
¿Y Cuco?	E	8	Rigby	Arbol de Lit/Let's Get Togt.
Gregoria el gigante gruñón	H	14	Rigby	Arbol de Lit/Out & About
La piel	F	11	Rigby	Arbol de Lit/Safe & Sound
Pizza Par Cenar	F	10	Rigby	Arbol de Lit/Out & About
¡Qué Barbaridad!	H	14	Rigby	Arbol de Lit/Out & About
Las fotos de la familia	G	12	Rigby	Arbol de Lit/Safe & Sound
Si te gustan las fresas, no leas este libro	G	12	Rigby	Arbol de Lit/Safe & Sound
Feliz cumpleaños patito	F	10	Rigby	Arbol de Lit/Times & Seasons
Un Amigo	F	10	Rigby	Arbol de Lit/Times & Seasons
Amarillo	B	2	Rigby	Arbol de Lit/Work & Play
Nuestra casa nueva	D	5	Rigby	Arbol de Lit/Work & Play
El Rancho	A	1	Rigby	Lit. 2000-Nivel 1
Un Zoológico	A	1	Rigby	Lit. 2000-Nivel 1
El fantasma	E	8	Rigby	Lit. 2000-Nivel 2
El árbol de Diego	E	9	Rigby	Lit. 2000-Nivel 3
Cuando Laura estuvo ausente	F	11	Rigby	Mary Cappelini
El enorme escarabajo negro	E	9	Rigby	Mary Cappelini
El goloso pulpo gris	G	13	Rigby	Mary Cappelini
El almuerzo de ranita	F	11	Scholastic	Beginning Literacy
En el Barrio	H	14	Scholastic	Beginning Literacy
Tortillas	F	10	Scholastic	Beginning Literacy
Una noche	F	10	Scholastic	Beginning Literacy
La cucaracha correlona	E	9	Scholastic	Cecilia Avalos-Iguana
Las Palomitas	A	1	Scholastic	Cecilia Avalos-Iguana
Día de Futbol	F	11	Seedling Publications	Mariana Robles
Recados de Mamá	H	14	Seedling Publications	Mariana Robles
Un dibujo	D	5	Shortland Publications	Augie Hunter
¿Qué es?	C	3	Shortland Publications	Dorothy Avery
El monstruo de la playa	F	10	Shortland Publications	Dot Meharry
Pintura Fresca	E	7	Shortland Publications	Edwin Johns
Los tres cabritos	F	9	Shortland Publications	Ian Douglas
Las Cuerdas	D	4	Shortland Publications	Jennifer Waters
Mi bebé	D	5	Shortland Publications	May Nelson
El coyote y mi Tata	B	2	SpanPress, Inc.	Arroz con Leche
Las Paredes de mi barrio	B	2	SpanPress, Inc.	Arroz con Leche
Sonrisas	B	2	SpanPress, Inc.	Arroz con Leche
Papa Noel y su sorpresa	E	9	Troll	Janet Craig
Federiquito el sapo	F	10	Troll	R. Greydanus
Gota a gota	E	9	Troll	Sharon Gordon
Un dinosauro en peligro	F	11	Troll	Sharon Gordon

Title	GR Level	RR Tutoring Level	Publisher	Author/Series
Abuelito, abuelito	G	12	Wright Group	La Caja de Cuentos
El cerdito	D	5	Wright Group	La Caja de Cuentos
El concierto de los animal	E	6	Wright Group	La Caja de Cuentos
El gigante hambriento	F	11	Wright Group	La Caja de Cuentos
El pastel de chocolate	B	2	Wright Group	La Caja de Cuentos
La rosa roja	E	9	Wright Group	La Caja de Cuentos
¿Quién pude ser mi mamá?	E	9	Wright Group	La Caja de Cuentos
La mamá gallina	D	4	Wright Group	Para leer juntos
Huggles hace un viaje	A	1	Wright Group	Sunshine - Set A
Nos Vestimos Como	A	1	Wright Group	Sunshine - Set AA
Mi perrito	B	2	Wright Group	Sunshine - Set B
Sopa Fuchi	B	2	Wright Group	Sunshine - Set B
Mi hogar	C	3	Wright Group	Sunshine - Set C
La granja	A	1	Wright Group	Sunshine - Set CC
Sopa	I	17	Wright Group	Sunshine Fiction
La confusa Señora Clara Cort	I	16	Wright Group	Sunshine Read Together
La Fiesta del Gato	G	12	Wright Group	Sunshine Read Together
Paco el raton gloton	H	14	Wright Group	Sunshine Read Together
Silencio en la biblioteca	E	9	Wright Group	Sunshine Read Together

Long-Lasting Literature

Aardema, V. (1975). *Why mosquitoes buzz in people's ears.* New York: Scholastic.

Ahlberg, J., & Ahlberg, A. (1986). *The jolly postman or other people's letters.* Boston: Little, Brown.

Andersen, H. C. (1965). *The ugly duckling* (R. P. Keigwin, Translator, & A. Adams, Illustrator). New York: Scribner.

Asbjornsen, P. C. (1973). *The three billy goats gruff* (P. Galdone, Illustrator). New York: Seaburry Press.

Avi, W. (1984). *The fighting ground.* Philadelphia: J. B. Lippincott.

Aylesworth, J. (1992). *Old black fly* (S. Gammell, Illustrator). New York: Holt.

Barrett, J. (1978). *Cloudy with a chance of meatballs* (R. Barrett, Illustrator). Hartford, CT: Atheneum.

Barrett, N. S. (1984). *Trucks* (T. Bryan, Illustrator). London, NY: F. Watts.

Barrett, N. S. (1989). *Spiders.* London, NY: F. Watts.

Base, G. (1986). *Animalia.* New York: Harry Abrams.

Battle-Lavert, G. (1994). *The barber's cutting edge.* Emeryville, CA: Children's Book Press.

Baum, L. F. (1972). *The Wizard of Oz.* Chicago: World.

Bonne, R. (1985). *I know an old lady.* New York: Scholastic.

Bourgeois, P., & Clark, B. (1986). *Franklin in the dark.* New York: Scholastic.

Boyd, C. D., & Cooper, F. (1995). *Daddy, Daddy, be there.* New York: Philomel Books.

Branley, F. (1983). *Saturn: The spectacular planet.* New York: HarperCollins.

Brown, M. (1947). *Stone soup.* New York: Scribner.

Bunting, E. (1990). *The wall.* New York: Clarion.

Burnford, S. (1960). *The incredible journey.* Boston: Little, Brown.

Byars, B. (1970). *The summer of the swans.* New York: Viking.

Byars, B. (1981). *The Cybil war.* New York: Viking.

Carle, E. (1986). *The grouchy ladybug.* New York: HarperCollins.

Carle, E. (1993). *Today is Monday.* New York: Philomel.

Chase, R. (1948). *Grandfather tales.* Boston: Houghton Mifflin.

Cherry, L. (1992). *A river ran wild: An environmental history.* San Diego: Gulliver/Harcourt Brace.

Christelow, E. (1992). *Don't wake up Mama! Another five little monkeys story.* New York: Clarion.

Cleary, B. (1952). *Henry and Beezus.* New York: William Morrow.

Clements, A., & Savadier, E. (1992). *Billy and the bad teacher.* New York: Simon & Schuster Books for Young Readers.

Cohn, A. L. (1994). *From sea to shining sea: A treasury of American folklore and folk songs.* New York: Scholastic.

Cole, J. (1992). *The magic school bus on the ocean floor* (B. Degen, Illustrator). New York: Scholastic.

Collier, J., & Collier, C. (1981). *Jump ship to freedom.* New York: Delacorte.

Collins, D. (1992). *Malcolm X: Black rage.* Minneapolis, MN: Dillon Press.

Cone, M. (1964). *A promise is a promise.* Boston: Houghton Mifflin.

Conroy, P. (1990). *The water is wide.* Atlanta, GA: Old New York Book Shop Press.

Cowley, J. (1980). *Hairy bear.* San Diego, CA: The Wright Group.

Cowley, J. (1982). *What a mess!* San Diego, CA: The Wright Group.

Dahl, R. (1961). *James and the giant peach: A children's story* (N. E. Burkert, Illustrator). New York: Alfred A. Knopf.

Dahl, R. (1964). *Charlie and the chocolate factory.* New York: Alfred A. Knopf.

Dakos, K. (1992). *Don't read this book, whatever you do! More poems about school* (G. B. Karas, Illustrator). New York: Four Winds.

Davis, D. (1990). *Listening for the crack of dawn.* Little Rock, AR: August House.

for Teachers

DeJong, M. (1953). *Hurry home, Candy.* New York: Harper.

Drew, D. (1989). *The life of the butterfly.* Crystal Lake, IL: Rigby.

Duke, K. (1992). *Aunt Isabel tells a good one.* New York: Dutton.

Fisher-Nagel, H. (1987). *The life of a butterfly.* Minneapolis, MN: Carolrhoda Books.

Fleischman, S. (1986). *The whipping boy.* Mahwah, NJ: Troll Associates.

Forbes, E. (1943). *Johnny Tremain.* Boston: Houghton Mifflin.

Fox, P. (1973). *The slave dancer.* New York: Bradbury.

Fox, P. (1986). *The moonlight man.* New York: Bradbury.

Garner, J. F. (1994). *Politically correct bedtime stories.* New York: Macmillan.

Gelman, R. G. (1976). *Why can't I fly?* (J. Kent, Illustrator). New York: Scholastic.

Gelman, R. G. (1977). *More spaghetti, I say!* New York: Scholastic.

Gelman, R. G. (1985). *Cats and mice.* New York: Scholastic.

George, J. (1972). *Julie of the wolves.* New York: HarperCollins.

The Gingerbread Man. (1985). (K. Schmidt, Illustrator.) New York: Scholastic.

Goble, P. (1993). *The lost children.* New York: Bradbury.

Gonzalez, L. M. (1997). *Senor Cat's romance.* New York: Scholastic Press.

Gwynne, F. (1970). *A chocolate moose for dinner.* New York: Windmill Books.

Gwynne, F. (1976). *The king who rained.* New York: Windmill Books.

Harlow, R., & Morgan, G. (1992). *Amazing nature experiments* (Kuo Kan Chen, Illustrator). New York: Random House.

Haskins, J. (1992). *I have a dream: The life and words of Martin Luther King, Jr.* Brookfield, CT: Millbrook.

Henwood, C. (1988). *Frogs* (B. Watts, Photographer). London, NY: Franklin Watts.

Herron, C. (1997). *Nappy hair.* New York: Alfred A. Knopf. (Author's note: Due to the rather sensitive nature of this topic, it is recommended for use by our African American teacher-colleagues only.)

Houston, J. (1977). *Frozen fire.* New York: Atheneum.

Hudson, W. (1998). *Anthony's big surprise.* East Orange, NJ: Just Us Books.

Hurwitz, J. (1985). *The adventures of Ali Babba Bernstein.* New York: Scholastic.

Jackson, G.N. (1993). *Garrett Morgan: Inventor.* Cleveland, OH: Modern Curriculum.

Johnson, D. W. (1976). *Jack and the beanstalk* (D. W. Johnson, Illustrator). Boston: Little, Brown.

Juster, N. (1961). *The phantom tollbooth.* New York: Random House.

Killilea, M. (1954). *Karen.* New York: Dodd, Mead.

Kinsey-Warnock, N., & Kinsey, H. (1993). *The bear that heard crying.* New York: Cobblehill.

Krauss, R. (1945). *The carrot seed* (C. Johnson, Illustrator). New York: Scholastic.

Krumgold, J. (1953). *... and now Miguel.* New York: Harper Trophy.

L'Engle, M. (1962). *A wrinkle in time.* New York: Dell.

Lewis, C. S. (1961). *The lion, the witch, and the wardrobe.* New York: Macmillan.

Lisle, J. T. (1989). *Afternoon of the elves.* New York: Franklin Watts.

The Little Red Hen. (1985). (L. McQueen, Illustrator). New York: Scholastic.

Littlejohn, C. (1988). *The lion and the mouse.* New York: Dial Books for Young Readers.

Lobel, A. (1981). *On Market Street* (Anita Lobel, Illustrator). New York: Scholastic.

Lock, S. (1980). *Hubert hunts his hum* (J. Newnham, Illustrator). Sydney, Australia: Ashton Scholastic.

Lowry, L. (1993). *The giver.* Boston: Houghton Mifflin.

Martin, B. (1983). *Brown Bear, Brown Bear, what do you see?* (E. Carle, Illustrator). New York: Henry Holt.

Martin, J. R., & Marx, P. (1993). *Now everybody really hates me* (R. Chast, Illustrator). New York: HarperCollins.

Math, I. (1981). *Wires and watts: Understanding and using electricity.* New York: Charles Scribner's Sons.

Mayer, M. (1976). *Ah-Choo.* New York: Dial Books for Young Readers.

Mayer, M. (1976). *Hiccup.* New York: Dial Books for Young Readers.

McKissack, P. C. (1986). *Flossie & the fox.* New York: Dial Books for Young Readers.

Monjo, F. N. (1970). *The drinking gourd.* New York: Harper & Row.

Myers, W. D. (1975). *Fast Sam, Cool Clyde, and Stuff.* New York: Puffin Books.

Numeroff, L. J. (1985). *If you give a mouse a cookie.* New York: Scholastic.

Palatini, M. (1995). *Piggie pie!* New York: Clarion.

Parish, P. (1980). *Good work, Amelia Bedelia* (L. Sweat, Illustrator). New York: Avon Books.

Paulsen, G. (1991). *The river.* New York: Delacourt.

Perlman, J. (1993). *Cinderella Penguin* (J. Perlman, Illustrator). New York: Viking.

Pfeffer, S. B. (1989). *Claire at sixteen.* New York: Bantam Books.

Polacco, P. (1992). *Chicken Sunday.* New York: Scholastic.

Potter, B. (1953). *The tale of Peter Rabbit* (R. Ruth, Illustrator). Racine, WI: Golden Press.

Provensen, A., & Provensen, M. (1983). *The glorious flight: Across the channel with Louis Bleriot.* New York: Viking Penguin.

Reuter, E. (1993). *Best friends* (A. Becker, Illustrator). Pitspopany Press.

Rice, J. (1992). *Texas night before Christmas.* Gretna, LA: Pelican.

Rich, E. S. (1964). *Hannah Elizabeth.* New York: HarperCollins.

Ross, T. (1986). *I want my potty.* Brooklyn, NY: Kane/Miller.

Schwartz, D. M. (1985). *How much is a million?* Richard Hill, Ontario: Scholastic-TAB.

Scieszka, J. (1989). *The true story of the 3 little pigs! By A. Wolf.* New York: Viking Kestrel.

Scieszka, J. (1992). *The stinky cheese man and other fairly stupid tales* (L. Smith, Illustrator). New York: Viking.

Sendak, M. (1962). *Chicken soup with rice.* New York: Scholastic.

Sendak, M. (1963). *Where the wild things are.* New York: HarperCollins.

Seuss, D. (1954). *Horton hears a Who!* New York: Random House.

Seuss, D. (1998). *Hooray for Diffendoofer Day!* New York: Alfred A. Knopf.

Sharmat, M. W. (1980). *Gila monsters meet you at the airport.* New York: Aladdin.

Skaar, G. (1972). *What do the animals say?* New York: Scholastic.

Smith, K. A. (1989). *A checkup with the doctor.* New York: McDougal, Littell.

Smith, R. K. (1981). *Jelly belly.* New York: Dell.

Speare, E. G. (1958). *The witch of Blackbird Pond.* New York: Dell.

Sperry, A. (1940). *Call it courage.* New York: Macmillan.

Spier, P. (1977). *Noah's ark.* Garden City, NY: Doubleday.

Steele, W. O. (1958). *The perilous road.* Orlando, FL: Harcourt, Brace.

Steinbeck, J. (1937). *The red pony.* New York: Bantam Books.

Stolz, M. (1963). *Bully on Barkham Street.* New York: Harper.

Thaler, M. (1989). *The teacher from the black lagoon.* New York: Scholastic.

Thompson, C. (1992). *The paper bag prince.* New York: Knopf.

Van Allsburg, C. (1985). *The polar express.* Boston: Houghton Mifflin.

Van Allsburg, C. (1987). *The Z was zapped.* Boston: Houghton Mifflin.

Viorst, J. (1972). *Alexander and the terrible horrible no good very bad day* (R. Cruz, Illustrator). New York: Atheneum.

Vozar, D. (1993). *Yo, hungry wolf!* (B. Lewin, Illustrator). Garden City, NY: Doubleday/Bantam Doubleday Dell.

Wells, R. (1973). *Noisy Nora.* New York: Scholastic.

White, E. B. (1952). *Charlotte's web.* New York: HarperCollins.

White, E. B. (1970). *The trumpet of the swan.* New York: HarperCollins.

Wood, A. (1984). *The napping house.* (D. Wood, Illustrator). San Diego: Harcourt Brace.

Wood, A. (1990). *Weird parents.* New York: Dial Books for Young Readers.

Young, E. (1992). *Seven blind mice.* New York: Philomel.

Alphabet Books

Anno, M. (1975). *Anno's alphabet: An adventure in imagination.* New York: Crowell.

Baldwin, R. M. (1972). *One hundred nineteenth-century rhyming alphabets in English.* Carbondale, IL: Southern Illinois University.

Brent, I. (1993). *An alphabet of animals.* Boston: Little, Brown.

Chwast, S. (1991). *Alphabet parade.* Fort Worth, TX: Harcourt Brace.

Crowther, R. (1978). *The most amazing hide-and-seek alphabet book.* New York: Viking.

Ehlert, L. (1989). *Eating the alphabet: Fruits and vegetables from A to Z.* Fort Worth, TX: Harcourt Brace.

Emberley, E. (1978). *Ed Emberley's ABC.* Boston: Little, Brown.

Feelings, M. (1974). *Jambo means Hello: Swahili alphabet book.* New York: Dial.

Hoban, T. (1987). *26 letters and 99 cents.* New York: Greenwillow.

Hughes, S, (1998). *Alfie's ABC.* New York: Lothrop, Lee & Shepard Books.

Hunt, J. (1989). *Illuminations.* New York: Bradbury.

Jonas, A. (1990). *Disembark.* New York: Greenwillow.

Kitchen, B. (1984). *Animal alphabet.* New York: Dial.

Lobel, A. (1990). *Alison's zinnia.* New York: Greenwillow.

McCurdy, M. (1998). *The sailor's alphabet.* Boston: Houghton Mifflin.

Merriam, E. (1987). *Halloween ABC.* New York: Macmillan.

Musgrove, M. (1976). *Ashanti to Zulu: African traditions.* New York: Dial.

Press, J. (1998). *Alphabet art: with A-Z animal art and fingerplays* (S. Dennen, Illustrator). Charlotte, VT: Williamson Publishing.

Provensen, A., & Provensen, M. (1978). *A peaceable kingdom: The Shaker abecedarius.* New York: Viking.

Ressmeyer, R. (1992). *Astronaut to zodiac.* New York: Crown.

Rosen, M. (1998). *Avalanche* (D. Butler, Illustrator). Cambridge, MA: Candlewick.

Thornhill, J. (1990). *The wildlife ABC: A nature alphabet book.* New York: Simon & Schuster.

Fantastic Fun and Facts

Burns, M. (1987). *The I hate mathematics book* (M. Hairston, Illustrator). Cambridge, MA: Cambridge University Press.

Cullinan, B. E. (1987). *Children's literature in the reading program.* Newark, DE: International Reading Association.

Kelley, L. (1998). *The scrambled states of America.* New York: Henry Holt.

Kobrin, B. (1988). *Eyeopeners!* New York: Penguin Books.

Lipson, E. R. (1988). *Parent's guide to the best books for children.* New York: Times Books.

McKenna, V. (1998). *Back to the blue* (I. Andrew, Illustrator). Brookfield, CT: Milbrook Press.

Norton, D. (1999). *Through the eyes of a child: An introduction to children's literature* (5th ed.). Upper Saddle River, NJ: Merrill/Prentice Hall.

Ohanian, S. (1984). Hot new item or same old stew? *Classroom Computer Learning, 5,* 30–31.

Reed, A. (1988). *Comics to classics.* Newark, DE: International Reading Association.

Trelease, J. (1989). *The new read-aloud handbook.* New York: Penguin Books.

Wankelman, W., Wigg, P., & Wigg, M. (1968). *A handbook of arts and crafts.* Dubuque, IA: W. C. Brown.

Wacky and Weighty Words

Hall, R. (1984). *Sniglets.* New York: Macmillan.

Levitt, P. M., Burger, D. A., & Guralnick, E. S. (1985). *The weighty word book.* Longmont, CO: Bookmakers Guild.

Mahy, M. (1997) *Boom, baby, boom, boom!* (P. MacCarthy, Illustrator). New York: Penguin books USA.

Nash, B., & Nash, G. (1980). *Pundles.* New York: Stone Song Press.

Poetry, Rhythm, and Rhyme

Adoff, A. (1991). *In for winter, out for spring.* Fort Worth, TX: Harcourt Brace.

Baracca, D., & Baracca, S. (1990). *Taxi dog.* New York: Dial.

Carle, E. (1989). *Eric Carle's animals, animals.* New York: Philomel.

Cassidy, S. (1987). *Roomrimes.* New York: Crowell.

Coe, W. (1979). *Dinosaurs and beasts of yore.* New York: Philomel Books.

Demi. (Ed.). (1992). *In the eyes of the cat. Japanese poetry for all seasons.* New York: Holt.

Fleishman, P. (1988). *Joyful noise: Poems for two voices.* New York: HarperCollins.

Florian, D. (1998). *Insectlopedia: Poems and Paintings.* San Diego, CA: Harcourt Brace.

Hoberman, M. (1998). *Miss Mary Mack: A handclapping rhyme.* Boston: Little Brown.

Hollyer, B. (1999). *Dreamtime: A book of lullabies* (R. Corfield, Illustrator). New York: Viking.

Hudson, W. (1993). *Pass it on: African-American poetry for children.* New York: Scholastic.

Kennedy, X. J., & Kennedy, D. (Eds.). (1982). *Knock at a star: A child's introduction to poetry.* Boston: Little, Brown.

Loveday, J. (Ed.). (1981). *Over the bridge: An anthology of new poems.* New York: Kestrel, Penguin.

Mahy, M. (1989). *Nonstop nonsense.* New York: Macmillan.

McCurdy, M. (1998). *The sailor's alphabet.* Boston: Houghton Mifflin.

O'Neill, M. (1961). *Hailstones and halibut bones.* Garden City, NY: Doubleday.

Poems teachers ask for. (1979). New York: Granger Book.

Prelutsky, J. (1984). *The new kid on the block.* New York: Greenwillow Books.

Prelutsky, J. (1976). *Nightmares: Poems to trouble your sleep.* New York: Greenwillow Books.

Prelutsky, J. (Ed.). (1983). *The Random House book of poetry for children.* New York: Random House.

Prelutsky, J. (1986). *Ride a purple pelican.* New York: Greenwillow Books.

Prelutsky, J. (1988). *Tyrannosaurus was a beast: Dinosaur poems.* New York: Greenwillow Books.

Prelutsky, J. (1990). *Something big has been here.* New York: Greenwillow Books.

Prelutsky, J. (1991). *For laughing out loud: Poems to tickle your funnybone.* New York: Alfred A. Knopf.

Schwartz, A. (1992). *And the green grass grew all around: Folk poetry from everyone.* New York: HarperCollins.

Silverstein, S. (1974). *Where the sidewalk ends.* New York: HarperCollins.

Silverstein, S. (1981). *A light in the attic.* New York: HarperCollins.

Sky-Peck, K. (Ed.). (1991). *Who has seen the wind? An illustrated collection of poetry for young people.* Boston: Museum of Fine Arts, Boston, & Rizzoli.

Yolen, J. (1998). *Here Be The Ghosts* (D. Wilgus, Illustrator). San Diego, CA: Harcourt Brace.

Yolen, J. (1998). *Snow, Snow: Winter Poems for Children.* Honesdale, PA: Wordsong/Boyds Miller Press.

Wordless Books

Anno, M. (1982). *Anno's Britain.* New York: Philomel.

Anno, M. (1980). *Anno's Italy.* New York: Collins.

Collington, P. (1987). *The angel and the soldier boy.* New York: Alfred A. Knopf.

dePaola, T. (1978). *Pancakes for breakfast.* Fort Worth, TX: Harcourt Brace.

Drescher, H. (1987). *The yellow umbrella.* New York: Bradbury.

Goodall, J. (1987). *The story of a main street.* New York: Macmillan.

Hoban, T. (1996). *Just look.* New York: Greenwillow Books.

McCully, E. A. (1987). *School.* New York: HarperCollins.

McCully, E. A. (1988). *New baby.* New York: HarperCollins.

Spier, P. (1977). *Noah's ark.* Garden City, NY: Doubleday.

Wiesner, D. (1988). *Free fall.* New York: Lothrop, Lee & Shepard.

Wiesner, D. (1991). *Tuesday.* New York: Clarion.

Almost Wordless Books

Dubanevich, A. (1983). *Pigs in hiding.* New York: Four Winds.

Martin, R. (1989). *Will's mammoth.* New York: Putnam.

Munro, R. (1987). *The inside-out book of Washington, D.C.* New York: E. P. Dutton.

Tafuri, N. (1983). *Early morning in the barn.* New York: Greenwillow.

Sing and Read Books

Bierhorst, J. (1979). *A cry from the earth: Music of the North American Indians.* New York: Four Winds.

Carroll, L. (1979). *Songs from* Alice. New York: Holiday House.

Cohn, A. L. (Ed.). (1993). *From sea to shining sea: A treasury of American folklore and folk songs.* New York: Scholastic.

Dallin, L., & Dallin, L. (1980). *Heritage songster.* Dubuque, IA: Wm. C. Brown.

Delacre, L. (1989). *Arroz con leche: Popular songs and rhymes from Latin America.* New York: Scholastic.

Fox, D. (Ed.). (1987). *Go in and out the window: An illustrated songbook for young people.* New York: Metropolitan Museum of Art & Holt, Rinehart & Winston.

Glazer, T. (1988). *Treasury of songs for children.* Garden City, NY: Doubleday.

Hollyer, B.; selections (1999). *Dreamtime: A book of lullabyes* (Robin Bell Corfield, Illustrator). New York: Viking.

Johnson, J. W. (1993). *Lift every voice and sing.* New York: Walker.

Keller, C. (1976). *The silly song book.* Englewood Cliffs, NJ: Prentice Hall.

Knight, H. (1981). *Hillary Knight's the twelve days of Christmas.* New York: Macmillan.

Nye, V. (1983). *Music for young children.* Dubuque, IA: Wm. C. Brown.

Pankake, M., & Pankake, J. (1988). *A Prairie Home Companion folk song book.* New York: Viking.

Peek, M. (1987). *The balancing act: A counting song.* New York: Clarion.

Rubin, R. (1980). *The all-year-long song book.* New York: Scholastic.

Seeger, R. C. (1948). *American folksongs for children—In home, school, and nursery school.* New York: Doubleday.

Spier, P. (1970). *The Erie canal.* New York: Doubleday.

Spier, P. (1970). *The fox went out on a chilly night.* New York: Doubleday.

Surplus, R. W. (1963). *The alphabet of music.* Minneapolis: Lerner.

Zinar, R. (1983). *Music in your classroom.* New York: Parker.

Chanting With Children

Cole, J., & Calmenson, S. (1990). *Mary Mack and other children's street rhymes.* New York: Morrow Junior Books.

Colgin, M. L. (Compiler). (1982). *Chants for children.* Manlius, NY: Colgin.

Dunn, S. (1987). *Butterscotch dreams.* Markham, Ontario: Pembroke.

Dunn, S. (1990). *Crackers and crumbs: Chants for whole language.* Portsmouth, NH: Heinemann.

Hoberman, M. (1998). *Miss Mary Mack: A hand-clapping rhyme.* Boston: Little Brown.

Literacy Learning

Kindergarten Literacy Milestones (English and Spanish)

Book and Print Awareness

K.BA.1	Knows parts of a book and their functions
K.BA.2	Follows print word by word when listening to familiar text read aloud

Phonemic Awareness

K. PA.1	Simple awareness that spoken words have individual sound parts
K. PA.2	Orally segmenting and blending simple compound words
K. PA.3	Orally segmenting and blending simple two-syllable words
K. PA.4	Orally segmenting and blending simple onsets and rimes
K. PA.5	Orally segmenting and blending sound by sound
K. PA.6	Oddity tasks and sound manipulation
K. PA.7	Produces a rhyming word when given a spoken word

Decoding and Word Recognition

K. D.1	Recognizes and names all uppercase and lowercase letters (an alphabetic principle component)
K. D.2	Knows that the sequence of written letters and the sequence of spoken sounds in a word are the same (an alphabetic principle component)
K. D.S.1	Applies letter sound knowledge of consonant-vowel patterns to produce syllables (Spanish only)

Spelling and Writing

K.S.1	Writes independently most uppercase and lowercase letters
K.S.2	Begins using phonemic awareness and letter knowledge to create simple "temporary" (invented) spellings

Oral Reading

K.OR.1	Recognizes some words by sight, including a few common "environmental print" words

Language Comprehension and Response to Text

K.C.1	Uses less new vocabulary and language in own speech
K.C.2	Distinguishes whether simple sentences do or don't make sense
K.C.3	Connects information and events in text to life experiences
K.C.4	Uses graphic organizers to comprehend text with guidance
K.C.5	Retells stories or parts of stories
K.C.6	Understands and follows oral directions
K.C.7	Demonstrates familiarity with a number of books and selections
K.C.8	Explains simple concepts from nonfiction text

First Grade Literacy Milestones (English and Spanish)

Decoding and Word Recognition

1.D.1	Can segment and blend simple compound words
1.D.2	Can segment and blend simple two syllable words
1.D.3	Can segment and blend a one-syllable word using its onset and rime
1.D.4	Decodes phonetically regular one-syllable words and nonsense words accurately

Cooter, R. B., Jr. & Cooter, K. S. (1999). *BLAST!: Balanced Literacy Assessment System and Training.* Chicago: Rigby.

Milestones for Grades K--3

1.D.5	Uses context clues to help identify unknown words in print
1.D.6	Uses context clues plus beginning, medial, and ending sounds in words to decode unknown words in print
1.D.7	Decodes two-syllable words using knowledge of sounds, letters, and syllables including consonants, vowels, blends, and stress (Spanish only)

Spelling and Writing

1.D.1	Spells three- and four-letter short vowel words correctly (English only)
1.D.2	Uses phonics to spell simple one- and two-syllable words independently (temporary and correct spellings)
1.D.3	Uses basic punctuation (periods, question marks, capitalization)
1.D.4	Uses simple graphic organizers to plan writing with guidance
1.D.5	Produces a variety of composition types such as stories, descriptions, and journal entries
1.D.S.1	Recognizes words that use specific spelling patterns such as r/rr, y/ll, s/c/z, q/c/k, g/j, j/x, b/v, ch, h, i/y, gue, and gui (Spanish only)
1.D.S.2	Spells words with two syllables using dieresis marks, accents, r/rr, y/ll, s/c/z, q/c/k, g/j, j/x, b/v, ch, h, and i/y accurately (Spanish only)
1.D.S.3	Uses verb tenses appropriately and consistently (Spanish only)

Oral Reading

1.OR.1	Reads aloud with fluency texts on his/her independent reading level
1.OR.2	Comprehends any text that is on his/her independent reading level
1.OR.3	Uses phonic knowledge to sound out unknown words when reading text
1.OR.4	Recognizes common, irregularly spelled words by sight

Language Comprehension and Response to Text

1.C.1	Reads and comprehends fiction and nonfiction that is appropriate for the second half of grade one
1.C.2	Notices difficulties in understanding text (early metacognition skills)
1.C.3	Connects information and events in text to life experiences
1.C.4	Reads and understands simple written directions
1.C.5	Predicts and justifies what will happen next in stories
1.C.6	Discusses *how, why,* and *what* questions in sharing nonfiction text
1.C.7	Describes new information in his/her own words
1.C.8	Distinguishes whether simple sentences are incomplete or do not make sense
1.C.9	Expands sentences in response to *what, when, where,* and *how* questions.
1.C.10	Uses new vocabulary and language in own speech and writing
1.C.11	Demonstrates familiarity with a number of genres including poetry, mysteries, humor, and everyday print sources such as newspapers, signs, phone books, notices, and labels
1.C.12	Summarizes the main points of a story

Reading Fluency and Rate (Minimum Expectations)

1.F.1	Frequent word-by-word reading
1.F.2	Some two- and three-word phrasing

1.F.3	May reread for problem solving or to clarify (strategic reading)
1.F.4	Shows some awareness of syntax and punctuation
1.F.5	Forty (40) words per minute reading rate (minimum)

Second Grade Literacy Milestones (English and Spanish)

Decoding and Word Recognition

2.D.1	Decodes phonetically regular two-syllable words and nonsense words
2.D.S.1	Decodes words with three or more syllables using knowledge of sounds, letters, and syllables including consonants, vowels, blends, and stress (Spanish only)
2.D.S.2	Uses structural cues to recognize words such as compounds, base words, and inflections such as -mente, -ito, and -ando (Spanish only)

Spelling and Writing

2.SW.1	Spells previously studied words and spelling patterns correctly in own writing (application)
2.SW.2	Begins to use formal language patterns in place of oral language patterns in own writing
2.SW.3	Uses revision and editing processes to clarify and refine own writing with assistance
2.SW.4	Writes informative, well-structured reports with organizational help
2.SW.5	Attends to spelling, mechanics, and presentation for final products
2.SW.6	Produces a variety of types of compositions such as stories, reports, and correspondence
2.SW.7	Uses information from nonfiction text in independent writing
2.SW.S.1	Spells words with three or more syllables using silent letters, dieresis marks, accents, verbs, r/rr, y/ll, s/c/z, q/c/k, g/j, j/x, b/v, ch, h, and i/y accurately (Spanish only)

Oral Reading

2.OR.1	Reads aloud with fluency any text that is appropriate for the first half of grade two
2.OR.2	Comprehends any text that is appropriate for the first half of grade two
2.OR.3	Uses phonic knowledge to sound out words, including multisyllable words, when reading text
2.OR.4	Reads irregularly spelled words, diphthongs, special vowel spellings, and common word endings accurately

Language Comprehension and Response to Text

2.C.1	Reads and comprehends both fiction and nonfiction that is appropriate for the second half of grade two
2.C.2	Rereads sentences when meaning is not clear
2.C.3	Interprets information from diagrams, charts, and graphs
2.C.4	Recalls facts and details of text
2.C.5	Reads nonfiction materials for answers to specific questions
2.C.6	Develops literary awareness of character traits, point of view, setting, problem, solution, and outcome

2.C.7	Connects and compares information across nonfiction selections
2.C.8	Poses possible answers to *how, why,* and *what-if* questions in interpreting nonfiction text
2.C.9	Explains and describes new concepts and information in own words
2.C.10	Identifies part of speech for concrete nouns, active verbs, adjectives, and adverbs
2.C.11	Uses new vocabulary and language in own speech and writing
2.C.12	Demonstrates familiarity with a number of read-aloud and independent reading selections, including nonfiction
2.C.13	Recognizes a variety of print resources and knows their contents, such as joke books, chapter books, dictionaries, atlases, weather reports, and *TV Guide*
2.C.14	Connects a variety of texts to literature and life experiences (language to literacy)
2.C.15	Summarizes a story, including the stated main idea

Reading Fluency and Rate (Minimum Skills)

2.F.1	Combination of word-by-word and fluent phrase reading
2.F.2	Some expressive phrasing
2.F.3	Shows attention to punctuation and syntax
2.F.4	Fifty (50) words per minute reading rate (minimum)

Third Grade Literacy Milestones (English and Spanish)

Decoding and Word Recognition

3.D.1	Uses context clues, phonic knowledge, and structural analysis to decode words

Spelling and Writing

3.SW.1	Spells previously studied words and spelling patterns correctly in own writing
3.SW.2	Uses the dictionary to check and correct spelling
3.SW.3	Uses all aspects of the writing process in compositions and reports with assistance, including

3.SW.3.1	Combines information from multiple sources in written reports
3.SW.3.2	Revises and edits written work independently on a level appropriate for first semester of third grade
3.SW.3.3	Produces a variety of written work (response to literature, reports, semantic maps)
3.SW.3.4	Uses graphic organizational tools with a variety of texts
3.SW.3.5	Incorporates elaborate descriptions and figurative language
3.SW.3.6	Uses a variety of formal sentence structures in own writing

3.SW.S.1	Writes proficiently using orthographic patterns and rules such as qu, use of n before v, m before b, m before p, and changing z to c when adding -es (Spanish only)

| 3.SW.S.2 | Spells words with three or more syllables using silent letters, dieresis marks, accents, verbs, r/rr, y/ll, s/c/z, q/c/k, g/j, j/x, b/v, ch, h, and i/y accurately (Spanish only) |

Oral Reading

| 3.OR.1 | Reads aloud with fluency any text that is appropriate for the first half of grade three |
| 3.OR.2 | Comprehends any text that is appropriate for the first half of grade three |

Language Comprehension and Response to Text

3.C.1	Reads and comprehends both fiction and nonfiction that is appropriate for grade three
3.C.2	Reads chapter books independently
3.C.3	Identifies specific words or phrases that are causing comprehension difficulties (metacognition)
3.C.4	Summarizes major points from fiction and nonfiction text
3.C.5	Can discuss similarities in characters and events across stories
3.C.6	Can discuss underlying theme or message when interpreting fiction
3.C.7	Distinguishes when interpreting nonfiction text between:
3.C.7.1	Cause and effect
3.C.7.2	Fact and opinion
3.C.7.3	Main idea and supporting details
3.C.8	Uses information and reasoning to evaluate opinions
3.C.9	Infers word meaning from roots, prefixes, and suffixes that have been taught
3.C.10	Uses dictionary to determine meanings and usage of unknown words
3.C.11	Uses new vocabulary in own speech and writing
3.C.12	Uses basic grammar and parts of speech correctly in independent writing
3.C.13	Shows familiarity with a number of read-aloud and independent reading selections, including nonfiction
3.C.14	Uses multiple sources to locate information
3.C.14.1	Tables of contents
3.C.14.2	Indexes
3.C.14.3	Internet search engines
3.C.15	Connects a variety of literary texts with life experiences

Reading Fluency

3.F.1	Very few word-by-word interruptions
3.F.2	Reads mostly in larger meaningful phrases
3.F.3	Reads with expression
3.F.4	Attends consistently to punctuation
3.F.5	Rereads to clarify or problem-solve
3.F.6	Sixty (60) words per minute reading rate (minimum)

Blank Miscue Grid

	MIS-PRONUN.	SUB-STITUTION	OMISSION	INSERTION	TCHR. ASSIST.	SELF-CORRECT.	MEANING DISRUPTION
TOTALS							

Notes:

	MIS- PRONUN.	SUB- STITUTION	OMISSION	INSERTION	TCHR. ASSIST.	SELF- CORRECT.	MEANING DISRUPTION
TOTALS							

Notes:

	MIS-PRONUN.	SUB-STITUTION	OMISSION	INSERTION	TCHR. ASSIST.	SELF-CORRECT.	MEANING DISRUPTION
TOTALS							

Notes:

References

Aardema, V. (1975). *Why mosquitoes buzz in people's ears.* New York: Scholastic.

Aaron, R. L., & Gillespie, C. (1990). Gates-MacGinitie Reading Tests, third edition [Test review]. In R. B. Cooter, Jr. (Ed.), *The teacher's guide to reading tests.* Scottsdale, AZ: Gorsuch Scarisbrick.

Adams, M. J. (1990a). *Beginning to read: Thinking and learning about print.* Cambridge, MA: MIT Press.

Adams, M. J. (1990b). *Beginning to read: Thinking and learning about print (Summary).* Urbana-Champaign, IL: Center for the Study of Reading.

Adams, M. J. (1994). *Beginning to read: Thinking and learning about print.* Cambridge, MA: MIT Press.

Adams, M. J., Allington, R. L., Chaney, J. H., Goodman, Y. M., Kapinus, B. A., McGee, L. M., Richgels, D. J., Schwartz, S. J., Shannon, P., Smitten, B., & Williams, J. P. (1991). Beginning to read: A critique by literacy professionals and a response by Marilyn Jager Adams. *The Reading Teacher, 44*(6), 370–395.

Ahlberg, J., & Ahlberg, A. (1986). *The jolly postman or other people's letters.* Boston: Little, Brown.

Alexander, J. E. (Ed.). (1983). *Teaching reading* (2nd ed.). Boston: Little, Brown.

Alexander, J. E., & Filler, R. C. (1976). *Attitudes and reading.* Newark, DE: International Reading Association.

Alexander, J. E., & Heathington, B. S. (1988). *Assessing and correcting classroom reading problems.* Glenview, IL: Scott, Foresman.

Allan, K. K. (1982). The development of young children's metalinguistic understanding of the word. *Journal of Educational Research, 76,* 89–93.

Allington, R. (1997, August/September). Commentary: Overselling phonics. *Reading Today,* 15–16.

Allington, R. L. (1977). If they don't read much, how they ever gonna get good? *Journal of Reading, 21,* 57–61.

Allington, R. L. (1980). Teacher interruption behaviors during primary grade oral reading. *Journal of Educational Psychology, 72,* 371–372.

Allington, R. L. (1983). The reading instruction provided readers of differing reading ability. *Elementary School Journal, 83,* 255–265.

Allington, R. L. (1997, August–September). Overselling phonics. *Reading Today, 14,* 15.

Allington, R. L., & Cunningham, P. M. (1996). *Schools that work: Where all children read and write.* New York: HarperCollins.

Altwerger, B., Edelsky, C., & Flores, B. M. (1987). Whole language: What's new? *The Reading Teacher, 41*(2), 144–154.

Altwerger, B., & Flores, B. (1989). Abandoning the basal: Some aspects of the change process. *Theory Into Practice, 28*(4), 288–294.

Alvermann, D. E. (1991). The discussion web: A graphic aid for learning across the curriculum. *The Reading Teacher, 45*(2), 92–99.

Alvermann, D. E., & Boothby, P. R. (1982). Text differences: Children's perceptions at the transition stage in reading. *The Reading Teacher, 36*(3), 298–302.

Alvermann, D. E., Dillon, D. R., & O'Brien, D. G. (1987). *Using discussion to promote reading comprehension.* Newark, DE: International Reading Association.

Alvermann, D. E., & Phelps, S. F. (1994). *Content reading and literacy.* Boston: Allyn & Bacon.

Alvermann, D. E., Smith, L. C., & Readence, J. E. (1985). Prior knowledge activation and the comprehension of compatible and incompatible text. *Reading Research Quarterly, 20*(4), 420–436.

Ancona, G. (1994). *The piñata maker: Piñatero.* San Diego, CA: Harcourt Brace.

Andersen, H. C. (1965). *The ugly duckling* (R. P. Keigwin, Trans., & A. Adams, Illustrator). New York: Scribner.

Anderson, L., Evertson, C., & Brophy, J. (1979). An experimental study of effective teaching in first-grade reading groups. *The Elementary School Journal, 79,* 193–222.

Anderson, R. C. (1970). Control of student mediating processes during verbal learning and instruction. *Review of Educational Research, 40,* 349–369.

Anderson, R. C., & Freebody, P. (1981). Vocabulary knowledge. In J. T. Guthrie (Ed.), *Comprehension and teaching: Research reviews* (pp. 80–82). Newark, DE: International Reading Association.

Anderson, R. C., Hiebert, E. F., Scott, J. A., & Wilkinson, I. A. G. (1985). *Becoming a nation of readers: The report of the commission on reading.* Washington, DC: The National Institute of Education.

Anderson, R. C., Mason, J., & Shirey, L. (1984). The reading group: An experimental investigation of a labyrinth. *Reading Research Quarterly, 20*(1), 6–38.

Anderson, R. C., Osborn, J., & Tierney, R. J. (1984). *Learning to read in American schools.* Hillsdale, NJ: Erlbaum.

Anderson, R. C., & Pearson, P. D. (1984). A schema-theoretic view of basic processes in reading. In D. P. Pearson (Ed.), *Handbook of reading research* (pp. 255–291). New York: Longman.

Anderson, R. C., Reynolds, R. E., Schallert, D. L., & Goetz, E. T. (1977). Frameworks for comprehending discourse. *American Educational Research Journal, 14,* 367–382.

Anderson, R. C., Wilson, P. T., & Fielding, L. G. (1988). Growth in reading and how children spend their time outside of school. *Reading Research Quarterly, 23*(3), 285–303.

Anderson, T. H., & Armbruster, B. B. (1980). Studying. In P. D. Pearson (Ed.), *Handbook of reading research* (pp. 657–680). New York: Longman.

Apple Computer. (1984). *Macwrite* [Computer program]. Cupertino, CA: Author.

Applebee, A. N. (1979). *The child's concept of story: Ages two to seventeen.* Chicago, IL: The University of Chicago Press.

Applebee, A. N., Langer, J. A., & Mullis, I. V. S. (1988). *Who reads best.* Princeton, NJ: Educational Testing Service.

Armbruster, B., & Anderson, T. (1981). *Content area textbooks* (Reading Education Report No. 23). Urbana-Champaign: University of Illinois at Urbana-Champaign, Center for the Study of Reading.

Armbruster, B. B. (1984). The problem of "inconsiderate text." In G. G. Duffy, L. R. Roehler, & J. Mason (Eds.), *Comprehension instruction: Perspective and suggestions.* New York: Longman.

Asbjornsen, P. C. (1973). *The three billy goats gruff* (Paul Galdone, Illustrator). New York: Seaburry Press.

Asch, F. (1993). *Moondance.* New York: Scholastic.

Asheim, L., Baker, D. P., & Mathews, V. H. (1983). *Reading and successful living: The family school partnership.* Hamden, CT: Library Professional.

Asher, S. R. (1977). *Sex differences in reading achievement.* (Reading Education Report No. 2). Urbana-Champaign: University of Illinois at Urbana-Champaign, Center for the Study of Reading.

Asher, S. R. (1980). Topic interest and children's reading comprehension. In Spiro, R. J., Bruce, B. C., & Brewer, W. F. (Eds.), *Theoretical issues in reading comprehension* (pp. 525–534). Hillsdale, NJ: Erlbaum.

Ashton-Warner, S. (1963). *Teacher.* New York: Touchstone Press.

Atwell, N. (1987). *In the middle: Writing, reading, and learning with adolescents.* Portsmouth, NH: Heinemann.

Au, K. H. (1993). *Literacy instruction in multicultural settings.* Fort Worth, TX: Harcourt Brace.

Aukerman, R. (1981). *The basal reader approach to reading.* New York: Wiley.

Ausubel, D. P. (1959). Viewpoints from related disciplines: Human growth and development. *Teachers College Record, 60,* 245–254.

Avi, W. (1984). *The fighting ground.* Philadelphia: Lippincott.

Bacharach, N., & Alexander, P. (1986). Basal reader manuals: What do teachers think of them? *Reading Psychology, 3,* 163–172.

Bader, L. A. (1984). Instructional adjustments to vision problems. *The Reading Teacher, 37*(7), 566–569.

Baker, L., & Brown, A. L. (1984). Cognitive monitoring in reading. In J. Flood (Ed.), *Understanding reading comprehension* (pp. 21–44). Newark, DE: International Reading Association.

Baldwin, R. S., & Kaufman, R. K. (1979). A concurrent validity study of the Raygor readability estimate. *Journal of Reading, 23,* 148–153.

Bank Street writer [Computer program]. (1990). Jefferson City, MO: Scholastic Software.

Bantam. (1985). *Choose your own adventure.* New York: Bantam.

Barker, R. (1978). Stream of individual behavior. In R. Barker & Associates (Eds.), *Habitats, environments, and human behavior* (pp. 3–16). San Francisco: Jossey-Bass.

Barracca, D., & Barracca, S. (1990). *Taxi dog.* New York: Dial Books.

Barrett, F. L. (1982). *A teacher's guide to shared reading.* Richmond Hill, Ontario, Canada: Scholastic-TAB.

Barrett, J. (1978). *Cloudy with a chance of meatballs* (R. Barrett, Illustrator). Hartford, CT: Atheneum.

Barrett, N. S. (1984). *Trucks* (Tony Bryan, Illustrator). London, NY: F. Watts.

Barrett, N. S. (1989). *Spiders.* London, NY: F. Watts.

Barrett, T. (1972). Taxonomy of reading comprehension. *Reading 360 Monograph.* Boston: Ginn.

Barron, R. F. (1969). The use of vocabulary as an advance organizer. In H. L. Herber & P. L. Sanders (Eds.), *Research in reading in the content areas: First year report.* Syracuse, NY: Reading and Language Arts Center, Syracuse University.

Bartlett, B. J. (1978). *Top-level structure as an organizational strategy for recall of classroom text.* Unpublished doctoral dissertation, Arizona State University.

Barton, D., Miller, R., & Macken, M. A. (1980). Do children treat clusters as one unit or two? *Papers and Reports on Child Language Development, 18,* 137.

Basal reading texts. What's in them to comprehend? (1984, November). *The Reading Teacher,* pp. 194–195.

Base, G. (1986). *Animalia.* New York: Harry N. Abrams.

Baum, L. F. (1972). *The Wizard of Oz.* World.

Baumann, J. F. (1992). Basal reading programs and the deskilling of teachers: A critical examination of the argument. *Reading Research Quarterly, 27*(4), 390–398.

Baumann, J. F. (1993). Letters to the editor: Is it "You just don't understand," or am I simply confused? A response to Shannon. *Reading Research Quarterly, 28*(2), 86–87.

Baumann, J. F. (1996). Do basal readers deskill teachers: A national survey of educators' use and opinions of basals. *Elementary School Journal, 96*(5), 511–526.

Baumann, J. F., Jones, L. A., & Siefert-Kessell, N. (1993). Using think alouds to enhance children's comprehension monitoring abilities. *The Reading Teacher, 47*(3), 184–193.

Baumann, J. F., & Stevenson, J. A. (1986). Teaching students to comprehend anaphoric relations. In J. W. Irwin (Ed.), *Understanding and teaching cohesion comprehension* (pp. 3–8). Newark, DE: International Reading Association.

Baylor, B. (1976). *Hawk, I'm your brother.* New York: Macmillan.

Bear, D. R., Templeton, S., Invernizzi, M., & Johnston, F. (1996). *Words their way: Word study for phonics, vocabulary, and spelling instruction.* Upper Saddle River, NJ: Merrill/Prentice Hall.

Beck, I. L. (1986). Using research on reading. *Educational Leadership, 43*(7), 13–15.

Beck, I. L., Armbruster, B., Raphael, T., McKeown, M. G., Ringler, L., & Ogle, D. (1989). *Reading today and tomorrow: Treasures. Level 3.* New York: Holt, Rinehart and Winston.

Beck, I. L., & McKeown, M. G. (1981). Developing questions that promote comprehension: The story map. *Language Arts, 58,* 913–918.

Beck, I. L., McKeown, M. G., Omanson, R. C., & Pople, M. T. (1984). Improving the comprehensibility of stories: The effects of revisions that improve coherence. *Reading Research Quarterly, 19,* 263–277.

Beck, I. L., Omanson, R. C., & McKeown, M. G. (1982). An instructional redesign of reading lessons: Effects on comprehension. *Reading Research Quarterly, 17,* 462–481.

Berlak, H. (1992). The need for a new science of assessment. In H. Berlak et al., *Toward a new science of educational testing and assessment.* New York: State University of New York Press.

Betts, E. A. (1946). *Foundation of reading instruction.* New York: American Book.

Bintz, W. P. (1991). Staying connected—Exploring new functions for assessment. *Contemporary Education, 62*(4), 307–312.

Bissex, G. L. (1980). *Gnys at wrk: A child learns to write and read.* Cambridge, MA: Harvard University Press.

Blachman, B. A. (1984). Relationship of rapid naming ability and language analysis skills to kindergarten and first-grade reading achievement. *Journal of Educational Psychology, 76,* 610–622.

Blachowicz, C. L. Z. (1977). Cloze activities for primary readers. *The Reading Teacher, 31*(3), 300–302.

Blachowicz, C. L. Z. (1986). Making connections: Alternatives to the vocabulary notebook. *Journal of Reading, 29*(7), 643–649.

Blackburn, L. (1997). *Whole music: A whole language approach to teaching music.* Westport, CT: Heinemann.

Blanchard, J., & Rottenberg, C. J. (1990). Hypertext and hypermedia: Discovering and creating meaningful learning environments. *The Reading Teacher, 43*(9), 656–661.

Blanchard, J. S., Mason, G. E., & Daniel, D. (1987). *Computer applications in reading.* Newark, DE: International Reading Association.

Blanton, W. E., & Moorman, G. B. (1985). *Presentation of reading lessons. Technical Report No. 1.* Boone, NC: Center for Excellence on Teacher Education, Appalachian State University.

Blanton, W. E., Moorman, G. B., & Wood, K. D. (1986). A model of direct instruction applied to the basal skills lesson. *The Reading Teacher, 40,* 299–305.

Blecher, S., & Jaffee, K. (1998). *Weaving in the arts: Widening the learning circle.* Westport, CT: Heinemann.

Bleich, D. (1978). *Subjective criticism.* Baltimore, MD: Johns Hopkins University Press.

Blevins, W. (1997). *Phonemic awareness activities for early reading success.* New York: Scholastic.

Blevins, W. (1998). *Phonics from A to Z.* New York: Scholastic.

Block, J. H. (1989). *Building effective mastery learning schools.* New York: Longman.

Bloom, A. (1987). *The closing of the American mind: How higher education has failed democracy and impoverished the souls of today's students.* New York: Simon & Schuster.

Bloom, B. (1956). *Taxonomy of educational objectives.* New York: David McKay.

Blum, I. (1995). Using audiotaped books to extend classroom literacy instruction into the homes of second-language learners. *Journal of Reading Behavior, 27*(4), 535–563.

Blume, J. (1972). *Tales of a fourth grade nothing.* New York: Dell.

Bohning, G. (1986). The McGuffey eclectic readers: 1836–1986. *The Reading Teacher, 40,* 263–269.

Bond, G. L., & Dykstra, R. (1967). The cooperative research program in first-grade reading instruction. *Reading Research Quarterly, 2,* 5–142.

Bonne, R. (1985). *I know an old lady.* New York: Scholastic.

Bonners, S. (1989). *Just in passing.* New York: Lothrop, Lee & Shepard.

Booth, J. (1985). *Impressions.* Toronto, Canada: Holt, Rinehart and Winston.

Bourgeois, P., & Clark, B. (1986). *Franklin in the dark.* New York: Scholastic.

Boyle, O. F., & Peregoy, S. F. (1990). Literacy scaffolds: Strategies for first- and second-language readers and writers. *The Reading Teacher, 44*(3), 194–200.

Brackett, G. (1989). *Super story tree.* Jefferson City, MO: Scholastic.

Branley, F. (1983). *Saturn: The spectacular planet.* New York: HarperCollins.

Bransford, J. C., & Johnson, M. K. (1972). Contextual prerequisites for understanding: Some investigations of comprehension and recall. *Journal of Verbal Learning and Verbal Behavior, 11,* 717–726.

Bransford, J. D., & Franks, J. J. (1971). The abstraction of linguistic ideas. *Cognitive Psychology, 2,* 331–350.

Braun, C. (1969). Interest-loading and modality effects on textual response acquisition. *Reading Research Quarterly, 4,* 428–444.

Brennan, J. (1994, September 3). Been there done that: Three John Grisham stories, one John Grisham plot. *Fort Worth Star Telegram,* p. 1E.

Bridge, C. (1978). Predictable materials for beginning readers. *Language Arts, 55,* 593–597.

Brigance, A. H. (1983). *Brigance® diagnostic comprehensive inventory of basic skills.* North Billerica, MA: Curriculum Associates.

Brigance, A. H. (1999). *Brigance® comprehensive inventory of basic skills-revised.* North Billerica, MA: Curriculum Associates.

Brimner, L. D. (1992). *A migrant family.* Minneapolis, MN: Lerner.

Bromley, K. D. (1991). *Webbing with literature: Creating story maps with children's books.* Boston: Allyn & Bacon.

Bronfenbrenner, U. (1977). Toward an experimental ecology of human development. *American Psychologist, 32,* 513–531.

Bronfenbrenner, U., McClelland, P., Wethington, E., Moen, P., & Ceci, S. J. (1996). *The state of Americans.* New York: Free Press.

Brown, A. (1982). Learning how to learn from reading. In J. A. Langer & M. T. Smith-Burke (Eds.), *Reader meets author: Bridging the gap* (pp. 26–54). Newark, DE: International Reading Association.

Brown, A., & Smiley, S. S. (1978). The development of strategies for studying texts. *Child Development, 49,* 1076–1088.

Brown, D. J., Engin, A. W., & Wallbrown, F. J. (1979). Developmental changes in reading attitudes during the intermediate grades. *Journal of Experimental Education, 47,* 262–279.

Brown, M. (1947). *Stone soup.* New York: Scribner.

Brown, T. (1986). *Hello, amigos.* New York: Holt, Rinehart and Winston.

Brozo, W. G., & Simpson, M. L. (1995). *Readers, teachers, learners: Expanding literacy in secondary schools.* Upper Saddle River, NJ: Merrill/Prentice Hall.

Bruner, J. (1986). *Actual minds, Possible worlds.* Cambridge, MA: Harvard University Press.

Burke, C. (1987). Burke reading interview. In Goodman, Y., Watson, D., & Burke, C. (Eds.), *Reading miscue inventory: Alternative procedures.* New York: Owen.

Burnford, S. (1960). *The incredible journey.* Boston: Little, Brown.

Burns, M. (1987). *The I hate mathematics book* (Martha Hairston, Illustrator). Cambridge, MA: Cambridge University Press.

Burns, P. C., Roe, B. D., & Ross, E. P. (1988). *Teaching reading in today's elementary schools* (4th ed.). Dallas: Houghton Mifflin.

Burns, P. C., Roe, B. D., & Ross, E. P. (1992). *Teaching reading in today's elementary schools* (5th ed.). Dallas: Houghton Mifflin.

Byars, B. (1970). *The summer of the swans.* New York: Viking.

Byars, B. (1981). *The Cybil war.* New York: Viking.

Byrne, B., & Fielding-Barnsley, R. (1989). Phonemic awareness and letter knowledge in the child's acquisition of the alphabetic principle. *Journal of Educational Psychology, 81,* 313–321.

Byrne, B., & Fielding-Barnsley, R. (1990). Acquiring the alphabetic principle: A case for teaching recognition of phoneme identity. *Journal of Educational Psychology, 82*(4), 805–812.

Byrne, B., Freebody, P., & Gates, A. (1992). Longitudinal data on the relations of word-reading strategies to comprehension, reading time, and phonemic awareness. *Reading Research Quarterly, 27*(2), 140–151.

Cafolla, R., Kauffman, D., & Knee, R. (1997). *World Wide Web for teachers: An interactive guide.* Boston: Allyn & Bacon.

California Department of Education. (1995). *Every child a reader: The report of the California Reading Task Force.* Sacramento, CA: California Department of Education.

California Reading Task Force. (1995). *Every child a reader.* Sacramento, CA: California Department of Education.

California State Department of Education. (1980). *Report on the special studies of selected ECE schools with increasing and decreasing reading scores.* (Available from Publication Sales, California State Department of Education, P.O. Box 271, Sacramento, CA 95802.)

Calkins, L. (1986). *The art of teaching writing.* Portsmouth, NH: Heinemann.

Calkins, L. (1994). *The art of teaching writing* (new ed.). Westport, CT: Heinemann.

Calkins, L. M. (1980). When children want to punctuate: Basic skills belong in context. *Language Arts, 57,* 567–573.

Calkins, L. M., & Harwayne, S. (1987). *The writing workshop: A world of difference* [Video]. Portsmouth, NH: Heinemann.

Cambourne, B. (1988). *The whole story: Natural learning and the acquisition of literacy in the classroom.* New York: Ashton-Scholastic.

Cambourne, B., & Turbill, J. (1990). Assessment in whole-language classrooms: Theory into practice. *Elementary School Journal, 90*(3), 337–349.

Canney, G., & Winograd, P. (1979). *Schemata for reading and reading comprehension performance* (Technical Report No. 120). Urbana-Champaign: University of Illinois at Urbana-Champaign, Center for the Study of Reading. (ERIC Document Reproduction Service No. ED 109 520)

Cantrell, S. C. (1999). Effective teaching and literacy learning: A look inside primary classrooms. *The Reading Teacher, 52*(4), 370–378.

Carbo, M. (1988). The evidence supporting reading styles: A response to Stahl. *Phi Delta Kappan, 70,* 323–327.

Carle, E. (1986). *The grouchy ladybug.* New York: HarperCollins.

Carr, E. (1985). The vocabulary overview guide: A metacognitive strategy to improve vocabulary comprehension and retention. *Journal of Reading, 28*(8), 684–689.

Carr, E., Dewitz, P., & Patberg, J. (1989). Using cloze for inference training with expository text. *The Reading Teacher, 43*(6), 380–385.

Carr, E., & Wixson, K. K. (1986). Guidelines for evaluating vocabulary instruction. *Journal of Reading, 29*(7), 588–589.

Carr, H. K. (1986). *Developing metacognitive skills: The key to success in reading and learning.* For the MERIT, Chapter 2 project, The School District of Philadelphia, H. K. Carr, MERIT supervisor. Philadelphia: School District of Philadelphia.

Carroll, J. B., Davies, P., & Richman, B. (1971). *Word frequency book.* Boston: Houghton Mifflin.

Carroll, L. (1872). *Through the looking glass.* New York: Macmillan.

Cassidy, J. (1981). Grey power in the reading program—a direction for the eighties. *The Reading Teacher, 35,* 287–291.

Cattell, J. M. (1885). Ueber die Zeit der Erkennung und Bennenung von Schriftzeichen, Bildern und Farben. *Philosophische Studien, 2,* 635–650.

Caverly, D. C., & Buswell, J. (1988). Computer assisted instruction that supports whole language instruction. *Colorado Communicator, 11*(3), 6–7.

Chall, J. S. (1967). *Learning to read: The great debate.* New York: McGraw-Hill.

Chall, J. S. (1979). The great debate: Ten years later, with a modest proposal for reading stages. In Resnick, L. B., & Weaver, P. A. (Eds.), *Theory and practice of early reading* (pp. 29–55). Hillsdale, NJ: Erlbaum.

Chall, J. S. (1983). *Stages of reading development.* New York: McGraw-Hill.

Chall, J. S. (1998). My life in reading. In E. Sturtevant, J. Dugan, P. Linder, & W. Linek (Eds.), *Literacy and community, the twentieth yearbook of the College Reading Association, USA,* 12–24.

Chapman, L. J., & Hoffman, M. (1977). *Developing fluent reading.* Milton Keynes, England: Open University Press.

Chase, R. (1948). *Grandfather tales.* Boston: Houghton Mifflin.

Chisom, F. P. (1989). *Jump start: The federal role in adult literacy.* Southport, CT: Southport Institute for Policy Analysis.

Choi, S. N. (1991). *Year of impossible goodbyes.* Boston: Houghton Mifflin.

Chomsky, C. (1971). Write first, read later. *Childhood Education, 47,* 230–237.

Chomsky, N. (1974). *Aspects of the theory of syntax.* Cambridge, MA: MIT Press.

Chomsky, N. (1975). *The logical structure of linguistic theory.* Chicago: The University of Chicago Press.

Chomsky, N. (1979). Human language and other semiotic systems. *Semiotica, 25,* 31–44.

Christopher, J. (1967). *The white mountains.* New York: Macmillan.

Clarke, M. A. (1989). Negotiating agendas: Preliminary considerations. *Language Arts, 66*(4), 370–380.

Clay, M. M. (1967). The reading behaviour of five year old children: A research report. *New Zealand Journal of Educational Studies, 2*(1), 11–31.

Clay, M. M. (1972). *Reading: The patterning of complex behaviour.* Exeter, NH: Heinemann.

Clay, M. M. (1975). *What did I write? Beginning writing behaviour.* Portsmouth, NH: Heinemann.

Clay, M. M. (1985). *The early detection of reading difficulties* (3rd ed.). Portsmouth, NH: Heinemann.

Clay, M. M. (1987). *Writing begins at home: Preparing children for writing before they go to school.* Portsmouth, NH: Heinemann.

Clay, M. M. (1990). What is and what might be in evaluation (Research currents). *Language Arts, 67*(3), 288–298.

Clay, M. M. (1993a). *An observation survey for early literacy achievement.* Portsmouth, NH: Heinemann.

Clay, M. M. (1993b). *Reading recovery: A guidebook for teachers in training.* Portsmouth, NH: Heinemann.

Cleary, B. (1952). *Henry and Beezus.* New York: William Morrow.

Cochrane, O., Cochrane, D., Scalena, D., & Buchanan, E. (1984). *Reading, writing and caring.* New York: Owen.

Cole, B. (1983). *The trouble with mom.* New York: Coward-McCann.

Cole, J. (1986). *This is the place for me.* New York: Scholastic.

Cole, J. (1990). *The magic school bus lost in the solar system.* New York: Scholastic.

Cole, J., & Calmenson, S. (1990). *Miss Mary Mack.* New York: Morrow Junior Books.

Collier, J., & Collier, C. (1981). *Jump ship to freedom.* New York: Delacorte.

Collins, A., & Smith, E. (1980). *Teaching the process of reading comprehension* (Tech. Rep. No. 182). Urbana-Champaign: University of Illinois at Urbana-Champaign, Center for the Study of Reading.

Collins, A. M., & Quillian, M. R. (1969). Retrieval time from semantic memory. *Journal of Verbal Learning and Verbal Behavior, 8,* 240–247.

Collis, B. (1988). Research windows. *The Computing Teacher, 15,* 15–16, 61.

Commeyras, M., & DeGroff, L. (1998). Literacy professionals' perspectives on professional development and pedagogy: A United States survey. *Reading Research Quarterly, 33*(4), 434–472.

Cone, M. (1964). *A promise is a promise.* Boston: Houghton Mifflin.

Cooter, R. B., Jr. (1988). Effects of Ritalin on reading. *Academic Therapy, 23,* 461–468.

Cooter, R. B., Jr. (Ed.). (1990). *The teacher's guide to reading tests.* Scottsdale, AZ: Gorsuch Scarisbrick, Publishers.

Cooter, R. B., Jr. (1993). *Improving oral reading fluency through repeated readings using simultaneous recordings.* Unpublished manuscript, PDS Urban Schools Project, Texas Christian University.

Cooter, R. B., Jr. (1994). Assessing affective and conative factors in reading. *Reading Psychology, 15*(2), 77–90.

Cooter, R. B., Jr. (1998). *Balanced literacy instructional strands.* Reading Research Report #91, Dallas, TX.

Cooter, R. B., Jr. (1999). *Realizing the dream: Meeting the literacy needs of Dallas children.* Dallas, TX: Unpublished manuscript.

Cooter, R. B., Jr., & Cooter, K. S. (1999). *BLAST!: Balanced Literacy Assessment System and Training.* Chicago: Rigby. (Prototype not yet in production)

Cooter, R. B., Jr., Diffily, D., Gist-Evans, D., & Sacken, M. A. (1994). *Literacy development milestones research project* (Report No. 94–100). Unpublished manuscript, Texas Christian University, Fort Worth, TX.

Cooter, R. B., Jr., & Flynt, E. S. (1989). Blending basal reader and whole language instruction. *Reading Horizons, 29*(4), 275–282.

Cooter, R. B., Jr., & Flynt, E. S. (1996). *Teaching reading in the content areas: Developing content literacy for all students.* Upper Saddle River, NJ: Merrill/ Prentice Hall.

Cooter, R. B., Jr., & Griffith, R. (1989). Thematic units for middle school: An honorable seduction. *Journal of Reading, 32*(8), 676–681.

Cooter, R. B., Jr., Jacobson, J. J., & Cooter, K. S. (1998). *Technically simple and socially complex: Three school-based attempts to improve literacy achievement.* Paper presented at The National Reading Conference Annual Convention, Austin, TX, December 5, 1998.

Cooter, R. B., Jr., Joseph, D. G., & Flynt, E. S. (1987). Eliminating the literal pursuit in reading comprehension. *Journal of Clinical Reading, 2*(1), 9–11.

Cooter, R. B., Jr., Mills-House, E., Marrin, P., Mathews, B., & Campbell, S. (in press for spring 1999). Family and community involvement: The bedrock of reading success. *The Reading Teacher.*

Cooter, R. B., Jr., & Reutzel, D. R. (1987). Teaching reading skills for mastery. *Academic Therapy, 23*(2), 127–134.

Cooter, R. B., Jr., & Reutzel, D. R. (1990). *Yakity-yak: A reciprocal response procedure for improving reading comprehension.* Unpublished manuscript, Brigham Young University, Department of Elementary Education, Provo, UT.

Cooter, R. B., Jr., Reutzel, D. R., & Cooter, K. S. (1998). *Sequence of development and instruction for phonemic awareness.* Unpublished paper.

Cornejo, R. (1972). *Spanish high frequency word list.* Austin, TX: Southwestern Educational Laboratory.

Corno, L., & Randi, J. (1997). Motivation, volition, and collaborative innovation in classroom literacy. In J. T. Guthrie & A. Wigfield (Eds.), *Reading engagement: Motivating readers through integrated instruction.* Newark, DE: International Reading Association.

Cousin, P. T., Weekly, T., & Gerard, J. (1993). The functional uses of language and literacy by students with severe language and learning problems. *Language Arts, 70*(7), 548–556.

Cowley, J. (1980). *Hairy bear.* San Diego, CA: The Wright Group.

Cowley, J. (1982). *What a mess!* San Diego, CA: The Wright Group.

Cox, C., & Zarillo, J. (1993). *Teaching reading with children's literature*. Upper Saddle River, NJ: Merrill/Prentice Hall.

Craft, H., & Krout, J. (1970). *The adventure of the American people*. Chicago, IL: Rand McNally.

Crist, B. I. (1975). One capsule a week-A painless remedy for vocabulary ills. *Journal of Reading, 19*(2), 147–149.

Cudd, E. T., & Roberts, L. L. (1987). Using story frames to develop reading comprehension in a 1st grade classroom. *The Reading Teacher, 41*(1), 74–81.

Cudd, E. T., & Roberts, L. L. (1993). A scaffolding technique to develop sentence sense and vocabulary. *Reading Teacher, 47*(4), 346–349.

Cunningham, A. E., & Stanovich, K. E. (1998). What reading does for the mind. *American Educator, 22,* 8–15.

Cunningham, P. (1980). Teaching were, with, what, and other "four-letter" words. *The Reading Teaching, 34,* 160–163.

Cunningham, P. M. (1995). *Phonics they use: Words for reading and writing* (2nd ed.). New York: HarperCollins.

D.E.S. (1975). *A language for life (The Bullock Report),* H.M.S.O.

Dahl, R. (1961). *James and the giant peach: A children's story* (Nancy Ekholm Burkert, Illustrator). New York: Alfred A. Knopf.

Dahl, R. (1964). *Charlie and the chocolate factory*. New York: Alfred A. Knopf.

Dale, E. (1969). *Audiovisual methods in teaching* (3rd ed.). New York: Holt, Rinehart and Winston.

Dallin, L., & Dallin, L. (1980). *Heritage songster*. Dubuque, IA: William C. Brown.

Dana, C. (1989). Strategy families for disabled readers. *Journal of Reading, 33*(1), 30–35.

Davis, D. (1990). *Listening for the crack of dawn*. Little Rock, AR: August House.

Day, K. C., & Day, H. D. (1979). Development of kindergarten children's understanding of concepts about print and oral language. In M. L. Damil & A. H. Moe (Eds.), *Twenty-eighth yearbook of the National Reading Conference* (pp. 19–22). Clemson, SC: National Reading Conference.

Dechant, E. V. (1970). *Improving the teaching of reading* (2nd ed.). Upper Saddle River, NJ: Prentice Hall.

DeFord, D., & Harste, J. C. (1982). Child language research and curriculum. *Language Arts, 59*(6), 590–601.

DeFord, D. E. (1985). Validating the construct of theoretical orientation in reading instruction. *Reading Research Quarterly, 20*(3), 351–367.

DeGroff, L. (1990). Is there a place for computers in whole language classrooms? *The Reading Teacher, 43*(8), 568–572.

DeJong, M. (1953). *Hurry home, Candy*. New York: Harper.

Delpit, L. D. (1988). The silenced dialogue: Power and pedagogy in educating other people's children. *Harvard Educational Review, 58*(3), 280–298.

dePaola, T. (1978). *The popcorn book*. New York: Holiday House.

Department of Education. (1985). *Reading in junior classes. Wellington, New Zealand*. New York: Owen.

Developmental Learning Materials. (1985). *The writing adventure*. Allen, TX: Developmental Learning Materials.

Devillar, R. A., Faltis, C. J., & Cummins, J. P. (1994). *Cultural diversity in schools: From rhetoric to practice*. Albany, NY: SUNY Press.

Dewey, J. (1913). *Interest and effort in education*. New York: Houghton Mifflin.

Dewey, J., & Bentley, A. F. (1949). *Knowing and the known.* Boston: Beacon Press.

Dewitz, P., & Carr, E. M. (1987, December). Teaching comprehension as a student directed process. In P. Dewitz (Chair), *Teaching reading comprehension, summarizing and writing in content area.* Symposium conducted at the National Reading Conference, Florida.

Dewitz, P., Stammer, J., & Jensen, J. (1980). *The development of linguistic awareness in young children from label reading to word recognition.* Paper presented at the annual meeting of the National Reading Conference, San Diego, CA.

Diffily, D. (1994, April). *Portfolio assessment in early literacy settings.* Paper presented at a professional development schools workshop at Texas Christian University, Fort Worth, TX.

Dillner, M. (1993–1994). Using hypermedia to enhance content area instruction. *Journal of Reading, 37*(4), 260–270.

Discoll, M. P. (1994). *Psychology of learning for instruction.* Boston, MA: Allyn & Bacon.

Doctorow, M., Wittrock, M. C., & Marks, C. (1978). Generative processes in reading comprehension. *Journal of Educational Psychology, 70*(2), 109–118.

D'Odorico, L. (1984). Nonsegmental features in prelinguistic communications: An analysis of some types of infant cry and noncry vocalizations. *Journal of Child Language, 11,* 17–27.

Dole, J. A., Rogers, T., & Osborn, J. (1987). Improving the selection of basal reading programs: A report of the textbook adoption guidelines project. *Elementary School Journal, 87,* 282–298.

Donelson, K. L., & Nilsen, A. P. (1985). *Literature for today's young adults.* Boston: Scott, Foresman.

Dowd, C. A., & Sinatra, R. (1990). Computer programs and the learning of text structure. *Journal of Reading, 34*(2), 104–112.

Dowhower, S. (1987). Effects of repeated readings on second-grade transitional readers' fluency and comprehension. *Reading Research Quarterly, 22,* 389–406.

Downing, J. (1977). How society creates reading disability. *The Elementary School Journal, 77,* 274–279.

Downing, J., & Oliver, P. (1973). The child's concept of a word. *Reading Research Quarterly, 9,* 568–582.

Downing, J., & Thomson, D. (1977). Sex role stereotypes in learning to read. *Research in the Teaching of English, 11,* 149–155.

Doyle, C. (1988). Creative applications of computer assisted reading and writing instruction. *Journal of Reading, 32*(3), 236–239.

Dreher, M. J., & Gambrell, L. B. (1985). Teaching children to use a self-questioning strategy for studying expository prose. *Reading Improvement, 22,* 2–7.

Drew, D. (1989). *The life of the butterfly.* Crystal Lake, IL: Rigby.

Drucker, P. F. (1998, August 24). The next information revolution. *Forbes ASAP,* 47–58.

Duffy, G. G., Roehler, L. R., & Putnam, J. (1987). Putting the teacher in control: Basal reading textbooks and instructional decision making. *The Elementary School Journal, 87*(3), 357–366.

Dunn, L., & Dunn, L. M. (1997). *Peabody picture vocabulary test—third edition* (PPVT-III). Circle Pines, MN: American Guidance Service.

Dunn, L., Lugo, D. E., Padilla, E. R., & Dunn, L. M. (1986). *Test de Vocabulario en Imágenes Peabody* (TVIP). Circle Pines, MN: American Guidance Service.

Dunn, L. M., & Markwardt, F. C. (1970). *Peabody individual achievement test.* Circle Pines, MN: American Guidance Service.

Dunn, R. (1988). Teaching students through their perceptual strengths or preferences. *Journal of Reading, 31,* 304–309.

Dunn, S. (1987). *Butterscotch dreams.* Markham, Ontario: Pembroke.

Durkin, D. (1966). *Children who read early: Two longitudinal studies.* New York: Teachers College Press.

Durkin, D. (1978). What classroom observations reveal about reading comprehension instruction. *Reading Research Quarterly, 14*(4), 482–533.

Durkin, D. (1981a). Reading comprehension in five basal reader series. *Reading Research Quarterly, 16*(4), 515–543.

Durkin, D. (1981b). What is the value of the new interest in reading comprehension? *Language Arts, 58,* 23–43.

Durkin, D. (1983). *Reading comprehension instruction: What the research says.* Presentation at the first annual Tarleton State University Reading Conference, Stephenville, TX.

Durkin, D. (1984). Is there a match between what elementary teachers do and what basal reader manuals recommend? *The Reading Teacher, 37,* 734–745.

Durkin, D. (1987). *Teaching young children to read* (4th ed.). New York: Allyn & Bacon.

Durkin, D. (1989). *Teaching them to read* (5th ed.). New York: Allyn & Bacon.

Durrell, D. D. (1940). *Improvement of basic reading abilities.* New York: World Book.

Duthie, J. (1986). The web: A powerful tool for the teaching and evaluation of the expository essay. *The History and Social Science Teacher, 21,* 232–236.

Eastlund, J. (1980). Working with the language deficient child. *Music Educators Journal, 67*(3), 60–65.

Eckhoff, B. (1983). How reading affects children's writing. *Language Arts, 60*(5), 607–616.

Edelsky, C. (1988). Living in the author's world: Analyzing the author's craft. *The California Reader, 21,* 14–17.

Edelsky, C., Altwerger, B., & Flores, B. (1991). *Whole language: What's the difference?* Portsmouth, NH: Heinemann.

Eder, D. (1983). Ability grouping and student's academic self-concepts: A case study. *The Elementary School Journal, 84,* 149–161.

Educational Testing Service. (1988). *Who reads best?* Princeton, NJ: Educational Testing Service.

Ehri, L. C. (1984). How orthography alters spoken language competencies in children. In J. Downing & R. Valtin (Eds.), *Language awareness and learning to read* (pp. 118–147). New York: Springer-Verlag.

Ehri, L. C., & Sweet, J. (1991). Fingerpoint-reading of memorized text: What enables beginners to process the print? *Reading Research Quarterly, 26,* 442–462.

Ehri, L. C., & Wilce, L. C. (1980). The influence of orthography on readers' conceptualization of the phonemic structure of words. *Applied Psycholinguistics, 1,* 371–385.

Ehri, L. C., & Wilce, L. C. (1985). Movement into reading: Is the first stage of printed word learning visual or phonetic? *Reading Research Quarterly, 20,* 163–179.

Ekwall, E. E., & Shanker, J. L. (1989). *Teaching reading in the elementary school* (2nd ed.). Upper Saddle River, NJ: Merrill/Prentice Hall.

Elbow, P. (1994). Will the virtues of portfolios blind us to their potential dangers? In L. Black, D. Daiker, J. Sommers, & G. Stygall (Eds.), *New directions in portfolio assessment* (pp. 40–55). Portsmouth, NH: Boynton/Cook.

Eldredge, J. L. (1990). Increasing the performance of poor readers in the third grade with a group assisted strategy. *Journal of Educational Research, 84*(2), 69–77.

Eldredge, J. L., & Quinn, D. W. (1988). Increasing reading performance of low-achieving second graders with dyad reading groups. *Journal of Educational Research, 82,* 40–46.

Eldredge, J. L., Reutzel, D. R., & Hollingsworth, P. M. (1996, Summer). Comparing the effectiveness of two oral reading practices: Round-robin reading and the shared book experience. *Journal of Literacy Research, 28*(2), 201–225.

Ellis, A. K., & Fouts, J. T. (1993). *Research on educational innovations.* Princeton Junction, NJ: Eye on Education.

Ellison, C. (1989, January). PCs in the schools: An American tragedy. *PC/Computing, 96–104.*

Engelmann, S., & Bruner, E. C. (1995). *Reading mastery I: Presentation book C* (Rainbow Edition) Columbus, OH: Science Research Associates/Macmillan/McGraw-Hill.

Ericson, L., & Juliebo, M. F. (1998). *The phonological awareness handbook for kindergarten and primary teachers.* Newark, DE: International Reading Association.

Ervin, J. (1982). *How to have a successful parents and reading program: A practical guide.* New York: Allyn & Bacon.

Esch, M. (1991, February, 17). Whole language teaches reading. *The Daily Herald* (Provo, UT), p. D1.

Estes, T. H., & Vaughn, J. L. (1978). *Reading and learning in the content classroom.* Boston: Allyn & Bacon.

Fader, D. N. (1976). *The new hooked on books.* New York: Berkley.

Farr, R. (1991). *Portfolios: Assessment in the language arts.* ED334603.

Farr, R., & Tone, B. (1994). *Portfolio and performance assessment.* Fort Worth, TX: Harcourt Brace.

Farr, R., & Tulley, M. (1989). State level adoption of basal readers: Goals, processes, and recommendations. *Theory Into Practice, 28*(4), 248–253.

Farr, R., Tulley, M. A., & Powell, D. (1987). The evaluation and selection of basal readers. *The Elementary School Journal, 87,* 267–281.

Farrar, M. T. (1984). Asking better questions. *The Reading Teacher, 38,* 10–17.

Fay, L. (1965). Reading study skills: Math and science. In J. A. Figurel (Ed.), *Reading and inquiry.* Newark, DE: International Reading Association.

Felmlee, D., & Eder, D. (1983). Contextual effects in the classroom: The impact of ability groups on student attention. *Sociology of Education, 56,* 77–87.

Ferreiro, E., & Teberosky, A. (1982). *Literacy before schooling.* Portsmouth, NH: Heinemann.

Fisher-Nagel, H. (1987). *The life of a butterfly.* Minneapolis: Carolrhoda Books.

Fitzgerald, J. (1993). Literacy and students who are learning English as a second language. *The Reading Teacher, 46*(8), 638–647.

Fitzgerald, J. (1994). Crossing boundaries: What do second-language-learning theories say to reading and writing teachers of English-as-a-second-language learners? *Reading Horizons, 34*(4), 339–355.

Fitzgerald, J. (1995). English-as-a-second-language reading instruction in the United States: A research review. *Journal of Reading Behavior, 27*(2), 115–152.

Fleischman, S. (1986). *The whipping boy.* Mahwah, NJ: Troll Associates.

Flesch, R. (1955). *Why Johnny can't read.* New York: HarperCollins.

Flesch, R. (1979, November 1). Why Johnny still can't read. *Family Circle, 26,* 43–46.

Flesch, R. (1981). *Why Johnny still can't read.* New York: HarperCollins.

Flood, J., & Lapp, D. (1986). Types of texts: The match between what students read in basals and what they encounter in tests. *Reading Research Quarterly, 21,* 284–297.

Flynt, E. S., & Cooter, R. B., Jr. (1993). *The Flynt/Cooter reading inventory for the classroom.* Scottsdale, AZ: Gorsuch Scarisbrick.

Flynt, E. S., & Cooter, R. B., Jr. (1995). *The Flynt/Cooter reading inventory for the classroom* (2nd ed.). Scottsdale, AZ: Gorsuch Scarisbrick.

Flynt, E. S., & Cooter, R. B., Jr. (1999). *The Flynt/Cooter English * Español reading inventory.* Upper Saddle River, NJ: Merrill/Prentice Hall.

Follett, R. (1985). The school textbook adoption process. *Book Research Quarterly, 1,* 19–23.

Foorman, B. R., et al. (1997). Early intervention for children with reading problems: Study designs and preliminary findings. *Learning Disabilities: A Multidisciplinary Journal, 8*(1), 63–71.

Forbes, E. (1943). *Johnny Tremain.* Boston: Houghton Mifflin.

Fountas, I. C., & Pinnell, G. S. (1996). *Guided reading instruction: Good first teaching for all children.* Portsmouth, NH: Heinemann.

Fowler, G. L. (1982). Developing comprehension skills in primary students through the use of story frames. *The Reading Teacher, 36*(2), 176–179.

Fox, B. J. (1996). *Strategies for word identification: Phonics from a new perspective.* Upper Saddle River, NJ: Merrill/Prentice Hall.

Fox, P. (1973). *The slave dancer.* New York: Bradbury.

Fox, P. (1986). *The moonlight man.* New York: Bradbury.

Fredericks, A. D., & Rasinski, T. V. (1990). Working with parents: Involving the uninvolved: How to. *The Reading Teacher, 43*(6), 424–425.

Freeman, D. E., & Freeman, Y. S. (1994). *Between worlds: Access to second language acquisition.* Portsmouth, NH: Heinemann.

Freeman, Y. S., & Freeman, D. E. (1992). *Whole language for second language learners.* Portsmouth, NH: Heinemann.

Freppon, P. A., & Dahl, K. L. (1998). Balanced instruction: Insights and considerations. *Reading Research Quarterly, 33*(2), 240–251.

Fry, E. (1977). Fry's readability graph: Clarifications, validity, and extension to level 17. *Journal of Reading, 21,* 242–252.

Fry, E. (1980). The new instant word list. *The Reading Teacher, 34,* 284–289.

Fry, E. B., Polk, J. K., & Fountoukidis, D. (1984). *The reading teacher's book of lists.* Upper Saddle River, NJ: Prentice Hall.

Gahn, S. M. (1989). A practical guide for teaching writing in the content areas. *Journal of Reading, 33,* 525–531.

Gall, M. D., Ward, B. A., Berliner, D. C., Cahen, L. S., Crown, K. A., Elashoff, J. D., Stanton, G. C., & Winne, P. H. (1975). *The effects of teacher use of questioning techniques on student achievement and attitude.* San Francisco: Far West Laboratory for Educational Research and Development.

Gallant, M. G. (1986). *More fun with Dick and Jane.* New York: Penquin Books.

Gallup, G. (1969). *The Gallup poll.* New York: American Institute of Public Opinion.

Gamberg, R., Kwak, W., Hutchings, M., & Altheim, J. (1988). *Learning and loving it: Theme studies in the classroom.* Portsmouth, NH: Heinemann.

Gambrell, L. B. (1985). Dialogue journals: Reading-writing instruction. *The Reading Teacher, 38*(6), 512–515.

Gambrell, L. B., & Marnak, B. A. (1997). Incentives and intrinsic motivation to read. In J. T. Guthrie & A. Wigfield (Eds.), *Reading engagement: Motivating readers through integrated instruction*. Newark, DE: International Reading Association.

Gambrell, L. B., Pfeiffer, W., & Wilson, R. (1985). The effects of retelling upon reading comprehension and recall of text information. *Journal of Educational Research, 78,* 216–220.

Gambrell, L. B., Wilson, R. M., & Gnatt, W. N. (1981). Classroom observations of task-attending behaviors of good and poor readers. *Journal of Educational Research, 74,* 400–404.

Garcia, S. B., & Malkin, D. H. (1993, Fall). Toward defining programs and services for culturally and linguistically diverse learners in special education. *Teaching Exceptional Children,* 52–58.

Gardener, H. (1993). *Frames of mind: The theory of multiple intelligences.* New York: Basic Books.

Garza, C. L. (1990). *Cuadros de familia: Family pictures.* San Francisco: Children's Book Press.

Gates, A. I. (1921). An experimental and statistical study of reading and reading tests (in three parts). *Journal of Educational Psychology, 12,* 303–314, 378–391, 445–465.

Gates, A. I. (1937). The necessary mental age for beginning reading. *Elementary School Journal, 37,* 497–508.

Gates, A. I. (1961). Sex differences in reading ability. *Elementary School Journal, 61,* 431–434.

Gelman, R. G. (1976). *Why can't I fly?* New York: Scholastic, Inc.

Gelman, R. G. (1977). *More spaghetti, I say!* New York: Scholastic.

Gelman, R. G. (1985). *Cats and mice.* New York: Scholastic.

Gentry, R. (1987). *Spel . . . is a four-letter word.* Portsmouth, NH: Heinemann.

George, J. (1972). *Julie of the wolves.* New York: HarperCollins.

Gibson, E. J., & Levin, H. (1975). *The psychology of reading.* Cambridge, MA: MIT Press.

Gillet, J. W., & Temple, C. (1986). *Understanding reading problems: Assessment and instruction.* Boston: Little, Brown.

Gipe, J. P. (1980). Use of a relevant context helps kids learn new word meanings. *The Reading Teacher, 33,* 398–402.

Gipe, J. P. (1987). *Corrective reading techniques for the classroom teacher.* Scottsdale, AZ: Gorsuch Scarisbrick.

Glatthorn, A. A. (1993). Outcome-based education: Reform and the curriculum process. *Journal of Curriculum and Supervision, 8*(4), 354–363.

Glazer, S. M. (1989). Oral language and literacy development. In D. S. Strickland & L. M. Morrow (Eds.), *Emerging literacy: Young children learn to read and write* (pp. 16–26). Newark, DE: International Reading Association.

Glazer, S. M., & Brown, C. S. (1993). *Portfolios and beyond: Collaborative assessment in reading and writing.* Norwood, MA: Christopher-Gordon.

Gleason, J. B. (1989). *The development of language* (2nd ed.) Upper Saddle River, NJ: Merrill/Prentice Hall.

Goetz, E. T., Reynolds, R. E., Schallert, D. L., & Radin, D. I. (1983). Reading in perspective: What real cops and pretend burglars look for in a story. *Journal of Educational Psychology, 75*(4), 500–510.

Golden, J. M. (1992). The growth of story meaning. *Language Arts, 69*(1), 22–27.

Good, T. (1979). Teacher effectiveness in the elementary school. *The Journal of Teacher Education, 30,* 52–64.

Goodman, K., Shannon, P., Freeman, Y., & Murphy, S. (1988). *Report card on basal readers.* Katona, NY: Owen.

Goodman, K., Smith, E. B., Meredith, R., & Goodman, Y. M. (1987). *Language and thinking in school: A whole-language curriculum.* Katona, NY: Owen.

Goodman, K. S. (1967). Reading: A psycholinguistic guessing game. *Journal of the Reading Specialist, 6,* 126–135.

Goodman, K. S. (1968). *Study of children's behavior while reading orally* (Final Report, Project No. S 425). Washington, DC: U.S. Department of Health, Education, and Welfare.

Goodman, K. S. (1976). Behind the eye: What happens in reading. In H. Singer & R. B. Ruddell (Eds.), *Theoretical models and processes of reading* (2nd ed., pp. 470–496). Newark, DE: International Reading Association.

Goodman, K. S. (1985). Unity in reading. In H. Singer & R. B. Ruddell (Eds.), *Theoretical models and processes of reading* (3rd ed.). Newark, DE: International Reading Association.

Goodman, K. S. (1986). *What's whole in whole language?* Ontario, Canada: Scholastic.

Goodman, K. S. (1987). Look what they've done to Judy Blume!: The "basalization" of children's literature. *The New Advocate, 1*(1), 29–41.

Goodman, K. S., & Goodman, Y. M. (1983). Reading and writing relationships: Pragmatic functions. *Language Arts, 60*(5), 590–599.

Goodman, Y. M. (1986). Children coming to know literacy. In W. H. Teale & E. Sulzby (Eds.), *Emergent literacy: Writing and reading* (pp. 1–14). Norwood, NJ: Ablex.

Goodman, Y. M., & Altwerger, B. (1981). *Print awareness in preschool children: A study of the development of literacy in preschool children.* Occasional paper, Program in Language and Literacy. Tucson, AZ: University of Arizona.

Gordon, C. J., & Braun, C. (1983). Using story schema as an aid to reading and writing. *The Reading Teacher, 37*(2), 116–121.

Gordon, N. (Ed.). (1984). *Classroom experiences: The writing process in action.* Exeter, NH: Heinemann.

Goswami, U., & Bryant, P. (1990). *Phonological skills and learning to read.* East Sussex, UK: Earlbaum.

Goswami, U., & Mead, F. (1992). Onset and rime awareness and analogies in reading. *Reading Research Quarterly, 27*(2), 152–163.

Gough, P. B. (1972). One second of reading. In J. F. Kavanagh & I. G. Mattingly (Eds.), *Language by ear and by eye.* Cambridge, MA: MIT Press.

Gove, M. K. (1983). Clarifying teacher's beliefs about reading. *The Reading Teacher, 37*(3), 261–268.

Graves, D. H. (1983). *Writing: Teachers and children at work.* Portsmouth, NH: Heinemann.

Greaney, V. (1994). World illiteracy. In F. Lehr & J. Osborn (Eds.), *Reading, language, and literacy: Instruction for the twenty-first century.* Hillsdale, NJ: Erlbaum.

Greene, F. P. (1973). *OPIN.* Unpublished paper, McGill University, Montreal, Quebec, Canada.

Griffith, P. L., & Olson, M. W. (1992). Phonemic awareness helps beginning readers break the code. *The Reading Teacher, 45,* 516–523.

Groff, P. J. (1984). Resolving the letter name controversy. *The Reading Teacher, 37*(4), 384–389.

Groom (1986). *Forrest Gump.* New York: Pocket Books.

Gross, A. D. (1978). The relationship between sex differences and reading ability in an Israeli kibbutz system. In D. Feitelson (Ed.), *Cross-cultural perspectives on reading and reading research* (pp. 72–88). Newark, DE: International Reading Association.

Guilfoile, E. (1957). *Nobody listens to Andrew.* Cleveland, OH: Modern Curriculum Press.

Gunderson, L. (1991). *ESL literacy instruction: A guidebook to theory and practice.* Upper Saddle River, NJ: Prentice Hall.

Guszak, F. J. (1967). Teacher questioning and reading. *The Reading Teacher, 21,* 227–234.

Guthrie, J. T. (1982). Effective teaching practices. *The Reading Teacher, 35*(7), 766–768.

Guthrie, J. T., & McCann, A. D. (1997). Characteristics of classrooms that promote motivations and strategies for learning. In J. T. Guthrie & A. Wigfield (Eds.), *Reading engagement: Motivating readers through integrated instruction.* Newark, DE: International Reading Association.

Guthrie, J. T., Seifert, M., Burnham, N. A., & Caplan, R. J. (1974). The maze technique to assess and monitor reading comprehension. *The Reading Teacher, 28*(2), 161–168.

Gwynne, F. (1970). *A chocolate moose for dinner.* New York: Windmill Books.

Gwynne, F. (1976). *The king who rained.* New York: Windmill Books.

Hagerty, P. (1992). *Reader's workshop: Real reading.* New York: Scholastic.

Haggard, M. R. (1986). The vocabulary self-collection strategy: Using student interest and world knowledge to enhance vocabulary growth. *Journal of Reading, 29*(7), 634–642.

Hagood, B. F. (1997). Reading and writing with help from story grammar. *Teaching Exceptional Children, 29*(4), 10–14.

Hall, M. A. (1978). *The language experience approach for teaching reading: A research perspective.* Newark, DE: International Reading Association.

Hall, M. A. (1981). *Teaching reading as a language experience* (3rd ed.). Upper Saddle River, NJ: Merrill/Prentice Hall.

Hall, N. (1987). *The emergence of literacy.* Portsmouth, NH: Heinemann.

Hall, R. (1984). *Sniglets.* Upper Saddle River, NJ: Merrill/Prentice Hall.

Haller, E. J., & Waterman, M. (1985). The criteria of reading group assignments. *The Reading Teacher, 38,* 772–781.

Halliday, M. A. K. (1975). *Learning how to mean: Explorations in the development of language.* London: Edward Arnold.

Hallinan, M. T., & Sorensen, A. B. (1985). Ability grouping and student friendships. *American Educational Research Journal, 22,* 485–499.

Hammill, D., & Larsen, S. C. (1974). The relationship of selected auditory perceptual skills and reading ability. *Journal of Learning Disabilities, 7,* 429–435.

Hansen, J. (1987). *When writers read.* Portsmouth, NH: Heinemann.

Harkrader, M. A., & Moore, R. (1997). Literature preferences of fourth graders. *Reading Research and Instruction, 36*(4), 325–339.

Harp, B. (1988). When the principal asks: "Why are your kids singing during reading time?" *The Reading Teacher, 41*(4), 454–457.

Harp, B. (1989a). What do we do in the place of ability grouping? *The Reading Teacher, 42,* 534–535.

Harp, B. (1989b). When the principal asks: "Why don't you ask comprehension questions?" *The Reading Teacher, 42*(8), 638–639.

Harris, A. J., & Sipay, E. R. (1990). *How to increase reading ability* (9th ed.). New York: Longman.

Harris, T., Matteoni, L., Anderson, L., & Creekmore, M. (1975). *Keys to reading.* Oklahoma City: Economy.

Harris, T. L., & Hodges, R. E. (Eds.). (1995). *The literacy dictionary: The vocabulary of reading and writing.* Newark, DE: International Reading Association.

Harste, J. C., & Burke, C. L. (1977). A new hypothesis for reading teacher research: Both the teaching and learning of reading are theoretically based. In Pearson, D. P. (Ed.). *Reading: Theory, research, and practice* (pp. 32–40). Clemson, SC: National Reading Conference.

Harste, J. C., Short, K. G., & Burke, C. (1988). *Creating classrooms for authors: The reading writing connection.* Portsmouth, NH: Heinemann.

Harste, J. C., Woodward, V. A., & Burke, C. L. (1984). *Language stories and literacy lessons.* Portsmouth, NH: Heinemann.

Harwayne, S. (1992). *Lasting impressions.* Portsmouth, NH: Heinemann.

Hasbrouck, J. E., & Tindal, G. (1992). Curriculum-based oral reading fluency for students in grades 2 through 5. *Teaching Exceptional Children, 24*(3), 41–44.

Hawking, S. W. (1988). *A brief history of time: From the big bang to black holes.* Toronto: Bantam.

Heald-Taylor, G. (1989). *The administrator's guide to whole language.* Katona, NY: Owen.

Heald-Taylor, G. (1991). *Whole language strategies for ESL students.* San Diego, CA: Dominie Press.

Heath. (no date). *Quill* [computer program]. Lexington, MA: Heath.

Heathington, B. S. (1990). Test review: Concepts about print test. In R. B. Cooter, Jr., (Ed.), *The teacher's guide to reading tests* (pp. 110–114). Scottsdale, AZ: Gorsuch Scarisbrick.

Heide, F. P., & Gilliland, J. H. (1990). *Day of Ahmed's secret.* New York: Lothrop, Lee & Shepard Books.

Heilman, A. W., Blair, T. R., & Rupley, W. H. (1990). *Principles and practices of teaching reading.* Upper Saddle River, NJ: Merrill/Prentice Hall.

Henk, W. A., & Holmes, B. C. (1988). Effects of content-related attitude on the comprehension and retention of expository text. *Reading Psychology, 9*(3), 203–225.

Hennings, K. (1974). Drama reading, an on-going classroom activity at the elementary school level. *Elementary English, 51,* 48–51.

Henwood, C. (1988). *Frogs* (Barrie Watts, Photographer). London, NY: Franklin Watts.

Herber, H. L. (1978). *Teaching reading in the content areas* (2nd ed.). Upper Saddle River, NJ: Prentice Hall.

Heymsfeld, C. R. (1989, March). Filling the hole in whole language. *Educational Leadership,* pp. 65–68.

Hiebert, E. (1978). Preschool children's understanding of written language. *Child Development, 49,* 1231–1241.

Hiebert, E. (1981). Developmental patterns and interrelationships of preschool children's print awareness. *Reading Research Quarterly, 16,* 236–260.

Hiebert, E. H. (1983). An examination of ability grouping for reading instruction. *Reading Research Quarterly, 18,* 231–255.

Hiebert, E. H., & Colt, J. (1989). Patterns of literature-based reading. *The Reading Teacher, 43*(1), 14–20.

Hiebert, E., & Ham, D. (1981). *Young children and environmental print.* Paper presented at the annual meeting of the National Reading Conference, Dallas, TX.

Hill, B., & Ruptic, C. (1994). *Practical aspects of authentic assessment: Putting the pieces together.* Norwood, MA: Christopher-Gordon.

Hill, S. (1990a). *Raps and rhymes.* Armadale, Victoria, Australia: Eleanor Curtain.

Hill, S. (1990b). *Readers theatre: Performing the text.* Armadale, Victoria, Australia: Eleanor Curtain.

Hirsch, E. D. (1987). *Cultural literacy: What every American needs to know.* Boston: Houghton Mifflin.

Hirschfelder, A. B., & Singer, B. R. (1992). *Rising voices: Writing of young Native Americans.* New York: Scribner's.

Hoffman, J. V. (1987). Rethinking the role of oral reading in basal instruction. *The Elementary School Journal, 87*(3), 367–374.

Hoffman, J. V., McCarthey, S. J., Abbott, J., Christian, C., Corman, L., Curry, C., Dressman, M., Elliott, B., Matherne, D., & Stahle, D. (1994). So what's new in the new basals? A focus on first grade. *Journal of Reading Behavior, 26*(1), 47–73.

Hoffman, J. V., & Segel, K. W. (1982). *Oral reading instruction: A century of controversy.* (ERIC Document Reproduction Service No. ED 239 277)

Hoffman, M. (1991). *Amazing grace.* New York: Dial Books for Young Readers.

Holdaway, D. (1979). *The foundations of literacy.* Exeter, NH: Heinemann.

Holdaway, D. (1981). Shared book experience: Teaching reading using favorite books. *Theory Into Practice, 21,* 293–300.

Holdaway, D. (1984). *Stability and change in literacy learning.* Portsmouth, NH: Heinemann.

Hollingsworth, P. H. (1978). An experimental approach to the impress method of teaching reading. *The Reading Teacher, 31,* 624–626.

Hollingsworth, P. M., & Reutzel, D. R. (1988). Get a grip on comprehension. *Reading Horizons, 29*(1), 71–78.

Holmes, J. A. (1953). *The substrata-factor theory of reading.* Berkeley, CA: California Book.

Homan, S. P., Klesius, J. P., & Hite, C. (1993). Effects of repeated readings and non-repetitive strategies on students' fluency and comprehension. *Journal of Educational Research, 87*(2), 94–99.

Hopkins, C. (1979). Using every-pupil response techniques in reading instruction. *The Reading Teacher, 33,* 173–175.

Hoskisson, K., & Tompkins, G. E. (1987). *Language arts: Content and teaching strategies.* Upper Saddle River, NJ: Merrill/Prentice Hall.

Houston, J. (1977). *Frozen fire.* New York: Atheneum.

Huck, C. S., Helper, S., & Hickman, J. (1987). *Children's literature in the elementary school.* New York: Holt, Rinehart and Winston.

Huck, C. S., & Kuhn, D. Y. (1968). *Children's literature in the elementary school.* New York: Holt, Rinehart and Winston.

Hughes, T. O. (1975). *Sentence-combining: A means of increasing reading comprehension.* Kalamazoo: Western Michigan University, Department of English.

Hull, M. A. (1989). *Phonics for the teacher of reading.* Upper Saddle River, NJ: Merrill/Prentice Hall.

Hunt, L. C. (1970). Effect of self-selection, interest, and motivation upon independent, instructional, and frustrational levels. *Reading Teacher, 24,* 146–151.

Hunter, M. (1984). Knowing, teaching and supervising. In P. L. Hosford (Ed.), *Using what we know about teaching.* Alexandria, VA: Association for Supervision and Curriculum Development.

Hymes, D. (Ed.). (1964). *Language in culture and society.* New York: HarperCollins.

Jachym, N. K., Allington, R. L., & Broikou, K. A. (1989). Estimating the cost of seatwork. *The Reading Teacher, 43,* 30–37.

Jacobs, H. H., & Borland, J. H. (1986). The interdisciplinary concept model: Theory and practice. *Gifted Child Quarterly, 30*(4), 159–163.

Jaffe, N. (1993). *The uninvited guest and other Jewish holiday tales.* New York: Scholastic.

Jenkins, R. (1990). *Whole language in Australia.* Scholastic Co. workshop at Brigham Young University, Provo, UT.

Jobe, F. W. (1976). *Screening vision in schools.* Newark, DE: International Reading Association.

Johns, J. L. (1980). First graders' concepts about print. *Reading Research Quarterly, 15,* 529–549.

Johns, J. L. (1986). Students: Perceptions of reading: Thirty years of inquiry. In D. B. Yaden, Jr. & S. Templeton (Eds.), *Awareness and beginning literacy: Conceptualizing what it means to read and write* (pp. 31–40). Portsmouth, NH: Heinemann.

Johns, J. L. , & Ellis, D. W. (1976). Reading: Children tell it like it is. *Reading World, 16,* 115–128.

Johns, J. L., & Johns, A. L. (1971). How do children in the elementary school view the reading process? *The Michigan Reading Journal, 5,* 44–53.

Johns, J. L., & Lunn, M. K. (1983). The informal reading inventory: 1910–1980. *Reading World, 23*(1), 8–18.

Johnson, D. (1989). *Pressing problems in world literacy: The plight of the homeless.* Paper presented at the 23rd annual meeting of the Utah Council of the International Reading Association, Salt Lake City, UT.

Johnson, D., & Pearson, P. D. (1984). *Teaching reading vocabulary.* New York: Holt, Rinehart and Winston.

Johnson, D. D. (1973). Sex differences in reading across cultures. *Reading Research Quarterly, 9*(1), 67–86.

Johnson, D. D., & Baumann, J. F. (1984). Word identification. In P. D. Pearson (Ed.), *Handbook of reading research* (pp. 583–608). New York: Longman.

Johnson, D. D., & Pearson. P. D. (1975). Skills management systems: A critique. *The Reading Teacher, 28,* 757–764.

Johnson, D. D., & Pearson, P. D. (1984). *Teaching reading vocabulary.* New York: Holt, Rinehart and Winston.

Johnson, D. W. (1976). *Jack and the beanstalk* (D. William Johnson, Illustrator). Boston: Little, Brown.

Johnson, D. W., Maruyama, G., Johnson, R. T., Nelson, D., & Skon, L. (1981). Effects of cooperative, competitive and individualistic goal structures on achievement: A meta-analysis. *Psychological Bulletin, 89,* 47–62.

Johnson, T. D., & Louis, D. R. (1987). *Literacy through literature.* Portsmouth, NH: Heinemann.

Jones, M. B., & Nessel, D. D. (1985). Enhancing the curriculum with experience stories. *The Reading Teacher, 39,* 18–23.

Jongsma, K. S. (1989). Questions & answers: Portfolio assessment. *The Reading Teacher, 43*(3), 264–265.

Jongsma, K. S. (1990). Collaborative Learning (Questions and Answers). *The Reading Teacher, 43*(4), 346–347.

Joseph, D. G., Flynt, E. S., & Cooter, R. B., Jr. (1987, March). *Diagnosis and correction of reading difficulties: A new model.* Paper presented at the National Association of School Psychologists annual convention, New Orleans, LA.

Juster, N. (1961). *The phantom tollbooth.* Random House.

Kagan, J. (1966). Reflection-impulsivity: The generality and dynamics of conceptual tempo. *Journal of Abnormal Psychology, 71,* 17–24.

Kang, H. W. (1994). Helping second language readers learn from content area text through collaboration and support. *The Journal of Reading, 37*(8), 646–652.

Karlsen, B., & Gardner, E. F. (1984). *Stanford diagnostic reading test* (3rd ed.). New York: Harcourt Brace.

Kaufman, A., & Kaufman, N. (1985). *Kaufman test of educational achievement.* Circle Pines, MN: American Guidance Service.

Kearsley, R. (1973). The newborn's response to auditory stimulation: A demonstration of orienting and defensive behavior. *Child Development, 44,* 582–590.

Keegan, M. (1991). *Pueblo boy: Growing up in two worlds.* New York: Cobblehill Books.

Keene, E. O., & Zimmerman, S. (1997). *Mosaic of thought.* Portsmouth, NH: Heinemann.

Keith, S. (1981). *Politics of textbook selection* (Research report No. 81-AT). Stanford, CA: Stanford University School of Education, Institute for Research on School Finance and Governance.

Kemp, M. (1987). *Watching children read and write.* Portsmouth, NH: Heinemann.

Kessen, W., Levine, J., & Wendrich, K. (1979). The imitation of pitch in infants. *Infant Behavior and Development, 2,* 93–100.

Killilea, M. (1954). *Karen.* New York: Dodd, Mead.

Kirsch, I. S., Jungeblut, A., Jenkins, L., & Kolstad, A. (1993). *Adult literacy in America: A first look at the results of the national adult literacy survey.* Washington, DC: National Center for Educational Statistics.

Klare, G. R. (1963). Assessing readability. *Reading Research Quarterly, 10,* 62–102.

Koskinen, P., Wilson, R., & Jensema, C. (1985). Closed-captioned television: A new tool for reading instruction. *Reading World, 24,* 1–7.

Koskinen, P. S., Blum, I. H., Bisson, S. A., Phillips, S. M., Creamer, T. S., & Baker, T. K. (1999). Shared reading, books, and audiotapes: Supporting diverse students in school and at home. *The Reading Teacher, 52*(5), 430–444.

Kownslar, A. O. (1977). *People and our world: A study of world history.* New York: Holt, Rinehart and Winston.

Kozol, J. (1985). *Illiterate America.* New York: New American Library.

Krashen, S. (1982). *Principles and practices in second language acquisition.* New York: Pergamon Press.

Krashen, S. (1992). *The power of reading.* Englewood, CO: Libraries Unlimited.

Krashen, S. (1993). *The power of reading: Insights from the research.* Englewood, CO: Libraries Unlimited.

Krashen, S., & Biber, D. (1988). *On course.* Sacramento, CA: CABE.

Krauss, R. (1945). *The carrot seed* (Crockett Johnson, Illustrator). New York: Scholastic.

Kuchinskas, G., & Radencich, M. C. (1986). *The semantic mapper.* Gainesville, FL: Teacher Support Software.

Kulik, C. C., & Kulik, J. A. (1982). Effects of ability grouping on secondary students: A meta-analysis of evaluation findings. *American Educational Research Journal, 19,* 415–428.

LaBerge, D., & Samuels, S. J. (1974). Toward a theory of automatic information processing in reading. *Cognitive Psychology, 6,* 293–323.

LaBerge, D., & Samuels, S. J. (1985). Toward a theory of automatic information processing in reading. In H. Singer & R. B. Ruddell (Eds.), *Theoretical models and processes of reading* (pp. 689–718). Newark, DE: International Reading Association.

Lamme, L. L., & Hysmith (1991). One school's adventure into portfolio assessment. *Language Arts, 68,* 629–640.

Lamoreaux, L., & Lee, D. M. (1943). *Learning to read through experience.* New York: Appleton-Century-Crofts.

Langer, J. (1981). From theory to practice: A prereading plan. *Journal of Reading, 25,* 152–156.

Langer, J. A. (1984). Examining background knowledge and text comprehension. *Reading Research Quarterly, 19,* 468–481.

Langer, P., Kalk, J. M., & Searls, D. T. (1984). Age of admission and trends in achievement: A comparison of blacks and Caucasians. *American Educational Research Journal, 21,* 61–78.

Larsen, N. (1994). *The publisher's chopping block: What happens to children's trade books when they are published in a basal reading series?* Unpublished master's project, Brigham Young University.

Lass, B., & Davis, B. (1985). *The remedial reading handbook.* Upper Saddle River, NJ: Prentice Hall.

Lathlaen, P. (1993). A meeting of minds: Teaching using biographies. *The Reading Teacher, 46*(6), 529–531.

Law, B., & Eckes, M. (1990). *The more than just surviving handbook: ESL for every classroom teacher.* Winnipeg, Canada: Peguis.

Leinhardt, G., Zigmond, N., & Cooley, W. (1981). Reading instruction and its effects. *American Educational Research Journal, 18,* 343–361.

Lemann, N. (1997, November). The reading wars. *The Atlantic Monthly, 280*(5), 128–134.

L'Engle, M. (1962). *A wrinkle in time.* New York: Dell.

Lenneberg, E. H. (1964). *New directions in the study of language.* Cambridge, MA: MIT Press.

Levin, J. R., Johnson, D. D., Pittelman, S. D., Levin, K., Shriberg, L. K., Toms-Bronowski, S., & Hayes, B. (1984). A comparison of semantic- and mnemonic-based vocabulary-learning strategies. *Reading Psychology, 5,* 1–15.

Levin, J. R., Levin, M. E., Glasman, L. D., & Nordwall, M. B. (1992). Mnemonic vocabulary instruction: Additional effectiveness evidence. *Contemporary Educational Psychology, 17,* 156–174.

Levine, S. S. (1976). *The effect of transformational sentence-combining exercises on the reading comprehension and written composition of third-grade children.* Unpublished doctoral dissertation, Hofstra University.

Lewis, C. S. (1961). *The lion, the witch, and the wardrobe.* New York: Macmillan.

Liberman, I. Y., Shankweiler, D., Liberman, A., Fowler, C., & Fischer, F. (1977). Phonetic segmentation and decoding in the beginning reader. In A. S. Reber & D. L. Scarborough (Eds.), *Toward a psychology of reading* (pp. 207–225). Hillsdale, NJ: Erlbaum.

Lima, C., & Lima, J. (1993). *A to zoo: A subject access to children's picture books.* New York: Bowker.

Lindsay, P. H., & Norman, D. A. (1977). *Human information processing: An introduction to psychology.* New York: Academic Press.

Lipson, M. Y. (1983). The influence of religious affiliation on children's memory for text information. *Reading Research Quarterly, 18*(4), 448–457.

Lipson, M. Y. (1984). Some unexpected issues in prior knowledge and comprehension. *The Reading Teacher, 37*(8), 760–764.

Lisle, J. T. (1989). *Afternoon of the elves.* New York: Franklin Watts.

Littlejohn, C. (1988). *The lion and the mouse.* New York: Dial Books for Young Readers.

Livingston, N., & Birrell, J. R. (1994). Learning about cultural diversity through literature. *BYU Children's Book Review, 54*(5), 1–6.

Lobel, A. (1981). *On Market Street* (Pictures by Anita Lobel). New York: Scholastic.

Lobel, A. (1983). *Fables.* New York: Harper & Row.

Lock, S. (1980). *Hubert hunts his hum* (J. Newnham, Illustrator). Sydney, Australia: Ashton Scholastic.

Lomax, R. G., & McGee, L. M. (1987). Young children's concepts about print and reading: Toward a model of word reading acquisition. *Reading Research Quarterly, 22*(2), 237–256.

Loughlin, C. E., & Martin, M. D. (1987). *Supporting literacy: Developing effective learning environments.* New York: Teachers College Columbia Press.

Lowery, L. F., & Grafft, W. (1967). Paperback books and reading attitudes. *The Reading Teacher, 21*(7), 618–623.

Lyman, F. (1988). Think-Pair-Share, Wait time two, and on . . . *Mid-Atlantic Association for Cooperation in Education Cooperative News, 2,* 1.

Lyon, G. R. (1997). Statement of G. Reid Lyon to The Committee on Education and the Workforce, U.S. House of Representatives (July 19, 1997). Washington, DC.

Lyon, G. R. (1998). Why reading is not a natural process. *Educational Leadership, 55*(6), 14–18.

Lyon, R. (1977). Auditory-perceptual training: The state of the art. *Journal of Learning Disabilities, 10,* 564–572.

MacGinitie, W. H. (1969). Evaluating readiness for learning to read: A critical review and evaluation of research. *Reading Research Quarterly, 4,* 396–410.

MacGinitie, W. H., & MacGinitie, R. K. (1989). *Gates-MacGinitie reading tests, third edition.* Chicago: Riverside.

Macmillan/McGraw-Hill. (1993). *Macmillan/McGraw-Hill reading/language: A new view.* New York: Author.

Manarino-Leggett, P., & Salomon, P. A. (1989, April–May). *Cooperation vs. competition: Techniques for keeping your classroom alive but not endangered.* Paper presented at the thirty-fourth annual convention of the International Reading Association, New Orleans, LA.

Mandler, J. M., & Johnson, N. S. (1977). Remembrance of things parsed: Story structure and recall. *Cognitive Psychology, 9,* 111–151.

Manzo, A. V. (1969). The request procedure. *The Journal of Reading, 13,* 123–126.

Manzo, A. V., & Manzo, U. C. (1990). *Content area reading: A heuristic approach.* Upper Saddle River, NJ: Merrill/Prentice Hall.

Marchionini, G. (1988). Hypermedia and learning: Freedom and chaos. *Educational Technology, 28,* 8–12.

Martin, B. (1990). *Brown Bear, Brown Bear, What do you see?* New York: Henry Holt.

Martin, B. (1991). *Polar Bear, Polar Bear, What do you hear?* New York: Henry Holt.

Martin, B., & Archaumbalt, J. (1987). *Knots on a counting rope.* New York: Holt, Rinehart and Winston.

Martin, J. H. (1987). *Writing to read* [Computer program]. Boca Raton, FL: IBM.

Martinez, M. (1993). Motivating dramatic story reenactments. *The Reading Teacher, 46*(8), 682–688.

Martinez, M., & Nash, M. F. (1990). Bookalogues: Talking about children's literature. *Language Arts, 67,* 576–580.

Martorella, P. H. (1985). *Elementary social studies.* Boston: Little, Brown.

Marzano, R. J. (1993–1994). When two world views collide. *Educational Leadership, 51*(4), 6–11.

Marzollo, J., & Marzollo, C. (1982). *Jed's junior space patrol: A science fiction easy to read.* New York: Dial.

Mason, J. (1983). An examination of reading instruction in third and fourth grades. *The Reading Teacher, 36*(9), 906–913.

Mason, J. M. (1980). When do children begin to read: An exploration of four-year-old children's letter and word reading competencies. *Reading Research Quarterly, 15,* 203–227.

Masonheimer, P. E., Drum, P. A., & Ehri, L. C. (1984). Does environmental print identification lead children into word reading? *Journal of Reading Behavior, 16,* 257–271.

Math, I. (1981). *Wires and watts: Understanding and using electricity.* New York: Charles Scribner's Sons.

Mathes, P. G. (1997). Cooperative story mapping. *Remedial and Special Education, 18*(1), 20–27.

Mathes, P. G., Simmons, D. C., & Davis, B. I. (1992). Assisted reading techniques for developing reading fluency. *Reading Research and Instruction, 31*(4), 70–77.

Mathewson, G. C. (1985). Toward a comprehensive model of affect in the reading process. In H. Singer & R. B. Ruddell (Eds.), *Theoretical models and processes of reading* (3rd ed., pp. 841–856). Newark, DE: International Reading Association.

Mathewson, G. C. (1994). Model of attitude influence upon reading and learning to read. In H. Singer & R. B. Ruddell (Eds.), *Theoretical models and processes of reading* (4th ed., pp. 1131–1161). Newark, DE: International Reading Association.

Maxim, G. (1989). *The very young: Guiding children from infancy through the early years* (3rd ed.). Upper Saddle River, NJ: Merrill/Prentice Hall.

May, F. B., & Elliot, S. B. (1978). *To help children read: Mastery performance modules for teachers in training* (2nd ed.). Upper Saddle River, NJ: Merrill/Prentice Hall.

Mayer, M. (1976a). *Ah-choo.* New York: Dial Books.

Mayer, M. (1976b). *Hiccup.* New York: Dial Books.

McCallum, R. D. (1988). Don't throw the basals out with the bath water. *The Reading Teacher, 42,* 204–209.

McCarthey, S. J., Hoffman, J. V., Christian, C., Corman, L., Elliott, B., Matherne, D., & Stahle, D. (1994). Engaging the new basal readers. *Reading Research and Instruction, 33*(3), 233–256.

McCormick, C. E., & Mason, J. (1986). Intervention procedures for increasing preschool children's interest in and knowledge about reading. In W. H. Teale & E. Sulzby (Eds.), *Emergent literacy: Writing and reading* (pp. 90–115). Norwood, NJ: Ablex Publishing.

McCormick, S. (1995). *Instructing students who have literacy problems.* Upper Saddle River, NJ: Merrill/Prentice Hall.

McCracken, R. A., & McCracken, M. J. (1978). Modeling is the key to sustained reading. *Reading Teacher, 31,* 406–408.

McDermott, G. (1993). *Raven: Trickster tale from the Pacific Northwest.* San Diego, CA: Harcourt Brace.

McGee, L. M., & Richgels, D. J. (1996). *Literacy's beginnings: Supporting young readers and writers* (2nd ed.). Boston: Allyn & Bacon.

McGee, L. M., Lomax, R. G., & Head, M. H. (1988). Young children's written language knowledge: What environmental and functional print reading reveals. *Journal of Reading Behavior, 20*(2), 99–118.

McGee, L. M., Ratliff, J. L., Sinex, A., Head, M., & LaCroix, K. (1984). Influence of story schema and concept of story on children's story compositions. In J. A. Niles & L. A. Harris (Eds.), *Thirty-third yearbook of the National Reading Conference* (pp. 270–277). Rochester, NY: Natonal Reading Conference.

McGuire, F. N. (1984). How arts instruction affects reading and language: Theory and research. *The Reading Teacher, 37*(9), 835–839.

McInnes, J. (1983). *Networks.* Toronto, Canada: Nelson of Canada.

McKee, D. (1990). *Elmer.* London: Red Fox.

McKeown, M. G., & Beck, I. L. (1988). Learning vocabulary: Different ways for different goals. *Remedial and Special Education, 9*(1), 42–52.

McKissack, P. C. (1986). *Flossie & the fox.* New York: Dial Books for Young Readers.

McKuen, R. (1990). Ten books on CD ROM. *MacWorld, 7*(12), 217–218.

McNeil, J. D. (1987). *Reading comprehension* (2nd ed.). Glenview, IL: Scott, Foresman.

McTighe, J., & Lyman, F. T. (1988). Cueing thinking in the classroom: The promise of theory-embedded tools. *Educational Leadership, 45*(7), 18–24.

Meade, E. L. (1973). The first R-A point of view. *Reading World, 12,* 169–180.

MECC. (1984). *Writing a narrative* [computer program]. St. Paul, MN: Minnesota Educational Computing Consortium.

Menyuk, P. (1988). *Language development knowledge and use.* Glenview, IL: Scott, Foresman/Little, Brown College Division.

Merrill Mathematics (Grade 5). (1985). Upper Saddle River, NJ: Merrill/Prentice Hall.

Merrill Science (Grade 3). (1989). Upper Saddle River, NJ: Merrill/Prentice Hall.

Meyer, B., Brandt, D., & Bluth, G. (1980). Use of top-level structure in text for reading comprehension of ninth-grade students. *Reading Research Quarterly, 16,* 72–103.

Meyer, B. J. (1979). Organizational patterns in prose and their use in reading. In M. L. Kamil & A. J. Moe (Eds.), *Reading research: Studies and applications* (pp. 109–117). Twenty-eighth Yearbook of the National Reading Conference.

Meyer, B. J. F., & Freedle, R. O. (1984). Effects of discourse type on recall. *American Educational Research Journal, 21*(1), 121–143.

Mezynski, K. (1983). Issues concerning the acquisition of knowledge: Effects of vocabulary training on reading comprehension. *Review of Educational Research, 53*(2), 253–279.

Miller, B. F., Rosenberg, E. B., & Stackowski, B. L. (1971). *Investigating your health.* Boston: Houghton Mifflin.

Mindplay. (1990). *Author! Author!* Danvers, MA: Methods and Solutions.

Moe, A. J., & Irwin, J. W. (1986). Cohesion, coherence, and comprehension. In J. W. Irwin (Ed.), *Understanding and teaching cohesion comprehension* (pp. 3–8). Newark, DE: International Reading Association.

Moffett, J. (1983). *Teaching the universe of discourse.* Boston: Houghton Mifflin.

Moffett, J., & Wagner, B. J. (1976). *Student-centered language arts and reading K–13. A handbook for teachers* (2nd ed.). Boston: Houghton Mifflin.

Monjo, F. N. (1970). *The drinking gourd.* New York: HarperCollins.

Mooney, M. E. (1990). *Reading to, with, and by children.* Katonah, NY: Owen.

Moore, M. A. (1991). Electronic dialoguing: An avenue to literacy. *The Reading Teacher, 45*(4), 280–286.

Morphett, M. V., & Washburne, C. (1931). When should children begin to read? *Elementary School Journal, 31,* 496–503.

Morrow, L. M. (1984). Reading stories to young children: Effects of story structure and traditional questioning strategies on comprehension. *Journal of Reading Behavior, 16,* 273–288.

Morrow, L. M. (1985). Retelling stories: A strategy for improving children's comprehension, concept of story structure and oral language complexity. *Elementary School Journal, 85,* 647–661.

Morrow, L. M. (1988a). Retelling as a diagnostic tool. In S. M. Glazer, L. W. Searfoss, & L. Gentile (Eds.), *Re-examining reading diagnosis: New trends and procedures in classrooms and clinics* (pp. 128–149). Newark, DE: International Reading Association.

Morrow, L. M. (1988b). Young children's responses to one-to-one story reading in school settings. *The Reading Teacher, 23*(1), 89–107.

Morrow, L. M. (1993). *Literacy development in the early years: Helping children read and write* (2nd ed). Boston, MA: Allyn & Bacon.

Morrow, L. M. (1995). *Family literacy: Connections in schools and communities.* Newark, DE: International Reading Association.

Morrow, L. M., & Rand, M. K. (1991). Promoting literacy during play by designing early childhood classroom environments. *The Reading Teacher, 44*(6), 396–402.

Mosenthal, P. B. (1989a). From random events to predictive reading models. *The Reading Teacher, 42*(7), 524–525.

Mosenthal, P. B. (1989b). The whole language approach: Teachers between a rock and a hard place. *The Reading Teacher, 42*(8), 628–629.

Moustafa, M. (1997). *Beyond traditional phonics: Research discoveries and reading instruction.* Portsmouth, NH: Heinemann.

Moustafa, M., & Maldonado-Colon, E. (1999). Whole-to-parts phonics instruction: Building on what children know to help them know more. *The Reading Teacher, 52*(5), 448–458.

Mullis, I. V. S., Campbell, J. R., & Farstrup, A. E. (Eds.). (1993). *NAEP 1992 reading report card for the nation and the states* (Report No. 23-ST06). Washington, DC: National Center for Education Statistics, USDOE.

Munsch, R. (1980). *The paper bag princess.* Toronto, Canada: Annick Press.

Muth, K. D. (1989). *Children's comprehension of text: Research into practice.* Newark, DE: International Reading Association.

Myers, W. D. (1975). *Fast Sam, Cool Clyde, and Stuff.* New York: Puffin Books.

NAEP (National Assessment of Educational Progress). (1996). *Results from the NAEP 1994 reading assessment—at a glance.* Washington, DC: National Center for Educational Statistics.

Nagy, W. (1988). *Teaching vocabulary to improve reading comprehension.* Unpublished manuscript, Champaign, IL: Center for the Study of Reading.

Nagy, W. E., & Anderson, R. C. (1984). How many words are there in printed school English? *Reading Research Quarterly, 19*(3), 304–330.

Nagy, W. E., Herman, P. A., & Anderson, R. C. (1985). Learning words from context. *Reading Research Quarterly, 20,* 233–253.

Naiden, N. (1976). Ratio of boys to girls among disabled readers. *The Reading Teacher, 29*(6), 439–442.

Namioka, L. (1992). *Yang the youngest and his terrible ear.* Boston: Little, Brown.

Nash, B., & Nash, G. (1980). *Pundles.* New York: Stone Song Press.

Naslund, J. C., & Samuel, J. S. (1992). Automatic access to word sounds and meaning in decoding written text. *Reading and Writing Quarterly, 8*(2), 135–156.

National Assessment of Educational Progress. (1990). *Learning to read in our nation's schools: Instruction and achievement in 1988 at grades 4, 8, and 12.* Princeton, NJ: Author.

National Association for the Education of Young Children. (1986). Position statement on developmentally appropriate practice in programs for 4- and 5-year-olds. *Young Children, 41*(6), 20–29.

National Commission on Teaching and America's Future. (1996). *What matters most: Teaching for America's future.* Woodbridge, VA: Author.

National Research Council. (1998). Preventing reading difficulties in young children. Washington, DC: U.S. Department of Education. (Note: An image version of this report is available in the Internet at *http://www.nap.edu/readingroom/ enter2.cgi?030906418X.html*)

Nelson, T. (1988, January). Managing immense storage. *Byte,* 225–238.

Neuman, S., & Koskinen, P. (1992). Captioned television as comprehensible input: Effects of incidental word learning from context for language minority students. *Reading Research Quarterly, 27*(3), 94–106.

Neuman, S., & Roskos, K. (1992). Literacy objects as cultural tools: Effects on children's literacy behaviors in play. *Reading Research Quarterly, 27*(3), 203–225.

Neuman, S. B. (1981). Effect of teaching auditory perceptual skill on reading achievement in first grade. *The Reading Teacher, 34,* 422–426.

Neuman, S. B., & Roskos, K. (1990). Play, print, and purpose: Enriching play environments for literacy development. *The Reading Teacher, 44*(3), 214–221.

Neuman, S. B., & Roskos, K. (1993). *Language and literacy learning in the early years: An integrated approach.* New York: Harcourt Brace.

Newman, J. M. (1985a). Yes, that's an interesting idea, but . . . In J. M. Newman (Ed.), *Whole language theory in use* (pp. 181–186). Portsmouth, NH: Heinemann.

Newman, J. M. (Ed.). (1985b). *Whole language: Theory in use.* Portsmouth, NH: Heinemann.

Nist, S. L., & Simpson, M. L. (1993). *Developing vocabulary concepts for college thinking.* Lexington, MA: Heath.

Nolan, E. A., & Berry, M. (1993). Learning to listen. *The Reading Teacher, 46*(7), 606–608.

Nordquist, V. M., & Twardosz, S. (1990). Preventing behavior problems in early childhood special education classrooms through environmental organization. *Education and Treatment of Children, 13*(4), 274–287.

Norton, D. E. (1993). *The effective teaching of language arts* (4th ed.). Upper Saddle River, NJ: Merrill/Prentice Hall.

Norton, D. E. (1998). *Through the eyes of a child: An introduction to children's literature* (5th edition). Upper Saddle River, NJ: Merrill/Prentice Hall.

Numeroff, L. J. (1985). *If you give a mouse a cookie.* New York: Scholastic.

Nurss, J. R., Hough, R. A., & Goodson, M. S. (1981). Prereading/language development in two day care centers. *Journal of Reading Behavior, 13,* 23–31.

Oakes, J. (1992). Can tracking research inform practice? *Educational Researcher, 21*(4), 12–21.

O'Bruba, W. S. (1987). Reading through the creative arts. *Reading Horizons, 27*(3), 170–177.

Ogle, D. M. (1986). K-W-L: A teaching model that develops active reading of expository text. *The Reading Teacher, 39*(6), 564–570.

Ohanian, S. (1984). Hot new item or same old stew? *Classroom Computer Learning, 5,* 30–31.

O'Huigin, S. (1988). *Scary poems for rotten kids.* New York: Firefly Books.

Olson, M. W., & Gee, T. C. (1988). Understanding narratives: A review of story grammar research. *Childhood Education, 64*(4), 302–306.

Olson, M. W., & Longnion, B. (1982). Pattern guides: A workable alternative for content teachers. *Journal of Reading, 25,* 736–741.

Osborn, J. (1984). The purposes, uses, and contents of workbooks and some guidelines for publishers. In R. C. Anderson, J. Osborn, & R. J. Tierney (Eds.), *Learning to read in American schools* (pp. 45–112). Hillsdale, NJ: Erlbaum.

Osborn, J. (1985). Workbooks: Counting, matching, and judging. In J. Osborn, P. T. Wilson, & R. C. Anderson (Eds.), *Reading education: Foundations for a literate America* (pp. 11–28). Lexington, MA: Lexington Books.

Otto, J. (1982). The new debate in reading. *The Reading Teacher, 36*(1), 14–18.

Palincsar, A., & Brown, A. (1985). Reciprocal teaching: A means to a meaningful end. In Osborn, J., Wilson, P. T., & Anderson, R. C. (Eds.), *Reading education: Foundations for a Literate America* (pp. 299–310). Lexington, MA: Heath.

Pankake, M., & Pankake, J. (1988). *A Prairie Home Companion folk song book.* New York: Viking.

Pappas, C. C., Kiefer, B. Z., & Levstik, L. S. (1990). *An integrated language perspective in the elementary school.* New York: Longman.

Paradis, E., & Peterson, J. (1975). Readiness training implications from research. *The Reading Teacher, 28*(5), 445–448.

Paradis, E. E. (1974). The appropriateness of visual discrimination exercises in reading readiness materials. *Journal of Educational Research, 67,* 276–278.

Paradis, E. E. (1984). *Comprehension: thematic units* [videotape]. University of Wyoming, Laramie.

Paris, S. G., Lipson, M. Y., & Wixson, K. K. (1983). Issues concerning the acquisition of knowledge: Effects of vocabulary training on reading comprehension. *Review of Educational Research, 53,* 293–316.

Parish, P. (1963). *Amelia Bedelia.* New York: HarperCollins.

Parker, A., & Paradis, E. (1986). Attitude development toward reading in grades one through six. *Journal of Educational Research, 79*(5), 313–315.

Parkes, B. (1986a). *The enormous watermelon.* Crystal Lake, IL: Rigby.

Parkes, B. (1986b). *Who's in the shed?* Crystal Lake, IL: Rigby.

Parsons, L. (1990). *Response journals.* Portsmouth, NH: Heinemann.

Paterson, K. (1977). *Bridge to Terabithia.* New York: Thomas Y. Crowell.

Pearson, P. D. (1974). The effects of grammatical complexity on children's comprehension, recall, and conception of certain semantic relations. *Reading Research Quarterly, 10*(2), 155–192.

Pearson, P. D. (1985). Changing the face of reading comprehension instruction. *The Reading Teacher, 38*(8), 724–738.

Pearson, P. D. (1989a). *Improving national reading assessment: The key to improved reading instruction.* Paper presented at the 1989 annual reading conference of the Utah Council of the International Reading Association, Salt Lake City, UT.

Pearson, P. D. (1989b). Reading the whole language movement. *Elementary School Journal, 90*(2), 231–242.

Pearson, P. D. (1989c). Whole language. *The Elementary School Journal, 90*(2), 231–242.

Pearson, P. D., & Fielding, L. (1982). Listening comprehension. *Language Arts, 59*(6), 617–629.

Pearson, P. D., & Gallagher, M. C. (1983). The instruction of reading comprehension. *Contemporary Educational Psychology, 8*(3), 317–344.

Pearson, P. D., & Johnson, D. D. (1978). *Teaching reading comprehension.* New York: Holt, Rinehart and Winston.

Pearson, P. D., Hansen, J., & Gordon, C. (1979). The effect of background knowledge on children's comprehension of implicit and explicit information. *Journal of Reading Behavior, 11*(3), 201–209.

Peregoy, S. F., & Boyle, O. F. (1993). *Reading, writing, and learning in ESL.* New York: Longman.

Perez, S. A. (1983). Teaching writing from the inside: Teachers as writers. *Language Arts, 60*(7), 847–850.

Perfetti, C. A., & Lesgold, A. M. (1977). Discourse comprehension and sources of individual differences. In M. A. Just & P. A. Carpenter (Eds.), *Cognitive processes in comprehension* (pp. 141–184). Hillsdale, NJ: Erlbaum.

Peterson, B. (1991). Selecting books for beginning readers. In D. E. DeFord, C. A. Lyons, & G. S. Pinnell (Eds.), *Bridges to literacy: Learning from reading recovery* (pp. 119–147). Portsmouth, NH: Heinemann.

Peterson, R., & Eeds, M. (1990). *Grand conversations: Literature groups in action.* New York: Scholastic.

Pfeffer, S. B. (1989). *Future forward.* New York: Holt.

Piaget, J. (1955). *The language and thought of the child.* New York: World.

Pikulski, J. J. (1985). Questions and answers. *The Reading Teacher, 39*(1), 127–128.

Pikulski, J. J., & Templeton, S. (1997). The role of phonemic awareness in learning to read. *Invitations to Literacy* [Monograph Series]. Boston: Houghton Mifflin.

Pinkney, A. D. (1993). *Alvin Ailey.* New York: Hyperion Books for Children.

Pinnell, G. S., & Fountas, I. C. (1997a). *A handbook for volunteers: Help America read.* Portsmouth, NH: Heinemann.

Pinnell, G. S., & Fountas, I. C. (1997b). *Help America read: Coordinator's guide.* Portsmouth, NH: Heinemann.

Pinnell, G. S., Fried, M. D., & Estice, R. M. (1990). Reading recovery: Learning how to make a difference. *The Reading Teacher, 43,* 282–295.

Pinnell, G. S., Lyons, C. A., DeFord, D. E., Bryk, A. S., & Seltzer, M. (1994). Comparing instructional models for the literacy education of high-risk first graders. *Reading Research Quarterly, 29*(1), 8–39.

Pino, E. (1978). *Schools are out of proportion to man.* Seminar on discipline, Utah State University, Logan, UT.

Point/counterpoint. The value of basal readers. (1989, August–September). *Reading Today, 7,* 18.

Pollack, P. (1982). *Keeping it secret.* New York: Putnam.

Potter, B. (1903). *The tale of Peter Rabbit.* New York: F. Warne.

Powell, D. A. (1986). *Retrospective case studies of individual and group decision making in district-level elementary reading textbook selection.* Unpublished doctoral dissertation, Indiana University, Bloomington, IN.

Prelutsky, J. (1976). *Nightmares: Poems to trouble your sleep.* New York: Greenwillow Books.

Prelutsky, J. (1984). *A new kid on the block.* New York: Greenwillow Books.

Prelutsky, J. (1990). *Something big has been here.* New York: Greenwillow Books.

Prelutsky, J. (1991). *Poems for laughing out loud.* New York: Alfred A. Knopf.

Prelutsky, J. (1996). *A pizza the size of the sun.* New York: Greenwillow Books.

Prince, A. T., & Mancus, D. S. (1987). Enriching comprehension: A schema altered basal reading lesson. *Reading Research and Instruction, 27,* 45–53.

Provensen, A., & Provensen, M. (1983). *The glorious flight: Across the channel with Louis Bleriot.* New York: Viking Penguin.

Puckett, M. B., & Black, J. K. (1994). *Authentic assessment of the young child.* Upper Saddle River, NJ: Merrill/Prentice Hall.

Pulver, C. J. (1986). Teaching students to understand explicit and implicit connectives. In J. W. Irwin (Ed.), *Understanding and teaching cohesion comprehension* (pp. 3–8). Newark, DE: International Reading Association.

Ramirez, G., & Ramirez, J. L. (1994). *Multiethnic literature.* Albany, NY: Delmar.

Raphael, T. E. (1982). Question-answering strategies for children. *The Reading Teacher, 36,* 186–191.

Raphael, T. E. (1986). Teaching question-answer relationships, revisited. *The Reading Teacher, 39*(6), 516–523.

Raphael, T. E., & Pearson, P. D. (1982). *The effect of metacognitive awareness training on children's question answering behavior* (Tech. Rep. No. 238). Urbana-Champaign: University of Illinois at Urbana-Champaign, Center for the Study of Reading.

Rasinski, T. (1990). Investigating measure of reading fluency. *Educational Research Quarterly, 14*(3), 37–44.

Rasinski, T. (1998, September). *Reading to learn: Vocabulary development strategies.* Paper presented at the Fall Session of the Dallas Reading Plan Grades 4–6 Professional Development Series, Dallas, TX.

Rasinski, T., & Padak, N. D. (1990). Multicultural learning through children's literature. *Language Arts, 69,* 14–20.

Rasinski, T. V. (1990). Effects of repeated reading and listening-while-reading on reading fluency. *Journal of Educational Research, 83,* 147–150.

Raskinski, T. V. (1995). *Parents and teachers: Helping children learn to read and write.* New York: Harcourt Brace.

Raskinski, T. V., & Fredericks, A. D. (1988). Sharing literacy: Guiding principles and practices for parent involvement. *The Reading Teacher, 41,* 508–512.

Rasinski, T. V., & Fredericks, A. D. (1989). Working with parents: What do parents think about reading in the schools? *The Reading Teacher, 43*(3), 262–263.

Raven, J. (1992). A model of competence, motivation, and behavior, and a paradigm for assessment. In H. Berlak, et al., *Toward a new science of educational testing and assessment.* New York: State University of New York Press.

Ravitch, D., & Finn, C. E., Jr. (1987). *What do our 17-year-olds know?* New York: HarperCollins.

Rawls, W. (1961). *Where the red fern grows.* New York: Doubleday.

Raygor, A. L. (1977). The Raygor readability estimate: A quick and easy way to determine difficulty. In P. D. Pearson (Ed.), *Reading: Theory, research and practice* (pp. 259–263). Clemson, SC: National Reading Conference.

Read, C. (1971). Preschool children's knowledge of English phonology. *Harvard Educational Review, 41,* 1–34.

Read, S. J., & Rosson, M. B. (1982). Rewriting history: The biasing effects of attitudes on memory. *Social Cognition, 1,* 240–255.

Reid, J. F. (1966). Learning to think about reading. *Educational Research, 9,* 56–62.

Reimer, B. L. (1983). Recipes for language experience stories. *The Reading Teacher, 36*(4), 396–401.

Reinking, D. (Ed.). (1987). *Computers and reading: Issues for theory and practice.* New York: Teachers College Press.

Reinking, D., & Rickman, S. S. (1990). The effects of computer-mediated texts on the vocabulary learning and comprehension of intermediate-grade readers. *Journal of Reading Behavior, 22*(4), 395–409.

Reutzel, D. R. (1985a). Reconciling schema theory and the basal reading lesson. *The Reading Teacher, 39,* 194–197.

Reutzel, D. R. (1985b). Story maps improve comprehension. *The Reading Teacher, 38*(4), 400–405.

Reutzel, D. R. (1991). Understanding and using basal readers effectively. In Bernard L. Hayes (Ed.), *Reading instruction and the effective teacher* (pp. 254–280). New York: Allyn & Bacon.

Reutzel, D. R. (1992). Breaking the letter a week tradition: Conveying the alphabetic principle to young children. *Childhood Education, 69*(1), 20–23.

Reutzel, D. R. (1995). Fingerpoint-reading and beyond: Learning about print strategies (LAPS). *Reading Horizons, 35*(4), 310–328.

Reutzel, D. R. (1996a). A balanced reading approach. In J. Baltas & S. Shafer (Eds.), *Scholastic guide to balanced reading: Grade 3–6,* 7–11. New York: Scholastic.

Reutzel, D. R.(1996b). A balanced reading approach. In J. Baltas & S. Shafer (Eds.), *Scholastic guide to balanced reading: K–2.* New York: Scholastic, 6–12.

Reutzel, D. R. (1999a). On balanced reading. *The Reading Teacher, 52*(4), 2–4.

Reutzel, D. R. (1999b). Organizing literacy instruction: Effective grouping strategies and organizational plans. In L. M. Morrow, L. B. Gambrell, S. Neuman, &

M. Pressley (Eds.), *Best practices for literacy instruction.* New York: Guilford Press. (In press for 1999)

Reutzel, D. R., & Cooter, R. B., Jr. (1990). Whole language: Comparative effects on first-grade reading achievement. *Journal of Educational Research, 83,* 252–257.

Reutzel, D. R., & Cooter, R. B., Jr. (1991). Organizing for effective instruction: The reading workshop. *The Reading Teacher, 44*(8), 548–555.

Reutzel, D. R., & Cooter, R. B., Jr. (1999). *Balanced reading strategies and practices: Assessing and assisting readers with special needs.* Upper Saddle River, NJ: Merrill/Prentice Hall.

Reutzel, D. R., & Daines, D. (1987a). The instructional cohesion of reading lessons in seven basal reading series. *Reading Psychology, 8,* 33–44.

Reutzel, D. R., & Daines, D. (1987b). The text-relatedness of seven basal reading series. *Reading Research and Instruction, 27,* 26–35.

Reutzel, D. R., & Fawson, P. C. (1989). Using a literature webbing strategy lesson with predictable books. *The Reading Teacher, 43*(3), 208–215.

Reutzel, D. R., & Fawson, P. C. (1990). Traveling tales: Connecting parents and children in writing. *The Reading Teacher, 44,* 222–227.

Reutzel, D. R., & Fawson, P. C. (1991). Literature webbing predictable books: A prediction strategy that helps below-average, first-grade readers. *Reading Research and Instruction, 30*(4), 20–30.

Reutzel, D. R., & Fawson, P. C. (1998). Global literacy connections: Stepping into the future. *Think, 8*(2), 32–34.

Reutzel, D. R., & Gali, K. (1998). The art of children's book selection: A labyrinth unexplored. *Reading Psychology, 19*(3), 3–50.

Reutzel, D. R., & Hollingsworth, P. M. (1988a). Highlighting key vocabulary: A generative-reciprocal procedure for teaching selected inference types. *Reading Research Quarterly, 23*(3), 358–378.

Reutzel, D. R., & Hollingsworth, P. M. (1988b). Whole language and the practitioner. *Academic Therapy, 23*(4), 405–416.

Reutzel, D. R., & Hollingsworth, P. M. (1991a). Investigating the development of topic-related attitude: Effect on children's reading and remembering text. *Journal of Educational Research, 84*(5), 334–344.

Reutzel, D. R., & Hollingsworth, P. M. (1991b). Reading comprehension skills: Testing the skills distinctiveness hypothesis. *Reading Research and Instruction, 30*(2), 32–46.

Reutzel, D. R., & Hollingsworth, P. (1991c). Reading time in school: Effect on fourth graders' performance on a criterion-referenced comprehension test. *Journal of Educational Research, 84*(3), 170–176.

Reutzel, D. R., & Hollingsworth, P. M. (1991d). Using literature webbing for books with predictable narrative: Improving young readers' predictions, comprehension, & story structure knowledge. *Reading Psychology, 12*(4), 319–333.

Reutzel, D. R., & Hollingsworth, P. M. (1993). Effects of fluency training on second grader's reading comprehension. *Journal of Educational Research, 86*(6), 325–331.

Reutzel, D. R., Hollingsworth, P. M., & Eldredge, J. L. (1994). Oral reading instruction: The impact on student reading development. *Reading Research Quarterly, 23*(1), 40–62.

Reutzel, D. R., & Morgan, B. C. (1990). Effects of prior knowledge, explicitness, and clause order on children's comprehension of causal relationships. *Reading Psychology: An International Quarterly, 11,* 93–114.

Reutzel, D. R., Oda, L. K., & Moore, B. H. (1989). Developing print awareness: The effect of three instructional approaches on kindergartners: Print awareness, reading readiness, and word reading. *Journal of Reading Behavior, 21*(3), 197–217.

Reutzel, D. R., & Sabey, B. (1995). Teacher beliefs about reading and children's conceptions: Are there connections? *Reading Research and Instruction, 35*(4), 323–342.

Reutzel, D. R., & Wolfersberger, M. (1996). An environmental impact statement: Designing supportive literacy classrooms for young children. *Reading Horizons, 36*(3), 266–282.

Rhodes, L. K., & Dudley-Marling, C. (1988). *Readers and writers with a difference.* Portsmouth, NH: Heinemann.

Rhodes, L. K., & Shanklin, N. (1993). *Windows into literacy: Assessing learners K–8.* Portsmouth, NH: Heinemann.

Ribowsky, H. (1985). *The effects of a code emphasis approach and a whole language approach upon emergent literacy of kindergarten children* (Report No. CS-008-397). (ERIC Document Reproduction Service No. ED 269 720)

Rice, P. E. (1991). Novels in the news. *The Reading Teacher, 45*(2), 159–160.

Rich, E. S. (1964). *Hannah Elizabeth.* New York: HarperCollins.

Richek, M. A. (1978). Readiness skills that predict initial word learning using 2 different methods of instruction. *Reading Research Quarterly, 13,* 200–222.

Richgels, D. J., & Wold, L. S. (1998). Literacy on the road: Backpacking partnerships between school and home. *The Reading Teacher, 52*(1), 18–29.

Riley, R. E. (1993). *Adult literacy in America.* Washington, DC: United States Department of Education.

Roberts, B. (1992). The evolution of the young child's concept of word as a unit of spoken and written language. *Reading Research Quarterly, 27*(2), 124–139.

Roberts, T. (1975). Skills of analysis and synthesis in the early stages of reading. *British Journal of Educational Psychology, 45,* 3–9.

Robinson, B. (1972). *The best Christmas pageant ever.* New York: HarperCollins.

Robinson, F. (1946). *Effective study.* New York: Harper Brothers.

Robinson, H. M. (1972). Perceptual training—does it result in reading improvement? In R. C. Aukerman (Ed.), *Some persistent questions on beginning reading* (pp. 135–150). Newark, DE: International Reading Association.

Romero, G. G. (1983). *Print awareness of the preschool bilingual Spanish English speaking child.* Unpublished doctoral dissertation, University of Arizona Tucson.

Rosenbaum, J. (1980). *Making inequality: The hidden curriculum of high school tracking.* New York: Wiley.

Rosenblatt, L. M. (1978). *The reader, the text, and the poem.* Carbondale, IL: Southern Illinois University Press.

Rosenshine, B. V. (1980). Skill hierarchies in reading comprehension. In Spiro, R. J., Bruce, B. C., & Brewer, W. F. (Eds.), *Theoretical issues in reading comprehension* (pp. 535–554). Hillsdale, NJ: Erlbaum.

Roser, N. L., Hoffman, J. V., & Farest, C. (1990). Language, literature, and at-risk children. *The Reading Teacher, 43*(8), 554–561.

Routman, R. (1988). *Transitions: From literature to literacy.* Portsmouth, NH: Heinemann.

Routman, R. (1996). *Literacy at the crossroads: Crucial talk about reading, writing, and other teaching dilemmas.* Portsmouth, NH: Heinemann.

Rowe, M. B. (1974). Wait-time and rewards as instructional variables, their influence on language, logic, and fate control: Part one—wait time. *Journal of Research in Science Teaching, 11,* 81–94.

Ruddell, R. (1974). *Reading-language instruction: Innovative practices.* Upper Saddle River, NJ: Prentice Hall.

Ruddell, R. B., & Ruddell, M. R. (1995). *Teaching children to read and write: Becoming an influential teacher.* Boston, MA: Allyn & Bacon.

Ruddell, R. B., & Unrau, N. J. (1997). The role of responsive teaching in focusing reader intention and developing reader motivation. In J. T. Guthrie & A. Wigfield (Eds.), *Reading engagement: Motivating readers through integrated instruction.* Newark, DE: International Reading Association.

Rumelhart, D. E. (1975). Notes on a schema for stories. In D. G. Bobrow & A. Collins (Eds.), *Representation and understanding: Studies in cognitive science* (pp. 211–236). New York: Academic Press.

Rumelhart, D. E. (1980). Schemata: The building blocks of cognition. In R. J. Spiro (Ed.), *Theoretical issues in reading comprehension* (pp. 33–58). Hillsdale, NJ: Erlbaum.

Rumelhart, D. E. (1981). Schemata: The building blocks of cognition. In Guthrie, J. T. (Ed.), *Comprehension and teaching: Research reviews* (pp. 3–26). Newark, DE: International Reading Association.

Rumelhart, D. E. (1984). Understanding understanding. In J. Flood (Ed.), *Understanding reading comprehension* (pp. 1–20). Newark, DE: International Reading Association.

Rupley, W., & Blair, T. (1987). Assignment and supervision of reading seatwork: Looking in on 12 primary teachers. *The Reading Teacher, 40*(4), 391–393.

Rupley, W. H., & Blair, T. R. (1978). Teacher effectiveness in reading instruction. *The Reading Teacher, 31,* 970–973.

Rye, J. (1982). *Cloze procedure and the teaching of reading.* Portsmouth, NH: Heinemann.

Sadow, M. W. (1982). The use of story grammar in the design of questions. *The Reading Teacher, 35,* 518–523.

Samuels, S. J. (1967). Attentional process in reading: The effect of pictures on the acquisition of reading responses. *Journal of Educational Psychology, 58,* 337–342.

Samuels, S. J. (1970). Effects of pictures on learning to read, comprehension, and attitudes. *Review of Educational Research, 40,* 397–408.

Samuels, S. J. (1979). The method of repeated readings. *The Reading Teacher, 32*(4), 403–408.

Sanford, A. J., & Garrod, S. C. (1981). *Understanding written language.* New York: Wiley.

Santa, C. (1990). *Reporting on the Montana Teacher Change Project: Kallispell reading/language initiative.* Utah Council of the International Reading Association, Salt Lake City, UT.

Santa, C. M. (1997). School change and literacy engagement: Preparing teaching and learning environments. In J. T. Guthrie & A. Wigfield (Eds.), *Reading engagement:*

Motivating readers through integrated instruction. Newark, DE: International Reading Association.

Savage, J. F. (1994). *Teaching reading using literature.* Madison, WI: Brown & Benchmark.

Scholastic. (1986). *Talking text* [computer program]. Jefferson City, MO: Scholastic.

Scholastic. (1990). *Bank Street writer III* [computer program]. Jefferson City, MO: Scholastic Software.

Scholastic. (1995). *Literary place program.* New York: Author.

Schreiber, A., & Tuchman, G. (1997). *Scholastic Phonics Readers® The Big Hit: Book 14.* New York, NY: Scholastic Inc.

Schwartz, D. M. (1985). *How much is a million?* Richard Hill, Ontario: Scholastic-TAB.

Schwartz, R. M., & Raphael, T. E. (1985). Concept of definition: A key to improving students' vocabulary. *The Reading Teacher, 39*(2), 198–205.

Scieszka, J. (1989). *The true story of the 3 little pigs: By A. Wolf.* New York: Viking Kestrel.

Searfoss, L. W. (1975). Radio reading. *Reading Teacher, 29,* 295–296.

Searfoss, L. W., & Readence, J. E. (1989). *Helping children learn to read* (2nd ed.). Upper Saddle River, NJ: Prentice Hall.

Seefeldt, C., & Barbour, N. (1986). *Early childhood education: An introduction.* Upper Saddle River, NJ: Merrill/Prentice Hall.

Sendak, M. (1962). *Chicken soup with rice.* New York: Scholastic.

Sendak, M. (1963). *Where the wild things are.* New York: HarperCollins.

Senechal, M., & Cornell, E. H. (1993). Vocabulary acquisition through shared reading experiences. *Reading Research Quarterly, 28*(4), 361–373.

Seuss, D. (1954). *Horton hears a Who!* New York: Random House.

Shake, M. C., & Allington, R. L. (1985). Where do teacher's questions come from? *The Reading Teacher, 38,* 432–439.

Shanahan, T. (1984). Nature of the reading-writing relation: An exploratory multivariate analysis. *Journal of Educational Psychology, 76,* 466–477.

Shanahan, T., & Barr, R. (1995). Reading Recovery: An independent evaluation of the effects of an early intervention for at-risk learners. *Reading Research Quarterly, 30*(40), 958–996.

Shanahan, T., & Lomax, R. G. (1986). An analysis and comparison of theoretical models of the reading-writing relationship. *Journal of Educational Psychology, 78,* 116–123.

Shanklin, N. L., & Rhodes, L. K. (1989). Comprehension instruction as sharing and extending. *The Reading Teacher, 43*(7), 496–500.

Shannon, P. (1983). The use of commercial reading materials in American elementary schools. *Reading Research Quarterly, 19,* 68–85.

Shannon, P. (1989a). Basal readers: Three perspectives. *Theory Into Practice, 28*(4), 235–239.

Shannon, P. (1989b). *Broken promises.* Granby, MA: Bergin & Garvey.

Shannon, P. (1992). *Becoming political: Readings and writings in the politics of literacy education.* Portsmouth, NH: Heinemann.

Shannon, P. (1993). Letters to the editor: Comments on Baumann. *Reading Research Quarterly, 28*(2), 86.

Shannon, P., & Goodman, K. (1994). *Basal readers: A second look.* New York: Owen.

Sharmat, M. W. (1980). *Gila monsters meet you at the airport.* New York: Aladdin.

Shockley, B., Michalove, B., & Allen, J. (1995). *Engaging Families.* Portsmouth, NH: Heinemann.

Short, K. G., Harste, J. C., & Burke, C. (1996). *Creating classrooms for authors and inquirers.* Portsmouth, NH: Heinemann.

Siegel, M. (1983). *Reading as signification.* Unpublished doctoral dissertation, Indiana University.

Silvaroli, N. J. (1986). *Classroom reading inventory* (5th ed.). Dubuque, IA: William C. Brown.

Silverstein, S. (1974). *Where the sidewalk ends.* New York: HarperCollins.

Silverstein, S. (1996). *Falling Up.* New York: HarperCollins.

Singer, H. (1960). *Conceptual ability in the substrata-factor theory of reading.* Unpublished doctoral dissertation, University of California at Berkeley.

Singer, H. (1978a). Active comprehension: From answering to asking questions. *The Reading Teacher, 31,* 901–908.

Singer, H. (1978b). Research in reading that should make a difference in classroom instruction. In *What research has to say about reading instruction* (pp. 57–71). Newark, DE: International Reading Association.

Singer, H., & Donlan, D. (1989). *Reading and learning from text* (2nd ed.). Hillsdale, NJ: Erlbaum.

Sippola, A. E. (1994). Holistic analysis of basal readers: An assessment tool. *Reading Horizons, 34*(3), 234–246.

Skaar, G. (1972). *What do the animals say?* New York: Scholastic.

Slaughter, H. B. (1988). Indirect and direct teaching in a whole language program. *The Reading Teacher, 42*(1), 30–35.

Slavin, R. E. (1988). Cooperative learning and student achievement. *Educational Leadership, 45,* 31–33.

Slavin, R. E. (1991). Are cooperative learning and "untracking" harmful to the gifted? *Education Leadership, 48*(6), 68–71.

Slavin, R. E. (1995). *Cooperative learning: Theory, research, and practice.* Needham Heights, MA: Allyn & Bacon.

Slavin, R. E., & Madden, N. (1995). Effects of success for all on the achievement of English language learners. Paper presented at the annual meeting of the American Educational Research Association, San Francisco, CA, April, 1995.

Slosson, R. L. (1971). *Slosson intelligence test.* East Aurora, NY: Slosson Educational Publications.

Sloyer, S. (1982). *Reader's theater: Story dramatization in the classroom.* Urbana, IL: National Council of Teachers of English.

Smith, D. E. P. (1967). *Learning to learn.* New York: Harcourt Brace.

Smith, E. B., Goodman, K. S., & Meredith, R. (1976). *Language and thinking in school* (2nd ed.). New York: Holt, Rinehart and Winston.

Smith, F. (1977). The uses of language. *Language Arts, 54*(6), 638–644.

Smith, F. (1983). *Essays into literacy.* Exeter, NH: Heinemann.

Smith, F. (1985). *Reading without nonsense* (2nd ed.). New York: Teachers College Press.

Smith, F. (1987). *Insult to intelligence.* New York: Arbor House.

Smith, F. (1988). *Understanding reading* (4th ed.). Hillsdale, NJ: Erlbaum.

Smith, K. A. (1989). *A checkup with the doctor.* New York: McDougal, Littell.

Smith, N. B. (1965). *American reading instruction.* Newark, DE: International Reading Association.

Smith, N. B. (1986). *American Reading Instruction.* Newark, DE: International Reading Association.

Smith, R. K. (1981). *Jelly belly.* New York: Dell.

Smoot, R. C., & Price, J. (1975). *Chemistry, a modern course.* Upper Saddle River, NJ: Merrill/Prentice Hall.

Snow, C. (1999). *Preventing reading difficulties.* Keynote address at the Second Annual Commissioner's Reading Day, Austin, TX.

Snow, C. E., Burns, M. S., & Griffin, P. (1998). *Preventing reading failure in young children.* Washington, DC: National Academy Press.

Soto, G. (1993). *Local news.* San Diego, CA: Harcourt Brace.

Spache, G., & Spache, E. (1977). *Reading in the elementary school* (4th ed.). Boston: Allyn & Bacon.

Spady, W., & Marshall, K. J. (1991). Beyond traditional outcome-based education. *Educational Leadership, 48,* 67–72.

Spangler, K. L. (1983). Reading interests vs. reading preferences: Using the research. *The Reading Teacher, 36*(9), 876–878.

Speare, E. G. (1958). *The witch of Blackbird Pond.* New York: Dell.

Sperry, A. (1940). *Call it courage.* New York: Macmillan.

Spiegel, D. L. (1981). Six alternatives to the directed reading activity. *Reading Teacher, 34,* 914–922.

Spier, P. (1977). *Noah's ark.* Garden City, NY: Doubleday.

Spinelli, J. (1991). Catching Maniac Magee. *The Reading Teacher, 45*(3), 174–176.

Spivak, M. (1973). Archetypal place. *Architectural Forum, 140,* 44–49.

Squire, J. R. (1983). Composing and comprehending: Two sides of the same basic process. *Language Arts, 60*(5), 581–589.

Squire, J. R. (1989). A reading program for all seasons. *Theory Into Practice, 28*(4), 254–257.

Stahl, S. A. (1986). Three principles of effective vocabulary instruction. *Journal of Reading, 29*(7), 662–668.

Stahl, S. A., Hare, V. C., Sinatra, R., & Gregory, J. F. (1991). Defining the role of prior knowledge and vocabulary in reading comprehension: The retiring of number 41. *Journal of Reading Behavior, 23*(4), 487–507.

Stahl, S. A., & Jacobson, M. G. (1986). Vocabulary difficulty, prior knowledge, and text comprehension. *Journal of Reading Behavior, 18*(4), 309–319.

Stahl, S. A., & Miller, P. D. (1989). Whole language and language experience approaches for beginning reading: A quantitative research synthesis. *Review of Educational Research, 59,* 87–116.

Standard for the English Language Arts. (1996). A project of The International Reading Association and National Council of Teachers of English. Newark, DE: International Reading Association.

Stanovich, K. (1980). Toward an interactive-compensatory model of individual differences in the development of reading fluency. *Reading Research Quarterly, 16*(1), 37–71.

Stauffer, R. G. (1969). *Directing reading maturity as a cognitive process.* New York: HarperCollins.

Stauffer, R. G. (1975). *Directing the reading-thinking process.* New York: HarperCollins.

Stayter, F. Z., & Allington, R. L. (1991). Fluency and the understanding of texts. *Theory Into Practice, 30*(3), 143–148.

Stedman, L. C., & Kaestle, C. E. (1987). Literacy and reading performance in the United States from 1880 to the present. *Reading Research Quarterly, 22,* 8–46.

Steele, W. O. (1958). *The perilous road.* Orlando, FL: Harcourt Brace.

Stein, N. L., & Glenn, C. G. (1979). An analysis of story comprehension in elementary school children. In R. O. Freedle (Ed.), *New directions in discourse processing* (pp. 53–120). Hillsdale, NJ: Erlbaum.

Steinbeck, J. (1937). *The red pony.* New York: Bantam Books.

Stenner, A. J. (1996). *Measuring reading comprehension with the Lexile framework.* Washington, DC: Paper presented at the 4th North American Conference on Adolescent/Adult Literacy.

Stenner, A. J., & Burdick, D. S. (1997). *The objective measurement of reading comprehension.* Durham, NC: MetaMetrics.

Steptoe, J. (1987). *Mufaro's beautiful daughters: An African tale.* New York: Lothrop, Lee, & Shepard Books.

Stern, D. N., & Wasserman, G. A. (1979). *Maternal language to infants.* Paper presented at a meeting of the Society for Research in Child Development.

Stevens, R., & Rosenshine, B. (1981). Advances in research on teaching. *Exceptional Education Quarterly, 2,* 1–9.

Stevens, R. J., Madden, N. A., Slavin, R. E., & Farnish, A. (1987a). *Cooperative integrated reading and composition: A brief overview of the CIRC program.* Johns Hopkins University, Center for Research on Elementary and Middle Schools.

Stevens, R. J., Madden, N. A., Slavin, R. E., & Farnish, A. M. (1987b). Cooperative integrated reading and composition: Two field experiments. *Reading Research Quarterly, 22*(4), 433–454.

Stevens, R. J., & Slavin, R. E. (1995). Effects of a cooperative learning approach in reading and writing on academically handicapped and nonhandicapped students. *Elementary School Journal, 95*(3), 241–262.

Stolz, M. (1963). *Bully on Barkham Street.* New York: HarperCollins.

Stoodt, B. D. (1989). *Reading instruction.* New York: HarperCollins.

Strickland, D. S. (1998). *Teaching phonics today: A primer for educators.* Newark, DE: International Reading Association.

Strickland, D. S., Feeley, J. T., & Wepner, S. B. (1987). *Using computers in the teaching of reading.* New York: Teachers College Press.

Sucher, F., & Allred, R. A. (1986). *Sucher-Allred group reading placement test.* Oklahoma City: Economy.

Sukhomlinsky, V. (1981). *To children I give my heart* (pp. 125–126). Moscow, USSR: Progress.

Sulzby, E. (1985). Children's emergent reading of favorite storybooks: A developmental study. *Reading Research Quarterly, 20*(4), 458–481.

Sulzby, E. (1991). Assessment of emergent literacy: Storybook reading. *The Reading Teacher, 44*(7), 498–500.

Sulzby, E., Hoffman, J., Niles, J., Shanahan, T., & Teale, W. (1989). *McGraw-Hill reading.* New York: McGraw-Hill.

Sunburst. (1987). *The puzzler.* Pleasantville, NY: Sunburst Communications.

Swafford, J. (1995). I wish all my groups were like this one: Facilitating peer interaction during group work. *Journal of Reading, 38*(8), 626–631.

Sweet, A. (1997). Teacher perceptions of student motivation and their relation to literacy learning. In J. T. Guthrie & A. Wigfield (Eds.), *Reading engagement: Motivating readers through integrated instruction.* Newark, DE: International Reading Association.

Taba, H. (1975). *Teacher's handbook for elementary social studies.* Reading, MA: Addison-Wesley.

Tarver, S. G., & Dawson, M. M. (1978). Modality preference and the teaching of reading: A review. *Journal of Learning Disabilities, 11*(1), 5–17.

Taxel, J. (1993). The politics of children's literature: Reflections on multiculturalism and Christopher Columbus. In V. J. Harris (Ed.), *Teaching multicultural literature in grades K–8* (pp. 1–36). Norwood, MA: Christopher Gordon.

Taylor, B., Harris, L. A., & Pearson, P. D. (1988). *Reading difficulties: Instruction and assessment.* New York: Random House.

Taylor, B. M., Frye, B. J., & Gaetz, T. M. (1990). Reducing the number of reading skill activities in the elementary classroom. *Journal of Reading Behavior, 22*(2), 167–180.

Taylor, D. (1983). *Family literacy: Young children learning to read and write.* Portsmouth, NH: Heinemann.

Taylor, D., & Strickland, D. S. (1986). *Family storybook reading.* Portsmouth, NH: Heinemann.

Taylor, G. C. (1981). ERIC/RCS report: Music in language arts instruction. *Language Arts, 58,* 363–368.

Taylor, M. D. (1990). *Road to Memphis.* New York: Dial Books.

Taylor, N. E. (1986). Developing beginning literacy concepts: Content and context. In D. B. Yaden, Jr., & S. Templeton (Eds.), *Metalinguistic awareness and beginning literacy* (pp. 173–184). Portsmouth, NH: Heinemann.

Taylor, N. E., Blum, I. H., & Logsdon, M. (1986). The development of written language awareness: Environmental aspects and program characteristics. *Reading Research Quarterly, 21*(2), 132–149.

Taylor, W. L. (1953). Cloze procedure: A new tool for measuring readability. *Journalism Quarterly, 30,* 415–433.

Teale, W. H. (1987). Emergent literacy: Reading and writing development in early childhood. In Readence, J. E., Baldwin, R. S., Konopak, J. P., & Newton, H. (Eds.), *Research in literacy: Merging perspectives* (pp. 45–74). Rochester, NY: National Reading Conference.

Teale, W. H., & Sulzby, E. (1986). *Emergent literacy: Writing and reading.* Norwood, NJ: Ablex.

Temple, C., & Gillet, J. (1996). *Language and literacy: A lively approach.* New York: HarperCollins.

Temple, C., Nathan, R., Burris, N., & Temple, F. (1988). *The beginnings of writing* (2nd ed.). Newton, MA: Allyn & Bacon.

Templeton, S. (1995). Children's literacy: Contexts for meaningful learning. Princeton, NJ: Houghton Mifflin.

Thaler, M. (1989). *The teacher from the Black Lagoon.* New York: Scholastic.

Tharpe, R. G., & Gallimore, R. (1988). *Rousing minds to life.* Cambridge, MA: Cambridge University Press.

The American people (Grade 6). (1982). New York: American.

The bilingual writing center. (1992). Fremont, CA: The Learning Company (Aidenwood Tech Park, 493 Kaiser Drive, Fremont, CA 94555, (800) 852-2255).

The gingerbread man. (1985). K. Schmidt, Illustrator. New York: Scholastic.

Thelen, J. N. (1984). *Improving reading in science.* Newark, DE: International Reading Association.

The little red hen. (1985). L. McQueen, Illustrator. New York: Scholastic.

The United States and the other Americas (Grade 5). (1980). Upper Saddle River, NJ: Merrill/Prentice Hall.

The United States: Its history and neighbors (Grade 5). (1985). San Diego, CA: Harcourt Brace.

Thomas, D. G., & Readence, J. E. (1988). Effects of differential vocabulary instruction and lesson frameworks on the reading comprehension of primary children. *Reading Research and Instruction, 28,* 1–13.

Thorndike, R. L. (1973). *Reading comprehension education in fifteen countries: An empirical study.* New York: Wiley.

Thorndyke, P. N. (1977). Cognitive structure in comprehension and memory of narrative discourse. *Cognitive Psychology, 9*(1), 77–110.

Tierney, R. J. (1992). Setting a new agenda for assessment. *Learning, 21*(2), 61–64.

Tierney, R. J., Carter, M. A., & Desai, L. E. (1991). *Portfolio assessment in the reading-writing classroom.* Norwood, MA: Christopher-Gordon.

Tierney, R. J., & Cunningham, J. W. (1984). Research on teaching reading comprehension. In P. D. Pearson (Ed.), *Reading research handbook* (pp. 609–656). New York: Longman.

Tierney, R. J., & Pearson, P. D. (1983). Toward a composing model of reading. *Language Arts, 60*(5), 568–580.

Tierney, R. J., Readence, J. E., & Dishner, E. K. (1985). *Reading strategies and practices: A compendium* (2nd ed.). Boston: Allyn & Bacon.

Tomasello, M. (1996). Piagetian and Vygotskian approaches to language acquisition. *Human Development, 39,* 269–276.

Tompkins, G. E. (1990). *Teaching writing: Balancing process and product.* Upper Saddle River, NJ: Merrill/Prentice Hall.

Tompkins, G. E. (1994). *Teaching writing: Balancing process and product* (2nd ed.). Upper Saddle River, NJ: Merrill/Prentice Hall.

Tompkins, G. E., & Hoskisson, K. (1991). *Language arts: Content and teaching strategies.* Upper Saddle River, NJ: Merrill/Prentice Hall.

Tompkins, G. E., & Hoskisson, K. (1995). *Language arts: Content and teaching strategies* (3rd ed.). Upper Saddle River, NJ: Merrill/Prentice Hall.

Topping, K. (1989). Peer tutoring and paired reading: Combining two powerful techniques. *The Reading Teacher, 42,* 488–494.

Torrey, J. W. (1979). Reading that comes naturally. In G. Waller & G. E. MacKinnon (Eds.), *Reading research: Advance in theory and practice* (Vol. 1, pp. 115–144). New York: Academic Press.

Tovey, D. R., & Kerber, J. E. (Eds.). (1986). *Roles in literacy learning.* Newark, DE: International Reading Association.

Towers, J. M. (1992). Outcome-based education: Another educational bandwagon. *Educational Forum, 56*(3), 291–305.

Towle, (1993). *The real McCoy: The life of an African American inventor.* New York: Scholastic.

Treiman, R. (1985). Onsets and rimes as units of spoken syllables: Evidence from children. *Journal of Experimental Child Psychology, 39,* 161–181.

Trelease, J. (1995). *The new read-aloud handbook, 4th Edition.* New York: Penguin.

Tunnell, M. O., & Jacobs, J. S. (1989). Using "real" books: Research findings on literature based reading instruction. *The Reading Teacher, 42,* 470–477.

Tutolo, D. (1977). The study guide: Types, purpose and value. *Journal of Reading, 20,* 503–507.

Vacca, J. L., Vacca, R. T., & Gove, M. K. (1987). *Reading and learning to read.* Boston: Little, Brown.

Vacca, J. L., Vacca, R. T., & Gove, M. K. (1991). *Reading and learning to read* (2nd ed.). Boston: Little, Brown.

Vacca, J. L., Vacca, R. T., & Gove, M. K. (1995). *Reading and learning to read* (3rd ed.). Boston: Little, Brown.

Vacca, R. T., & Vacca, J. L. (1989). *Content area reading* (3rd ed.). Glenview, IL: Scott, Foresman.

Valencia, S. (1990). A portfolio approach to classroom reading assessment: The whys, whats, and hows. *The Reading Teacher, 43*(4), 338–340.

Valencia, S. (1998). *Portfolios in action.* New York: HarperCollins.

Valencia, S., McGinley, W., & Pearson, P. D. (1990). *Assessing reading and writing: Building a more complete picture for middle school assessment* (Tech. Rep. No. 500). Urbana, IL: Center for the Study of Reading. (ERIC Document Reproduction Service No. ED 320 121)

Valencia, S., & Pearson, P. D. (1987). Reading assessment: Time for a change. *The Reading Teacher, 40*(8), 726–733.

Vallecorsa, A. L., & deBettencourt, L. U. (1997). Using a mapping procedure to teach reading and writing skills to middle grade students with learning disabilities. *Education and the Treatment of Children, 20*(2), 173–188.

Van Allsburg, C. (1985). *The polar express.* Boston: Houghton Mifflin.

Van Allsburg, C. (1987). *The Z was zapped.* Boston: Houghton Mifflin.

Van Manen, M. (1986). *The tone of teaching.* Ontario, Canada: Scholastic.

Varble, M. E. (1990). Analysis of writing samples of students taught by teachers using whole language and traditional approaches. *The Journal of Educational Research, 83*(5), 245–251.

Veatch, J. (1968). *How to teach reading with children's books.* New York: Owen.

Veatch, J. (1978). *Reading in the elementary school* (2nd ed.). New York: Owen.

Veatch, J., & Cooter, R. B., Jr. (1986). The effect of teacher selection on reading achievement. *Language Arts, 63*(4), 364–368.

Viorst, J. (1972). *Alexander and the terrible horrible no good very bad day* (R. Cruz, Illustrator). New York: Atheneum.

Voltz, D. L., & Demiano-Lantz, M. (1993, Summer). Developing ownership in learning. *Teaching Exceptional Children,* pp. 18–22.

Vygotsky, L. S. (1939). Thought and speech. *Psychiatry, 2,* 29–54.

Vygotsky, L. S. (1962). *Thought and language.* Cambridge, MA: MIT Press.

Vygotsky, L. S. (1978). *Mind in society.* Cambridge, MA: Harvard University Press.

Walker, J. E. (1991, May). *Affect in naturalistic assessment: Implementation and implications.* Paper presented at the 36th annual convention of the International Reading Association, Las Vegas, NV.

Wallach, L., Wallach, M. A., Dozier, M. G., & Kaplan, N. E. (1977). Poor children learning to read do not have trouble with auditory discrimination but do have trouble with phoneme recognition. *Journal of Educational Psychology, 69,* 36–39.

Walley, C. (1993). An invitation to reading fluency. *The Reading Teacher, 46*(6), 526–527.

Walters, K., & Gunderson, L. (1985). Effects of parent volunteers reading first language (L1) books to ESL students. *The Reading Teacher, 39*(1), 66–69.

Wasik, B. A. (1998). Using volunteers as reading tutors: Guidelines for successful practices. *The Reading Teacher, 51*(7), 562–573.

Watson, D., & Crowley, P. (1988). How can we implement a whole-language approach? In C. Weaver (Ed.), *Reading process and practice* (pp. 232–279). Portsmouth, NH: Heinemann.

Watson, S. (1976). *No man's land.* New York: Greenwillow.

Weaver, C. (1994). *Reading process and practice: From socio-psycholinguistics to whole language, 2nd ed.* Portsmouth, NH: Heinemann.

Weaver, C. (1998). *Reconsidering a balanced approach to reading.* Urbana, IL: National Council of Teachers of English.

Weaver, C., Chaston, J., & Peterson, S. (1993). *Theme exploration: A voyage of discovery.* Portsmouth, NH: Heinemann.

Webb, K., & Willoughby, N. (1993). An analytic rubric for scoring graphs. *The Texas School Teacher, 22*(3), 14–15.

Webb, M., & Schwartz, W. (1988, October). Children teaching children: A good way to learn. *PTA Today,* pp. 16–17.

Weimans, E. (1981). *Which way courage?* New York: Atheneum.

Weinstein, R. S. (1976). Reading group membership in first grade: Teacher behaviors and pupil experience over time. *Journal of Educational Psychology, 68,* 103–116.

Weintraub, S., & Denny, T. P. (1965). What do beginning first graders say about reading? *Childhood Education, 41,* 326–327.

Wells, R. (1973). *Noisy Nora.* New York: Scholastic.

Wepner, S. B. (1990). Holistic computer applications in literature-based classrooms. *The Reading Teacher, 44*(1), 12–19.

Wepner, S. B. (1992). Technology and text sets. *The Reading Teacher, 46*(1), 68–71.

Wepner, S. B. (1993). Technology and thematic units: An elementary example on Japan. *The Reading Teacher, 46*(5), 442–445.

Wepner, S. B., & Feeley, J. T. (1993). *Moving forward with literature: Basals, books, and beyond.* Upper Saddle River, NJ: Merrill/Prentice Hall.

Wepner, S. B., Feeley, J. T., & Strickland, D. S. (1995). *The administration and supervision of reading programs* (2nd ed). New York: Teacher's College Columbia Press.

Wessells, M. G. (1990). *Computer, self, and society.* Upper Saddle River, NJ: Prentice Hall.

Whaley, J. F. (1981). Readers' expectations for story structures. *Reading Research Quarterly, 17,* 90–114.

Wharton-McDonald, R., Pressley, M., Rankin, J., Mistretta, J., Yokoi, L., & Ettenberger, S. (1997). Effective primary-grades literacy instruction = balanced literacy instruction. *The Reading Teacher 50*(6), 518–521.

What matters most: Teaching for America's future. (1996). Report of the National Commission on Teaching and America's Future, New York: Teacher's College Columbia University.

Wheatley, E. A., Muller, D. H., & Miller, R. B. (1993). Computer-assisted vocabulary instruction. *Journal of Reading, 37*(2), 92–102.

Whitaker, B. T., Schwartz, E., & Vockell, E. (1989). *The computer in the reading curriculum.* New York: McGraw-Hill.

White, C. S. (1983). Learning style and reading instruction. *The Reading Teacher, 36,* 842–845.

White, E. B. (1952). *Charlotte's web.* New York: HarperCollins.

White, E. B. (1970). *The trumpet of the swan.* New York: HarperCollins.

Wiesendanger, W. D. (1986). Durkin revisited. *Reading Horizons, 26,* 89–97.

Wigfield, A. (1997). Motivations, beliefs, and self-efficacy in literacy development. In J. T. Guthrie & A. Wigfield (Eds.), *Reading engagement: Motivating readers through integrated instruction.* Newark, DE: International Reading Association.

Wiggins, R. A. (1994). Large group lesson/small group follow-up: Flexible grouping in a basal reading program.*The Reading Teacher, 47*(6), 450–460.

Wilde, S. (1997). *What's a schwa sound anyway?* Portsmouth, NH: Heinemann.

Wilson, R. M., & Gambrell, L. B. (1988). *Reading comprehension in the elementary school.* Boston: Allyn & Bacon.

Winograd, P. (1989). Improving basal reading instruction: Beyond the carrot and the stick. *Theory Into Practice, 28*(4), 240–247.

Winograd, P. N. (1989). Introduction: Understanding reading instruction. In Winograd, P. N., Wixson, K. K., & Lipson, M. Y. (Eds.). *Improving basal reader instruction* (pp. 1–20). New York: Teachers College Press.

Winograd, P. N., Paris, S., & Bridge, C. (1991). Improving the assessment of literacy. *The Reading Teacher, 45*(2), 108–116.

Winograd, P. N., Wixson, K. K., & Lipson, M. Y. (Eds.). (1989). *Improving basal reader instruction.* New York: Teachers College Press.

Wiseman, D. L. (1992). *Learning to read with literature.* Boston: Allyn & Bacon.

Wittrock, M. C. (1974). Learning as a generative process. *Educational Psychologist, 11,* 87–95.

Wixson, K. K., Peters, C. W., Weber, E. M., & Roeber, E. D. (1987). New directions in statewide reading assessment. *The Reading Teacher, 40*(8), 749–755.

Wong, J. W., & Au, K. H. (1985). The concept-text-application approach: Helping elementary students comprehend expository text. *The Reading Teacher, 38*(7), 612–618.

Wood, A. (1984). *The napping house* (Don Wood, Illustrator). San Diego, CA: Harcourt Brace.

Wood, A. (1990). *Weird parents.* New York: Dial Books for Young Readers.

Wood, K. D. (1983). A variation on an old theme: 4-way oral reading. *The Reading Teacher, 37*(1), 38–41.

Wood, K. D. (1987). Fostering cooperative learning in middle and secondary level classrooms. *Journal of Reading, 31,* 10–18.

Woodcock, R., Mather, N., & Barnes, E. K. (1987). *Woodcock reading mastery tests-revised.* Circle Pines, MN: American Guidance Service.

Woodcock, R. W., & Muñoz-Sandoval, A. F. (1993). *Woodcock-Muñoz language survey* (WMLS), English and Spanish forms. Chicago: Riverside.

Worby, D. Z. (1980). *An honorable seduction: Thematic studies in literature.* Arlington, VA: ERIC Document Reproduction Service. (ERIC Document Reproduction Service No. ED 100 723)

Worthy, J., Moorman, M., & Turner, M. (1999). What Johnny likes to read is hard to find in school. *Reading Research Quarterly, 34*(1), 12–27.

Yaden, D. B., Jr. (1982). A multivariate analysis of first graders' print awareness as related to reading achievement, intelligence, and gender. *Dissertation Abstracts International, 43,* 1912A. (University Microfilms No. 82–25, 520)

Yashima, T. (1983). *Crow boy.* New York: Viking.

Yellin, D., & Blake, M. E. (1994). *Integrating language arts: A holistic approach.* New York: HarperCollins.

Yep, L. (1989). *The rainbow people.* New York: HarperCollins.

Ylisto, I. P. (1967). An empirical investigation of early reading responses of young children (doctoral dissertation, The University of Michigan, 1967). *Dissertation Abstracts International, 28,* 2153A. (University Microfilms No. 67–15, 728)

Yolen, J. (1976). *An invitation to a butterfly ball: A counting rhyme.* New York: Philomel.

Yolen, J. (1988). *The devil's arithmetic.* New York: Viking Kestrel.

Yopp, H. K. (1988). The validity and reliability of phonemic awareness tests. *Reading Research Quarterly, 23,* 159–177.

Yopp, H. K. (1992). Developing phonemic awareness in young children. *The Reading Teacher, 45*(9), 696–703.

Yopp, H. K., & Troyer, S. (1992). *Training phonemic awareness in young children.* Unpublished manuscript.

Young, E. (1989). *Lon Po Po.* New York: Philomel Books.

Young, T. A., & Vardell, S. (1993). Weaving readers theatre and nonfiction into the curriculum. *Reading Teacher, 46,* 396–406.

Zarillo, J. (1989). Teachers' interpretations of literature-based reading. *The Reading Teacher, 43*(1), 22–29.

Zemelman, S., Danieals, H., & Hyde, A. (1993). *Best practice: New standards for teaching and learning in America's schools.* Portsmouth, NH: Heinemann.

Zentall, S. S. (1993). Research on the educational implications of attention deficit hyperactivity disorder. *Exceptional Children, 60*(2), 143–153.

Zintz, M. V., & Maggart, Z. R. (1989). *The reading process: The teacher and the learner.* Dubuque, IA: William C. Brown.

Zlatos, B. (1993). Outcomes-based outrage. *Executive Educator, 15*(9), 12–16.

Zutell, J., & Rasinski, T. (1991). Training teachers to attend to their students' oral reading fluency. *Theory Into Practice, 30*(3), 211–217.

Name Index

Subject Index